American History Teacher's
BOOK OF LISTS

—Fay R. Hansen—

**THE CENTER FOR APPLIED
RESEARCH IN EDUCATION**
West Nyack, New York 10994

Library of Congress Cataloging-in-Publication Data

Hansen, Fay R.
 The American history teacher's book of lists: a compendium of
important lists, chronologies, and documents on political, military,
social, economic, intellectual, and cultural events in the U.S./
Fay R. Hansen.
  p. cm.
 ISBN 0-13-081927-1 (spiral wire) ISBN 0-13-092572-1 (paper)
 1. United States--History--Study and teaching handbooks, manuals,
etc. 2. United States--History miscellanea. I. Title.
E175.8.H297 1999
973'.02'02--dc21   99-36172
                                                     CIP

© 2000 by The Center for Applied Research in Education

Printed in the United States of America

10 9 8 7 6 5 4 3 2 1   *10 9 8 7 6 5 4 3 2 1*
ISBN 0-13-081927-1 (spiral wire) ISBN 0-13-092572-1 (paper)

THE CENTER FOR APPLIED RESEARCH IN EDUCATION
West Nyack, NY 10994
On the World Wide Wed at http://www.phdirect.com

Acknowledgments

I want to thank Ivy Greenstein for her extensive research on the intellectual and cultural history lists, Colin Doolittle for his work on the pre-Columbian populations and explorers and Michelle Gardiner for her research assistance on the foreign policy and military history sections. I would also like to thank my editor at Prentice Hall, Connie Kallback, for her sharp skills, calm support, and wonderful sense of balance. Every writer should be so lucky as to have her as an editor.

About the Author

Fay Hansen received a B.A. in political science from New College, an M.A. in American History from Florida State University, and an M.A. in European History from Cornell University. After years of teaching at the University of South Florida and at Cornell University, she is now a writer and editor specializing in books, articles, and research reports on political and economic trends. Ms. Hansen also works as a research analyst for state legislative reforms and prepares white paper reports for national organizations and federal agencies.

Her history and social sciences teacher's resource, *Ready-to-Use Citizenship Activities for Grades 5–12,* was published by The Center for Applied Research in Education in the fall of 1998.

America was discovered accidentally by a great seaman who was looking for something else; when discovered it was not wanted; and most of the exploration for the next fifty years was done in the hope of getting through or around it. America was named after a man who discovered no part of the New World. History is like that, very chancy.

Samuel Eliot Morison

About This Resource

American History Teacher's Book of Lists is a reference work designed to help teachers capture their students' interest in the past and direct them in building a working knowledge of our world. This comprehensive resource includes lists of people and events plus original documents, statistics and chronologies for teachers to reproduce and distribute to students or to use as their own reference for preparing class materials. The lists—ranging from pre-Columbian populations to the rise of digital technology—are divided into six major parts and grouped by topic and chronologically within each section:

Beginnings: Early populations and explorers, natural history, the colonies, Puritanism, the American Revolution, expansion, the Constitution, and early political documents.

Political History: The presidency, cabinet departments, federal agencies, electoral politics, Congress and congressional leaders, the judiciary, Supreme Court cases, the balance of powers, and state government.

Diplomacy and Military History: Treaties, foreign policy, slavery and the Civil War, nineteenth century conflicts, World War I, World War II, the Korean, Vietnam, and Persian Gulf Wars, the United Nations, the armed forces, major weapons, military costs, and casualties.

Economic History: Industrial and technological development, the Great Depression, the New Deal, the public debt and deficits, economic growth, inflation, employment, the work force, trade unions, business leaders, and corporations.

Social History: Population trends, urbanization, income trends, poverty, public health, education, crime rates and the prison system, ethnic groups, the civil rights movement, the women's rights movement, American Indian populations, notable families, and religious life.

Intellectual and Cultural History: Literature—novelists, poets and playwrights—journalism, visual arts, architecture, academic disciplines, performing arts, radio and television, popular music, and public libraries.

HOW TO USE THESE LISTS

These lists are resources that can be used in a number of ways. Some are reference tools designed to give the teacher basic information and background. Others can be copied and given to students to use as study guides or in assignments. All of them can be used to guide discussions and debates, create classroom activities and assignments, and launch research projects.

These lists can help students build their knowledge of American history—the rise of political institutions, the emergence of social problems and values that still affect our well-being, the territorial and economic expansion of the nation, and the blossoming of intellectual and artistic communities. Although the primary purpose of the lists is to impart information, they can also help students develop broader analytical skills:

- *Thinking through historical issues.* Perhaps the greatest value of the lists found here is their ability to impart a great deal of information in a small amount of space and time, and to leave students free to pursue the meaning of the information according to their own interests. From the annotated lists of historic Supreme Court decisions, for example, students will find at least one case of interest that will lead them to a deeper understanding of how the court works and how it has struggled with the pressing issues of different eras.

- *Understanding the magnitude of events.* Some lists will certainly grab students' attention and bring them to realizations that lectures and textbooks may not. Few sights are as sobering as the simple list of war casualties. The sheer magnitude of the numbers, reported without long accounts of battles or detailed explanations of alliances, helps students grasp the real importance of events.

- *Gaining historical perspective.* Other lists provide perspective. They offer students a chance to view the events of their own era in the context of what has gone before. The AIDS epidemic of our own time may seem almost unimaginably tragic until it appears in the list of major epidemics, some of which claimed an even greater number of lives.

- *Understanding the pace of change.* Yet other lists can be used to help students understand just how much life has changed, or how much remains the same. For example, the list of the largest manufacturing plants in 1900 is notable primarily because so few of these plants still operate today. In this particular aspect of American life—the history of manufacturing—change has been quick, deep, and visible, while other types of change are much slower. Few students can read the chronology of the women's rights movement without reaching a new understanding of the roots of social change in our own time and the deep and sometimes centuries-long struggle required to achieve fundamental social goals.

- *Stimulating questions of causality.* Many of the lists in this resource document sweeping shifts in demographics, economic trends, and social institutions. All of them force the inevitable question of why significant changes occur. When change over time is so obvious, as it is in the table on women in the work force, for example, students immediately begin to search for explanations.

- *Encouraging critical reading.* Many of the brief chronologies provided here raise questions about the traditional assumptions we make about the past and historians' conflicting interpretations. The lists, chronologies, and documents spur students to think for themselves about the past. What is it about the Monroe Doctrine, a relatively brief and simple text prepared in 1823, that placed it at the center of debates about expansionism? Although many students may not be able to read the entire text of *Moby Dick,* the excerpts included here may be sufficient to give them some sense of why many critics believe that the book is the greatest American novel ever penned.

- *Developing research topics.* Working from the lists of colonial capitals or important abolitionists, or from the chronologies of the railroad industry or the development of the atomic bomb, students can select specific topics for research projects. They can use the data on population density or poverty to begin more lengthy investigations into major trends, or refer to the chronology of public education to explore additional reading.

- *Building citizenship.* The lists on voter rights, the chronology of conscription, and the description of the electoral college are just a few examples of the materials provided to help generate class discussions about the role of government and the role of citizens in a democracy.

WHY THESE LISTS?

In any book of lists, the inevitable question arises: Why these lists, and not others? Some are included here for obvious reasons. No American history book of lists would be complete without noting all the presidents and Supreme Court justices, major battles, important business leaders and influential writers. Other lists are included for less obvious reasons—because they may spark an idea that is otherwise difficult to reach. The list of works of Henry James, for example, provide at a glance the unparalleled prolificacy of a generation of American writers who were truly "men of letters." Some lists appear because they impart a sense of the past that is difficult to create in today's classrooms. The chronology of Emerson's life, for example, reveals in a brief space the ongoing personal tragedies that marked the lives of most people living in Emerson's time.

Some lists are designed to give the grand sweep of an era or an event, while others document details. The short chronology of the Civil War, for example, shows only the barest outline of the struggle. The detailed list of Civil War battles allows students to look at the war in their own state or town and may encourage them to pursue their study of the war at the local history level.

Some entries may appear to be purely whimsical, such as the best-selling books in the 1960s. But this list speaks volumes about a society that read J.D. Salinger along with Billy Graham, Henry Miller along with Douglas MacArthur. The diverse and contradictory messages of the decade, which are often difficult to describe, are clearly reflected there. The list of spies and espionage from 1775-1999 makes for interesting reading, but it can also be used to launch a discussion on national interests.

Although historians tend to focus on political and military history, this resource includes information from economic history, which is increasingly recognized as a crucial field of inquiry, and from social, cultural, and intellectual history—important parts of the past and precisely the parts that students often find to be the best doorway to the whole.

Some original documents are included simply because they are so essential to understanding particular eras and because no list could begin to communicate the same sense of the past that original documents provide. No list of Puritan ministers or chronology of Puritan theology can convey the beauty and the terror that forms the center of Puritan thinking and is so immediately evident in a few pages from Jonathan Edwards' "Sinners in the Hands of an Angry God." In the same manner, Franklin Roosevelt's address to the nation in 1941 helps students understand the significance of America's entry into World War II in a way that simple chronologies of the event cannot explain.

References are provided for lists where the sources might be difficult to identify. Virtually all of the statistical information comes from official government sources, such as the U.S. Census Bureau, the Department of Labor, and the Commerce Department. Other lists are taken from major reference works and monographs by professional historians cited in the footnotes.

Contents

PART V   SOCIAL HISTORY / 327

Section 14   Demographics—329

Section 15   Public Institutions—354

Section 16   Ethnic, Social and Religious Groups—374

PART VI   INTELLECTUAL AND CULTURAL HISTORY / 423

Section 17   American Writers—425

I

BEGINNINGS

1. Pre-Columbian Populations, Exploration and Natural History

2. The Colonies

3. American Revolution and the New Nation

SECTION 1

Pre-Columbian Populations, Exploration and Natural History

1.1 Pre-Columbian Population Groups
of North America

Tribe	Language Group	Pre-Columbian Locations
Eastern Woodlands		
Abnaki	Algonquin	Maine
Cayuga	Iroquoian	New York
Cherokee	Iroquoian	Tennessee, North Carolina, South Carolina, Georgia
Chicksaw	Muskogean	Mississippi
Chippewa	Algonquin	North Dakota, Montana, Wisconsin
Choctaw	Muskogean	Mississippi
Creek	Muskogean	Alabama, Georgia
Delaware	Algonquin	New Jersey, Pennsylvania, Delaware
Illinois	Algonquin	Illinois, Iowa, Missouri, Wisconsin
Lenape	Algonquin	New Jersey, Pennsylvania
Massachusett	Algonquin	Massachusetts, New Hampshire
Menominee	Algonquin	Wisconsin
Miami	Algonquin	Illinois, Indiana, Michigan, Wisconsin, Ohio
Mohawk	Iroquoian	New York
Mohegan	Algonquin	Connecticut
Mohican (Mahican)	Algonquin	New York
Munsee	Algonquin	New York, Pennsylvania, New Jersey
Narragansett	Algonquin	Massachusetts, Rhode Island
Natchez	Natchez	Louisiana, Mississippi
Nauset	Algonquin	Massachusetts
Oneida	Iroquoian	New York
Onondaga	Iroquoian	New York
Passamaquoddy	Algonquin	Maine
Penobscot	Algonquin	Maine
Pequot	Algonquin	Connecticut, Massachusetts, Rhode Island
Phoenician	Semitic	Massachusetts
Potawatami	Algonquin	Illinois, Michigan, Wisconsin
Powhatan	Algonquin	Virginia, West Virginia
Sauk	Algonquin	Iowa, Illinois, Wisconsin
Seminole	Muskogean	Florida, Georgia
Seneca	Iroquoian	New York
Shawnee	Algonquin	Kentucky, Ohio, Pennsylvania, West Virginia
Tuscarora	Iroquoian	North Carolina
Wampanoag	Algonquin	Massachusetts
Winnebago	Siouan	Wisconsin, Missouri
Plains		
Arapaho	Algonquin	Colorado, Wyoming
Arikara	Caddoan	North Dakota
Assiniboin	Siouan	Minnesota
Atsina	Algonquin	North Dakota, South Dakota
Blackfoot	Algonquin	Montana
Caddo	Caddoan	Texas, Louisiana, Arkansas
Cheyenne	Algonquin	Minnesota, North Dakota
Comanche	Uto-Aztecan	Colorado, Texas, Kansas
Crow	Siouan	Wyoming, Montana

<u>Tribe</u>	<u>Language Group</u>	<u>Pre-Columbian Locations</u>

Plains (Cont'd.)

Hidatsa	Siouan	North Dakota
Iowa	Siouan	Iowa
Kansa	Siouan	Kansas
Kiowa	Kiowa	Colorado, Oklahoma
Mandan	Siouan	North Dakota, South Dakota
Osage	Siouan	Missouri, Arkansas, Oklahoma
Pawnee	Caddoan	Nebraska
Quapaw	Siouan	Arkansas
Sioux	Siouan	North Dakota, South Dakota, Minnesota, Montana

Southwest

Apache	Athapascan	Arizona, New Mexico, Colorado
Hopi	Uto-Aztecan	Arizona
Mohave	Yuma	Arizona, California
Navaho	Athapascan	Arizona, New Mexico
Pima	Uto-Aztecan	Arizona
Yaqui	Uto-Aztecan	Arizona
Yuma	Yuma	Arizona, California
ZuÒi	ZuÒian	New Mexico

California/Great Basin/Plateau

Bannock	Uto-Aztecan	Idaho, Wyoming
Flathead	Salish	Montana
Klamath	Lutuamian	California, Oregon
Kutenai	Kutenai	Idaho, Montana
Maidu	Maidu	California
Modoc	Lutuamian	California, Oregon
Nez PercÈ	Sahaptin	Idaho, Oregon, Washington
Paiute	Uto-Aztec	Arizona, California, Nevada, Utah
Pomo	Pomo	California
Shoshone	Uto-Aztecan	Idaho, Nevada, Wyoming
Ute	Uto-Aztecan	Colorado, New Mexico, Utah
Walla Walla	Sahaptin	Washington
Yakama	Sahaptin	Oregon, Washington

Pacific Northwest

Chinook	Chinookan	Oregon, Washington
Haida	Haida	Alaska
Nootka	Wakashan	Washington
Tsimshian	Tsimshian	Alaska
Tlingit	Tlingit	Alaska
Yurok	Algonquin	California

Arctic

Aleut	Eskimoan	Alaska
Inuit	Eskimoan	Alaska
Yuit	Eskimoan	Alaska

Hawaii

Hawaiians	Polynesian	Hawaii

1.2   Early Overseas Explorers in North America

Explorer	Nationality	Main Achievements	Date
Balboa, Vasco Nunez de	Spanish	Led expedition across isthmus of Panama; sighted Pacific Ocean.	1513
Cabeza de Vaca, Alvar Nunez	Spanish	Explored Gulf Plains from Texas to Mexico.	1528-1536
Cabot, John	Italian	Sailed across the North Atlantic to what is now Canada.	1497–1498
Cartier, Jacques	French	Sailed up the St. Lawrence River.	1535
Columbus, Christopher	Italian	Made four voyages to the West Indies and Caribbean lands.	1492–1504
Coronado, Francisco de	Spanish	Explored the American Southwest.	1540–1542
De Soto, Hernando	Spanish	Explored American Southeast; reached Mississippi River.	1539–1542
Frobisher, Sir Martin	English	Searched North American coast for a Northwest Passage.	1576–1578
Onate, Juan de	Spanish	Explored American Southwest.	1598-1605
Ponce de Leon, Juan	Spanish	Explored Florida.	1513
Verrazano, Giovanni da	Italian	Searched for a Northwest Passage.	1524

1.3   Internal Exploration of the United States

Explorer	Year(s)	Country Represented	Area of Exploration
Hanno[1]	c. 425 b.c.	Carthage	New England
Leif Ericson	c. 1000	Viking	Atlantic Coastline
Henry Sinclair[2]	1380-1398	Scotland	New England
Juan Ponce de León	1513	Spain	Florida
Giovanni da Verrazano	1524	France	New York Bay
Cabeza de Vaca[3]	1528-36	Spain	Texas, Gulf coast
Hernando de Soto	1539-42	Spain	Southeastern US
Francisco de Coronado	1540-42	Spain	Southwestern US
Juan de Cabrillo	1542-43	Spain	California coast
Juan Pardo	1566-67	Spain	Southeastern US
Francis Drake	1578	England	California coast
Samuel de Champlain	1608-16	France	New York, New England
Henry Hudson	1609	England	Mid-Atlantic region
Jean Nicolet	1634	France	Great Lakes
Pierre Radisson	1654-1660	France	Great Lakes, Hudson Bay
Jacques Marquette and Louis Jolliet	1673	France	Mississippi River
Henry Woodward	1674-82	England	Southeast US
Robert La Salle	1678-82	France	Great Lakes, Mississippi River
Henri de Tonti	1679-82	France	Mississppi River, Great Lakes
Arnout Viele	1692-94	Netherlands	Pennsylvania, Ohio
Pierre Le Moyne	1699-1700	France	Mississippi River, Louisiana
Pierre le Sueur	1700	France	Mississippi
John Lawson	1701	England	North Carolina
Vitus Bering	1740-41	Russia	Alaska
Thomas Walker	1750	England	Kentucky
Christopher Gist	1750-52	England	Ohio River, Pennsylvania
George Croghan	1765	England	Ohio
Daniel Boone	1769-71	England	Kentucky
James Cook	1778	England	Alaskan coast, Hawaii
David Thompson	1789-1812	England	Northwest US
Meriwether Lewis and William Clark	1804-6	United States	Pacific Northwest, Great Plains
Zebulon Pike	1805-7	United States	New Mexico, Rocky Mountains
Jedediah Strong Smith	1824-29	United States	Rocky Mountains
John Charles Fremont	1842-46	United States	Rocky Mountains, Oregon

[1] Extent of exploration not known. There is evidence of Carthaginian/Phoenecian exploration and settlements all over the Americas dating back to 450 b.c.

[2] Extent of exploration not known.

[3] Originally led by Panfilio de Narveaz from 1527-28.

1.4   Grant for Christopher Columbus, 1492

Privileges and Prerogatives Granted by Their Catholic Majesties to Christopher Columbus: 1492 FERDINAND and ISABELLA, by the Grace of God, King and Queen of Castile, of Leon, of Arragon, of Sicily, of Granada, of Toledo, of Valencia, of Galicia, of Majorca, of Minorca, of Sevil, of Sardinia, of Jaen, of Algarve, of Algezira, of Gibraltar, of the Canary Islands, Count and Countess of Barcelona, Lord and Lady of Biscay and Molina, Duke and Duchess of Athens and Neopatria. Count and Countess of Rousillion and Cerdaigne, Marquess and Marchioness of Oristan and Gociano, & c.

For as much of you, Christopher Columbus, are going by our command, with some of our vessels and men, to discover and subdue some Islands and continent in the ocean, and it is hoped that by God's assistance, some of the said Islands and continent in the ocean will be discovered and conquered by your means and conduct, therefore it is but just and reasonable, that since you expose yourself to such danger to serve us, you should be rewarded for it. And we being willing to honour and favour you for the reasons aforesaid: our will is, that you, Christopher Columbus, after discovering and conquering the said Islands and continent in the said ocean, or any of them, shall be our Admiral of the said Islands and continent you shall so discover and conquer; and that you be our Admiral, Vice-Roy, and Governor in them, and that for the future, you may call and style yourself, D. Christopher Columbus, and that your sons and successors in the said employment, may call themselves Dons, Admirals, Vice-Roys, and Governors of them; and that you may exercise the office of Admiral, with the charge of Vice-Roy and Governor of the said Islands and continent, which you and your lieutenants shall conquer, and freely decide all causes, civil and criminal, appertaining to the said employment of Admiral, Vice-Roy, and Governor, as you shall think fit in justice, and as the Admirals of our kingdoms use to do; and that you have power to punish offenders; and you and your lieutenants exercise the employments of Admiral, Vice-Roy, and Governor, in all things belonging to the said offices, or any of them; and that you enjoy the perquisites and salaries belonging to the said employments, and to each of them, in the same manner as the High Admiral of our kingdoms does.

And by this, our letter, or a copy of it signed by a Public Notary: we command Prince John, our most dearly beloved son, the infants, dukes, prelates, marquesses, great masters and military orders, priors, commendaries, our counsellors, judges, and other officers of justice whatsoever, belonging courts, and chancery, and constables of castles, strong houses, and others; and all corporations, bayliffs, governors, judges, commanders, sea officers; and the aldermen, common council, officers, and good people of all cities, lands, and places in our kingdoms and dominions, and in those you shall conquer and subdue, and the captains, masters, mates, and other officers and sailors, our natural subjects now being, or that shall be for the time to come, and any of them that when you shall have discovered the said Islands and continent in the ocean; and you, or any that shall have your commission, shall have taken the usual oath in such cases, that they for the future, look upon you as long as you live, and after you, your son and heir, and so from one heir to another forever, as our Admiral on our said ocean, and as Vice-Roy and Governor of the said Islands and continent, by you, Christopher Columbus, discovered and conquered; and that they treat you and your lieutenants, by you appointed, for executing the employments of Admiral, Vice-Roy, and Governor, as such in all respects, and give you all the perquisites and other things belonging and appertaining to the said offices; and allow, and cause to be allowed you, all the honours, graces, concessions, prehaminences, prerogatives, immunities, and other things, or any of them which are due to you, by virtue of your commands of Admiral, Vice-Roy, and Governor, and to be observed completely, so that nothing be diminished; and that they make no objection to this, or any part of it, nor suffer it to be made; forasmuch as we from this time forward, by this our letter, bestow on you the employments of Admiral, Vice-Roy, and perpetual Governor forever; and we put you into possession of the said offices, and of every of them, and full power to use and exercise them, and to receive the perquisites and salaries belonging to them, or any of them, as was said above.

Concerning all which things, if it be requisite, and you shall desire it, we command our chancellor, notaries, and other officers, to pass, seal, and deliver to you, our Letter of Privilege, in such form and legal manner, as you shall require or stand in need of. And that none of them presume to do anything to the contrary, upon pain of our displeasure, and forfeiture of 30 ducats for each offense. And we command him, who shall show them this our letter, that he summon them to appear before us at our Court, where we shall then be, within fifteen days after such summons, under the said penalty. Under which same, we also command any public notary whatsoever, that he give to him that shows it him, a certificate under his seal, that we may know how our command is obeyed.

GIVEN at Granada, on the 30th of April, in the year of our Lord, 1492.

I, THE KING, I, THE QUEEN. By their Majesties Command, John Coloma, Secretary to the King and Queen. Entered according to order. RODERICK. Doctor. SEBASTIAN DOLONA, FRANCIS DE MADRID, Councellors.

1.5   Geographic Profile of the United States

Highest point: Mt. McKinley, Alaska	20,320 ft. (6,198 m)
Lowest point: Death Valley, Calif.	282 ft. (86 m) below sea level
Approximate mean elevation	2,500 ft. (763 m)
Points farthest apart (50 states): Log point, Elliot Key, Fla., and Kure Island, Hawaii	5,859 mi. (9,429 km)
Geographic center (50 states): in Buttle County, S.D. (west of Castle Rock)	44 58 N lat.103 46 w long.
Geographic center (48 conterminous states): in Smith County, Kan. (near Lebanon)	39 50 N lat. 98 35 w long.

Boundaries

Between Alaska and Canada	1,538 mi. (2,475 km)
Between the 48 contiguous states and Canada (including Great Lakes)	3,987 mi. (6,416 km)
Between the United States and Mexico	1,933 mi (3,111 km)

Extreme Points of the United States (50 states)

Extreme Point	Lattitude	Longitude
Northernmost point: Point Barrow, Alaska	71 23 N	156 29 W
Easternmost point: West Quoddy Head, Me.	44 49 N	66 57 W
Southernmost point: Ka Lae (South Cape), Hawaii	18 55 N	155 41 W
Westernmost point: Cape Wrangell, Alaska (Attu Island)	52 55 N	172 27 E

Source: U.S. Geological Survey.

1.6   Notable Rivers of the U.S.

River	Source	Mouth	Length
Alabama	Alabama	Alabama, Gulf of Mexico	315 miles
Allegheny	Pennsylvania	Pennsylvania, Ohio River	325 miles
Arkansas	Colorado	Arkansas, Mississippi River	1,450 miles
Canadian	New Mexico	Oklahoma, Arkansas River	906 miles
Colorado	Colorado	Mexico, Gulf of California	1,370 miles
Colorado	Texas	Texas, Gulf of Mexico	840 miles
Columbia	Canada	Oregon/Washington, Pacific Ocean	1,214 miles
Connecticut	New Hampshire, Connecticut	Long Island Sound	407 miles
Cumberland	Kentucky	Kentucky, Ohio River	687 miles
Delaware	New York	New Jersey/Delaware, Delaware Bay	300 miles
Detroit	Lake Saint Clair	Michigan/Canada, Lake Erie	28 miles
Gila	New Mexico	Arizona, Colorado River	630 miles
Green	Kentucky	Kentucky, Ohio River	360 miles
Housatonic	Massachusetts	Connecticut, Long Island Sound	148 miles
Hudson	New York	New York/New Jersey, Atlantic Ocean	306 miles
Illinois	Illinois	Illinois, Mississippi River	273 miles
James	Virginia	Virginia, Chesapeake Bay	340 miles
Kennebec	Maine	Maine, Atlantic Ocean	164 miles
Kentucky	Kentucky	Kentucky, Ohio River	250 miles
Klamath	Oregon	California, Pacific Ocean	250 miles
Minnesota	South Dakota	Minnesota, Mississippi River	332 miles
Mississippi	Minnesota	Louisiana, Gulf of Mexico	2,350 miles
Missouri	Montana	Missouri, Mississippi River	2,315 miles
Mohawk	New York	New York, Hudson River	148 miles
Monongahela	West Virginia	Pennsylvania, Ohio River	178 miles
Niagara	Lake Erie	New York/Canada, Lake Ontario	34 miles
Ohio	Pennsylvania	Illinois/Kentucky, Mississippi River	981 miles
Pecos	New Mexico	Texas, Rio Grande	800 miles
North Platte	Colorado	Nebraska, Platte River	618 miles
Platte	Nebraska	Nebraska, Missouri River	310 miles
South Platte	Colorado	Nebraska, Platte River	424 miles
Potomac	Virginia	Maryland/Virginia, Chesapeake Bay	287 miles
Red River	Texas	Louisiana, Mississippi River	1,215 miles
Red River of the North	North Dakota	Canada, Lake Winnipeg	533 miles
Rio Grande	Colorado	Texas/Mexico, Gulf of Mexico	1,885 miles
Sabine	Texas	Texas/Louisiana, Gulf of Mexico	578 miles
Sacramento	California	California, San Francisco Bay	382 miles
San Joaquin	California	California, San Francisco Bay	350 miles
Savannah	South Carolina	South Carolina/Georgia, Atlantic Ocean	341 miles
Schuylkill	Pennsylvania	Pennsylvania, Delaware River	131 miles
Shenandoah	Virginia	West Virginia, Potomac River	170 miles
Snake	Wyoming	Washington, Columbia River	1,039 miles
Susquehanna	New York	Maryland, Chesapeake Bay	444 miles
St. Lawrence	Lake Ontario	Canada, Gulf of St. Lawrence	1,945 miles
Tennessee	Tennessee	Kentucky, Ohio River	652 miles
Wabash	Ohio	Illinois/Indiana, Ohio River	475 miles
Yellowstone	Wyoming	North Dakota, Missouri River	672 miles
Yukon	Yukon Territory	Alaska, Bering Sea	1,979 miles

1.7   Major U.S. Lakes

Lake	Location	Size
Lake Champlain	New York, Vermont, Canada	431 square miles
Crater Lake	The crater of Mt. Mazma, Oregon	20 square miles
Lake Erie	Michigan, Ohio, Pennsylvania, New York, Canada	9,940 square miles
Lake George	New York	44 square miles
Great Salt Lake	Utah	969-2,300 square miles
Lake Huron	Michigan, Canada	23,010 square miles
Lake Itasca	Minnesota	2 square miles
Lake Mead	Arizona, Nevada	228.83 square miles
Lake Michigan	Illinois, Michigan, Indiana, Wisconsin	22,400 square miles
Mono Lake	California	87 square miles
Moosehead Lake	Maine	120 square miles
Lake Okeechobee	Florida	730 square miles
Lake Ontario	New York, Canada	7,520 square miles
Lake Onieda	New York	79.8 square miles
Lake of the Ozarks	Missouri	93 square miles
Lake Placid	New York	4.37 square miles
Lake Pontchartrain	Louisiana	625 square miles
Lake Powell	Arizona, Utah	250 square miles
Lake Saint Clair	Michigan, Canada	460 square miles
Salton Sea	California	300 square miles
Lake Superior	Minnesota, Wisconsin, Michigan, Canada	31,800 square miles
Lake Tahoe	California, Nevada	187 square miles
Lake Tear of the Clouds	New York	Less than 1 square mile
Utah Lake	Utah	140 square miles
Lake Winnebago	Wisconsin	215 square miles
Lake Winnipesaukee	New Hampshire	72 square miles
Lake of the Woods	Minnesota, Canada	1,485 square miles
Yellowstone Lake	Wyoming	137 square miles

1.8   Primeval Forests, 1800

Dimensions of trees in Vermont in the year 1800

	Diameter	**Height**
Pine	6 feet	250 feet
Maple	5 3/4 feet	From 100 to 200 feet
Buttonwood	5 1/2 feet	From 100 to 200 feet
Elm	5 1/2 feet	From 100 to 200 feet
Hemlock	4 3/4 feet	From 100 to 200 feet
Oak	4 3/4 feet	From 100 to 200 feet
Basswood	4 3/4 feet	From 100 to 200 feet
Ash	4 3/4 feet	From 100 to 200 feet
Birch	4 3/4 feet	From 100 to 200 feet

Today, the largest trees in these Vermont villages are rarely three feet in diameter, which is roughly half the girth of the largest trees two centuries ago.

Source: Alice Outwater, *Water: A Natural History* (New York: Basic Books, 1996).

1.9   American Trees

Ash, black
Ash, white
Aspen, large toothed
Basswood
Beech, American
Birch, black/sweet
Birch, paper/white
Birch, yellow
Cedar, eastern red
Cedar, northern white
Cedar, western red
Cherry, black
Corkwood
Cottonwood, eastern
Cypress, bald
Dogwood, flowering

Elm, American
Fir, balsam
Fir, Douglas
Gum, black/sour
Gum, tupelo
Hemlock, eastern
Hemlock, western
Hickory, shagbark
Ironwood, black
Locust, black/yellow
Magnolia, cucumber
Maple, red
Maple, sugar
Oak, live
Oak, northern red
Oak, white

Pine, eastern white
Pine, loblolly
Pine, longleaf
Pine, ponderosa
Pine, red
Pine, western white
Poplar, yellow/tulip
Redwood
Sassafras
Spruce, Engelmann
Spruce, red/yellow
Spruce, white
Spruce, Sitka
Sycamore, American
Tamarack, American
Walnut, black

1.10 National Parks of the United States

<u>Location, description, date established</u>

Acadia; Maine; 170 sq km (66 sq mi); Mount Desert Island and Atlantic coast; established 1919

American Samoa; American Samoa; 36 sq km (14 sq mi); rain forest preserves and a coral reef; authorized 1988

Arches; Utah; 297 sq km (115 sq mi); natural arches formed by wind erosion; established 1971

Badlands; South Dakota; 982 sq km (379 sq mi); wind-eroded formations, fossils, and prairie grassland; established 1978

Big Bend; Texas; 3,242 sq km (1,252 sq mi); mountain and desert scenery along the Rio Grande; established 1944

Biscayne; Florida; 700 sq km (270 sq mi); 33 keys in a north-south chain, mostly reef and water; established 1980

Bryce Canyon; Utah 145 sq km (56 sq mi); colorful eroded pinnacles; established 1928

Canyonlands; Utah; 1,366 sq km (527 sq mi); rock spires and mesas; established 1964

Capitol Reef; Utah; 979 sq km (378 sq mi); gorges, fossils, and cliff dwelling; established 1971

Carlsbad Caverns; New Mexico; 189 sq km (73 sq mi); among largest natural caves yet discovered; established 1930

Channel Islands; California; 1,009 sq km (390 sq mi); five Pacific islands, sea birds, sea lion rookeries, plants; established 1980

Crater Lake; Oregon; 741 sq km (286 sq mi); lake in crater of extinct volcano; established 1902

Death Valley; California and Nevada; approx. 13,759 sq km (5,312 sq mi); wilderness area and geological formations, and lowest point in Western Hemisphere; established 1994

Denali (also preserve); Alaska; 20,234 sq km (7,813 sq mi); highest mountain in North America (Mt. McKinley), glaciers; established 1980

Dry Tortugas; Florida; 262 sq km (101 sq mi); site of Fort Jefferson, largest all masonry fortification in the Western world and bird and marine life refuge; established 1992

Everglades; Florida; 6,097 sq km (2,354 sq mi); subtropical wilderness with abundant wildlife; authorized 1934

Gates of the Arctic (also preserve); Alaska; 30,448 sq km (11,756 sq mi); tundra wilderness, wild rivers, lakes; established 1980

Glacier; Montana; 4,102 sq km (1,584 sq mi); glaciers, lakes, and wildlife in Rocky Mountains; established 1910

Glacier Bay (also preserve); Alaska; 13,052 sq km (5,039 sq mi); tidewater glaciers, rain forest, large variety of wildlife; established 1980

Grand Canyon; Arizona; 4,926 sq km (1,902 sq mi); canyon of the Colorado River; established 1919

Grand Teton; Wyoming; 1,255 sq km (484 sq mi); Teton Range of the Rocky Mountains; established 1929

Great Basin; Nevada; 312 sq km (120 sq mi); scrubland, meadows, mountains, glacial lakes, bristlecone pine habitat; established 1986

Great Smoky Mountains; Tennessee and North Carolina; 2,105 sq km (813 sq mi); Appalachian uplands; established 1930

Guadalupe Mountains; Texas; 350 sq km (135 sq mi); mountains and limestone fossil reef; established 1972

Haleakala; Hawaii; 114 sq km (44 sq mi); extinct volcanic crater on Maui island; established 1960

Hawaii Volcanoes; Hawaii; 927 sq km (358 sq mi); active volcanoes on Hawaii Island; established 1916

Hot Springs; Arkansas; 24 sq km (9 sq mi); 47 hot springs in the Ouachita Mountains; established 1921

Isle Royale; Michigan; 2,314 sq km (893 sq mi); island in Lake Superior; authorized 1931

Joshua Tree; California; approx. 3,213 sq km (1,241 sq mi); Joshua trees and desert wildlife, including desert bighorn; established 1994

Katmai (also preserve); Alaska; 15,038 sq km (5,806 sq mi); lakes, forest volcanoes, marshlands, wildlife; established 1980

Kenai Fjords; Alaska; 2,710 sq km (1,046 sq mi); major U.S. icecap, glaciers, fjords, islands, rain forest; established 1980

Kings Canyon; California; 1,869 sq km (722 sq mi); canyons of the Kings River, Sierra Nevada peaks; established 1890

Kobuk Valley; Alaska; 7,084 sq km (2,735 sq mi); archaeological remains, sand dunes, Arctic wildlife; established 1980

Lake Clark (also preserve); Alaska; 10,671 sq km (4,120 sq mi); Coast Ranges, wildlife, fishing area, volcanoes; established 1980

Lassen Volcanic; California; 430 sq km (166 sq mi); active volcano, hot springs, and geysers; established 1916

Mammoth Cave; Kentucky; 213 sq km (82 sq mi); cave system; established 1941

Mesa Verde; Colorado; 211 sq km (81 sq mi); prehistoric cliff dwellings; established 1906

Mount Rainier; Washington; 953 sq km (368 sq mi); glacier system on volcanic peak; established 1899

North Cascades; Washington; 2,043 sq km (789 sq mi); glaciers, waterfalls, and lakes; established 1968

Olympic; Washington; 3,734 sq km (1,442 sq mi); mountain wilderness, glaciers, and Pacific Ocean coast; established 1938

Petrified Forest; Arizona; 379 sq km (146 sq mi); petrified trees, parts of the Painted Desert, American Indian ruins, and petroglyphs; established 1962

Redwood; California; 446 sq km (172 sq mi); redwood forest and Pacific Ocean coast; established 1968

Rocky Mountain; Colorado; 1,075 sq km (415 sq mi); Front Range of Rocky Mountains; established 1915

Saguaro; Arizona; 77 sq km (30 sq mi); site of the giant saguaro cacti in the Sonoran Desert, established 1994

Sequoia; California; 1,629 sq km (629 sq mi); giant sequoia groves and Mount Whitney; established 1890

Shenandoah; Virginia; 795 sq km (307 sq mi); Blue Ridge Mountains and Skyline Drive; established 1935

Theodore Roosevelt; North Dakota; 285 sq km (110 sq mi); badlands along the little Missouri River; established 1978

Virgin Islands; Virgin Islands; 59 sq km (23 sq mi); beaches and nearby hills on St. Johns; authorized 1956

Voyageurs; Minnesota; 882 sq km (341 sq mi); connecting lakes and forests; established 1975

Wind Cave; South Dakota; 115 sq km (44 sq mi); limestone caverns in Black Hills; established 1903

Wrangell-Saint Elias (also preserve); Alaska; 33,717 sq km (13,018 sq mi); glaciers, mountains, rare wildlife; established 1980

Yellowstone; Wyoming, Montana, and Idaho; 8,983 sq km (3,468 sq mi); geysers, hot springs, lakes and waterfalls, and canyon of the Yellowstone River; established 1872

Yosemite; California; 3081 sq km (1,189 sq mi); peaks, domes, and sequoia groves of the Sierra Nevada; established 1890

Zion; Utah; 593 sq km (229 sq mi); colorful canyon and mesas; established 1919

1.11 Major National Monuments

<u>Location, description, date established</u>

Agate Fossil; Nebraska; 12.4 sq km (4.8 sq mi); quarries, mammal fossils, collection of Indian artifacts; authorized 1965

Alibates Flint; Texas; 5.5 sq km (2.1 sq mi); Pre-Columbian Indians quarry site for making tools; authorized 1965

Bandelier; New Mexico; 133 sq km (51 sq mi); Pueblo Indian cliff dwellings; proclaimed 1916

Black Canyon of the Gunnison; Colorado; 84 sq km (32 sq mi); ancient rocks in this canyon, carved by the Gunnison River; proclaimed 1933

Booker T. Washington Home; Virginia; 0.9 sq km (0.35 sq mi); birthplace and early childhood home of the black educator; authorized 1956

Cabrillo; California; 0.6 sq km (0.2 sq mi); memorial to the Portuguese explorer who claimed the area for Spain in 1542

Canyon de Chelly; Arizona; 339 sq km (131 sq mi); Indian remains in cliffs and caves; authorized 1931

Cape Krusenstern; Alaska; 2,670 sq km (1,031 sq mi); archeological Eskimo sites dating back 4,000 years; proclaimed 1978

Casa Grande Ruins; Arizona; 1.9 sq km (0.7 sq mi); Indian ruins of the Gila Valley; proclaimed 1918

Castillo de San Marcos; Florida; 0.08 sq km (0.03 sq mi); Saint Augustine masonry fort, oldest in the continental United States; proclaimed 1924

Craters of the Moon; Idaho; 217 sq km (84 sq mi); volcanic formations; proclaimed 1924

Devils Postpile; California; 3.2 sq km (1.2 sq mi); ancient lava formations of basalt columns; proclaimed 1911

Devils Tower; Wyoming; 5.5 sq km (2.1 sq mi); this first national monument is a tower of columnar rock, the remains of a volcanic intrusion, proclaimed 1906

Dinosaur; Utah and Colorado; 853 sq km (329 sq mi); canyons and fossil remains; proclaimed 1915

Effigy Mounds; Iowa; 6 sq km (2.3 sq mi); prehistoric Indian mounds, some in shapes of birds and bears; proclaimed 1949

El Morro; New Mexico; 5.2 sq km (2 sq mi); inscribed sandstone monolith, Pre-Columbian petroglyphs, and Indian ruins; proclaimed 1906

Fort McHenry; Maryland; 0.2 sq km (0.07 sq mi); successful defense of this fort in the War of 1812 inspired the writing of "The Star-Spangled Banner"; authorized 1925

Fort Stanwix; New York; 0.06 sq km (0.02 sq mi); reconstructed American Revolutionary War fort; authorized 1935

Fort Sumter; South Carolina; 0.78 sq km (0.3 sq mi); Civil War fortress; authorized 1948

George Washington Birthplace; Virginia; 2.2 sq km (0.8 sq mi); birthplace of the first U.S. president; established 1930

George Washington Carver; Missouri; 0.85 sq km (0.33 sq mi); birthplace and childhood home of George Washington Carver; authorized 1943

Gila Cliff Dwellings; New Mexico; 2.2 sq km (0.8 sq mi); Indian cliff dwellings; proclaimed 1907

Grand Portage; Minnesota; 2.9 sq km (1.1 sq mi); portage link to the Northwest, with reconstruction of the Grand Portage post of the North West Company; redesignated 1958

Great Sand Dunes; Colorado; 157 sq km (61 sq mi); among the highest and largest U.S. dunes; proclaimed 1932

Homestead National Monument of America; Nebraska; 0.8 sq km (0.3 sq mi); memorial to the pioneers who settled the West; authorized 1936

Hovenweep; Colorado; 3.2 sq km (1.2 sq mi); towers, pueblos, and cliff dwellings of Pre-Columbian Indians; proclaimed 1923

Lava Beds; California; 188 sq km (73 sq mi); volcanic activity formed a rugged landscape of molten rock and lava; proclaimed 1925

Little Bighorn Battlefield; Montana; 3.1 sq km (1.2 sq mi); battlefield where Gen. George Custer was defeated in 1876 by the Sioux and Cheyenne; redesignated 1946

Montezuma Castle; Arizona; 3.5 sq km (1.3 sq mi); Indian cliff dwelling; proclaimed 1906

Muir Woods; California; 2.2 sq km (0.9 sq mi); virgin stand of coastal redwoods; proclaimed 1908

Navajo; Arizona; 1.5 sq km (0.6 sq mi); Kayenta Anasazi cliff dwellings; proclaimed 1909

Oregon Caves; Oregon; 2 sq km (0.8 sq mi); cave passages and flowstone formations from groundwater dissolving marble bedrock; proclaimed 1909

Organ Pipe Cactus; Arizona; 1,338 sq km (517 sq mi); plants and animals of the Sonoran Desert; proclaimed 1937

Russell Cave; Alabama; 1.3 sq km (0.5 sq mi); archaeological site, records about 9,000 years of human habitation to 1650; proclaimed 1961

Salinas Pueblo Missions; New Mexico; 4.5 sq km (1.7 sq mi); Spanish mission churches and Pueblo Indian villages; proclaimed 1909

White Sands; New Mexico; 582 sq km (225 sq mi); gypsum sand dunes; proclaimed 1933

Wupatki; Arizona; 143 sq km (55 sq mi); Pueblo red sandstone

1.12 Chronology of Notable Natural Disasters, 1643-1999

July 5, 1643: What may be New England's first tornado is recorded by Gov. John Winthrop in Essex County, Massachusetts. Toll: one death

August 27, 1667: First recorded U.S. hurricane, in Jamestown, Virginia. Toll: unrecorded amount of property damage and deaths

July 29-31, 1715: Hurricane strikes the waters off Miami, Florida, sinking ten Spanish ships laden with millions of gold and silver pesos, gold bars, and gems en route from Havana to Spain. Toll: 1,000 deaths

November 18, 1755: Violent earthquake strikes just north of Boston. Its impact extends from Maryland's Chesapeake Bay to Nova Scotia, Canada.

June 5, 1805: The Midwest's first recorded tornado hits southern Illinois

September 10, 1811: Violent tornado whips through Charleston, South Carolina. Toll: destruction of large areas of the city and over 500 deaths

December 6, 1811-February 7, 1812: Series of earthquakes strikes the Midwest's Mississippi Valley, sending shock waves felt by two-thirds of the then United States. New lakes are created, the course of the Mississippi River is altered, landslides occur and land levels are changed. Toll: loss of 150,000 acres of timberland and farmland and the destruction of the town of New Madrid, Missouri

August 25, 1814: Tornado strikes Washington, D.C., injuring and killing British troops who were there laying siege to the city

September 23, 1815: New England is hit by a devastating hurricane known as The "Great September Gale"

July 27-28, 1819: Powerful hurricane touches down in Mobile, Alabama, destroying buildings and ships. Toll: more than 200 deaths

1824: Hurricane on St. Simons Island, Georgia floods slaves working in plantation fields. Toll: 83 deaths

August 31, 1835: Hurricane wipes out several villages in the Florida Keys. Toll: 100 deaths

May 7, 1840: In the worst storm of the pre-Civil War period, a deadly tornado hits Natchez, Mississippi, wiping out a large part of the city's residential area within five minutes. Toll: over 300 deaths, $1 million in damages and 100 injuries

September 1841: Powerful hurricane destroys the entire bayou town of St. Jo, near Apalachicola, Florida. Toll: 4,000 deaths

August 10, 1856: Hurricane submerges Dernieres Island, Louisiana. Toll: 137 deaths

1869: Hurricane hits the Northeast coast, striking hardest in Boston. Toll: 50 deaths

1871: Torrential winds spread Wisconsin logging fires across 4.25 million acres, destroying the town of Peshtigo and marking the country's greatest wildfire to date. Toll: 1,500 deaths

April 1874: In Baton Rouge, Louisiana, thawed snow and spring rains cause the Mississippi River to overflow its banks all along its valley, submerging land and people. Toll: 250 deaths

April 18, 1880: 24 tornadoes level the city of Marshfield, Missouri as they spiral across Arkansas to Wisconsin. Toll: $2 million in damages and over 100 deaths

1882: Mount Rainier erupts in the Cascade Mountains

February 9-19, 1884: A series of tornadoes rips through the Midwest from the Gulf of Mexico to Illinois. Toll: 600 deaths

August 19, 1886: Hurricane strikes Indianola, Texas, a small town on the Gulf Coast. Toll: 250 deaths and damage or destruction of almost every home in the town.

August 31, 1886: Powerful earthquake rocks Charleston, South Carolina for eight minutes. Aftershocks, felt from Boston and Milwaukee to New Orleans, are reported for a year. Toll: 100 deaths

March 12-13, 1888: Blizzard paralyzes New York City, breaking gas and water pipes and freezing its citizens. Toll: 400 deaths

May 31, 1889: In Johnstown, Pennsylvania, the world's largest earth dam at the time, the South Fork reservoir dam, breaks. A 125 feet high wall of water pours down onto the Johnstown valley, washing away several towns. Toll: 7,000 deaths

1892: Broken pipelines in a flooded Oil City, Pennsylvania cover the water with a thick layer of oil. As the oil catches fire, flames spread throughout the city, consuming every building in their wake. Toll: 130 deaths

August 27, 1893: Powerful hurricane sweeps along the coasts of Georgia and South Carolina, submerging islands and damaging cities and towns. Toll: property damage of $10 million and over 1,000 deaths

October 1, 1893: Gulf coast hurricane unleashes 13-foot high wave onto unsuspecting Port Eads, Louisiana. Toll: 2,000 deaths

May 27, 1896: Tornado hits St. Louis, Missouri, destroying a heavily populated area of the city in 20 minutes. Toll: $12 million in property damage, 2,500 injuries and 300 deaths

September 10, 1899: Earthquake strikes uninhabited Yakutat Bay, Alaska, shattering and reversing the direction of glaciers. The western shoreline of Disenchantment Bay is raised by over 47 feet in the largest vertical surface displacement caused by a single earthquake event.

September 8, 1900: Violent hurricane strikes Galveston, obliterating half of Texas's most important port city. Toll: 2,600 homes destroyed, 10,000 citizens left homeless, and 6,000 deaths

May 16-June 1, 1903: Heavy rains in the Midwest raise water levels and cause extensive flooding along the Missouri, Kansas, and Des Moines rivers. Every Missouri River bridge in Kansas City, Missouri is destroyed and the animals in the stockyards drowned. Toll: property damage of $20 million, 8,000 left homeless and 200 deaths

June 15, 1903: Violent storm in Oregon's Blue Mountains sparks a flashflood, washing away the town of Heppner. Toll: 325 deaths

April 18, 1906: Historic earthquake strikes San Francisco, collapsing buildings within a 400 square mile area. Fires caused by broken gas and electrical lines result in greatest damage, destroying three-quarters of the city including scores of landmark buildings. Toll: damages of up to $400 million, 300,000 people left homeless and over 500 deaths

September 10-21, 1909: Hurricane rages across four southeast states, devastating the town of Warrington, Florida and flooding New Orleans with waters from the Mississippi. Toll: $5 million in property damage and 350 deaths

March 1, 1910: Avalanche in the Cascade Mountains in Wellington, Washington carries three passenger trains, several carriages and the station house into a 150-foot gorge. Toll: 118 deaths

June 6, 1912: Mount Katmai erupts in eastern Alaska, the largest volcanic eruption in North America history. The explosion is heard almost 1,000 miles away and a dense cloud of ashes darkens the state. Toll: a 50-square mile valley of empty woods is transformed into the "Valley of 10,000 Smokes" (later to be used as a training ground for astronauts)

March 25-26, 1913: Severe Midwest rains cause destructive flooding. The Ohio River submerges Dayton under 13 feet of water. Toll: $100 million in damages and 500-700 deaths

August 5-25, 1915: Violent hurricane strikes Galveston, Texas. The huge seawall built after the deadly storm of 1900 holds against the waves, but the city still suffers tremendous damage. Toll: $50 million in damages and 275 deaths

March 23-27, 1917: Series of tornadoes tears through Tennessee, Kentucky, Indiana and Illinois. Toll: 211 deaths

October 12, 1918: Brush fires spread in and around Cloquet, Minnesota, consuming over 25 towns and villages. Toll: damage of $175 million and over 800 deaths

1921: Record rainfall deluges San Antonio, Texas in minutes. Toll: 51 deaths

1923: Raging fires destroy much of Berkeley, California. Toll: 24 deaths

March 18, 1925: Traveling 220 miles in three and a half hours, the fastest, longest lasting, and most destructive tornado on record rips through Missouri, Illinois and Indiana. Toll: 1,980 injuries, 689 deaths

September 18, 1926: Violent hurricane almost wipes out newly built Miami, Florida. Toll: $76 million in damages, 40,000 left homeless, 115 deaths

April 1927: In its greatest flood to date, in and around Cairo, Illinois, the Mississippi River submerges 17 million acres of farmland under water. Toll: $300 million in damages, 670,000 left homeless, 300 deaths

September 16-17, 1928: Hurricane hits south-central Florida, collapsing Lake Okeechobee's dikes and devastating the state. Toll: millions in damages and 2,500 deaths

March 21, 1932: Tornadoes rip through the South, bearing down primarily in rural central Alabama. Toll: 8,000 homeless, 1,000 injuries and 268 deaths

1932-1940: Drought and dust storms plague the Midwest, destroying farms and livelihoods and causing lung disease and starvation. Toll: millions of acres of farmland lost, 350,000 citizens forced to abandon the area and deaths in the thousands

January-February, 1935: One and a half trillion tons of rain fall over the Midwest, overflowing rivers in twelve states. Toll: 75,000 homes damaged or destroyed, over $300 million in damages and 250-900 flood-related deaths

September 2, 1935: Hurricane hits the Florida Keys. Huge waves flood the causeway, destroying the islands' rail system and isolating its citizens from the mainland. Toll: $6 million in damages and over 400 deaths

April 5-6, 1936: Tornadoes touch down in six southern states, hitting hardest in Tupelo, Mississippi and Gainesville, Georgia. Toll: $13 million in damages, 1,800 injuries and 400 deaths

September 10-22, 1938: Hurricane strikes the entire Eastern Seaboard, ravaging Long Island and putting downtown Providence, Rhode Island under 13 feet of water. Toll: $400 million in damages, 14,000 homes destroyed, 63,000 left homeless, 2,000 injuries and over 500 deaths

April 1, 1946: Seismic waves caused by an earthquake in the Aleutian Trench travel down the Pacific coast. Fifty-foot high tsunami crashes into the Hawaiian Islands. Toll: $25 million in property damages, 163 injuries, 173 deaths.

December 26, 1947: Worst blizzard in over fifty years hits New York City, stranding commuters and leaving 25.8 inches of snow on the streets of Manhattan. Toll: 77 deaths

July 1951: Storm floods the Kansas River basin in Kansas and Missouri, submerging much of Kansas City and driving hundreds of thousands of people from area homes. Toll: 850,000 acres of cropland affected, a record $1 billion in damages and 41 deaths

March 21-22, 1952: Thirty-one tornadoes hit six south-central states. Toll: $15 million in property damages, 1,400 injuries and 343 deaths

May 17, 1953: Tornado destroys downtown Waco, Texas. Toll: $39 million in damages, 114 deaths.

June 8, 1953: Several tornadoes ravage northern Ohio and southeastern Michigan, hitting hardest in Flint. Toll: over $19 million in damages, 867 injuries and 113 deaths

June 9, 1953: Devastating tornado hits Worcester, Massachusetts. Toll: $52 million in damages, 738 injuries and 62 deaths

August 25-31, 1954: Hurricane Carol strikes ten eastern states, severely damaging Newport, Rhode Island and racking up record amount of damages. Toll: $461 million in damages, 1,000 injuries and 60 deaths

October 5-18, 1954: Hurricane Hazel belts the Atlantic seaboard. Toll (from the Caribbean to Canada): $1 billion in damages and up to 1,200 deaths

August 17-19, 1955: Hurricane Diane batters the northeast from Pennsylvania to New England. It strikes a Putnam, Connecticut magnesium plant, sending exploding barrels of burning magnesium out into the streets.

Following on the heels of Hurricane Connie, Diane is the most expensive natural disaster in American history to date and leaves six eastern states declared disaster areas. Toll: $1.5 billion of damages and 310 deaths

June 27, 1957: Hurricane Audrey hits Louisiana's Gulf Coast, destroying the town of Cameron. Toll: 500 deaths

February 15-16, 1958: The worst snowfall in U.S. history blankets Allentown, Pennsylvania and the entire Northeast. Toll: $500 million in damages, 500 deaths

May 22, 1960: Twenty-foot high tsunami wave smashes into Hilo, Hawaii, sweeping garbage, sewage and mud into the city's downtown. Toll: 230 buildings collapsed, $20 million in damages and 61 deaths

March 27, 1964: 8.6 magnitude earthquake, centered in Anchorage, Alaska, is the worst in U.S. history. Landslides, rock slides and avalanches are triggered, thirty blocks of buildings in downtown Anchorage are destroyed and far-reaching tsunamis wipe out Eskimo villages along the Gulf of Eskimo and kill six people in Crescent, California. Toll: $500 million in damages and 118 deaths

April 11, 1965: Forty tornadoes and fifty thunderstorms hit fives states in the Midwest on a single day. Toll: $200 million in damages, 5,000 injuries and 271 deaths

January 18-26, 1969: Nine days of heavy rains in Los Angeles result in massive landslides. Toll: hundreds of homes destroyed, $31 million in property damages and 95 deaths

August 14-22, 1969: Hurricane Camille roars from the Gulf Coast up through the Mid-Atlantic states, bringing with it torrential rain and winds up to 200 miles per hour. Toll: $1.5 billion in damages and 225 deaths

June 9, 1972: Heavy rains cause the Canyon Lake Dam above Rapid City, South Dakota to break open. Toll: 80 city blocks and 1,200 homes destroyed, damages of $100 million and 236 deaths

June 14-23, 1972: Hurricane Agnes rages through seven Atlantic states, causing the worst flooding in the country's history. Toll: 300,000 people left homeless, $4.5 billion of damages and 100 deaths

December 2, 1972: Largest sinkhole ever reported in the United States, measuring 425 long, 350 feet wide and 150 deep, collapses near Montevallo, Alabama.

January 16, 1974: 400 foot long, 125 foot wide mudslide on the wall of Canyon Creek, Oregon sweeps a concrete relay station into the creek and fills the canyon with mud. Toll: 9 deaths

April 3-4, 1974: Over one hundred tornadoes strike thirteen midwestern states in a record eighteen hours. Toll: $500 million in damages, 5,500 injuries and 315 deaths

July 31, 1976: Flash flood raises the level of the Colorado Rockies' Big Thompson River by twenty feet, destroying bridges and highways and sweeping away visiting vacationers. Toll: 139 deaths.

January-February 1977: Buffalo, New York, buried in 35 inches of snow left by 40 days of snowfall, is hit by a four-day Canadian blizzard. Toll: 17,000 people trapped at work and 29 deaths

July 20, 1977: Heavy rainfall again floods Johnstown, Pennsylvania. Toll: 500 homes destroyed, $200 million in damages and 77 deaths

February 6, 1978: A hurricane-force blizzard roars through Massachusetts, dumping a record 27.1 inches of snow on Boston in 32 hours. Toll: millions of dollars in damages, 100,000 people left homeless and 29 deaths

April 10, 1979: Three tornadoes strike southern Oklahoma and north-central Texas, destroying 2,000 homes in Wichita Falls. Toll: $400 million in property damage, 800 injuries and 60 deaths

May 18, 1980: In Washington State's Cascade Mountains, Mount St. Helens spews 1.3 billion cubic yards of material into the atmosphere, erupting in the most violent volcanic event in the area that is now the United States in 4,500 years. 150 square miles around the volcano are flattened, rivers and valleys flooded with mud, and tons of ash and dust dumped on neighboring states. Toll: $800 million in damages, thousands of wildlife killed and 34 deaths

June 21, 1981: A massive wall of ice and rock breaks off the face of Mount Rainier in Washington State, burying mountain climbers 70 feet deep. Toll: 11 deaths

Spring/Summer 1988: Drought in mid-section of the United States. Toll: costliest devastation of farms and ranches in U.S. history

August 22-26, 1992: Hurricane Andrew strikes the coast of Florida, leaving behind massive weckage as it moves across the state to Louisiana's Gulf Coast. Toll: $20 billion in damages, 63,000 homes destroyed and over 60 deaths.

March 13-14, 1993: "Storm of the Century" hits the eastern seaboard with hurricane-force winds, freezing temperatures, massive ocean swells, and huge amounts of rain and snow, closing every major airport and wreaking havoc from Florida to New England. Toll: $3 billion in damages and 243 deaths

July-August 1993: Massive rainfall results in the flooding of 31,000 square miles of land as the Mississippi, Missouri, and other midwestern rivers reach record water levels. Toll: 20 million acres of ruined farmland, $12 billion in damages, 70,000 left homeless and 50 deaths

January 17, 1994: Earthquake measuring 6.8 hits Los Angeles, California, raising surrounding mountains by a foot and destroying nine raised highways and over 10,000 buildings in 30 seconds. Toll: 60 deaths

February 23-24, 1998: Series of tornadoes cause devastation in Central Florida, leaving residents battered and homeless. Toll: 260 injuries, 38 deaths

May 4, 1999: Tornadoes in Oklahoma and Kansas with winds recorded at 318 mph—the highest ever recorded. Toll: 30 deaths, hundreds injured, and 2,000 homes flattened

1.13 Famous American Undersea Explorers

Explorer	Main Achievements	Date
Anderson, William R.	Commanded U.S. Navy submarine Nautilus during voyage under Arctic Waters to the North Pole.	1958
Beebe, William	Descended one-half mile (0.8 kilometer) into the ocean in a bathy-sphere.	1934
Walsh, Don	Descended into the Mariana Trench with Jacques Piccard.	1960

1.14 Famous American Polar Explorers

Explorer	Main Achievements	Date
Bartlett, Robert A.	Explored Alaska, Greenland, Labrador and Siberia.	1897-1941
Byrd, Richard Evelyn	Flew over North Pole; flew over South Pole.	1926-1929
Henson, Matthew A.	Member of first expedition credited with reaching the North Pole.	1909
Perry, Robert Edwin	Led first expedition credited with reaching North Pole.	1909
Stefansson, Vilhjalmur	Explored many parts of the Arctic.	1906-1918
Wilkes, Charles	Explored the coast of Antarctica.	1840

SECTION 2

The Colonies

2.1   Chronology of the 1600s and 1700s

1607   Jamestown founded, the first permanent British settlement.
1613   The Articles of Confederation of the United Colonies of New England signed.
1620   Plymouth Colony, Massachusetts, founded; Mayflower Compact signed.
1621   Charter of the Dutch West India Company.
1622   Province of Maine granted to Sir Ferdinando Gorges and John Mason.
1626   Manhattan purchased by the Dutch from Indians.
1629   Charter of the Colony of New Plymouth granted to William Bradford
1634   Maryland founded as Catholic colony with religious tolerance.
1635   Founding of Providence, Rhode Island.
1641   Government of Rhode Island established.
1660   British parliament passed Navigation Act.
1662   Charter of Connecticut granted.
1663   Charter of Carolina granted.
1664   England took control of New Netherland and New Sweden.
1681   Philadelphia founded.
1683   William Penn signs treaty with Indians for Pennsylvania lands.
1699   French establish settlements in Mississippi and Louisiana.
1701   Charter of Privileges granted by William Penn to the inhabitants of Pennsylvania and Territories.
1725   Explanatory Charter of Massachusetts Bay.
1734   Great Awakening.
1754   Albany Plan of Union.
1763   Britain defeats France in the French and Indian War and gains control of eastern North America.
1764   Britain passes Sugar Act to tax certain goods in the colonies.
1765   Britain passes Stamp Act to tax newspapers and legal documents in the colonies.
1767   Britain passes Townsend Acts to tax glass, lead, paper and tea.
1770   American civilians killed by British troops in the Boston Massacre.
1773   Colonists stage the Boston Tea Party.
1774   The Intolerable Acts close Boston Harbor. The First Continental Congress meets.
1775   The Revolutionary War begins.
1776   Constitution of New Hampshire.
1776   Virginia Declaration of Rights.
1776   Declaration of Independence adopted. Articles of Confederation and Perpetual Union adopted.
1778   Treaties of 1778 with France.
1778   Treaty with the Delawares.
1781   Articles of Confederation.
1781   Americans defeat British at Yorktown in last battle of Revolutionary War.
1783   Treaty of Paris officially ends Revolutionary War and recognizes the U.S. as an independent nation.
1787   Northwest Ordinance.
1787   United States Constitution.
1789   Resolution of the First Congress submitting twelve amendments to the Constitution.
1794   Whiskey Rebellion.
1794   Jay Treaty.
1798   Alien and Sedition Acts.
1799   Second Great Awakening.

2.2 Mayflower Compact, 1620

The Mayflower Compact was signed by 41 of the passengers on board the Mayflower as it lay anchored in the harbor near what is now Provincetown, Massachusetts.

Agreement Between the Settlers at New Plymouth:

IN THE NAME OF GOD, AMEN. We, whose names are underwritten, the Loyal Subjects of our dread Sovereign Lord King James, by the Grace of God, of Great Britain, France, and Ireland, King, Defender of the Faith, &c. Having undertaken for the Glory of God, and Advancement of the Christian Faith, and the Honour of our King and Country, a Voyage to plant the first Colony in the northern Parts of Virginia; Do by these Presents, solemnly and mutually, in the Presence of God and one another, covenant and combine ourselves together into a civil Body Politick, for our better Ordering and Preservation, and Furtherance of the Ends aforesaid: And by Virtue hereof do enact, constitute, and frame, such just and equal Laws, Ordinances, Acts, Constitutions, and Officers, from time to time, as shall be thought most meet and convenient for the general Good of the Colony; unto which we promise all due Submission and Obedience. IN WITNESS whereof we have hereunto subscribed our names at Cape-Cod the eleventh of November, in the Reign of our Sovereign Lord King James, of England, France, and Ireland, the eighteenth, and of Scotland the fifty-fourth, Anno Domini; 1620.

Mr. John Carver	Digery Priest
Mr. William Bradford	Thomas Williams
Mr Edward Winslow	Gilbert Winslow
Mr. William Brewster	Edmund Margesson
Isaac Allerton	Peter Brown
Myles Standish	Richard Britteridge
John Alden	George Soule
John Turner	Edward Tilly
Francis Eaton	John Tilly
James Chilton	Francis Cooke
John Craxton	Thomas Rogers
John Billington	Thomas Tinker
Joses Fletcher	John Ridgdale
John Goodman	Edward Fuller
Mr. Samuel Fuller	Richard Clark
Mr. Christopher Martin	Richard Gardiner
Mr. William Mullins	Mr. John Allerton
Mr. William White	Thomas English
Mr. Richard Warren	Edward Doten
John Howland	Edward Liester
Mr. Steven Hopkins	

2.3   The Articles of Confederation of the United Colonies of New England, 1613

The Articles of Confederation between the Plantations under the Government of the Massachusetts, the Plantations under the Government of New Plymouth, the Plantations under the Government of Connecticut, and the Government of New Haven with the Plantations in Combination therewith:

1. Whereas we all came into these parts of America with one and the same end and aim, namely, to advance the Kingdom of our Lord Jesus Christ and to enjoy the liberties of the Gospel in purity with peace; and whereas in our settling (by a wise providence of God) we are further dispersed upon the sea coasts and rivers than was at first intended, so that we can not according to our desire with convenience communicate in one government and jurisdiction; and whereas we live encompassed with people of several nations and strange languages which hereafter may prove injurious to us or our posterity. And forasmuch as the natives have formerly committed sundry Insolence and outrages upon several Plantations of the English and have of late combined themselves against us: and seeing by reason of those sad distractions in England which they have heard of, and by which they know we are hindered from that humble way of seeking advice, or reaping those comfortable fruits of protection, which at other times we might well expect. We therefore do conceive it our bounded duty, without delay to enter into a present Consociation amongst ourselves, for mutual help and strength in all our future concernments: That, as in nation and religion, so in other respects, we be and continue one according to the tenor and true meaning of the ensuing articles: Wherefore it is fully agreed and concluded by and between the parties or Jurisdictions above named, and they jointly and severally do by these presents agree and conclude that they all be and henceforth be called by the name of the United Colonies of New England.

2. The said United Colonies for themselves and their posterities do jointly and severally hereby enter into a firm and perpetual league of friendship and amity for offence and defence, mutual advice and succor upon all just occasions both for preserving and propagating the truth and liberties of the Gospel and for their own mutual safety and welfare.

3. It is further agreed that the Plantations which at present are or hereafter shall be settled within the limits of the Massachusetts shall be forever under the Massachusetts and shall have peculiar jurisdiction among themselves in all cases as an entire body, and that Plymouth, Connecticut, and New Haven shall each of them have like peculiar jurisdiction and government within their limits; and in reference to the Plantations which already are settled, or shall hereafter be erected, or shall settle within their limits respectively; provided no other Jurisdiction shall hereafter be taken in as a distinct head or member of this Confederation, nor shall any other Plantation or Jurisdiction in present being, and not already in combination or under the jurisdiction of any of these Confederates, be received by any of them; nor shall any two of the Confederates join in one Jurisdiction without consent of the rest, which consent to be interpreted as is expressed in the sixth article ensuing.

4. It is by these Confederates agreed that the charge of all just wars, whether offensive or defensive, upon what part or member of this Confederation soever they fall, shall both in men, provisions and all other disbursements be borne by all the parts of this Confederation in different proportions according to their different ability in manner following, namely, that the Commissioners for each Jurisdiction from time to time, as there shall be occasion, bring a true account and number of all their males in every Plantation, or any way belonging to or under their several Jurisdictions, of what quality or condition soever they be, from sixteen years old to threescore, being inhabitants there. And that according to the different numbers which from time to time shall be found in each Jurisdiction upon a true and just account, the service of men and all charges of the war be borne by the poll: each Jurisdiction or Plantation being left to their own just course and custom of rating themselves and people according to their different estates with due respects to their qualities and exemptions amongst themselves though the Confederation take no notice of any such privilege: and that according to their different charge of each Jurisdiction and Plantation the whole advantage of the war (if it please God so to bless their endeavors) whether it be in lands, goods, or persons, shall be proportionately divided among the said Confederates.

5. It is further agreed, that if any of these Jurisdictions or any Plantation under or in combination with them, be invaded by any enemy whomsoever, upon notice and request of any three magistrates of that Jurisdiction so invaded, the rest of the Confederates without any further meeting or expostulation shall forthwith send aid to the Confederate in danger but in different proportions; namely, the Massachusetts an hundred men sufficiently armed and provided for such a service and journey, and each of the rest, forty-five so armed and provided, or any less number, if less be re-

quired according to this proportion. But if such Confederate in danger may be supplied by their next Confederates, not exceeding the number hereby agreed, they may crave help there, and seek no further for the present: the charge to be borne as in this article is expressed: and at the return to be victualled and supplied with powder and shot for their journey (if there be need) by that Jurisdiction which employed or sent for them; but none of the Jurisdictions to exceed these numbers until by a meeting of the Commissioners for this Confederation a greater aid appear necessary. And this proportion to continue till upon knowledge of greater numbers in each Jurisdiction which shall be brought to the next meeting, some other proportion be ordered. But in any such case of sending men for present aid, whether before or after such order or alteration, it is agreed that at the meeting of the Commissioners for this Confederation, the cause of such war or invasion be duly considered: and if it appear that the fault lay in the parties so invaded then that Jurisdiction or Plantation make just satisfaction, both to the invaders whom they have injured, and bear all the charges of the war themselves, without requiring any allowance from the rest of the Confederates towards the same. And further that if any Jurisdiction see any danger of invasion approaching, and there be time for a meeting, that in such a case three magistrates of the Jurisdiction may summon a meeting at such convenient place as themselves shall think meet, to consider and provide against the threatened danger; provided when they are met they may remove to what place they please; only whilst any of these four Confederates have but three magistrates in their Jurisdiction, their requests, or summons, from any two of them shall be accounted of equal force with the three mentioned in both the clauses of this article, till there be an increase of magistrates there.

6. It is also agreed, that for the managing and concluding of all Affairs and concerning the whole Confederation two Commissioners shall be chosen by and out of each of these four Jurisdictions: namely, two for the Massachusetts, two for Plymouth, two for Connecticut, and two for New Haven, being all in Church-fellowship with us, which shall bring full power from their several General Courts respectively to hear, examine, weigh, and determine all affairs of our war, or peace, leagues, aids, charges, and numbers of men for war, division of spoils and whatsoever is gotten by conquest, receiving of more Confederates for Plantations into combination with any of the Confederates, and all things of like nature, which are the proper concomitants or consequents of such a Confederation for amity, offense, and defence: not intermeddling with the government of any of the Jurisdictions, which by the third article is preserved entirely to themselves. But if these eight Commissioners when they meet shall not all agree yet it [is] concluded that any six of the eight agreeing shall have power to settle and determine the business in question. But if six do not agree, that then such propositions with their reasons so far as they have been debated, be sent and referred to the four General Courts; namely, the Massachusetts, Plymouth, Connecticut, and New Haven; and if at all the said General Courts the business so referred be concluded, then to be prosecuted by the Confederates and all their members. It is further agreed that these eight Commissioners shall meet once every year besides extraordinary meetings (according to the fifth article) to consider, treat, and conclude of all affairs belonging to this Confederation, which meeting shall ever be the first Thursday in September. And that the next meeting after the date of these presents, which shall be accounted the second meeting, shall be at Boston in the Massachusetts, the third at Hartford, the fourth at New Haven, the fifth at Plymouth, the sixth and seventh at Boston; and then Hartford, New Haven, and Plymouth, and so on course successively, if in the meantime some middle place be not found out and agreed on, which may be commodious for all the Jurisdictions.

7. It is further agreed that at each meeting of these eight Commissioners, whether ordinary or extraordinary, they or six of them agreeing as before, may choose their President out of themselves whose office work shall be to take care and direct for order and a comely carrying on of all proceedings in the present meeting: but he shall be invested with no such power or respect, as by which he shall hinder the propounding or progress of any business, or any way cast the scales otherwise than in the precedent article is agreed.

8. It is also agreed that the Commissioners for this Confederation hereafter at their meetings, whether ordinary or extraordinary, as they may have commission or opportunity, do endeavor to frame and establish agreements and orders in general cases of a civil nature, wherein all the Plantations are interested, for preserving of peace among themselves, for preventing as much as may be all occasion of war or differences with others, as about the free and speedy passage of justice in every Jurisdiction, to all the Confederates equally as to their own, receiving those that remove from one Plantation to another without due certificate, how all the Jurisdictions may carry it towards the Indians, that they neither grow insolent nor be injured without due satisfaction, lest war break in upon the Confederates through such miscarriages. It is also agreed that if any servant run away from his master into any other of these confederated Jurisdictions, that in such case, upon the ceritficate of one magistrate in the Jurisdiction out of which the said servant fled, or upon other due proof; the said servant shall be delivered, either to his master, or any other that pursues and brings such certificate or proof. And that upon the escape of any prisoner whatsoever, or fugitive for any criminal cause, whether breaking prison, or getting from the officer, or otherwise escaping, upon the certificate of two magistrates of the Jurisdiction out of which the escape is made, that he was a prisoner, or such an offender at the time of the escape, the magis-

trates, or some of them of that Jurisdiction where for the present the said prisoner or fugitive abideth, shall forthwith grant such a warrant as the case will bear, for the apprehending of any such person, and the delivery of him into the hands of the officer or other person who pursues him. And if there be help required, for the safe returning of any such offender, then it shall be granted to him that craves the same, he paying the charges thereof.

9. And for that the justest wars may be of dangerous consequence, especially to the smaller Plantations in these United Colonies, it is agreed that neither the Massachusetts, Plymouth, Connecticut, nor New Haven, nor any of the members of them, shall at any time hereafter begin, undertake, or engage themselves, or this Confederation, or any part thereof in any war whatsoever (sudden exigencies, with the necessary consequents thereof excepted), which are also to be moderated as much as the case will permit, without the consent and agreement of the forementioned eight Commissioners, or at least six of them, as in the sixth article is provided: and that no charge be required of any of the Confederates, in case of a defensive war, till the said Commissioners have met, and approved the justice of the war, and have agreed upon the sum of money to be levied, which sum is then to be paid by the several Confederates in proportion according to the fourth article.

10. That in extraordinary occasions, when meetings are summoned by three magistrates of any Jurisdiction, or two as in the fifth article, any of the Commissioners come not, due warning being given or sent, it is agreed that four of the Commissioners shall have power to direct a war which cannot be delayed, and to send for due proportions of men out of each Jurisdiction, as well as six might do if all met; but not less than six shall determine the justice of the war, or allow the demands or bills of charges, or cause any levies to be made for the same.

11. It is further agreed that if any of the Confederates shall hereafter break any of these present articles, or be any other ways injurious to any one of the other Jurisdictions; such breach of agreement or injury shall be duly considered and ordered by the Commissioners for the other Jurisdictions, that both peace and this present Confederation may be entirely preserved without violation.

12. Lastly, this perpetual Confederation, and the several articles and agreements thereof being read and seriously considered, both by the General Court for the Massachusetts, and by the Commissioners for Plymouth, Connecticut, and New Haven, were fully allowed and confirmed by three of the forenamed Confederates, namely, the Massachusetts, Connecticut, and New Haven; only the Commissioners for Plymouth having no commission to concludes desired respite until they might advise with their General Court; whereupon it was agreed and concluded by the said Court of the Massachusetts, and the Commissioners for the other two Confederates, that, if Plymouth consent, then the whole treaty as it stands in these present articles is, and shall continue, firm and stable without alteration: but if Plymouth come not in yet the other three Confederates do by these presents confirm the whole Confederation, and all the articles thereof; only in September next when the second meeting of the Commissioners is to be at Boston, new consideration may be taken of the sixth article, which concerns number of Commissioners for meeting and concluding the affairs of this Confederation to the satisfaction of the Court of the Massachusetts, and the Commissioners for the other two Confederates, but the rest to stand unquestioned. In testimony whereof, the General Court of the Massachusetts by their Secretary, and the Commissioners for Connecticut and New Haven, have subscribed these present articles of this nineteenth of the third month, commonly called May, Anno Domini 1643.

At a meeting of the Commissioners for the Confederation held at Boston the 7th of September, it appearing that the General Court of New Plymouth and the several townships thereof have read, considered, and approved these Articles of Confederation, as appeareth by commission of their General Court bearing date the 29th of August, 1643, to Mr. Edward Winslow and Mr. William Collier to ratify and confirm the same on their behalf: we therefore, the Commissioners for the Massachusetts, Connecticut, and New Haven, do also from our several Governments subscribe unto them.

2.4   Colonies and Founders

Colony	Founder	Date Founded
Roanoke	Sir Walter Raleigh	1585
Virginia	John Smith	1607
Plymouth	William Bradford	1620
New York	Peter Minuit	1626
Massachusetts Bay	John Winthrop	1630
New Hampshire	John Mason	1630
Maryland	George Calvert	1634
Connecticut	Thomas Hooker	1636
Rhode Island	Roger Williams	1636
Delaware	Peter Minuit	1638
North Carolina	Group of proprietors	1653
New Jersey	Lord Berkeley	1660
South Carolina	Group of proprietors	1670
Pennsylvania	William Penn	1682
Georgia	James Oglethorpe	1733

2.5   Colonial Capitals

Colony	Capital
Virginia	Jamestown (1607-1699) Williamsburg (1699-1776)
Plymouth	Plymouth (1620-1691)
New Netherlands	New Amsterdam (1626-1664)
Massachusetts Bay	Boston (1630-1776)
Maryland	St. Marys (1632-1694) Annapolis (1694-1776)
Rhode Island (and Providence Plantation)	Providence (1636-1776)
Connecticut	Hartford (1636-1776)
New Haven	New Haven (1638-1664)
New Sweden	Fort Christina (1638-1655)
New York	New York (1664-1776)
East New Jersey	Elizabeth (1668-1683) Perth Amboy (1683-1702)
West New Jersey	Elizabeth (1674-1683) Burlington (1683-1702)
New Jersey	Elizabeth (1668-1674) Perth Amboy & Burlington (1702-1776)
Carolina	Albemarle (1663-1670) Charleston (1670-1729)
North Carolina	Albermarle (1729-1746) New Bern (1746-1776)
South Carolina	Charleston (1729-1776)
Pennsylvania	Philadelphia (1682-1776)
Delaware	New Castle (1704-1776)
New Hampshire	Portsmouth (1679-1776)
Georgia	Savannah (1733-1776)
East Florida	St. Augustine (1762-1783)
West Florida	Pensacola (1762-1781)

2.6   Colonial Cities

City	Year Founded	Location	Founding Country
San Miguel	1526	North Carolina	Spain
Charlesfort	1562	South Carolina	France
St. Augustine	1565	Florida	Spain
Guale	1566	Georgia	Spain
Roanoke	1585	North Carolina	England
Jamestown	1607	Virginia	England
Fort St. George	1607	Maine	England
Santa Fé	1609	New Mexico	Spain
Plymouth	1620	Massachusetts	England
Fort Nassau	1623	New York	Netherlands
Fort Orange (Albany)	1624	New York	Netherlands
New Amsterdam (New York)	1626	New York	Netherlands
Naumkeag (Salem)	1626	Massachusetts	England
Boston	1630	Massachusetts	England
St. Mary's	1634	Maryland	England
Saybrook (Old Saybrook)	1635	Connecticut	England
Providence	1636	Rhode Island	England
Hartford	1636	Connecticut	England
New Haven	1638	Connecticut	England
Fort Christina (Wilmington)	1638	Pennsylvania	Sweden
Newport	1639	Rhode Island	England
Tinicum Island	1643	Pennsylvania	Sweden
Breukelen (Brooklyn)	1646	New York	Netherlands
Providence (Annapolis)	1649	Maryland	England
New Amstel (New Castle)	1651	Delaware	Netherlands
Fort Niagra	1668	New York	France
Charles Town (Charleston)	1670	South Carolina	England
Philadelphia	1682	Pennsylvania	England
Pensacola	1698	Florida	Spain
Williamsburg	1699	Virginia	England
Biloxi	1699	Mississippi	France
Fort Détroit (Detroit)	1701	Michigan	France
Fort Condé	1711	Alabama	France
New Orleans	1718	Louisiana	France
San Antonio	1718	Texas	Spain
Savannah	1733	Georgia	England
Augusta	1736	Georgia	England
Alexandria	1749	Virginia	England
Fort Duquesne	1754	Pennsylvania	France
Pittsburgh	1763	Pennsylvania	England
St. Louis	1764	Missouri	France
San Diego	1769	California	Spain
Monterey	1770	California	Spain
San Gabriel (Los Angeles)	1771	California	Spain
San Francisco	1776	California	Spain
Tucson	1776	Arizona	Spain
Fort Ross	1812	California	Russia

2.7   Population of the Colonies in 1700

The best estimates of the population of the English colonies in 1700 are as follows:

New Hampshire	10,000
Massachusetts Bay	80,000
Rhode Island	10,000
Connecticut	30,000
Total New England	**130,000**
New York	30,000
New Jersey	15,000
Pennsylvania and Delaware	20,000
Total Middle Colonies	**65,000**
Maryland	32,258
Virginia	55,000
Total Chesapeake Colonies	**87,258**
North Carolina	5,000
South Carolina	7,000
Total The Carolinas	**12,000**
Jamaica[1]	50,000
Barbados[2]	71,000
Total West Indies	**121,000**

[1] Of this number, only 5,000 were white.
[2] Probably 60,000 of these were slaves. There must have been some 2,000 more English and 10,000 more slaves in the Leeward Islands, but no figures are available.
Source: Samuel Eliot Morison, *The Oxford History of the American People,* New York: Oxford University Press, 1965.

2.8   Colonial Population Estimates, 1610-1800

Year	Population	Year	Population
1610	350	1710	331,700
1620	2,300	1720	466,200
1630	4,600	1730	629,400
1640	26,600	1740	905,600
1650	50,400	1750	1,170,800
1660	75,100	1760	1,593,600
1670	111,900	1770	2,148,100
1680	151,500	1780	2,780,400
1690	210,400	1790	3,929,214
1700	250,900	1800	5,308,483

2.9   Largest U.S. Cities in 1790

Philadelphia	42,444
New York	33,131
Boston	18,038
Charlestown	16,359
Baltimore	13,503
Salem	7,921
Newport	6,716

2.10   Slave Population in 1790

New Hampshire	157
Rhode Island	958
Connecticut	2,648
New York	21,193
New Jersey	11,423
Pennsylvania	3,707
Delaware	8,887
Maryland	103,036
Virginia	292,627
North Carolina	100,783
South Carolina	107,094
Georgia	29,264
Kentucky	12,430
Southwest Territory	3,417
UNITED STATES	697,624

2.11 Chronology of Slavery in the Colonies

1440s   Portuguese begin to capture Africans off the coast of Mauritania and the Sengambia region.

1619   First Africans are brought to English colonies, to Jamestown, Virginia.

1626   New Amsterdam is founded by the Dutch. Eleven Africans, all indentured servants, are among the settlers.

1638   The New England slave trade begins in Boston Massachusetts.

1641   Jonathan Winthrop records first documented baptism of a slave in New England.

1660   Charles II of England urges the Council for Foreign Plantations to christianize slaves.

1661   Black Codes give statutory recognition to the institution of slavery in the colony of Virginia.

1667   Virginia Assembly passes a law denying that baptism grants worldly freedom to slaves.

1680s   Colonial governors in North America are instructed by England to convert slaves and Indians to Christianity.

1688   Members of the Society of Friends (Quakers) protest slavery in Germantown, Pennsylvania.

1693   Society of Negroes is founded in Boston, Massachusetts.

1694   A group of ministers attempts to persuade the court of Massachusetts to pass a bill permitting slave holders to retain baptized slaves.

1700   More than 100,000 slaves are at work on plantations in the West Indies.

1700s   Many North American slave holders fear that christianizing their slaves will lead to rebellion.

1706   Puritan leader Cotton Mather publishes *The Negro Christianized,* arguing that blacks are, indeed, human. He writes, "Man, Thy Negro is thy Neighbor."

1712   Slave insurrection in New York City.

1750s-early 1800s. Small, independent, black congregations begin to emerge in the south, the first gatherings of slaves in the area.

1775   A group of Quakers organize the first Abolition Society in Philadelphia.

1777   Slavery is abolished in Vermont.

1778   Virginia prohibits external slave trade.

1778   Pennsylvania passes a law that allows for the gradual abolition of slavery.

1780-1810   Almost as many slaves are brought into the Unites States as had been brought in over the previous 160 years.

1783   Slavery abolished in Massachusetts.

1784   "The Christmas Conference" of the Methodist Church passes a resolution against slave holding.

1790   Slave population in U.S. reaches 700,000.

1799   Second Great Awakening begins with the Cane Ridge camp meeting. Many slaves convert to Christianity.

2.12   Chronology of the Life of Jonathan Edwards

*Perhaps the greatest of all the Puritan theologians and one of America's first notable philosophers,
Jonathan Edwards produced a significant number of works while carrying on the duties of a New England
minister, as this chronology demonstrates.*

1703   Born October 5, at East Windsor, Connecticut.

1716-20   Undergraduate at Yale College.

1720-22   Studies theology and earns MA from Yale.

1722-23   Ministers in a Presbyterian Church in New York and begins writing his "Diary," "Resolutions,"
            "Miscellanies," and completes "The Mind."

1724-26   Tutors at Yale.

1726   Becomes Associate Minister in Northampton, Massachusetts, under his grandfather, Solomon
            Stoddard.

1727   Marries Sarah Pierpont.

1729   Becomes full pastor of the First Church of Northampton upon the death of Solomon Stoddard.

1734   Revival breaks out in Northampton with Edwards' "Justification by Faith."

1737   Edwards publishes "A Faithful Narrative of the Surprising Work of God," defending the revival.

1740   The Great Awakening gathers momentum. Whitefield first visits New England.

1741   Edwards preaches "Sinners in the Hands of an Angry God" in Enfield, Connecticut.

1746   Edwards writes "A Treatise Concerning Religious Affections."

1750   Edwards is dismissed as pastor of the Church in Northampton by a 20-2 margin.

1751   Edwards becomes pastor and missionary to the Indians in Stockbridge, Massachusetts. While in
            Stockbridge, Edwards does some of his greatest writing, including "Freedom of the Will," "Con-
            cerning the End for Which God Created the World," "The Nature of True Virtue," and "Original
            Sin."

1758   Edwards accepts the Presidency of the College of New Jersey (Princeton) in January, and dies of
            a smallpox inoculation on March 22.

2.13 Edwards' "Sinners in the Hands of an Angry God," 1741

Excerpts from Jonathan Edwards' sermon, "Sinners in the Hands of an Angry God," delivered in 1741 in Enfield, Connecticut.

-Their foot shall slide in due time- Deut. xxxii. 35

In this verse is threatened the vengeance of God on the wicked unbelieving Israelites, who were God's visible people, and who lived under the means of grace; but who, notwithstanding all God's wonderful works towards them, remained (as ver. 28.) void of counsel, having no understanding in them. Under all the cultivations of heaven, they brought forth bitter and poisonous fruit; as in the two verses next preceding the text. The expression I have chosen for my text, Their foot shall slide in due time, seems to imply the following doings, relating to the punishment and destruction to which these wicked Israelites were exposed. . . .

The observation from the words that I would now insist upon is this. "There is nothing that keeps wicked men at any one moment out of hell, but the mere pleasure of God." By the mere pleasure of God, I mean his sovereign pleasure, his arbitrary will, restrained by no obligation, hindered by no manner of difficulty, any more than if nothing else but God's mere will had in the least degree, or in any respect whatsoever, any hand in the preservation of wicked men one moment.

So that, whatever some have imagined and pretended about promises made to natural men's earnest seeking and knocking, it is plain and manifest, that whatever pains a natural man takes in religion, whatever prayers he makes, till he believes in Christ, God is under no manner of obligation to keep him a moment from eternal destruction.

So that, thus it is that natural men are held in the hand of God, over the pit of hell; they have deserved the fiery pit, and are already sentenced to it; and God is dreadfully provoked, his anger is as great towards them as to those that are actually suffering the executions of the fierceness of his wrath in hell, and they have done nothing in the least to appease or abate that anger, neither is God in the least bound by any promise to hold them up one moment; the devil is waiting for them, hell is gaping for them, the flames gather and flash about them, and would fain lay hold on them, and swallow them up; the fire pent up in their own hearts is struggling to break out; and they have no interest in any Mediator, there are no means within reach that can be any security to them. In short, they have no refuge, nothing to take hold of, all that preserves them every moment is the mere arbitrary will, and uncovenanted, unobliged forbearance of an incensed God.

The use of this awful subject may be for awakening unconverted persons in this congregation. This that you have heard is the case of every one of you that are out of Christ. That world of misery, that lake of burning brimstone, is extended abroad under you. There is the dreadful pit of the glowing flames of the wrath of God; there is hell's wide gaping mouth open; and you have nothing to stand upon, nor any thing to take hold of, there is nothing between you and hell but the air; it is only the power and mere pleasure of God that holds you up.

You probably are not sensible of this; you find you are kept out of hell, but do not see the hand of God in it; but look at other things, as the good state of your bodily constitution, your care of your own life, and the means you use for your own preservation. But indeed these things are nothing; if God should withdraw his hand, they would avail no more to keep you from falling, than the thin air to hold up a person that is suspended in it.

Your wickedness makes you as it were heavy as lead, and to tend downwards with great weight and pressure towards hell; and if God should let you go, you would immediately sink and swiftly descend and plunge into the bottomless gulf, and your healthy constitution, and your own care and prudence, and best contrivance, and all your righteousness, would have no more influence to uphold you and keep you out of hell, than a spider's web would have to stop a falling rock. Were it not for the sovereign pleasure of God, the earth would not bear you one moment; for you are a burden to it; the creation groans with you; the creature is made subject to the bondage of your corruption, not willingly; the sun does not willingly shine upon you to give you light to serve sin and Satan; the earth does not willingly yield her increase to satisfy your lusts; nor is it willingly a stage for your wickedness to be acted upon; the air does not willingly serve you for breath to maintain the flame of life in your vitals, while you spend your life in the service of God's enemies. God's creatures are good, and were made for men to serve God with, and do not willingly subserve to any other purpose, and groan when they are abused to purposes so directly contrary to their nature and end. And the world would spew you out, were it not for the sovereign hand of him who hath subjected it in hope. There are black clouds of God's wrath now hanging directly over your heads, full of the dreadful storm, and big with thunder; and were it not for the restraining hand of God, it would immediately burst forth upon you. The sovereign pleasure of God, for the present, stays his rough wind; otherwise it would come with fury, and your destruction would come like a whirlwind, and you would be like the chaff of the summer threshing floor.

The wrath of God is like great waters that are dammed for the present; they increase more and more, and rise higher and higher, till an outlet is given; and the longer the stream is stopped, the more rapid and mighty is its course, when once it is let loose. It is true, that judgment against your evil works has not been executed hitherto; the floods of God's vengeance have been withheld; but your guilt in the mean time is constantly increasing, and you are every day treasuring up more wrath; the waters are constantly rising, and waxing more and more mighty; and there is nothing but the mere pleasure of God, that holds the waters back, that are unwilling to be stopped, and press hard to go forward. If God should only withdraw his hand from the flood-gate, it would immediately fly open, and the fiery floods of the fierceness and wrath of God, would rush forth with inconceivable fury, and would come upon you with omnipotent power; and if your strength were ten thousand times greater than it is, yea, ten thousand times greater than the strength of the stoutest, sturdiest devil in hell, it would be nothing to withstand or endure it.

The bow of God's wrath is bent, and the arrow made ready on the string, and justice bends the arrow at your heart, and strains the bow, and it is nothing but the mere pleasure of God, and that of an angry God, without any promise or obligation at all, that keeps the arrow one moment from being made drunk with your blood. Thus all you that never passed under a great change of heart, by the mighty power of the Spirit of God upon your souls; all you that were never born again, and made new creatures, and raised from being dead in sin, to a state of new, and before altogether unexperienced light and life, are in the hands of an angry God. However you may have reformed your life in many things, and may have had religious affections, and may keep up a form of religion in your families and closets, and in the house of God, it is nothing but his mere pleasure that keeps you from being this moment swallowed up in everlasting destruction. However unconvinced you may now be of the truth of what you hear, by and by you will be fully convinced of it. Those that are gone from being in the like circumstances with you, see that it was so with them; for destruction came suddenly upon most of them; when they expected nothing of it, and while they were saying, Peace and safety: now they see, that those things on which they depended for peace and safety, were nothing but thin air and empty shadows.

The God that holds you over the pit of hell, much as one holds a spider, or some loathsome insect over the fire, abhors you, and is dreadfully provoked: his wrath towards you burns like fire; he looks upon you as worthy of nothing else, but to be cast into the fire; he is of purer eyes than to bear to have you in his sight; you are ten thousand times more abominable in his eyes, than the most hateful venomous serpent is in ours. You have offended him infinitely more than ever a stubborn rebel did his prince; and yet it is nothing but his hand that holds you from falling into the fire every moment. It is to be ascribed to nothing else, that you did not go to hell the last night; that you were suffered to awake again in this world, after you closed your eyes to sleep. And there is no other reason to be given, why you have not dropped into hell since you arose in the morning, but that God's hand has held you up. There is no other reason to be given why you have not gone to hell, since you have sat here in the house of God, provoking his pure eyes by your sinful wicked manner of attending his solemn worship. Yea, there is nothing else that is to be given as a reason why you do not this very moment drop down into hell.

O sinner! Consider the fearful danger you are in: it is a great furnace of wrath, a wide and bottomless pit, full of the fire of wrath, that you are held over in the hand of that God, whose wrath is provoked and incensed as much against you, as against many of the damned in hell. You hang by a slender thread, with the flames of divine wrath flashing about it, and ready every moment to singe it, and burn it asunder; and you have no interest in any Mediator, and nothing to lay hold of to save yourself, nothing to keep off the flames of wrath, nothing of your own, nothing that you ever have done, nothing that you can do, to induce God to spare you one moment. . . .

And now you have an extraordinary opportunity, a day wherein Christ has thrown the door of mercy wide open, and stands in calling and crying with a loud voice to poor sinners; a day wherein many are flocking to him, and pressing into the kingdom of God. Many are daily coming from the east, west, north and south; many that were very lately in the same miserable condition that you are in, are now in a happy state, with their hearts filled with love to him who has loved them, and washed them from their sins in his own blood, and rejoicing in hope of the glory of God. How awful is it to be left behind at such a day! To see so many others feasting, while you are pining and perishing! To see so many rejoicing and singing for joy of heart, while you have cause to mourn for sorrow of heart, and howl for vexation of spirit! How can you rest one moment in such a condition? Are not your souls as precious as the souls of the people at Suffield*, where they are flocking from day to day to Christ?

Are there not many here who have lived long in the world, and are not to this day born again? And so are aliens from the commonwealth of Israel, and have done nothing ever since they have lived, but treasure up wrath against the day of wrath? Oh, sirs, your case, in an especial manner, is extremely dangerous. Your guilt and hardness of heart is extremely great. Do you not see how generally persons of your years are passed over and left, in the present remarkable and wonderful dispensation of God's mercy? You had need to consider yourselves, and awake thoroughly out of sleep. You cannot bear the fierceness and wrath of the infinite God. And you, young men, and young women, will you neglect this precious season which you now enjoy, when so many others of your age are renouncing all youthful vanities, and flocking to Christ? You especially have now an extraordinary opportunity; but if you neglect it, it will soon be with you as with those persons who spent all the precious days of youth in sin, and are now come to such a dreadful pass in blindness and hardness. And you, children, who are unconverted, do not you know that you are going down to hell, to bear the dreadful wrath of that God, who is now angry with you every day and every night? Will you be content to be the children of the devil, when so many other children in the land are converted, and are become the holy and happy children of the King of kings?

And let every one that is yet out of Christ, and hanging over the pit of hell, whether they be old men and women, or middle aged, or young people, or little children, now harken to the loud calls of God's word and providence. This acceptable year of the Lord, a day of such great favours to some, will doubtless be a day of as remarkable vengeance to others. Men's hearts harden, and their guilt increases apace at such a day as this, if they neglect their souls; and never was there so great danger of such persons being given up to hardness of heart and blindness of mind. God seems now to be hastily gathering in his elect in all parts of the land; and probably the greater part of adult persons that ever shall be saved, will be brought in now in a little time, and that it will be as it was on the great out-pouring of the Spirit upon the Jews in the apostles' days; the election will obtain, and the rest will be blinded. If this should be the case with you, you will eternally curse this day, and will curse the day that ever you were born, to see such a season of the pouring out of God's Spirit, and will wish that you had died and gone to hell before you had seen it. Now undoubtedly it is, as it was in the days of John the Baptist, the axe is in an extraordinary manner laid at the root of the trees, that every tree which brings not forth good fruit, may be hewn down and cast into the fire.

Therefore, let every one that is out of Christ, now awake and fly from the wrath to come. The wrath of Almighty God is now undoubtedly hanging over a great part of this congregation: Let every one fly out of Sodom: "Haste and escape for your lives, look not behind you, escape to the mountain, lest you be consumed."

* A town in the neighborhood.

SECTION 3

American Revolution and the New Nation

3.1   Chronology of the American Revolution, 1764-1788

<u>1764</u>

Sugar Act. Parliament, desiring revenue from its North American colonies, passed the first law specifically aimed at raising colonial money for the Crown. The act increased duties on non-British goods shipped to the colonies.

Currency Act. This act prohibited American colonies from issuing their own currency, angering many American colonists.

Beginnings of Colonial Opposition. American colonists responded to the Sugar Act and the Currency Act with protest. In Massachusetts, participants in a town meeting cried out against taxation without proper representation in Parliament, and suggested some form of united protest throughout the colonies. By the end of the year, many colonies were practicing nonimportation, a refusal to use imported English goods.

<u>1765</u>

Quartering Act. The British further angered American colonists with the Quartering Act, which required the colonies to provide barracks and supplies to British troops.

Stamp Act. Parliament's first direct tax on the American colonies, this act, like those passed in 1764, was enacted to raise money for Britain. It taxed newspapers, almanacs, pamphlets, broadsides, legal documents, dice, and playing cards. Issued by Britain, the stamps were affixed to documents or packages to show that the tax had been paid.

Organized Colonial Protest. American colonists responded to Parliament's acts with organized protest. Throughout the colonies, a network of secret organizations known as the Sons of Liberty was created, aimed at intimidating the stamp agents who collected Parliament's taxes. Before the Stamp Act could even take effect, all the appointed stamp agents in the colonies had resigned.

  The Massachusetts Assembly suggested a meeting of all the colonies to work for the repeal of the Stamp Act. All but four colonies were represented. The Stamp Act Congress passed a "Declaration of Rights and Grievances," which claimed that American colonists were equal to all other British citizens, protested taxation without representation, and stated that, without colonial representation in Parliament, it could not tax colonists. In addition, the colonists increased their nonimportation efforts.

<u>1766</u>

Repeal of the Stamp Act. Although some in Parliament thought the army should be used to enforce the Stamp Act (1765), others commended the colonists for resisting a tax passed by a legislative body in which they were not represented. The act was repealed, and the colonies abandoned their ban on imported British goods.

Declaratory Act. The repeal of the Stamp Act did not mean that Great Britain was surrendering any control over its colonies. The Declaratory Act, passed by Parliament on the same day the Stamp Act was repealed, stated that Parliament could make laws binding the American colonies "in all cases whatsoever."

Resistance to the Quartering Act in New York. New York served as headquarters for British troops in America, so the Quartering Act (1765) had a great impact on New York City. When the New York Assembly refused to assist in quartering troops, a skirmish occurred in which one colonist was wounded. Parliament suspended the Assembly's powers but never carried out the suspension, since the Assembly soon agreed to contribute money toward the quartering of troops.

<u>1767</u>

Townshend Acts. To help pay the expenses involved in governing the American colonies, Parliament passed the Townshend Acts, which initiated taxes on glass, lead, paint, paper, and tea.

Nonimportation. In response to new taxes, the colonies again decided to discourage the purchase of British imports.

"Letters from a Farmer in Pennsylvania to the Inhabitants of the British Colonies." Originally published in a newspaper, this widely reproduced pamphlet by John Dickinson declared that Parliament could not tax the colonies, called the Townshend Acts unconstitutional, and denounced the suspension of the New York Assembly as a threat to colonial liberties.

1768

Massachusetts Circular Letter. Samuel Adams wrote a statement, approved by the Massachusetts House of Representatives, which attacked Parliament's persistence in taxing the colonies without proper representation, and which called for unified resistance by all the colonies. Many colonies issued similar statements. In response, the British governor of Massachusetts dissolved the state's legislature.

British Troops Arrive in Boston. Although the Sons of Liberty threatened armed resistance to arriving British troops, none was offered when the troops stationed themselves in Boston.

1769

Virginia's Resolutions. The Virginia House of Burgesses passed resolutions condemning Britain's actions against Massachusetts, and stating that only Virginia's governor and legislature could tax its citizens. The members also drafted a formal letter to the King, completing it just before the legislature was dissolved by Virginia's royal governor.

1770

Townshend Acts Cut Back. Because of the reduced profits resulting from the colonial boycott of imported British goods, Parliament withdrew all of the Townshend Acts (1767) taxes except for the tax on tea.

An End to Nonimportation. In response to Parliament's relaxation of its taxation laws, the colonies relaxed their boycott of British imported goods (1767).

Conflict between Citizens and British Troops in New York. After a leading New York Son of Liberty issued a broadside attacking the New York Assembly for complying with the Quartering Act (1765), a riot erupted between citizens and soldiers, resulting in serious wounds but no fatalities.

Boston Massacre. The arrival of troops in Boston provoked conflict between citizens and soldiers. On March 5, a group of soldiers surrounded by an unfriendly crowd opened fire, killing three Americans and fatally wounding two more. A violent uprising was avoided only with the withdrawal of the troops to islands in the harbor. The soldiers were tried for murder, but convicted only of lesser crimes; noted patriot John Adams was their principal lawyer.

1772

Attack on the "Gaspee." After several boatloads of men attacked a grounded British customs schooner near Providence, Rhode Island, the royal governor offered a reward for the discovery of the men, planning to send them to England for trial. The removal of the "Gaspee" trial to England outraged American colonists.

Committees of Correspondence. Samuel Adams called for a Boston town meeting to create committees of correspondence to communicate Boston's position to the other colonies. Similar committees were soon created throughout the colonies.

1773

Tea Act. By reducing the tax on imported British tea, this act gave British merchants an unfair advantage in selling their tea in America. American colonists condemned the act, and many planned to boycott tea.

Boston Tea Party. When British tea ships arrived in Boston harbor, many citizens wanted the tea sent back to England without the payment of any taxes. The royal governor insisted on payment of all taxes. On December 16, a group of men disguised as American Indians boarded the ships and dumped all the tea in the harbor.

1774

Coercive Acts. In response to the Boston Tea Party, Parliament passed several acts to punish Massachusetts. The Boston Port Bill banned the loading or unloading of any ships in Boston harbor. The Administration of Justice Act offered protection to royal officials in Massachusetts, allowing them to transfer to England all court cases against them involving riot suppression or revenue collection. The Massachusetts Government Act put the election of most government officials under the control of the Crown, essentially eliminating the Massachusetts charter of government.

Quartering Act. Parliament broadened its previous Quartering Act (1765). British troops could now be quartered in any occupied dwelling.

The Colonies Organize Protest. To protest Britain's actions, Massachusetts suggested a return to nonimportation, but several states preferred a congress of all the colonies to discuss united resistance. The colonies soon named delegates to a congress—the First Continental Congress—to meet in Philadelphia on September 5.

First Continental Congress. Twelve of the thirteen colonies sent a total of fifty-six delegates to the First Continental Congress. Only Georgia was not represented. One accomplishment of the Congress was the Association of 1774, which urged all colonists to avoid using British goods, and to form committees to enforce this ban.

New England Prepares for War. British troops began to fortify Boston, and seized ammunition belonging to the colony of Massachusetts. Thousands of American militiamen were ready to resist, but no fighting occurred. Massachusetts created a Provincial Congress, and a special Committee of Safety to decide when the militia should be called into action. Special groups of militia, known as Minute Men, were organized to be ready for instant action.

1775

New England Restraining Act. Parliament passed an act banning trade between the New England colonies and any other country besides Great Britain.

New England Resists. British troops continued to attempt to seize colonial ammunition, but were turned back in Massachusetts, without any violence. Royal authorities decided that force should be used to enforce recent acts of Parliament; war seemed unavoidable.

Lexington and Concord. British troops planned to destroy American ammunition at Concord. When the Boston Committee of Safety learned of this plan, it sent Paul Revere and William Dawes to alert the countryside and gather the Minute Men. On April 19, Minute Men and British troops met at Lexington, where a shot from a stray British gun lead to more British firing. The Americans only fired a few shots; several Americans were killed. The British marched on to Concord and destroyed some ammunition, but soon found the countryside swarming with militia. At the end of the day, many were dead on both sides.

Second Continental Congress. The Second Continental Congress convened in Philadelphia on May 10. John Hancock was elected president of Congress.

George Washington Is Named Commander-In-Chief. On June 10, John Adams proposed that Congress consider the forces in Boston a continental army, and suggested the need for a general. He recommended George Washington for the position. Congress began to raise men from other colonies to join the army in New England, and named a committee to draft military rules. On June 15, Washington was nominated to lead the army; he accepted the next day. To pay for the army, Congress issued bills of credit, and the twelve colonies represented in the Congress promised to share in repaying the bills.

Bunker Hill. On June 12, British General Gage put martial law in effect, and stated that any person helping the Americans would be considered a traitor and rebel. When Americans began to fortify a hill against British forces, British ships in the harbor discovered the activity and opened fire. British troops—2,400 in number—arrived shortly after. Although the Americans—1,000 in number—resisted several attacks, eventually they lost the fortification.

Olive Branch Petition. Congress issued a petition declaring its loyalty to the king, George III, and stating its hope that he would help arrange a reconciliation and prevent further hostilities against the colonies. Four months later, King George III rejected the petition and declared the colonies in rebellion.

Congress Treats with the Indians. Acting as an independent government, Congress appointed commissioners to create peace treaties with the Indians.

Congress Creates a Navy. Congress began to plan for aggressive action against British ships stocked with ammunition. It authorized the building of four armed ships, and began to formulate rules for a navy. On December 22, Congress named Esek Hopkins commodore of the fledgling American navy. Soon after, Congress authorized privateering, and issued rules for dealing with enemy vessels and plunder.

Congress Searches for Foreign Aid. When a congressional committee began to investigate the possibility of foreign aid in the war against Great Britain, France expressed interest.

1776

"Common Sense." Thomas Paine moved many to the cause of independence with his pamphlet titled "Common Sense." In a direct, simple style, he cried out against King George III and the monarchical form of government.

The British Evacuate Boston. American General Henry Knox arrived in Boston with cannons he had moved with great difficulty from Fort Ticonderoga, New York. Americans began to entrench themselves around Boston, planning to attack the British. British General William Howe planned an attack, but eventually retreated from Boston.

Congress Authorizes the Colonies to Write Constitutions. In May, the Second Continental Congress adopted a resolution authorizing the colonies to adopt new constitutions; the former colonial governments had dissolved with the outbreak of war.

Congress Declares Independence. When North Carolina and Virginia empowered their delegates to vote for American independence, Virginian Richard Henry Lee offered a resolution stating that the colonies "are, and of right ought to be, free and independent States." A committee was appointed to draft a declaration of independence, and Thomas Jefferson was chosen to write it. On July 2, Congress voted in favor of independence, and on July 4, the Declaration of Independence was approved. Copies were sent throughout the colonies to be read publicly.

Battle of Long Island. After leaving Boston, British General Howe planned to use New York as a base. The British captured Staten Island and began a military build-up on Long Island in preparation for an advance on Brooklyn. Washington succeeded in saving his army by secretly retreating onto Manhattan Island. Washington eventually retreated from Manhattan, fearing the prospect of being trapped on the island, and the British occupied New York City.

Congress Names Commissioners to Treat with Foreign Nations. Congress sent a delegation of three men to Europe—Silas Deane, Benjamin Franklin, and Arthur Lee—to prepare treaties of commerce and friendship, and to attempt to secure loans from foreign nations.

The Battle of White Plains. British and American forces met at White Plains, New York, where the British captured an important fortification. Washington once again retreated, still attempting to save his army from the full force of the British army.

Retreat through New Jersey. Washington and his army retreated across New Jersey, crossing the Delaware River into Pennsylvania. Congress, fearing a British attack on Philadelphia, fled to Baltimore.

Battle of Trenton. On December 26, Washington launched a surprise attack against a British fortification at Trenton, New Jersey, that was staffed by Hessian soldiers. After one hour of confused fighting, the Hessians surrendered. Only five American soldiers were killed.

1777

Battle of Princeton. British General Howe reacted to the Battle of Trenton by sending a large force of men to New Jersey. At Princeton, Washington once again launched a surprise attack, and succeeded in defeating the British. His efforts cleared most of New Jersey of enemy forces, and greatly boosted American morale.

American Flag. On June 14, Congress declared that the flag of the United States would consist of thirteen alternating red and white stripes, and a blue field with thirteen white stars.

The British Attack Philadelphia. British and Americans met at Brandywine Creek, Pennsylvania. The Americans retreated, and the British soon occupied Philadelphia, forcing Congress once again to flee the city. After retreating further during the Battle of Germantown, Washington settled his army for the winter in Valley Forge—a winter of extreme cold and great hunger.

Saratoga. On October 7, British and American troops engaged in New York. Fatigued from battle and short of supplies, British General John Burgoyne's troops were repulsed by American forces under General Horatio Gates. On October 8, Burgoyne retreated to Saratoga; by October 13th, he asked for terms of surrender. The "Convention of Saratoga" called for Burgoyne's army to be sent back to England, and for each soldier to pledge not to serve again in the war against the colonies.

The "Conway Cabal." Many in Congress were unhappy with Washington's leadership; some murmured the name of General Horatio Gates as a possible replacement. Thomas Conway, the army's inspector general, wrote a critical letter to Gates about Washington, leading many to believe there was an organized effort to replace Washington. Conway resigned from the army, and eventually apologized to Washington.

Articles of Confederation. When Richard Henry Lee made a motion for independence (1776), he also proposed a formal plan of union among the states. After a discussion lasting more than a year, the Articles of Confederation were adopted by Congress, although the states did not ratify the Articles until 1781.

1778

France and America Become Allies. France and America formed an alliance, negotiated by Benjamin Franklin, stating that each would consider the other a "most favored nation" for trade and friendship; France would be obligated to fight for American independence; and America would be obligated to stand by France if war should occur between France and Great Britain. Within four months, France and Great Britain were at war.

The British Attempt to Make Peace. Threatened by the alliance between France and America, Parliament proposed the repeal of the Tea Act (1773) and Coercive Acts (1774), pledged not to tax the colonies, and sent peace commissioners to America. However, most Americans were interested only in British recognition of American independence. When a British commissioner tried to bribe congressmen Joseph Reed, Robert Morris, and Francis Dana, Americans became even less interested in reconciliation. Competing for support from the American people, both Congress and the desperate commissioners appealed directly to them with broadsides, but the British commissioners soon returned to Great Britain, their mission a failure.

John Paul Jones Wins Victories. Although Esek Hopkins was never very successful with the American navy, Captain John Paul Jones won several victories against the British with his ship, the "Ranger."

Battle of Monmouth. When the British headed for New York, Washington left Valley Forge to follow. At the Battle of Monmouth, American General Charles Lee gave several confused orders, and then ordered a sudden retreat. Washington's arrival on the scene saved the battle, although the British escaped to New York during the night. Lee was later court-martialed.

1779

The British Attack in North and South. Fighting continued in both the northern and southern states. In the frontier settlements of Pennsylvania, Loyalists and Indians led by Mohawk Joseph Brant attacked American settlers. The Loyalists soon were defeated, and Americans went on to destroy many Indian villages whose residents were fighting on the side of the British.

Spain Joins the War. Spain asked Britain for Gibraltar as a reward for joining the war on the British side.

© 2000 by The Center for Applied Research in Education

When Britain refused, Spain joined with France in its war against Britain, although refusing to recognize American independence.

1780

The British Take Charleston. After a brief fight, the British took Charleston, capturing 5,400 men and four American ships in the harbor. It was the worst American defeat of the war.

Mutiny in the Continental Army. When the value of Continental currency sank to a new low, Congress had problems supplying the American army. Great shortages of food led to a short-lived mutiny among some Connecticut soldiers at Washington's camp in New Jersey.

The Treason of Benedict Arnold. American General Benedict Arnold, ambitious and frustrated, began dealing with British General Sir Henry Clinton. After he was promised the command at West Point by General Washington, Arnold told Clinton that he would give the strategic American fortification to the British. But when British Major John Andre, acting as messenger, was captured, Arnold fled to a British ship, revealing his involvement in the treasonous plan. Andre was executed as a spy, and Arnold was made a brigadier general in the British army.

1781

Congress Creates a Department of Finance. American finances were in such dire straits that Congress saw the need for a separate department of finance. Robert Morris was appointed Superintendent of Finance.

The Articles of Confederation Are Ratified. With the ratification of the Articles of Confederation, under discussion since 1777, Congress assumed a new title, "The United States in Congress Assembled."

Battle of Yorktown. French and American forces joined at Yorktown, on land and at sea, and attacked British fortifications. Key British points were soon held by the Americans and French, and British General Cornwallis surrendered almost 8,000 men. With this defeat, Britain lost hope of winning the war in America.

1782

Peace Negotiations Begin in Paris. British, French, and American commissioners met in Paris to discuss peace. The United States sent Benjamin Franklin, John Adams, and John Jay. By November, the commissioners had drafted a peace treaty. Its terms called for Great Britain to recognize American independence and provide for the evacuation of all British troops. Great Britain also gave up its territory between the Mississippi River and the Allegheny Mountains, doubling the size of the new nation.

1783

The Army Complains. When a delegation of army officers complained to Congress about their unpaid salaries and pensions, Congress had no quick solution. An anonymous letter urged officers to unite and attempt one last appeal to Congress. If its attempt was ignored, the army was prepared to revolt against Congress. Washington, addressing the army in person at its headquarters in Newburgh, New York, convinced them to be patient, and not to dishonor themselves after their glorious victory. Visibly moved, the officers adopted resolutions to present to Congress, and pledged not to threaten violence or rebellion.

Congress Ratifies the Preliminary Articles of Peace. After Spain, France, and Britain successfully came to terms, the treaty between France, Britain, and America was put into effect, and warfare formally ceased. Congress ratified the Articles of Peace on April 15.

The Loyalists and British Evacuate New York. New York City was the last Loyalist refuge in America. Starting in April, nearly 30,000 Loyalists, knowing that the British soon would leave New York, packed their belongings and sailed to Canada and England, followed shortly by the British army. In November, when the British sailed away, Washington entered the city and formally bade farewell to his officers. Soon after, he resigned his commission.

The American Army Disbands. In June, most of Washington's army disbanded and headed for home just before the British evacuated New York. A small force remained until all the British had departed.

Congress Is Threatened. A group of soldiers from Pennsylvania marched on Congress, demanding their pay. Armed and angry, they surrounded Independence Hall. The members of Congress eventually were allowed to leave the building; they fled to Princeton, New Jersey.

1784

The Western Territories. Thomas Jefferson headed a committee that proposed a plan for dividing the western territories, providing a temporary government for the West, and devising a method for new western states to enter the Union on an equal basis with the original states. The plan was adopted, but not put into effect.

Congress Creates a Board of Finance. When Robert Morris resigned as Superintendent of Finance, he was replaced by a Board of Finance consisting of three commissioners.

New York the Temporary Capital. Congress decided to make New York City the temporary capital of the United States, until the location of a permanent federal city was decided upon.

1785

Congress Lacks Power over Commerce. When American commissioners attempted to make trade arrangements with Britain, the British Ambassador refused, because any state could decline to abide by Congress's trade regulations. The inability of Congress to regulate commerce on a national scale led to the formation of a committee dedicated to appealing to the states to grant Congress enlarged powers over commerce. Despite these attempts, no effective action was taken.

Conference at Mount Vernon. Several commissioners from Virginia and Maryland met at Mount Vernon, the home of George Washington, to discuss regulation of trade between the two states. At the meeting's conclusion, the commissioners suggested that all the states meet at a convention in Annapolis to discuss common commercial problems.

Basic Land Ordinance. Congress arranged for surveys to divide the western territories into townships, with one lot in each town set aside as a site for a public school.

1786

The Virginia Statute for Religious Freedom. The Virginia House of Burgesses passed a statute, written by Thomas Jefferson in 1779 and sponsored by James Madison, declaring that no person should be discriminated against because of religious belief, or compelled to join or support any church. This statute helped shape the First Amendment of the United States Constitution.

Attempts to Revise the Articles of Confederation. In Congress, Charles Pinckney proposed a revision of the Articles of Confederation. A committee debated the question, and recommended several changes, including granting Congress power over foreign and domestic commerce, and enabling Congress to collect money owed by the states. Under the Articles, unanimous approval from all thirteen states would be necessary to pass the suggested changes. Doubting that all the states would ever agree, Congress never acted.

Annapolis Convention. Nine states agreed to send delegates to Annapolis to discuss commerce, but only five state delegations arrived on time. Because of the poor attendance, the delegates decided to invite the states to another convention. Alexander Hamilton drafted an address to the states, inviting them to a convention to be held in Philadelphia in 1787, to discuss not only commerce, but all matters necessary to improve the federal government. After debate, on February 21, 1787, Congress endorsed the plan to revise the Articles of Confederation.

1787

The Constitutional Convention. Every state but Rhode Island sent delegates to the Constitutional Convention in Philadelphia. The gathering included some of the most respected and talented men in America. George Washington was named president.

Edmund Randolph proposed the "Virginia Plan," drafted by James Madison—a plan that recommended an entirely new form of government, including an executive, a judiciary, and a legislature composed of two houses and including a number of representatives from each state based on their population.

Opposition came from the small states, which feared domination by the more populous states in the legislature. William Paterson proposed the "New Jersey Plan," which essentially revised the Articles of Confederation, preserving equal representation of the states. After much debate, the Convention rejected the New Jersey Plan, deciding instead to work toward an entirely new form of government.

The issue of representation in the two houses of the new national legislature became a major sticking point for the Convention. Roger Sherman was helpful in framing the "Connecticut Compromise," a plan that suggested representation in the lower house (the House of Representatives) based on population, and equal representation in the upper house (the Senate). With this compromise, the Convention succeeded in completing a rough draft of a constitution.

A Committee of Style was appointed to create a final draft; Gouverneur Morris was chosen to write it. After carefully reviewing the draft, the Convention approved the Constitution on September 17. After signing it and sending it to Congress, the Convention adjourned.

Northwest Ordinance. While the Constitutional Convention debated a new government, Congress decided upon a plan for governing all western territories north of the Ohio River. The Northwest Ordinance provided for a plan of government, the creation of states, the acceptance of each new state as an equal of the original states, freedom of religion, right to a trial by jury, public support of education, and the prohibition of slavery. Arthur St. Clair was named first governor of the territory.

Congress Receives the Constitution. Although some congressmen were displeased at the Convention for doing far more than revising the Articles of Confederation, on September 28 Congress agreed to pass the Constitution on to the states, so each could debate it in separate ratifying conventions. Nine states had to agree to the new Constitution for it to go into effect.

The Federalist Papers. Supporters of the Constitution—Federalists—and opponents of the Constitution—Antifederalists—fought fiercely in the press. Seventy-seven essays, written anonymously by "Publius," appeared in New York newspapers, explaining and defending the new Constitution. These essays, published in book form with eight additional essays, were titled The Federalist. Written by Alexander Hamilton, James Madison, and John Jay, The Federalist was the most organized, coherent effort to defend the Constitution.

1788

The Constitution Is Ratified by Nine States. On June 21, New Hampshire became the ninth state to ratify the new Constitution, making its adoption official. Preceding New Hampshire were Delaware, Pennsylvania, New Jersey, Georgia, Connecticut, Massachusetts, Maryland, and South Carolina. Virginia and New York ratified shortly after New Hampshire, followed by North Carolina in November 1789. Rhode Island was last to ratify, not joining the Union until May 1790.

Congress Steps Aside for a New Government. On July 2, Congress announced that the Constitution had been adopted. By September, a committee had prepared for the change in government, naming New York City as the temporary official capital, and setting dates for elections and for the meeting of the first Congress under the new Constitution. Congress completed its business on October 10. Its last action was the granting of ten square miles of land to Congress for a federal town.

Source: U.S. Congressional Library.

3.2   Continental Congresses

The First Continental Congress met in Philadelphia on September 5, 1774, and was attended by representatives of all the colonies except Georgia. This Congress, which adjourned October 26, 1774, passed intercolonial resolutions calling for an extensive boycott by the colonies against British trade. The following year, most of the delegates from the colonies were chosen by popular election to attend the Second Continental Congress, which assembled in Philadelphia on May 10. On June 15, 1775, George Washington was elected to command the Continental army. Congress adjourned December 12, 1776.

Other Continental Congresses were held in Baltimore (1776-1777), Philadelphia (1777), Lancaster, Pa. (1777), York, Pa. (1777-1778), and Philadelphia (1778-1781).

In 1781, the Articles of Confederation provided for the continuance of Congress. Known thereafter as the Congress of the Confederation, it held sessions in Philadelphia (1781-1783), Princeton, N.J. (1783), Annapolis, Md. (1783-1784), and Trenton, N.J. (1784). Five sessions were held in New York City between the years 1785 and 1789.

The Congress of the United States, established by the ratification of the Constitution, held its first meeting on March 4, 1789, in New York City. Several sessions of Congress were held in Philadelphia, and the first meeting in Washington, D.C., was on Nov. 17, 1800.

Presidents of the Continental Congresses

Name	Elected
Peyton Randolph, Va.	9/5/1774
Henry Middleton, S.C.	10/22/1774
Peyton Randolph, Va.	5/10/1775
John Hancock, Mass.	5/24/1775
Henry Laurens, S.C.	11/1/1777
John Jay, N.Y.	12/10/1778
Samuel Huntington, Conn.	9/28/1779
Thomas McKean, Del.	7/10/1781
John Hanson, Md.	11/5/1781
Elias Boudinot, N.J.	11/4/1782
Thomas Miffin, Pa.	11/3/1783
Richard Henry Lee, Va.	11/30/1784
John Hancock, Mass.	11/23/1785
Nathaniel Gorham, Mass.	6/6/1786
Arthur St. Clair, Pa.	2/21/1787
Cyrus Griffin, Va.	1/22/1788

3.3   Patrick Henry: "Give Me Liberty or Give Me Death," 1775

March 23, 1775

No man thinks more highly than I do of the patriotism, as well as abilities, of the very worthy gentlemen who have just addressed the House. But different men often see the same subject in different lights; and, therefore, I hope it will not be thought disrespectful to those gentlemen if, entertaining as I do opinions of a character very opposite to theirs, I shall speak forth my sentiments freely and without reserve. This is no time for ceremony. The questing before the House is one of awful moment to this country. For my own part, I consider it as nothing less than a question of freedom or slavery; and in proportion to the magnitude of the subject ought to be the freedom of the debate. It is only in this way that we can hope to arrive at truth, and fulfill the great responsibility which we hold to God and our country. Should I keep back my opinions at such a time, through fear of giving offense, I should consider myself as guilty of treason towards my country, and of an act of disloyalty toward the Majesty of Heaven, which I revere above all earthly kings.

Mr. President, it is natural to man to indulge in the illusions of hope. We are apt to shut our eyes against a painful truth, and listen to the song of that siren till she transforms us into beasts. Is this the part of wise men, engaged in a great and arduous struggle for liberty? Are we disposed to be of the number of those who, having eyes, see not, and, having ears, hear not, the things which so nearly concern their temporal salvation? For my part, whatever anguish of spirit it may cost, I am willing to know the whole truth; to know the worst, and to provide for it.

I have but one lamp by which my feet are guided, and that is the lamp of experience. I know of no way of judging of the future but by the past. And judging by the past, I wish to know what there has been in the conduct of the British ministry for the last ten years to justify those hopes with which gentlemen have been pleased to solace themselves and the House. Is it that insidious smile with which our petition has been lately received? Trust it not, sir; it will prove a snare to your feet. Suffer not yourselves to be betrayed with a kiss. Ask yourselves how this gracious reception of our petition comports with those warlike preparations which cover our waters and darken our land. Are fleets and armies necessary to a work of love and reconciliation? Have we shown ourselves so unwilling to be reconciled that force must be called in to win back our love? Let us not deceive ourselves, sir. These are the implements of war and subjugation; the last arguments to which kings resort. I ask gentlemen, sir, what means this martial array, if its purpose be not to force us to submission? Can gentlemen assign any other possible motive for it? Has Great Britain any enemy, in this quarter of the world, to call for all this accumulation of navies and armies? No, sir, she has none. They are meant for us: they can be meant for no other. They are sent over to bind and rivet upon us those chains which the British ministry have been so long forging. And what have we to oppose to them? Shall we try argument? Sir, we have been trying that for the last ten years. Have we anything new to offer upon the subject? Nothing. We have held the subject up in every light of which it is capable; but it has been all in vain. Shall we resort to entreaty and humble supplication? What terms shall we find which have not been already exhausted? Let us not, I beseech you, sir, deceive ourselves. Sir, we have done everything that could be done to avert the storm which is now coming on. We have petitioned; we have remonstrated; we have supplicated; we have prostrated ourselves before the throne, and have implored its interposition to arrest the tyrannical hands of the ministry and Parliament. Our petitions have been slighted; our remonstrances have produced additional violence and insult; our supplications have been disregarded; and we have been spurned, with contempt, from the foot of the throne! In vain, after these things, may we indulge the fond hope of peace and reconciliation. There is no longer any room for hope. If we wish to be free—if we mean to preserve inviolate those inestimable privileges for which we have been so long contending—if we mean not basely to abandon the noble struggle in which we have been so long engaged, and which we have pledged ourselves never to abandon until the glorious object of our contest shall be obtained—we must fight! I repeat it, sir, we must fight! An appeal to arms and to the God of hosts is all that is left us!

They tell us, sir, that we are weak; unable to cope with so formidable an adversary. But when shall we be stronger? Will it be the next week, or the next year? Will it be when we are totally disarmed, and when a British guard shall be stationed in every house? Shall we gather strength by irresolution and inaction? Shall we acquire the means of effectual resistance by lying supinely on our backs and hugging the delusive phantom of hope, until our enemies shall have bound us hand and foot? Sir, we are not weak if we make a proper use of those means which the God of nature hath placed in our power. The millions of people, armed in the holy cause of liberty, and in such a country as that which we possess, are invincible by any force which our enemy can send against us. Besides, sir, we shall not fight our battles alone. There is a just God who presides over the destinies of nations, and who will raise up friends to fight our battles for us. The battle, sir, is not to the strong alone; it is to the vigilant, the active, the brave. Besides, sir, we have no election. If we were base enough to desire it, it is now too late to retire from the contest. There is no retreat but in submission and slavery! Our chains are forged! Their clanking may be heard on the plains of Boston! The war is inevitable—and let it come! I repeat it, sir, let it come.

It is in vain, sir, to extenuate the matter. Gentlemen may cry, Peace, Peace—but there is no peace. The war is actually begun! The next gale that sweeps from the north will bring to our ears the clash of resounding arms! Our brethren are already in the field! Why stand we here idle? What is it that gentlemen wish? What would they have? Is life so dear, or peace so sweet, as to be purchased at the price of chains and slavery? Forbid it, Almighty God! I know not what course others may take; but as for me, give me liberty or give me death!

3.4   Major Battles in the Revolutionary War

Battle	Date	Place	Importance
Lexington-Concord	April 1775	Massachusetts	First armed conflict.
Ft. Ticonderoga	May 1775	Lake Champlain	Ethan Allen captured fort.
Bunker Hill	June 1775	Boston	Only battle in long siege of Boston.
Dorchester Heights	March 1776	Boston	British forced to evacuate New England.
Long Island	August 1776	New York	U.S. forces forced to retreat to Manhattan, then New Jersey.
Trenton	December 1776	New Jersey	Hessian army crushed in Washington's raid across the Delaware River.
Princeton	January 1777	New Jersey	U.S. recovers New Jersey from British in 10 days. British retreat to New York.
Brandywine Creek Germantown	September 1777 October 1777	Philadelphia	British seize Philadelphia after these victories.
Saratoga	October 17, 1777	Upstate New York	Turning point of war. Convinced French of U.S. strength.
Monmouth	June 1778	New Jersey	U.S. army almost captured British but British forces escape.
Savannah	December 1778	Georgia	Beginning of British push in the South.
Charleston	December 1779	South Carolina	British gain control of South.
Yorktown	October 19, 1781	Virginia	Cornwallis surrenders to Washington.

3.5   Virginia's Declaration of Rights, 1776

Virginia's Declaration of Rights was drawn upon by Thomas Jefferson for the opening paragraphs of the Declaration of Independence. It was widely copied by the other colonies and became the basis of the Bill of Rights. Written by George Mason, it was adopted by the Virginia Constitutional Convention on June 12, 1776.

A DECLARATION OF RIGHTS made by the representatives of the good people of Virginia, assembled in full and free convention which rights do pertain to them and their posterity, as the basis and foundation of government.

Section 1. That all men are by nature equally free and independent and have certain inherent rights, of which, when they enter into a state of society, they cannot, by any compact, deprive or divest their posterity; namely, the enjoyment of life and liberty, with the means of acquiring and possessing property, and pursuing and obtaining happiness and safety.

Section 2. That all power is vested in, and consequently derived from, the people; that magistrates are their trustees and servants and at all times amenable to them.

Section 3. That government is, or ought to be, instituted for the common benefit, protection, and security of the people, nation, or community; of all the various modes and forms of government, that is best which is capable of producing the greatest degree of happiness and safety and is most effectually secured against the danger of maladministration. And that, when any government shall be found inadequate or contrary to these purposes, a majority of the community has an indubitable, inalienable, and indefeasible right to reform, alter, or abolish it, in such manner as shall be judged most conducive to the public weal.

Section 4. That no man, or set of men, is entitled to exclusive or separate emoluments or privileges from the community, but in consideration of public services; which, nor being descendible, neither ought the offices of magistrate, legislator, or judge to be hereditary.

Section 5. That the legislative and executive powers of the state should be separate and distinct from the judiciary; and that the members of the two first may be restrained from oppression, by feeling and participating the burdens of the people, they should, at fixed periods, be reduced to a private station, return into that body from which they were originally taken, and the vacancies be supplied by frequent, certain, and regular elections, in which all, or any part, of the former members, to be again eligible, or ineligible, as the laws shall direct.

Section 6. That elections of members to serve as representatives of the people, in assembly ought to be free; and that all men, having sufficient evidence of permanent common interest with, and attachment to, the community, have the right of suffrage and cannot be taxed or deprived of their property for public uses without their own consent or that of their representatives so elected, nor bound by any law to which they have not, in like manner, assembled for the public good.

Section 7. That all power of suspending laws, or the execution of laws, by any authority, without consent of the representatives of the people, is injurious to their rights and ought not to be exercised.

Section 8. That in all capital or criminal prosecutions a man has a right to demand the cause and nature of his accusation, to be confronted with the accusers and witnesses, to call for evidence in his favor, and to a speedy trial by an impartial jury of twelve men of his vicinage, without whose unanimous consent he cannot be found guilty; nor can he be compelled to give evidence against himself; that no man be deprived of his liberty except by the law of the land or the judgment of his peers.

Section 9. That excessive bail ought not to be required, nor excessive fines imposed, nor cruel and unusual punishments inflicted.

Section 10. That general warrants, whereby an officer or messenger may be commanded to search suspected places without evidence of a fact committed, or to seize any person or persons not named, or whose offense is not particularly described and supported by evidence, are grievous and oppressive and ought not to be granted.

Section 11. That in controversies respecting property, and in suits between man and man, the ancient trial by jury is preferable to any other and ought to be held sacred.

Section 12. That the freedom of the press is one of the great bulwarks of liberty, and can never be restrained but by despotic governments.

Section 13. That a well-regulated militia, composed of the body of the people, trained to arms, is the proper, natural, and safe defense of a free state; that standing armies, in time of peace, should be avoided as dangerous to liberty; and that in all cases the military should be under strict subordination to, and governed by, the civil power.

Section 14. That the people have a right to uniform government; and, therefore, that no government separate from or independent of the government of Virginia ought to be erected or established within the limits thereof.

Section 15. That no free government, or the blessings of liberty, can be preserved to any people but by a firm adherence to justice, moderation, temperance, frugality, and virtue and by frequent recurrence to fundamental principles.

Section 16. That religion, or the duty which we owe to our Creator, and the manner of discharging it, can be directed only by reason and conviction, not by force or violence; and therefore all men are equally entitled to the free exercise of religion, according to the dictates of conscience; and that it is the mutual duty of all to practise Christian forbearance, love, and charity toward each other.

3.6 Declaration of Independence, 1776

IN CONGRESS, July 4, 1776.

The unanimous Declaration of the thirteen united States of America,

When in the Course of human events, it becomes necessary for one people to dissolve the political bands which have connected them with another, and to assume among the powers of the earth, the separate and equal station to which the Laws of Nature and of Nature's God entitle them, a decent respect to the opinions of mankind requires that they should declare the causes which impel them to the separation.

We hold these truths to be self-evident, that all men are created equal, that they are endowed by their Creator with certain unalienable Rights, that among these are Life, Liberty and the pursuit of Happiness.—That to secure these rights, Governments are instituted among Men, deriving their just powers from the consent of the governed,—That whenever any Form of Government becomes destructive of these ends, it is the Right of the People to alter or to abolish it, and to institute new Government, laying its foundation on such principles and organizing its powers in such form, as to them shall seem most likely to effect their Safety and Happiness. Prudence, indeed, will dictate that Governments long established should not be changed for light and transient causes; and accordingly all experience hath shewn, that mankind are more disposed to suffer, while evils are sufferable, than to right themselves by abolishing the forms to which they are accustomed. But when a long train of abuses and usurpations, pursuing invariably the same Object evinces a design to reduce them under absolute Despotism, it is their right, it is their duty, to throw off such Government, and to provide new Guards for their future security.—Such has been the patient sufferance of these Colonies; and such is now the necessity which constrains them to alter their former Systems of Government. The history of the present King of Great Britain is a history of repeated injuries and usurpations, all having in direct object the establishment of an absolute Tyranny over these States. To prove this, let Facts be submitted to a candid world.

He has refused his Assent to Laws, the most wholesome and necessary for the public good.

He has forbidden his Governors to pass Laws of immediate and pressing importance, unless suspended in their operation till his Assent should be obtained; and when so suspended, he has utterly neglected to attend to them.

He has refused to pass other Laws for the accommodation of large districts of people, unless those people would relinquish the right of Representation in the Legislature, a right inestimable to them and formidable to tyrants only.

He has called together legislative bodies at places unusual, uncomfortable, and distant from the depository of their public Records, for the sole purpose of fatiguing them into compliance with his measures.

He has dissolved Representative Houses repeatedly, for opposing with manly firmness his invasions on the rights of the people.

He has refused for a long time, after such dissolutions, to cause others to be elected; whereby the Legislative powers, incapable of Annihilation, have returned to the People at large for their exercise; the State remaining in the mean time exposed to all the dangers of invasion from without, and convulsions within.

He has endeavoured to prevent the population of these States; for that purpose obstructing the Laws for Naturalization of Foreigners; refusing to pass others to encourage their migrations hither, and raising the conditions of new Appropriations of Lands.

He has obstructed the Administration of Justice, by refusing his Assent to Laws for establishing Judiciary powers.

He has made Judges dependent on his Will alone, for the tenure of their offices, and the amount and payment of their salaries.

He has erected a multitude of New Offices, and sent hither swarms of Officers to harrass our people, and eat out their substance.

He has kept among us, in times of peace, Standing Armies without the Consent of our legislatures.

He has affected to render the Military independent of and superior to the Civil power.

He has combined with others to subject us to a jurisdiction foreign to our constitution, and unacknowledged by our laws; giving his Assent to their Acts of pretended Legislation:

For Quartering large bodies of armed troops among us:

For protecting them, by a mock Trial, from punishment for any Murders which they should commit on the Inhabitants of these States:

For cutting off our Trade with all parts of the world:

For imposing Taxes on us without our Consent:

For depriving us in many cases, of the benefits of Trial by Jury:

For transporting us beyond Seas to be tried for pretended offences:

For abolishing the free System of English Laws in a neighbouring Province, establishing therein an Arbitrary government, and enlarging its Boundaries so as to render it at once an example and fit instrument for introducing the same absolute rule into these Colonies:

For taking away our Charters, abolishing our most valuable Laws, and altering fundamentally the Forms of our Governments:

For suspending our own Legislatures, and declaring themselves invested with power to legislate for us in all cases whatsoever.

He has abdicated Government here, by declaring us out of his Protection and waging War against us.

He has plundered our seas, ravaged our Coasts, burnt our towns, and destroyed the lives of our people.

He is at this time transporting large Armies of foreign Mercenaries to compleat the works of death, desolation and tyranny, already begun with circumstances of Cruelty & perfidy scarcely paralleled in the most barbarous ages, and totally unworthy the Head of a civilized nation.

He has constrained our fellow Citizens taken Captive on the high Seas to bear Arms against their Country, to become the executioners of their friends and Brethren, or to fall themselves by their Hands.

He has excited domestic insurrections amongst us, and has endeavoured to bring on the inhabitants of our frontiers, the merciless Indian Savages, whose known rule of warfare, is an undistinguished destruction of all ages, sexes and conditions.

In every stage of these Oppressions We have Petitioned for Redress in the most humble terms: Our repeated Petitions have been answered only by repeated injury. A Prince whose character is thus marked by every act which may define a Tyrant, is unfit to be the ruler of a free people.

Nor have We been wanting in attentions to our British brethren. We have warned them from time to time of attempts by their legislature to extend an unwarrantable jurisdiction over us. We have reminded them of the circumstances of our emigration and settlement here. We have appealed to their native justice and magnanimity, and we have conjured them by the ties of our common kindred to disavow these usurpations, which, would inevitably interrupt our connections and correspondence. They too have been deaf to the voice of justice and of consanguinity. We must, therefore, acquiesce in the necessity, which denounces our Separation, and hold them, as we hold the rest of mankind, Enemies in War, in Peace Friends.

We, therefore, the Representatives of the United States of America, in General Congress, Assembled, appealing to the Supreme Judge of the world for the rectitude of our intentions, do, in the Name, and by Authority of the good People of these Colonies, solemnly publish and declare, That these United Colonies are, and of Right ought to be Free and Independent States; that they are Absolved from all Allegiance to the British Crown, and that all political connection between them and the State of Great Britain, is and ought to be totally dissolved; and that as Free and Independent States, they have full Power to levy War, conclude Peace, contract Alliances, establish Commerce, and to do all other Acts and Things which Independent States may of right do. And for the support of this Declaration, with a firm reliance on the protection of divine Providence, we mutually pledge to each other our Lives, our Fortunes and our sacred Honor.

The 56 signatures on the Declaration:

Georgia
    Button Gwinnett
    Lyman Hall
    George Walton
North Carolina
    William Hooper
    Joseph Hewes
    John Penn
South Carolina
    Edward Rutledge
    Thomas Heyward, Jr.
    Thomas Lynch, Jr.
    Arthur Middleton
Maryland
    Samuel Chase
    William Paca
    Thomas Stone
    Charles Carroll of Carrollton
Virginia
    George Wythe
    Richard Henry Lee
    Thomas Jefferson
    Benjamin Harrison
    Thomas Nelson, Jr.
    Francis Lightfoot Lee
    Carter Braxton

Pennsylvania
    Robert Morris
    Benjamin Rush
    Benjamin Franklin
    John Morton
    George Clymer
    James Smith
    George Taylor
    James Wilson
    George Ross
Delaware
    Caesar Rodney
    George Read
    Thomas McKean
New York
    William Floyd
    Philip Livingston
    Francis Lewis
    Lewis Morris
New Jersey
    Richard Stockton
    John Witherspoon
    Francis Hopkinson
    John Hart
    Abraham Clark

New Hampshire
    Josiah Bartlett
    William Whipple
    Matthew Thornton
Massachusetts
    John Hancock
    Samuel Adams
    John Adams
    Robert Treat Paine
    Elbridge Gerry
Rhode Island
    Stephen Hopkins
    William Ellery
Connecticut
    Roger Sherman
    Samuel Huntington
    William Williams
    Oliver Wolcott

3.7 Delegates to the Constitutional Convention, 1787

On February 21, 1787, the Continental Congress resolved that:

. . . it is expedient that on the second Monday in May next a Convention of delegates who shall have been appointed by the several States be held at Philadelphia for the sole and express purpose of revising the Articles of Confederation. . . .

The original states, except Rhode Island, collectively appointed 70 individuals to the Constitutional Convention, but a number did not accept or could not attend. Those who did not attend included Richard Henry Lee, Patrick Henry, Thomas Jefferson, John Adams, Samuel Adams, and John Hancock.

In all, 55 delegates attended the Constitutional Convention sessions, but only 39 actually signed the Constitution. The delegates ranged in age from Jonathan Dayton, aged 26, to Benjamin Franklin, aged 81, who was so infirm that he had to be carried to sessions in a sedan chair.

(*indicates delegates who did not sign the Constitution)

Connecticut
Oliver Ellsworth (Elsworth)*
William S. Johnson
Roger Sherman

Delaware
Richard Bassett (Basset)
Gunning Bedford, Jr.
Jacob Broom
John Dickinson
George Read

Georgia
Abraham Baldwin
William Few
William Houstoun*
William L. Pierce*

Maryland
Daniel Carroll
Daniel Jenifer of St. Thomas
Luther Martin*
James McHenry
John F. Mercer*

Massachusetts
Elbridge Gerry*
Nathaniel Gorham
Rufus King
Caleb Strong*

New Hampshire
Nicholas Gilman
John Langdon

New Jersey
David Brearly (Brearley)
Jonathan Dayton
William C. Houston*
William Livingston
William Paterson (Patterson)

New York
Alexander Hamilton
John Lansing, Jr.*
Robert Yates*

North Carolina
William Blount
William R. Davie*
Alexander Martin*
Richard D. Spaight
Hugh Williamson

Pennsylvania
George Clymer
Thomas Fitzsimons
    (FitzSimons; Fitzsimmons)
Benjamin Franklin
Jared Ingersoll
Thomas Mifflin
Gouverneur Morris
Robert Morris
James Wilson

South Carolina
Pierce Butler
Charles Pinckney
Charles Cotesworth Pinckney
John Rutledge

Rhode Island
Rhode Island did not send
    any delegates to the
    Constitutional Convention.

Virginia
John Blair
James Madison
George Mason*
James McClurg*
Edmund J. Randolph*
George Washington
George Wythe*

3.8   States Voting to Adopt the Constitution

The plan for the Constitution said that if nine of the thirteen states approved it, the Constitution would become law. The following chart shows the results of votes by the representatives sent to state meetings.

State	For	Against	Decision
Delaware	30	0	for
Pennsylvania	46	23	for
New Jersey	38	0	for
Georgia	26	0	for
Connecticut	128	40	for
Massachusetts	187	168	for
Maryland	63	11	for
South Carolina	149	73	for
New Hampshire	57	47	for
Virginia	89	79	for
New York	30	27	for
North Carolina	194	77	for
Rhode Island	34	32	for

3.9 Bill of Rights, 1791

The following text is a transcription of the first ten amendments to the Constitution in their original form. These amendments were ratified December 15, 1791, and form what is known as the "Bill of Rights."

Amendment I

Congress shall make no law respecting an establishment of religion, or prohibiting the free exercise thereof; or abridging the freedom of speech, or of the press; or the right of the people peaceably to assemble, and to petition the Government for a redress of grievances.

Amendment II

A well regulated Militia, being necessary to the security of a free State, the right of the people to keep and bear Arms, shall not be infringed.

Amendment III

No Soldier shall, in time of peace be quartered in any house, without the consent of the Owner, nor in time of war, but in a manner to be prescribed by law.

Amendment IV

The right of the people to be secure in their persons, houses, papers, and effects, against unreasonable searches and seizures, shall not be violated, and no Warrants shall issue, but upon probable cause, supported by Oath or affirmation, and particularly describing the place to be searched, and the persons or things to be seized.

Amendment V

No person shall be held to answer for a capital, or otherwise infamous crime, unless on a presentment or indictment of a Grand Jury, except in cases arising in the land or naval forces, or in the Militia, when in actual service in time of War or public danger; nor shall any person be subject for the same offence to be twice put in jeopardy of life or limb; nor shall be compelled in any criminal case to be a witness against himself, nor be deprived of life, liberty, or property, without due process of law; nor shall private property be taken for public use, without just compensation.

Amendment VI

In all criminal prosecutions, the accused shall enjoy the right to a speedy and public trial, by an impartial jury of the State and district wherein the crime shall have been committed, which district shall have been previously ascertained by law, and to be informed of the nature and cause of the accusation; to be confronted with the witnesses against him; to have compulsory process for obtaining witnesses in his favor, and to have the Assistance of Counsel for his defence.

Amendment VII

In suits at common law, where the value in controversy shall exceed twenty dollars, the right of trial by jury shall be preserved, and no fact tried by a jury, shall be otherwise reexamined in any Court of the United States, than according to the rules of the common law.

Amendment VIII

Bail shall not be required, nor excessive fines imposed, nor cruel and unusual punishments inflicted.

Amendment IX

The enumeration in the Constitution, of certain rights, shall not be construed to deny or disparage others retained by the people.

Amendment X

The powers not delegated to the United States by the Constitution, nor prohibited by it to the States, are reserved to the States respectively, or to the people.

3.10 Northwest Ordinance, 1787

Northwest Ordinance, July 13, 1787: An Ordinance for the government of the Territory of the United States northwest of the River Ohio.

Section 1. Be it ordained by the United States in Congress assembled, That the said territory, for the purposes of temporary government, be one district, subject, however, to be divided into two districts, as future circumstances may, in the opinion of Congress, make it expedient.

Section 2. Be it ordained by the authority aforesaid, That the estates, both of resident and nonresident proprietors in the said territory, dying intestate, shall descent to, and be distributed among their children, and the descendants of a deceased child, in equal parts; the descendants of a deceased child or grandchild to take the share of their deceased parent in equal parts among them: And where there shall be no children or descendants, then in equal parts to the next of kin in equal degree; and among collaterals, the children of a deceased brother or sister of the intestate shall have, in equal parts among them, their deceased parents' share; and there shall in no case be a distinction between kindred of the whole and half blood; saving, in all cases, to the widow of the intestate her third part of the real estate for life, and one third part of the personal estate; and this law relative to descents and dower, shall remain in full force until altered by the legislature of the district. And until the governor and judges shall adopt laws as hereinafter mentioned, estates in the said territory may be devised or bequeathed by wills in writing, signed and sealed by him or her in whom the estate may be (being of full age), and attested by three witnesses; and real estates may be conveyed by lease and release, or bargain and sale, signed, sealed and delivered by the person being of full age, in whom the estate may be, and attested by two witnesses, provided such wills be duly proved, and such conveyances be acknowledged, or the execution thereof duly proved, and be recorded within one year after proper magistrates, courts, and registers shall be appointed for that purpose; and personal property may be transferred by delivery; saving, however to the French and Canadian inhabitants, and other settlers of the Kaskaskies, St. Vincents and the neighboring villages who have heretofore professed themselves citizens of Virginia, their laws and customs now in force among them, relative to the descent and conveyance, of property.

Section 3. Be it ordained by the authority aforesaid, That there shall be appointed from time to time by Congress, a governor, whose commission shall continue in force for the term of three years, unless sooner revoked by Congress; he shall reside in the district, and have a freehold estate therein in 1,000 acres of land, while in the exercise of his office.

Section 4. There shall be appointed from time to time by Congress, a secretary, whose commission shall continue in force for four years unless sooner revoked; he shall reside in the district, and have a freehold estate therein in 500 acres of land, while in the exercise of his office. It shall be his duty to keep and preserve the acts and laws passed by the legislature, and the public records of the district, and the proceedings of the governor in his executive department, and transmit authentic copies of such acts and proceedings, every six months, to the Secretary of Congress: There shall also be appointed a court to consist of three judges, any two of whom to form a court, who shall have a common law jurisdiction, and reside in the district, and have each therein a freehold estate in 500 acres of land while in the exercise of their offices; and their commissions shall continue in force during good behavior.

Section 5. The governor and judges, or a majority of them, shall adopt and publish in the district such laws of the original States, criminal and civil, as may be necessary and best suited to the circumstances of the district, and report them to Congress from time to time: which laws shall be in force in the district until the organization of the General Assembly therein, unless disapproved of by Congress; but afterwards the Legislature shall have authority to alter them as they shall think fit.

Section 6. The governor, for the time being, shall be commander in chief of the militia, appoint and commission all officers in the same below the rank of general officers; all general officers shall be appointed and commissioned by Congress.

Section 7. Previous to the organization of the general assembly, the governor shall appoint such magistrates and other civil officers in each county or township, as he shall find necessary for the preservation of the peace and good order in the same: After the general assembly shall be organized, the powers and duties of the magistrates and other civil officers shall be regulated and defined by the said assembly; but all magistrates and other civil officers not herein otherwise directed, shall during the continuance of this temporary government, be appointed by the governor.

Section 8. For the prevention of crimes and injuries, the laws to be adopted or made shall have force in all parts of the district, and for the execution of process, criminal and civil, the governor shall make proper divisions thereof; and he shall proceed from time to time as circumstances may require, to lay out the parts of the district in which the Indian titles shall have been extinguished, into counties and townships, subject, however, to such alterations as may thereafter be made by the legislature.

Section 9. So soon as there shall be five thousand free male inhabitants of full age in the district, upon giving proof thereof to the governor, they shall receive authority, with time and place, to elect a representative from their counties or townships to represent them in the general assembly: Provided, That, for every five hundred free male inhabitants, there shall be one representative, and so on progressively with the number of free male inhabitants shall the right of representation increase, until the number of representatives shall amount to twenty five; after which, the number and proportion of representatives shall be regulated by the legislature: Provided, That no person be eligible or qualified to act as a representative unless he shall have been a citizen of one of the United States three years, and be a resident in the district, or unless he shall have resided in the district three years; and, in either case, shall likewise hold in his own right, in fee simple, two hundred acres of land within the same; Provided, also, That a freehold in fifty acres of land in the district, having been a citizen of one of the states, and being resident in the district, or the like freehold and two years residence in the district, shall be necessary to qualify a man as an elector of a representative.

Section 10. The representatives thus elected, shall serve for the term of two years; and, in case of the death of a representative, or removal from office, the governor shall issue a writ to the county or township for which he was a member, to elect another in his stead, to serve for the residue of the term.

Section 11. The general assembly or legislature shall consist of the governor, legislative council, and a house of representatives. The Legislative Council shall consist of five members, to continue in office five years, unless sooner removed by Congress; any three of whom to be a quorum: and the members of the Council shall be nominated and appointed in the following manner, to wit: As soon as representatives shall be elected, the Governor shall appoint a time and place for them to meet together; and, when met, they shall nominate ten persons, residents in the district, and each possessed of a freehold in five hundred acres of land, and return their names to Congress; five of whom Congress shall appoint and commission to serve as aforesaid; and, whenever a vacancy shall happen in the council, by death or removal from office, the house of representatives shall nominate two persons, qualified as aforesaid, for each vacancy, and return their names to Congress; one of whom congress shall appoint and commission for the residue of the term. And every five years, four months at least before the expiration of the time of service of the members of council, the said house shall nominate ten persons, qualified as aforesaid, and return their names to Congress; five of whom Congress shall appoint and commission to serve as members of the council five years, unless sooner removed. And the governor, legislative council, and house of representatives, shall have authority to make laws in all cases, for the good government of the district, not repugnant to the principles and articles in this ordinance established and declared. And all bills, having passed by a majority in the house, and by a majority in the council, shall be referred to the governor for his assent; but no bill, or legislative act whatever, shall be of any force without his assent. The governor shall have power to convene, prorogue, and dissolve the general assembly, when, in his opinion, it shall be expedient.

Section 12. The governor, judges, legislative council, secretary, and such other officers as Congress shall appoint in the district, shall take an oath or affirmation of fidelity and of office; the governor before the president of congress, and all other officers before the Governor. As soon as a legislature shall be formed in the district, the council and house assembled in one room, shall have authority, by joint ballot, to elect a delegate to Congress, who shall have a seat in Congress, with a right of debating but not voting during this temporary government.

Section 13. And, for extending the fundamental principles of civil and religious liberty, which form the basis whereon these republics, their laws and constitutions are erected; to fix and establish those principles as the basis of all laws, constitutions, and governments, which forever hereafter shall be formed in the said territory: to provide also for the establishment of States, and permanent government therein, and for their admission to a share in the federal councils on an equal footing with the original States, at as early periods as may be consistent with the general interest:

Section 14. It is hereby ordained and declared by the authority aforesaid, That the following articles shall be considered as articles of compact between the original States and the people and States in the said territory and forever remain unalterable, unless by common consent, to wit:

Article 1. No person, demeaning himself in a peaceable and orderly manner, shall ever be molested on account of his mode of worship or religious sentiments, in the said territory.

Article 2. The inhabitants of the said territory shall always be entitled to the benefits of the writ of habeas corpus, and of the trial by jury; of a proportionate representation of the people in the legislature; and of judicial proceedings according to the course of the common law. All persons shall be bailable, unless for capital offenses, where the proof shall be evident or the presumption great. All fines shall be moderate; and no cruel or unusual punishments shall be inflicted. No man shall be deprived of his liberty or property, but by the judgment of his peers or the law of the land; and, should the public exigencies make it necessary, for the common preservation, to take any person's property, or to demand his particular services, full compensation shall be made for the same. And, in the just preservation of rights and property, it is understood and declared, that no law ought ever to be made, or have force in the said territory, that shall, in any manner whatever, interfere with or affect private contracts or engagements, bona fide, and without fraud, previously formed.

Article 3. Religion, morality, and knowledge, being necessary to good government and the happiness of mankind, schools and the means of education shall forever be encouraged. The utmost good faith shall always be observed towards the Indians; their lands and property shall never be taken from them without their consent; and, in their property, rights, and liberty, they shall never be invaded or disturbed, unless in just and lawful wars authorized by Congress; but laws founded in justice and humanity, shall from time to time be made for preventing wrongs being done to them, and for preserving peace and friendship with them.

Article 4. The said territory, and the States which may be formed therein, shall forever remain a part of this Confederacy of the United States of America, subject to the Articles of Confederation, and to such alterations therein as shall be constitutionally made; and to all the acts and ordinances of the United States in Congress assembled, conformable thereto. The inhabitants and settlers in the said territory shall be subject to pay a part of the federal debts contracted or to be contracted, and a proportional part of the expenses of government, to be apportioned on them by Congress according to the same common rule and measure by which apportionments thereof shall be made on the other States; and the taxes for paying their proportion shall be laid and levied by the authority and direction of the legislatures of the district or districts, or new States, as in the original States, within the time agreed upon by the United States in Congress assembled. The legislatures of those districts or new States, shall never interfere with the primary disposal of the soil by the United States in Congress assembled, nor with any regulations Congress may find necessary for securing the title in such soil to the bona fide purchasers. No tax shall be imposed on lands the property of the United States; and, in no case, shall nonresident proprietors be taxed higher than residents. The navigable waters leading into the Mississippi and St. Lawrence, and the carrying places between the same, shall be common highways and forever free, as well to the inhabitants of the said territory as to the citizens of the United States, and those of any other States that may be admitted into the confederacy, without any tax, impost, or duty therefor.

Article 5. There shall be formed in the said territory, not less than three nor more than five States; and the boundaries of the States, as soon as Virginia shall alter her act of cession, and consent to the same, shall become fixed and established as follows, to wit: The western State in the said territory, shall be bounded by the Mississippi, the Ohio, and Wabash Rivers; a direct line drawn from the Wabash and Post Vincents, due North, to the territorial line between the United States and Canada; and, by the said territorial line, to the Lake of the Woods and Mississippi. The middle State shall be bounded by the said direct line, the Wabash from Post Vincents to the Ohio, by the Ohio, by a direct line, drawn due north from the mouth of the Great Miami, to the said territorial line, and by the said territorial line. The eastern State shall be bounded by the last mentioned direct line, the Ohio, Pennsylvania, and the said territorial line: Provided, however, and it is further understood and declared, that the boundaries of these three States shall be subject so far to be altered, that, if Congress shall hereafter find it expedient, they shall have authority to form one or two States in that part of the said territory which lies north of an east and west line drawn through the southerly bend or extreme of Lake Michigan. And, whenever any of the said States shall have sixty thousand free inhabitants therein, such State shall be admitted, by its delegates, into the Congress of the United States, on an equal footing with the original States in all respects whatever, and shall be at liberty to form a permanent constitution and State government: Provided, the constitution and government so to be formed, shall be republican, and in conformity to the principles contained in these articles; and, so far as it can be consistent with the general interest of the confederacy, such admission shall be allowed at an earlier period, and when there may be a less number of free inhabitants in the State than sixty thousand.

Article 6. There shall be neither slavery nor involuntary servitude in the said territory, otherwise than in the punishment of crimes whereof the party shall have been duly convicted: Provided, always, That any person escaping into the same, from whom labor or service is lawfully claimed in any one of the original States, such fugitive may be lawfully reclaimed and conveyed to the person claiming his or her labor or service as aforesaid.

Be it ordained by the authority aforesaid, That the resolutions of the 23rd of April, 1784, relative to the subject of this ordinance, be, and the same are hereby repealed and declared null and void.

Done by the United States, in Congress assembled, the 13th day of July, in the year of our Lord 1787, and of their sovereignty and independence the twelfth.

3.11   Slave Trade Statute, 1794

An Act to Prohibit the Carrying on the Slave Trade from the United States to any Foreign Place or Country

Section 1. Be it enacted by the Senate and House of Representatives of the United States of America in Congress assembled, That no citizen or citizens of the United States, or foreigner, or any other persons coming into, or residing within the same, shall, for himself or any other person whatsoever, either as master, factor or owner, build, fit, equip, load or otherwise prepare any ship or vessel, within any port or place of the said United States nor shall cause any ship or vessel to sail from any port or place within the same, for the purpose of carrying on any trade or traffic in slaves, to any foreign country; or for the purpose of procuring, from any foreign kingdom, place or country, the Inhabitants of such kingdom, place or country, to be transported to any foreign country, port, or place whatever, to be sold or disposed of, as slaves And if any ship or vessel shall be so fitted out, as aforesaid, for the said purposes, or shall be caused to sail, so as aforesaid, every such ship or vessel her tackle, furniture, apparel and other appurtenances, shall be forfeited to the United States; and shall be liable to be seized, prosecuted and condemned, in any of the circuit courts, or district court for the district where the said ship or vessel may be found and seized.

Section 2. And be it further enacted, That all and every person, so building, fitting out, equipping, loading, or otherwise preparing, or sending away, any ship or vessel, knowing or intending that the same shall be employed in such trade or business, contrary to the true intent and meaning of this act, or any ways aiding or abetting therein, shall severally forfeit and pay the sum of two thousand dollars, one moiety thereof to the use of the United States, and the other moiety thereof to the use of him or her who shall sue for and prosecute the same.

Section 3. And be it further enacted, That the owner, master or factor of each and every foreign ship or vessel, clearing out for any of the coasts or kingdoms of Africa, or suspected to be intended for the slave trade, and the suspicion being declared to the officer of the customs, by any citizen, on oath or affirmation, and such information being to the satisfaction of the said officer, shall first give bond with sufficient sure ties, to the treasurer of the United States, that none of the natives of Africa, or any other foreign country or place, shall be taken on board the said ship or vessel, to be transported, or sold as slaves, in any other foreign port or place whatever, within nine months thereafter.

Section 4. And be it further enacted, That if any citizen or citizens of the United States shall, contrary to the true intent and meaning of this act, take on board, receive or transport any such persons, as above described, in this act, for the purpose of selling them as slaves, as adores said, he or they shall forfeit and pay, for each and every person, so received on board, transported, or sold as aforesaid, the sum of two hundred dollars, to be recovered in any court of the United States pro per to try the same; the one moiety thereof to the use of the United States, and the other moiety to the use of such person or persons, who shall sue for and prosecute the same.

APPROVED. March 22, 1794.

3.12   State Requirements for Voting Rights, 1790 and 1828

Year	States where voters had to own property	States where voters had to be taxpayers	States where voters did not have to be property owners
1790 (13 states in the Union)	Massachusetts Rhode Island Connecticut New York New Jersey Delaware Maryland Virginia North Carolina	Pennsylvania South Carolina New Hampshire Georgia	
1828 (24 states in the Union)	Rhode Island New Jersey Virginia North Carolina Tennessee	Pennsylvania Delaware Ohio Louisiana Connecticut Mississippi Massachusetts	Vermont Kentucky New Hampshire Georgia South Carolina Maryland Indiana Illinois Alabama Maine New York Missouri

3.13   Chronology of the War of 1812

Event	Date	Importance
Napoleon excludes British goods from "fortress Europe"	1806	American ships caught in middle as British respond with blockade. British seize 1,000 U.S. ships.
British impress American sailors	1803-1812	British captains take American citizens to man ships
Chesapeake-Leopard fight off Virginia coast	June 1807	*Chesapeake* fired on by *Leopard* after refusing to be boarded. Three Americans killed, 18 wounded
Embargo Act	December 1807	Jefferson's attempt at "peaceful coercion" results in economic disaster for merchants
Hawks elected to Congress	1810	Calhoun, Clay, others bothered by insults to U.S.
Battle of Tippecanoe	1811	Tecumseh's brother leads attack on Harrison's army of 1,000 in Ohio River valley
Congress declares war	June 18, 1812	Pushed by War Hawks, Madison asks for declaration. All Federalists oppose it.
Invasion attempts of Canada	1812	Three attempts to invade border—all fail
Battle of York (Toronto)	April 1813	U.S. troops take control of Great Lakes, burn York
Battle of Lake Erie	September 1813	Capt. Perry repulses British naval attack
Battle of Thames	October 1813	Tecumseh killed in U.S. victory in Ontario. Indians weakened by battle.
Battle of Horseshoe Bend	March 1814	Andrew Jackson defeats Creek Indians in Mississippi Territory.
British plan invasion of U.S.: Chesapeake Bay, Lake Champlain, and mouth of Mississippi River	1814	British burn capital Washington, D.C., buildings, but are turned back at Baltimore harbor
Battle of Plattsburgh	September 1814	U.S. secures northern Lake Champlain border with victory over larger British force
Hartford Convention	December 15, 1814	Group of Federalists discuss secession in Connecticut
Treaty of Ghent	December 24, 1814	British and American diplomats reach agreement in Ghent, Belgium
Battle of New Orleans	January 1815	Jackson's forces defeat British.

3.14 Key's "The Star-Spangled Banner"

"The Star-Spangled Banner," now the national anthem, was also called "The Defense of Fort McHenry." It was written by Francis Scott Key and dated September 20, 1814.

Oh, say can you see, by the dawn's early light,
What so proudly we hailed at the twilight's last gleaming?
Whose broad stripes and bright stars, through the perilous fight,
O'er the ramparts we watched, were so gallantly streaming?
And the rockets' red glare, the bombs bursting in air,
Gave proof through the night that our flag was still there.
O say, does that star-spangled banner yet wave
O'er the land of the free and the home of the brave?

On the shore, dimly seen through the mists of the deep,
Where the foe's haughty host in dread silence reposes,
What is that which the breeze, o'er the towering steep,
As it fitfully blows, now conceals, now discloses?
Now it catches the gleam of the morning's first beam,
In full glory reflected now shines on the stream:
'Tis the star-spangled banner! O long may it wave
O'er the land of the free and the home of the brave.

And where is that band who so vauntingly swore
That the havoc of war and the battle's confusion
A home and a country should leave us no more?
Their blood has wiped out their foul footstep's pollution.
No refuge could save the hireling and slave
From the terror of flight, or the gloom of the grave:
And the star-spangled banner in triumph doth wave
O'er the land of the free and the home of the brave.

Oh! thus be it ever, when freemen shall stand
Between their loved homes and the war's desolation!
Blest with victory and peace, may the heaven-rescued land
Praise the Power that hath made and preserved us a nation.
Then conquer we must, for our cause it is just,
And this be our motto: "In God is our trust."
And the star-spangled banner forever shall wave
O'er the land of the free and the home of the brave!

3.15 Population by State, 1800

State	Population
Connecticut	251,002
Delaware	64,273
Georgia	162,686
Kentucky	220,955
Maryland	341,543
Massachusetts	422,845
New Hampshire	183,858
New Jersey	211,149
New York	586,182
North Carolina	478,103
Pennsylvania	602,365
Rhode Island	69,122
South Carolina	345,591
Tennessee	105,602
Vermont	154,465
Virginia	885,171

3.16 Chronology of the Life of Benjamin Franklin

Printer, publisher, author, postmaster, educator, scientist, statesman, diplomat, philosopher, abolitionist—
Benjamin Franklin's life is an example of the range of talents that marked many of the nation's founders.

1706	Born in Boston on January 17
1718	Begins an apprenticeship in his brother James' printing shop in Boston
1723	Leaves his family and moves to Philadelphia
1724	Moves to London, continuing his training as a printer
1726	Returns to Philadelphia
1728	Opens his own printing office in Philadelphia
1729	Becomes owner and publisher of the Pennsylvania *Gazette*
1730	Marries Deborah Read Rogers
1731	Birth of son William; founds the first Circulating Library
1732	Birth of son Francis
1732	Begins annual publication of *Poor Richard: An Almanack,* which appears each year until 1758
1736	Death of son Francis; founds the Union Fire Company in Philadelphia
1737	Appointed Postmaster of Philadelphia
1742	Proposes establishment of the University of Pennsylvania
1743	Birth of daughter Sarah
1745	Death of father, Josiah Franklin
1747	First writings on electricity; organizes the first militia
1748	Sells printing office, retiring from business
1751	His book *Experiments and Observations on Electricity* is published in London
1752	In June, performs famous kite experiment; death of mother, Abiah Folger Franklin; founds first American fire insurance company
1757-62	In London as representative of the Pennsylvania Assembly
1762	Returns to Philadelphia
1764	Travels to London
1767	Travels to France
1769	Elected president of the American Philosophical Society
1774	The Hutchinson Letters affair damages Franklin's reputation; wife dies
1775	Returns to Philadelphia from London; elected to Continental Congress; submits Articles of Confederation of United Colonies
1776	Signs the Declaration of Independence; presides at Pennsylvania Constitutional Convention; goes to France as American Commissioner
1778	Negotiates and signs Treaty of Alliance with France
1779	Appointed Minister to France
1782	Negotiates, with John Adams and John Jay, the Treaty of Peace with Great Britain
1784	Negotiates treaties with Prussia and other European countries
1785	Returns to Philadelphia
1787	Elected president of the Pennsylvania Society for Promoting the Abolition of Slavery; delegate to the Constitutional Convention
1790	Dies in Philadelphia on April 17

II

POLITICAL HISTORY

SECTION 4

The Presidency and Electoral Politics

4.1   Chronology of the Right to Vote, 1620-1975

1620—The Mayflower Compact declares that only those *Mayflower* passengers who signed the Compact will be allowed to vote in Plymouth Colony. Future newcomers to the Colony will be granted voting privileges only if they are members of the Puritan Church.

Colonial era—Voting is restricted to middle and upper class voters, with property and personal assets the main criteria for voting privileges. While laws vary from colony to colony and are subject to change, the general intent is to keep the vote in the hands of prosperous adult white male Protestants and away from Catholics, Jews, blacks, women, servants and strangers. The "sovereign" status imposed upon American Indians means that their voting rights are not to be considered at all until well into the 19th century.

Late 1600s—The Massachusetts Bay and the Connecticut Colonies limit voting rights to men who are either worth forty (English) pounds or whose land provides an income of forty (English) shillings per year.

1699—New York raises the required land value for voting rights from forty shillings to forty pounds.

1700s—The Virginia legislature passes a law requiring voters to own fifty acres of land or twenty-five acres with a house on it or valuables worth fifty pounds. In Rhode Island, the right to vote can be inherited as property.

1719—Apprentices and sailors are denied the vote in South Carolina.

1725—The New Jersey assembly writes a suffrage law specifying that only men who own a freehold worth fifty pounds can vote. In 1776, this requirement is changed from land to any valuables worth fifty pounds.

1728—New Hampshire voters must own real estate worth fifty pounds.

1752—Georgia voters must own fifty acres of land.

1759—Voters in South Carolina must own one hundred acres of land.

Mid-1700s—By this time, all thirteen original colonies pass laws requiring ownership of a minimum amount of property or personal worth in exchange for voting rights. As long as they meet this restriction, free blacks, with the exception of those living in South Carolina and Georgia, are permitted to vote.

Revolutionary War era—In writing their constitutions, most states do away with earlier black voting rights. Of the original colonies, only Massachusetts, New Hampshire and Rhode Island now allow blacks to vote. Except for Vermont and Maine, no new states entering the Union give blacks the right to vote until after the Civil War.

During the War, demand for voting reform rises, particularly in relation to property requirements. Young soldiers object to being asked to fight for their country while being barred from voting and taxpayers begin to demand voting representation. Many states respond either by reducing property requirements or by substituting other restrictions.

1775—New Hampshire eliminates its property requirement, giving the vote to all free male taxpayers over twenty-one who can pay a poll tax.

1776—Pennsylvania's new state constitution gives the vote to any taxpaying male over age twenty-one who has lived in the state for one year.

1777—Vermont does away with both property and taxpaying restrictions and declares every adult male eligible to vote.

1787—The new United States Constitution gives each state the right to determine voting qualifications for both state and federal elections.

1790—New Jersey grants all free citizens the right to vote.

1791—Vermont is admitted to the Union as the only state to allow all white men who have a year's residency to vote without property or taxpaying restrictions.

1807—New Jersey rewrites its voting qualifications to exclude women

1810—Maryland gives the vote to all qualified free white male residents with no property restrictions.

Mid-19th century—By now, most states have dropped property-holding and taxpaying requirements and have granted suffrage to all native-born free white males over age twenty-one. Some states still have restrictions that specifically withhold voting rights from women, blacks, Indians, Chinese, Catholics and Jews.

1848—The fight for women's suffrage officially begins at the Seneca Falls (NY) Convention attended by three hundred people. Elizabeth Cady Stanton's "Declaration of Sentiments," modeled on the Declaration of Independence, is the first American document to present the women's suffrage demand.

1850—The first National Woman's Rights Convention takes place in Worcester, Massachusetts.

1860s—Civil war soldiers protest the tradition of twenty-one being the minimum age for voting rights.

1866—The Civil Rights Act of 1866 grants citizenship, with all its inherent rights, to ex-slaves.

1867—The Reconstruction Act of 1867 gives blacks the opportunity to vote.

1868—The Fourteenth Amendment to the Constitution, defining citizens as all people born or naturalized in the United States and subject to its jurisdiction, gives citizenry to blacks but does not necessarily grant them voting rights. As for American Indians, arguments remain that those who live in "Indian country" are "sovereign citizens," not subject to United States jurisdiction and therefore ineligible to vote. The Fourteenth Amendment also reinforces the individual states' tradition of establishing twenty-one as the minimum voting age.

1869—The Wyoming Territory adopts a constitution granting universal suffrage to both sexes, marking the first time women in the modern world win the right to unrestricted voting. When Wyoming achieves statehood in 1890, women's suffrage is written into its state constitution.

1870—The Fifteenth Amendment to the Constitution declares that the right of citizens of the United States or of any state cannot be denied on the basis of race, color or previous conditions of servitude. This does not necessarily mean, however, that blacks must be *allowed* to vote and states are still free to set their own qualifications. Moreover, the right of women to vote is still unclear and American Indians are still disenfranchised.

1870—The Territory of Utah enfranchises women.

1874—In ruling that an official in St. Louis is free to refuse to register a woman to vote, the U.S. Supreme Court's *Minor v. Happersett* decision rules that the Fifteenth Amendment does not grant suffrage to women.

1875—Women win the right to vote in school elections in Michigan and Minnesota.

1876—In *United States v. Cuikshank,* the United States Supreme Court rules that voting is not an automatic right of citizens. States are now free to set their own suffrage requirements. In accordance with the Fifteenth Amendment, however, these requirements must apply to everyone.

1878—The Sixteenth Amendment to the Constitution, known as the "Anthony Amendment" in honor of women's suffrage leader Susan B. Anthony, has its first Senate Committee hearing. Introduced by Senator Aaron Sargent of California, the proposal reads: "The rights of citizens of the United States to vote shall not be denied or abridged by the United States or any state on account of sex."

1887—The Senate votes on the proposed Sixteenth Amendment for the first time. It is defeated by a vote of more than two to one against.

1887—Congress denies the vote previously given Utah women.

1890—The National American Women Suffrage Association determines its goal must be to win the right to vote state by state in order to gain enough political clout to push the Anthony Amendment through Congress.

1890-1920—Except for Texas and Arkansas, all southern states rewrite their constitutions' suffrage requirements. Ability to pass a literacy test and, for some states, the ability to pay a poll tax, now determine one's right to vote.

1893—Colorado becomes the second state to give the vote to women.

1896—Idaho, Indiana and Utah give women the vote.

1898—In *Williams v. Mississippi,* the United States Supreme Court strikes down challenges to literacy tests, declaring them legal. While these tests do apply to both black and white voters, several states adopt "grandfather clauses" exempting anyone whose forebears had voted prior to 1867 from taking the test; thus, whites are largely unaffected by the requirement. For black voters in the South, however, the Supreme Court ruling is a deathblow. In the face of intimidating and unfair oral literacy tests, the number of registered black voters drops dramatically. In two years' time, Mississippi's registered black voters drop from almost seventy percent of those eligible to less than six percent. Louisiana's registered black voters fall from 130,000 in 1896 to less than 1,500 by 1904. The ruling also upholds the constitutionality of poll taxes, applicable to everyone. Many states, primarily southern, soon pass similar laws.

1909—The National Association for the Advancement of Colored People is founded, largely to combat unfair suffrage laws.

1910—Washington State grants women suffrage.

1913—Illinois is the first state east of the Mississippi to enfranchise women.

1913—A pro-suffrage parade of 8,000 people lines Washington, D.C.'s Pennsylvania Avenue the day before President-elect Woodrow Wilson's inauguration. As angry men attack the marchers, the parade turns into a near-riot and federal troops are called in. This episode marks the beginning of newer, more militant battles for women's suffrage.

1914—The Senate votes again on the proposed women's suffrage amendment. Although the votes in favor actually exceed those against, the proposal fails to win the necessary two-thirds majority for passage.

1915—In *Guinn v. United States,* the U.S. Supreme Court rules that grandfather clauses, designed to exempt whites from taking literacy tests, are illegal.

1915—The House of Representatives' vote on the Anthony Amendment is defeated 204 to 174.

Nov. 1916—Hundreds of women picket the White House to demand support from newly re-elected President Wilson for the suffrage amendment. Violence and arrests ensue and many women are jailed. In prison, some are forced to perform rough labor while others are put in solitary confinement or are physically mistreated. Ultimately, Wilson demands the inmates be unconditionally released. Later, the D.C. Court of Appeals rules that the arrests, convictions and inprisonments are unconstitutional.

Jan. 1918—President Wilson publicly comes out in favor of the suffrage amendment and urges Congress to pass it. The House of Representatives secures the necessary two-thirds majority, but it is opposed by the Senate.

June 1919—The House of Representatives re-passes the proposed amendment and the Senate finally votes to accept with necessary majority. The Anthony Amendment is submitted to the states for ratification.

1919—An act passed by Congress confers citizenship on those American Indians who had served in the armed forces during World War I.

August 1920—Tennessee becomes the 36th and last state (Wisconsin being the first) to ratify the Nineteenth Amendment to the Constitution (first proposed as the Sixteenth). The proclamation granting American women the right to vote is signed into law by Secretary of State Bainbridge Colby.

1920—North Carolina drops its poll tax requirement.

1920s—A movement to lower the voting age from twenty-one, voiced most recently during World War I, fails to gain momentum.

1924—The Indian Citizenship Act grants full citizenship to all American Indians born in the United States. However, in the coming years, the same barriers prohibiting blacks from voting, such as poll taxes, grandfather clauses and literacy tests, will also often be used to bar American Indian voters.

1934—Louisiana drops its poll tax requirement.

1937—Florida drops its poll tax requirement.

1941—In the *United States v. Classic,* the U.S. Supreme Court declares that primary elections are actual elections if they are "integral" to the political system. This ruling ends the practice of excluding blacks from participating in what are, in effect, primary elections in southern states, where, because of the dominance of the whites-only Democratic party, the winner of the general election is invariably chosen in the primary.

1942—Jennings Randolph of West Virginia introduces a resolution in the House to amend the United States Constitution by lowering the voting age to eighteen. The bill goes no further than congressional hearings. In the years that follow, more than one hundred and fifty versions of the proposed resolution will be introduced in Congress.

1942-1949—Congress passes five laws against poll taxes; all of them are killed in the Senate.

1943—Georgia Governor Ellis Arnall leads a state drive to lower the voting age. The amendment is overwhelmingly approved by the voters, making Georgia the first (and for the next twelve years, the only) state to allow eighteen year olds to vote.

1944—In its *Smith v. Allwright* decision, the U.S. Supreme Court rules in favor of a black man from Texas who had been denied a ballot for a congressional primary election, effectively declaring the white primary to be unconstitutional.

1947—Only about one percent of eligible blacks in Alabama and Mississippi and only about two percent in Louisiana are registered voters. President Truman sets up a President's Committee on Civil Rights to address the problem.

1948—The United States Supreme Court rules that the State of Alabama, in a suit brought against it by the N.A.A.C.P. and the Voters and Veterans Association, had used its oral literacy tests in a discriminatory manner and that tests given had to be "uniform" and "objective," thus ushering in the use of written literacy tests.

1954—After years of Congressional attempts, the proposed constitutional amendment to lower the voting age to eighteen gains momentum. President Dwight D. Eisenhower speaks in favor of the proposal during his January State of the Union message and in March the debate is brought to the Senate floor for the first time. The amendment fails, five votes shy of the required two-third's majority. It is voted down mostly by Southern senators who resent federal intervention in state voting matters.

1955—Kentucky lowers its voting age to eighteen.

1957—The Civil Rights Act of 1957, designed to encourage black voting, establishes a new Commission on Civil Rights and gives the U.S. Attorney General the right to go to court to enforce voting laws.

1960—The Civil Rights Act of 1960 gives the federal government greater authority to protect blacks' voting rights and enforce voting laws.

1964—The Civil Rights Act of 1964 makes a sixth grade education sufficient proof of literacy and sparks voter registration drives in the South.

1964—The Twenty-Fourth Amendment to the Constitution is ratified, striking down the use of poll taxes in federal elections.

Jan. 1965—Dr. Martin Luther King, Jr. leads a black voter registration drive in Selma, Alabama. He is arrested, along with thousands of others, on such charges as "unlawful assembly."

March 1965—Dr. King leads a non-violent march from Selma to Montgomery, Alabama to protest restrictions against black voters. State troopers and local law officials attack the marchers with whips, tear gas, nightsticks, and electric cattle prods.

1965—The Voting Rights Bill of 1965 bans literacy tests and allows the government to use federal registrars to enforce minority—in particular, black and American Indian—voter registration. Within two years of the bill's passage, almost half a million blacks are added to voting lists in the South.

1966—The U.S. Supreme Court declares that all poll taxes are illegal, including those levied for state and local elections, as they violate the Fourteenth Amendment. Affected are Alabama, Arkansas, Mississippi, Texas, and Virginia, all of which still impose poll taxes for local and state elections.

1968—Indiana Senator Birch Bayh chairs hearings by the Senate Subcommittee on Constitutional Amendments to re-address the issue of lowering the voting age. A lowered voting age is favored by many leading politicians, including outgoing President Lyndon B. Johnson and presidential candidates Richard Nixon and Hubert Humphrey, as well as by the thousands of young people who rally, petition and lobby for it throughout the country. Despite such support, however, it seems that winning the three-fourths approval of the states necessary to ratify the amendment will be a long, hard-fought battle.

1970—As a means of side-stepping the lengthy amendment ratification process, Senator Mike Mansfield of Montana introduces a rider to the Voting Rights Act of 1970, proposing a lowering of the voting age to eighteen in all federal, state and local elections. The act passes House and Senate approval. With misgivings, for he believes a constitutional amendment is the preferred process, President Richard Nixon signs the bill into law in order to avoid vetoing the attached Voting Rights Act. Later in the year, in a split decision, the Supreme Court rules that the eighteen-year-old vote applies only to national elections and that states still have the right to determine voter qualifications in state and local contests.

1971—The proposed Twenty-Sixth Amendment to the Constitution is once again bought to a vote in the Senate. This time, the approval is 94 to 0. The vote in the House is 400 to 19 in favor of. Minutes after congressional passage, Minnesota becomes the first state to ratify the amendment. A record three months later, on June 30, 1971, Ohio becomes the last to ratify. Eighteen- to twenty-year-old United States citizens are finally given the right to vote.

1975—The 1965 Voting Rights Act is expanded to require states to provide bilingual ballots and voting information where Spanish, Asian and American Indian languages and dialects are spoken by large numbers of voters.

4.2   Comparative Voter Participation Levels

Actual voter turnout rates for recent elections in selected countries:

Country	Year	Type of Election	% Turnout of Eligible Voters
United States	**1996**	**Presidential**	**65.97**
Algeria	1995	Presidential	75.69
Argentina	1995	Presidential	80.9
Australia	1996	Parliamentary	96.3
Austria	1995	Parliamentary	82.74
Belgium	1995	Parliamentary	91.15
Bulgaria	1996	Presidential	49.79
Canada	1993	Prime Min.	73
Croatia	1995	Legislative	68.79
Cyprus	1996	Legislative	90.13
Czech Republic	1996	Legislative	76.29
Ecuador	1996	Presidential	73
Germany	1994	Parliamentary	71
Ghana	1996	Presidential	78.21
Greece	1996	Parliamentary	76.34
Japan	1995	Parliamentary	44.5
Nicaragua	1996	Presidential	76.38
Russia	1996	Presidential	69.56
Slovenia	1996	Parliamentary	73.67
Sweden	1994	Parliamentary	87.3
Taiwan	1996	Presidential	75.2
Turkey	1995	Parliamentary	85.2
Zambia	1996	Presidential	58.23
Zimbabwe	1995	Parliamentary	31.8

Source: International Foundation for Election Systems.

4.3 Voter Turnout in U.S. Federal Elections, 1960-1996

Year	Voting Age Population	Registration	Turnout	% T/O of VAP
1996	196,511,000	146,211,960	96,456,345	49.08%
1994	193,650,000	130,292,822	75,105,860	38.78
1992	189,529,000	133,821,178	104,405,155	55.09
1990	185,812,000	121,105,630	67,859,189	36.52
1988	182,778,000	126,379,628	91,594,693	50.11
1986	178,566,000	118,399,984	64,991,128	36.40
1984	174,466,000	124,150,614	92,652,680	53.11
1982	169,938,000	110,671,225	67,615,576	39.79
1980	164,597,000	113,043,734	86,515,221	52.56
1978	158,373,000	103,291,265	58,917,938	37.21
1976	152,309,190	105,037,986	81,555,789	53.55
1974	146,336,000	96,199,020[1]	55,943,834	38.23
1972	140,776,000	97,328,541	77,718,554	55.21
1970	124,498,000	82,496,747[2]	58,014,338	46.60
1968	120,328,186	81,658,180	73,211,875	60.84
1966	116,132,000	76,288,283[3]	56,188,046	48.39
1964	114,090,000	73,715,818	70,644,592	61.92
1962	112,423,000	65,393,751[4]	53,141,227	47.27
1960	109,159,000	64,833,096[5]	68,838,204	63.06

Definitions: % T/O of VAP = Percent Turnout of Voting Age Population
[1]Registrations from Iowa not included.
[2]Registrations from Iowa and Missouri not included.
[3]Registrations from IA, KS, MS, MO, NE, and WY not included. D.C. had no independent status.
[4]Registrations from AL, AK, DC, IA, KS, KY, MS, MO, NE, NC, ND, SD, TN, WI, and WY not included.
[5]Registrations from AL, AK, DC, IA, KS, KY, MS, MO, NE, NM, NC, ND, OK, SD, WI, and WY not included.
Source: Congressional Research Service reports, Election Data Services Inc., and State Election Offices.

4.4   The Workings of the Electoral College

U.S. presidents are selected by the electoral college made up of electors from each state. Each state is allocated a number of electors equal to the number of its U.S. Senators (always two) plus the number of its U.S. Representatives (which may change each decade according to the size of each state's population as determined in the census).

The political parties (or independent candidates) in each state submit to the state's chief election official a list of individuals pledged to their candidate for president and equal in number to the state's electoral vote. Usually, the major political parties select these individuals either in their state party conventions or through appointment by their state party leaders while third parties and independent candidates merely designate theirs.

After their caucuses and primaries, the major parties nominate their candidates for president and vice president in their national conventions traditionally held in the summer preceding the election. Third parties and independent candidates follow different procedures according to the individual state laws. The names of the duly nominated candidates are then officially submitted to each state's chief election official so that they might appear on the general election ballot.

On the Tuesday following the first Monday of November in years divisible by four, the people in each state cast their ballots for the party slate of electors representing their choice for president and vice president. Whichever party slate wins the most popular votes in the state becomes that state's electors—so that, in effect, whichever presidential ticket gets the most popular votes in a state wins all the electors of that state. (The two exceptions to this are Maine and Nebraska where two electors are chosen by statewide popular vote and the remainder by the popular vote within each Congressional district.)

On the Monday following the second Wednesday of December each state's electors meet in their respective state capitals and cast their electoral votes—one for president and one for vice president. In order to prevent electors from voting only for "favorite sons" of their home state, at least one of their votes must be for a person from outside their state. The electoral votes are then sealed and transmitted from each state to the President of the Senate who, on the following January 6, opens and reads them before both houses of the Congress.

The candidate for president with the most electoral votes, provided that it is an absolute majority (one over half of the total), is declared president. Similarly, the vice presidential candidate with the absolute majority of electoral votes is declared vice president.

In the event no one obtains an absolute majority of electoral votes for president, the U.S. House of Representatives (as the chamber closest to the people) selects the president from among the top three contenders with each state casting only one vote and an absolute majority of the states being required to elect. Similarly, if no one obtains an absolute majority for vice president, then the U.S. Senate makes the selection from among the top two contenders for that office. At noon on January 20, the duly elected president and vice president are sworn into office.

Source: Congressional Research Service.

4.5 Presidential Elections, 1789-1996

Year	President	Party	Popular Vote Total %	Electoral Vote
1789	George Washington (Va.)	No party designations		69
	John Adams (Mass.)			34
	Others			35
1792	George Washington (Va.)	No party designations		132
	John Adams (Mass.)			77
	George Clinton (N.Y.)			50
	Thomas Jefferson (Va.)		4	
	Aaron Burr (N.Y.)		1	
1796	John Adams (Mass.)	Federalist		71
	Thomas Jefferson (Va.)	Democratic-Republican	68	
	Thomas Pinckney (S.C.)	Federalist	59	
	Aaron Burr (N.Y.)	Democratic-Republican	30	
	Others		48	
1800	Thomas Jefferson (Va.)	Democratic-Republican	73	
	Aaron Burr (N.Y.)	Democratic-Republican	73	
	John Adams (Mass.)	Federalist		65
	Charles C. Pinckney (S.C.)	Federalist		64
	John Jay (N.Y.)	Federalist	1	
1804	Thomas Jefferson (Va.)	Democratic-Republican	162	
	and George Clinton (N.Y.)			162
	Charles C. Pinckney (S.C.)	Federalist		14
	and Rufus King (N.Y.)		14	
1808	James Madison (Va.)	Democratic-Republican		122
	and George Clinton (N.Y.)			113
	Charles C. Pinckney (S.C.)	Federalist		47
	and Rufus King (N.Y.)		47	
	George Clinton (N.Y.)	Democratic-Republican		6
1812	James Madison (Va.)	Democratic-Republican		128
	and Elbridge Gerry (Mass.)			131
	DeWitt Clinton (N.Y.)	Federalist		89
	and Jared Ingersoll (Pa.)		86	
1816	James Monroe (Va.)	Democratic-Republican		183
	and Daniel Tompkins (N.Y.)			183
	Rufus King (N.Y.)	Federalist	3	
	and John Howard (Md.)			22
1820	James Monroe (Va.)	Democratic-Republican		231
	and Daniel Tompkins (N.Y.)			218
	John Quincy Adams (Mass.)	Democratic-Republican		1
1824	John Quincy Adams (Mass.)	Democratic-Republican	30.92	84
	Andrew Jackson (Tenn.)	Democratic-Republican	41.34	99
	William H. Crawford (Ga.)	Democratic-Republican	11.17	41
	Henry Clay (Ky.)	Democratic-Republican	12.99	37
	Others		3.57	—

Year	President	Party	Popular Vote Total %	Electoral Vote
1828	Andrew Jackson (Tenn.)	Democratic	55.97	178
	and John C. Calhoun (S.C.)			171
	John Quincy Adams (Mass.)	National-Republican	43.63	83
	and Richard Rush (Pa.)			
	Others		0.40	—
1832	Andrew Jackson (Tenn.)	Democratic	54.23	219
	and Martin Van Buren (N.Y.)			189
	Henry Clay (Ky.)	National-Republican	37.42	49
	and John Sereant (Pa.)			49
	John Floyd (Va.)	Independent	N/A	11
	and Henry Lee (Mass.)			11
	William Wirt (Md.)	Anti-Masonic	7.78	7
	and Amos Ellmaker (Pa.)			7
	Others		0.56	—
1836	Martin Van Buren (N.Y.)	Democratic	50.83	170
	and Richard M. Johnson (Ky.)			147
	William H. Harrison (Ohio)	Whig	36.63	73
	Hugh L. White (Tenn.)	Whig	9.72	26
	Daniel Webster (Mass.)	Whig	2.74	14
	W.P. Mangum (N.C.)	Independent	N/A	11
	Others		0.08	—
1840	William H. Harrison (Ohio)	Whig	52.88	234
	and John Tyler (Va.)			
	Martin Van Buren (N.Y.)	Democratic	46.81	60
	James G. Birney (N.Y.)	Liberty	0.28	—
	Others		0.03	—
1844	James K. Polk (Tenn.)	Democratic	49.54	170
	and George M. Dallas (Pa.)			
	Henry Clay (Ky.)	Whig	48.08	105
	and Theodore Frelinghuysen (N.J.)			
	James G. Birney (N.Y.)	Liberty	2.30	—
	Others		0.08	—
1848	Zachary Taylor (La.)	Whig	47.28	163
	and Millard Fillmore (N.Y.)			
	Lewis Cass (Mich.)	Democratic	42.49	127
	and William O. Butler (Ky.)			
	Martin Van Buren (N.Y.)	Free-Soil	10.12	—
	and Charles Francis Adams (Mass.)			
	Others		0.10	—
1852	Franklin Pierce (N.H.)	Democratic	50.84	254
	and William King (Ala.)			
	Winfield Scott (Va.)	Whig	43.87	42
	and William A. Graham (N.C.)			
	John P. Hale (N.H.)	Free-Soil	4.91	—
	and George Washington Julian (Ind.)			
	Others		0.38	—
1856	James Buchanan (Pa.)	Democratic	45.28	174
	and John C. Breckinridge (Ky.)			

Year	President	Party	Popular Vote Total %	Electoral Vote
	John C. Fremont (Calif.) and William L. Dayton (N.J.)	Republican	33.11	114
	Millard Fillmore (N.Y.) and Andrew J. Donelson (Tenn.)	American (Know-Nothing)	21.53	8
	Others		0.08	—
1860	Abraham Lincoln (Ill.) and Hannibal Hamlin (Maine)	Republican	39.82	180
	Stephen A. Douglas (Ill.) and Herschel V. Johnson (Ga.)	Democratic	29.46	12
	John C. Breckinridge (Ky.) and Joseph Lane (Oreg.)	Southern Democratic	18.09	72
	John Bell (Tenn.) and Edward Everett (Mass.)	Constitutional Union	12.61	39
	Others		0.01	—
1864	Abraham Lincoln (Ill.) and Andrew Johnson (Tenn.)	Republican	55.02	212
	George B. McClellan (N.Y.) and George Pendleton (Ohio)	Democratic	44.96	21
	Others		0.02	—
1868	Ulysses S. Grant (Ohio) and Schuyler Colfax (Ind.)	Republican	52.66	214
	Horatio Seymour (N.Y.) and Francis P. Blair (Mo.)	Democratic	47.3	80
	Others		—	—
1872	Ulysses S. Grant (Ohio) and Henry Wilson (Mass.)	Republican	55.63	286
	Horace Greeley (N.Y.) and Benjamin Gratz Brown (Mo.)	Democratic, Liberal Republican	43.83	
	Charles O'Conor (N.Y.) and John Quincy Adams II (Mass.)	"Straight" Democratic	0.29	—
	Others		0.25	

(Greeley died shortly after the popular election and before the meeting of the presidential electors. The electors supporting him divided their 66 votes among minor candidates.)

Year	President	Party	Popular Vote Total %	Electoral Vote
1876	Rutherford B. Hayes (Ohio) and William A. Wheeler (N.Y.)	Republican	47.95	185
	Samuel J. Tilden (N.Y.) and Thomas Hendrix (Ind.)	Democratic	50.97	184
	Peter Cooper (N.Y.)	Greenback	0.90	—
	Others		0.17	—
1880	James A. Garfield (Ohio) and Chester A. Arthur (N.Y.)	Republican	48.27	214
	Winfield S. Hancock (Pa.) and William English (Ind.)	Democratic	48.25	155
	James B. Weaver (Iowa) and Benjamin J. Chambers (Tex.)	Greenback-Labor	3.32	—
	Others		0.15	
1884	Grover Cleveland (N.Y.) and Thomas A. Hendricks (Ind.)	Democratic	48.50	219

Year	President	Party	Popular Vote Total %	Electoral Vote
	James G. Blaine (Maine) and John A. Logan (Ill.)	Republican	48.25	182
	Benjamin F. Butler (Mass.)	Greenback-Labor	1.74	—
	John P. St. John (Kans.)	Prohibition	1.47	—
	Others		0.04	—
1888	Benjamin Harrison (Ind.) and Levi. P. Morton (N.Y.)	Republican	47.82	233
	Grover Cleveland (N.Y.) and Allen G. Thurman (Ohio)	Democratic	48.62	168
	Clinton B. Fish (N.J.)	Prohibition	2.19	—
	Alson J. Streeter (Ill.)	Union Labor	1.29	—
	Others		0.07	—
1892	Grover Cleveland (N.Y.) and Adlai E. Stevenson (Ill.)	Democratic	46.05	277
	Benjamin Harrison (Ind.) and Whitelaw Reid (N.Y.)	Republican	42.96	145
	James B. Weaver (Iowa) and James G. Field (Va.)	Populist	8.50	22
	John Bidwell (Calif.)	Prohibition	2.25	—
	Others		0.25	—
1896	William McKinley (Ohio) and Garret Hobart (Va.)	Republican	51.01	271
	William Jennings Bryan (Nebr.) and Arthur Sewall (Maine)	Democratic	46.73	176 149
	William Jennings Bryan (endorsed) and Thomas E. Watson (Ga.)	Populist		—
	John M. Palmer (Ill.)	National-Democratic	0.96	—
	Joshua Levering (Md.)	Prohibition	0.90	—
	Others		0.41	—
1900	William McKinley (Ohio) and Theodore Roosevelt (N.Y.)	Republican	51.67	292
	William Jennings Bryan (Nebra.) and Adlai E. Stevenson (Ill.)	Democratic Populist	45.51	155
	John C. Woolley (Ill.)	Prohibition	1.50	—
	Eugene V. Debs (Ind.)	Socialist	0.62	—
	Others		0.70	
1904	Theodore Roosevelt (N.Y.) and Charles Fairbanks (Ind.)	Republican	56.41	336
	Alton B. Parker (N.Y.) and Henry G. Davis (W.Va.)	Democratic	37.60	140
	Eugene V. Debs (Ind.)	Socialist	2.98	—
	Silas C. Swallow (Pa.)	Prohibition	1.91	—
	Others		1.10	
1908	William H. Taft (Ohio) and James Sherman (N.Y.)	Republican	51.58	321
	William Jennings Bryan (Nebra.) and John W. Kern (Ind.)	Democratic	43.05	162
	Eugene V. Debs (Ind.)	Socialist	2.82	—

Year	President	Party	Popular Vote Total %	Electoral Vote
	Eugene W. Chafin (Ill.)	Prohibition	1.70	—
	Others		0.85	
1912	Woodrow Wilson (N.J.) and Thomas Marshall (Ind.)	Democratic	41.84	435
	Theodore Roosevelt (N.Y.) and Hiram Johnson (Calif.)	Progressive	27.39	88
	William Howard Taft (Ohio) and James Sherman (N.Y.)	Republican	23.18	8
	Eugene V. Debs (Ind.)	Socialist	5.99	—
	Others		1.61	
1916	Woodrow Wilson (N.J.) and Thomas Marshall (Ind.)	Democratic	49.24	277
	Charles Evans Hughes (N.Y.) and Charles W. Fairbanks (Ind.)	Republican	46.11	254
	A.L. Benson (N.Y.)	Socialist	3.18	—
	James Hanley (Ind.)	Prohibition	1.19	—
	Others		0.28	—
1920	Warren G. Harding (Ohio) and Calvin Coolidge (Mass.)	Republican	60.30	404
	James M. Cox (Ohio) and Franklin D. Roosevelt (N.Y.)	Democratic	34.17	127
	Eugene V. Debs (Ind.)	Socialist	3.42	—
	Parley P. Christensen (Utah)	Farmer Labor	0.99	—
	Others		1.13	—
1924	Calvin Coolidge (Mass.) and Charles Dawes (Ohio)	Republican	54.00	382
	John W. Davis (N.Y.) and Charles W. Bryan (Nebr.)	Democratic	28.84	136
	Robert M. La Follette (Wis.) and Burton K. Wheeler (Mont.)	Progressive	16.56	13
	Others		0.55	—
1928	Herbert C. Hoover (Calif.) and Charles Curtis (Kans.)	Republican	58.20	444
	Alfred E. Smith (N.Y.) and Joseph Robison (Ariz.)	Democratic	40.77	87
	Norman M. Thomas (N.Y.)	Socialist	0.72	—
	William Foster (Ill.)	Communist	0.13	
	Others		0.17	—
1932	Franklin D. Roosevelt (N.Y.) and John Nance Garner (Tex.)	Democratic	57.42	472
	Herbert C. Hoover (Calif.) and Charles Curtis (Kans.)	Republican	39.64	59
	Norman M. Thomas (N.Y.)	Socialist	2.22	—
	William Foster (Ill.)	Communist	0.26	—
	Others		0.45	—
1936	Franklin D. Roosevelt (N.Y.) and John Nance Garner (Tex.)	Democratic	60.79	523

Year	President	Party	Popular Vote Total %	Electoral Vote
	Alfred M. Landon (Kans.) and Frank Knox (Ill.)	Republican	36.54	8
	William Lemke (N.Dak.)	Union	1.96	—
	Norman M. Thomas (N.Y.)	Socialist	0.41	—
	Others		0.30	—
1940	Franklin D. Roosevelt (N.Y.) and Henry A. Wallace (Iowa)	Democratic	54.70	449
	Wendell L. Wilkie (Ind.) and Charles McNary (Oreg.)	Republican	44.82	82
	Norman M. Thomas (N.Y.)	Socialist	0.23	—
	Roger W. Babson (Mass.)	Prohibition	0.12	—
	Others		0.13	
1944	Franklin D. Roosevelt (N.Y.) and Harry S. Truman (Mo.)	Democratic	53.39	432
	Thomas E. Dewey (N.Y.) and John W. Bricker (Ohio)	Republican	45.89	99
	Norman Thomas (N.Y.)	Socialist	0.16	—
	Claude A. Watson (Calif.)	Prohibition	0.16	—
	Others		0.41	
1948	Harry S. Truman (Mo.) and Alben Barkley (Ky.)	Democratic	49.51	303
	Thomas E. Dewey (N.Y.) and Earl Warren (Calif.)	Republican	45.12	189
	J. Strom Thurmond (S.C.) and Fielding Wright (Miss.)	State's Rights Democratic	2.40	39
	Henry A. Wallace (Iowa) and Glen Taylor (Idaho)	Progressive	2.38	—
	Others		0.60	
1952	Dwight D. Eisenhower (Kans.) and Richard M. Nixon (Calif.)	Republican		
	Adlai E. Stevenson (Ill.) and John J. Sparkman	Democratic		442
				89
1956	Dwight D. Eisenhower (Kans.) and Richard M. Nixon (Calif.)	Republican		457
	Adlai E. Stevenson (Ill.) and Estes Kefauver (Tenn.)	Democratic		73
1960	John F. Kennedy (Mass.) and Lyndon Johnson (Tex.)	Democratic	49.7	
	Richard M. Nixon (Calif.) and Henry Cabot Lodge (Mass.)	Republican		303
				219
1964	Lyndon Johnson (Tex.) and Hubert H. Humphrey (Minn.)	Democratic		486
	Barry M. Goldwater (Ariz.) and William E. Miller	Republican		52
1968	Richard M. Nixon (Calif.) and Spiro T. Agnew (Md.)	Republican	43.4	301
	Hubert H. Humphrey (Minn.) and Edmund S. Muskie (Minn.)	Democratic		191

Year	President	Party	Popular Vote Total %	Electoral Vote
	George C. Wallace (Ala). and Curtis F. LeMay	American Independent		46
1972	Richard M. Nixon (Calif.) and Spiro T. Agnew (Md.)	Republican		520
	George McGovern (Mass.) and Sargent Shriver	Democratic		17
1976	Jimmy Carter (Ga.) and Walter Mondale (Minn.)	Democratic		297
	Gerald R. Ford (Mich.) and Robert J. Dole (Kans.)	Republican		240
1980	Ronald Reagan (Calif.) and George Bush (Tex.)	Republican		489
	Jimmy Carter (Ga.) and Walter F. Mondale (Minn.)	Democratic		40
1984	Ronald Reagan (Calif.) and George Bush (Tex.)	Republican		525
	Walter F. Mondale (Minn.) and Geraldine A. Ferraro (N.Y.)	Democratic		13
1988	George Bush (Tex.) and Dan Quayle (Ind.)	Republican		426
	Michael S. Dukakis (Mass.) and Lloyd Bentsen (Tex.)	Democratic		111
1992	Bill Clinton (Ark.) and Al Gore, Jr. (Tenn.)	Democratic	43.0	370
	George Bush (Tex.) and Dan Quayle (Ind.)	Republican		168
	H. Ross Perot (Tex.) and James B. Stockdale (Calif.)	Independent	8.0	0
1996	Bill Clinton (Ark.) and Al Gore, Jr. (Tenn.)	Democratic	49.0	379
	Robert J. Dole (Kans.) and Jack F. Kemp (N.Y.)	Republican	41.0	159
	H. Ross Perot (Tex.) and Pat Choate (Okla.)	Independent		0

4.6   Qualifications for Federal Office

	PRESIDENT	VICE-PRES	SENATOR	REPRESENTATIVE
AGE	35+	35+	30+	25+
CITIZEN	born in US	born in US	9+ years	7+ years
RESIDENCE	14+ years	14+ years	in state	in state
TERM	4 years	4 years	6 years	2 years
LIMIT	2 terms	none	none	none
NUMBER OF	1	1	100	435

4.7   Federal Campaign Contribution Limits

An individual may give a maximum of:

- $1,000 per election to a Federal candidate or the candidate's campaign committee. The limit applies separately to each election. Primaries, runoffs and general elections are considered separate elections.

- $5,000 per calendar year to a PAC or State party committee. This limit applies to a PAC (political action committee) or a State (or local) party committee that supports Federal candidates. (PACs are neither party committees nor candidate committees. Some PACs are sponsored by corporations and unions and trade, industry and labor PACs. Other PACs, often ideological, do not have a corporate or labor sponsor and are therefore called non-connected PACs.) Party committees and PACs use individuals' contributions to make their own contributions to Federal candidates to fund other election-related activities.

- $20,000 per calendar year to a national party committee. This limit applies separately to a party's national committee, House campaign committee and Senate campaign committee.

- $25,000 total per calendar year. This annual limit places a ceiling on total contributions.

- $100 in currency (cash) to any political committee. (Anonymous cash contributions may not exceed $50.) Contributions exceeding $100 must be made by check, money order or other written instrument.

4.8   Presidents and Vice Presidents, 1789-1999

Year	President and Vice President	Party
1789	George Washington (Va.) John Adams (Mass.)	No party designations
1792	George Washington (Va.) John Adams (Mass.)	No party designations
1796	John Adams (Mass.) Thomas Jefferson (Va.)	Federalist Democratic-Republican
1800	Thomas Jefferson (Va.) Aaron Burr (N.Y.)	Democratic-Republican
1804	Thomas Jefferson (Va.) and George Clinton (N.Y.)	Democratic-Republican
1808	James Madison (Va.) and George Clinton (N.Y.)	Democratic-Republican
1812	James Madison (Va.) and Elbridge Gerry (Mass.)	Democratic-Republican
1816	James Monroe (Va.) and Daniel Tompkins (N.Y.)	Democratic-Republican
1820	James Monroe (Va.) and Daniel Tompkins (N.Y.)	Democratic-Republican
1824	John Quincy Adams (Mass.) and Andrew Jackson (Tenn.)	Democratic-Republican
1828	Andrew Jackson (Tenn.) and John C. Calhoun (S.C.)	Democratic
1832	Andrew Jackson (Tenn.) and Martin Van Buren (N.Y.)	Democratic
1836	Martin Van Buren (N.Y.) and Richard M. Johnson (Ky.)	Democratic
1840	William H. Harrison (Ohio) and John Tyler (Va.)	Whig
1841	John Tyler (Va.) (no Vice President)	Whig
1844	James K. Polk (Tenn.) and George M. Dallas (Pa.)	Democratic
1848	Zachary Taylor (La.) and Millard Fillmore (N.Y.)	Whig
1850	Milard Filmore (N.Y.) (no Vice President)	Whig
1852	Franklin Pierce (N.H.) and William King (Ala.)	Democratic
1856	James Buchanan (Pa.) and John C. Breckinridge (Ky.)	Democratic
1860	Abraham Lincoln (Ill.) and Hannibal Hamlin (Maine)	Republican
1864	Abraham Lincoln (Ill.) and Andrew Johnson (Tenn.)	Republican
1865	Andrew Johnson (Tenn.) (no Vice President)	Republican

<u>Year</u>	<u>President</u>	<u>Party</u>
1868	Ulysses S. Grant (Ohio) and Schuyler Colfax (Ind.)	Republican
1872	Ulysses S. Grant (Ohio) and Henry Wilson (Mass.)	Republican
1876	Rutherford B. Hayes (Ohio) and William A. Wheeler (N.Y.)	Republican
1880	James A. Garfield (Ohio) and Chester A. Arthur (N.Y.)	Republican
1881	Chester A. Arthur (N.Y.) (no Vice President)	Republican
1884	Grover Cleveland (N.Y.) and Thomas A. Hendricks (Ind.)	Democratic
1888	Benjamin Harrison (Ind.) and Levi. P. Morton (N.Y.)	Republican
1892	Grover Cleveland (N.Y.) and Adlai E. Stevenson (Ill.)	Democratic
1896	William McKinley (Ohio) and Garret Hobart (Va.)	Republican
1900	William McKinley (Ohio) and Theodore Roosevelt (N.Y.)	Republican
1901	Theodore Roosevelt (N.Y.) (no Vice President)	Republican
1904	Theodore Roosevelt (N.Y.) and Charles Fairbanks (Ind.)	Republican
1908	William H. Taft (Ohio) and James Sherman (N.Y.)	Republican
1912	Woodrow Wilson (N.J.) and Thomas Marshall (Ind.)	Democratic
1916	Woodrow Wilson (N.J.) and Thomas Marshall (Ind.)	Democratic
1920	Warren G. Harding (Ohio) and Calvin Coolidge (Mass.)	Republican
1924	Calvin Coolidge (Mass.) and Charles Dawes (Ohio)	Republican
1928	Herbert C. Hoover (Calif.) and Charles Curtis (Kans.)	Republican
1932	Franklin D. Roosevelt (N.Y.) and John Nance Garner (Tex.)	Democratic
1936	Franklin D. Roosevelt (N.Y.) and John Nance Garner (Tex.)	Democratic
1940	Franklin D. Roosevelt (N.Y.) and Henry A. Wallace (Iowa)	Democratic
1944	Franklin D. Roosevelt (N.Y.) and Harry S. Truman (Mo.)	Democratic
1945	Harry S. Truman (Mo.) (no Vice President)	Democratic
1948	Harry S. Truman (Mo.) and Alben Barkley (Ky.)	Democratic
1952	Dwight D. Eisenhower (Kans.) and Richard M. Nixon (Calif.)	Republican

Year	President	Party
1956	Dwight D. Eisenhower (Kans.) and Richard M. Nixon (Calif.)	Republican
1960	John F. Kennedy (Mass.) and Lyndon Johnson (Tex.)	Democratic
1963	Lyndon Johnson (Tex.) (no Vice President)	Democratic
1964	Lyndon Johnson (Tex.) and Hubert H. Humphrey (Minn.)	Democratic
1968	Richard M. Nixon (Calif.) and Spiro T. Agnew (Md.)	Republican
1972	Richard M. Nixon (Calif.) and Spiro T. Agnew (Md.)	Republican
1974	Gerald R. Ford (Mich.) and Nelson Rockefeller (N.Y.)	Republican
1976	Jimmy Carter (Ga.) and Walter Mondale (Minn.)	Democratic
1980	Ronald Reagan (Calif.) and George Bush (Tex.)	Republican
1984	Ronald Reagan (Calif.) and George Bush (Tex.)	Republican
1988	George Bush (Tex.) and Dan Quayle (Ind.)	Republican
1992	Bill Clinton (Ark.) and Al Gore, Jr. (Tenn.)	Democratic
1996	Bill Clinton (Ark.) and Al Gore, Jr. (Tenn.)	Democratic

4.9 First Ladies

	Birth–Death Dates
Martha Dandridge Washington	1731-1802
Abigail Smith Adams	1744-1818
Dolley Payne Madison	1768-1849
Elizabeth Kortright Monroe	1768-1830
Louisa Catherine Adams	1775-1852
Anna Symmes Harrison	1775-1864
Letitia Christian Tyler	1790-1842
Julia Gardiner Tyler	1820-1889
Sarah Childress Polk	1803-1891
Margaret Smith Taylor	1788-1852
Abigail Powers Fillmore	1798-1853
Jane Appleton Pierce	1806-1863
Mary Todd Lincoln	1818-1882
Eliza McCardle Johnson	1810-1876
Julia Dent Grant	1826-1902
Lucy Webb Hayes	1831-1889
Lucretia Rudolph Garfield	1832-1918
Frances Folsom Cleveland	1864-1947
Caroline Scott Harrison	1832-1892
Ida Saxton McKinley	1847-1907
Edith Carow Roosevelt	1861-1948
Helen Herron Taft	1861-1943
Ellen Axson Wilson	1860-1914
Edith Bolling Wilson	1872-1961
Florence Kling Harding	1860-1924
Grace Goodhue Coolidge	1879-1957
Lou Henry Hoover	1875-1944
Anna Eleanor Roosevelt	1884-1962
Elizabeth Wallace Truman	1885-1982
Mary Doud Eisenhower	1896-1979
Jacqueline Bouvier Kennedy	1929-1994
Claudia Taylor Johnson	1912
Thelma Ryan Nixon	1912-1993
Elizabeth Bloomer Ford	1918
Rosalynn Smith Carter	1927
Anne Davis Reagan	1921
Barbara Pierce Bush	1925
Hillary Rodham Clinton	1947

4.10   First Ladies Who Have Addressed Congress

No First lady has ever delivered an address before a joint meeting of Congress. However, three first ladies have testified before congressional committees, as have three Vice Presidents' wives. Below is a complete list of first ladies and Vice Presidents' wives who have addressed Congress.

Hillary Rodham Clinton:
September 30, 1993: Senate Finance on health care reform
September 29, 1993: Senate Labor and Human Resources on health care reform
September 29, 1993: House Education and Labor on health care reform
September 28, 1993: House Energy and Commerce on health care reform
September 28, 1993: House Ways and Means on health care reform

Rosalynn Carter:
February 7, 1979: Senate Labor and Human Resources on funding of mental health programs
April 30, 1979: House Science and Technology Committee on technology oversight

Eleanor Roosevelt:
December 10, 1940: House Select Committee on interstate Migration of Destitute Citizens on migrant laborers
January 14, 1942: House Select Committee on National Defense Migration on citizens migrating to urban centers to find work in defense industries

Tipper Gore:
May 13, 1993: Senate Labor and Human Resources on mental health care

Marilyn Quayle:
April 23, 1990: House Energy and Commerce on women's health issues
May 16, 1990: House Select Committee on Aging on breast cancer

Joan Mondale:
June 26, 1979: Senate Labor and Human Resources on arts, humanities, and museums
September 25, 1979: Senate Governmental Affairs Committee on art in architecture
February 7, 1980: House Select Committee on Aging on arts and senior citizen programs
March 3, 1980: House Education and Labor on arts, humanities, and museum services

4.11   Order of Succession to the President

Vice President
Speaker of the House of Representatives
President Pro Tempore of the Senate
Secretary of State
Secretary of Treasury
Secretary of Defense
Attorney General
Secretary of Interior
Secretary of Agriculture
Secretary of Commerce
Secretary of Labor
Secretary of Health and Human Services
Secretary of Housing and Urban Development
Secretary of Transportation
Secretary of Energy
Secretary of Education

4.12 Creation of Cabinet Departments

All departments are headed by a secretary, except the Justice Department, which is headed by the Attorney General.

Department of Agriculture
Created in 1862.

Department of Commerce
Created in 1903. The Department of Commerce and Labor split into two separate departments in 1913.

Department of Defense
The Department of Defense was established in 1947 by combining the Department of War (established in 1789), the Department of the Navy (established in 1798) and the Department of the Air Force (established in 1947).

Department of Education
Created in 1979. Formerly part of the Department of Health, Education and Welfare.

Department of Energy
Created in 1977.

Department of Health and Human Services
Created in 1979, when the Department of Health, Education and Welfare (created in 1953) was split into separate entities.

Department of Housing and Urban Development
Created in 1965.

Department of the Interior
Created in 1849.

Department of Justice
Created in 1870. Between 1789 and 1870, the Attorney General was a member of the Cabinet, but not the head of a department.

Department of Labor
Created in 1913.

Department of State
Created in 1789.

Department of Transportation
Created in 1966.

Department of the Treasury
Created in 1789.

Department of Veterans Affairs
Created in 1988. Formerly the Veterans Administration, now elevated to Cabinet level.

4.13   Chronology of the Life of William Clinton

1942   Bill Clinton's parents, Virginia Cassidy and William Blythe, are married.

1946   Clinton's father is killed and Clinton is born four months later.

1950   Virginia marries Roger Clinton when Bill is 4 and moves back to Hope, Arkansas.

1963   Bill Clinton meets President John F. Kennedy at a Boys Nation American Legion convention in Washington D.C.

1964   Clinton graduates from Hot Springs High School and enters Georgetown School of Foreign Service in the fall.

1964-1966   Clinton works for Senator J. William Fulbright in Washington, D.C.

1968   Clinton wins Rhodes Scholarship to Oxford.

1970   Clinton enters Yale Law School, where he meets Hillary Rodham.

1972   Clinton manages George McGovern's campaign in Texas.

1973   Clinton graduates with a degree in law and moves to Fayetteville to join the Faculty of Law at the University of Arkansas in the fall of 1973.

1974   Clinton runs for Congress and is defeated.

1975   Clinton runs for state Attorney General and wins.

1978   Clinton runs for Governor of Arkansas and wins.

1980   Ronald Reagan is elected president. The Clinton's daughter, Chelsea, is born.

1982   Clinton is re-elected to his second term as Governor. He launches major education reforms initiative.

1984   Clinton is elected to his third term as Governor. He launches a successful program of economic development.

1986   Clinton is named chairman of the National Governors Association (NGA). He is elected to his fourth term as Governor.

1990   The Democratic Leadership Council names Clinton as its chairman. That fall, he is re-elected to an unprecedented fifth term as Governor.

1991   Clinton declares his candidacy for President on October 3rd.

1992   Clinton wins more than 2,400 delegates to gain a first-ballot victory at the Democratic National Convention in New York City. Clinton defeats George Bush.

1996   Clinton wins a second term as President.

1999   Clinton is impeached by the House of Representatives for perjury and obstruction of justice. After a trial by the Senate, he is acquitted.

4.14 Franklin D. Roosevelt's First Inaugural Address, 1933

March 4, 1933

I am certain that my fellow Americans expect that on my induction into the Presidency I will address them with a candor and a decision which the present situation of our Nation impels. This is preeminently the time to speak the truth, the whole truth, frankly and boldly. Nor need we shrink from honestly facing conditions in our country today. This great nation will endure as it has endured, will revive and will prosper. So, first of all, let me assert my firm belief that the only thing we have to fear is fear itself—nameless, unreasoning, unjustified terror which paralyzes needed efforts to convert retreat into advance. In every dark hour of our national life a leadership of frankness and vigor has met with that understanding and support of the people themselves which is essential to victory. I am convinced that you will again give that support to leadership in these critical days.

In such a spirit on my part and on yours we face our common difficulties. They concern, thank God, only material things. Values have shrunken to fantastic levels; taxes have risen; our ability to pay has fallen; government of all kinds is faced by serious curtailment of income; the means of exchange are frozen in the currents of trade; the withered leaves of industrial enterprise lie on every side; farmers find no markets for their produce; the savings of many years in thousands of families are gone.

More important, a host of unemployed citizens face the grim problem of existence, and an equally great number toil with little return. Only a foolish optimist can deny the dark realities of the moment.

Yet our distress comes from no failure of substance. We are stricken by no plague of locusts. Compared with the perils which our forefathers conquered because they believed and were not afraid, we have still much to be thankful for. Nature still offers her bounty and human efforts have multiplied it. Plenty is at our doorstep, but a generous use of it languishes in the very sight of the supply. Primarily this is because the rulers of the exchange of mankind's goods have failed, through their own stubbornness and their own incompetence, have admitted their failure, and abdicated. Practices of the unscrupulous money changers stand indicted in the court of public opinion, rejected by the hearts and minds of men.

True they have tried, but their efforts have been cast in the pattern of an outworn tradition. Faced by failure of credit they have proposed only the lending of more money. Stripped of the lure of profit by which to induce our people to follow their false leadership, they have resorted to exhortations, pleading tearfully for restored confidence. They know only the rules of a generation of self-seekers. They have no vision, and when there is no vision the people perish.

The money changers have fled from their high seats in the temple of our civilization. We may now restore that temple to the ancient truths. The measure of the restoration lies in the extent to which we apply social values more noble than mere monetary profit.

Happiness lies not in the mere possession of money; it lies in the joy of achievement, in the thrill of creative effort. The joy and moral stimulation of work no longer must be forgotten in the mad chase of evanescent profits. These dark days will be worth all they cost us if they teach us that our true destiny is not to be ministered unto but to minister to ourselves and to our fellow men.

Recognition of the falsity of material wealth as the standard of success goes hand in hand with the abandonment of the false belief that public office and high political position are to be valued only by the standards of pride of place and personal profit; and there must be an end to a conduct in banking and in business which too often has given to a sacred trust the likeness of callous and selfish wrongdoing. Small wonder that confidence languishes, for it thrives only on honesty, on honor, on the sacredness of obligations, on faithful protection, on unselfish performance; without them it cannot live.

Restoration calls, however, not for changes in ethics alone. This Nation asks for action, and action now.

Our greatest primary task is to put people to work. This is no unsolvable problem if we face it wisely and courageously. It can be accomplished in part by direct recruiting by the Government itself, treating the task as we would treat the emergency of a war, but at the same time, through this employment, accomplishing greatly needed projects to stimulate and reorganize the use of our natural resources.

Hand in hand with this we must frankly recognize the overbalance of population in our industrial centers and, by engaging on a national scale in a redistribution, endeavor to provide a better use of the land for those best fitted for the land. The task can be helped by definite efforts to raise the values of agricultural products and with this the power to purchase the output of our cities. It can be helped by preventing realistically the tragedy of the growing loss through foreclosure of our small homes and our farms. It can be helped by insistence that the Federal, State, and local governments act forthwith on the demand that their cost be drastically reduced. It can be helped by the unifying of relief activities which today are often scattered, uneconomical, and unequal. It can be helped by national planning for and supervision of all forms of transportation and of communications and other utilities which have a definitely public character. There are many ways in which it can be helped, but it can never be helped merely by talking about it. We must act and act quickly.

Finally, in our progress toward a resumption of work we require two safeguards against a return of the evils of the old order; there must be a strict supervision of all banking and credits and investments; there must be an end to speculation with other people's money, and there must be provision for an adequate but sound currency.

There are the lines of attack. I shall presently urge upon a new Congress in special session detailed measures for their fulfillment, and I shall seek the immediate assistance of the several states.

Through this program of action we address ourselves to putting our own national house in order and making income balance outgo. Our international trade relations, though vastly important, are in point of time and necessity secondary to the establishment of a sound national economy. I favor as a practical policy the putting of first things first. I shall spare no effort to restore world trade by international economic readjustment, but the emergency at home cannot wait on that accomplishment.

The basic thought that guides these specific means of national recovery is not narrowly nationalistic. It is the insistence, as a first consideration, upon the interdependence of the various elements in all parts of the United States—a recognition of the old and permanently important manifestation of the American spirit of the pioneer. It is the way to recovery. It is the immediate way. It is the strongest assurance that the recovery will endure.

In the field of world policy I would dedicate this nation to the policy of the good neighbor—the neighbor who resolutely respects himself and, because he does so, respects the rights of others— the neighbor who respects his obligations and respects the sanctity of his agreements in and with a world of neighbors.

If I read the temper of our people correctly, we now realize as we have never realized before our interdependence on each other; that we cannot merely take but we must give as well; that if we are to go forward, we must move as a trained and loyal army willing to sacrifice for the good of a common discipline, because without such discipline no progress is made, no leadership becomes effective. We are, I know, ready and willing to submit our lives and property to such discipline, because it makes possible a leadership which aims at a larger good. This I propose to offer, pledging that the larger purposes will bind upon us all as a sacred obligation with a unity of duty hitherto evoked only in time of armed strife.

With this pledge taken, I assume unhesitatingly the leadership of this great army of our people dedicated to a disciplined attack upon our common problems.

Action in this image and to this end is feasible under the form of government which we have inherited from our ancestors. Our Constitution is so simple and practical that it is possible always to meet extraordinary needs by changes in emphasis and arrangement without loss of essential form. That is why our constitutional system has proved itself the most superbly enduring political mechanism the modern world has produced. It has met every stress of vast expansion of territory, of foreign wars, of bitter internal strife, of world relations.

It is to be hoped that the normal balance of executive and legislative authority may be wholly adequate to meet the unprecedented task before us. But it may be that an unprecedented demand and need for undelayed action may call for temporary departure from that normal balance of public procedure.

I am prepared under my constitutional duty to recommend the measures that a stricken nation in the midst of a stricken world may require. These measures, or such other measures as the Congress may build out of its experience and wisdom, I shall seek, within my constitutional authority, to bring to speedy adoption.

But in the event that the Congress shall fail to take one of these two courses, and in the event that the national emergency is still critical, I shall not evade the clear course of duty that will then confront me. I shall ask the Congress for the one remaining instrument to meet the crisis—broad Executive power to wage a war against the emergency, as great as the power that would be given to me if we were in fact invaded by a foreign foe.

For the trust reposed in me I will return the courage and the devotion that befit the time. I can do no less.

We face the arduous days that lie before us in the warm courage of the national unity; with the clear consciousness of seeking old and precious moral values; with the clean satisfaction that comes from the stern performance of duty by old and young alike. We aim at the assurance of a rounded and permanent national life.

We do not distrust the future of essential democracy. The people of the United States have not failed. In their need they have registered a mandate that they want direct, vigorous action. They have asked for discipline and direction under leadership. They have made me the present instrument of their wishes. In the spirit of the gift I take it.

In this dedication of a nation we humbly ask the blessing of God. May He protect each and every one of us. May He guide me in the days to come.

4.15 John F. Kennedy's Inaugural Address, 1961

January 20, 1961

Vice President Johnson, Mr. Speaker, Mr. Chief Justice, President Eisenhower, Vice President Nixon, President Truman, reverend clergy, fellow citizens, we observe today not a victory of party, but a celebration of freedom—symbolizing an end, as well as a beginning—signifying renewal, as well as change. For I have sworn before you and Almighty God the same solemn oath our forebears prescribed nearly a century and three-quarters ago.

The world is very different now. For man holds in his mortal hands the power to abolish all forms of human poverty and all forms of human life. And yet the same revolutionary beliefs for which our forebears fought are still at issue around the globe—the belief that the rights of man come not from the generosity of the state, but from the hand of God.

We dare not forget today that we are the heirs of that first revolution. Let the word go forth from this time and place, to friend and foe alike, that the torch has been passed to a new generation of Americans—born in this century, tempered by war, disciplined by a hard and bitter peace, proud of our ancient heritage—and unwilling to witness or permit the slow undoing of those human rights to which this Nation has always been committed, and to which we are committed today at home and around the world.

Let every nation know, whether it wishes us well or ill, that we shall pay any price, bear any burden, meet any hardship, support any friend, oppose any foe, in order to assure the survival and the success of liberty.

This much we pledge—and more.

To those old allies whose cultural and spiritual origins we share, we pledge the loyalty of faithful friends. United, there is little we cannot do in a host of cooperative ventures. Divided, there is little we can do—for we dare not meet a powerful challenge at odds and split asunder.

To those new States whom we welcome to the ranks of the free, we pledge our word that one form of colonial control shall not have passed away merely to be replaced by a far more iron tyranny. We shall not always expect to find them supporting our view. But we shall always hope to find them strongly supporting their own freedom—and to remember that, in the past, those who foolishly sought power by riding the back of the tiger ended up inside.

To those peoples in the huts and villages across the globe struggling to break the bonds of mass misery, we pledge our best efforts to help them help themselves, for whatever period is required—not because the Communists may be doing it, not because we seek their votes, but because it is right. If a free society cannot help the many who are poor, it cannot save the few who are rich.

To our sister republics south of our border, we offer a special pledge—to convert our good words into good deeds—in a new alliance for progress—to assist free men and free governments in casting off the chains of poverty. But this peaceful revolution of hope cannot become the prey of hostile powers. Let all our neighbors know that we shall join with them to oppose aggression or subversion anywhere in the Americas. And let every other power know that this Hemisphere intends to remain the master of its own house.

To that world assembly of sovereign states, the United Nations, our last best hope in an age where the instruments of war have far outpaced the instruments of peace, we renew our pledge of support—to prevent it from becoming merely a forum for invective—to strengthen its shield of the new and the weak—and to enlarge the area in which its writ may run.

Finally, to those nations who would make themselves our adversary, we offer not a pledge but a request: that both sides begin anew the quest for peace, before the dark powers of destruction unleashed by science engulf all humanity in planned or accidental self-destruction.

We dare not tempt them with weakness. For only when our arms are sufficient beyond doubt can we be certain beyond doubt that they will never be employed.

But neither can two great and powerful groups of nations take comfort from our present course—both sides overburdened by the cost of modern weapons, both rightly alarmed by the steady spread of the deadly atom, yet both racing to alter that uncertain balance of terror that stays the hand of mankind's final war.

So let us begin anew—remembering on both sides that civility is not a sign of weakness, and sincerity is always subject to proof. Let us never negotiate out of fear. But let us never fear to negotiate.

Let both sides explore what problems unite us instead of belaboring those problems which divide us.

Let both sides, for the first time, formulate serious and precise proposals for the inspection and control of arms—and bring the absolute power to destroy other nations under the absolute control of all nations.

Let both sides seek to invoke the wonders of science instead of its terrors. Together let us explore the stars, conquer the deserts, eradicate disease, tap the ocean depths, and encourage the arts and commerce.

Let both sides unite to heed in all corners of the earth the command of Isaiah—to "undo the heavy burdens . . . and to let the oppressed go free."

And if a beachhead of cooperation may push back the jungle of suspicion, let both sides join in creating a new endeavor, not a new balance of power, but a new world of law, where the strong are just and the weak secure and the peace preserved.

All this will not be finished in the first 100 days. Nor will it be finished in the first 1,000 days, nor in the life of this Administration, nor even perhaps in our lifetime on this planet. But let us begin.

In your hands, my fellow citizens, more than in mine, will rest the final success or failure of our course. Since this country was founded, each generation of Americans has been summoned to give testimony to its national loyalty. The graves of young Americans who answered the call to service surround the globe.

Now the trumpet summons us again—not as a call to bear arms, though arms we need; not as a call to battle, though embattled we are—but a call to bear the burden of a long twilight struggle, year in and year out, "rejoicing in hope, patient in tribulation"—a struggle against the common enemies of man: tyranny, poverty, disease, and war itself.

Can we forge against these enemies a grand and global alliance, North and South, East and West, that can assure a more fruitful life for all mankind? Will you join in that historic effort?

In the long history of the world, only a few generations have been granted the role of defending freedom in its hour of maximum danger. I do not shrink from this responsibility—I welcome it. I do not believe that any of us would exchange places with any other people or any other generation. The energy, the faith, the devotion which we bring to this endeavor will light our country and all who serve it—and the glow from that fire can truly light the world.

And so, my fellow Americans: ask not what your country can do for you—ask what you can do for your country.

My fellow citizens of the world: ask not what America will do for you, but what together we can do for the freedom of man.

Finally, whether you are citizens of America or citizens of the world, ask of us the same high standards of strength and sacrifice which we ask of you. With a good conscience our only sure reward, with history the final judge of our deeds, let us go forth to lead the land we love, asking His blessing and His help, but knowing that here on earth God's work must truly be our own.

4.16   U.S. Secretaries of State, 1789-1999

Year appointed		Year appointed	
1789	Thomas Jefferson	1893	Walter Q. Gresham
1794	Edmund Randolph	1895	Richard Olney
1795	Timothy Pickering	1897	John Sherman
1800	John Marshall	1898	William R. Day
1801	James Madison	1898	John Hay
1809	Robert Smith	1905	Elihu Root
1811	James Monroe	1909	Robert Bacon
1817	John Quincy Adams	1909	Philander C. Knox
1825	Henry Clay	1913	William J. Bryan
1829	Martin Van Buren	1915	Robert Lansing
1831	Edward Livingston	1920	Bainbridge Colby
1833	Louis McLane	1921	Charles E. Hughes
1834	John Forsyth	1925	Frank B. Kellogg
1841	Daniel Webster	1929	Henry L. Stimson
1843	Abel P. Upshur	1933	Cordell Hull
1844	John C. Calhoun	1944	E.R. Stettinius, Jr.
1845	James Buchanan	1945	James F. Byrnes
1849	John M. Clayton	1947	George C. Marshall
1850	Daniel Webster	1949	Dean G. Acheson
1852	Edward Everett	1953	John Foster Dulles
1853	William L. Marcy	1959	Christian A. Herter
1857	Lewis Cass	1961	Dean Rusk
1860	Jeremiah S. Black	1969	William P. Rogers
1861	William H. Seward	1973	Henry A. Kissinger
1869	Elihu B. Washburne	1977	Cyrus R. Vance
1869	Hamilton Fish	1980	Edmund S. Muskie
1877	William M. Evarts	1981	Alexander M. Haig
1881	James G. Blaine	1982	George P. Shultz
1881	F.T. Frelinghuysen	1989	James Baker, 3d
1885	Thomas F. Bayard	1993	Warren M. Christopher
1889	James G. Blaine	1997	Madeleine K. Albright
1892	John W. Foster		

4.17 Federal Agencies and Commissions

Advisory Council on Historic Preservation
Arms Control and Disarmament Agency
Central Intelligence Agency
Consumer Product Safety Commission
Corporation for National Service
Commodity Futures Trading Commission
Environmental Protection Agency
Federal Communications Commission
Federal Deposit Insurance Corporation
Federal Election Commission
Federal Emergency Management Agency
Federal Housing and Finance Board
Federal Trade Commission
General Services Administration
Institute of Museum Services
US Merit Systems Protection Board
National Aeronautics and Space Administration
National Archives and Records Administration
National Commission on Libraries and Information Sciences
National Endowment for the Arts
National Endowment for the Humanities
National Performance Review
National Science Foundation
National Security Agency
National Technology Transfer Center
Nuclear Regulatory Commission
Peace Corps
President's Commission to Study Capital Budgeting
President's Council on Physical Fitness
President's Council on Sustainable Development
President's Interagency Council on Women
Railroad Retirement Board
Securities and Exchange Commission
Selective Service System
Small Business Administration
Smithsonian Institution
Social Security Administration
United States Advisory Commission on Public Diplomacy
US Agency For International Development
US Information Agency
US International Trade Commission
United States Office of Government Ethics
United States Postal Service
Voice of America
White House Fellows

4.18 Presidents Elected with Less than Half the Votes

Year	President	Popular Percent
1824	John Q. Adams	29.8%
1844	James K. Polk (D)	49.3
1848	Zachary Taylor (W)	47.3
1856	James Buchanan (D)	45.3
1860	Abraham Lincoln (R)	39.9
1876	Rutherford B. Hayes (R)	47.9
1880	James A. Garfield (R)	48.3
1884	Grover Cleveland (D)	48.8
1888	Benjamin Harrison (R)	47.8
1892	Grover Cleveland (D)	46.0
1912	Woodrow Wilson (D)	41.8
1916	Woodrow Wilson (D)	49.3
1948	Harry S. Truman (D)	49.5
1960	John F. Kennedy (D)	49.7
1968	Richard M. Nixon (R)	43.4
1992	William J. Clinton (D)	43.0
1996	William J. Clinton (D)	49.0

4.19   Presidential Vetoes, 1789-1996

Since the beginning of the federal government in 1789, 41 Presidents have exercised their veto authority 2,532 times. Of that total number, 1,465 have been regular vetoes—i.e., the rejected legislation was returned to the congressional house of origin, while it was in session, with a presidential message of explanation— and 1,067 were pocket vetoes, or rejected while Congress was adjourned. Congress has challenged the President's veto 306 times and succeeded in overriding on 105 occasions.

President	Congress	Total Vetoes	President	Congress	Total Vetoes
Washington	1st-4th	2	Arthur	47th-48th	12
Adams	5th-6th	—	Cleveland	49th-50th	414
Jefferson	7th-10th	—	McKinley	55th-57th	42
Madison	11th-14th	7	T. Roosevelt	57th-60th	82
Monroe	15th-18th	1	Taft	61st-62nd	39
J.Q. Adams	19th-20th	—	Wilson	63rd-66th	44
Jackson	21st-24th	12	Harding	67th	6
Van Buren	25th-26th	1	Coolidge	68th-70th	50
Harrison	27th	—	Hoover	71st-72nd	37
Tyler	27th-28th	10	F.D. Roosevelt	73rd-79th	635
Polk	29th-30th	3	Truman	79th-82nd	250
Taylor	31st	—	Eisenhower	83rd-86th	181
Fillmore	31st-32nd	—	Kennedy	87th-88th	21
Pierce	33rd-34th	9	Johnson	88th-90th	30
Buchanan	35th-36th	7	Nixon	91st-93rd	43
Lincoln	37th-39th	7	Ford	93rd-94th	66
A. Johnson	39th-40th	29	Carter	95th-96th	31
Grant	41st-44th	93	Reagan	97th-100th	78
Hayes	45th-46th	13	Bush	101st-102nd	46
Garfield	47th	—	Clinton	103rd-105th	17
			Total		**2,532**

Sources: U.S. Congress, Secretary of the Senate. Presidential Vetoes, 1789-1996.

4.20 Chronology of the Watergate Crisis

November 1960—Kennedy defeats Nixon in 1960 presidential race. In an extremely close election, Vice President Nixon loses to JFK.

November 1962—Pat Brown defeats Nixon in 1962 California gubernatorial race.

November 1968—Nixon defeats Humphrey and Wallace for president.

May 1969—Nixon orders wiretaps to discover leaks of secret bombing of Cambodia.

June 13, 1971—Pentagon Papers published by *New York Times.* Daniel Ellsberg is indicted for theft, conspiracy, and espionage for leaking papers that expose the government's plans in Vietnam, though the Supreme Court refuses to stop publishing papers.

June 1971—Plumbers unit created to discredit Ellsberg. Secret White House group assigned to ruin Ellsberg's reputation breaks into psychiatrist's office in Beverly Hills but finds nothing embarrassing.

June 17, 1972—Watergate burglars arrested after Plumbers break into Democratic National Committee offices to repair wiretap bug.

September 1972—Hush money paid to Watergate burglars in exchange for promise of silence.

November 1972—Nixon defeats McGovern.

May 1973—Senate Watergate hearings. Senator Irvine conducts three months of televised hearings which report enemies lists, money drops, illegally obtained campaign funds, and harassment by IRS of political enemies. Most importantly, a secret tape-recording system in the White House is discovered.

August 1973—Vice President Agnew accused of income-tax evasion, bribery, conspiracy and extortion. Agnew eventually resigns. Gerald Ford becomes Vice President in October.

October 1973—Court rules Nixon must present tapes to Special Prosecutor Archibold Cox.

October 20, 1973—Saturday Night Massacre. Nixon offers summaries of tapes to Cox, who demands actual tapes. Nixon orders Richardson to fire Cox, who refuses and resigns. Assistant Attorney General Ruckelshaus also refuses and resigns. Finally, Robert Bork fires Cox.

March 1974—Eight former White House aides are indicted by grand jury for conspiring in cover-up. Mitchell, Haldeman, Ehrlichmann and others accused of obstructing justice and perjury. Nixon is named as an unindicted co-conspirator.

April 1974—Nixon releases heavily edited tape transcripts. A key 18-minute section of a June 20, 1972 meeting is inexplicably missing.

July 1974—House Committee recommends impeachment hearings. Judiciary Committee votes 27-11 to impeach Nixon for cover-up, abuse of power and failure to abide by subpoenas.

July 24, 1974—In *U.S. v. Richard Nixon,* Supreme Court rules that Nixon must hand over tapes.

August 8, 1974—Nixon resigns. Ford succeeds Nixon.

September 1974—Ford pardons Nixon.

SECTION 5

Congress

5.1 20th Century Congressional Leaders

Nelson W. Aldrich (1841-1915)
Conservative Republican from Rhode Island; considered most influential Senator of his time; helped control first powerful party leadership organization in Senate which prevented passage of President Theodore Roosevelt's progressive policies.

Joseph Martin (1884-1968)
Republican from Massachusetts; led the House from 1929-59 as minority leader; Speaker of the House 1947-49 and 1953-55; only Republican Speaker between 1931 and 1993; chaired Republican National Committee.

Huey P. Long (1893-1935)
Democrat from Louisiana; Governor from 1928-31; elected to Senate in 1932; populist champion of the poor; opposed FDR's New Deal as not radical enough; proposed a Share Our Wealth Society limiting personal wealth; declared presidential candidacy and was assassinated in 1935.

Mike Mansfield (1903-)
Montana Democrat; elected to House in 1942; Foreign Affairs Committee; elected to Senate in 1953; Foreign Relations Committee; majority Whip in 1957; Majority Leader after Johnson 1961-77, longest run in Senate history; known as the "gentle persuader;" led efforts to cut funds for Vietnam war, forcing Nixon into negotiations to end it.

Lyndon B. Johnson (1908-1973)
Democrat from Texas; elected to Senate in 1948; on Senate Armed Services Committee; elected Whip in 1950; Minority Floor Leader in 1952; Majority Leader in 1954; led passage of first civil rights bill since Reconstruction in 1957; Vice President in 1960 with John F. Kennedy; President in 1963 after Kennedy's assassination; elected to full-term in 1964; initiated Great Society bills.

Thomas P. O'Neill, Jr. (1912-1994)
Known as "Tip," this Massachusetts Democrat was Majority Whip in 1971; Majority Leader in 1973; Speaker from 1976-87; strongly partisan and a symbol of his party.

John F. Kennedy (1917-1963)
Massachusetts Democrat from a politically influential and wealthy Boston family; elected to House in 1947, Senate in 1953; Foreign Relations Committee; critical of foreign policy of Eisenhower; lost Vice Presidential nomination in 1956; elected President in 1960 over Nixon; assassinated in 1963.

Russell B. Long (1918 -)
Democrat from Louisiana; son of Huey Long; elected to Senate in 1948; Finance Committee in 1953, chair from 1965-81; Majority Whip in 1965; removed from whip position in 1969; retired in 1987.

Robert Byrd (1918 -)
Democrat from West Virginia; elected to House in 1952; elected to Senate in 1958; secretary of the Democratic Conference 1967; Majority Whip in 1971, replacing Edward M. Kennedy; Majority Leader in 1977, replacing Mike Mansfield; Minority Leader from 1977-89; Majority Leader again in 1987; chaired Appropriations Committee in 1989; President Pro Tempore; most senior member of the majority party in 1989; trusted insider to President Carter.

Jim Wright (1922-)

Texas Democrat; elected to House in 1953, Public Works Committee; Majority Leader in 1976; Speaker in 1987; investigation of his personal finances led to his resignation; first Speaker to be forced out by scandal; his one year as Speaker was of the most legislatively productive terms.

Robert Dole (1923-)

Kansas Republican; elected to House in 1961, Senate in 1969; committee chair of the Finance Committee; Gerald Ford's vice presidential running mate in 1976; oversaw President Reagan's sweeping tax-cut program and Social Security overhaul in 1981; Minority Leader; helped win approval for Gulf War; failed presidential bids in 1980 and 1988.

Robert Michel (1923-)

Illinois Republican; elected to House in 1956; House Appropriations Committee for 25 years; Minority Whip in 1974; Minority Leader; led divided house to give President George Bush authority to use military force against Iraq.

Thomas S. Foley (1929-)

Democrat from Washington; elected to House in 1964; supported Johnson's Great Society programs; 1981- Majority Whip; 1987- Majority Leader; Permanent Select Committee on Intelligence and Budget Committee; elected Speaker in 1989 after Jim Wright's resignation; dealt with Iran-Contra Affair; defeated in 1994 election; appointed by President Bill Clinton as Chairman of the President's Foreign Intelligence Advisory Board in 1996; respected for fairness.

Richard Gephardt (1941-)

Missouri Democrat; elected to Congress in 1974; sat on Ways and Means Committee; helped found Democratic Leadership Council; chaired House Democratic Caucus; unsuccessful presidential bid in 1988; House Majority Leader in 1989, ex officio seat on House Budget Committee.

Source: Congressional Quarterly, Inc.; U.S. Senate.

5.2   Standing Committees of Congress

HOUSE:

Agriculture
Appropriations
Armed Services
Banking, Finance and Urban Affairs
Budget
District of Columbia
Education and Labor
Energy and Commerce
Foreign Affairs
Government Operations
House Administration
Interior and Insular Affairs
Judiciary
Merchant Marine and Fisheries
Post Office and Civil Service
Public Works and Transportation
Rules
Science, Space and Technology
Small Business
Standards of Official Conduct
Veterans' Affairs
Ways and Means

SENATE:

Agriculture, Nutrition and Forestry
Appropriations
Armed Services
Banking, Finance and Urban Affairs
Budget
Commerce, Science and Transportation
Energy and Natural Resources
Environment and Public Works
Finance
Foreign Relations
Governmental Affairs
Judiciary
Labor and Human Resources
Rules and Administration
Small Business
Veterans' Affairs

Source: U.S. Senate.

5.3 Major Filibusters, 1789-1999

1789	Delaying tatics first used in the Senate by opponents of a bill to locate the nation's capital on the Susquehanna River.
1841	First full-fledged filibusters—Democrats and Whigs argued over the appointment of official Senate printers, then over the establishment of a national bank.
Civil War	Numerous filibusters took place over slavery, the Civil War, Reconstruction, and blacks' voting rights.
1915-1917	Republican filibusters killed two of President Woodrow Wilson's proposals to prepare for World War I.
1917	Senate adopts rule limiting debate if two-thirds of the Senators present voted to end it. First cloture rule.
1919	First successful use of cloture rule ended debate on the Treaty of Versailles following World War I.
1920-27	Nine more cloture votes taken; three successful.
1927-62	Sixteen cloture votes taken.
1935	Democrat from Louisiana, Huey Long, filibustered for 15 hours and 30 minutes with his thoughts on the Constitution and recipes for turnip greens and corn bread.
1949	Cloture rule modified to ban the limitation of debate on proposals to change the Senate rules, including the cloture rule itself. Cloture could now be invoked by two-thirds of the full Senate membership.
1957	Strom Thurmond, South Carolina Democrat, spoke for 24 hours and 18 minutes on a civil rights bill. Longest speech in Senate history.
1959	Bipartisan leadership group pushed through change in the cloture rule. New version of the rule allowed cloture to be invoked by two-thirds of those present and voting and also applied to proposals for changes in the rules.
1960	Eighteen southerners formed teams of two and talked in non-stop relays on a civil rights bill. Majority Leader at the time, Lyndon B. Johnson, a Texas Democrat, tried to end the filibuster by keeping the Senate going for nine days around the clock in the longest-ever session. Bill ultimately abandoned for a weaker version.
1962	First successful cloture vote since 1927, on a communications satellite bill.
1964	Senate invoked cloture rule for the first time on a civil rights bill after the longest filibuster in history—74 days.
1965 and 1968	More civil rights filibusters broken. Liberal supporters of civil rights, who had tried often to tighten debate controls, were less eager for cloture reform after these victories.
1970s	Liberals filibuster against Nixon administration policies for the Vietnam War, defense weapons systems and anti-busing proposals.
1979	Senate agrees to set an absolute limit of 100 hours on post-cloture filibusters.
1986	Live televised coverage of Senate proceedings prompts members to think more about their public images and filibustering becomes less popular. Revised rules cut down the limit from 100 hours to 30 hours of time allowed to debate, procedural moves and roll-call votes after the Senate has invoked cloture to end a filibuster.
1992	Republicans filibuster on anti-crime legislation and a bill to ban replacement of striking workers. Both bills were shelved when attempts at ending the filibusters failed.
1990s	Some Senate leaders call for additional limits on filibusters, but many are reluctant to end this Senate tradition.

Source: Congressional Quarterly, Inc.

5.4   Special Sessions of Congress

Article II, Section 3, of the Constitution grants the President authority to call for an extraordinary, or "special" session of Congress after it has already adjourned. The President can state the reason for calling Congress into session and place before Congress his request. Congress still retains the authority as an independent branch of government to act or not act on the President's request, and to transact other business if it so wishes.

Twenty-seven sessions of Congress have been convened by Presidents in the history of Congress. President John Adams was the first President to call the Congress into special session in 1797 over suspending relations with France. The last President to convene Congress was Harry Truman, in 1948, who did so to urge enactment of his domestic legislative agenda expanding New Deal programs.

Here are the reasons given by past Presidents for calling Congress into extraordinary session:

President Adams
  Relations with France
President Jefferson
  (1) Louisiana Purchase from France (2) U.S.-British Relations
President Madison
  War with Britain
President Tyler
  Financial condition of the country
President Pierce
  Appropriations for the Army
President Lincoln
  Civil War
President Hayes
  Appropriations for the Army
President Cleveland
  Repeal of Silver Purchase
President McKinley
  Special Tariff
President Roosevelt
  Trade treaty with Cuba
President Taft
  (1) Special Tariff (2) Trade with Canada
President Wilson
  (1) World War I (2) Federal Reserve Act (3) Cost of Living
President Harding
  (1) Emergency Tariff (2) Merchant Marine
President Hoover
  Smoot-Hawley Tariff
President Roosevelt
  (1) New Deal legislative agenda (2) Wage and Hours Act (3) Neutrality
President Truman
  Domestic issue agenda

5.5 Salaries for the President, Congress, Cabinet Officers, and Court Justices, 1999

Congressional leaders receive a higher salary than the rank-and-file Members and Senators, who receive an annual salary of $133,600.

PRESIDENT*
$200,000

CONGRESS
Senate
President Pro Tempore $148,400
Majority Leader $148,400
Minority Leader $148,400
House
Speaker of the House $171,500
Majority Leader $148,400
Minority Leader $148,400

EXECUTIVE BRANCH
Cabinet Officers $148,400

JUDICIAL BRANCH
Supreme Court, Chief Justice $171,500
Supreme Court, Justices $164,100
Circuit Judges $141,700
U.S. District Judges $133,600

* The President's salary was set at $25,000 for George Washington in 1789; raised to $50,000 for Ulysses S. Grant's second term; raised to $75,000 for William H. Taft in 1909; raised to $100,000 for Harry S. Truman's second term; and then set at $200,000 in 1969 when Richard M. Nixon took office.

5.6 Members of the 105th Congress Who Were Governors of Their States

Out of 100 Senators, 13 were Governors. In the House, out of 435 Members and 5 non-voting delegates, 2 were once Governors. They are listed here with their dates of service.

Senate

John Ashcroft (R-Missouri), 1985-1993
Kit Bond (R-Missouri), 1973-1977 and 1981-1985
Richard Bryan (D-Nevada), 1983-1989
Dale Bumpers (D-Arksansas), 1970-1974
John Chafee (R-Rhode Island), 1963-1969
Wendell Ford (D-Kentucky), 1971-1974
Bob Graham (D-Florida), 1978-1986
Judd Gregg (R-New Hampshire), 1988-1992
Fritz Hollings (D-South Carolina), 1959-1963
Bob Kerrey (D-Nebraska), 1983-1987
Charles Robb (D-Virginia), 1982-1986
Jay Rockefeller (D-West Virginia), 1976-1984
Strom Thurmond (R-South Carolina), 1947-1951

House

Michael Castle (R-Delaware), 1985-1993
Carlos Romero-Barcelo (D-Puerto Rico), 1976-1984

5.7 Party Leaders in Congress

Although party divisions sprang up almost from the first Congress, the formally structured party leadership organizations now taken for granted are a relatively modern development. Constitutionally specified leaders, namely the Speaker of the House and the President Pro Tempore of the Senate, can be identified since the first Congress. Other leadership posts, however, were not officially recognized until about the middle of the 19th century, and some are 20th century creations.

The Senate was later than the House in developing a separate, identifiable party leadership. Records of party conferences in the 19th century Senate are not available. Memoirs and other secondary sources reveal the identities of party conference or caucus chairmen for some, but not all, Congresses after about 1850, but these posts carried very little authority. It was not uncommon for Senators to publicly declare that within the Senate parties there was no single leader. Rather, through the turn of the 20th century individuals who led the Senate achieved their position through recognized personal attributes, including persuasion and oratory skills, rather than election or appointment to official leadership posts.

The development of Senate party floor leaders was, like in the House, one of slow evolution, linked for the most part to the post of conference chairman. Not until 1945 did Senate Republicans specify that the conference chairmanship and floor leader posts must be held by separate Senators. Among Senate Democrats, the floor leader is also chairman of the conference.

Official congressional documents (the House Journal and Senate Journal, and the Congressional Record and predecessor publications) can be used to document the tenure of the constitutionally specified leaders. However, the actions of the party organizations in choosing other leaders, such as floor leaders, whips, or caucus or conference chairmen, frequently went unacknowledged in these sources.

In the frequent absence of party caucus records in the latter half of the 19th century, scholars have had to rely on secondary sources, such as memoirs and correspondence, for evidence of party leadership position-holding. Other problems are caused by the changing nature of congressional leadership. For example, it was the common practice of President Jefferson and his immediate successors to designate a member of the House as principal legislative spokesman. Often these spokesmen held no other formal leadership position in the House, and presidents frequently designated new spokesmen, or even specialized spokesmen for individual measures, as their terms progressed.

Most historians who study the 19th century House acknowledge that an informal "positional leadership" system emerged possibly as early as the "War Hawk" Congress (1811-13) under Speaker Clay. Under this system, the Speaker—who at the time designated the chairmen of the standing committees—would name his principal lieutenant to be chairman of the Ways and Means Committee. After the Appropriations Committee was split from the Ways and Means Committee in 1865, the Speaker's principal floor lieutenant received either of these chairmanships. Sometimes, the Speaker chose a rival for the speakership to chair one of these committees in an effort to resolve intra-party disputes. It is somewhat inaccurate, however, to consider these early floor leaders to be Majority Leaders in the modern sense.

The position of chairman of the Appropriations or Ways and Means Committee inevitably made the incumbent a powerful congressional figure because of the important legislation reported from these committees. But these chairmen were not chosen by the full party organization as the majority or minority House Leaders are now. Furthermore, other leading congressional figures, such as the Republican Leader Thomas Brackett Reed, achieved their positional influence within the House by service on other committees, such as—in Reed's case—the post-1880 Rules Committee.

Source: U.S. Congress.

5.8 Speakers of the House of Representatives, 1789-1998

© 2000 by The Center for Applied Research in Education

Speaker	Party–State	Congress	Dates
Frederick A.C. Muhlenberg	NA*—PA	1st	Apr. 1, 1789-Mar. 3, 1791
		3rd	Dec. 2, 1793-Mar. 3, 1795
Jonathan Trumbull	NA—CT	2nd	Oct. 24, 1791-Mar. 3, 1793
Jonathan Dayton	NA—NJ	4th-5th	Dec. 7, 1795-Mar. 3, 1797
Theodore Sedgwick	NA—MA	6th	Dec. 2, 1799-Mar. 3, 1801
Nathaniel Macon	NA—NC	7th-9th	Dec. 7, 1801-Mar. 3, 1807
Joseph B. Varnum	NA—MA	10th-11th	Oct. 26, 1807-Mar. 3, 1811
Langdon Cheves	R—SC	13th	Jan. 19, 1814-Mar. 3, 1815
Henry Clay	R—KY	12th-13th	Nov. 4, 1811-Jan. 19, 1814[1]
		14th-16th	Dec. 4, 1815-Oct. 28, 1820
		18th	Dec 3, 1823-Mar. 6, 1825[2]
Philip Barbour	R—VA	17th	Dec. 4, 1821-Mar. 3, 1823
John W. Taylor	R—NY	16th	Nov. 15, 1820-Mar. 3, 1821
		19th	Dec. 5, 1825-Mar. 3, 1827
Andrew Stevenson	NA—VA	20th-23rd	Dec. 3, 1927-June 2, 1834
John Bell	NA—TN	23rd	June 2, 1834-Mar. 3, 1835
James K. Polk	Jacksonian—TN	24th-25th	Dec. 7, 1835-Mar. 3, 1839
Robert M.T. Hunter	Whig—VA	26th	Dec. 16, 1839-Mar. 3, 1841
John White	W—KY	27th	May 31, 1841-Mar. 3, 1843
John W. Jones	D—VA	28th	Dec. 4, 1843-Mar. 3, 1845
John W. Davis	D—IN	29th	Dec. 1, 1845-Mar. 3, 1847
Robert C. Winthrop	W—MA	30th	Dec. 6, 1847-Mar. 3, 1849
Howell Cobb	D—GA	31st	Dec. 22, 1849-Mar. 3, 1851
Linn Boyd	D—KY	32nd-33rd	Dec. 1, 1851-Mar. 3, 1855
Nathaniel P. Banks	American Party—MA[3]	34th	Feb. 2, 1856-Mar. 3, 1857[3]
James L. Orr	D—SC	35th	Dec. 7, 1857-Mar. 3, 1859
William Pennington	R—NJ	36th	Feb. 1, 1860-Mar. 3, 1861
Galusha A. Grow	R—PA	37th	July 4, 1861-Mar. 3, 1863
Schuyler Colfax	R—IN	38th-40th	Dec. 7, 1863-Mar. 3, 1869
Theodore Pomeroy	R—NY	40th	Mar. 3, 1869[4]
James G. Blaine	R—ME	41st-43rd	Mar. 4, 1869-Mar. 3, 1875
Michael C. Kerr	D—IN	44th	Dec. 6, 1875-Aug. 19, 1876[5]
Samuel J. Randall	D—PA	44th-46th	Dec. 4, 1876-Mar. 3, 1881
J. Warren Keifer	R—OH	47th	Dec. 5, 1881-Mar. 3, 1883
John G. Carlisle	D—KY	48th-50th	Dec. 3, 1883-Mar. 3, 1889

Speaker	Party—State	Congress	Dates
Charles F. Crisp	D—GA	52nd-53rd	Dec. 7, 1891-Mar. 3, 1895
Thomas B. Reed	R—ME	51st	Dec. 2, 1889-Mar. 3, 1891
		54th-55th	Dec. 2, 1895-Mar. 3, 1899
David B. Henderson	R—IA	56th-57th	Dec. 4, 1899-Mar. 3, 1903
Joseph G. Cannon	R—IL	58th-61st	Nov. 9, 1903-Mar. 3, 1911
James B. (Champ) Clark	D—MO	62nd-65th	Apr. 4, 1911-Mar. 3, 1919
Frederick H. Gillett	R—MA	66th-68th	May 19, 1919-Mar. 3, 1925
Nicholas Longworth	R—OH	69th-71st	Dec. 7, 1925-Mar. 3, 1931
John N. Garner	D—TX	72nd	Dec. 7, 1931-Mar. 3, 1933
Henry T. Rainey	D—IL	73rd	Mar. 9, 1933-Aug. 19, 1934[6]
Joseph W. Byrns	D—TN	74th	Jan. 3, 1935-June 4, 1936[7]
William B. Bankhead	D—AL	74th-76th	June 4, 1936-Sept. 15, 1940[8]
Joseph W. Martin, Jr.	R—MA	80th	Jan. 3, 1947-Jan. 3, 1949
Sam T. Rayburn	D—TX	76th-79th	Sept. 16, 1940-Jan. 3, 1947
		81st-82nd	Jan. 3, 1949-Jan. 3, 1953
		83rd	Jan. 3, 1953-Jan. 3, 1955
		84th-87th	Jan. 5, 1955-Nov. 16, 1961[9]
John W. McCormack	D—MA	87th-91st	Jan. 10, 1962-Jan. 3, 1971
Carl Albert	D—OK	92nd-94th	Jan. 21, 1971-Jan. 3, 1977
Thomas P. O'Neill, Jr.	D—MA	95th-99th	Jan. 4, 1977-Jan. 3, 1987
James C. Wright, Jr.	D—TX	100th-101st	Jan. 6, 1987-June 6, 1989[10]
Thomas S. Foley	D—WA	101st-103rd	June 6, 1989-Jan. 3, 1995
Newt Gingrich	R—GA	104th	Jan. 4, 1995-1998

* No formal party affiliation recorded.

[1] Resigned from office, January 19, 1814.

[2] Resigned from office, March 6, 1825.

[3] Speaker Banks served in the House three separate times under three different party designations. In the 34th Congress, he served as an American Party Member.

[4] Elected Speaker, March 3, 1869 and served one day.

[5] Died in office, August 19, 1876.

[6] Died in office, August 19, 1934.

[7] Died in office, June 4, 1936.

[8] Died in office, September 15, 1940.

[9] Died in office, November 16, 1961.

[10] Wright resigned the speakership on June 6, 1989, then resigned from the House on June 30, 1989.

5.9 House Democratic Floor Leaders, 1899-1999

Floor Leader	State	Congress	Dates
James D. Richardson	TN	56th-57th	1899-1903
John Sharp Williams	MS	58th-60th	1903-1908
Oscar W. Underwood	AL	*62nd-63rd	1911-1915
James B. (Champ) Clark	MO	60th-61st	1908-1911
		66th	1919-1921
Claude Kitchin	NC	*64th-65th	1915-1919
		67th	1921-1923
Finis J. Garrett	IN	68th-70th	1923-1929
John N. Garner	TX	71st	1929-1931
Henry T. Rainey	IL	*72nd	1931-1933
Joseph W. Byrns	TN	*73rd	1933-1935
William B. Bankhead	AL	*74th	1935-June 4, 1936[1]
Sam T. Rayburn	TX	*75th-76th	1937-Sept. 16, 1940[2]
		80th	1947-1949
		83rd	1953-1955
John W. McCormack	MA	*76th-79th	Sept. 16, 1940-1947[3]
		*81st-82nd	1949-1953
		* 84th-87th	1955-Jan. 10, 1962[4]
Carl Albert	OK	*87th-91st	Jan. 10, 1962-1971[5]
Thomas Hale Boggs	LA	*92nd	1971-1973[6]
Thomas P. O'Neill, Jr.	MA	*93rd-94th	1973-1977
James Wright	TX	*95th-99th	1977-1987
Thomas S. Foley	WA	*100th-101st	1987-June 6, 1989[7]
Richard A. Gephardt	MO	*101st-106th	June 14, 1989-1999[8]

* Indicates Congresses in which the floor leader was also Majority Leader.

[1] Elected Speaker, filling the vacancy caused by the death of Speaker Byrns. Records indicate that Representative John J. O'Connor of New York, Chairman of the House Rules Committee, served as acting Majority Leader during the fourteen remaining days of the 74th Congress. However, he does not appear to have been formally elected Majority Leader at that time and is not included in this list. At the commencement of the 75th Congress, Representatives Rayburn, O'Connor, John Rankin, and others competed for the post of Majority Leader, with Rayburn ultimately elected by the Democratic Caucus.

[2] Elected Speaker following the death of Speaker Bankhead.

[3] Elected Majority Leader on September 16, 1940, to fill post made vacant by the election of Sam Rayburn as Speaker.

[4] Elected Speaker at the start of the 87th Congress, 2nd Session following the death of Sam Rayburn.

[5] Elected Majority Leader at commencement of the 87th Congress, 2nd Session when Majority Leader John McCormack was elected Speaker to succeed Speaker Rayburn.

[6] Disappeared on a campaign flight from Anchorage to Juneau, Alaska, October 16, 1972. Presumed dead pursuant to House Resolution 1, 93rd Congress.

[7] Elected Speaker on June 6, 1989 following Speaker Wright's resignation from that post on the same date.

[8] Elected Majority Leader on June 14, 1989, to fill the post made vacant by the election of Thomas S. Foley to be Speaker on June 6, 1989.

5.10 House Republican Floor Leaders, 1899-1999

Floor Leader	State	Congress	Dates
Sereno E. Payne	NY	*56th-61st	1899-1911
James R. Mann	IL	62nd-65th	1911-1919
Franklin W. Mondell	WY	*66th-67th	1919-1923
Nicholas Longworth	OH	*68th	1923-1925
John Q. Tilson	CT	*69th-71st	1925-1931
Bertrand H. Snell	NY	72nd-75th	1931-1939
Joseph W. Martin, Jr.	MA	76th-79th	1939-1947
		81st-82nd	1949-1953
		84th-85th	1955-1959
Charles Halleck	IN	*80th	1947-1949
		*83rd	1953-1955
		86th-88th	1959-1965
Gerald R. Ford	MI	89th-93rd	1965-Dec. 6, 1973[1]
John J. Rhodes	AZ	93rd-96th	Dec. 7, 1973-1981
Robert H. Michel	IL	97th-103rd	1981-1995
Richard K. Armey	TX	*104th-106th	1995-1999

* Indicates Congresses in which the floor leader was also Majority Leader.

[1] Resigned from the House having been nominated to become Vice President to fill the post vacated by the resignation of Spiro T. Agnew.

5.11 House Democratic Whips, 1901-1999

Whip	State	Congress	Dates
Oscar W. Underwood	AL	56th	1901
James T. Lloyd	MO	57th-60th	1901-1908[1]
		61st-62nd	1909-1913
Thomas M. Bell	GA	63rd	1913-1915
		64th-66th	1915-1921
William A. Oldfield	AR	67th-70th	1921-Nov. 19, 1928[2]
John McDuffie	AL	70th-72nd	1928-1933
Arthur Greenwood	IN	73rd	1933-1935
Patrick J. Boland	PA	74th-77th	1935-May 18, 1942[3]
Robert Ramspeck	GA	77th-79th	1942-Dec. 31, 1945[4]
John J. Sparkman	AL	79th	1946-1947
John W. McCormack	MA	80th	1947-1949
		83rd	1953-1955
J. Percy Priest	TN	81st-82nd	1949-1953
Carl Albert	OK	84th-87th	1955-1962
Thomas Hale Boggs	LA	87th-91st	1962-1971
Thomas P. O'Neill, Jr.	MA	92nd	1971-1973
John J. McFall	CA	93rd-94th	1973-1977
John W. Brademas	IN	95th-96th	1977-1981
Thomas S. Foley	WA	97th-99th	1981-1987
Tony Coelho	CA	100th-101st	1987-June 14, 1989[5]
William H. Gray, III	PA	101st-102nd	June 14, 1989[6]-Sept. 11, 1991[7]
David E. Bonior	MI	102nd-	Sept. 11, 1991[8]

[1] Resigned from post, 1908

[2] Died in office, November 19, 1928.

[3] Died in office, May 18, 1942.

[4] Resigned from office, December 31, 1945.

[5] Representative Coelho was the first elected Democratic Whip; previously Democratic Whips were appointed.

[6] Representative Gray was elected Whip on June 14, 1989, one day before Representative Coelho resigned from the House.

[7] Resigned from the House, September 11, 1991.

[8] Elected July 11, 1991, but did not assume office until September 11, 1991.

5.12 House Republican Whips, 1897-1999

Whip	State	Congress	Dates
James A. Tawney	MN	55th-58th	1897-1905
James E. Watson	IN	59th-60th	1905-1909
John W. Dwight	NY	61st-62nd	1909-1913
Charles H. Burke	SD	63rd	1913-1915
Charles M. Hamilton	WY	64th-65th	1915-1919
Harold Knutson	MN	66th-67th	1919-1923
Albert H. Vestal	IN	68th-71st	1923-1931
Carl G. Bachmann	WV	72nd	1931-1933
Harry L. Englebright	CA	73rd-78th	1933-May 13, 1943[1]
Leslie C. Arends	IL	78th-93rd	1943-1975
Robert H. Michel	IL	94th-96th	1975-1981
Trent Lott	MS	97th-100th	1981-1989
Dick Cheney	WY	101st	1989-Mar. 17, 1989[2]
Newt Gingrich	GA	101st-103rd	Mar. 22, 1989-1995[2]
Tom Delay	TX	104th	1995-1999

[1] Died in office, May 13, 1943.

[2] Representative Gingrich was elected Whip on March 22, 1989, following Representative Cheney's resignation from the House on March 17, 1989, to become Secretary of Defense.

5.13   Presidents Pro Tempore of the Senate, 1789-1997[1]

President Pro Tempore	Party–State	Congress	Dates[2]
John Langdon	NA*—NH	1st	Apr. 6, 1789
Richard Henry Lee	NA—VA	2nd	Apr. 18, 1792
John Langdon	F—NH	2nd	Nov. 5, 1792
Ralph Izard	NA—SC	3rd	May 31, 1794
Henry Tazewell	NA—VA	3rd	Feb. 20, 1795
Henry Tazewell	NA—VA	4th	Dec. 7, 1795
Samuel Livermore	F—NH	4th	May 6, 1796
William Bingham	F—PA	4th	Feb. 16, 1797
William Bradford	NA—RI	5th	July 6, 1797
Jacob Read	F—SC	5th	Nov. 22, 1797
Theodore Sedgwick	F—MA	5th	June 27, 1798
John Laurance	NA—NY	5th	Dec. 6, 1798
James Ross	F—PA	5th	Mar. 1, 1799
Samuel Livermore	F—NH	6th	Dec. 12, 1799
Uriah Tracy	F—CT	6th	May 14, 1800
John E. Howard	F—MD	6th	Nov. 21, 1800
James Hillhouse	NA—CT	6th	Feb. 28, 1801
Abraham Baldwin	NA—GA	7th	Dec. 7, 1801
Stephen R. Bradley	NA—VT	7th	Dec. 14, 1802
John Brown	NA—KY	8th	Oct. 17, 1803
Jesse Franklin	R—NC	8th	Mar. 10, 1804
Joseph Anderson	NA—TN	8th	Jan. 15, 1805
Samuel Smith	R—MD	9th	Dec. 2, 1805
Samuel Smith	R—MD	10th	Apr. 17, 1808
Stephen R. Bradley	NA—VT	10th	Dec. 28, 1808
John Milledge	NA—GA	10th	Jan. 30, 1809
Andrew Gregg	R—PA	11th	June 26, 1809
John Gaillard	R—SC	11th	Feb. 28, 1810
John Pope	R—KY	11th	Feb. 23, 1811
William H. Crawford	NA—GA	12th	Mar. 24, 1812
Joseph B. Varnum	R—MA	13th	Dec. 6, 1813
John Gaillard	R—SC	13th	Apr. 18, 1814
John Gaillard	R—SC	14th[3]	
John Gaillard	R—SC	15th	Mar. 6, 1817
James Barbour[4]	—VA	15th	Feb. 15, 1819
John Gaillard	R—SC	16th	Jan. 25, 1820
John Gaillard	R—SC	17th	Feb. 1, 1822
John Gaillard	R—SC	18th	May 21, 1824
John Gaillard	R—SC	19th	Mar. 9 1825
Nathaniel Macon	R—SC	19th	May 20, 1826
Samuel Smith	R—MD	20th	May 15, 1828
Samuel Smith	R—MD	21st	Mar. 13, 1829
Littleton Tazewell	NA—VA	22nd	July 9, 1832
Hugh L. White	Jacksonian—TN	22nd	Dec. 3, 1832
George Poindexter	D—MS	23rd	June 28, 1834
John Tyler	R—VA	23rd	Mar. 3, 1835

President Pro Tempore	Party–State	Congress	Dates[2]
William R. King	R—AL	24th	July 1, 1836
William R. King	R—AL	25th	Mar. 7, 1837
William R. King	R—AL	26th	July 3, 1840
William R. King	R—AL	27th	Mar. 4, 1841
Samuel L. Southard	W—NJ	27th	Mar. 11, 1841
Willie P. Mangum	W—NC	27th	May 31, 1842[5]
Willie P. Mangum	W—NC	28th	[no election, incumbent remains]
Ambrose Sevier	D—AR	29th	Dec. 27, 1845[6]
David R. Atchison	D—MO	29th	Aug. 8, 1846
David R. Atchison	D—MO	30th	Feb. 2, 1848
David R. Atchison	D—MO	31st	Mar. 5, 1849
William R. King	R—AL	31st	May 6, 1850
William R. King	R—AL	32nd	[no election, incumbent remains]
David R. Atchison	D—MO	32nd	Dec. 20,1852[7]
David R. Atchison	D—MO	33rd	Mar. 4, 1853
Lewis Cass	D—MI	33rd	Dec. 4, 1853[8]
Jesse D. Bright	D—IN	33rd	Dec. 5, 1853
Jesse D. Bright	D—IN	34th	[no election, incumbent remains]
Charles E. Stuart	D—MI	34th	June 9, 1856
James M. Mason	D—VA	34th	Jan. 6, 1857
James M. Mason	D—VA	35th	Mar. 4, 1857
Thomas J. Rusk	D—TX	35th	Mar. 14, 1857
Benjamin Fitzpatrick	D—AL	35th	Dec. 7, 1857
Benjamin Fitzpatrick	D—AL	36th	Mar. 9, 1859
Jesse D. Bright	D—IN	36th	June 12, 1860
Solomon Foot	R—VT	36th	Feb. 16, 1861
Solomon Foot	R—VT	37th	Mar. 23, 1861
Solomon Foot	R—VT	38th	Mar. 4, 1863
Daniel Clark	R—NH	38th	Apr. 26, 1864
Lafayette S. Foster	R—CT	39th	Mar. 7, 1865
Benjamin F. Wade	R—OH	39th	Mar. 2, 1867
Benjamin F. Wade	R—OH	40th	[no election, incumbent remains]
Henry B. Anthony	R—RI	41st	Mar. 23, 1869
Henry B. Anthony	R—RI	42nd	Mar. 10, 1871
Matthew H. Carpenter	R—WI	43rd	Mar. 12, 1873
Henry B. Anthony	R—RI	43rd	Jan. 25, 1875
Thomas W. Ferry	R—MI	44th	Mar. 9, 1875
Thomas W. Ferry	R—MI	45th	Mar. 5, 1877
Allen G. Thurman	D—OH	46th	Apr. 15, 1879
Thomas F. Bayard	D—DE	47th	Oct. 10, 1881
David Davis	Independent—IL	47th	Oct. 13, 1881
George F. Edmunds	R—VT	47th	Mar. 3, 1883
George F. Edmunds	R—VT	48th	Jan. 14, 1884
John Sherman	R—OH	49th	Dec. 7, 1885
John J. Ingalls	R—KS	49th	Feb. 25, 1887[9]
John J. Ingalls	R—KS	50th	[no election, incumbent remains]
John J. Ingalls	R—KS	51st	Mar. 7, 1889
Charles F. Manderson[10]	R—NE	51st-53rd	Mar. 2, 1891-Mar. 22, 1893
Isham Harris	D—TN	53rd	Mar. 22, 1893-Jan. 7, 1895
Matt W. Ransom	D—NC	53rd	Jan. 7, 1895-Jan. 10, 1895
Isham Harris	D—TN	53rd-54th	Jan. 10, 1895-Feb. 7, 1896
William P. Frye	R—ME	54th-62nd	Feb. 7, 1896-Apr. 27, 1911

President Pro Tempore	Party–State	Congress	Dates[2]
Charles Curtis	R—KS	62nd	Dec. 4, 1911-Dec. 12, 1911
Augustus O. Bacon	D—GA	62nd[11]	
Jacob H. Gallinger	R—NH	62nd[11]	
Henry Cabot Lodge	R—MA	62nd[11]	
Frank B. Brandegee	R—CT	62nd[11]	
James P. Clarke	D—AR	63rd-64th	Mar. 13, 1913-Oct. 1, 1916
Willard Saulsbury	D—DE	64th-65th	Dec. 14, 1916-Mar. 3, 1919
Albert B. Cummins	R—IA	66th-69th	May 19, 1919-Mar. 6, 1925
George H. Moses	R—NH	69th-72nd	Mar. 6, 1925-Mar. 3, 1933
Key Pittman	D—NV	73rd-76th	Mar. 9, 1933-Nov. 18, 1940
William H. King	D—UT	76th	Nov. 19, 1940-Jan. 3, 1941
Pat Harrison	D—MS	77th	Jan. 6, 1941-June 22, 1941
Carter Glass	D—VA	77th-78th	July 10, 1941-Jan. 3, 1945
Kenneth McKellar	D—TN	79th	Jan. 6, 1945-Jan. 3, 1947
Arthur H. Vandenberg	R—MI	80th	Jan. 4, 1947-Jan. 3, 1949
Kenneth McKellar	D—TN	81st-82nd	Jan. 3, 1949-Jan. 3, 1953
Styles Bridges	R—NH	83rd	Jan. 3, 1953-Jan. 3, 1955
Walter F. George	D—GA	84th	Jan. 5, 1955-Jan. 3, 1957
Carl Hayden	D—AZ	85th-90th	Jan. 3, 1957-Jan. 3, 1969
Richard B. Russell	D—GA	91st-92nd	Jan. 3, 1969-Jan. 21, 1971
Allen J. Ellender	D—LA	92nd	Jan. 22, 1971-July 27, 1971
James O. Eastland	D—MS	92nd-95th	July 28, 1971-Jan. 3, 1979
Warren G. Magnuson	D—WA	96th	Jan. 15, 1979-Jan. 3, 1981
Strom Thurmond	R—SC	97th-99th	Jan. 5, 1981-Jan. 3, 1987
John C. Stennis	D—MS	100th	Jan. 6, 1987-Jan. 3, 1989
Robert C. Byrd	D—WV	101st-103rd	Jan. 3, 1989-Jan. 4, 1995
Strom Thurmond	R—SC	104th	Jan. 4, 1995-

[*] NA = No formal party affiliation recorded.

[1] Until 1890, the Senate elected a President Pro Tempore whenever the Vice President was not in attendance, whether for a day, or permanently as in the case of the Vice President's death or resignation. When the Vice President returned, the Pro Tempore lost his place. Then, when the Vice President was again absent, the Senate again elected a President Pro Tempore, in many cases the same Senator who had been chosen before. By the standing order agreed to on March 12, 1890, the Senate declared that the President Pro Tempore shall hold office during "the pleasure of the Senate and until another is elected, and shall execute the duties thereof during all future absences of the Vice President until the Senate does otherwise order." For the period before 1890, this table lists only the first date in each Congress in which a particular Senator was elected President Pro Tempore.

[2] Prior to 1890, dates reflect only the date of elections. Following 1890, dates are inclusive of service.

[3] Senator Gaillard was elected President Pro Tempore on November 25, 1814, upon the death, in the 13th Congress, of Vice President Gerry. He served continuously in the post for the remainder of the 13th Congress, the entire 14th Congress, and for nearly all Senate daily sessions of the 15th Congress.

[4] Anti-Democrat and State Rights candidate.

[5] Senator Southard resigned as President Pro Tempore, and Senator Mangum was chosen in his place. The vice presidency being vacant upon John Tyler's succession to the presidency on April 4, 1841, Mangum continued in office until Vice President Dallas took the oath on March 4, 1845, officially in the 29th Congress.

[6] Senator Sevier's name appears in Senator Byrd's history, but the 1911 Senate document quotes the Senate Journal as stating Sevier was only "permitted to occupy" the chair that day and was not elected President Pro Tempore.

[7] Senator Atchison was chosen on various days to serve; the Senate Journal notes Senator King designated him.

[8] The Senate Journal notes that Senator Cass "by unanimous consent" was chosen President Pro Tempore "for this day."

[9] The Senate Journal notes that Senator Ingalls was elected on January 25, 1887, but did not take the oath until Senator Sherman's resignation became effective on February 26, 1887.

[10] Senator Manderson was the first President Pro Tempore to be elected under the Standing Order of March 12, 1890, which stated that a President Pro Tempore would hold office until another was elected. Thus, since then a President Pro Tempore has held the post continuously, whether or not the Vice President was absent.

[11] Senators Bacon, Gallinger, Lodge, and Brandegee rotated in the position for the remainder of the 62nd Congress, with none serving more than three months.

5.14   Senate Whips, 1913-1996

Democrats

Whip	State	Congress	Dates
James Hamilton Lewis	IL	63rd-65th	1913-1919
Peter Gerry	RI	66th-70th	1919-1929
Morris Sheppard	TX	71st-72nd	1929-1933
James Hamilton Lewis	IL	73rd-75th	1933-1939
Sherman Minton	IN	76th	1939-1941
Lister Hill	AL	77th-79th	1941-1947
Scott W. Lucas	IL	80th	1947-1949
Francis J. Myers	PA	81st	1949-1951
Lyndon B. Johnson	TX	82nd	1951-1953
Earle Clements	KY	83rd-84th	1953-1957
Mike Mansfield	MT	85th-86th	1957-1961
Hubert H. Humphrey	MN	87th-88th	1961-1965
Russell W. Long	LA	89th-90th	1965-1969
Edward M. Kennedy	MA	91st	1969-1971
Robert C. Byrd, Jr.	WV	92nd-94th	1971-1977
Alan Cranston	CA	95th-101st	1977-1991
Wendell H. Ford	KY	102nd-	1991-

Republicans

Whip[1]	State	Congress	Dates
James W. Wadsworth	NY	64th	1915
Charles Curtis	KS	64th-68th	1915-1924
Wesley L. Jones	WA	68th-70th	1924-1929
Simeon D. Fess	OH	71st-72nd	1929-1933
Felix Hebert	RI	73rd	1933-1935
Kenneth S. Wherry	NE	78th-80th	1944-1949
Leverett Saltonstall	MA	81st-84th	1949-1957
Everett Dirksen	IL	85th	1957-1959
Thomas Kuchel	CA	86th-90th	1959-1969
Hugh Scott	PA	91st	1969
Robert Griffin	MI	91st-94th	1969-1977
Ted Stevens	AK	95th-98th	1977-1985
Alan Simpson	WY	99th-103rd	1985-1995
Trent Lott	MS	104th	1995-June 12, 1996[2]
Don Nickles	OK	104th-	June 12, 1996[3]

[1] Between 1936 and 1943 the post of Republican Whip was filled by informal, irregular appointment by the Republican Leader.
[2] Elected Majority Leader, June 12, 1996.
[3] Elected to replace Trent Lott, June 12, 1996.

5.15   Checks and Balances

Traditional means for checks and balances among the three branches of government:

- Congress can pass federal legislation
- President can veto federal bills
- Supreme Court can declare new laws unconstitutional
- President can appoint federal judges
- Senate can refuse to confirm presidential appointments
- Congress can impeach federal judges
- President can make foreign treaties
- Congress can override a presidential veto
- Supreme Court interprets the law
- Congress can propose constitutional amendments to overturn judicial decisions
- Congress can declare executive acts unconstitutional

5.16   Steps in the Legislative Process

The legislative process comprises a number of steps:

1. Introducing Legislation.
The work of Congress is initiated by the introduction of a proposal in one of four principal forms: the bill, the joint resolution, the concurrent resolution, and the simple resolution. A bill is the form used for most legislation. A bill originating in the House of Representatives is designated by the letters "H.R.", signifying "House of Representatives", followed by a number that it retains throughout all its parliamentary stages. Bills are presented to the President for action when approved in identical form by both the House of Representatives and the Senate.

2. Referral to Committee
Any Member in the House of Representatives may introduce a bill at any time while the House is in session by simply placing it in the "hopper" provided for the purpose at the side of the Clerk's desk in the House Chamber. The sponsor's signature must appear on the bill. A public bill may have an unlimited number of co-sponsoring members. The bill is assigned its legislative number by the Clerk and referred to the appropriate committee by the Speaker, with the assistance of the Parliamentarian. The bill is then printed in its introduced form. An important phase of the legislative process is the action taken by committees. It is during committee action that the most intense consideration is given to the proposed measures; this is also the time when the people are given their opportunity to be heard. Each piece of legislation is referred to the committee that has jurisdiction over the area affected by the measure.

3. Consideration by Committee
Usually the first step in this process is a public hearing, where the committee members hear witnesses representing various viewpoints on the measure. After hearings are completed, the bill is considered in a session that is popularly known as the "mark-up" session. Members of the committee study the viewpoints presented in detail. Amendments may be offered to the bill, and the committee members vote to accept or reject these changes.

4. Committee Action
At the conclusion of deliberation, a vote of committee or subcommittee members is taken to determine what action to take on the measure. It can be reported, with or without amendment, or tabled, which means no further action on it will occur. If the committee has approved extensive amendments, they may decide to report a new bill incorporating all the amendments. This is known as a "clean bill," which will have a new number. If the committee votes to report a bill, the Committee Report is written. This report describes the purpose and scope of the measure and the reasons for recommended approval. House Report numbers are prefixed with "H.Rpt." and then a number indicating the Congress.

5. House Floor Consideration
Consideration of a measure by the full House can be a simple or very complex operation. In general, a measure is ready for consideration by the full House after it has been reported by a committee. Under certain circumstances, it may be brought to the Floor directly. The consideration of a measure may be governed by a "rule." A rule is itself a simple resolution, which must be passed by the House, that sets out the particulars of debate for a specific bill—how much time will be allowed for debate, whether amendments can be offered, and other matters. Debate time for a measure is normally divided between proponents and opponents. Each side yields time to those members who wish to speak on the bill. When amendments are offered, these are also debated and voted upon. After all debate is concluded and amendments decided upon, the House is ready to vote on final passage.

6. Resolving Differences

After a measure passes in the House, it goes to the Senate for consideration. A bill must pass both bodies in the same form before it can be presented to the President for signature into law. If the Senate changes the language of the measure, it must return to the House for concurrence or additional changes. This back-and-forth negotiation may occur on the House floor, with the House accepting or rejecting Senate amendments or complete Senate text. Often a conference committee will be appointed with both House and Senate members. This group will resolve the differences in committee and report the identical measure back to both bodies for a vote. Conference committees also issue reports outlining the final version of the bill.

7. Final Step

Votes on final passage, as well as all other votes in the House, may be taken by the electronic voting system which registers each individual member's response. These votes are referred to as Yea/Nay votes or recorded votes, and are available in House Votes by Bill number, roll call vote number or words describing the reason for the vote. Votes in the House may also be by voice vote, and no record of individual responses is available. After a measure has been passed in identical form by both the House and Senate, it is considered "enrolled." It is sent to the President who may sign the measure into law, veto it and return it to Congress, let it become law without signature, or at the end of a session, pocket-veto it.

5.17 Chronology of Development of Congressional Staffs

Mid-1800s—House Committees were authorized to hire staff.

1946—Legislative Reorganization Act of 1946 marked beginning of modern staffing system; authorized permanent complement of 10 staff members per standing committee.

Post World War II—House used as many as 7 select committees; additional staff authorized for most standing committees either by law or resolution.

1970—Legislative Reorganization Act of 1970 increased maximum number of staff for each standing committee from 10 to 12; established procedure by which additional staff could be added.

1974—Committee Reform Amendments of 1974—raised staff allotment from 12 to 30.

1975—Congress replaced 1974 funding provisions with a new rule authorizing each subcommittee chair and ranking minority member to appoint one staff person which helped guarantee independent staffing of House subcommittees.

1979—House standing committee staff nearly three times larger than in 1970, from 700 in 1900.

1983—House's only current select committee, the Permanent Select Committee on Intelligence, obtained authority to receive funding for 30 statutory staff.

1980s-early 90s—Committees, party caucuses and individual members explored the following issues: The appropriate levels of funds and staff for all House committees; the amount of committee resources allotted to minority party members on committees; pay equity for male and female committee aids; combining statutory and investigative funds for committees; and switching from an annual to a biennial funding cycle.

Source: Congressional Research Service.

SECTION 6

The Judiciary

6.1 Justices of the U.S. Supreme Court, 1789-1999

Justice	Dates*	Appointed by
John Jay+	1789-95	George Washington
William Cushing	1789-1810	George Washington
James Wilson	1789-98	George Washington
John Blair	1789-96	George Washington
James Iredell	1790-99	George Washington
Thomas Johnson	1791-93	George Washington
William Paterson	1793-1806	George Washington
John Rutledge#	1790-91; 1795	George Washington
Samuel Chase	1796-1811	George Washington
Oliver Ellsworth+	1796-99	George Washington
Bushrod Washington	1798-1829	John Adams
Alfred Moore	1799-1804	John Adams
John Marshall+	1801-35	John Adams
William Johnson	1804-34	Thomas Jefferson
H. B. Livingston	1806-23	Thomas Jefferson
Thomas Todd	1807-26	Thomas Jefferson
Joseph Story	1811-45	James Madison
Gabriel Duval	1811-35	James Madison
Smith Thompson	1823-43	James Monroe
Robert Trimble	1826-28	John Quincy Adams
John McLean	1829-61	Andrew Jackson
Henry Baldwin	1830-44	Andrew Jackson
James M. Wayne	1835-67	Andrew Jackson
Roger B. Taney+	1836-64	Andrew Jackson
Philip P. Barbour	1836-41	Andrew Jackson
John Catron	1837-65	Andrew Jackson
John McKinley	1837-52	Martin Van Buren
Peter V. Daniel	1841-60	Martin Van Buren
Samuel Nelson	1845-72	John Tyler
Levi Woodbury	1845-51	James K. Polk
Robert C. Grier	1846-70	James K. Polk
Benjamin R. Curtis	1851-57	Millard Fillmore
John A. Campbell	1853-61	Franklin Pierce
Nathan Clifford	1858-81	James Buchanan
Noah H. Swayne	1862-81	Abraham Lincoln
Samuel F. Miller	1862-90	Abraham Lincoln
David Davis	1862-77	Abraham Lincoln
Stephen J. Field	1863-97	Abraham Lincoln
Salmon P. Chase+	1864-73	Abraham Lincoln
William Strong	1870-80	Ulysses S. Grant

<u>Justice</u>	<u>Dates*</u>	<u>Appointed by</u>
Joseph P. Bradley	1870-92	Ulysses S. Grant
Ward Hunt	1872-82	Ulysses S. Grant
Morrison R. Waite+	1874-88	Ulysses C. Grant
John Marshall Harlan	1877-1911	Rutherford B. Hayes
William B. Woods	1880-87	Rutherford B. Hayes
Stanley Matthews	1881-89	James A. Garfield
Horace Gray	1881-1902	Chester A. Arthur
Samuel Blatchford	1882-93	Chester A. Arthur
Lucius Q. C. Lamar	1888-93	Grover Cleveland
Melville W. Fuller+	1888-1910	Grover Cleveland
David J. Brewer	1889-1910	Benjamin Harrison
Henry B. Brown	1890-1906	Benjamin Harrison
George Shiras	1892-1903	Benjamin Harrison
Howell E. Jackson	1893-95	Benjamin Harrison
Edward D. White	1894-1910	Grover Cleveland
Rufus W. Peckham	1895-1909	Grover Cleveland
Joseph McKenna	1898-1925	William McKinley
Oliver W. Holmes	1902-32	Theodore Roosevelt
William R. Day	1903-22	Theodore Roosevelt
William H. Moody	1906-10	Theodore Roosevelt
Horace H. Lurton	1910-14	William H. Taft
Charles Evans Hughes	1910-16	William H. Taft
Edward D. White+	1910-21	William H. Taft
W. Van Devanter	1910-37	William H. Taft
Joseph R. Lamar	1911-16	William H. Taft
Mahlon Pitney	1912-22	William H. Taft
James C. McReynolds	1914-41	Woodrow Wilson
Louis O. Brandeis	1916-39	Woodrow Wilson
John H. Clarke	1916-22	Woodrow Wilson
William Howard Taft	1921-30	Warren G. Harding
George Sutherland	1922-38	Warren G. Harding
Pierce Butler	1922-39	Warren G. Harding
Edward T. Sanford	1923-30	Warren G. Harding
Harlan F. Stone	1925-41	Calvin Coolidge
Charles Evans Hughes+	1930-41	Herbert Hoover
Owen J. Roberts	1930-45	Herbert Hoover
Benjamin N. Cardozo	1932-38	Herbert Hoover
Hugo L. Black	1937-71	Franklin D. Roosevelt
Stanley Reed	1938-57	Franklin D. Roosevelt
Felix Frankfurter	1939-62	Franklin D. Roosevelt

Justice	Dates*	Appointed by
William O. Douglas	1939-75	Franklin D. Roosevelt
Frank Murphy	1940-49	Franklin D. Roosevelt
James F. Byrnes	1941-42	Franklin D. Roosevelt
Harlan E. Stone+	1941-46	Franklin D. Roosevelt
Robert H. Jackson	1941-54	Franklin D. Roosevelt
Wiley Rutledge	1943-49	Franklin D. Roosevelt
Harold H. Burton	1945-58	Harry S. Truman
Frederick M. Vinson+	1946-53	Harry S. Truman
Tom C. Clark	1949-67	Harry S. Truman
Sherman Minton	1949-56	Harry S. Truman
Earl Warren+	1953-69	Dwight D. Eisenhower
John Marshall Harlan	1955-71	Dwight D. Eisenhower
William J. Brennan, Jr.	1956-90	Dwight D. Eisenhower
Charles E. Whittaker	1957-62	Dwight D. Eisenhower
Potter Stewart	1958-81	Dwight D. Eisenhower
Byron R. White	1962-93	John Kennedy
Arthur J. Goldberg	1962-65	John Kennedy
Abe Fortas#	1965-69	Lyndon Johnson
Thurgood Marshall	1967-91	Lyndon Johnson
Warren E. Burger+	1969-86	Richard Nixon
Harry A. Blackmun	1970-94	Richard Nixon
Lewis F. Powell Jr.	1972-87	Richard Nixon
William Rehnquist	1972-86	Richard Nixon
John P. Stevens	1976-	Gerald Ford
Sandra D. O'Connor	1981-	Ronald Reagan
William Rehnquist+	1986-	Ronald Reagan
Antonin Scalia	1986-	Ronald Reagan
Anthony M. Kennedy	1987-	Ronald Reagan
David H. Souter	1990-	George Bush
Clarence Thomas	1991-	George Bush
Ruth Bader Ginsburg	1993-	Bill Clinton
Stephen G. Breyer	1994-	Bill Clinton

* Dates begin with year of nomination.
+Chief justices.
Never confirmed by the Senate as Chief Justice.

6.2 Chief Justices of the U.S. Supreme Court, 1789-1999

Justice	Years on Court	President Who Nominated	Party
John Jay	1789-1795	George Washington	F
John Rutledge*	1795	George Washington	F
Oliver Ellsworth	1796-1800	George Washington	F
John Marshall	1801-1835	John Adams	F
Roger B. Taney	1836-1864	Andrew Jackson	D
Salmon P. Chase	1864-1873	Abraham Lincoln	R
Morrison R. Waite	1874-1888	Ulysses S. Grant	R
Melville W. Fuller	1888-1910	Grover Cleveland	D
Edward D. White**	1910-1921	William H. Taft	D
William H. Taft	1921-1930	Warren G. Harding	R
Charles E. Hughes	1930-1940	Herbert Hoover	R
Harlan F. Stone	1941-1946	Franklin D. Roosevelt	D
Frederick M. Vinson	1946-1953	Harry S. Truman	D
Earl Warren	1953-1969	Dwight D. Eisenhower	R
Warren E. Burger	1969-1986	Richard M. Nixon	R
William H. Rehnquist**	1986-	Ronald Reagan	R

* Appointed to replace John Jay; served without confirmation Aug. 12-Dec. 15, 1795, while Congress was in recess. Senate refused to confirm his nomination.
** Former associate justice.
D = Democrat; F = Federalist; R = Republican

6.3 Major Cases of the Marshall Court, 1801-1835

Cases expanding the authority of the Supreme Court:

Marbury v. Madison (1803) gave the Court the power of judicial review.

U.S. v. Peters (1809) established the Court's right to coerce a state legislature.

Martin v. Hunter's Lessee (1816) confirmed the Court's right to overrule a state court.

Cohens v. Virginia (1821). States were no longer sovereign in all respects since they had ratified the Constitution. State courts must submit to federal jurisdiction.

Cases expanding the powers of Congress:

McCullough v. Maryland (1819) upheld the right of Congress to charter a national bank, thus putting into national law the doctrine of implied powers.

Gibbons v. Ogden (1824) gave the national government undisputed control over interstate commerce by ruling invalid a steamboat monopoly chartered by New York State. This freed internal transportation from state restraint.

Cases weakening the states:

Fletcher v. Peck (1810) established the principle that state laws were invalid when in conflict with the Constitution.

Dartmouth College v. Woodward (1819) by forbidding the state legislature to alter the college charter, established the principle that charters were contracts which could not be impaired.

Martin v. Mott (1827) denied a state the right to withhold its militia from service.

6.4   Profiles of Supreme Court Justices, 1999

WILLIAM M. REHNQUIST
Appointed by: Nixon in 1971 and elevated to the position of Chief Justice by Reagan in 1986.
Background: Practiced law in Phoenix before going to work for the Nixon administration as Assistant Attorney General for the Justice Department.

JOHN PAUL STEVENS
Appointed by: Ford in 1975.
Background: Practiced anti-trust law in Chicago before being appointed to the 7th U.S. Circuit Court of Appeals by Nixon.

SANDRA DAY O'CONNOR
Appointed by: Reagan in 1981.
Background: Practiced law in California and Arizona. Served as Republican state senator in Arizona, and later sat on the Arizona Court of Appeals.

ANTONIN SCALIA
Appointed by: Reagan in 1986.
Background: Served as general counsel in Nixon administration, and Assistant Attorney General in the Ford administration. Appointed to U.S. Court of Appeals for the District of Columbia by Reagan.

ANTHONY M. KENNEDY
Appointed by: Reagan in 1988.
Background: Practiced law in San Francisco, later appointed to U.S. Court of Appeals for the 9th Circuit by Ford.

DAVID H. SOUTER
Appointed by: Bush in 1990.
Background: Assistant Attorney General and Deputy Attorney General in New Hampshire. Served as associate justice of New Hampshire's highest court, and appointed to the 1st Circuit U.S. Court of Appeals by Bush.

CLARENCE THOMAS
Appointed by: Bush in 1991.
Background: Assistant secretary of civil rights in the Education Department under Reagan, and head of the Equal Employment Opportunity Commission. Appointed to U.S. Court of Appeals for the District of Columbia by Bush. Appointment tarnished by sexual harassment charges by Anita Hill.

RUTH BADER GINSBURG
Appointed by: Clinton in 1993.
Background: Law professor at Rutgers University Law School in Newark, where she assisted the New Jersey American Civil Liberties Union and later the National ACLU. Law professor at Columbia Law School. Appointed to U.S. Court of Appeals for the District of Columbia by Carter.

STEPHEN G. BREYER
Appointed by: Clinton in 1994.
Background: Professor at Harvard Law School. Served as assistant special prosecutor in the Watergate Investigation, and worked for the Senate Judiciary Committee. Appointed to U.S. Court of Appeals.

6.5 U.S. Circuit Courts

The intermediate appellate courts in the federal judicial system are the courts of appeals. Twelve of these courts have jurisdiction over cases from certain geographic areas. The Court of Appeals for the Federal Circuit has national jurisdiction over specific types of cases. The U.S. Court of Appeals for the Federal Circuit and the 12 regional courts of appeals are often referred to as circuit courts. The First through Eleventh Circuits each include three or more states. The U.S. Court of Appeals for the District of Columbia hears cases arising in the District of Columbia and has appellate jurisdiction assigned by Congress in legislation concerning many departments of the federal government.

First Circuit	Maine, Massachusetts, New Hampshire, Rhode Island, and Puerto Rico
Second Circuit	Connecticut, New York, and Vermont
Third Circuit	Delaware, New Jersey, Pennsylvania, and the Virgin Islands
Fourth Circuit	Maryland, North Carolina, South Carolina, Virginia, and West Virginia
Fifth Circuit	Louisiana, Mississippi, and Texas
Sixth Circuit	Kentucky, Michigan, Ohio, and Tennessee
Seventh Circuit	Illinois, Indiana, and Wisconsin
Eighth Circuit	Arkansas, Iowa, Minnesota, Missouri, Nebraska, North Dakota, South Dakota, Alaska, Arizona, and California
Ninth Circuit	Hawaii, Idaho, Montana, Nevada, Oregon, Washington, Guam, and the Northern Mariana Islands
Tenth Circuit	Colorado, Kansas, New Mexico, Oklahoma, Utah, and Wyoming
Eleventh Circuit	Alabama, Florida, and Georgia

6.6   Common Legal Terms in U.S. Courts

acquittal: Judgment that a criminal defendant has not been proved guilty beyond a reasonable doubt.

affidavit: A written statement of facts confirmed by the oath of the party making it, before a notary or officer having authority to administer oaths.

affirmed: In the practice of the appellate courts, the decree or order is declared valid and will stand as rendered in the lower court.

answer: The formal written statement by a defendant responding to a civil complaint and setting forth the grounds for defense.

appeal: A request made after a trial, asking another court (usually the court of appeals) to decide whether the trial was conducted properly. To make such a request is "to appeal" or "to take an appeal." One who appeals is called the appellant.

appellate: About appeals; an appellate court has the power to review the judgment of another lower court or tribunal.

arraignment: A proceeding in which an individual who is accused of committing a crime is brought into court, told of the charges, and asked to plead guilty or not guilty.

bail: Security given for the release of a criminal defendant or witness from legal custody (usually in the form of money) to secure his appearance on the day and time appointed.

bankruptcy: Refers to statutes and judicial proceedings involving persons or businesses that cannot pay their debts and seek the assistance of the court in getting a fresh start. Under the protection of the bankruptcy court, debtors may discharge their debts, perhaps by paying a portion of each debt. Bankruptcy judges preside over these proceedings.

bench trial: Trial without a jury in which a judge decides the facts.

brief: A written statement submitted by the lawyer for each side in a case that explains to the judges why they should decide the case or a particular part of a case in favor of that lawyer's client.

chambers: A judge's office.

capital offense: A crime punishable by death.

case law: The law as laid down in the decisions of the courts in previous cases.

charge to the jury: The judge's instructions to the jury concerning the law that applies to the facts of the case on trial.

chief judge: The judge who has primary responsibility for the administration of a court but also decides cases; chief judges are determined by seniority.

circumstantial evidence: All evidence except eyewitness testimony.

clerk of court: An officer appointed by the court to work with the chief judge in overseeing the court's administration, especially to assist in managing the flow of cases through the court and to maintain court records.

common law: The legal system that originated in England and is now in use in the United States. It is based on judicial decisions rather than legislative action.

complaint: A written statement by the plaintiff stating the wrongs allegedly committed by the defendant.

contract: An agreement between two or more persons that creates an obligation to do or not to do a particular thing.

conviction: A judgment of guilt against a criminal defendant.

counsel: Legal advice; a term used to refer to lawyers in a case.

counterclaim: A claim that a defendant makes against a plaintiff.

court: Government entity authorized to resolve legal disputes. Judges sometimes use "court" to refer to themselves in the third person, as in "the court has read the briefs."

court reporter: A person who makes a word-for-word record of what is said in court and produces a transcript of the proceedings upon request.

damages: Money paid by defendants to successful plaintiffs in civil cases to compensate the plaintiffs for their injuries.

default judgment: A judgment rendered because of the defendant's failure to answer or appear.

defendant: In a civil suit, the person complained against; in a criminal case, the person accused of the crime.

deposition: An oral statement made before an officer authorized by law to administer oaths. Such statements are often taken to examine potential witnesses, to obtain discovery, or to be used later in trial.

discovery: Lawyers' examination, before trial, of facts and documents in possession of the opponents to help the lawyers prepare for trial.

docket: A log containing brief entries of court proceedings.

en banc: "In the bench" or "full bench." Refers to court sessions with the entire membership of a court participating rather than the usual quorum. U.S. courts of appeals usually sit in panels of three judges, but may expand to a larger number in certain cases. They are then said to be sitting en banc.

evidence: Information presented in testimony or in documents that is used to persuade the fact finder (judge or jury) to decide the case for one side or the other.

federal question: Jurisdiction given to federal courts in cases involving the interpretation and application of the U.S. Constitution, acts of Congress, and treaties.

felony: A crime carrying a penalty of more than a year in prison.

file: To place a paper in the official custody of the clerk of court to enter into the files or records of a case.

grand jury: A body of citizens who listen to evidence of criminal allegations presented by the government, and determine whether there is probable cause to believe the offense was committed. As it is used in federal criminal cases, "the government" refers to the lawyers of the U.S. attorney's office who are prosecuting the case.

habeas corpus: A writ that is usually used to bring a prisoner before the court to determine the legality of his imprisonment. It may also be used to bring a person in custody before the court to give testimony, or to be prosecuted.

hearsay: Statements by a witness who did not see or hear the incident in question but heard about it from someone else. Hearsay is usually not admissible as evidence in court.

impeachment: (1) The process of calling something into question, as in "impeaching the testimony of a witness." (2) The constitutional process whereby the House of Representatives may "impeach" (accuse of misconduct) high officers of the federal government for trial in the Senate.

indictment: The formal charge issued by a grand jury stating that there is enough evidence that the defendant committed the crime to justify having a trial; it is used primarily for felonies.

in forma pauperis: In the manner of a pauper. Permission given to a person to sue without payment of court fees on claim of indigence or poverty.

information: A formal accusation by a government attorney that the defendant committed a misdemeanor.

injunction: An order of the court prohibiting (or compelling) the performance of a specific act to prevent irreparable damage or injury.

instructions: Judge's explanation to the jury before it begins deliberations of the questions it must answer and the law governing the case.

interrogatories: Written questions asked by one party of an opposing party, who must answer them in writing under oath; a discovery device in a lawsuit.

issue: (1) The disputed point in a disagreement between parties in a lawsuit. (2) To send out officially, as in to issue an order.

judge: Government official with authority to decide lawsuits brought before courts. Other judicial officers in the U.S. courts system are Supreme Court justices.

judgment: The official decision of a court finally determining the respective rights and claims of the parties to a suit.

jurisdiction: (1) The legal authority of a court to hear and decide a case. Concurrent jurisdiction exists when two courts have simultaneous responsibility for the same case. (2) The geographic area over which the court has authority to decide cases.

jurisprudence: The study of law and the structure of the legal system.

jury: Persons selected according to law and sworn to inquire into and declare a verdict on matters of fact.

lawsuit: A legal action started by a plaintiff against a defendant based on a complaint that the defendant failed to perform a legal duty, resulting in harm to the plaintiff.

litigation: A case, controversy, or lawsuit. Participants (plaintiffs and defendants) in lawsuits are called litigants.

magistrate judges: Judicial officers who assist U.S. district judges in getting cases ready for trial, who may decide some criminal and civil trials when both parties agree to have the case heard by a magistrate judge instead of a judge.

misdemeanor: Usually a petty offense, a less serious crime than a felony, punishable by less than a year of confinement.

mistrial: An invalid trial, caused by fundamental error. When a mistrial is declared, the trial must start again from the selection of the jury.

nolo contendere: No contest—has the same effect as a plea of guilty, as far as the criminal sentence is concerned, but may not be considered as an admission of guilt for any other purpose.

opinion: A judge's written explanation of a decision of the court or of a majority of judges. A dissenting opinion disagrees with the majority opinion because of the reasoning and/or the principles of law on which the decision is based. A concurring opinion agrees with the decision of the court but offers further comment.

oral argument: An opportunity for lawyers to summarize their position before the court and also to answer the judges' questions.

panel: (1) In appellate cases, a group of judges (usually three) assigned to decide the case; (2) In the jury selection process, the group of potential jurors.

parties: Plaintiffs and defendants (petitioners and respondents) to lawsuits, also known as appellants and appellees in appeals, and their lawyers.

petit jury (or trial jury): A group of citizens who hear the evidence presented by both sides at trial and determine the facts in dispute. Federal criminal juries consist of 12 persons. Federal civil juries consist of six persons.

plaintiff: The person who files the complaint in a civil lawsuit.

plea: In a criminal case, the defendant's statement pleading "guilty" or "not guilty" in answer to the charges, a declaration made in open court.

pleadings: Written statements of the parties in a civil case of their positions. In the federal courts, the principal pleadings are the complaint and the answer.

precedent: A court decision in an earlier case with facts and law similar to a dispute currently before a court. Precedent will ordinarily govern the decision of a later similar case, unless a party can show that it was wrongly decided or that it differed in some significant way.

pretrial conference: A meeting of the judge and lawyers to discuss which matters should be presented to the jury, to review evidence and witnesses, to set a timetable, and to discuss the settlement of the case.

probation: A sentencing alternative to imprisonment in which the court releases convicted defendants under supervision as long as certain conditions are observed.

procedure: The rules for the conduct of a lawsuit; there are rules of civil, criminal, evidence, bankruptcy, and appellate procedure.

pro se: A Latin term meaning "on one's own behalf"; in courts, it refers to persons who present their own cases without lawyers.

prosecute: To charge someone with a crime. A prosecutor tries a criminal case on behalf of the government.

record: A written account of all the acts and proceedings in a lawsuit.

remand: When an appellate court sends a case back to a lower court for further proceedings.

reverse: When an appellate court sets aside the decision of a lower court because of an error. A reversal is often followed by a remand.

sentence: The punishment ordered by a court for a defendant convicted of a crime.

sequester: To separate. Sometimes juries are sequestered from outside influences during their deliberations.

service of process: The service of writs or summonses to the appropriate party.

settlement: Parties to a lawsuit resolve their difference without having a trial. Settlements often involve the payment of compensation by one party in satisfaction of the other party's claims.

sidebar: A conference between the judge and lawyers held out of earshot of the jury and spectators.

statute: A law passed by a legislature.

statute of limitations: A law that sets the time within which parties must take action to enforce their rights.

subpoena: A command to a witness to appear and give testimony.

subpoena duces tecum: A command to a witness to produce documents.

summary judgment: A decision made on the basis of statements and evidence presented for the record without a trial. It is used when there is no dispute as to the facts of the case, and one party is entitled to judgment as a matter of law.

temporary restraining order: Prohibits a person from an action that is likely to cause irreparable harm. This differs from an injunction in that it may be granted immediately, without notice to the opposing party, and without a hearing. It is intended to last only until a hearing can be held.

testimony: Evidence presented orally by witnesses during trials or before grand juries.

tort: A civil wrong or breach of a duty to another person, as outlined by law. A very common tort is negligent operation of a motor vehicle that results in property damage and personal injury in an automobile accident.

transcript: A written, word-for-word record of what was said, either in a proceeding such as a trial or during some other conversation, as in a transcript of a hearing or oral deposition.

uphold: The decision of an appellate court not to reverse a lower court decision.

U.S. attorney: A lawyer appointed by the President in each judicial district to prosecute and defend cases for the federal government.

venue: The geographical location in which a case is tried.

verdict: The decision of a petit jury or a judge.

voir dire: The process by which judges and lawyers select a petit jury from among those eligible to serve, by questioning them to determine knowledge of the facts of the case and a willingness to decide the case only on the evidence presented in court. "Voir dire" is a phrase meaning "to speak the truth."

warrant: A written order directing the arrest of a party. A search warrant orders that a specific location be searched for items, which if found, can be used in court as evidence.

witness: A person called upon by either side in a lawsuit to give testimony before the court or jury.

writ: A formal written command, issued from the court, requiring the performance of a specific act.

writ of certiorari: An order issued by the Supreme Court directing the lower court to transmit records for a case which it will hear on appeal.

6.7   Important U.S. Supreme Court Cases

Marbury v. Madison, 5 U.S. 137 (1803)
Judicial v. executive power; judicial review

At issue was the question of whether the Supreme Court of the United States has the power, under Article III, Section 2, of the Constitution, to interpret the constitutionality of a law or statute passed by Congress. The Court decided that the federal law in question in the case contradicted the Constitution, and since the Constitution is the Supreme Law of the Land, it must reign supreme. Through this case, Chief Justice John Marshall established the power of judicial review: the power of the Court not only to interpret the constitutionality of a law or statute but also to carry out the process and enforce its decision.

McCulloch v. Maryland, 17 U.S. 316 (1819)
Federal v. state rights

At issue in this case was whether the state of Maryland had the right to tax a federal agency which was properly set up by the United States Congress. In a unanimous decision, the Supreme Court of the United States ruled that the "power to tax involves the power to destroy," and that the federal government's national bank was immune to state taxation.

Gibbons v. Ogden, 22 U.S. 1 (1824)
Interstate commerce; federal v. state rights

At issue in this case was whether the New York statute that prohibited vessels licensed by the United States from navigating the waters of New York was unconstitutional and, therefore, void. In this case, the Court put forth the position that Congress can legislate and regulate all matters of interstate commerce as long as there is some commercial connection with another state. While interstate commerce is regulated by Congress, power to regulate "completely internal" commerce (trade carried on in a state that does not affect other states) is reserved to the states.

Dred Scott v. Sanford, 60 U.S. 393 (1857)
Slavery and citizenship v. Fifth Amendment and property rights

Dred Scott, a slave, was taken by his owner, Sanford, into northern federal territory. Scott felt that he was free because of the Missouri Compromise of 1820, which excluded slavery from specified portions of United States territories. When he came back to Missouri, Scott sued his owner for his freedom. The Supreme Court ruled that slaves were property, not citizens and, therefore, Dred Scott was not entitled to use the courts. Justice Taney said that freeing Scott would be a clear violation of the Fifth Amendment because it would amount to depriving Sanford of his property without due process of law. He also said that Congress had no power to prohibit slavery in the territory and that the Missouri Compromise was unconstitutional.

Munn v. Illinois, 94 U.S. 113 (1877)
Public v. private property; state rights

At issue was whether the regulation of railroad rates by the state of Illinois deprived the railroad companies of property without due process of law. The Court upheld the Illinois law because the movement and storage of grain were considered to be closely related to public interest. This type of economic activity could be governed by state legislatures, whereas purely private contracts could only be governed by the courts.

In Re Debs, 158 U.S. 564 (1895)
Union strikes; commerce clause v. First and Fourteenth Amendments

At issue was whether the federal government has the constitutional authority to stop railroad workers from striking. The Court upheld the authority of the federal government to halt the strike. The Court reasoned that the federal government has "enumerated powers" found in Article 1, Section 8, to "regulate commerce . . . among the several states," and to establish post offices and post roads. When the American Railway Union struck, it interfered with the railroad's ability to carry commerce and mail which benefited the needs and "general welfare" of all Americans.

© 2000 by The Center for Applied Research in Education

Plessy v. Ferguson, 163 U.S. 537 (1896)
Separate but equal; equal protection v. state rights
The question here was whether laws which provided for the separation of races violated the rights of blacks as guaranteed by the equal protection clause of the fourteenth amendment. The Court held that the Louisiana Act, which stated that "all railway companies were to provide equal but separate accommodations for white and black races," did not violate the Constitution. The law did not violate the Fourteenth Amendment, which gave all blacks citizenship, and forbade states from passing any laws which would deprive blacks their constitutional rights. [The Plessy doctrine of "separate but equal" was overturned by *Brown v. Board of Education of Topeka,* 347 U.S. 483 (1954), which held "separate but equal" to be unconstitutional.]

Lochner v. New York, 198 U.S. 45 (1905)
Individual property rights v. state police powers
At issue was whether a law which limited the number of hours bakery employees were allowed to work interfered with the bakery owner's right to make employer/employee contracts. The Court held that even though states have the power to regulate in the areas of health, safety, morals, and public welfare, the New York law in question was not within the limits of these "police powers" of the State. This decision marked the beginning of the "substantive due process" era, in which the Court struck down a number of state laws that interfered with an individual's economic and property rights. It was overturned twelve years later in *Bunting v. Oregon,* 243 U.S. 426 (1917).

Muller v. Oregon, 208 U.S. 412 (1908)
Employee-employer contracts; Tenth Amendment v. Fourteenth Amendment
The state of Oregon passed a law prohibiting women from working in factories or laundries more than ten hours in any day. At question in this case was whether Oregon, through its regulation of women's work hours, violated the "privileges and immunities" clause of the Fourteenth Amendment by forbidding the employment of women for more than ten hours a day in laundries and factories. The Court held that the Oregon law that barred women from certain factory and laundry work to be correct and sustained the legislation.

Debs v. United States, 249 U.S. 211 (1919)
Clear and present danger; free speech
Eugene v. Debs, a well-known socialist, gave a public speech intended to interfere with recruiting for the armed forces. Debs was arrested and charged with violating the Espionage Act of 1917. The Court refused to grant Debs protection under the First Amendment freedom of speech clause because his speech represented a "clear and present danger" to the safety of the United States.

Schechter Poultry Corp. v. United States, 295 U.S. 495 (1935)
Congressional v. presidential power
At issue was whether the National Industrial Recovery Act, which gave the President the authority to regulate certain aspects of commerce during the Depression, was an unconstitutional delegation of presidential power. The Court held that the delegation of power made by the NIRA was unconstitutional. The Court held that Congress cannot delegate legislative power to the President, even under the extraordinary conditions of the Depression. The NIRA was declared unconstitutional because it exceeded the commerce power that had been given to Congress by the Constitution.

Korematsu v. United States, 323 U.S. 214 (1944)
Japanese relocation; equal protection v. executive powers
Exclusion Order #34 and Executive Order #9066 of 1942, which had been issued to protect the West Coast from acts of espionage and sabotage, required all Japanese-Americans living in restricted areas to go to inland relocation centers. At issue was whether this violated the Fourteenth Amendment right to equal protection of the law and the Fifth Amendment right to life, liberty, and property. The Court ruled that the government was permitted to deny the Japanese-Americans, their constitutional rights because of military considerations. Such exclusion was not beyond the war powers of Congress and the President since their interest in national security was "compelling."

Dennis v. United States, 341 U.S. 494 (1951)

Free speech v. national security

Eugene Dennis, a leader of the Communist Party in the United States, was arrested for violation of the "Smith Act." The Act prohibited advocacy of the overthrow of the United States Government by force and violence. The Court found that the Smith Act did not violate Dennis' First Amendment right to free speech. Although free speech is a guaranteed right, it is not unlimited. The right to free speech may be lifted if the speech presents a clear and present danger to overthrow any government in the United States by force or violence. Since the speech made by Dennis advocated his position that the government should be overthrown, it represented a clear and present danger to the national security of the United States.

Brown v. Board of Education of Topeka, 347 U.S. 483 (1954)

School segregation; equal protection v. state rights

The issue before the Court was whether the segregation of children in public schools denies black children their Fourteenth Amendment right of equal protection under the law. The Supreme Court looked not to the "tangible" factors but the effect of segregation itself on public education. The Court decided unanimously that segregation of black children in the public school system was a direct violation of the equal protection clause of the Fourteenth Amendment. It rejected the "separate but equal" doctrine of *Plessy v. Ferguson*, 164 U.S. 537 (1896), and stated that this doctrine had no place in education. According to the Court, even if the facilities were physically equal, the children of the minority group would still receive an inferior education. Separate educational facilities were held to be "inherently unequal."

Watkins v. United States, 354 U.S.178 (1957)

Self-incrimination

Watkins had been summoned to testify before the House Committee on Un-American Activities. He refused to answer questions about whether other persons were members of the Communist Party. The Court held that congressional committees are required to uphold the Bill of Rights and must grant citizens the freedom of speech. Such committees are restricted to the areas of investigation delegated to the committees, and no witness can be made to testify on matters outside those areas.

Mapp v. Ohio, 367 U.S. 643 (1961)

Searches

At issue was the Fourth Amendment right to be secure from search and seizure. The Supreme Court ruled that both the Fourth and Fourteenth Amendments protected persons from unwarranted federal and state intrusion of their private property.

Gideon v. Wainwright, 372 U.S. 335 (1963)

Right to counsel

At issue was whether the state of Florida violated Gideon's Sixth Amendment right to counsel, made applicable to the states by the Fourteenth Amendment, by not providing him with the assistance of counsel for his criminal defense. The Court ruled unanimously in Gideon's favor, and held that the Fourteenth Amendment included state as well as federal defendants. The Court said that all states must provide an attorney in all felony and capital cases for people who cannot afford one themselves. Through the Fourteenth Amendment due process clause, the Sixth Amendment guarantee of the right to counsel applies to the states.

Escobedo v. Illinois, 378 U.S. 478 (1964)

Self-incrimination

At issue was whether the state of Illinois violated Escobedo's Fourteenth Amendment protections, his Fifth Amendment right to remain silent, and his Sixth Amendment right to assistance of counsel by denying his request to speak to a lawyer before questioning.The Court found that the denial by the police of Escobedo's right to counsel and their failure to inform him of his right to remain silent were unconstitutional. Furthermore, the Court held that incriminating statements made by defendants are inadmissible as evidence unless the accused is informed of his rights before making the statements.

Heart of Atlanta Motel, Inc. v. United States, 379 U.S. 241 (1964)
Discrimination

The Civil Rights Act of 1964 prohibited racial discrimination and segregation in public accommodations. At issue in this case was whether Congress, under its authority to regulate interstate commerce, has the power to require private businesses within a state to comply with the Civil Rights Act of 1964. The Court held that the Civil Rights Act was constitutional and that the commerce clause of the Constitution empowers Congress to regulate both commercial and non-commercial interstate travel. A motel's refusal to accommodate blacks posed a potential obstruction to their freedom of movement across state lines.

Miranda v. Arizona, 384 U.S. 436 (1966)
Rights of the accused

At issue was whether the state of Arizona violated the constitutional rights of Miranda under the Fifth, Sixth, and Fourteenth Amendments when they interrogated him without advising him of his constitutional right to remain silent. The Court ruled that the police were in error. The Court held that the police must inform suspects that they have the right to remain silent, that anything they say may be used against them, and that they have the right to counsel before the police may begin to question those held in custody. This case established the "Miranda Warning" which police now give when someone is arrested.

New York Times Co. v. United States, 403 U.S. 713 (1971)
Free press v. executive power

The question in this case was whether the President had the power to stop the publication of historical news that might have an impact on the Vietnam War. The Supreme Court of the United States said that prior restraints (prohibiting information from being published or aired) are almost never valid. The government must strongly justify any abridgement of a newspaper's freedom of speech. In this situation, the Court found that the government's attempt at censorship was unconstitutional.

Roe v. Wade, 410 U.S. 113 (1973)
Abortion rights

A Texas law made it a crime to procure or attempt an abortion except when the mother's life would be in danger if she remained pregnant. The Court ruled that states could regulate abortions only in certain circumstances but otherwise women did have a right to privacy and reproductive autonomy. The woman's right to privacy was held to be a fundamental right which could only be denied if a compelling state interest existed. Once the fetus reaches a "viable" stage of development, such a compelling point is reached because the unborn child is now given constitutional protection.

University of California Regents v. Bakke, 438 U.S. 265 (1978)
Affirmative action

At issue was whether the University's special admissions program, which accepted minority students with significantly lower scores than white students, violated the white students' Fourteenth Amendment equal protection rights; and whether the University was permitted to take race into account as a factor in its future admissions decisions. In six separate opinions, the Court invalidated the University's special admissions program, but held that institutions of higher learning may take race into account to remedy disadvantages cast on minorities by past racial prejudice.

6.8 Important Supreme Court Cases by Topic

Abortion Rights

Roe v. Wade, 410 U.S. 113 (1973)
Bigelow v. Virginia, 421 U.S. 809 (1975)
Planned Parenthood of Central Missouri v. Danforth, 428 U.S. 52 (1976)
Maher v. Roe, 432 U.S. 464 (1977)
Beal v. Doe, 432 U.S. 438 (1977)
Poelker v. Doe, 432 U.S. 519 (1977)
Harris v. McRae, 448 U.S. 297 (1980)
Akron v. Akron Center for Reproductive Health, Inc., 462 U.S. 416 (1983)
Thornburgh v. American College of Obstetricians & Gynecologists, 476 U.S. 747 (1986)
Frisby v. Schultz, 487 U.S. 474 (1988)
Webster v. Reproductive Health Services, 492 U.S. 490 (1989)
Hodgson v. Minnesota, 497 U.S. 417 (1990)
Rust v. Sullivan, 500 U.S. 173 (1991)
Planned Parenthood of Southeastern Pennsylvania v. Casey, 505 U.S. 833 (1992)

Capital Punishment

Palko v. Connecticut, 302 U.S. 319 (1937)
Louisiana ex rel. Francis v. Resweber, 329 U.S. 459 (1947)
United States v. Jackson, 390 U.S. 570 (1968)
Witherspoon v. Illinois, 391 U.S. 510 (1968)
Bumper v. North Carolina, 391 U.S. 543 (1968)
Furman v. Georgia, 408 U.S. 238 (1972)
Schick v. Reed, 419 U.S. 256 (1974)
Gregg v. Georgia, 428 U.S. 153 (1976)
Proffitt v. Florida, 428 U.S. 242 (1976)
Jurek v. Texas, 428 U.S. 262 (1976)
Woodson v. North Carolina, 428 U.S. 280 (1976)
Coker v. Georgia, 433 U.S. 584 (1977)
Lockett v. Ohio, 438 U.S. 586 (1978)
Bell v. Ohio, 438 U.S. 637 (1978)
Eddings v. Oklahoma, 455 U.S. 104 (1982)
Enmund v. Florida, 458 U.S. 782 (1982)
Pulley v. Harris, 465 U.S. 37 (1984)
Lockhart v. McCree, 476 U.S. 162 (1986)
Ford v. Wainwright, 477 U.S. 399 (1986)
McCleskey v. Kemp, 481 U.S. 279 (1987)

Civil Rights

Scott v. Sandford, 60 U.S. 393 (1856)
Plessy v. Ferguson, 163 U.S. 537 (1896)
Gitlow v. People, 268 U.S. 652 (1925)
Brown v. Board of Education, 347 U.S. 483 (1954)
Brown v. Board of Education, 349 U.S. 294 (1955)

Heart of Atlanta Motel, Inc. v. United States, 379 U.S. 241 (1964)
Katzenbach v. McClung, 379 U.S. 294 (1964)
Cox v. Louisiana, 379 U.S. 536 (1965)
Washington v. Davis, 426 U.S. 229 (1976)
Martin v. Wilks, 490 U.S. 755 (1989)

Due Process

Munn v. Illinois, 94 U.S. 113 (1876)
Lochner v. New York, 198 U.S. 45 (1905)
Muller v. Oregon, 208 U.S. 412 (1908)
Village of Euclid v. Ambler Realty Co., 272 U.S. 365 (1926)
Tyson & Brother v. Banton, 273 U.S. 418 (1927)
Nebbia v. New York, 291 U.S. 502 (1934)
Norris v. Alabama, 294 U.S. 587 (1935)
West Coast Hotel Co. v. Parrish, 300 U.S. 379 (1937)
Chambers v. Florida, 309 U.S. 227 (1940)
Kent v. Dulles, 357 U.S. 116 (1958)
Bartkus v. Illinois, 359 U.S. 121 (1959)
In re Gault, 387 U.S. 1 (1967)
Loving v. Virginia, 388 U.S. 1 (1967)
Fuentes v. Shevin, 407 U.S. 67 (1972)
Board of Regents of State Colleges v. Roth, 408 U.S. 564 (1972)
Perry v. Sindermann, 408 U.S. 593 (1972)
Goss v. Lopez, 419 U.S. 565 (1975)
Paul v. Davis, 424 U.S. 693 (1976)
Hampton v. Mow Sun Wong, 426 U.S. 88 (1976)
Young v. American Mini Theatres, Inc., 427 U.S. 50 (1976)

Freedom of Religion

Selective Draft Law Cases, 245 U.S. 366 (1918)
Pierce v. Society of Sisters, 268 U.S. 510 (1925)
Cantwell v. Connecticut, 310 U.S. 296 (1940)
Minersville School District v. Board of Education, 310 U.S. 586 (1940)
West Virginia State Board of Education v. Barnette, 319 U.S. 624 (1943)
Marsh v. Alabama, 326 U.S. 501 (1946)
Everson v. Board of Education of the Township of Ewing, 330 U.S. 1 (1947)
Illinois ex rel. McCollum v. Board of Education of School District, 333 U.S. 203 (1948)
Zorach v. Clauson, 343 U.S. 306 (1952)
Joseph Burstyn, Inc. v. Wilson, 343 U.S. 495 (1952)
Engel v. Vitale, 370 U.S. 421 (1962)
School District of Abington Township, Pennsylvania v. Schempp, 374 U.S. 203 (1963)
Sherbert v. Verner, 374 U.S. 398 (1963)
Board of Education v. Allen, 392 U.S. 236 (1968)
Epperson v. Arkansas, 393 U.S. 97 (1968)
Welsh v. United States, 398 U.S. 333 (1970)
Lemon v. Kurtzman, 403 U.S. 602 (1971)
Johnson v. Robison, 415 U.S. 361 (1974)
McDaniel v. Paty, 435 U.S. 618 (1978)
Harris v. McRae, 448 U.S. 297 (1980)

Freedom of the Press

Schenck v. United States, 249 U.S. 47 (1919)
Abrams v. United States, 250 U.S. 616 (1919)
Gitlow v. People, 268 U.S. 652 (1925)
Near v. Minnesota, 283 U.S. 697 (1931)
Grosjean v. American Press Co., Inc., 297 U.S. 233 (1936)
Thornhill v. Alabama, 310 U.S. 88 (1940)
Marsh v. Alabama, 326 U.S. 501 (1946)
Joseph Burstyn, Inc. v. Wilson, 343 U.S. 495 (1952)
Yates v. United States, 354 U.S. 298 (1957)
New York Times Co. v. Sullivan, 376 U.S. 254 (1964)
Aptheker v. Secretary of State, 378 U.S. 500 (1964)
Curtis Publishing Co. v. Butts, 388 U.S. 130 (1967)
Brandenburg v. Ohio, 395 U.S. 444 (1969)
Rosenbloom v. Metromedia, 403 U.S. 29 (1971)
New York Times Co. v. United States, 403 U.S. 713 (1971)
Branzburg v. Hayes, 408 U.S. 665 (1972)
Pittsburgh Press Co. v. Pittsburgh Commission on Human Relations, 413 U.S. 376 (1973)
Communist Party of Indiana v. Whitcomb, 414 U.S. 441 (1974)
Miami Herald Publishing Co. v. Tornillo, 418 U.S. 241 (1974)
Gertz v. Robert Welch, Inc., 418 U.S. 323 (1974)

Judicial Review

Marbury v. Madison, 5 U.S. 137 (1803)
Martin v. Hunter's Lessee, 14 U.S. 304 (1816)
Cohens v. Virginia, 19 U.S. 264 (1821)
South Carolina v. Katzenbach, 383 U.S. 301 (1966)
Kent v. United States, 383 U.S. 541 (1966)
Bond v. Floyd, 385 U.S. 116 (1966)
Johnson v. Robison, 415 U.S. 361 (1974)
United States v. Nixon, 418 U.S. 683 (1974)
Warth v. Seldin, 422 U.S. 490 (1975)
Mathews v. Eldridge, 424 U.S. 319 (1976)
Minnesota v. Clover Leaf Creamery Co., 449 U.S. 456 (1981)

Separation of Powers

Calder v. Bull, 3 U.S. 386 (1798)
Kendall v. United States, 37 U.S. 524 (1838)
Prize Cases, 67 U.S. 635 (1862)
Ex parte McCardle, 74 U.S. 506 (1868)
United States v. Klein, 80 U.S. 128 (1871)
Kilbourn v. Thompson, 103 U.S. 168 (1880)
McCray v. United States, 195 U.S. 27 (1904)
Standard Oil Co. of New Jersey v. United States, 221 U.S. 1 (1911)
Selective Draft Law Cases, 245 U.S. 366 (1918)
Block v. Hirsh, 256 U.S. 135 (1921)
Myers v. United States, 272 U.S. 52 (1926)
The Pocket Veto Case, 279 U.S. 655 (1929)

A. L. A. Schechter Poultry Corp. v. United States, 295 U.S. 495 (1935)
Humphrey's Executor v. United States, 295 U.S. 602 (1935)
Youngstown Sheet & Tube Co. v. Sawyer, 343 U.S. 579 (1952)
Wiener v. United States, 357 U.S. 349 (1958)
Baker v. Carr, 369 U.S. 186 (1962)
Wesberry v. Sanders, 376 U.S. 1 (1964)
United States v. Brown, 381 U.S. 437 (1965)
South Carolina v. Katzenbach, 383 U.S. 301 (1966)

Sex Discrimination

Muller v. Oregon, 208 U.S. 412 (1908)
West Coast Hotel Co. v. Parrish, 300 U.S. 379 (1937)
Hoyt v. Florida, 368 U.S. 57 (1961)
Reed v. Reed, 404 U.S. 71 (1971)
Frontiero v. Richardson, 411 U.S. 677 (1973)
Orr v. Orr, 440 U.S. 268 (1979)
Michael M. v. Superior Court, 450 U.S. 464 (1981)
Meritor Savings Bank v. Vinson, 477 U.S. 57 (1986)
Johnson v. Transportation Agency, 480 U.S. 616 (1987)
Board of Directors, Rotary International v. Rotary Club of Duarte, 481 U.S. 537 (1987)
Price Waterhouse v. Hopkins, 490 U.S. 228 (1989)
International Union, United Automobile, Aerospace & Agricultural Implement Workers of America, UAW v. Johnson Controls, Inc., 499 U.S. 187 (1991)
Franklin v. Gwinnett County Public Schools, 503 U.S. 60 (1992)

State Rights and Powers

Georgia v. Brailsford, 3 U.S. 1 (1794)
Fletcher v. Peck, 10 U.S. 87 (1810)
Trustees of Dartmouth College v. Woodward, 17 U.S. 518 (1819)
Proprietors of Charles River Bridge v. Proprietors of Warren Bridge, 36 U.S. 420 (1837)
Luther v. Borden, 48 U.S. 1 (1849)
Kentucky v. Dennison, 65 U.S. 66 (1860)
Texas v. White, 74 U.S. 700 (1868)
Slaughterhouse Cases, 83 U.S. 36 (1872)
Munn v. Illinois, 94 U.S. 113 (1876)
Holden v. Hardy, 169 U.S. 366 (1898)
Stearns v. Minnesota, 179 U.S. 223 (1900)
Lochner v. New York, 198 U.S. 45 (1905)
Muller v. Oregon, 208 U.S. 412 (1908)
Coyle v. Smith, 221 U.S. 559 (1911)
Pacific States Telephone and Telegraph Company v. Oregon, 223 U.S. 118 (1912)
State of Missouri v. Holland, 252 U.S. 416 (1920)
Village of Euclid v. Ambler Realty Co., 272 U.S. 365 (1926)
Tyson & Brother v. Banton, 273 U.S. 418 (1927)
Home Building & Loan Assn. v. Blaisdell, 290 U.S. 398 (1934)
Nebbia v. New York, 291 U.S. 502 (1934)
West Coast Hotel Co. v. Parrish, 300 U.S. 379 (1937)
South Carolina State Highway Department v. Barnwell Brothers, Inc., 303 U.S. 177 (1938)
Erie Railroad Co. v. Tompkins, 304 U.S. 64 (1938)

Southern Pacific Co. v. Arizona, 325 U.S. 761 (1945)
International Shoe v. State of Washington, 326 U.S. 310 (1945)
Marsh v. Alabama, 326 U.S. 501 (1946)
Shelley v. Kraemer, 334 U.S. 1 (1948)
Terry v. Adams, 345 U.S. 461 (1953)
Williams v. Lee, 358 U.S. 217 (1959)
Bibb v. Navajo Freight Lines, Inc., 359 U.S. 520 (1959)
Shelton v. Tucker, 364 U.S. 479 (1960)
Monroe v. Pape, 365 U.S. 167 (1961)
Engel v. Vitale, 370 U.S. 421 (1962)
Sherbert v. Verner, 374 U.S. 398 (1963)
Katzenbach v. Morgan, 384 U.S. 641 (1966)
Dandridge v. Williams, 397 U.S. 471 (1970)
Roe v. Wade, 410 U.S. 113 (1973)
United States Trust Company of New York v. New Jersey, 431 U.S. 1 (1977)
Hunt v. Washington State Apple Advertising Commission, 432 U.S. 333 (1977)
Hicklin v. Orbeck, 437 U.S. 518 (1978)

Trial By Jury

Strauder v. West Virginia, 100 U.S. 303 (1879)
Hurtado v. California, 110 U.S. 516 (1884)
Maxwell v. Dow, 176 U.S. 581 (1900)
Patton v. United States, 281 U.S. 276 (1930)
Norris v. Alabama, 294 U.S. 587 (1935)
Apodaca v. Oregon, 406 U.S. 404 (1972)
Lockett v. Ohio, 438 U.S. 586 (1978)

War Powers

Selective Draft Law Cases, 245 U.S. 366 (1918)
Block v. Hirsh, 256 U.S. 135 (1921)
Ashwander v. Tennessee Valley Authority, 297 U.S. 288 (1936)
Korematsu v. United States, 323 U.S. 214 (1944)
Woods v. Cloyd W. Miller Co., 333 U.S. 138 (1948)
Youngstown Sheet & Tube Co. v. Sawyer, 343 U.S. 579 (1952)
Trop v. Dulles, 356 U.S. 86 (1958)

SECTION 7

State Governments

7.1 Admission of the 13 Original States

State	Date of Admission
1. Delaware	December 7, 1787
2. Pennsylvania	December 12, 1787
3. New Jersey	December 18, 1787
4. Georgia	January 2, 1788
5. Connecticut	January 9, 1788
6. Massachusetts	February 6, 1788
7. Maryland	April 28, 1788
8. South Carolina	May 23, 1788
9. New Hampshire	June 21, 1788
10. Virginia	June 25, 1788
11. New York	July 26, 1788
12. North Carolina	November 21, 1789
13. Rhode Island	May 29, 1790

7.2 Territorial Expansion and the Creation of States, 1791-1999

1791	Vermont. Explored 1609; settled 1724. First new state after original 13.
1792	Kentucky. Explored c. 1750; settled 1775.
1796	Tennessee. Explored 1540; settled 1769.
1803	Ohio. Explored 1600s; settled 1788.
1812	Louisiana. Explored 1528; settled c. 1715.
1816	Indiana. Explored 1679; settled c. 1700.
1817	Mississippi. Explored 1540; settled 1699.
1818	Illinois. Explored 1673; settled c. 1680.
1819	Alabama. Explored 1528; settled 1702.
1820	Maine. Possibly explored by Norsemen 11th century; settled 1624.
1821	Missouri. Explored 1683; settled c. 1735.
1836	Arkansas. Explored 1514; settled 1686.
1837	Michigan. Explored 1618; settled 1668.
1845	Florida. Explored 1513; settled 1565 by Spanish at St. Augustine.
1845	Texas. Explored c. 1530; settled 1682.
1846	Iowa. Explored 1673; settled c. 1790.
1848	Wisconsin. Explored 1634; settled c. 1670.
1850	California. Explored 1541; settled 1769.
1858	Minnesota. Explored c. 1660; settled c. 1815.
1859	Oregon. Explored 1579; settled 1811.
1861	Kansas. Explored 1541; settled 1727.
1863	West Virginia. Explored 1670s; settled 1726.
1864	Nevada. Explored c. 1770; settled c. 1850.
1867	Midway Islands (territory). Acquired by annexation.
1867	Nebraska. Explored 1541; settled 1847.
1876	Colorado. Explored 1500s; settled, 1858.
1889	North Dakota. Explored 1738; settled 1812.
1889	South Dakota. Explored c. 1742; settled 1817.
1889	Montana. Explored 1742; settled 1807.
1889	Washington. Explored c. 1540s; settled 1845.
1890	Idaho. Explored 1805; settled 1860.
1890	Wyoming. Explored 1700s; settled 1834.
1896	Utah. Explored 1540; settled 1847 by Mormons at Salt Lake City.
1898	Guam (territory). Acquired from Spain.
1898	Puerto Rico. Acquired from Spain; became self-governing 1952.
1898	Wake Island (territory). Acquired by annexation.
1899	American Samoa (territory). Acquired by treaty.
1903	Canal Zone (territory). Leased from Panama; control largely returned in 1978.
1907	Oklahoma. Explored 1541; settled 1796.
1912	New Mexico. Explored c. 1530; settled 1598.
1912	Arizona. Explored c. 1535; settled 1600s.
1917	Virgin Islands (territory). Acquired from Denmark.
1959	Alaska. Explored 1741; settled 1784. Gained territorial status 1912.
1959	Hawaii. Explored 1778; settled 1800s. Annexed by United States 1898 with Hawaiian indigenous government consent.
1999	Active discussion of statehood for Puerto Rico continues.

7.3 Secession and Readmission of States

State	Date of Secession	Date of Readmission
1. South Carolina	December 20, 1860	June 25, 1868
2. Mississippi	January 9, 1861	February 23, 1870
3. Florida	January 10, 1861	June 25, 1868
4. Alabama	January 11, 1861	June 25, 1868
5. Georgia	January 19, 1861	June 25, 1868*
6. Louisiana	January 26, 1861	June 25, 1868
7. Texas	February 1, 1861	March 30, 1870
8. Virginia	April 17, 1861	January 26, 1870
9. Arkansas	May 6, 1861	June 22, 1868
10. North Carolina	May 20, 1861	June 25, 1868
11. Tennessee	June 8, 1861	July 24, 1866

* Readmitted a second time July 15, 1870.

7.4 State Name Origins

Alabama   Originally the name for "tribal town," the territory of Alabama was later the home of the Alabama, or Alibamon, Indians of the Creek confederacy.

Alaska   The Russians adopted the word meaning "great lands" or "land that is not an island" from the Aleutian word *alakshak.*

Arizona   The Spanish coined the name either from the Pima Indian word meaning "little spring place" or from the Aztec *arizuma,* meaning "silver-bearing."

Arkansas   Once the territory of the Siouan Quapaw (downstream people), *Arkansas* is the French derivative of this Indian name.

California   The name of a fictitious earthly paradise in *Las Serged de Esplandian,* a sixteenth-century Spanish romance. It is believed that Spanish conquistadors named this state.

Colorado   Spanish word for "red." The name *Colorado* first referred to the Colorado River.

Connecticut   The Algonquin and Mohican Indian word for "long river place."

Delaware   This version of the name of Lord De La Warr, a governor of Virginia, was first used to name the Delaware River and later adopted by the Europeans to rename the local natives, originally called the Lene Lenape.

District of Columbia   Named for Christopher Columbus in 1791.

Florida   In his search for the "Fountain of Youth" Ponce de Leon named this region "flowery Easter" or "feast of flowers" on Easter Sunday, 1513.

Georgia   Named for King George II of England who granted James Oglethorpe a charter to found the colony of Georgia in 1732.

Hawaii   Commonly believed to be an English adaptation of the native word for "homeland," *hawaiki* or *owhyhee.*

Idaho   A name coined by the state meaning "gem of the mountains" or "light on the mountains." Originally the name *Idaho* was to be used for the Pike's Peak mining territory in Colorado, and later for the mining territory of the Pacific Northwest. Others believe the name derives from the Kiowa Apache word for the Comanche.

Illinois   From the French version of the Algonquin word meaning "men" or "soldiers," *Illini.*

Indiana   English-speaking settlers named the territory to mean "land of the Indians."

Iowa   From the Siouan *Ouaouia,* meaning "one who puts to sleep."

Kansas   Derived from the Siouan *Kansa* or *Kaw,* meaning "people of the south wind," who lived south of the settlements of the northern Great Plains.

Kentucky   Originally the term for the Kentucky Plains in Clark County, *Kentucky* is believed to derive from the American Indian word meaning "dark and bloody ground," "meadow land," or "land of tomorrow."

Louisiana   Present-day Louisiana is just a fraction of the territory that was named for the French king Louis XIV by Sieur de La Salle.

Maine   Originally a French territory, *Maine* was the ancient French word for "province." It is also believed that it refers to the mainland, as distinct from the many islands off the state's coast.

Maryland   Named for the Queen Henrietta Maria, wife of Charles I of England.

Massachusetts   The name of the native tribe that lived near Milton, Massachusetts, meaning "large hill place."

Michigan   Believed to be from the Chippewa word *micigama,* meaning "great water," after Lake Michigan, although Alouet defined it in 1672 as designating a clearing.

Minnesota   Named from the Sioux description of the Minnesota River, "sky-tinted water" or "muddy water."

Mississippi   Most likely derived from the Chippewa words *mici* (great) and *zibi* (river), it was first written by La Salle's lieutenant Henri de Tonti as "Michi Sepe."

Missouri   The Siouan word meaning "muddy water."

Montana   Derived from the Latin word meaning "mountainous."

Nebraska   From the Omaha or Oto word for "flat water" or "spreading water," describing the Platte and Nebraska rivers.

Nevada   Spanish word meaning "snow-clad."

New Hampshire   Captain John Mason named this colony for his home county in England in 1629.

New Jersey   Named after the Isle of Jersey in England by John Berkeley and Sir George Carteret.

New Mexico   Named by the Spanish for the territory north and west of the Rio Grande.

New York   Originally named New Netherland, New York was later named after the Duke of York and Albany, who received a patent to the region from his brother Charles II of England and captured it from the Dutch in 1644.

North Carolina   From the Latin name *Carolus,* meaning "Charles." The colony was originally given to Sir Robert Heath by Charles I and was to be called Province of Carolana. Carolana was divided into North and South Carolina in 1710.

North Dakota   From the Sioux word meaning "friend" or "ally."

Ohio   From an Iroquois word variously meaning "great," "fine," or "good river."

Oklahoma   The Choctaw word meaning "red man," which was coined by the Reverend Allen Wright, a Choctaw-speaking American Indian.

Oregon   Although its exact origin is unclear, one theory maintains that it may have been a variation on the name of the Wisconsin River, which was called *Ouaricon-sint* on a French map dated 1715. Later, the English explorer Major Robert Rogers named a river "called by the Indians Ouragon" in his request to seek a Northwest Passage from the Great Lakes. Another theory derives the word from the Algonquin *wauregan,* meaning "beautiful water."

Pennsylvania   Named after the colony's founder, the Quaker William Penn. The literal translation is "Penn's woods."

Rhode Island   Possibly named by Giovanni de Verrazano, who charted an island about the size of an island of the same name in the Mediterranean. Another theory suggests Rhode Island was named Roode Eylandt by Dutch explorer Adrian Block because of its red clay.

South Carolina   See North Carolina.

South Dakota   See North Dakota.

Tennessee   The state of Franklin, or Frankland, from 1784 to 1788, it was finally named after the Cherokee villages called *tanasi* on the Little Tennessee River.

Texas   Also written *texias, tejas,* and *teysas,* Texas is a variation on the Caddo word for "friend" or "ally."

Utah   Meaning "upper" or "higher," *Utah* is derived from a name used by the Navajos (Utes) to designate a Shoshone tribe.

Vermont   It is believed Samuel de Champlain coined the name from the French words *vert* (green) and *mont* (mountain). Later, Dr. Thomas Young proposed this name when the state was formed in 1777.

Virginia   Named for the Virgin Queen of England, Queen Elizabeth I, by Sir Walter Raleigh, who first visited its shores in 1584.

Washington   Originally named the Territory of Columbia, it was changed to *Washington* in honor of the first U.S. President because of the already existing District of Columbia.

West Virginia   Named when this area refused to secede from the Union in 1863.

Wisconsin   A Chippewa word that was spelled *Ouisconsin* and *Mesconsing* by early explorers. Wisconsin was formally named by Congress when it became a state.

Wyoming   The Algonquin word meaning "large prairie place," the name was adopted from Wyoming Valley, Pennsylvania, the site of an Indian massacre. It was widely known from Thomas Campbell's poem "Gertrude of Wyoming."

7.5   States and Their Capitals

State	Capital	State	Capital
Alabama	Montgomery	Montana	Helena
Alaska	Juneau	Nebraska	Lincoln
Arizona	Phoenix	Nevada	Carson City
Arkansas	Little Rock	New Hampshire	Concord
California	Sacramento	New Jersey	Trenton
Colorado	Denver	New Mexico	Santa Fe
Connecticut	Hartford	New York	Albany
Delaware	Dover	North Carolina	Raleigh
Florida	Tallahassee	North Dakota	Bismarck
Georgia	Atlanta	Ohio	Columbus
Hawaii	Honolulu	Oklahoma	Oklahoma City
Idaho	Boise	Oregon	Salem
Illinois	Springfield	Pennsylvania	Harrisburg
Indiana	Indianapolis	Rhode Island	Providence
Iowa	Des Moines	South Carolina	Columbia
Kansas	Topeka	South Dakota	Pierre
Kentucky	Frankfort	Tennessee	Nashville
Louisiana	Baton Rouge	Texas	Austin
Maine	Augusta	Utah	Salt Lake City
Maryland	Annapolis	Vermont	Montpelier
Massachusetts	Boston	Virginia	Richmond
Michigan	Lansing	Washington	Olympia
Minnesota	St. Paul	West Virginia	Charleston
Mississippi	Jackson	Wisconsin	Madison
Missouri	Jefferson City	Wyoming	Cheyenne

7.6   Official State Birds, Trees, and Flowers

State	Bird	Tree	Flower
Alabama	Yellowhammer	Southern Pine	Camelia
Alaska	Willow Ptarmigan	Stitka Spruce	Forget-me-not
Arizona	Cactus Wren	Paloverde	Saguaro Cactus
Arkansas	Mockingbird	Pine	Apple Blossom
California	Valley Quail	Redwood	Golden Poppy
Colorado	Lark Bunting	Blue Spruce	Rocky Mountain Columbine
Connecticut	Robin	White Oak	Mountain Laurel
Delaware	Blue Hen Chicken	American Holly	Peach Blossom
Florida	Mockingbird	Sabal Palm	Orange Blossom
Georgia	Brown Thrasher	Live Oak	Cherokee Rose
Hawaii	Nene (Hawaiian Goose)	Kukui	Hibiscus
Idaho	Mountain Bluebird	White Pine	Syringa
Illinois	Cardinal	White Oak	Native Violet
Indiana	Cardinal	Tulip Tree	Peony
Iowa	American Goldfinch	Oak	Wild Rose
Kansas	Western Meadowlark	Cottonwood	Sunflower
Kentucky	Cardinal	Kentucky Coffee	Goldenrod
Louisiana	Eastern Brown Pelican	Bald Cypress	Magnolia
Maine	Chickadee	White Pine	Pine Cone & Tassel
Maryland	Baltimore Oriole	White Oak	Black-eyed Susan
Massachusetts	Chickadee	American Elm	Mayflower
Michigan	Robin	White Pine	Apple Blossom
Minnesota	Common Loon	Red Pine	Lady's Slipper
Mississippi	Mockingbird	Magnolia	Magnolia Blossom
Missouri	Bluebird	Dogwood	Hawthorn
Montana	Western Meadowlark	Ponderosa Pine	Bitterroot
Nebraska	Western Meadowlark	Cottonwood	Goldenrod
Nevada	Mountain Bluebird	Bristlecone Pine	Sagebrush
New Hampshire	Purple Finch	White Birch	Purple Lilac
New Jersey	American Goldfinch	Red Oak	Purple Violet
New Mexico	Roadrunner	Pinon	Yucca Flower

State	Bird	Tree	Flower
New York	Eastern Bluebird	Sugar Maple	Rose
North Carolina	Cardinal	Pine	Dogwood
North Dakota	Western Meadowlark	American Elm	Wild Prairie Rose
Ohio	Cardinal	Buckeye	Scarlet Carnation
Oklahoma	Scissor-tailed Flycatcher	Redbud	Mistletoe
Oregon	Western Meadowlark	Douglas Fir	Oregon Grape
Pennsylvania	Ruffed Grouse	Hemlock	Mountain Laurel
Rhode Island	R.I. Red Chicken	Red Maple	Violet
South Carolina	Carolina Wren	Palmetto	Yellow Jessamine
South Dakota	Ring-necked Pheasant	Black Hills Spruce	Pasqueflower
Tennessee	Mockingbird	Tulip Poplar	Iris
Texas	Mockingbird	Pecan	Bluebonnet
Utah	Sea Gull	Blue Spruce	Sego Lily
Vermont	Hermit Thrush	Sugar Maple	Red Clover
Virginia	Cardinal	Dogwood	Dogwood
Washington	Willow Goldfinch	Western Hemlock	Rhododendron
West Virginia	Cardinal	Sugar Maple	Big Rhododendron
Wisconsin	Robin	Sugar Maple	Wood Violet
Wyoming	Western Meadowlark	Cottonwood	Indian Paintbrush

7.7   Division of Federal, State, and Local Powers

federal government   makes laws for the entire country; deals with relations with other countries; resolves disputes between states; maintains basic rights for all citizens

state government   makes laws for one state; establishes educational system; regulates commerce within the state; regulates relations between citizens within the state

local government   makes laws for a small area within a state—city, county; enforces local laws and ordinances; provides police and fire protection

7.8   Three Branches of State Government

Legislative
Senate
House of Representatives or Assembly

• passes state laws
• approves state budget
terms are usually
Senate = 4 years
Representatives = 2 years

Executive
Governor
Lieutenant Governor

• is chief of National Guard
• suggests state laws
• can veto state laws
terms are usually
2 or 4 years

Judicial
State Supreme Court
hears appeals cases

State District or Superior or Circuit Courts
hear trial cases: civil and criminal

Local Courts
• hear special trial cases such as traffic, family, juvenile
• hear cases about state laws
• hear cases between citizens of the same state
• usually have a judge and jury at trial cases

7.9   Richest and Poorest States

The U.S. Department of Commerce collects a number of statistics on the states. The tables below show the 10 states with the highest per capita (per person) income in 1997, and the 9 states with the lowest.

<u>10 states with the highest per capita income in 1997:</u>

	Dollars		Rank	
	1996	1997	1996	1997
Connecticut	34,174	36,263	1	1
New Jersey	31,265	32,654	2	2
Massachusetts	29,808	31,524	3	3
New York	29,221	30,752	4	4
Delaware	27,782	29,022	5	5
Maryland	27,676	28,969	6	6
Illinois	26,855	28,202	7	7
New Hampshire	26,772	28,047	8	8
Colorado	25,740	27,051	10	9
Minnesota	25,699	26,797	11	10

<u>9 states with the lowest per capita income in 1997:</u>

	Dollars		Rank	
	1996	1997	1996	1997
Kentucky	19,773	20,657	42	41
Oklahoma	19,574	20,556	44	42
Idaho	19,865	20,478	41	43
Utah	19,384	20,432	45	44
North Dakota	20,479	20,271	38	45
Montana	19,278	20,046	46	46
New Mexico	18,814	19,587	48	47
Arkansas	18,967	19,585	47	48
West Virginia	18,225	18,957	49	49

DIPLOMACY AND MILITARY HISTORY

SECTION 8

Foreign Relations and Diplomacy

8.1   Major Treaties of the 19th Century

1800	Convention of Peace, Commerce and Navigation with France
1803	Louisiana Purchase
1814	Treaty of Ghent; peace with England
1815	Commercial convention of 1815 with England
1818	Convention of 1818 with England (Rush-Bagot Accord) established 49th parallel as northern-most boundary of U.S.
1819	Adams-Onis Treaty with Spain ceded Florida to U.S., set southern frontier of former French Louisiana leaving Texas and territories south of Oregon to Spain
1824	Treaty of 1824 with Russia fixed southern frontier of Alaska; one of the first effective applications of the Monroe Doctrine
1832	Treaties of commerce with Russia
1833	Treaties of commerce with Siam
1842	Webster-Ashburton Treaty redefined New Brunswick-Maine border
1845	Annexation of Texas
1846	Oregon Partition Treaty
1848	Treaty of Guadalupe Hidalgo
1850	Clayton-Bulwer Treaty with England
1853	Gadsen Purchase
1854	Marcy-Elgin Treaty with England
1854	Treaty of Kanawaga (Yokohama) Japan
1857-1858	Harris Treaties established U.S. diplomatic relations with Japan
1867	Alaska Purchase Treaty
1871	Treaty of Washington with Great Britain
1881	Madrid Conference
1892	International agreement on the suppression of the African slave trade
1897	Treaty of annexation of Hawaii
1898	Peace treaty with Spain ending Spanish-American War
1899	Treaty of Paris; annexation of the Philippines

8.2 Monroe Doctrine, 1823

The Monroe Doctrine was expressed during President Monroe's seventh annual message to Congress, December 2, 1823:

. . . At the proposal of the Russian Imperial Government, made through the minister of the Emperor residing here, full power and instructions have been transmitted to the minister of the United States at St. Petersburg to arrange by amicable negotiation the respective rights and interests of the two nations on the northwest coast of this continent. A similar proposal has been made by His Imperial Majesty to the Government of Great Britain, which has likewise been acceded to. The Government of the United States has been desirous by this friendly proceeding of manifesting the great value which they have invariably attached to the friendship of the Emperor and their solicitude to cultivate the best understanding with his Government. In the discussions to which this interest has given rise and in the arrangements by which they may terminate the occasion has been judged proper for asserting, as a principle in which the rights and interests of the United States are involved, that the American continents, by the free and independent condition which they have assumed and maintain, are henceforth not to be considered as subjects for future colonization by any European powers. . . .

It was stated at the commencement of the last session that a great effort was then making in Spain and Portugal to improve the condition of the people of those countries, and that it appeared to be conducted with extraordinary moderation. It need scarcely be remarked that the results have been so far very different from what was then anticipated. Of events in that quarter of the globe, with which we have so much intercourse and from which we derive our origin, we have always been anxious and interested spectators. The citizens of the United States cherish sentiments the most friendly in favor of the liberty and happiness of their fellow-men on that side of the Atlantic. In the wars of the European powers in matters relating to themselves we have never taken any part, nor does it comport with our policy to do so. It is only when our rights are invaded or seriously menaced that we resent injuries or make preparation for our defense. With the movements in this hemisphere we are of necessity more immediately connected, and by causes which must be obvious to all enlightened and impartial observers. The political system of the allied powers is essentially different in this respect from that of America.

This difference proceeds from that which exists in their respective Governments; and to the defense of our own, which has been achieved by the loss of so much blood and treasure, and matured by the wisdom of their most enlightened citizens, and under which we have enjoyed unexampled felicity, this whole nation is devoted. We owe it, therefore, to candor and to the amicable relations existing between the United States and those powers to declare that we should consider any attempt on their part to extend their system to any portion of this hemisphere as dangerous to our peace and safety. With the existing colonies or dependencies of any European power we have not interfered and shall not interfere. But with the Governments who have declared their independence and maintain it, and whose independence we have, on great consideration and on just principles, acknowledged, we could not view any interposition for the purpose of oppressing them, or controlling in any other manner their destiny, by any European power in any other light than as the manifestation of an unfriendly disposition toward the United States. In the war between those new Governments and Spain we declared our neutrality at the time of their recognition, and to this we have adhered, and shall continue to adhere, provided no change shall occur which, in the judgement of the competent authorities of this Government, shall make a corresponding change on the part of the United States indispensable to their security.

The late events in Spain and Portugal show that Europe is still unsettled. Of this important fact no stronger proof can be adduced than that the allied powers should have thought it proper, on any principle satisfactory to themselves, to have interposed by force in the internal concerns of Spain. To what extent such interposition may be carried, on the same principle, is a question in which all independent powers whose governments differ from theirs are interested, even those most remote, and surely none of them more so than the United States. Our policy in regard to Europe, which was adopted at an early stage of the wars which have so long agitated that quarter of the globe, nevertheless remains the same, which is, not to interfere in the internal concerns of any of its powers; to consider the government de facto as the legitimate government for us; to cultivate friendly relations with it, and to preserve those relations by a frank, firm, and manly policy, meeting in all instances the just claims of every power, submitting to injuries from none. But in regard to those continents circumstances are eminently and conspicuously different.

It is impossible that the allied powers should extend their political system to any portion of either continent without endangering our peace and happiness; nor can anyone believe that our southern brethren, if left to themselves, would adopt it of their own accord. It is equally impossible, therefore, that we should behold such interposition in any form with indifference. If we look to the comparative strength and resources of Spain and those new Governments, and their distance from each other, it must be obvious that she can never subdue them. It is still the true policy of the United States to leave the parties to themselves, in hope that other powers will pursue the same course. . . .

8.3 Major Treaties of the 20th Century

1900	1st and 2nd Hay-Pauncefote Treaty—Panama Canal
1903	Platt Amendment with Cuba over Panama
1904	Hay-Bunau-Varilla Treaty—Panama Canal Zone
1913-15	U.S. signs 30 treaties embodying Secretary of State William Jennings Bryan's "cooling off" policies
1919	Treaty of Versailles
1921	Four-Power Treaty on the Pacific
1922	Five-Power Naval Disarmament Treaty
1922	Nine-Power Treaty on China
1922-38	Numerous treaties signed with Latin American countries
1928	Pact of Paris (Kellogg-Briand Pact) signed by unprecedented 63 nations

Aid Accords

1940	Destroyer bases accord of Sept. 3, 1940—aid to England
1941	Lend-Lease Act—brought U.S. to forefront of world diplomacy
1945-48	Bilateral Aid Accords
1948	Marshall Plan
1949	Point Four
1950	Franco-American Mutual Aid Accord

Peace Treaties

1948	London convention—reconstitution of Germany
1949	Washington Accords
1951	San Francisco Peace Treaty
1953	Korean War armistice
1955	Treaty of Paris—ended occupation of Paris
1955	Austrian State Treaty—established its neutrality
1973	Vietnam War (executive agreement)

Treaties of Alliance

1945	Pact of Chapultepec
1947	UN-US Headquarters Agreement—charter of the United Nations is legally a multilateral treaty
1948	Charter of the Organization of American States
1949	North Atlantic Treaty—U.S., Canada and many European nations—reaction to Cold War
1951	Pacific Security Pact with Australia and New Zealand
1953	Bilateral mutual defense treaty with South Korea
1954	Bilateral mutual defense treaty with Pakistan
1954	Bilateral mutual defense treaty with Republic of China (Taiwan)
1954	Treaty of Manila—created Southeast Asia Treaty Organization (SEATO)
1963	Hotline Agreement—established direct communication link between U.S. and USSR

Treaties of Deterrence/Arms Control

1960	The Antartic Treaty—that area to be used for peaceful purposes only
1963	Treaty of Moscow—Test Ban Treaty with Soviet Union and the United Kingdom

1967	Treaty for the Prohibition of Nuclear Weapons in Latin America (U.S. signed in 1977)
1967	Outer Space Treaty
1968	Treaty on the Nonproliferation of Nuclear Arms
1969-1972	Strategic Arms Limitation Talks (SALT) treaties and accords
1971	Seabed Arms Control Treaty
1971	Accidents Measures Agreement—advance notification of planned launches if aimed in direction of the other—U.S. and USSR
1972	Treaty between the U.S. and USSR on the Limitation of Anti-Ballistic Missile Systems
1972	Incidents at Sea Agreement—calls for advance notice of missile launches in international waters—U.S. and USSR
1972	Nixon trip to Soviet Union—several economic and technologic accords
1973	Prevention of Nuclear War Agreement—Leonid Brezhnev trip to Washington
1974	Threshold Test Ban Treaty—Nixon trip to Moscow—agreements curbing nuclear testing
1974	Ford meeting with Brezhnev—document limiting strategic offensive arms for 10 years
1975	Ford to Helsinki summit meeting—accord regarding European boundaries and human rights
1975	Prohibition of Use of Asphyxiating, Poisonous or Other Gases, and of Bacteriological Methods of Warfare
1976	Treaty on Underground Nuclear Explosions for Peaceful Purposes—U.S. and USSR
1977	U.S. and USSR agree to uphold SALT agreements
1977	Prohibition of Military or Any Other Hostile Use of Environmental Modification Techniques
1978	Treaties with Panama—granting Panamanian sovereignty and jurisdiction in Canal Zone by 2000
1982	Strategic Arms Reduction Talks (START)—Reagan proposals for prior notification of Intercontinental and Submarine-Launched Ballistic Missile (ICBM & SLBM) launches
1985	South Pacific Nuclear Free Zone Treaty
1986	Document of the Stockholm conference on Confidence and Security Building Measures and Disarmament in Europe
1987	Treaty between the U.S. and USSR on the elimination of their Intermediate-Range and Shorter-Range Missiles (or INF-Intermediate-Range Nuclear Forces)
1988	Agreement on Advance Notification of ICBM and SLBM launches
1989	Treaty on the Conventional Armed Forces in Europe
1991	START I Treaty—advance notification of flight testing of ICBMs or SLBMs
1993	Convention on the Prohibition of the Development, Production, Stockpiling and Use of Chemical Weapons and on Their Destruction
1993	START II Treaty
1996-99	Comprehensive Test Ban Treaty—negotiated over 2 years
1997	Oslo Treaty—convention on the use, stockpiling, production and transfer of anti-personnel mines and their destruction

Other

1990	Treaty on the Final Settlement—German unity
1990	Charter of Paris for a New Europe
1994	Vienna Document

Sources: Encyclopedia of American Foreign Policy-Studies of the Principal Movements and Ideas, Alexander DeConde, ed.; U.S. State Department.

8.4   Truman Doctrine, 1947

President Harry S. Truman's address before a joint session of Congress, March 12, 1947:

Mr. President, Mr. Speaker, Members of the Congress of the United States:

The gravity of the situation which confronts the world today necessitates my appearance before a joint session of the Congress. The foreign policy and the national security of this country are involved.

One aspect of the present situation, which I wish to present to you at this time for your consideration and decision, concerns Greece and Turkey.

The United States has received from the Greek Government an urgent appeal for financial and economic assistance. Preliminary reports from the American Economic Mission now in Greece and reports from the American Ambassador in Greece corroborate the statement of the Greek Government that assistance is imperative if Greece is to survive as a free nation.

I do not believe that the American people and the Congress wish to turn a deaf ear to the appeal of the Greek Government.

Greece is not a rich country. Lack of sufficient natural resources has always forced the Greek people to work hard to make both ends meet. Since 1940, this industrious and peace-loving country has suffered invasion, four years of cruel enemy occupation, and bitter internal strife.

When forces of liberation entered Greece they found that the retreating Germans had destroyed virtually all the railways, roads, port facilities, communications, and merchant marine. More than a thousand villages had been burned. Eighty-five percent of the children were tubercular. Livestock, poultry, and draft animals had almost disappeared. Inflation had wiped out practically all savings.

As a result of these tragic conditions, a militant minority, exploiting human want and misery, was able to create political chaos which, until now, has made economic recovery impossible.

Greece is today without funds to finance the importation of those goods which are essential to bare subsistence. Under these circumstances the people of Greece cannot make progress in solving their problems of reconstruction. Greece is in desperate need of financial and economic assistance to enable it to resume purchases of food, clothing, fuel and seeds. These are indispensable for the subsistence of its people and are obtainable only from abroad. Greece must have help to import the goods necessary to restore internal order and security, so essential for economic and political recovery.

The Greek Government has also asked for the assistance of experienced American administrators, economists and technicians to insure that the financial and other aid given to Greece shall be used effectively in creating a stable and self-sustaining economy and in improving its public administration.

The very existence of the Greek state is today threatened by the terrorist activities of several thousand armed men, led by Communists, who defy the government's authority at a number of points, particularly along the northern boundaries. A Commission appointed by the United Nations security Council is at present investigating disturbing conditions in northern Greece and alleged border violations along the frontier between Greece on the one hand and Albania, Bulgaria, and Yugoslavia on the other.

Meanwhile, the Greek Government is unable to cope with the situation. The Greek army is small and poorly equipped. It needs supplies and equipment if it is to restore the authority of the government throughout Greek territory. Greece must have assistance if it is to become a self-supporting and self-respecting democracy.

The United States must supply that assistance. We have already extended to Greece certain types of relief and economic aid but these are inadequate.

There is no other country to which democratic Greece can turn.

No other nation is willing and able to provide the necessary support for a democratic Greek government.

The British Government, which has been helping Greece, can give no further financial or economic aid after March 31. Great Britain finds itself under the necessity of reducing or liquidating its commitments in several parts of the world, including Greece.

We have considered how the United Nations might assist in this crisis. But the situation is an urgent one requiring immediate action and the United Nations and its related organizations are not in a position to extend help of the kind that is required.

It is important to note that the Greek Government has asked for our aid in utilizing effectively the financial and other assistance we may give to Greece, and in improving its public administration. It is of the utmost importance that we supervise the use of any funds made available to Greece; in such a manner that each dollar spent will count toward making Greece self-supporting, and will help to build an economy in which a healthy democracy can flourish.

No government is perfect. One of the chief virtues of a democracy, however, is that its defects are always visible and under democratic processes can be pointed out and corrected. The Government of Greece is not perfect. Nevertheless it represents eighty-five per cent of the members of the Greek Parliament who were chosen in an election last year. Foreign observers, including 692 Americans, considered this election to be a fair expression of the views of the Greek people.

The Greek Government has been operating in an atmosphere of chaos and extremism. It has made mistakes. The extension of aid by this country does not mean that the United States condones everything that the Greek Government has done or will do. We have condemned in the past, and we condemn now, extremist measures of the right or the left. We have in the past advised tolerance, and we advise tolerance now.

Greece's neighbor, Turkey, also deserves our attention.

The future of Turkey as an independent and economically sound state is clearly no less important to the freedom-loving peoples of the world than the future of Greece. The circumstances in which Turkey finds itself today are considerably different from those of Greece. Turkey has been spared the disasters that have beset Greece. And during the war, the United States and Great Britain furnished Turkey with material aid.

Nevertheless, Turkey now needs our support.

Since the war Turkey has sought financial assistance from Great Britain and the United States for the purpose of effecting that modernization necessary for the maintenance of its national integrity.

That integrity is essential to the preservation of order in the Middle East.

The British government has informed us that, owing to its own difficulties, it can no longer extend financial or economic aid to Turkey.

As in the case of Greece, if Turkey is to have the assistance it needs, the United States must supply it. We are the only country able to provide that help.

I am fully aware of the broad implications involved if the United States extends assistance to Greece and Turkey, and I shall discuss these implications with you at this time.

One of the primary objectives of the foreign policy of the United States is the creation of conditions in which we and other nations will be able to work out a way of life free from coercion. This was a fundamental issue in the war with Germany and Japan. Our victory was won over countries which sought to impose their will, and their way of life, upon other nations.

To ensure the peaceful development of nations, free from coercion, the United States has taken a leading part in establishing the United Nations, The United Nations is designed to make possible lasting freedom and independence for all its members. We shall not realize our objectives, however, unless we are willing to help free peoples to maintain their free institutions and their national integrity against aggressive movements that seek to impose upon them totalitarian regimes. This is no more than a frank recognition that totalitarian regimes imposed on free peoples, by direct or indirect aggression, undermine the foundations of international peace and hence the security of the United States.

The peoples of a number of countries of the world have recently had totalitarian regimes forced upon them against their will. The Government of the United States has made frequent protests against coercion and intimidation, in violation of the Yalta agreement, in Poland, Rumania, and Bulgaria. I must also state that in a number of other countries there have been similar developments.

At the present moment in world history nearly every nation must choose between alternative ways of life. The choice is too often not a free one.

One way of life is based upon the will of the majority, and is distinguished by free institutions, representative government, free elections, guarantees of individual liberty, freedom of speech and religion, and freedom from political oppression.

The second way of life is based upon the will of a minority forcibly imposed upon the majority. It relies upon terror and oppression, a controlled press and radio; fixed elections, and the suppression of personal freedoms.

I believe that it must be the policy of the United States to support free peoples who are resisting attempted subjugation by armed minorities or by outside pressures.

I believe that we must assist free peoples to work out their own destinies in their own way.

I believe that our help should be primarily through economic and financial aid which is essential to economic stability and orderly political processes.

The world is not static, and the status quo is not sacred. But we cannot allow changes in the status quo in violation of the Charter of the United Nations by such methods as coercion, or by such subterfuges as political infiltration. In helping free and independent nations to maintain their freedom, the United States will be giving effect to the principles of the Charter of the United Nations.

It is necessary only to glance at a map to realize that the survival and integrity of the Greek nation are of grave importance in a much wider situation. If Greece should fall under the control of an armed minority, the effect upon its neighbor, Turkey, would be immediate and serious. Confusion and disorder might well spread throughout the entire Middle East.

Moreover, the disappearance of Greece as an independent state would have a profound effect upon those countries in Europe whose peoples are struggling against great difficulties to maintain their freedoms and their independence while they repair the damages of war.

It would be an unspeakable tragedy if these countries, which have struggled so long against overwhelming odds, should lose that victory for which they sacrificed so much. Collapse of free institutions and loss of independence would be disastrous not only for them but for the world. Discouragement and possibly failure would quickly be the lot of neighboring peoples striving to maintain their freedom and independence.

Should we fail to aid Greece and Turkey in this fateful hour, the effect will be far reaching to the West as well as to the East.

We must take immediate and resolute action.

I therefore ask the Congress to provide authority for assistance to Greece and Turkey in the amount of $400,000,000 for the period ending June 30, 1948. In requesting these funds, I have taken into consideration the maximum amount of relief assistance which would be furnished to Greece out of the $350,000,000 which I recently requested that the Congress authorize for the prevention of starvation and suffering in countries devastated by the war.

In addition to funds, I ask the Congress to authorize the detail of American civilian and military personnel to Greece and Turkey, at the request of those countries, to assist in the tasks of reconstruction, and for the purpose of supervising the use of such financial and material assistance as may be furnished. I recommend that authority also be provided for the instruction and training of selected Greek and Turkish personnel.

Finally, I ask that the Congress provide authority which will permit the speediest and most effective use, in terms of needed commodities, supplies, and equipment, of such funds as may be authorized.

If further funds, or further authority, should be needed for purposes indicated in this message, I shall not hesitate to bring the situation before the Congress. On this subject the Executive and Legislative branches of the Government must work together.

This is a serious course upon which we embark.

I would not recommend it except that the alternative is much more serious. The United States contributed $341,000,000,000 toward winning World War II. This is an investment in world freedom and world peace.

The assistance that I am recommending for Greece and Turkey amounts to little more than 1 tenth of 1 percent of this investment. It is only common sense that we should safeguard this investment and make sure that it was not in vain.

The seeds of totalitarian regimes are nurtured by misery and want. They spread and grow in the evil soil of poverty and strife. They reach their full growth when the hope of a people for a better life has died. We must keep that hope alive.

The free peoples of the world look to us for support in maintaining their freedoms.

If we falter in our leadership, we may endanger the peace of the world—and we shall surely endanger the welfare of our own nation.

Great responsibilities have been placed upon us by the swift movement of events.

I am confident that the Congress will face these responsibilities squarely.

8.5 Universal Declaration of Human Rights, 1948

Written at the United Nations in 1948:

Preamble

WHEREAS recognition of the inherent dignity and of the equal and inalienable rights of all members of the human family is the foundation of freedom, justice and peace in the world,

WHEREAS disregard and contempt for human rights have resulted in barbarous acts which have outraged the conscience of mankind, and the advent of a world in which human beings shall enjoy freedom of speech and belief and freedom from fear and want has been proclaimed as the highest aspiration of the common people,

WHEREAS it is essential, if man is not to be compelled to have recourse, as a last resort, to rebellion against tyranny and oppression, that human rights should be protected by the rule of law,

WHEREAS it is essential to promote the development of friendly relations between nations,

WHEREAS the peoples of the United Nations have in the Charter reaffirmed their faith in fundamental human rights, in the dignity and worth of the human person and in the equal rights of men and women and have determined to promote social progress and better standards of life in larger freedom,

WHEREAS Member States have pledged themselves to achieve, in co-operation with the United Nations, the promotion of universal respect for and observance of human rights and fundamental freedoms,

WHEREAS a common understanding of these rights and freedoms is of the greatest importance for the full realization of this pledge,

Now, Therefore,

The General Assembly

proclaims

This Universal Declaration of Human Rights

as a common standard of achievement for all peoples and all nations, to the end that every individual and every organ of society, keeping this Declaration constantly in mind, shall strive by teaching and education to promote respect for these rights and freedoms and by progressive measures, national and international, to secure their universal and effective recognition and observance, both among the peoples of Member States themselves and among the peoples of territories under their jurisdiction.

Article 1. All human beings are born free and equal in dignity and rights. They are endowed with reason and conscience and should act towards one another in a spirit of brotherhood.

Article 2. Everyone is entitled to all the rights and freedoms set forth in this Declaration, without distinction of any kind, such as race, colour, sex, language, religion, political or other opinion, national or social origin, property, birth or other status.

Furthermore, no distinction shall be made on the basis of the political, jurisdictional or international status of the country or territory to which a person belongs, whether it be independent, trust, non-self-governing or under any other limitation of sovereignty.

Article 3. Everyone has the right to life, liberty and security of person.

Article 4. No one shall be held in slavery or servitude; slavery and the slave trade shall be prohibited in all their forms.

Article 5. No one shall be subjected to torture or to cruel, inhuman or degrading treatment or punishment.

Article 6. Everyone has the right to recognition everywhere as a person before the law.

Article 7. All are equal before the law and are entitled without any discrimination to equal protection of the law. All are entitled to equal protection against any discrimination in violation of this Declaration and against any incitement to such discrimination.

Article 8. Everyone has the right to an effective remedy by the competent national tribunals for acts violating the fundamental rights granted him by the constitution or by law.

Article 9. No one shall be subjected to arbitrary arrest, detention or exile.

Article 10. Everyone is entitled in full equality to a fair and public hearing by an independent and impartial tribunal, in the determination of his rights and obligations and of any criminal charge against him.

Article 11. (1) Everyone charged with a penal offense has the right to be presumed innocent until proved guilty according to the law in a public trial at which he has had all the guarantees necessary for his defense. (2) No one shall be held guilty of any penal offense on account of any act or omission which did not constitute a penal offense, under national or international law, at the time when it was committed. Nor shall a heavier penalty be imposed than the one that was applicable at the time the penal offense was committed.

Article 12. No one shall be subjected to arbitrary interference with his privacy, family, home or correspondence, nor to attacks upon his honour and reputation. Everyone has the right to the protection of the law against such interference or attacks.

Article 13. (1) Everyone has the right to freedom of movement and residence within the borders of each State.

(2) Everyone has the right to leave any country, including his own, and to return to his country.

Article 14. (1) Everyone has the right to seek and to enjoy in other countries asylum from persecution.

(2) This right may not be invoked in the case of prosecutions genuinely arising from non-political crimes or from acts contrary to the purposes and principles of the United Nations.

Article 15. (1) Everyone has the right to a nationality.

(2) No one shall be arbitrarily deprived of his nationality nor denied the right to change his nationality.

Article 16. (1) Men and women of full age, without any limitation due to race, nationality or religion, have the right to marry and to found a family. They are entitled to equal rights as a marriage, during marriage and at its dissolution.

(2) Marriage shall be entered into only with the free and full consent of the intending spouses.

(3) The family is the natural and fundamental group unit of society and is entitled to protection by society and the State.

Article 17. (1) Everyone has the right to own property alone as well as in association with others.

(2) No one shall be arbitrarily deprived of his property.

Article 18. Everyone has the right to freedom of thought, conscience and religion; this right includes freedom to change his religion or belief, and freedom, either alone or in community with others and in public or private, to manifest his religion or belief in teaching, practice, worship and observance.

Article 19. Everyone has the right to freedom of opinion and expression; this right includes freedom to hold opinions without interference and to seek, receive and impart information and ideas through any media and regardless of frontiers.

Article 20. (1) Everyone has the right to freedom of peaceful assembly and association.

(2) No one may be compelled to belong to an association.

Article 21. (1) Everyone has the right to take part in the government of his country, directly or through freely chosen representatives.

(2) Everyone has the right of equal access to public service in his country.

(3) The will of the people shall be the basis of the authority of the government; this will shall be expressed in periodic and genuine elections which shall be by universal and equal suffrage and shall be held by secret vote or by equivalent free voting procedures.

Article 22. Everyone, as a member of society, has the right to social security and is entitled to realization, through national effort and international co-operation and in accordance with the organization and resources of each State, of the economic, social and cultural rights indispensible for his dignity and the free development of his personality.

Article 23. (1) Everyone has the right to work, to free choice of employment, to just and favourable conditions of work and to protection against unemployment.

(2) Everyone, without any discrimination, has the right to equal pay for equal work.

(3) Everyone who works has the right to just and favourable remuneration ensuring for himself and his family an existence worthy of human dignity, and supplemented, if necessary, by other means of social protection.

(4) Everyone has the right to form and to join trade unions for the protection of his interests.

Article 24. Everyone has the right to rest and leisure, including reasonable limitation of working hours and periodic holidays with pay.

Article 25. (1) Everyone has the right to a standard of living adequate for the health and well-being of himself and of his family, including food, clothing, housing, and medical care and necessary social services, and the right to security in the event of unemployment, sickness, disability, widowhood, old age, or other lack of livelihood in circumstances beyond his control.

(2) Motherhood and childhood are entitled to special care and assistance. All children, whether born in or out of wedlock, shall enjoy the same social protection.

Article 26. (1) Everyone has the right to education. Education shall be free, at least in the elementary and fundamental stages. Elementary education shall be compulsory. Technical and professional education shall be made generally available and higher education shall be equally accessible to all on the basis of merit.

(2) Education shall be directed to the full development of the human personality and to the strengthening of respect for human rights and fundamental freedoms. It shall promote understanding, tolerance and friendship among all nations, racial or religious groups, and shall further the activities of the United Nations for the maintenance of peace.

(3) Parents have a prior right to choose the kind of education that shall be given to their children.

Article 27. (1) Everyone has the right freely to participate in the cultural life of the community, to enjoy the arts and to share in scientific advancement and its benefits.

(2) Everyone has the right to the protection of the moral and material interests resulting from any scientific, literary or artistic production of which he is the author.

Article 28. Everyone is entitled to a social and international order in which the rights and freedoms set forth in this Declaration can be fully realized.

Article 29. (1) Everyone has duties to the community in which alone the free and full development of his personality is possible.

(2) In the exercise of his rights and freedoms, everyone shall be subject only to such limitations as are determined by law solely for the purpose of securing due recognition and respect for the rights and freedoms of others and of meeting the just requirements of morality, public order and the general welfare in a democratic society.

(3) These rights and freedoms may in no case be exercised contrary to the purposes and principles of the United Nations.

Article 30. Nothing in this Declaration may be interpreted as implying for any State, group or person any right to engage in any activity or to perform any act aimed at the destruction of any of the rights and freedoms set forth herein.

8.6   Membership of the United Nations, 1996

Member	Date of Admission	Member	Date of Admission
Afghanistan	Nov. 19, 1946	Ecuador*	Dec. 21, 1945
Albania	Dec. 14, 1955	Egypt*	Oct. 24, 1945
Algeria	Oct. 8, 1962	El Salvador*	Oct. 24, 1945
Andorra	July 28, 1993	Equatorial Guinea	Nov. 12, 1968
Angola	Dec. 1, 1976	Eritrea	May 28, 1993
Antigua and Barbuda	Nov. 11, 1981	Estonia	Sept. 17, 1991
Argentina*	Oct. 24, 1945	Ethiopia*	Nov. 13, 1945
Armenia	Mar. 2, 1992	Fiji	Oct. 13, 1970
Australia*	Nov. 1, 1945	Finland	Dec. 14, 1955
Austria	Dec. 14, 1955	France*	Oct. 24, 1945
Azerbaijan	Mar. 2, 1992	Gabon	Sept. 20, 1960
Bahamas	Sept. 18, 1973	Gambia	Sept. 21, 1965
Bahrain	Sept. 21, 1971	Georgia	Mar. 2, 1992
Bangladesh	Sept. 17, 1974	Germany++	Sept. 18, 1973
Barbados	Dec. 9, 1966	Ghana	Mar. 8, 1957
Belarus*	Oct. 24, 1945	Greece*	Oct. 25, 1945
Belgium*	Dec. 27, 1945	Grenada	Sept. 17, 1974
Belize	Sept. 25, 1981	Guatemala*	Nov. 21, 1945
Benin (formerly Dahomey)	Sept. 20, 1960	Guinea	Dec. 12, 1958
Bhutan	Sept. 21, 1971	Guinea-Bissau	Sept. 17, 1974
Bolivia*	Nov. 14, 1945	Guyana	Sept. 20, 1966
Bosnia and Hercegovina	May 22, 1992	Haiti*	Oct. 24, 1945
Botswana	Oct. 17, 1966	Honduras*	Dec. 17, 1945
Brazil*	Oct. 24, 1945	Hungary	Dec. 14, 1955
Brunei	Sept. 21, 1984	Iceland	Nov. 19, 1946
Bulgaria	Dec. 14, 1955	India*	Oct. 30, 1945
Burkina Faso (formerly Upper Volta)	Sept. 20, 1960	Indonesia	Sept. 28, 1950
Burundi	Sept. 18, 1962	Iran*	Oct. 24, 1945
Cambodia	Dec. 14, 1955	Iraq*	Dec. 21, 1945
Cameroon	Sept. 20, 1960	Ireland	Dec. 14, 1955
Canada*	Nov. 9, 1945	Israel	May 11, 1949
Cape Verde	Sept. 16, 1975	Italy	Dec. 14, 1955
Central African Republic	Sept. 20, 1960	Ivory Coast	Sept. 20, 1960
Chad	Sept. 20, 1960	Jamaica	Sept. 18, 1962
Chile*	Oct. 24, 1945	Japan	Dec. 18, 1956
China*+	Oct. 24, 1945	Jordan	Dec. 14, 1955
Colombia*	Nov. 5, 1945	Kazakhstan	Mar. 2, 1992
Comoros	Nov. 12, 1975	Kenya	Dec. 16, 1963
Congo	Sept. 20, 1960	Korea, North	Sept. 17, 1991
Costa Rica*	Nov. 2, 1945	Korea, South	Sept. 17, 1991
Croatia	May 22, 1992	Kuwait	May 14, 1963
Cuba*	Oct. 24, 1945	Kyrgyzstan	Mar. 2, 1992
Cyprus	Sept. 20, 1960	Laos	Dec. 14, 1955
Czech Republic**	Jan. 19, 1993	Latvia	Sept. 17, 1991
Denmark*	Oct. 24, 1945	Lebanon*	Oct. 24, 1945
Djibouti	Sept. 20, 1977	Lesotho	Oct. 17, 1966
Dominica	Sept. 18, 1978	Liberia*	Nov. 2, 1945
Dominican Republic*	Oct. 24, 1945	Libya	Dec. 14, 1955

Member	Date of Admission	Member	Date of Admission
Liechtenstein	Sept. 18, 1990	Samoa	Dec. 15, 1976
Lithuania	Sept. 17, 1991	San Marino	Mar. 2, 1992
Luxembourg*	Oct. 24, 1945	Sao Tome and Principe	Sept. 16, 1975
Macedonia	Apr. 8, 1993	Saudi Arabia*	Oct. 24, 1945
Madagascar (Malagasy Republic)	Sept. 20, 1960	Senegal	Sept. 28, 1960
Malawi	Dec. 1, 1964	Seychelles	Sept. 21, 1976
Malaysia	Sept. 17, 1957	Sierra Leone	Sept. 27, 1961
Maldives	Sept. 21, 1965	Singapore	Sept. 21, 1965
Mali	Sept. 28, 1960	Slovakia**	Jan. 19, 1993
Malta	Dec. 1, 1964	Slovenia	May 22, 1992
Marshall Islands	Sept. 17, 1991	Solomon Islands	Sept. 19, 1978
Mauritania	Oct. 27, 1961	Somalia	Sept. 20, 1960
Mauritius	Apr. 24, 1968	South Africa*	Nov. 7, 1945
Mexico*	Nov. 7, 1945	Spain	Dec. 14, 1955
Micronesia	Sept. 17, 1991	Sri Lanka	Dec. 14, 1955
Moldova	Mar. 2, 1992	Sudan	Nov. 12, 1956
Monaco	May 28, 1993	Suriname	Dec. 4, 1975
Mongolia	Oct. 27, 1961	Swaziland	Sept. 24, 1968
Morocco	Nov. 12, 1956	Sweden	Nov. 19, 1946
Mozambique	Sept. 16, 1975	Syrian Arab Republic*	Oct. 24, 1945
Namibia	Apr. 23, 1990	Tajikistan	Mar. 2, 1992
Nepal	Dec. 14, 1955	Tanzania	Dec. 14, 1961
Netherlands*	Dec. 10, 1945	Thailand	Dec. 16, 1946
New Zealand*	Oct. 24, 1945	Togo	Sept. 20, 1960
Nicaragua*	Oct. 24, 1945	Trinidad and Tobago	Sept. 18, 1962
Niger	Sept. 20, 1960	Tunisia	Nov. 12, 1956
Nigeria	Oct. 7, 1960	Turkey*	Oct. 24, 1945
Norway*	Nov. 27, 1945	Turkmenistan	Mar. 2, 1992
Oman	Oct. 7, 1971	Uganda	Oct. 25, 1962
Pakistan	Sept. 30, 1947	Ukraine*	Oct. 24, 1945
Palau	Dec. 15, 1994	United Arab Emirates	Dec. 9, 1971
Panama*	Nov. 13, 1945	United Kingdom of Great Britain and Northern Ireland*	Oct. 24, 1945
Papua New Guinea	Oct. 10, 1975		
Paraguay*	Oct. 24, 1945	United States of America*	Oct. 24, 1945
Peru*	Oct. 31, 1945	Uruguay*	Dec. 18, 1945
Philippines*	Oct. 24, 1945	Uzbekistan	Mar. 2, 1992
Poland*	Oct. 24, 1945	Vanuatu	Sept. 15, 1981
Portugal	Dec. 14, 1955	Venezuela*	Nov. 15, 1945
Qatar	Sept. 21, 1971	Vietnam	Sept. 20, 1977
Romania	Dec. 14, 1955	Western Samoa	Dec. 15, 1976
Russia*x	Oct. 24, 1945	Yemen	Sept. 30, 1947
Rwanda	Sept. 18, 1962	Yugoslavia*+++	Oct. 24, 1945
Saint Kitts and Nevis	Sept. 23, 1983	Zaire	Sept. 20, 1960
Saint Lucia	Sept. 18, 1979	Zambia	Dec. 1, 1964
Saint Vincent and the Grenadines	Sept. 16, 1980	Zimbabwe	Aug. 25, 1980

*Original member

**xRussia now has the seat formerly occupied by the Union of Soviet Socialist Republics.

+The Republic of China (Taiwan) represented China until 1971, when the UN voted to have China represented by the People's Republic of China.

**Czech Republic and Slovakia admitted on Jan. 19, 1993; Czechoslovakia was a founding member.

++Date of admission of East Germany and West Germany.

+++Yugoslavia's membership is under suspension.

8.7   Representatives of the U.S. to the United Nations, 1946-1999

The U.S. Mission to the United Nations was formally established, with that title, by Executive Order 9844 on April 28, 1947. The U.S. representatives follow with their years of service:

Edward R. Stettinius, Jr., April 1946

Warren R. Austin, 1947-1953

Henry Cabot Lodge, Jr., 1953-1960

James J. Wadsworth, 1960-1961

Adlai E. Stevenson, 1961-1965

Arthur J. Goldberg, 1965-1968

George W. Ball, 1968

James Russell Wiggins, 1968-1969

Charles W. Yost, 1969-1971

George Bush, 1971-1973

John A. Scali, 1973-1975

Daniel P. Moynihan, 1975-1976

William W. Scranton, 1976-1977

Andrew J. Young, 1977-1979

Donald F. McHenry, 1979-1981

Jeane J. Kirkpatrick, 1981-1985

Vernon A. Walters, 1985-1989

Thomas R. Pickering, 1989-1992

Edward Joseph Perkins, 1992-1993

Madeleine K. Albright, 1993-1997

Bill Richardson, 1997-present

8.8   Women in the U.S. Foreign Service

1922   Lucile Atcherson—secretary in the Diplomatic Service.

1925   Pattie H. Field—Vice Consul at Amsterdam, first woman to enter the Foreign Service after the passage of the Rogers Act.

1933   Ruth Bryan Owen—daughter of William Jennings Bryan; first woman to be chief of a U.S. Diplomatic Mission—Minister to Denmark.

1949   Eugenie Moore Anderson—first woman to hold rank of Ambassador—Denmark.

1953   Francis E. Willis—first woman Foreign Service Officer to become an Ambassador—Switzerland, later Norway, Ceylon (now Sri Lanka).

1973   Carol C. Laise—first woman to become an Assistant Secretary of State (for Public Affairs), later served as Director General of the Foreign Service.

1977   Lucy Wilson Benson—first woman Under Secretary of State (for Security Assistance, Science and Technology).

1985   Rozanne L. Ridgway—first woman to head one of the regional bureaus, Assistant Secretary of State for European and Canadian Affairs. Also the first woman to serve as Counselor of the Department of State.

1997   Madeline K. Albright—first woman appointed Secretary of State.

Source: U.S. State Department.

8.9   Organization of a U.S. Diplomatic Mission

Chief of Mission

> Deputy Chief of Mission
> Home Agency
> > Mission Staff

U.S. Information Agency

> Public Affairs Officer

Agency for International Development

> AID Mission Director

Department of State

> Consul-General
> Administrative Counselor
> Economic Counselor
> Political Counselor

Department of Defense

> Defense Attaché
> Military Group Leader

Department of Agriculture

> Agricultural Trade Office Representative
> Agricultural Counselor

Department of Commerce

> Commercial Counselor

8.10 Chronology of the Evolution of the Foreign Service

1790s	President George Washington's distrust of foreign entanglements led to a downplaying of the importance of U.S. ambassadors abroad who were referred to only as "charges d'affaires." Early diplomats, who included Benjamin Franklin, Thomas Jefferson, John Adams, John Jay, and James Monroe, had to pay most of their own expenses.
1792	First Act of Congress providing for U.S. Consuls abroad was passed. Consuls received no salary and were not required to be U.S. citizens.
1800s-early 1900s	Spoils System—appointment and promotion on a political basis—dominated. Diplomatic positions served as rewards for service and frequently went to unqualified political associates and wealthy people who were campaign contributors.
1856	Act of Congress established two levels of consular posts. The first group was paid more, but could not engage in business, the second was paid less, but could maintain their outside means of income. Non-citizens could still be appointed to consular posts, but could not receive fees. The Act also provided for "consular pupils" who would be assigned to consulates; this was repealed at the next session of Congress.
1864-1896	Congress authorized thirteen consular clerks in 1864. Between 1864 and 1896, sixty-four consular clerks were appointed. Eight were appointed to consul; most preferred a small salary and the security of maintaining their businesses to make money and save for an uncertain future.
1895	President Grover Cleveland issued an executive order that required consular appointees with salaries between $1,000-$2,000 to be either a qualified officer of the Department or to pass a written exam.
1905 and 1906	President Theodore Roosevelt issued executive orders that instituted examinations for the lower grades of the Consular Service and for Secretaries in the Diplomatic Service.
1924	The Rogers Act combined the Diplomatic and Consular Services into a unified U.S. Foreign Service. The Act also established difficult examinations for Foreign Service career officers, put promotion on a merit, rather than on a political basis, established the first retirement and disability pay system and installed the system of extra allowances so that qualified people who were not wealthy could accept overseas appointments.
1946	The Foreign Service Act of 1946 gave ambassadors and ministers their first pay raises in almost 100 years and set up a new class system for the Foreign Service.
1980	The Foreign Service Act of 1980 established the Senior Foreign Service and increased Foreign Service salaries to make them comparable with Civil Service salaries of the same levels, set up an office to improve job placement and retirement and survivors benefits for spouses of Foreign Service members.

Source: U.S. State Department.

8.11 African Americans in the State Department and Foreign Service

1845	William A. Leidesdorff appointed as Vice Consul at Yerba Buena (now San Francisco).
1869-1877	Ebenezer Don Carlos Basset appointed the first African American diplomat. He was Minister Resident and Consul-General in Haiti.
1925	Clifton R. Wharton was the first African American to join the Foreign Service.
1953	Jessie D. Locker was the first African American appointed Ambassador. He served in Liberia until he died there in 1955.
1958	Clifton R. Wharton was the first African American Foreign Service Officer to become chief of a Diplomatic Mission when he was appointed Minister to Romania and then Ambassador to Norway in 1961.
1965	Patricia Roberts Harris became the first African American woman to become an Ambassador when she was appointed to that post in Luxembourg.
1968	Barbara M. Watson became the first African American woman to be chief of a State Department Bureau when she became Administrator of the Bureau of Security and Consular Affairs.
1977	Barbara M. Watson was appointed Assistant Secretary of State for Consular Affairs.
1993	Clifton R. Wharton, Jr., son of pioneering Foreign Service Officer, Clifton R. Wharton, became the highest-ranking African American in the Department of State when he became the Deputy Secretary of State—the second-ranking position in the Department.

Source: U.S. State Department.

8.12 American Nobel Peace Prize Winners, 1906-1999

1906	Theodore Roosevelt, peace negotiator in Russo-Japanese War.
1912	Elihu Root, organizer of Central American Peace Conference.
1919	Woodrow Wilson, for work on League of Nations.
1925	G. Dawes, originator of plan for payment of German reparations.
1929	Frank Billings Kellogg, negotiator of Kellogg-Briand Peace Pact.
1931	Jane Addams, for work on Women's International League for Peace and Freedom, and Nicholas M. Butler, for work with Carnegie Endowment for International Peace.
1945	Cordell Hull, who worked for peace as Secretary of State.
1946	John R. Mott, for YMCA and refugee work, and Emily Greene Blach, who worked with Women's International League for Peace and Freedom.
1950	Ralph J. Búnche, UN mediator in Palestine.
1953	George C. Marshall, pioneer of European Recovery Program.
1962	Linus Pauling, for work toward ban on nuclear weapons tests.
1964	Martin Luther King, Jr., for non-violent campaign for racial equality.
1970	Norman E. Borlaug, who developed high-yield cereals for Third World countries.
1973	Henry Kissinger, negotiator of cease-fire in Vietnam.
1986	Elie Wiesel, for work on the behalf of the victims of racism.

8.13   Chronology of Foreign Diplomacy, 1776-1999

1776-1783 Diplomacy of the American Revolution
Benjamin Franklin in Paris
John Jay in Madrid
John Adams in Holland
Francis Dana in Russia
Robert Livingston—1st Secretary of State for Foreign Affairs
French Resistance to American Cause
Treaty of Paris (1783)

1784-1800 Diplomacy of the New Republic
Department of State founded—Thomas Jefferson was first Secretary of State (1790-93)
John Jay's Treaty
Washington's Farewell Address called for isolationism to protect new nation

1801-1829 Jeffersonian Diplomacy
Louisiana Purchase
Barkany Pirates
War of 1812
Acquisition of Florida
Monroe Doctrine—President James Monroe in Congressional address

1830-1860 Diplomacy and Westward Expansion
Manifest Destiny I—the annexation of Texas
Manifest Destiny II—adding the Oregon Territory
Manifest Destiny III—Nicholas Trist and the American southwest
Cushing and Perry open Asia
John Quincy Adams and the Amistad case
Webster-Ashburton Treaty—settling U.S.-Canadian dispute
Monroe Doctrine—previously just a policy, its ideals became more popular and increasingly used

1861-1865 Diplomacy and the Civil War
William H. Seward—Secretary of State
Charles Francis Adams and British neutrality
Trent Affair
Alabama claims
Foreign Relations of the U.S.—series established by Seward to publish record of American diplomacy

1866-1913 Rise to Global Power
James G. Blaine—Secretary of State
Seward and the Alaska Purchase
Blaine and Pan-Americanism—interest in Latin America
Venezuela boundary dispute
Annexation of Hawaii
War with Spain
Open Door Policy with China
Teddy Roosevelt and World Order
Dollar Diplomacy (1909-1913)—policy of President William H. Taft and Secretary of State, Philander C.
   Knox, to create world stability and order using private funds
Anti-imperialism (1898-1921)

1914-1920 Diplomacy of World War I
William Jennings Bryan—Secretary of State
Wilson at Versailles
League of Nations controversy

1921-1936 Diplomacy and Isolationism

Allied loans and war reparations

Rogers Act of 1924

Stimson Doctrine—non-recognition

Smoot-Hawley Tariff

Good Neighbor Policy

Disarmament

Internationalism—new approach—participation with other nations in Five Power Treaty and Kellogg-Briand
 Peace Pact didn't prevent forces leading to World War II

1937-1945 Diplomacy of World War II

Cooperation with Allies

Neutrality Acts

Lend-Lease

Wartime Conferences—Bretton Woods, Dumbarton Oaks, Yalta—most important and controversial

Potsdam—pre-Cold War tensions arise

Atlantic Charter

Formation of the United Nations

1946-1968 Diplomacy and the Cold War

Foreign Service Act of 1946

National Security Act of 1947

Kennan and containment

Regional Collective Security Pacts

Marshall Plan—1948—plan to rebuild Western Europe. Eastern Europe and the Soviet Union's lack of
 participation worsens East/West tensions leading up to Cold War

Political attacks on Department of State

Castro and Cuban Missile Crisis

Anti-Communist crusades in the Third World

Peace Corps and Alliance for Progress

1969-1989 Detente and the waining of the Cold War

Detente

Kissinger and Shuttle Diplomacy

Terrorism

START

Nixon Doctrine

Camp David Peace Accords—1977—Egyptian president Anwar el Sadat and Israeli prime minister
 Menachem Begin

Egyptian/Israeli Peace Treaty

Communism in crisis

Iran-Contra Affair

Panama Canal

1990-1999 Diplomacy in a Multipolar World

Regional peace-keeping efforts

Middle East Peace Accords

Gulf War Coalition

Dayton Peace Accords—Shuttle Diplomacy

Open Door Policy—1997—Secretary of State Madeline Albright

Talks with Yugoslavia fail and result in NATO bombing of Yugoslavia

Source: U.S. State Department.

8.14 Spies and Espionage, 1775-1999

1775-1783 Revolutionary War. George Washington's network of spies obtained intelligence and information for the Continental Army during the Revolutionary War. American Secret Service operations were directed by Major Benjamin Tallmadge.

Nathan Hale (1755-1776). A graduate of Yale College, Hale volunteered to spy on the British, but was captured and hanged the next day. His famous last words are reported as, "I only regret that I have but one life to lose for my country."

Benedict Arnold (1741-1801). Distinguished officer during the first part of the Revolutionary War who helped Ethan Allen take Fort Ticonderoga. Agreed to surrender fort at West Point, where he was commandant, to the British in exchange for money and a commission in the British Army. Arnold fled to the British after the plot was exposed by the captured British Major John Andre. As a British officer, Arnold conducted raids in the South and among former neighbors in Connecticut. He died in England.

1861-1865 Civil War. Allan Pinkerton directed espionage and counter-espionage for the Union Army. Lafayette C. Baker succeeded Pinkerton; later a Bureau of Information carried on this work.

Harriet Tubman (1820-1913). During the Civil War she served as a spy and scout for the Union Army. Born a slave, this famous abolitionist established the "Underground Railroad" helping hundreds of slaves to freedom in the North.

Belle Boyd (1844-1900). Spied for Confederacy by carrying letters across enemy lines. Ironically, she married a Union Naval Officer before the end of the war.

Early 1900s—World War I. Second section of Army General staff (G-2) had its latent intelligence responsibilities reactivated and the Office of Naval Intelligence (ONI), organized in 1882, was given more scope to safeguard secret military information, but not authorized for espionage.

Espionage Act of 1917. Prohibited spying for a foreign country and provided for heavy penalties for doing so. Amended in 1940 and 1978, it is still in effect. More than 1500 convictions were made during World War I under this act.

Sedition Act of 1918. Banned spoken or printed attacks on the U.S. government, Constitution or flag. Repealed in 1921.

1919 U.S. Supreme Court. Justices Oliver Wendel Holmes, Jr., and Louis Brandeis stated that unpatriotic speech and press were only illegal if they posed a "clear and present danger" to national security.

1939-1945 World War II. The Office of Strategic Services (OSS) was founded under Colonel William J. Donovan to conduct government overseas espionage and intelligence operations.

    Revision of the Espionage Act (1940). Penalties for violations of the act were increased.

    Pearl Harbor bombing (1941). Considered a great intelligence failure for U.S., but spurred the postwar growth of the massive intelligence machine in the U.S.

    Application of Espionage Act (1944). Application of this act to "mere" propaganda was limited by a Supreme Court decision. Only about 160 people were convicted under the act during the World War II period.

1947 U.S. Central Intelligence Agency (CIA). Congress establishes the CIA to coordinate government intelligence activities that may bear on national security and to carry on its own operations. CIA became a world force, known for its pervasive international surveillance.

Alger Hiss (1948-1950). When his case began in 1948, Hiss was president of the Carnegie Endowment for International Peace, and had been a lawyer for two White House Departments. He was accused by Whittaker Chambers, a respected writer and former editor of Time magazine, of transmitting classified documents to the USSR. Chambers testified before the Committee on Un-American Activities (led by Senator Joseph McCarthy) that he himself was a former Communist who had once been a courier with Hiss. Hiss was convicted and served 4 years of his 5-year sentence, always maintaining his innocence.

1951 Julius and Ethel Rosenberg. Convicted of treason, in the first trial by a civil court under the Espionage Act, for passing information regarding the building of nuclear weapons to the USSR during World War II. Questions arose about the fairness of the trial and international pleas for clemency erupted for these first Americans executed for treason during peacetime. Both were executed in 1953.

1954 Espionage Act. Act is modified to call a crime of peacetime espionage, previously punishable by 20 years imprisonment, a capital offense.

1950s-1960s Cold War. FBI and CIA concentrated efforts primarily on the Soviet KGB or Committee of State Security.

1958 Colonel Rudolf Abel. A high-ranking Soviet Officer, Abel had operated in the U.S. as a spy for years. Arrested in 1958.

1960s-1970s. Role of CIA questioned in the era of disillusionment with the Vietnam War, the Watergate scandal and the policies of detente. Media disclosures about intelligence agency wrong-doings instigated investigations. The role of the CIA continues to be under question.

1974. Congress passed the Foreign Assistance Act, known as the Hughes-Ryan Amendment, which required that the President report to Congress any covert CIA operations in a foreign country other than for intelligence collection.

1975. The Church Committee and the Rockefeller Commission begin extensive investigations into the operations of the CIA.

1976. President Gerald Ford issued the first Executive Order on intelligence and a new intelligence Oversight Board was established within the Executive Office of the President.

1977-1980. Continued investigations, limitations and restrictions on intelligence operations.

1981. President Ronald Reagan issued Executive Order which reaffirmed the functions of intelligence agencies and generally allowed the CIA greater latitude.

1985 The Year of the Spy. Former CIA officer, Edward Lee Howard, defected. Arrested were John A. Walker, Jr. and Jerry A. Whitworth, navy personnel with access to highly sensitive information; CIA employees, Sharon Scranage and Larry Wu-Tai-Chin; former NSA employee, Ronald W. Pelton; FBI agent, Richard Miller and an employee of Naval intelligence, Jonathan J. Pollard. Whitworth, Pelton and Howard cases dealt serious blows to U.S. intelligence.

1986. Goldwater-Nicholas Act reorganized the Department of Defense and shifted authority from the military departments to the Joint Chiefs.

1986 Iran-Contra Affair. Congress learned that representatives of the Reagan Administration, contrary to announced policies of the Government, had sold arms to Iran in return for its help in getting release of U.S. hostages held in Lebanon. Some of the money from the sale of arms went to support the anti-communist rebels in Nicaragua.

1986-1989. Investigations and legislation was enacted to prevent a repeat of the Iran-Contra Affair debacle; newly elected President George Bush, a former Director of Central Intelligence, assured Congress that it would not happen again.

1988-1989. Congressional intelligence committees investigated problems with intelligence operations. No legislation was enacted, however, partly because of the fall of the Berlin Wall and the changes taking place in the Soviet Union which lessened the intensity of focusing on problems with spies.

1989-1995. End of the Cold War—Berlin Wall came down, Communist regimes of Eastern Europe collapsed; Iraq invaded Kuwait. Intelligence leaders reorganized, streamlined and refocused on transnational threats.

1991 Gulf War. The war highlighted the need to expand the link between intelligence and combat systems. The Joint Intelligence Center was created. Problems arose with differing CIA and military assessments of the damage of allied bombing.

1991 Gates Task Force. Director of Central Intelligence, Robert Gates, examined the post-Cold War intelligence community.

1992-1993. Intelligence Organization Act and Intelligence Authorization Act defined, for the first time, the intelligence community by law.

1993. President Bill Clinton issued an Executive Order to merge the Intelligence Oversight Board with the President's Foreign Intelligence Advisory Board.

1994. Aldrich H. Ames, a 30-year CIA employee, was charged with spying for the Soviet Union since 1985. He pled guilty to having exposed many of the CIA's Soviet agents, many of whom were later executed or imprisoned. Ames and his wife went to prison; public confidence in the CIA's abilities were seriously eroded.

1994. Legislation was enacted to improve counterintelligence and security operations in the intelligence community, especially improving coordination between CIA and FBI.

1995 Intelligence Authorization Act of 1995. Established a commission to study the roles and capabilities of intelligence agencies in the post-Cold War era and to make recommendations for change.

1998-1999 Chinese Spy Controversy. Congressional investigation of theft of U.S. atomic secrets by Chinese spies at national weapons laboratories.

8.15   Chronology of Foreign Aid, 1939-1999

1939-1945. Large scale foreign aid begins.

1940-1945 Lend Lease Program. U.S. gave over $50 billion in supplies and equipment to Allies; technical and development assistance for Latin America; funds to war relief programs.

1946-1948. UN Relief and Rehabilitation Administration (UNRRA), funded mostly by U.S. grants, helped provide food and shelter for millions in post-war Europe and Asia. U.S. foreign assistance is shaped by emergence of Soviet Union as an increasingly powerful nation.

1947 Truman Doctrine. Formulated in response to Communist pressure in Turkey and Greece; $400 million in military and economic aid given to those two countries to help resist Communism.

1948 Marshall Plan (European Recovery Program). U.S.'s first broad reconstruction program—$13 billion to Western Europe for rebuilding over four years; part of emerging policy of Truman's of containment of Communist nations. Containment policy shifts emphasis from some countries to entire underdeveloped world as Asia, Africa, and Latin America emerge as apparent stages upon which Cold War will be played out.

1949 North Atlantic Treaty Organization (NATO). Formed by the U.S. and 11 other nations to stop spread of Communism by China and the Soviet Union in countries including Greece, Laos, South Korea, South Vietnam, Taiwan, and Turkey. U.S. also gave aid to India, Pakistan, and others considered of major political importance.

1950 Point Four Program. President Harry Truman's $35 million technical assistance program to promote the economic development and military security of developing countries in Africa, Asia, and Latin America, in part a response to the Communist take-over of China in 1949.

1954 Agricultural Trade Development and Assistance Act. Authorized sale of surplus farm commodities for foreign currencies to be then granted or lent back to developing country as development assistance (Food for Peace). Between 1954-1990 this program assisted countries with $43 billion worth of commodities.

1955 Organization for Economic Cooperation and Development (OECD). Offered foreign assistance increasing from an annual average of $4.2 billion between 1955-60 to $6.1 billion in the 1961-65 period. U.S. economic assistance to developing nations consisted of loans and grants for long run economic development and supporting assistance to help establish internal and external security.

1957 Development Loan Fund. Created as a source of assistance for development projects.

1959 Inter-American Development Bank (IDB). Founded to make long-term loans to Latin American countries. Financed mainly by U.S.

Early 1960s. Presidents Kennedy and then Johnson strongly supported technical assistance and economic development programs.
—Food for Peace Program gave $1.5 billion a year in food shipments to needy nations.
—Congress established the Agency for international Development (AID) to administer bilateral aid programs.
—U.S. and 19 Latin American countries established the Alliance for Progress to promote economic and social reform in Latin America with aid going primarily to Brazil, Chile, Columbia, and Peru.
—Kennedy established the Peace Corps.

1965 Asian Development Bank. Established to lend money to governments and private enterprises in Asia. Originally financed by U.S., Japan, India, and Australia and headquartered in the Philippines.

Late 1960s. White House task force studied future of U.S. policies towards underdeveloped countries. Development assistance shifted from project to program aid. Main goals were to help nations maintain independence and develop into self-supporting countries to ensure long-run security and peace for the U.S.

Early 1970s. U.S. reduced foreign aid program; public support softened; international politics no longer dominated by bipolarity of the U.S. and USSR.
—Money redirected to military and domestic programs.
—U.S. tried to end balance of payments deficit.

Mid-1970s. Foreign aid was on the rise, especially to Egypt and Israel.

1980s. Portion of Gross National Product (GNP) allocated to foreign aid (in 1989) dipped to 0.2%, down from more than 2% in the 1940s. Many other countries allocated more than the U.S.
—Majority of U.S. aid went to Asia and the Middle East.
—Europe received about 13% of U.S. aid disbursed from 1945-90.
—South Asia and Middle East received more than 37% during this period, Latin America received 8%.
—Since the end of the Marshall Plan, South Vietnam, Israel, South Korea, India, Egypt, Turkey, Pakistan and Taiwan received bulk of U.S. aid. Israel received the most—$47 billion.
—Congress passed legislation requiring the Department of State to report on how much support the U.S. receives in the United Nations from countries that benefit from American Aid.

1990s European Bank for Reconstruction and Development. Established to make loans to Eastern European countries and to help them switch from Communist to free-market economics. Financed by 40 countries from around world and by two institutions of the former European Community (EC).
—Political support for foreign aid diminished.
—With break-up of Soviet Union, Russia and the Ukraine were among top recipients of U.S. aid.

1995. Survey respondents believed that 15% of the federal budget went to foreign aid; only 1% did.

Mid-1990s. Policy makers passed several proposals to restrict foreign aid to organizations that supported abortions in foreign countries.

Late 1990s. Some policy makers argue that aid to countries of the former USSR would help the peace initiative in the world; others appeal to the moral imperative to help others.

8.16   Agencies of the United Nations

General Agreement on Tarriffs and Trade (GATT)

Food and Agriculture Organization (FAO)

International Atomic Energy Agency (IAEA)

International Bank for Reconstruction and Development (World Bank)

International Civil Aviation Organization (ICAO)

International Development Association (IDA)

International Finance Corporation (IFC)

International Fund for Agricultural Development (IFAD)

International Labor Organization (ILO)

International Marine Organization (IMO)

International Monetary Fund (IMF)

International Telecommunication Union (ITU)

United Nations Educational, Scientific and Cultural Organization (UNESCO)

United Nations Industrial Development Organization (UNIDO)

Universal Postal Union (UPU)

World Health Organization (WHO)

World Intellectual Property Organization (WIPO)

World Meterological Organization (WMO)

8.17   United Nations Secretaries General

Secretary General Elected	Country
Trygve Lie 1946	Norway
Dag Hammarskjold 1953	Sweden
U Thant 1961	Burma
Kurt Waldheim 1972	Austria
Javier Perez de Cuellar 1982	Peru
Boutros Ghali 1992	Egypt

SECTION 9

Conflicts of the 19th Century

9.1   Major Conflicts in U.S. History

1775-1781	American Revolution
1812-1815	War of 1812
1846-1848	Mexican War
1861-1865	Civil War
1898	Spanish-American War
1914-1918	World War I
1939-1945	World War II
1950-1953	Korean War
1957-1975	Vietnam War
1990-1991	Persian Gulf War

9.2   Chronology of Conscription in the U.S., Colonial Era to 1999

Colonial Era—In times of need, each colony calls to arms all adult male citizens who group together to form colonial militias.

Revolutionary War Era—A regular army is raised by offering enlisted men cash bonuses and a promise of free western land after the war is over. This system, however, does not attract enough men and enlistments often run out before battles are over. General George Washington is forced to call on state militias, made up of poorly trained and led citizens who often leave service at inopportune times to return home and tend to their farms. Once he becomes president, Washington tries to remedy the inadequacy of the nation's military system by proposing legislation that men be registered for service and assigned to military units for training. Congress passes neither this nor similar such legislation later proposed by Presidents Adams, Jefferson, and Madison.

War of 1812—A regular army is authorized by Congress. Recruitment efforts include thirteen-month enlistment periods, a sixteen-dollar sign-up bonus and the promise of three months' pay and one hundred sixty acres of land upon discharge. Despite these enticements, the army is never effectively recruited and Congress authorizes President James Monroe to call up one hundred thousand state militia. Some states refuse to order any men to be sent out and the soldiers who do serve are largely untrained and frequently unwilling to face the enemy.

Mexican War—The one-year enlistment period of large numbers of American troops under General Winfield Scott expires just as he is moving into Mexico City. Military action must wait until replacement troops arrive.

Civil War—The Confederate Army enlists volunteer troops for one-year stints while troops for the North enlist for periods of three or nine months. Again, this often means loss of precious manpower at inopportune moments. Eventually, each side turns to conscription as a means of keeping its armies in place after enlistment periods end.

> **North**—In March, 1863, the Northern Army begins its Civil War conscription when Congress gives President Lincoln the authority to require draft registration by all able-bodied men between the ages of twenty and forty-five, regardless of their marital status or profession. To avoid military service, however, substitute soldiers are permitted to be hired and for a $300 fee, draft exemptions can be bought, proving the sys-

© 2000 by The Center for Applied Research in Education

tem to be unfair and unpopular. Many northern businessmen whose livelihoods benefit from southern slavery resist service and the Governor of New York, Horatio Seymour, himself declares the conscription act unconstitutional.

On July 13, 1863, an angry mob sets off the four-day New York City Draft Riots by seizing the 2nd Avenue Armory and interrupting the selection of registrants' names. Abolitionists' homes, conscription offices and city buildings are burned, shops are looted, and blacks, along with anyone refusing to join the marauders, are tortured. About one thousand people die. New York troops are called back from Gettysburg to quell the riot and Gov. Seymour finally urges compliance with the draft.

In 1864, the Northern draft is amended to allow buyouts by conscientious objectors only.

South—The Confederacy passes their conscription law in April 1862. Three years of military service is required from all white men between the ages of eighteen and thirty-five, excepting those legally exempted. Exemptions are numerous, leading to widespread non-compliance of the draft; substitutes are allowed to be hired at any set price. Poor morale and insufficient numbers of troops result. Later, the age limit for draftees is amended to include men between seventeen and fifty and in 1865, the Confederate Army begins to conscript slaves.

1898 (Spanish-American War)—Congress declares that all males between eighteen and forty-five are subject to military duty.

May 1917—Congress passes the Selective Service Act, establishing local, district, state and territorial civilian boards to register, classify, examine and either induct and ship out or defer men between the ages of twenty-one and thirty for service in World War I. There is much opposition to this draft: during the first drawing, 50,000 men apply for exemptions and over 250,000 fail to register at all. In one round-up held in New York City in 1918 to catch those who failed to report, 16,000 men are arrested. After the war's end, efforts to set up standard military training and service are defeated in Congress.

1920—The National Defense Act establishes a system of voluntary recruitment.

Nov. 1940—Congress enacts the Selective Training and Service Act. All males between the ages of twenty-one and thirty-five are ordered to register for the draft and the first national lottery is held. Draftees are shipped to army induction centers in the country's first peacetime draft. Later, as World War II progresses, the draft age is lowered to eighteen and men are called to service not by lottery number but by age, with the oldest going first.

1941—Following the attack on Pearl Harbor, Congress gives the President power to send draftees anywhere in the world, removing the distinctions between draftees, regulars, National Guardsmen and Reservists, and creating one army made up of all.

Jan. 1947—President Harry S. Truman recommends to Congress that the 1940 Selective Training and Service Act expire and that the level of required military forces be maintained by means of voluntary enlistments.

Mar. 1948—In the wake of the escalating Cold War, President Truman asks that the draft be reinstated as the level of military forces falls below necessary numbers. The new Selective Service Act provides for the drafting of men between nineteen and twenty-six for twelve months of active service.

1950—The Korean War draft, which exempts World War II veterans, calls up men between the ages of eighteen and a half and thirty five for terms of duty averaging two years.

June 1951—The Universal Military Training and Service Act is passed, requiring males between eighteen and twenty-six to register.

1952—Congress enacts the Reserve Forces Act, compelling every man who is drafted or enlisted to an eight-year obligation to military service. After a term of active duty is completed, one is assigned to standby reserve and can be called back to active duty upon a declaration of war or national emergency.

1965—Opposition to the war in Vietnam leads to calls for draft reform and/or the complete elimination of Selective Service. For the first time since the Civil War, anti-draft demonstrations, particularly on college campuses and at induction centers, surface and proliferate. In its *U.S. v. Seeger* decision, the Supreme Court broadens the definition of conscientious objection to include religious beliefs nontraditional and nontheistic in nature.

1966—In response to anti-war sentiment, President Lyndon Johnson appoints a special study commission to recommend changes in the Selective Service structure.

1967-70—During this period, the number of conscientious objectors recognized by Selective Service grows two and a half times and thousands of young men either destroy their draft cards or leave the country to avoid the draft.

1969—President Nixon orders the "nineteen year old draft": if a young man is not drafted at age nineteen, he will be exempt from future military service except in the event of war or national emergency. Deferrals are allowed for hardship cases, certain occupations, conscientious objectors, clergymen, and high school and college students. Student deferments are a loaded issue and one year later, Nixon will argue in favor of ending them.

1969—President Nixon orders a "random selection" lottery system for selecting men to serve in the war in Vietnam, changing the previous system of drafting according to age.

1970—In *U.S. v. Welsh,* the Supreme Court adds sincerely held ethical and moral beliefs to the definition of allowable grounds for conscientious draft objection.

1973—The 1967 Selective Service Act, extended through an act of Congress in 1971, expires, ending the authority to induct draft registrants.

1980—The Selective Service System again becomes active, following the passage of legislation to reinstate draft registration without authorizing induction.

Present—At this time, the U.S. operates under an all-volunteer armed forces policy. All male citizens between the ages of eighteen and twenty-six, however, are required to register for the draft and are liable for training and service until the age of thirty-five.

9.3   Chronology of the 1800s

1800   Washington, D.C., becomes the national capital.

1803   Louisiana Purchase.

1804   Lewis and Clark expedition.

1812-15   War of 1812 against Britain.

1819   Spain surrendered Florida to U.S.

1820   The Missouri Compromise.

1823   Monroe Doctrine established.

1825   Erie Canal opened.

1836   Mexicans attack the Alamo in San Antonio.

1842   Oregon Trail opened.

1845   Texas joined the U.S.

1848   Gold Rush began in California.

1850   California admitted to Union September 9.

1854   Kansas-Nebraska Act passed.

1857   *Dred Scott* decision by U.S. Supreme Court.

1860   Abraham Lincoln elected President.

1861-65   Civil War.

1862   Homestead Act.

1863   Emancipation Proclamation.

1865   The 13th Amendment outlawed slavery throughout the U.S.

1867   U.S. bought Alaska from Russia.

1869   Transcontinental railroad completed.

1875   Civil Rights Act passed.

1898   Spanish-American War.

9.4 Chronology of Slavery, 1800-1865

1800   Gabriel's Rebellion is attempted in Richmond, Virginia. Slave revolts in South Carolina, North Carolina, George, Louisiana and Mississippi follow.

1800   The state of Virginia passes a law forbidding African Americans to assemble between sunset and sunrise for religious worship or for instruction.

1805   The North Joy Street African Baptist Church of Boston is organized.

1814   An African Methodist Episcopal Church forms in Philadelphia.

1816   Several African Methodist churches meet at Bethel Church in Philadelphia in April and form a unified African Methodist Episcopal Church.

1822   Denmark Vesey, a former slave to Captain Joseph Vesey, leads a slave insurrection in South Carolina. Vessey and his men are arrested before they have a chance to put their plan into action.

1827   First African American newspaper, *Freedom's Journal,* begins publication in New York.

1829   David Walker publishes the first edition of his *Appeal to the Coloured Citizens of the World* and distributes the work to African Americans in the South.

1831   Nat Turner leads a revolt in Southampton County, Virginia, killing at least 57 whites.

1838   Presbyterians divide over slavery.

1844   Methodists divide over slavery.

1852   Harriet Beecher Stowe's *Uncle Tom's Cabin* is published.

1852   Josiah Priest publishes Bible defense of slavery.

1856   Booker T. Washington is born in Franklin County, Virginia, on April 5. Washington later becomes a leader in the educational, social and political realms of African American life.

1857   On March 6, the Supreme Court decides that an African American cannot be a citizen of the U.S. and has no rights of citizenship.

1860   Abraham Lincoln is elected the 16th President on November 6.

1861   Civil War begins.

1862   Slavery is abolished in the District of Columbia.

1863   The Emancipation Proclamation takes effect January 1, legally freeing slaves in areas of the South in rebellion.

1865   On January 31, Congress approves the Thirteenth Amendment outlawing slavery in the United States.

1865   Civil War ends.

9.5   Chronology of the Mexican-American War, 1845-1848

1836 Texas becomes independent. U.S. recognizes an independent Texas in 1837; Mexico refuses to recognize its independence.

1845 Texas is annexed and is admitted as a state. Mexico regards this as equivalent to a declaration of war.

September 1845 Mexico refuses U.S. offer to purchase land. President Polk instructs John Slidell to offer Mexico up to $25 million for New Mexico and California. Insulted Mexicans refuse to meet.

January 1846 Troops sent in. Zachary Taylor and 4,000 men are sent to disputed territory. Conflict with Mexican troops results in 16 American casualties.

May 1846 Congress declares war. Polk asks for war with Mexico. Northern Whigs fear victory would add more slave states to U.S. Declaration passes 40-2 in Senate, 174-14 in House.

June 1846 Bear Flag Republic established. John C. Fremont and volunteers capture town of Sonoma and hoist California Bear Flag.

July 1846 Americans capture Monterey. American troops capture Mexico's California capital.

August 1846 Americans capture Santa Fe. Stephen Kearny's 1,700 men take key Mexican trading post.

December 1846 Battle of San Diego. In fierce fighting, Kearny's California forces barely survive attack of Mexican troops.

January 1847 Battle of San Gabriel. American forces cross San Gabriel River and take Los Angeles.

February 1847 Battle of Buena Vista. Despite a much larger army, Santa Ana is unable to defeat Taylor's American forces.

March 1847 Americans capture Vera Cruz. General Winfred Scott captures fort on path to Mexico City.

September 1847 Mexico gives up all claim to Texas. U.S. pays Mexico $15 million and agrees to assume all American claims against Mexico. By the end of the War, 13,000 Americans had been killed in battle or were dead from disease. Northern Mexico and Texas were added to United States—virtually half of Mexico's territory.

February 1848 Treaty of peace signed at Guadalupe Hidalgo. Nicholas P. Trist negotiates for President Polk a major expansion of U.S. territory.

9.6 Events Preceding Civil War

1850s Economic expansion and sectionalism

Northern Mexico and Texas added to U.S. by 1848 peace treaty, fueling westward expansion and debate over slavery in the West.
Economic prosperity and expansion of railroads to 30,000 miles by 1860.
Bessemer process allows mass production of steel.
Telegraph revolutionizes communications.

North:
—Northern industrial growth, with market expansion for northeast manufacturers. Railroads open domestic markets as clipper ships and steamships opened European markets.
—California gold rush of 1848 added capital.
—Expansion of labor supply as more workers move to cities and immigrants arrive from from Ireland and Germany as a result of famines and unrest in Europe.
—Dominant social groups centered in commerce, industry, and finance.

South:
—Spread of plantation system. Slavery seen as indispensable for South's prosperity.
—Expansion of cotton production.
—Expansion of tobacco market.
—Dominant social groups centered in agriculture and foreign trade.

West:
—Western agriculture expanded as a result of railroad growth and opening of European markets.
—Westerners became aware of world hostility to slavery.
—Westerners became convinced of importance of Northeast to their prosperity rather than the South which purchased a much smaller share of their produce.

1850s Growth of slavery controversy
—Fear of slave insurrections grows.
—Compromise of 1850 angered extremists on both sides.
—Admission of California as a free state.
—Remaining western territories organized with no restriction on slavery.
—Congress ends all slave trade in the District of Columbia.
—Strict federal fugitive slave law.
—Southerners look for new potential slave regions.
—Cuba: U.S. sought to purchase Cuba from Spain.
—Mexico: Gadsden Purchase in SW Arizona territory in 1853 for $10 million for possible railroad route.
—Harriet Beecher Stowe's *Uncle Tom's Cabin* (1852) convinced many northerners of the evil of slavery.

1854 Kansas-Nebraska Act
—Stephen Douglas proposed that Kansas and Nebraska territories be divided into two sections.
—Missouri Compromise to be repealed, with settlers in each territory choosing whether or not they wanted slavery.
—Party realignments—Whig Party collapsed; Know-Nothing Party emerged; Republican Party, organized in support of keeping slavery out of the territories, gained strength.
—Bleeding Kansas violence as pro- and anti-slavery forces rushed in to Kansas territory.

1857 Dred Scott

—In *Dred Scott v. Sanford,* U.S. Supreme Court Chief Justice Taney ruled that Scott could not sue for his freedom.
—Missouri Compromise of 1820-1821 is found to be unconstitutional (Congress had no right to restrict slavery from territories).
—Constitution and citizenship did not apply to blacks.

1858 Lincoln-Douglas debates and Illinois Senate election

—Stephen Douglas and Abraham Lincoln debated throughout the state, focusing on slavery and its expansion.
—Freeport Doctrine (Douglas): people could keep slavery out by refusing to enact black codes and other laws necessary for its survival.
—Lincoln: "A house divided against itself cannot stand." Slavery should not be extended into territories.
—Lincoln loses election, but gains national prominence for his arguments.

1859 John Brown's raid

—Brown and his followers planned a slave insurrection to begin at Harper's Ferry but are quickly captured, tried and hanged.
—Northern abolitionists promote Brown as a martyr, taking action against the evil of slavery.
—Southerners see Brown and northern support for him as a threat.

1860 Presidential election

—Democrats split into northern and southern factions and nominated two candidates (Douglas and Breckenridge). Breckenridge carried the South.
—Former Whigs nominated Bell in an attempt to preserve Union with Constitutional Union Party. Strong only in Virginia and upper South. Bell wins three states—Virgina, Kentucky, Tennessee.
—Republicans nominated Lincoln as a moderate compromise candidate. Lincoln carried the northern states and won the electoral vote, though earning only 1.9 million votes out of 4.7 million cast.

1860 Secession

—On December 20, with the news of Lincoln's election, South Carolina becomes the first of the southern states to secede from the United States. By February 1861, seven states are planning secession.

1861 War breaks out

—On February 4, the Confederacy is established at Montgomery Convention. Jefferson Davis becomes president.
—Confederates bombard Fort Sumter to force its surrender on April 13. Civil War begins.

9.7 Influential Abolitionists

John Woolman (1720-1772)
Led Quakers in antislavery efforts. Wrote first public proclamations by a religious body of the evils of slavery.

Elias Hicks (1748-1830)
Liberal Quaker minister. Endorsed boycott of all goods produced by slave labor and advocated establishment of a homeland for freed slaves.

James Forten (1776-1842)
Son of free African American parents, served in the American Navy during the Revolutionary War, fortune amassed as a sailmaker supported abolition, African American and women's rights, and temperance.

Benjamin Lundy (1789-1837)
American Quaker who founded an abolitionist journal for Scotish-Irish, Moravians and Quakers, persuaded William Lloyd Garrison to be co-editor of the *Genius,* starting the career of that famous abolitionist.

David Walker (1785-1830)
African American abolitionist and Boston correspondent for an antislavery newspaper. Wrote controversial piece on abortion that may have led to his death by poisoning.

Sarah Moore Grimke (1792-1873) and Angelina Emily (1805-1879)
Sarah converted to Quakerism, went north with her sister, Angelina, and lectured for the American Anti-Slavery Society. Published what was probably the first written works advocating women's rights in the U.S. Angelina married fellow abolitionist, Theodore Weld.

Lucretia Coffin Mott (1793-1880)
Quaker preacher, abolitionist and women's rights activist. Was at the first meeting of the American Anti-Slavery Society; established the Anti-Slavery Convention of American Women.

Sojourner Truth (1797-1883)
Preacher, abolitionist, feminist and leading African American woman orator. Born into slavery as Isabelle Spelling, ran away when master refused to recognize New York's Emancipation Act of 1827, renamed herself Sojourner Truth to symbolize her emancipation struggle.

Lydia Maria Child (1802-1880)
With her husband she edited the weekly, *National Anti-Slavery Standard,* and helped to convert William Ellery Channing, Thomas Wentworth Higginson, and Charles Sumner to the antislavery cause.

Prudence Crandall (1803-1890)
Educator and abolitionist who opened the first school for African American girls in New England after an uproar over her admittance of an African American girl to her previous school. Arrested, tried and convicted for establishing a school for nonresident African Americans. Married fellow abolitionist, Reverend Calvin Phillo.

William Lloyd Garrison (1805-1879)
Considered personification of American abolitionist movement. Opposed slavery as an abomination in God's

sight. Edited anti-slavery publication, *The Liberator.* The American Anti-Slavery Society supported his radical views, including calling for the immediate release of all slaves. Was nonviolent until his later years when he condoned violent resistance to the 1850 Fugitive Slave Law and the Harper's Ferry raid.

John Greenleaf Whittier (1807-1892)
An American poet and Quaker from New England who began as a journalist for William Lloyd Garrison and was committed to the abolitionist cause.

Cassius M. Clay (1810-1903)
American politician, diplomat, and abolitionist who ran for office on anti-slavery ticket, founded newspaper *True American* (later *The Examiner*), and was a friend of Abraham Lincoln.

Charles Sumner (1811-1874)
Lawyer, legal scholar, Senator, and passionate abolitionist, leader of the "Conscience Wings," active organizer of the Free Soil Movement, fought for equal rights for former slaves during post-Civil War reconstruction.

Wendell Phillips (1811-1884)
Harvard Law School graduate, aristocrat turned radical slavery opponent and supporter of women's right, labor reform, and temperance, regarded as the movement's most eloquent speaker, married Ann Terry Greene, disciple of William Lloyd Garrison, a leader of the American Anti-Slavery Society, supported violence as a means to an immediate end to slavery.

Harriet Beecher Stowe (1811-1896)
Author of *Uncle Tom's Cabin* (1852), an anti-slavery novel of such power that is often cited as a cause of the Civil War.

Frederick Douglass (1817-1895)
One of America's greatest orators, advisor to Abraham Lincoln, published autobiographical account of life as a slave to prove his lineage since, because he was such an eloquent speaker, people doubted he had even been a slave. Held several public offices after Civil War, including U.S. Minister to Haiti.

James Russell Lowell (1819-1891)
One of the most-distinguished poets and literary critics of his time, married abolitionist Maria White and went on to write many pieces on abolition.

Lucy Stone (1818-1893)
Great orator and supporter of women's rights and the anti-slavery movement.

9.8   Chronology of the Civil War, 1861-1865

© 2000 by The Center for Applied Research in Education

1861

February 1861—The South secedes and forms a government.

The South Carolina legislature called a state convention and the delegates voted to remove the state of South Carolina from the United States of America. The secession of South Carolina was followed by the secession of six more states—Mississippi, Florida, Alabama, Georgia, Louisiana, and Texas. At a convention in Montgomery, Alabama, the seven seceding states created the Confederate Constitution and Jefferson Davis was named provisional president of the Confederacy. Four more states soon proclaimed secession—Virginia, Arkansas, Tennessee, and North Carolina, making eleven states in the Confederate States of America.

February 1861—The South seizes federal forts.

When President Buchanan refused to surrender southern federal forts to the seceding states, southern state troops seized them. At Fort Sumter, South Carolina's troops repulsed a supply ship trying to reach federal forces based in the fort.

March 1861—Lincoln's inauguration.

At his inauguration on March 4, Lincoln announced that he would not accept secession.

April 1861—Attack on Fort Sumter.

On April 12, the Civil War began with shots fired on Fort Sumter, which was eventually surrendered to South Carolina. Later in the month, after Virginia's secession, Richmond was named the Confederate capitol.

June 1861—West Virginia created.

Residents of the western counties of Virginia did not wish to secede along with the rest of the state. This section of Virginia was admitted into the Union as the state of West Virginia on June 20, 1863.

July 1861—First Bull Run.

General-in-Chief Winfield Scott advanced on the South before adequately training his untried troops. Confederate reinforcements fought in what became a Southern victory and a chaotic retreat toward Washington by federal troops.

July 1861—Blockade of the South.

An effective blockade by the federal navy was in place. The South responded by building small, fast ships that could outmaneuver Union vessels.

1862

January 1862—Lincoln orders action.

On January 27, President Lincoln issued a war order authorizing the Union to launch a unified aggressive action against the Confederacy. General McClellan ignored the order.

March 1862—Peninsular Campaign begins.

On March 8, President Lincoln—impatient with General McClellan's inactivity—issued an order reorganizing the Army of Virginia and relieving McClellan of supreme command. McClellan was given command of the Army of the Potomac and ordered to attack Richmond, beginning the Peninsular Campaign.

March 1862—First naval engagement.

Confederate engineers converted a scuttled Union frigate, the U.S.S. *Merrimac*, into an iron-sided vessel rechristened the C.S.S. *Virginia*. On March 9, in the first naval engagement between ironclad ships, the Union's *Monitor* fought the *Virginia* to a draw, but not before the *Virginia* had sunk two wooden Union warships off Norfolk, Virginia.

April 1862—The Battle of Shiloh.

On April 6, Confederate forces attacked Union forces under General Ulysses S. Grant at Shiloh, Tennessee. By the end of the day, the federal troops were almost defeated. Yet, during the night, reinforcements arrived, and by the next morning the Union commanded the field. Casualties were heavy—13,000 out of 63,000 Union soldiers died, and 11,000 of 40,000 Confederate troops were killed.

April 1862—New Orleans.

Flag Officer David Farragut led an assault up the Mississippi River. By April 25, he was in command of New Orleans.

April 1862—The Peninsular Campaign.

In April, General McClellan's troops left northern Virginia and by May 4, they occupied Yorktown, Virginia.

May 1862—Jackson defeats Union forces.

Confederate General Thomas J. "Stonewall" Jackson, commanding forces in the Shenandoah Valley, attacked Union forces in late March, forcing them to retreat across the Potomac. As a result, Union troops were rushed to protect Washington, D.C.

June 1862—The Battle of Seven Pines (Fair Oaks).

On May 31, the Confederate army attacked federal forces at Seven Pines, almost defeating them; last-minute reinforcements saved the Union from a serious defeat. Confederate commander Joseph E. Johnston was severely wounded, and command of the Army of Northern Virginia fell to Robert E. Lee.

July 1862—Battles of the Seven Days.

Between June 25 and July 2, Union and Confederate forces fought a series of battles: Mechanicsville (June 26-27), Gaines's Mill (June 27), Savage's Station (June 29), Frayser's Farm (June 30), and Malvern Hill (July 1). On July 2, the Confederates withdrew to Richmond, ending the Peninsular Campaign.

July 1862—Halleck commands Union army.

On July 11, Major-General Henry Halleck was named general-in-chief of the Union army.

August 1862—Second Bull Run.

Union General John Pope was defeated at the Second Battle of Bull Run on August 29-30. General Fitz-John Porter was held responsible for the defeat because he had failed to commit his troops to battle quickly enough; he was forced out of the army by 1863.

September 1862—Harper's Ferry.

Union General McClellan defeated Confederate General Lee at South Mountain and Crampton's Gap in September, but did not move quickly enough to save Harper's Ferry, which fell to Confederate General Jackson on September 15, along with a great number of men and a large body of supplies.

September 1862—Antietam.

On September 17, Confederate forces under General Lee were caught by General McClellan near Sharpsburg, Maryland. This battle proved to be the bloodiest day of the war; 2,108 Union soldiers were killed and

9,549 wounded—2,700 Confederates were killed and 9,029 wounded. The battle had no clear winner, but because General Lee withdrew to Virginia, McClellan was considered the victor. The battle convinced the British and French—who were contemplating official recognition of the Confederacy—to reserve action, and gave Lincoln the opportunity to announce his Preliminary Emancipation Proclamation (September 22), which would free all slaves in areas rebelling against the United States, effective January 1, 1863.

December 1862—The Battle of Fredericksburg.

Lincoln replaced McClellan with Major-General Ambrose E. Burnside, but Burnside's forces were defeated in a series of attacks against Confederate forces at Fredericksburg, Virginia, and Burnside was replaced with General Joseph Hooker.

1863

January 1863—Emancipation Proclamation.

In 1861, Congress had passed an act stating that all slaves employed against the Union were to be considered free and in 1862, another act stated that all slaves of men who supported the Confederacy were to be considered free. Lincoln issued the Emancipation Proclamation on January 1, 1863, declaring that all slaves in areas still in rebellion were, in the eyes of the federal government, free.

March 1863—The First Conscription Act.

Because of recruiting difficulties, an act was passed making all men between the ages of 20 and 45 liable to be called for military service. Service could be avoided by paying a fee or finding a substitute. The act was seen as unfair to the poor, and riots in working-class sections of New York City broke out in protest. A similar conscription act in the South provoked a similar reaction.

May 1863—The Battle of Chancellorsville.

Union General Hooker crossed the Rappahannock River to attack General Lee's forces. Lee split his army, attacking a surprised Union army in three places and almost completely defeating them.

May 1863—The Vicksburg Campaign.

Union General Grant won several victories around Vicksburg, Mississippi, the fortified city considered essential to the Union's plans to regain control of the Mississippi River. On May 22, Grant began a siege of the city. The Confederates surrendered, giving up the city and 30,000 men.

July 1863—Gettysburg.

On July 1, a chance encounter between Union and Confederate forces began the Battle of Gettysburg. The Union won the battle, ending Confederate hopes of formal recognition by foreign governments. On November 19, President Lincoln dedicated a portion of the Gettysburg battlefield as a national cemetery, and delivered his memorable "Gettysburg Address."

1864

May 1864—Grant's Wilderness Campaign.

General Grant, commander of the Union armies, led an inconclusive three-day battle in the Virginia wilderness. Lee inflicted more casualties on the Union forces than his own army incurred, but unlike Grant, he had no replacements.

June 1864—The Battle of Cold Harbor.

Grant again attacked Confederate forces at Cold Harbor, losing over 7,000 men in twenty minutes. Although Lee suffered fewer casualties, his army never recovered from Grant's continual attacks.

June 1864—The Siege of Petersburg.

Grant hoped to take Petersburg, below Richmond, and then approach the Confederate capital from the South. The attempt failed, resulting in a ten-month siege and the loss of thousands of lives on both sides.

July 1864—Confederates march toward Washington, D.C.

Confederate General Jubal Early led his forces into Maryland to relieve the pressure on Lee's army. Early got within five miles of Washington, D.C., but on July 13, he was driven back to Virginia.

August 1864—Sherman's Atlanta Campaign.

Without much to stop him, Sherman marched toward Atlanta and General Hood surrendered the city on September 1; Sherman occupied the city the next day.

November 1864—Sherman's March to the Sea.

General Sherman continued his march through Georgia to the sea. In the course of the march, he cut himself off from his source of supplies, planning for his troops to live off the land. His men cut a path 300 miles in length and 60 miles wide as they passed through Georgia, destroying everything.

November 1864—Lincoln is re-elected.

President Abraham Lincoln and Andrew Johnson ran on the Republican Party ticket, defeating the Democratics' General George B. McClellan for President, and George Pendleton for Vice President.

1865

January 1865—Battle of Fort Fisher.

Wilmington, NC was the last seaport through which the Confederates could supply the war effort. The U.S. Navy and federal troops coordinated actions to take Wilmington, capturing 2,000 Confederate prisoners and leaving Lee without supplies for his army.

April 1865—Surrender at Appomattox.

On April 9, after four years of war, Lee had failed to escape with what little was left of his army, and federal troops surrounded him. Sheridan's calvary and infantry blocked Lee's retreat on one side and Grant and Meade advanced from the rear. Grant sent a note advising Lee to surrender and Lee agreed. At the Appomattox Courthouse, Lee accepted Grant's generous terms for a general pardon and sent his troops home. Sherman and the Confederate General Johnston signed a similar agreement on April 18.

Source: U.S. Congressional Library.

9.9 Worst Civil War Battles

Battle/dates	Casualties[*]
Gettysburg, July 1-3, 1863	51,116
Battles of the Seven Days, June 25-July 2, 1862	36,463
Chickamauga, Sept. 19-20, 1863	34,624
Chancellorsville/Fredericksburg, May 1-4, 1863	29,609
Wilderness, May 5-7, 1862	25,416[#]
Manassas/Chantilly, Aug. 27-Sept. 2, 1862	25,340
Stone's River, Dec. 31, 1862-Jan. 1, 1863	24,645
Shiloh, April 6-7, 1862	23,741
Antietam, Sept. 17, 1862	22,726
Fredericksburg, Dec. 13, 1862	17,962

[*] Killed, missing, and wounded.
[#] Confederate totals estimated.

9.10   The Battle Hymn of the Republic

By Julia Ward Howe

Mine eyes have seen the glory of the coming of the Lord
He is trampling out the vintage where the grapes of wrath are stored,
He has loosed the fateful lightening of His terrible swift sword
His truth is marching on.

> Glory! Glory! Hallelujah!
> Glory! Glory! Hallelujah!
> Glory! Glory! Hallelujah!
> His truth is marching on.

I have seen Him in the watch-fires of a hundred circling camps
They have builded Him an altar in the evening dews and damps
I can read His righteous sentence by the dim and flaring lamps
His day is marching on.

> Glory! Glory! Hallelujah!
> Glory! Glory! Hallelujah!
> Glory! Glory! Hallelujah!
> His truth is marching on.

I have read a fiery gospel writ in burnishd rows of steel,
"As ye deal with my contemners, So with you my grace shall deal;"
Let the Hero, born of woman, crush the serpent with his heel
Since God is marching on.

> Glory! Glory! Hallelujah!
> Glory! Glory! Hallelujah!
> Glory! Glory! Hallelujah!
> His truth is marching on.

He has sounded forth the trumpet that shall never call retreat
He is sifting out the hearts of men before His judgment-seat
Oh, be swift, my soul, to answer Him! be jubilant, my feet!
Our God is marching on.

> Glory! Glory! Hallelujah!
> Glory! Glory! Hallelujah!
> Glory! Glory! Hallelujah!
> His truth is marching on.

He has sounded forth the trumpet that shall never call retreat
He is sifting out the hearts of men before His judgment-seat
Oh, be swift, my soul, to answer Him! be jubilant, my feet!
Our God is marching on.

> Glory! Glory! Hallelujah!
> Glory! Glory! Hallelujah!
> Glory! Glory! Hallelujah!
> His truth is marching on.

In the beauty of the lilies Christ was born across the sea,
With a glory in His bosom that transfigures you and me:
As He died to make men holy, let us die to make men free,
While God is marching on.

> Glory! Glory! Hallelujah!
> Glory! Glory! Hallelujah!
> Glory! Glory! Hallelujah!
> His truth is marching on.

9.11 Executive Cabinet of the Confederate States of America, 1861-1865

President Jefferson Davis of Confederate States of America created an official Cabinet:

Secretaries of State

Robert Toombs (21 February 1861-25 July 1861)
R.M.T. Hunter (25 July 1861-1 February 1862)
William M. Brown (1 February 1862-18 March 1862)
Judah P. Benjamin (18 March 1862-4 May 1865)

Attorneys General

Judah P. Benjamin (25 February 1861-17 September 1861)
Wade Keyes (17 September 1861-21 November 1861)
Thomas Bragg (21 November 1861-18 March 1862)
Thomas Watts (18 March 1862-1 October 1863)
Wade Keyes (1 October 1863-2 January 1864)
George Davis (2 January 1864-April 1865)

Secretaries of the Treasury

Christopher Memminger (21 February 1861-18 July 1864)
George Trenholm (18 July 1864-27 April 1865)

Secretary of the Navy

Stephen Mallory (2 March 1861-4 May 1865)

Postmaster General

John Reagan (6 March 1861-10 May 1865)

Secretaries of War

Leroy Pope Walker (21 February 1861-17 September 1861)
Judah Benjamin (17 September 1861-18 March 1862)
Brig. Gen. George Randolph (18 March 1862-17 November 1862)
Maj. Gen. Gustavus Smith (17 November 1862-21 November 1862)
James Seddon (21 November 1862-6 February 1865)
Maj. Gen. John C. Breckinridge (6 February 1865-4 May 1865)

9.12   Civil War Battles by Campaign

Main Eastern Theater

1861

Blockade of the Chesapeake Bay [May-June 1861]

- Sewell's Point (VA)
- Aquia Creek (VA)
- Big Bethel (VA)

Operations in Western Virginia [June-December 1861]

- Philippi (WV)
- Rich Mountain (WV)
- Kessler's Cross Lanes (WV)
- Carnifex Ferry (WV)
- Cheat Mountain (WV)
- Greenbrier River (WV)
- Camp Alleghany (WV)

Manassas Campaign [July 1861]

- Hoke's Run (WV)
- Blackburn's Ford (VA)
- Manassas I (VA)

Blockade of the Carolina Coast [August 1861]

- Hatteras Inlet Batteries (NC)

McClellan's Operations in Northern Virginia [October-December 1861]

- Ball's Bluff (VA)
- Dranesville (VA)

1862

Blockade of the Potomac River [October 1861-January 1862]

- Cockpit Point (VA)

Jackson's Operations Against the B&O Railroad [January 1862]

- Hancock (MD)

Burnside's North Carolina Expedition [February-June 1862]

- Roanoke Island (NC)
- New Berne (NC)
- Fort Macon (NC)
- South Mills (NC)
- Tranter's Creek (NC)

Jackson's Valley Campaign [March-June 1862]

- Kernstown I (VA)
- McDowell (VA)
- Front Royal (VA)
- Winchester I (VA)
- Cross Keys (VA)
- Port Republic (VA)

Peninsula Campaign [March-July 1862]

- Hampton Roads (VA)
- Yorktown (VA)
- Williamsburg (VA)
- Eltham's Landing (VA)
- Drewry's Bluff (VA)
- Hanover Courthouse (VA)
- Seven Pines (VA)
- Oak Grove (VA)
- Beaver Dam Creek (VA)
- Gaines' Mill (VA)
- Garnetts & Goldings Farm (VA)
- Savage's Station (VA)
- White Oak Swamp (VA)
- Glendale (VA)
- Malvern Hill (VA)

Northern Virginia Campaign [August 1862]

- Cedar Mountain (VA)
- Rappahannock Station I (VA)
- Manassas Station Operations (VA)
- Thoroughfare Gap (VA)
- Manassas II (VA)
- Chantilly (VA)

Maryland Campaign [September 1862]

- Harpers Ferry (WV)
- South Mountain (MD)
- Antietam (MD)
- Shepherdstown (WV)

Fredericksburg Campaign [November-December 1862]

- Fredericksburg (VA)

Goldsboro Expedition [December 1862]

- Kinston (NC)
- White Hall Ferry (NC)
- Goldsboro Bridge (NC)

1863

Longstreet's Tidewater Operations [March-April 1863]

- Fort Anderson (NC)
- Washington (NC)
- Norfleet House/Suffolk (VA)
- Hill's Point/Suffolk (VA)

Cavalry Operations along the Rappahannock [March 1863]

- Kelly's Ford (VA)

Chancellorsville Campaign [April-May 1863]

- Chancellorsville (VA)
- Fredericksburg II (VA)
- Salem Church (VA)

Gettysburg Campaign [June-July 1863]

- Brandy Station (VA)
- Winchester (VA)
- Aldie (VA)
- Middleburg (VA)
- Upperville (VA)
- Hanover (PA)
- Gettysburg (PA)
- Williamsport (MD)
- Boonsborough (MD)
- Manassas Gap (VA)

Bristoe Campaign [October-November 1863]

- Auburn (VA)
- Bristoe Station (VA)
- Buckland Mills (VA)
- Rappahannock Station II (VA)

Averell's Raid on the Virginia & Tennessee Railroad [November 1863]

- Droop Mountain (WV)

Mine Run Campaign [November-December 1863]

- Mine Run (VA)

1864

Demonstration on the Rapidan River [February 1864]

- Morton's Ford (VA)

Kilpatrick-Dahlgren Raid [March 1864]

- Mantapike Hill [Walkerton] (VA)

Operations Against Plymouth [April-May 1864]

- Plymouth (NC)
- Albemarle Sound (NC)

Crook-Averell Raid on the Virginia & Tennessee Railroad [May 1864]

- Cloyd's Mountain (VA)
- Cove Mountain (VA)

Bermuda Hundred Campaign [May 1864]

- Port Walthall Junction (VA)
- Swift Creek (VA)
- Chester Station (VA)
- Proctor's Creek (VA)
- Ware Bottom Church (VA)

Grant's Overland Campaign [May-June 1864]

- Wilderness (VA)
- Spotsylvania Court House (VA)
- Yellow Tavern (VA)
- Wilson's Wharf (VA)
- Haw's Shop (VA)
- North Anna (VA)
- Totopotomy Creek/Bethesda Church (VA)
- Old Church (VA)
- Cold Harbor (VA)
- Trevilian Station (VA)
- Saint Mary's Church (VA)

Lynchburg Campaign [May-June 1864]

- New Market (VA)
- Piedmont (VA)
- Lynchburg (VA)

Early's Raid and Operations Against the B&O Railroad [June-August 1864]

- Monocacy (MD)
- Fort Stevens (DC)
- Cool Spring (VA)
- Rutherford's Farm (VA)
- Kernstown II (VA)
- Folck's Mill (MD)
- Moorefield (WV)

Richmond-Petersburg Campaign [June-December 1864]

- Petersburg I (VA)
- Petersburg II (VA)
- Jerusalem Plank Road (VA)
- Staunton River Bridge (VA)
- Sappony Church (VA)
- Ream's Station I (VA)

- Deep Bottom I (VA)
- Crater (VA)
- Deep Bottom II (VA)
- Globe Tavern (VA)
- Ream's Station II (VA)
- Chaffin's Farm and New Market Heights (VA)
- Peebles' Farm (VA)
- Darbytown and New Market Roads (VA)
- Darbytown Road (VA)
- Fair Oaks and Darbytown Road (VA)
- Boydton Plank Road (VA)

Sheridan's Valley Campaign [August-October 1864]

- Guard Hill (VA)
- Summit Point (WV)
- Smithfield Crossing (WV)
- Berryville (VA)
- Opequon (VA)
- Fisher's Hill (VA)
- Tom's Brook (VA)
- Cedar Creek (VA)

Expedition Against Fort Fisher [December 1864]

- Fort Fisher (NC)

1865

Operations Against Fort Fisher and Wilmington [January-February 1865]

- Fort Fisher (NC)
- Wilmington (NC)

Richmond-Petersburg Campaign Continued [January-March 1865]

- Hatcher's Run (VA)
- Fort Stedman (VA)

Sheridan's Expedition to Petersburg [March 1865]

- Waynesboro (VA)

Appomattox Campaign [March-April 1865]

- Lewis's Farm (VA)
- White Oak Road (VA)
- Dinwiddie Court House (VA)
- Five Forks (VA)
- Petersburg III (VA)
- Sutherland's Station (VA)
- Namozine Church (VA)
- Amelia Springs (VA)
- Sayler's Creek (VA)
- Rice's Station (VA)

- Cumberland Church (VA)
- High Bridge (VA)
- Appomattox Station (VA)
- Appomattox Court House (VA)

Lower Seaboard Theater and Gulf Approach

1861

Operations in Charleston Harbor [April 1861]

- Fort Sumter (SC)

Operations of the Gulf Blockading Squadron [October 1861]

- Santa Rosa Island (FL)

1862

Operations Against Fort Pulaski [April 1862]

- Fort Pulaski (GA)

Expedition to, and Capture of, New Orleans [April-May 1862]

- Forts Jackson & Phillip (LA)
- New Orleans (LA)

Operations Against Charleston [June 1862]

- Secessionville (SC)
- Simmon's Bluff (SC)

Operations Against Tampa [June-July 1862]

- Tampa (FL)

Operations Against Baton Rouge [July-August 1862]

- Baton Rouge (LA)
- Donaldsonville (LA)

Expedition to St. John's Bluff [September-October 1862]

- Saint John's Bluff (FL)

Operations in LaFourche District [October 1862]

- Georgia Landing (LA)

1863

Naval Attacks on Fort McAllister [March 1863]

- Fort McAllister (GA)

Operations in West Louisiana [April 1863]

- Fort Bisland (LA)
- Irish Bend (LA)
- Vermillion Bayou (LA)

Operations Against the Defenses of Charleston [April-September 1863]

- Charleston Harbor (SC)
- Fort Wagner (SC)
- Grimball's Landing (SC)
- Fort Wagner, Morris Island (SC)
- Fort Sumter (SC)
- Charleston Harbor (SC)

Siege of Port Hudson [May-July 1863]

- Plains Store (LA)
- Port Hudson (LA)

Taylor's Operations in West Louisiana [June-September 1863]

- LaFourche Crossing (LA)
- Donaldsonville (LA)
- Kock's Plantation (LA)
- Stirling's Plantation (LA)

Expedition to Hillsboro River [October 1863]

- Fort Brooke (FL)

1864

Florida Expedition [February 1864]

- Olustee (FL)

1865

Operations near Saint Mark's [March 1865]

- Natural Bridge (FL)

Main Western Theater

1861

Operations in Eastern Kentucky [September-December 1861]

- Barbourville (KY)
- Camp Wild Cat (KY)
- Ivy Mountain (KY)
- Rowlett's Station (KY)

Operations at the Ohio and Mississippi River Confluence [November 1861]

- Belmont (MO)

1862

Offensive in Eastern Kentucky [January 1862]

- Middle Creek (KY)
- Mill Springs (KY)

Federal Penetration up the Cumberland and Tennessee Rivers [February-June 1862]

- Fort Henry (TN)
- Fort Donelson (TN)
- Shiloh (TN)
- Corinth (MS)

Joint Operations Against New Madrid, Island No. 10, and Memphis [February-June 1862]

- New Madrid (MO)
- Island No. 10 (MO)
- Memphis (TN)

Confederate Heartland Offensive [June-October 1862]

- Chattanooga (TN)
- Murfreesborough (TN)
- Richmond (VA)
- Munfordville (KY)
- Perryville (KY)

Iuka and Corinth Operations [September-October 1862]

- Iuka (MS)
- Corinth (MS)
- Hatchie's Bridge (TN)

1863

Stones River Campaign [December 1862-January 1863]

- Hartsville (TN)
- Stones River (TN)

Forrest's Expedition into West Tennessee [December 1862-January 1863]

- Jackson (TN)
- Parker's Cross Roads (TN)

Operations Against Vicksburg [December 1862-January 1863]

- Chickasaw Bayou (MS)
- Arkansas Post (AR)

Grant's Operations Against Vicksburg [March-July 1863]

- Grand Gulf (MS)
- Snyder's Bluff (MS)
- Jackson (MS)
- Port Gibson (MS)
- Raymond (MS)
- Champion Hill (MS)
- Big Black River Bridge (MS)
- Vicksburg (MS)
- Milliken's Bend (LA)
- Goodrich's Landing (LA)
- Helena (AR)

Middle Tennessee Operations [February-April 1863]

- Dover (TN)
- Thompson's Station (TN)
- Vaught's Hill (TN)
- Brentwood (TN)
- Franklin (TN)

Streight's Raid in Alabama and Georgia [April 1863]

- Day's Gap (AL)

Tullahoma or Middle Tennessee Campaign [June 1863]

- Hoover's Gap (TN)

Morgan's Raid in Kentucky, Indiana, and Ohio [July 1863]

- Corydon (IN)
- Buffington Island (OH)
- Salineville (OH)

Chickamauga Campaign [August-September 1863]

- Chattanooga (TN)
- Davis' Cross-Roads (GA)
- Chickamauga (GA)

East Tennessee Campaign [September-October 1863]

- Blountsville (TN)
- Blue Springs (TN)

Reopening the Tennessee River [October 1863]

- Wauhatchie (TN)

Operations on the Memphis & Charleston Railroad [November 1863]

- Collierville (TN)

Chattanooga-Ringgold Campaign [November 1863]

- Chattanooga (TN)
- Ringgold Gap (GA)

Longstreet's Knoxville Campaign [November-December 1863]

- Campbell's Station (TN)
- Fort Sanders (TN)
- Bean's Station (TN)

Operations about Dandridge [December 1863-January 1864]

- Mossy Creek (TN)
- Dandridge (TN)
- Fair Garden (TN)

1864

Operations in North Alabama [January 1864]

- Athens (AL)

Meridian and Yazoo River Expeditions [February 1864]

- Meridian (MS)
- Okolona (MS)

Demonstration on Dalton [February 1864]

- Dalton I (GA)

Forrest's Expedition into West Tennessee and Kentucky [March-April 1864]

- Paducah (KY)
- Fort Pillow (TN)

Atlanta Campaign [May-September 1864]

- Rocky Face Ridge (GA)
- Resaca (GA)
- Adairsville (GA)
- New Hope Church (GA)
- Dallas (GA)
- Pickett's Mills (GA)
- Pine Mountain(GA)
- Gilgal Church (GA)
- Noonday Creek (GA)
- Kolb's Farm (GA)
- Kennesaw Mountain (GA)
- Ruff's Mill (GA)

© 2000 by The Center for Applied Research in Education

- Peachtree Creek (GA)
- Atlanta (GA)
- Ezra Church (GA)
- Utoy Creek (GA)
- Dalton II (GA)
- Lovejoy's Station (GA)
- Jonesborough (GA)

Morgan's Raid into Kentucky [June 1864]

- Cynthiana (KY)

Forrest's Defense of Mississippi [June-August 1864]

- Tupelo (MS)
- Brice's Cross Roads (MS)
- Memphis (TN)

Operations in Mobile Bay [August 1864]

- Mobile Bay (AL)

Franklin-Nashville Campaign [September-December 1864]

- Allatoona (GA)
- Decatur (AL)
- Johnsonville (TN)
- Columbia (TN)
- Spring Hill (TN)
- Franklin (TN)
- Murfreesborough (TN)
- Nashville (TN)

Burbridge's Raid into Southwest Virginia [October 1864]

- Saltville (VA)

Breckenridge's Advance into East Tennessee [November 1864]

- Bull's Gap (TN)

Savannah Campaign [November-December 1864]

- Griswoldville (GA)
- Buck Head Creek (GA)
- Honey Hill (SC)
- Waynesborough (GA)
- Fort McAllister (GA)

Stoneman's Raid into Southwest Virginia [December 1864]

- Marion (VA)
- Saltville (VA)

1865

Carolinas Campaign [February-March 1865]

- Rivers' Bridge (SC)
- Wyse Fork (NC)
- Monroe's Cross-Roads (NC)
- Averasborough (NC)
- Bentonville (NC)

Mobile Campaign [March-April 1865]

- Spanish Fort (AL)
- Fort Blakely (AL)

Wilson's Raid in Alabama and Georgia [April 1865]

- Selma (AL)

Trans-Mississippi Theater

1861

Operations to Control Missouri [June-October 1861]

- Booneville (MO)
- Carthage (MO)
- Wilson's Creek (MO)
- Dry Wood Creek (MO)
- Lexington (MO)
- Liberty or Blue Mills (MO)
- Fredericktown (MO)
- Springfield (MO)

Operations in the Indian Territory [November-December 1861]

- Round Mountain (OK)
- Chusto-Talasah (OK)
- Chustenahlah (OK)

Operations in Northeast Missouri [December 1861]

- Mount Zion Church (MO)
- Roan's Tan Yard (MO)

1862

Sibley's New Mexico Campaign [February-March 1862]

- Valverde (NM)
- Glorieta Pass (NM)

Pea Ridge Campaign [March 1862]

- Pea Ridge (AR)

Operations on the White River [June 1862]

- Saint Charles (AR)

Operations near Cache River, Arkansas [July 1862]

- Hill's Plantation (AR)

Operations North of Boston Mountains [August-November 1862]

- Clark's Mill (MO)
- Kirksville (MO)
- Independence (MO)
- Lone Jack (MO)
- Newtonia (MO)
- Old Fort Wayne (OK)

Operations to Suppress the Sioux Uprising [August-September 1862]

- Fort Ridgely (MN)
- Wood Lake (MN)

Operations to Blockade the Texas Coast [September 1862-January 1863]

- Sabine Pass (TX)
- Galveston (TX)

Prairie Grove Campaign [November 1862]

- Canehill (AR)
- Prairie Grove (AR)

Operations Against Galveston [December 1862-January 1863]

- Galveston (TX)

1863

Marmaduke's First Expedition into Missouri [January 1863]

- Springfield (MO)
- Hartville (MO)

Marmaduke's Second Expedition into Missouri [April-May 1863]

- Cape Girardeau (MO)
- Chalk Bluff (AR)

Operations to Control Indian Territory [June-September 1863]

- Cabin Creek (OK)
- Honey Springs (OK)
- Devil's Backbone (AR)

Operations Against the Sioux in North Dakota [July 1863]

- Big Mound (ND)
- Dead Buffalo Lake (ND)
- Stony Lake (ND)
- Whitestone Hill (ND)

Quantrill's Raid into Kansas [August 1863]

- Lawrence (KS)

Operations to Blockade the Texas Coast [September 1863)

- Sabine Pass II (TX)

Advance on Little Rock [September-October 1863]

- Bayou Fourche or Little Rock (AR)
- Pine Bluff (AR)

Occupation of Indian Territory North of the Arkansas River [October 1863]

- Baxter Springs (KS)

1864

Red River Campaign [March-April 1864]

- Fort De Russy (LA)
- Mansfield (LA)
- Pleasant Hill (LA)
- Blair's Landing (LA)
- Monett's Ferry (LA)
- Mansura (LA)
- Yellow Bayou (LA)

Camden Expedition [April 1864]

- Elkin's Ferry (AR)
- Prairie D'Ane (AR)
- Poison Spring (AR)
- Marks' Mills (AR)
- Jenkins' Ferry (AR)

Expedition to Lake Village [June 1864]

- Old River Lake (AR)

Sully's Expedition Against the Sioux in Dakota Territory [July 1864]

- Killdeer Mountain (ND)

Price's Missouri Expedition [September-October 1864]

- Fort Davidson (MO)
- Glasgow (MO)

- Lexington (MO)
- Little Blue River (MO)
- Independence (MO)
- Byram's Ford (MO)
- Westport (MO)
- Marais des Cygnes (KS)
- Marmiton River (MO)
- Mine Creek (KS)
- Newtonia (MO)

Sand Creek Campaign [November 1864]

- Sand Creek (CO)

1865

Expedition from Brazos Santiago [May 1865]

- Palmeto Ranch (TX)

9.13 Chronology of the Spanish-American War, 1895-1899

February 24, 1895	Second Cuban revolution starts. For the second time, Cuba attempts to overthrow Spanish colonial control. American investments in Cuba suffer; destruction of sugar and tobacco crops reduce trade between U.S. and Cuba.
February 16, 1896	Spain defeats Cuban revolutionaries. Most are herded off to concentration camps.
April 7, 1896	Cleveland administration attempts to start talks between the Cuban rebels and the Spanish, but resists pressure for direct intervention.
August 26, 1896	The Philippines rebel against Spain.
March 4, 1897	President William McKinley is inaugurated for the first of two terms. McKinley had promised in his campaign that he would protect American business and free the Cuban people.
April 6, 1897	Theodore Roosevelt is appointed as Secretary of the Navy.
June 30, 1897	U.S. Navy prepares for a war with Spain.
December 6, 1897	President McKinley formally denounces the Spanish policy of concentration camps and threatens he will "intervene with force."
January 1, 1898	Cuba is granted limited autonomy under Spanish rule.
January 12, 1898	Pro-Spanish militants riot in Havana protesting autonomy.
January 25, 1898	U.S.S. *Maine* arrives in Havana.
February 9, 1898	Spanish ambassador de Lome writes critical letter to McKinley. The letter is published in newspapers and the ambassador resigns.
February 15, 1898	U.S.S. *Maine* explodes in Havana, killing 268 Americans. Anti-Spanish and pro-war sentiment spreads throughout the U.S. Popular press calls for war and speculates about a Spanish plot.
April 11, 1898	McKinley asks Congress for power to use the military to end Spanish presence in Cuba.
April 19, 1898	Congress recognizes independence of Cuba.
April 21, 1898	U.S. Navy begins blockade of Cuba.
April 23, 1898	Spain declares war on the U.S.
May 1, 1898	The U.S. Asiatic Squadron under the command of Admiral George Dewey defeats the Spanish fleet in Manila and blockades the city.
June 22, 1898	First Americans land in Cuba near Santiago, led by Theodore Roosevelt.
June 24, 1898	Battle of Las Guásimas; U.S. victorious.
July 1, 1898	Battles of San Juan Hill and El Caney; Santiago is captured.
July 3, 1898	Spanish fleet under the command of Admiral Cervera tries to break through the American blockade and is destroyed.
July 17, 1898	General Toro officially surrenders Santiago.

July 25, 1898	General Miles invades Puerto Rico, gaining complete control of the island two weeks later.
August 12, 1898	Preliminary protocols of peace are signed in Madrid. Fighting ends.
August 13, 1898	Admiral Dewey and General Wesley Merrit attack Manila and capture the city. Spanish surrender the Philippines.
December 10, 1898	Treaty of Paris is signed, ending the war. Spain cedes Puerto Rico and Guam to the U.S., sells the Philippines to the U.S. for $20 million and grants sovereignty to Cuba.
April 1, 1899	Treaty of Peace is signed by Spain and U.S.

Outcome of war:

—385 American battle deaths; several thousand deaths from disease
—Total cost: $250,000,000
—U.S. acquired Puerto Rico, Guam, Philippine Islands (100,000 sq. miles, 10 million people) for $20 million
—Teller Amendment pledged that U.S. would guarantee self-rule to Cubans
—U.S. becomes major player in international affairs, particularly in the Caribbean and the Far East

9.14   Indian Wars of 1854-1900

The Sioux Wars (1854-90)

Minnesota 1862: Hundreds of settlers massacred in Sioux uprising.
Wyoming 1868: Red Cloud forces government to give up three forts.
Montana 1876: Crazy Horse defeats Crook at battle of Rosebud.
S. Dakota 1876: Crazy Horse and Sitting Bull defeat Custer at battle of Little Bighorn.
N. Dakota 1890: Soldiers massacre 153 Sioux, battle of Wounded Knee.

The Southern Plains (1860-79)

Colorado 1864: Sand Creek Massacre: U.S. army kills peaceful Cheyenne and Arapaho.
Missouri 1874: Red River War: General Sheridan wins campaign after 14 battles.

The Nez Perce War (1877)

Montana 1877: Chief Joseph leads his people in 800 mi. (500 km) retreat while trying to reach Canada.

Navaho Conflicts (1846-64)

Arizona 1863-64: Navaho defeated by troops led by Kit Carson.

Apache Warfare (1861-1900)

Arizona 1886: Apache chief Geronimo leads one of last major uprisings against U.S. government.

9.15 Important American Indian Chiefs and Leaders

American Horse (Sioux)

Black Elk (Lakota)

Big Bear (Cree)

Bigfoot (Lakota)

Abel Bosum (Cree)

Joseph Brant (Mohawk)

Cochise (Apache)

Choncape

Chou-man-i-case

Corn Planter

Crazy Horse/Tashunkewitko (Lakota)

Dan George

Dull Knife (Cheyenne)

Eagle of Delight

Frank Fools Crow

Gall (Hunkpapa Sioux)

Geronimo/Goyathlay (Apache)

He-Dog

Little Wolf (Lakota)

Hole-in-the-Day (Ojibway)

John Ross (Cherokee)

Joseph (Nez Perce)

Keokuk

Little Crow (Kaposia Sioux)

Little Turtle (Miami)

Little Wolf (Cheyenne)

Low-Dog (Lakota)

Mougo

Ohiyesa/Dr. Charles Alexander Eastman (Santee Sioux)

Pontiac (Ottawa)

Pope (Tewa)

Potalesharo

Quanah Parker (Comanche)

Rain-in-the-Face (Sioux)

Red Cloud (Lakota)

Red Jacket (Seneca)

Roman Nose (Cheyenne)

Santana (Kiowa)

Sequoya (Cherokee)

Sitting Bull (Hunkpapa Sioux)

Spotted Tail (Brule Sioux)

Standing Bear (Lakota)

Tamahay (Sioux)

Tecumseh (Shawnee)

Two Strike/Tashunkekokipapi (Sioux)

Washakie (Shoshoni)

Wicked Chief

Wolf Robe (Cheyenne)

Wovoka (Paiute)

9.16 Famous Americans on the Western Frontier

Martha Jane Canary (Calamity Jane) (1852-1903)—She was a good shot, often dressed as a man, and drove wagon teams for the Union Pacific Railroad. Romantically linked to Wild Bill Hickok and buried next to him in Deadwood, Arizona.

Christopher (Kit) Carson (1809-1868)—Fur trapper, explorer, scout, and Indian fighter.

Cochise (c. 1800-1874)—Renegade chief of the Chiricahua Apaches who led his warriors in raids on settlers and miners throughout Arizona.

William F. Cody (Buffalo Bill) (1846-1917)—Pony Express rider and army scout. In 1883, he began his famous Wild West Show.

Samuel Colt (1814-1862)—Designed a new, more reliable six-shooter by adapting the trigger and hammer action of the old five-shot revolver. His .45 "Peacemaker" was one of the most widely used guns in the West.

Crazy Horse (Tashunka Witco) (1842-1877)—One of the most aggressive Dakota chiefs, he fought at Rosebud and Little Big Horn.

John Deere (1804-1886)—Inventor of the self-polishing steel plow, used by the settlers on the plains. Founder of Deere & Co., a farm machinery company still operating today.

Wyatt Earp (1848-1929)—Lawman in Wichita, Dodge City, and Tombstone.

Captain John Charles Fremont (1813-1890)—Early explorer of the West, nicknamed "Great Pathfinder." Kit Carson was his guide.

Pat F. Garrett (1850-1908)—Former buffalo hunter and cowboy, he was Sheriff of Lincoln County when he killed Billy the Kid.

Geronimo (Goyathly) (1829-1909)—Chiricahua Apache who led his people against both Mexicans and Americans. He finally surrendered.

Sam Houston (1793-1863)—Led the Texans at San Jacinto in the military drive to gain Texan independence from Mexico. First president of the Republic of Texas.

Chief Joseph (1840-1904)—Chief of the Nez Perces, pursued by the U.S. Army in a three-month battle.

James W. Marshall (1810-1885)—At Sutter's Mill, California, Marshall discovered gold, setting off the Gold Rush of 1849.

William Barclay (Bat) Masterson (1853-1921)—Canadian lawman and gambler who became Dodge City marshal.

Annie Oakley (1860-1926)—Rider in Buffalo Bill's Wild West Show; known as top marksman.

Isaac Parker (1838-1896)—An Arizona judge whose handling of outlaws soon earned him the nickname of the "Hanging Judge."

Red Cloud (1822-1909)—Dakota chief who successfully defended his land and became leader of the reservation Indians.

Sacajawea (1787-1812)—A Shoshono Indian who was a guide and interpreter for Lewis and Clark,1804-1806.

William Techumseh Sherman (1820-1891)—Union general in charge of the U.S. army between 1869 and 1884; led U.S. soldiers in many of the Indian wars.

William Matthew Tilghman (1854-1924)—Buffalo hunter and crack shot who became Dodge City's first marshal.

Brigham Young (1801-1877)—Religious leader who led the Mormons from Nauvoo, Illinois, where they were being persecuted for their beliefs, to Utah to settle on the shores of the Great Salt Lake.

9.17 Major Weapons, 1750-1999

1750-1800
Flintlock musket
Rifle
Light guns
408012 pounder guns
6-Inch howitzers
M1857 gun howitzer (the "Napolean")
Descendant of Gribeaval's 12-pounder
Artillery shell—Henry Shrapnel
Muskets with interchangeable parts—first mass
    production of weapons—Eli Whitney
Military observation balloon

1800-1850
Percussion cap pistol—led to invention of rifle
Minie bullet
Muzzle loading rifle
Rocket—Sir William Congreve

1850-1900
Breech loading artillery pieces
Anti-personnel projectiles—armor-piercing
Explosive shells replace shot
Smoothbore cannon replaces rifled gun
Disappearing gun—on ships
Repeating magazine rifle replaces single shot
    muzzle loader
Elongated conical bullet replaces Minie bullet
Machine gun
Field mines and booby traps (Civil War)
Submarine mines (Civil War)
Battleship
Torpedo—boat destroyer
Advanced explosives

1900-1925—World War I
Machine gun
Modern artillery piece
Barbed wire
Tank
Poison gas
Airplane
Paris gun
Long-range gun (German)

1925-1945—World War II
Proximity fuse
Shaped charges
Bazookas
Recoilless rifles
Rockets (return from a century of non-use)
Tanks
Tank destroyers
Cross-country vehicles
8-mm antiaircraft gun (German)
Landing Ship Tank (LST)
Landing Ship Infantry (LSI)
Bomber and torpedo aircraft
Warship
Submarine
Radar/Sonar
Bomb sight with superior accuracy

1945-Present
Nuclear or high-explosive warheads
Intercontinental Ballistic Missiles (ICBMs)
    with worldwide range
Submarine-Launched Ballistic Missiles (SLBMs)
Multiple Independently Targetable Reentry
    Vehicles (MIRVs)
Rocket missiles—surface-to-surface, surface-to-air,
    air-to-surface, air-to-air
Chemical and biological, radiological weapons
Helicopter
Tank
Nuclear-powered submarine—Polaris-type
    missiles, tube artillery
Delivery systems, nuclear warheads

Source: *Encyclopedia of Military History from 3500 BC to Present.*

SECTION 10

Conflicts of the 20th Century

10.1   Commissioned Ranks in the U.S. Military

Army	Navy	Air Force
General of the Army	Fleet Admiral	General of the Air Force
General	Admiral	Lieutenant General
Lieutenant General	Vice Admiral	Major General
Major General	Rear Admiral	Brigadier General
Brigadier General	Commodore	Colonel
Colonel	Captain	Lieutenant Colonel
Lieutenant Colonel	Commander	Major
Major	Lieutenant Commander	Captain
Captain	Lieutenant	First Lieutenant
First Lieutenant	Lieutenant Junior Grade	Second Lieutenant
Second Lieutenant	Acting Sub Lieutenant	

10.2   Elements of the Armed Forces

Armies: The largest operational unit consisting of two or more corps and usually commanded by full general, general, or major general. In the Civil War, union armies might contain over one hundred thousand men. Confederate armies were generally considerably smaller. In the Revolutionary War, Washington's army often had less than ten thousand men.

Battalion: Five hundred men from two or more companies commanded by a lieutenant colonel. Battalions were common in the Revolution but not in the Civil War.

Brigade: Two thousand men from two or more regiments and commanded by a brigadier general.

Company: Formed from a number of platoons to give strength of one hundred men. Commanded by a captain.

Corps: Two or more divisions commanded by a major general in the Union army; often a lieutenant general in the Confederate army. Corps strength was around ten thousand. In the Confederate army, the corps as well as divisions and brigades were often named after their commander but in the Union army they were designated by numerals.

Detachment: A relatively small body of soldiers, usually commanded by an officer, sent on a specific assignment.

Division: The smallest unit capable of independent operation; included infantry and/or cavalry supported by artillery, engineers, and medical. Commanded by a major general; divisional strength in the Civil War was usually between six and nine thousand men. In the Revolution it was often as few as one or two thousand.

Platoon: About forty soldiers commanded by a lieutenant.

Regiment: Composed of a number of companies to give it a strength of around one thousand. Commanded by a lieutenant colonel or full colonel.

Squad: Generally less than ten solders; commanded by a sergeant.

Source: Hubbard Cobb, *American Battlefields.* New York: Macmillan, Inc., 1995.

10.3   America's Relative Economic Position on the Eve of World War I

National income, population, and per capita income of the major powers in 1914.

	National Income	Population	Per Capita Income
United States	$37 billion	98 million	$377
Britain	11	45	244
France	6	39	153
Japan	2	55	36
Germany	12	65	184
Italy	4	37	108
Russia	7	171	41
Austria-Hungary	3	52	57

Source: Paul Kennedy, *The Rise and Fall of the Great Powers.* New York: Random House, 1987.

10.4   Warring Nations of World War I

Dates indicate when nation entered the war.

Allies

Belgium (Aug. 4, 1914)
Brazil (Oct. 26, 1917)
British Empire (Aug. 4. 1914)
China (Aug. 14, 1917)
Costa Rica (May 23, 1918)
Cuba (April 7, 1917)
France (Aug. 3, 1914)
Greece (July 2, 1917)
Guatemala (April 23, 1918)
Haiti (July 12, 1918)
Honduras (July 19, 1918)
Italy (May 23, 1915)
Japan (Aug. 23, 1914)
Liberia (Aug. 4, 1917)
Montenegro (Aug. 5, 1914)
Nicaragua (May 8, 1918)
Panama (April 7, 1917)
Portugal (March 9, 1916)
Russia (Aug. 1, 1914)
San Marino (June 3, 1915)
Serbia (July 28, 1914)
Siam (July 22, 1917)
United States (April 6, 1917)

Central Powers

Austria-Hungary (July 28, 1914)
Bulgaria (Oct. 14, 1915)
Germany (Aug. 1, 1914)
Ottoman Empire (Oct. 31, 1914)

10.5   Major Events of World War I

1914

June 28	Archduke Francis Ferdinand was assassinated in Bosnia by Serbian nationalists.
July 28	Austria-Hungary declared war on Serbia. Several other declarations of war followed during the next week.
Aug. 4	Germany invaded Belgium and started the fighting.
Aug. 10	Austria-Hungary invaded Russia, opening the fighting on the Eastern Front.
Aug. 23	Japan declares war on Germany.
Sept. 6-9	The Allies stopped the Germans in France in the First Battle of the Marne.
Oct. 10	Germans capture Antwerp.
Dec. 6	Germans advance through Poland.
Dec. 18	British declare protectorate over Egypt and move in to protect Suez Canal.

1915

Feb. 18	Germany began to blockade Great Britain.
April 25	Allied troops landed on the Gallipoli Peninsula.
May 7	A German submarine sank the liner *Lusitania*; 1,195 are killed.
May 23	Italy declared war on Austria-Hungary, and an Italian Front soon developed.
Aug. 4	Germany begins second major offensive on Eastern Front, capturing nearly all of Poland, Lithuania, and Kurland.

1916

Feb. 21	The Germans opened the Battle of Verdun.
May 31-June 1	The British fleet fought the German fleet in the Battle of Jutland.
July 1	The Allies launched the Battle of the Somme.
Nov. 28	German airplane raids on Britain launched.

1917

Feb. 1	Germany resumed unrestricted submarine warfare.
April 6	The United States declared war on Germany after Germany announces it will attack merchant ships.
June 24	American troops began landing in France under General John J. Pershing.
July 6	Col. T. E. Lawrence inspires Arab revolt against Turkish occupation.
Dec. 15	Russia signed an armistice with Germany, ending the fighting on the Eastern Front.

1918

Jan. 8	President Woodrow Wilson announced his Fourteen Points as the basis for peace.
March 3	Russia signed the Treaty of Brest-Litovsk.
March 21	Germany launched the first of its final three offensives on the Western Front.
July 15	French turn back German troops at Marne in a decisive battle.
Sept. 18	Final British offensive in Palestine; British and their Arab allies capture Damascus and Beirut.
Sept. 26	The Allies began their final offensive on the Western Front.
Nov. 11	Germany signed an armistice ending World War I.

10.6   Major Battles of World War I

Western Front

1st Battle of the Marne—September 1914
Battles of Ypres—October-November 1914, April 1915
Battle of Verdun—February-July 1916
Battle of the Somme—July-November 1916
Vimy Ridge—April 1917
Hindenburg Line—April 1917
Nivelle's Offensive—April-May 1917
Passchendaele—July-November 1917

Italian Front

Trentino Offensive—May 1915
Eleven Battles of the Isonzo—June 1915-September 1917
Asiago Offensive—May 1916
Caporetto—October 1917
Piave River—June 1918
Vittorio Veneto—October 1918
Seizure of Trieste—November 3, 1918

Eastern Front

Tannenburg—August 1914
Invasion of East Prussia—August-September 1914
Invasion of Galicia—August-September 1914
Masurian Lakes—September 1914
Invasion of Serbia—August 1914-September 1915
Lodz—November 1914
Central Powers breakthrough—May-September 1915
Invasion of Russia—May-September 1915
Russian Offensive—June 1916
Invasion of Romania—September 1916-January 1917

10.7   Major Weapons of World War I

Tanks

The British designed these machines during World War I to rip through barbed wire and cross trenches. Crews inside gunned down enemy troops.

Airplanes

First used in combat during World War I.

Machine Guns

The gun's rapid fire slaughtered attacking infantrymen, making World War I more deadly than earlier wars.

Poison Gas

British develop gas and deploy it against German troops.

Submarines

Firing torpedoes that struck surface ships and then exploded, the submarine proved its value as a warship during World War I. German subs challenged the great power of the British Navy.

10.8   Military Casualties in World War I, 1914-1918

The Allies	Dead	Wounded
Belgium	14,000	44,700
British Empire	908,400	2,090,200
France	1,385,000+	4,266,000
Greece	5,000	21,000
Italy	650,000	947,000
Portugal	7,200	13,800
Romania	335,700+	120,000
Russia	1,700,000	4,950,000
Serbia & Montenegro	48,000	143,000
United States	116,516#	234,428#

The Central Powers		
Austria-Hungary	1,200,000	3,620,000
Bulgaria	87,500	152,400
Germany	1,773,000	4,216,000
Ottoman Empire	325,000	400,000

Note: Except for the United States, all figures are approximate.
+Includes missing.
#Official U.S. government figure.

10.9   Warring Nations of World War II

Dates indicate when country entered war.

The Allies

Argentina (March 27, 1945)
Australia (Sept. 3, 1939)
Belgium (May 10, 1940)
Bolivia (April 7, 1943)
Brazil (Aug. 22, 1942)
Canada (Sept. 10, 1939)
Chile (Feb. 14, 1945)
China (Dec. 9, 1941)
Columbia (Nov. 26, 1943)
Costa Rica (Dec. 8, 1941)
Cuba (Dec. 9, 1941)
Czechoslovakia (Dec. 16, 1941)
Denmark (April 9, 1940)
Dominican Republic (Dec. 8, 1941)
Ecuador (Feb. 2, 1945)
Egypt (Feb. 24, 1945)
El Salvador (Dec. 8, 1941)
Ethiopia (Dec. 1, 1942)
France (Sept. 3, 1939)
Great Britain (Sept. 3, 1939)
Greece (Oct. 28, 1940)
Guatemala (Dec. 9, 1941)
Haiti (Dec. 8, 1941)
Honduras (Dec. 8, 1941)
India (Sept. 3, 1939)
Iran (Sept. 9, 1943)
Iraq (Jan. 16, 1943)
Lebanon (Feb. 27, 1945)
Liberia (Jan. 26, 1944)
Luxembourg (May 10, 1940)

Mexico (May 22, 1942)
Mongolian People's Republic (Aug. 9, 1945)
Netherlands (May 10, 1940)
New Zealand (Sept. 3, 1939)
Nicaragua (Dec. 8, 1941)
Norway (April 9, 1940)
Panama (Dec. 7, 1941)
Paraguay (Feb. 8, 1945)
Peru (Feb. 11, 1945)
Poland (Sept. 1, 1939)
San Marino (Sept. 24, 1944)
Saudi Arabia (March 1, 1945)
South Africa (Sept. 6, 1939)
Soviet Union (June 22, 1941)
Syria (Feb. 26, 1945)
Turkey (Feb. 23, 1945)
United States (Dec. 8, 1941)
Uruguay (Feb. 22, 1945)
Venezuela (Feb. 16, 1945)
Yugoslavia (April 6, 1941)

The Axis

Albania (June 15, 1940)
Bulgaria (April 6, 1941)
Finland (June 25, 1941)
Germany (Sept. 1, 1939)
Hungary (April 10, 1941)
Italy (June 10, 1940)
Japan (Dec. 7, 1941)
Romania (June 22, 1941)
Thailand (Jan. 25, 1942)

10.10   Major Events of World War II

© 2000 by The Center for Applied Research in Education

1939

Sept. 1	Germany invaded Poland, starting World War II.
Sept. 3	Britain and France declared war on Germany.
Sept. 15	Japan and USSR signed nonaggression pact.
Sept. 17	Soviets, allied with Germany, invade Poland from East.
Nov. 10	U.S. begins supplying arms to Britain and France on cash-and-carry basis.

1940

April 9	Germany invaded Denmark and Norway.
May 10	Germany invaded Belgium and the Netherlands.
June 10	Italy declared war on France and Great Britain.
June 22	France signed an armistice with Germany.
July 10	Battle of Britain began.
Sept. 2	Japanese occupy French Indochina.
Oct. 28	Italy invaded Greece.

1941

Mar. 11	Lend-Lease Act signed, providing critical supplies to Britain.
April 6	Germany invaded Greece and Yugoslavia.
June 22	Germany invaded the Soviet Union.
Sept. 8	German troops completed the blockade of Leningrad, lasting until January 1944.
Dec. 7	Japan bombed U.S. military bases at Pearl Harbor, Hawaii.
Dec. 8	The United States, Great Britain, and Canada declared war on Japan.

1942

Feb. 15	Singapore fell to the Japanese.
Feb. 26-28	Japan defeated an Allied naval force in the Battle of the Java Sea.
April 9	U.S. and Philippine troops on Bataan Peninsula surrendered.
April 18	U.S. Bombers hit Tokyo in the Doolittle raid.
May 4-8	The Allies checked a Japanese assault in the Battle of the Coral Sea.
May 26	USSR joins Allies after being invaded by Germany.
June 4-6	The Allies defeated Japan in the Battle of Midway.
Aug. 7	U.S. Marines landed on Guadalcanal.
Aug. 25	Hitler ordered his forces to capture Stalingrad.
Oct. 23	Britain attacked the Axis at El Alamein in Egypt.
Nov. 8	Allied troops landed in Algeria and Morocco.

1943

Feb. 2	The last Germans surrendered at Stalingrad.
May 13	Axis forces in Northern Africa surrendered.
July 4	Germany opened an assault near the Soviet city of Kursk.
July 10	Allied forces invaded Sicily.
Sept. 3	Italy secretly surrendered to the Allies.
Sept. 9	Allied troops landed at Salerno, Italy.
Nov. 20	U.S. forces invaded Tarawa.

1944

June 6	Allied troops landed in Normandy in the D-Day invasion of northern France, an effort to re-take continental Europe.
June 19-20	A U.S. naval force defeated the Japanese in the Battle of the Philippine Sea.
July 18	Japan's Prime Minister Tojo resigned.
July 20	A plot to assassinate Hitler failed.
Oct. 20	The Allies began landing in the Philippines.
Oct. 23-26	The Allies defeated Japan's navy in the Battle of Gulf in the Philippines.
Dec. 16	The Germans struck back at U.S. troops in the Battle of the Bulge.

1945

March 16	U.S. Marines captured Iwo Jima.
April 30	Hitler killed himself in Berlin.
May 7	Germany surrendered unconditionally to the Allies in Reims, France, ending World War II in Europe.
June 21	Allied forces captured Okinawa.
Aug. 6	U.S. drops atomic bomb on Hiroshima.
Aug. 8	The Soviet Union declared war on Japan.
Aug. 9	U.S. drops atomic bomb on Nagasaki.
Aug. 14	Japan agreed to surrender unconditionally.
Sept. 2	Japan signed surrender terms aboard the battleship U.S.S. Missouri in Tokyo Bay.

10.11   Major Battles of World War II

Europe and North Africa

Battle of Britain—July 1940-May 1941
El Alamein—July-October 1941
Kasserine Pass—February 1943
Kursk—July 1943
Invasion of Sicily—July-August 1943
Salerno—September 1943
Cassino—November 1943
Anzio—January 1944
Invasion of Normandy—June 6, 1944
Battle of the Bulge—December 1944

Asia and the Pacific

Pearl Harbor—December 7, 1941
Bataan—December 1941-April 1942
Java Sea—February 1942
Doolittle Raid—April 1942
Coral Sea—May 1942
Battle of Midway—June 1942
Guadalcanal—August 1942-February 1943
Tarawa—November 1943
Kwajalein—January-February 1944
Enewetak—February 1944
Bouganville—March 1944
Saipan—June 1944
Philippine Sea—June 1944
Guam—July-August 1944
Peleliu—September 1944
Leyte Gulf—October 1944
Iwo Jima—February-March 1945
Okinawa—April-June 1945

10.12   World War II U.S. Military Leaders

Henry H. Arnold (1886-1950) Five-Star General; Chief of the U.S. Army Air Forces; Joint Chief of Staff; commanded new 20th Air Force bombing of Japan.

Omar N. Bradley (1893-1991) U.S. Army General; invasion of North Africa; capture of Sicily; Normandy Invasion; Liberation of Paris; commanded 12th Army Group (1 million men).

Claire L. Chennault (1890-1958) Major General U.S. Army; Air Forces; led Flying Tigers.

Mark W. Clark (1896-1984) General U.S. Army; Chief of Staff; Allied Commander in Italy.

James Doolittle (1896-1993) General U.S. Army Air Corps; Commanded U.S. Air Forces in North Africa and Europe; led first bombing raid over Tokyo.

Dwight D. Eisenhower (1890-1969) General U.S. Army; Supreme Commander Western Allied Forces; Chief of Staff, U.S. Army.

William F. Halsey (1882-1959) Fleet Admiral U.S. Navy; successful campaigns in Pacific theater; Solomon Islands; commanded U.S. Third Fleet in defeat of Japanese fleet.

Oveta C. Hobby (1905-1995) Organized and directed Women's Auxiliary Army Corps; first woman to receive Distinguished Service Medal.

Curtis E. Lemay (1906-1990) Four-Star General U.S. Army; Bomber Commander in Europe and India; Architect of U.S. strategic air power after WW II.

Douglas MacArthur (1880-1964) Five-Star General U.S. Army; Commander of all U.S. Army forces in Pacific; Medal of Honor recipient; accepted surrender of Japanese aboard USS *Missouri*.

George C. Marshall (1880-1959) General U.S. Army; Chief of Staff.

Chester W. Nimitz (1885-1966) Fleet Admiral U.S. Navy; planned naval war against Japan; led all major naval battles of the war; signer of Japanese surrender.

George S. Patton (1885-1945) General U.S. Army; leader of Normandy Invasion, Battle of the Bulge.

Matthew B. Ridgway (1895-1993) General U.S. Air Force; Commander 82nd Airborne Division; planned and led first major airborne attack in American military history (Sicily).

Franklin D. Roosevelt (1882-1945) U.S. President and Commander in Chief; with Winston Churchill, personally determined Allied military and naval strategy in the West.

Carl Spaatz (1891-1974) First Chief of Staff of the newly formed U.S. Air Force; commanded 8th Air Force in England; conquest of Tunisia; invasion of Sicily; led U.S. Strategic Air Forces' final assault on Germany; went to Pacific to bomb Japan.

Raymond A. Spruance (1886-1969) Admiral U.S. Navy; Battle of Midway; Commander of Pacific fleet after Nimitz.

Joseph W. Stilwell (1883-1946) General U.S. Army; Chief of Staff for Generalissimo Chiang-Kai-shek; Commander of U.S. troops in China, Burma, India theater.

Maxwell D. Taylor (1901-1987) General U.S. Army Airborne; helped organize 82nd Division (first U.S. airborne division), infiltrated Axis lines to confer with Italian officials before Allied invasion; commanded 101st Airborne Division.

Jonathan M. Wainwright (1883-1953) General U.S. Army; took command of forces in Philippines from MacArthur; Japanese POW; Medal of Honor recipient upon return.

10.13   Major Weapons of World War II

Atomic Bomb
Based on atomic fission, the atom bomb developed by the U.S. brought about a quick Japanese surrender in the final year of the war.

Spitfire
Fast and agile British fighter plane that could outmaneuver most German planes. In 1940, Spitfires helped defeat Germany in the Battle of Britain.

B-17
Widely used U.S. bombers famous for daytime raids over Germany. Called the flying fortresses because of their heavy armor and many guns. German planes were no longer a threat after 1944.

DUKW
Nicknamed "Duck," it was an American six-wheeled truck that traveled over water and land, carrying men and supplies from transport ships to enemy shores in amphibious landings. First used in the invasion of Sicily in July 1943 and later in amphibious operations in the Pacific.

Tanks
Used primarily by Germany, the tank played a key role in combat. Germany, whose Panzer tanks could out-gun almost all Allied tanks, took advantage of their mobility and firepower, often massing the tanks and smashing through enemy battle lines in surprise attacks.

Aircraft Carriers
A floating airfield that became the backbone of the U.S. Navy during the war. Carrier-based planes took part in many Pacific battles and helped defeat Japan. Sometimes the carriers would have irregular patterns painted on them to make it hard for enemy submarines to determine the ship's course.

10.14   World War II Casualties

Country	Wartime Pop.	Forces Peak	Forces Killed/ Missing	Forces Wounded	Civilians Killed/Missing
U.S.A.	132m	16.4m	292,000	675,000	N.A.
Australia	7.1m	680,000	34,000	181,000	100
Belgium	8.1m	800,000	10,000	15,000	90,000
Canada	11.4m	780,000	43,000	53,000	N.A.
China	541m	5m	1.5m	2m	20m
France	41.9m	5m	245,000	390,000	173,000
Germany*	79.4m	10m	3.5m	2m	2m
India	388.8m	2.4m	48,000	65,000	N.A.
Italy**	45.4m	4.5m	380,000	225,000	180,000
Japan**	73.1m	6m	2.6m	326,000	953,000
Netherlands	9m	500,000	14,000	2,000	242,000
Poland	35m	1m	600,000	530,000	6m
Romania	20m	600,000	73,000	49,000	465,000
U.K.***	47.8m	4.7m	420,000	377,000	70,000
U.S.S.R.	193m	20m	13.6m	5m	7.7m
Yugoslavia	16.3m	3.7m	305,000	425,000	1.4m

  * Figures include Austria.
  ** Figures include colonies and mandated territories.
 *** Figures for killed and wounded include colonies other than India.
N.A. = not available.

10.15   Atlantic Charter, 1941

August 14, 1941

The President of the United States of America and the Prime Minister, Mr. Churchill, representing His Majesty's Government in the United Kingdom, being met together, deem it right to make known certain common principles in the national policies of their respective countries on which they base their hopes for a better future for the world.

First, their countries seek no aggrandizement, territorial or other;

Second, they desire to see no territorial changes that do not accord with the freely expressed wishes of the peoples concerned;

Third, they respect the right of all peoples to choose the form of government under which they will live; and they wish to see sovereign rights and self government restored to those who have been forcibly deprived of them;

Fourth, they will endeavor, with due respect for their existing obligations, to further the enjoyment by all States, great or small, victor or vanquished, of access, on equal terms, to the trade and to the raw materials of the world which are needed for their economic prosperity;

Fifth, they desire to bring about the fullest collaboration between all nations in the economic field with the object of securing, for all, improved labor standards, economic advancement and Social Security;

Sixth, after the final destruction of the Nazi tyranny, they hope to see established a peace which will afford to all nations the means of dwelling in safety within their own boundaries, and which will afford assurance that all the men in all lands may live out their lives in freedom from fear and want;

Seventh, such a peace should enable all men to traverse the high seas and oceans without hindrance;

Eighth, they believe that all of the nations of the world, for realistic as well as spiritual reasons must come to the abandonment of the use of force. Since no future peace can be maintained if land, sea or air armaments continue to be employed by nations which threaten, or may threaten, aggression outside of their frontiers, they believe, pending the establishment of a wider and permanent system of general security, that the disarmament of such nations is essential. They will likewise aid and encourage all other practicable measure which will lighten for peace-loving peoples the crushing burden of armaments.

Franklin D. Roosevelt
Winston S. Churchill

10.16 Franklin D. Roosevelt's Address to the Nation, 1941

Radio address by President Franklin D. Roosevelt broadcast from the White House, December 9, 1941, two days after the Japanese attack on Pearl Harbor:

Fellow Citizens:

The sudden criminal attacks perpetrated by the Japanese in the Pacific provide the climax of a decade of international immorality.

Powerful and resourceful gangsters have banded together to make war upon the whole human race. Their challenge has now been flung at the United States of America. The Japanese have treacherously violated the long-standing peace between us. Many American soldiers and sailors have been killed by enemy action. American ships have been sunk, American airplanes have been destroyed.

The Congress and the people of the United States have accepted that challenge.

Together with other free peoples, we are now fighting to maintain our right to live among our world neighbors in freedom and in common decency, without fear of assault.

I have prepared the full record of our past relations with Japan, and it will be submitted to the Congress. It begins with the visit of Commodore Perry to Japan 88 years ago. It ends with the visit of two Japanese emissaries to the Secretary of State last Sunday, an hour after Japanese forces had loosed their bombs and machine guns against our flag, our forces, and our citizens.

I can say with utmost confidence that no Americans today or a thousand years hence, need feel anything but pride in our patience and our efforts through all the years toward achieving a peace in the Pacific which would be fair and honorable to every nation, large or small. And no honest person, today or a thousand years hence, will be able to suppress a sense of indignation and horror at the treachery committed by the military dictators of Japan under the very shadow of the flag of peace borne by their special envoys in our midst.

The course that Japan has followed for the past 10 years in Asia has paralleled the course of Hitler and Mussolini in Europe and Africa. Today, it has become far more than a parallel. It is collaboration so well calculated that all the continents of the world, and all the oceans, are now considered by the Axis strategists as one gigantic battlefield.

In 1931, Japan invaded Manchukuo without warning.

In 1935, Italy invaded Ethiopia without warning.

In 1938, Hitler occupied Austria without warning.

In 1939, Hitler invaded Czechoslovakia without warning.

Later in 1939, Hitler invaded Poland without warning.

In 1940, Hitler invaded Norway, Denmark, Holland, Belgium, and Luxembourg without warning.

In 1940, Italy attacked France and later Greece without warning.

In 1941, the Axis Powers attacked Yugoslavia and Greece and they dominated the Balkans without warning.

In 1941, Hitler invaded Russia without warning.

And now Japan has attacked Malaya and Thailand and the United States without warning.

It is all of one pattern.

We are now in this war. We are all in it all the way. Every single man, woman, and child is a partner in the most tremendous undertaking of our American history. We must share together the bad news and the good news, the defeats and the victories the changing fortunes of war.

So far, the news has all been bad. We have suffered a serious set-back in Hawaii. Our forces in the Philippines, which include the brave people of that commonwealth, are taking punishment, but are defending themselves vigorously. The reports from Guam and Wake and Midway Islands are still confused, but we must be prepared for the announcement that all these three outposts have been seized.

The casualty lists of these first few days will undoubtedly be large. I deeply feel the anxiety of all families of the men in our armed forces and the relatives of people in cities which have been bombed. I can only give them my solemn promise that they will get news just as quickly as possible.

This government will put its trust in the stamina of the American people, and will give the facts to the public as soon as two conditions have been fulfilled: First, that the information has been definitely and officially confirmed; and, second, that the release of the information at the time it is received will not prove valuable to the enemy, directly or indirectly.

Most earnestly I urge my countrymen to reject all rumors. These ugly little hints of complete disaster fly thick and fast in wartime. They have to be examined and appraised.

As an example, I can tell you frankly that until further surveys are made, I have not sufficient information to state the exact damage which has been done to our naval vessels at Pearl Harbor. Admittedly the damage is serious. But no one can say how serious, until we know how much of this damage can be repaired and how quickly the necessary repairs can be made.

I cite as another example a statement made on Sunday night that a Japanese carrier had been located and sunk in the Canal Zone. And when you hear statements that are attributed to what they call "an authoritative source," you can be reasonably sure that under these war circumstances the "authoritative source" was not any person in authority.

Many rumors and reports which we now hear originate with enemy sources. For instance, today the Japanese are claiming that as a result of their one action against Hawaii they have gained naval supremacy in the Pacific. This is an old trick of propaganda which has been used innumerable times by the Nazis. The purposes of such fantastic claims are, of course, to spread fear and confusion among us, and to goad us into revealing military information which our enemies are desperately anxious to obtain.

Our government will not be caught in this obvious trap and neither will our people.

It must be remembered by each and every one of us that our free and rapid communication must be greatly restricted in wartime. It is not possible to receive full, speedy, accurate reports from distant areas of combat. This is particularly true where naval operations are concerned. For in these days of the marvels of radio it is often impossible for the commanders of various units to report their activities by radio, for the very simple reason that this information would become available to the enemy, and would disclose their position and their plan of defense or attack.

Of necessity there will be delays in officially confirming or denying reports of operations but we will not hide facts from the country if we know the facts and if the enemy will not be aided by their disclosure.

To all newspapers and radio stations, all those who reach the eyes and ears of the American people, I say this: You have a most grave responsibility to the Nation now and for the duration of this war.

If you feel that your government is not disclosing enough of the truth, you have every right to say so. But in the absence of all the facts, as revealed by official sources you have no right to deal out unconfirmed reports in such a way as to make people believe they are gospel truth.

Every citizen, in every walk of life, shares this same responsibility.

The lives of our soldiers and sailors—the whole future of this Nation—depend upon the manner in which each and every one of us fulfills his obligation to our country.

Now a word about the recent past and the future. A year and a half has elapsed since the fall of France, when the whole world first realized the mechanized might which the Axis nations had been building for so many years. America has used that year and a half to great advantage. Knowing that the attack might reach us in all too short a time, we immediately began greatly to increase our industrial strength and our capacity to meet the demands of modern warfare.

Precious months were gained by sending vast quantities of our war materials to the nations of the world still able to resist Axis aggression. Our policy rested on the fundamental truth that the defense of any country resisting Hitler or Japan was, in the long run, the defense of our own country. That policy has been justified. It has given us time, invaluable time, to build our American assembly lines of production.

Assembly lines are now in operation. Others are being rushed to completion. A steady stream of tanks and planes, of guns and ships, of shells and equipment that is what these 18 months have given us.

But it is all only a beginning of what has to be done. We must be set to face a long war against crafty and powerful bandits. The attack at Pearl Harbor can be repeated at any one of many points in both oceans and along both our coast lines and against all the rest of the hemisphere.

It will not only be a long war, it will be a hard war. That is the basis on which we now lay all our plans. That is the yardstick by which we measure what we shall need and demand money, materials, doubled and quadrupled production, ever increasing. The production must be not only for our own Army and Navy and air forces. It must reinforce the other armies and navies and air forces fighting the Nazis and the war lords of Japan throughout the Americas and the world.

I have been working today on the subject of production. Your government has decided on two broad policies.

The first is to speed up all existing production by working on a 7-day-week basis in every war industry, including the production of essential raw materials.

The second policy, now being put into form, is to rush additions to the capacity of production by building more new plants, by adding to old plants, and by using the many smaller plants for war needs.

Over the hard road of the past months we have at times met obstacles and difficulties, divisions and disputes, indifference and callousness. That is now all past and, I am sure, forgotten.

The fact is that the country now has an organization in Washington built around men and women who are recognized experts in their own fields. I think the country knows that the people who are actually responsible in each and every one of these many fields are pulling together with a teamwork that has never before been excelled.

On the road ahead there lies hard work—grueling work day and night, every hour and every minute.

I was about to add that ahead there lies sacrifice for all of us.

But it is not correct to use that word. The United States does not consider it a sacrifice to do all one can, to give one's best to our Nation when the Nation is fighting for its existence and its future life.

It is not a sacrifice for any man, old or young, to be in the Army or the Navy of the United States. Rather is it a privilege.

It is not a sacrifice for the industrialist or the wage earner, the farmer or the shopkeeper, the trainman or the doctor, to pay more taxes, to buy more bonds, to forego extra profits, to work longer or harder at the task for which he is best fitted. Rather is it a privilege.

It is not a sacrifice to do without many things to which we are accustomed if the national defense calls for doing without.

A review this morning leads me to the conclusion that at present we shall not have to curtail the normal articles of food. There is enough food for all of us and enough left over to send to those who are fighting on the same side with us.

There will be a clear and definite shortage of metals of many kinds for civilian use, for the very good reason that in our increased program we shall need for war purposes more than half of that portion of the principal metals which during the past year have gone into articles for civilian use. We shall have to give up many things entirely.

I am sure that the people in every part of the Nation are prepared in their individual living to win this war. I am sure they will cheerfully help to pay a large part of its financial cost while it goes on. I am sure they will cheerfully give up those material things they are asked to give up.

I am sure that they will retain all those great spiritual things without which we cannot win through.

I repeat that the United States can accept no result save victory, final and complete. Not only must the shame of Japanese treachery be wiped out, but the sources of international brutality, wherever they exist, must be absolutely and finally broken.

In my message to the Congress yesterday I said that we "will make very certain that this form of treachery shall never endanger us again." In order to achieve that certainty, we must begin the great task that is before us by abandoning once and for all the illusion that we can ever again isolate ourselves from the rest of humanity.

In these past few years and, most violently, in the past few days we have learned a terrible lesson.

It is our obligation to our dead; it is our sacred obligation to their children and our children that we must never forget what we have learned.

And what we all have learned is this:

There is no such thing as security for any nation or any individual in a world ruled by the principles of gangsterism.

There is no such thing as impregnable defense against powerful aggressors who sneak up in the dark and strike without warning.

We have learned that our ocean-girt hemisphere is not immune from severe attack that we cannot measure our safety in terms of miles on any map.

We may acknowledge that our enemies have performed a brilliant feat of deception, perfectly timed and executed with great skill. It was a thoroughly dishonorable deed, but we must face the fact that modern warfare as conducted in the Nazi manner is a dirty business. We don't like it, we didn't want to get in it, but, we are in it, and we're going to fight it with everything we've got.

I do not think any American has any doubt of our ability to administer proper punishment to the perpetrators of these crimes.

Your government knows that for weeks Germany has been telling Japan that if Japan did not attack the United States, Japan would not share in dividing the spoils with Germany when peace came. She was promised by Germany that if she came in she would receive the complete and perpetual control of the whole of the Pacific area and that means not only the Far East, not only all of the islands in the Pacific, but also a stranglehold on the west coast of North, Central, and South America.

We also know that Germany and Japan are conducting their military and naval operations in accordance with a joint plan. That plan considers all peoples and nations which are not helping the Axis Powers as common enemies of each and every one of the Axis Powers.

That is their simple and obvious grand strategy. That is why the American people must realize that it can be matched only with similar grand strategy. We must realize, for example, that Japanese successes against the United States in the Pacific are helpful to German operations in Libya; that any German success against the Caucasus is inevitably an assistance to Japan in her operations against the Dutch East Indies; that a German attack against Algiers or Morocco opens the way to a German attack against South America.

On the other side of the picture we must learn to know that guerrilla warfare against the Germans in Serbia helps us; that a successful Russian offensive against the Germans helps us; and that British successes on land or sea in any part of the world strengthen our hands.

Remember always that Germany and Italy, regardless of any formal declaration of war, consider themselves at war with the United States at this moment just as much as they consider themselves at war with Britain and Russia. And Germany puts all the other republics of the Americas into the category of enemies. The people of the hemisphere can be honored by that.

The true goal we seek is far above and beyond the ugly field of battle. When we resort to force, as now we must, we are determined that this force shall be directed toward ultimate good as well as against immediate evil. We Americans are not destroyers; we are builders.

We are now in the midst of a war, not for conquest, not for vengeance, but for a world in which this Nation, and all that this Nation represents, will be safe for our children. We expect to eliminate the danger from Japan, but it would serve us ill if we accomplished that and found that the rest of the world was dominated by Hitler and Mussolini.

We are going to win the war, and we are going to win the peace that follows.

And in the dark hours of this day and through dark days that may yet to come we will know that the vast majority of the members the human race are on our side. Many of them are fighting with us. All of them are praying for us. For, in representing our cause, we represent theirs as well, our hope and their hope for liberty under God.

10.17 Chronology of the Development of the Atomic Bomb

1895   The Atomic Age begins when Wilhelm K. Roentgen of Germany discovers X-rays.

1896   Prompted to find more high-energy rays like the X-ray, Antoine Henri Becquerel of France discovers that uranium gives off radiation.

1898   Marie and Pierre Curie, in search for more radioactive elements, isolate thorium and radium.

1904   Becquerel, the Curies and Ernest Rutherford of New Zealand discover three types of radioactive rays: alpha, beta and gamma.

1905   Albert Einstein develops the Theory of Relativity, saying energy and mass are related.

1911   Rutherford publishes his theory of atomic structure. He is the first to recognize that an atom is made of a nucleus surrounded by much lighter electrons.

1912   Frederick Soddy of Britain theorizes isotopes of elements. Isotopes are heavier versions of an element with more neutrons in its nucleus.

1919   An atom is artificially split when Rutherford splits a proton off a nitrogen atom.

1930   The first cyclotron (atom smasher) is invented by Ernest O. Lawrence of the U.S.

1932   James Chadwick of Great Britain discovers the neutron.

1934   Enrico Fermi of Italy bombards several kinds of atoms with neutrons. The neutrons are usually captured by the atoms and give off a beta particle (an electron). The neutron then became a proton and a new element is formed.

1938   Otto Han and Fritz Strassmann of Germany repeat Fermi's experiment and find that when one bombards a uranium atom, it splits into two lighter atoms. Some energy is also given off: this is nuclear fission.

1939   Lise Meitner and Otto Frisch of Germany explain Fermi's experiment and develop the nuclear fission theory.

1939   Einstein writes his fateful letter explaining to President Franklin Roosevelt the military possibilities of atomic power and suggesting that the government pursue it.

1941   After entering World War II, the U.S. hears Germany is trying to develop the atomic bomb. Preliminary preparations begin for the development of an atomic bomb.

1942   The Manhattan Project begins and the U.S. begins full-scale development of the atomic bomb. Three cities are built by the government to develop the bomb. Hanford, Washington and Oak Ridge, Tennessee are to produce the fuel for the bomb. Los Alamos, New Mexico, is the capital of the project and was in charge of producing and assembling the bomb itself.

The German bomb effort fails and is officially ended. The Allies however, are unaware of this.

The first nuclear chain reaction takes place at the University of Chicago, run by Enrico Fermi.

1943   J. Robert Oppenheimer is selected to direct the development, construction and testing of the atomic bomb at Los Alamos in New Mexico. Great Britain joins the Manhattan Project. Many scientists, exiled from Germany, come to the U.S. from Britain to help with development of the bomb.

July 16, 1945   First test of an atomic bomb takes place at Alamogordo Air Base in New Mexico.

August 6, 1945   First use of an atomic bomb in war, the bomb is dropped on Hiroshima, Japan.

August 9, 1945   Second and last use of an atomic bomb in war, Nagasaki, Japan, is bombed.

1946   Two atomic bombs are detonated by the U.S. in the Bikini atoll. They are used as tests to discover the strategic effectiveness of atomic bombs under several different conditions.

1949   The Soviet Union detonates its first atomic bomb.

1951   Electricity is first generated by atomic energy in Arco, Idaho.Using hydrogen fusion, the process of two hydrogen atoms fusing into helium, the U.S. develops the hydrogen bomb.

1955   The Soviet Union detonates its first hydrogen bomb.

1957   The first atomic bomb with a megaton-class explosion is detonated.

1961   Russia sets off a hydrogen bomb that produces a 50-megaton explosion.

10.18   Major Events of the Korean War

1948

Aug. 5   U.S.-backed Republic of South Korea was proclaimed; People's Democratic Republic of Korea was proclaimed in the North under Communist leadership.

1949

Sept. 2   United Nations' attempt to promote peaceful reunification failed.

1950

June 25   North Korean Communist troops invaded South Korea. The UN demanded that North Korea halt the action.

June 27   President Truman ordered U.S. air and naval forces to help defend South Korea. The UN asked member nations to aid South Korea.

June 30   Truman ordered U.S. ground troops to South Korea.

Sept. 8   Allied troops stopped the deepest Communist advance, at the Pusan Perimeter in southeastern South Korea.

Sept. 15   Allied troops landed behind the enemy lines at Inchon.

Sept. 26   General Douglas MacArthur, commander of UN forces, announced the capture of Seoul, the South Korean capitol.

Oct. 19   The allies captured Pyongyang, the capital of North Korea.

Oct. 25   China entered the war on the side of North Korea.

Nov. 26   The Allies began to retreat after an attack by the Chinese.

1951

Jan. 4   The Communists occupied Seoul.

March 14   The Allies re-occupied Seoul after ending their retreat.

April 11   Truman removed MacArthur and replaced him with General Matthew B. Ridgway.

July 10   Truce talks began, but fighting continued.

1952

April 28   Communist negotiators rejected a proposal for voluntary repatriation of prisoners.

Oct. 8   The truce talks were broken off.

1953

March 28   The Communists accepted a UN proposal to exchange sick and wounded prisoners.

April 26   The truce talks were resumed.

July 26   An armistice agreement was signed, and the fighting ended. Boundary for a divided Korea was drawn along battle lines.

10.19 Major Events of the Cold War

1946-48	Communists take over Eastern Europe. Soviets drop the "Iron Curtain" over Eastern Europe.
1947	Truman Doctrine allows for military and economic aid to Turkey and Greece.
1947	Marshall Plan outlines the reconstruction of Western Europe.
1948	Communists overturn the democratic government of Czechoslovakia.
1948-49	Berlin blockade set up by the Soviet Union.
1949	NATO Pact signed by 12 countries; establishes military counterweight to Soviet forces in Europe.
1949	Communists win control of China.
1950-53	Korean War—first use of United Nations troops in battle.
1953	Death of Stalin alters Cold War.
1955	Warsaw Treaty Organization established in response to the re-arming of Western Germany.
1955	Summit conference held in Geneva.
1960	Soviet Union downs U-2 spy plane.
1961	German Communists build Berlin Wall.
1961	Castro announces his Communism.
1962	Cuban Missile Crisis.
1963	Nuclear Test Ban Treaty.
1964	United States bombs bases in North Vietnam.
1972-74	Strategic Arms Limitation Talks (SALT) agreements culminate the detente efforts (begun in the mid-60s) of President Richard Nixon and his principle foreign policy advisor, Henry Kissinger.
1975	Communists win North Vietnam.
1977-81	U.S.-Soviet relations deteriorate during Carter Administration.
1979	Soviet Union invades Afghanistan.
1981-84	Fueled by Soviet support of Nicaraguan Sandanista rebels and the U.S.'s declared intention to develop an anti-nuclear Strategic Defense Initiative, U.S.-Soviet relations continue to suffer during the Reagan Administration.
1985	Soviet leader, Mikhail Gorbachev, rises to power with policies of domestic reform and reconciliation with the West.
1989	Communist rule comes to an end in several Eastern European countries.
1989	German Communists open the Berlin Wall.
1991	End of the Cold War and the Soviet satellite system with new policies of self-determination for the former Soviet countries.

10.20   Chronology of the Vietnam War

1957   The Viet Cong began to rebel against the South Vietnamese government headed by President Ngo Dinh Diem.

1959   (July 8) First U.S. military advisers die in Vietcong attack.

1960   (Dec.) Communists form National Liberation Front (NLF).

1961   (June 16) U.S. agrees to increase its 685-member advisor group and to arm and supply 20,000 South Vietnamese troops.

1962   Number of U.S. troops in Vietnam reaches 12,000.

1963   (Nov. 1) South Vietnamese generals overthrew the Diem government, and Diem was killed the next day.

1964   (Aug. 7) Congress passed the Tonkin Gulf Resolution, which gave the President power to take "all necessary measures" and "to prevent further aggression."

1964   (Dec. 11) U.S. announced massive aid increase to counter Hanoi's support of Vietcong.

1965   (March 6) President Lyndon B. Johnson sent U.S. Marines to Da Nang, South Vietnam. The Marines were the first U.S. ground troops in the war.

1966   (April 12) First bombing raid by B-52s. U.S. troops in Vietnam number 389,000 by year's end.

1967   U.S. B-52s stationed in Thailand. U.S. troops in Vietnam number 480,000 by year's end.

1968   (Jan. 30) North Vietnam and the Vietcong launched a major campaign against South Vietnamese cities.

1968   (Mar. 16) About 200 Vietnamese villagers massacred by U.S. troops at My Lai. Year-long cover-up followed.

1968   (May 10) Start of Paris peace talks.

1969   (June 8) President Richard M. Nixon announced that U.S. troops would begin to withdraw from Vietnam. Troop number peaks at 543,000.

1970   U.S. troops involved in fighting in Cambodia and Laos.

1971   (June) Publication of Pentagon Papers fuels antiwar sentiment in U.S.

1971   (Aug. 11) U.S. turned over all ground-combat responsibilities to South Vietnamese.

1972   (May 8) Nixon ordered mining of North Vietnamese ports. U.S. troops have been reduced to 24,200 by year's end.

1973   (Jan. 27) The United States, North and South Vietnam, and the Vietcong signed a cease-fire agreement.

1973   (March 29) The last U.S. ground troops left Vietnam.

1975   (April 30) South Vietnam surrendered.

10.21 Tonkin Gulf Incident, 1964

President Johnson's Message to Congress August 5, 1964:

Last night I announced to the American people that the North Vietnamese regime had conducted further deliberate attacks against U.S. naval vessels operating in international waters, and I had therefore directed air action against gunboats and supporting facilities used in these hostile operations. This air action has now been carried out with substantial damage to the boats and facilities. Two U.S. aircraft were lost in the action.

After consultation with the leaders of both parties in the Congress, I further announced a decision to ask the Congress for a resolution expressing the unity and determination of the United States in supporting freedom and in protecting peace in southeast Asia.

These latest actions of the North Vietnamese regime have given a new and grave turn to the already serious situation in southeast Asia. Our commitments in that area are well known to the Congress. They were first made in 1954 by President Eisenhower. They were further defined in the Southeast Asia Collective Defense Treaty approved by the Senate in February 1955.

This treaty with its accompanying protocol obligates the United States and other members to act in accordance with their constitutional processes to meet Communist aggression against any of the parties or protocol states.

Our policy in southeast Asia has been consistent and unchanged since 1954. I summarized it on June 2 in four simple propositions:

1. America keeps her word. Here as elsewhere, we must and shall honor our commitments.
2. The issue is the future of southeast Asia as a whole. A threat to any nation in that region is a threat to all, and a threat to us.
3. Our purpose is peace. We have no military, political, or territorial ambitions in the area.
4. This is not just a jungle war, but a struggle for freedom on every front of human activity. Our military and economic assistance to South Vietnam and Laos in particular has the purpose of helping these countries to repel aggression and strengthen their independence.

The threat to the free nations of southeast Asia has long been clear. The North Vietnamese regime has constantly sought to take over South Vietnam and Laos. This Communist regime has violated the Geneva accords for Vietnam. It has systematically conducted a campaign of subversion, which includes the direction, training, and supply of personnel and arms for the conduct of guerrilla warfare in South Vietnamese territory. In Laos, the North Vietnamese regime has maintained military forces, used Laotian territory for infiltration into South Vietnam, and most recently carried out combat operations—all in direct violation of the Geneva Agreements of 1962.

In recent months, the actions of the North Vietnamese regime have become steadily more threatening.

As President of the United States I have concluded that I should now ask the Congress, on its part, to join in affirming the national determination that all such attacks will be met, and that the United States will continue in its basic policy of assisting the free nations of the area to defend their freedom.

As I have repeatedly made clear, the United States intends no rashness, and seeks no wider war. We must make it clear to all that the United States is united in its determination to bring about the end of Communist subversion and aggression in the area. We seek the full and effective restoration of the international agreements signed in Geneva in 1954, with respect to South Vietnam, and again in Geneva in 1962, with respect to Laos.

Tonkin Resolution

Joint Resolution of Congress H.J. RES 1145 August 7, 1964:

Resolved by the Senate and House of Representatives of the United States of America in Congress assembled,

That the Congress approves and supports the determination of the President, as Commander in Chief, to take all necessary measures to repel any armed attack against the forces of the United States and to prevent further aggression.

The United States regards as vital to its national interest and to world peace the maintenance of international peace and security in southeast Asia. Consonant with the Constitution of the United States and the Charter of the United Nations and in accordance with its obligations under the Southeast Asia Collective Defense Treaty, the United States is, therefore, prepared, as the President determines, to take all necessary steps, including the use of armed force, to assist any member or protocol state of the Southeast Asia Collective Defense Treaty requesting assistance in defense of its freedom.

This resolution shall expire when the President shall determine that the peace and security of the area is reasonably assured by international conditions created by action of the United Nations or otherwise, except that it may be terminated earlier by concurrent resolution of the Congress.

10.22   U.S. Military Casualties in Southeast Asia, 1957-1995

	Army	Navy	Air Force	Marines	Coast Guard	Total
1957	1	0	0	0	0	1
1958	0	0	0	0	0	0
1959	2	0	0	0	0	2
1960	0	4	1	0	0	5
1961	7	1	8	0	0	16
1962	27	3	18	5	0	53
1963	73	4	31	10	0	118
1964	147	15	39	5	0	206
1965	1,079	114	162	508	0	1,863
1966	3,755	279	246	1,862	2	6,144
1967	6,467	583	317	3,786	0	11,153
1968	10,596	598	345	5,048	2	16,589
1969	8,186	426	305	2,694	3	11,614
1970	4,972	219	201	691	0	6,083
1971	2,131	55	90	81	0	2,357
1972	373	77	172	18	0	640
1973	34	52	75	7	0	168
1974	49	23	80	26	0	178
1975	23	22	83	32	0	160
1976	29	6	29	13	0	77
1977	29	24	39	4	0	96
1978	158	42	219	28	0	447
1979	38	3	101	6	0	148
1980-1995	25	5	22	14	0	66
TOTAL DEATHS	38,201	2,555	2,583	14,838	7	58,184

* Year of death may either be actual or based on a presumptive finding of death (originally declared missing and later declared dead).
Source: U.S. Department of Defense.

10.23 Events of the Gulf War, 1990-1991

1990

July 17	Sadam Hussein accuses Kuwait of oil overproduction and theft of oil from the Rumailia Oil Field.
July 25	U.S. Ambassador to Iraq, April Glaspie, tells Hussein that the Iraq/Kuwait dispute is an Arab matter, not one that affects the United States.
Aug. 2	Hussein invades Kuwait.
	—President Bush freezes Iraqi and Kuwati assets.
	—The United Nations calls on Hussein to withdraw.
Aug. 6	Economic sanctions are authorized.
Aug. 7	Secretery of Defense Cheny visits Saudi Arabia. The 82nd Airborne and several fighter squadrons are dispatched.
Aug. 8	Iraq annexes Kuwait.
Aug. 9	The UN declares Iraq's annexation invalid.
Aug. 12	The U.S. announces interdiction program of Iraqi shipping.
Aug. 22	President Bush authorizes call up of reserves.
Aug. 25	Military interdiction authorized by the UN.
Sept. 14	Iraqi forces storm a number of diplomatic missions in Kuwait City.
Nov. 8	Bush orders aditional deployments to give "offensive option" to U.S. forces.
Nov. 20	Forty-five Democrats file suit in Washington to have President Bush first seek Congressional approval of military operations—eventually thrown out.
Nov. 22	President Bush visits the troops for Thanksgiving.
Nov. 29	UN Security Council authorizes force if Iraq doesn't withdraw from Kuwait by midnight EST Jan. 15.
Nov. 30	Bush invites Tariq Aziz to Washington and offers to send Secretary of State James Baker to Baghdad.

1991

Jan. 9	Baker and Aziz meet in Geneva for 6 hours with no results.
Jan. 12	Congress votes to allow U.S. troops to be used in offensive operations.
Jan. 15	The deadline set by the UN Resolution 678 for Iraq to withdraw. First U.S. government statement of Operation Desert Storm made.
Jan. 16	Marlin Fitzwater announces, "The liberation of Kuwait has begun. . . ." U.S. warplanes attack Baghdad, Kuwait and other military targets in Iraq.
Jan. 17	Iraq launches first SCUD missile attack.
Jan. 30	U.S. forces in the Gulf exceed 500,000.
Feb. 6	Jordan King Hussein lashes out against American bombardments and supports Iraq.
Feb 13	U.S. Bombers destroy a bunker complex in Baghdad with several hundred citizens inside. Nearly 300 die.
Feb. 17	Tariq Aziz travels to Moscow to discuss possible negotiated end to the war.
Feb. 22	President Bush issues an ultimatum of Feb. 23 for Iraqi troops to withdraw from Kuwait.
Feb. 23	Ground war begins with Marines, Army and Arab forces moving into Iraq and Kuwait.
Feb. 25	Iraqi SCUD missile hits U.S. barracks in Saudi Arabia killing 27.
Feb. 26	Kuwaiti resistence leaders declare they are in control of Kuwait City.
Feb. 27	President Bush orders a cease-fire effective at midnight Kuwaiti time.
Mar. 3	Iraqi leaders formally accept cease-fire terms.
Mar. 4	Ten Allied POWs freed.
Mar. 5	35 POWs released.
Mar. 8	First U.S. combat forces return home.

10.24   Allies in the Persian Gulf War

Bangladesh
Britain
Egypt
France
Kuwait
Morocco
Oman
Pakistan
Qatar
Saudi Arabia
Syria
United Arab Emirates
United States

10.25   U.S. Wars: Percentage of Population in Military

Conflict	Population (millions)	Enrolled (thousands)	Percentage of population in military
Revolutionary War	3.5	200.0	5.7
War of 1812	7.6	286.0	3.8
Mexican War	21.1	78.7	0.4
Civil War:			
Union	26.2	2,803.3	10.7
Confederate	8.1	1,064.2	13.1
Combined	34.3	3,867.5	11.1
Spanish-American War	74.6	306.8	0.4
World War I	102.8	4,743.8	4.6
World War II	133.5	16,353.7	12.2
Korean War	151.7	5,764.1	3.8
Vietnam War	204.9	8,744.0	4.3
Gulf War	260.0	2,750.0	1.1

The percentage in the military is the percentage of people under arms.

The figure "Enrolled" represents the number of personnel maintained in the service. It includes all personnel ever in the service during the conflict.

10.26   U.S. Wars: Casualties

Conflict	Enrolled	Deaths				Ratio	Percentages			Duration	
		Combat	Other	Wounded	Total		KIA	Dead	Casualty	Months	KIA/Month
Revolutionary War	200.0	4,435	*	6,188	10,623	2.4	2.2	2.2	5.3	80	55
War of 1812	286.0	2,260	*	4,505	6,765	3.0	0.8	0.8	2.4	30	75
Mexican War	78.7	1,733	11,550	4,152	17,435	1.3	2.2	16.9	22.2	20	87
Civil War:											
Union	2,803.3	110,070	249,458	275,175	634,703	1.8	3.9	12.8	22.6	48	2,293
Confederate	1,064.2	74,524	124,000	137,000+	335,524	1.7	7.0	18.7	31.5	48	1,553
Combined	3,867.5	184,594	373,458	412,175+	970,227	1.7	4.8	14.4	25.1	48	3,846
Spanish-American War	306.8	385	2,061	1,662	4,108	1.7	0.1	0.8	1.3	4	96**
World War I	4,743.8	53,513	63,195	204,002	320,710	2.7	1.1	2.5	6.8	19	2,816
World War II	16,353.7	292,131	115,185	670,846	1,078,162	2.6	1.8	2.5	6.6	44	6,639
Korean War	5,764.1	33,651	*	103,284	136,935	4.1	0.6	0.6	2.4	37	909
Vietnam War	8,744.0	47,369	10,799	153,303	211,471	3.6	0.5	0.7	2.4	90	526
Gulf War	2,750.0	148	145	467^	760	2.6	0.0	0.0	0.0	1	148

"Combat deaths" refers to troops killed in action or dead of wounds. "Other" includes deaths from disease, privation, and accidents, and includes losses among prisoners of war. "Wounded" excludes those who died of their wounds, who are included under "Combat Deaths." "Ratio" is the proportion of wounded in action to combat deaths. Note that the wounded figures do not include cases of disease. Under "Percentages," "KIA" refers to the percent of those enrolled killed in action, "Dead" to the percent dead from all causes, and "Casualty" to the percent killed or injured. "KIA/Month," killed in action per month, gives a fair indication of the intensity of combat.

Notes:
* Non-battle deaths not known for these wars.
+ Confederate non-battle deaths and wounded estimated.
** Actually only six weeks of sustained combat.
^ There was only one month of combat.

10.27   U.S. Wars: Costs

Conflict	Cost in $Billions		Per Capita Costs
	Current	$1990s	(in $1990)
Revolutionary War (1775-1783)	$ .10	$ 1.2	$ 342.86
War of 1812 (1812-1815)	.09	0.7	92.11
Mexican War (1846-1848)	.07	1.1	52.13
Civil War (1861-1865):			
Union	3.20	27.3	1,041.98
Confederate	2.00	17.1	2,111.11
Combined	5.20	44.4	1,294.46
Spanish-American War (1898)	.40	6.3	84.45
World War I (1917-1918)	26.00	196.5	1,911.47
World War II (1941-1945)	288.00	2,091.3	15,655.17
Korea (1950-1953)	54.00	263.9	1,739.62
Vietnam (1964-1972)	111.00	346.7	1,692.04
Gulf War (1990-1991)	61.00	61.1	235.00

The table compares the cost of America's principal wars since 1775 on the basis of then current and 1990s dollars. Current dollars are the actual numbers spent at the time. Thus, a 1775-1783 dollar had the equivalent purchasing power of $10.75 in 1990s terms. Actually this conversion is only a rough guide, but at least gives some idea of the relative costs of the ten wars on an adjusted basis. The figures are for direct costs only, omitting pension costs, which tended to triple the ultimate outlays. The table also omits the cost of damage to the national infrastructure during those wars waged on American soil. Confederate figures are estimated.

10.28   U.S. Active Duty Military Deaths, 1980-1996

Selected Military Operations

MILITARY OPERATION/ INCIDENT	CASUALTY TYPE	ARMY	NAVY	AIR FORCE	MARINE CORPS	TOTAL
IRANIAN HOSTAGE RESCUE MISSION APRIL 25, 1980	NON-HOSTILE	0	0	5	3	8
LEBANON PEACEKEEPING, AUGUST 25, 1982-FEBRUARY 26, 1984	HOSTILE	3	19	0	234	256
	NON-HOSTILE	5	2	0	2	9
	TOTAL	8	21	0	236	265
URGENT FURY, GRENADA, 1983	HOSTILE	11	4	0	3	18
	NON-HOSTILE	1	0	0	0	1
	TOTAL	12	4	0	3	19
JUST CAUSE, PANAMA, 1989	HOSTILE	18	4	0	1	23
PERSIAN GULF WAR, 1990-1991						
DESERT SHIELD	NON-HOSTILE	21	36	9	18	84
DESERT STORM	HOSTILE	98	6	20	24	148
	NON-HOSTILE	105	14	6	26	151
	TOTAL	203	20	26	50	299
DESERT SHIELD/STORM	TOTAL	224	56	35	68	383
RESTORE HOPE/UNOSOM, SOMALIA, 1992-1994	HOSTILE	27	0	0	2	29
	NON-HOSTILE	4	0	8	2	14
	TOTAL	31	0	8	4	43
UPHOLD DEMOCRACY, HAITI, 1994-1996	NON-HOSTILE	3	0	0	1	4

Source: U.S. Department of Defense.

10.29 U.S. Strategic Nuclear Warheads, 1945-1996

Strategic Warheads					Strategic Warheads			
Year	ICBM	SLBM	Bombers	Total	Year	ICBM	SLBM	Bombers	Total
1945			6	6	1971	1,516	2,587	6,252	10,355
1946			11	11	1972	1,726	3,276	7,360	12,363
1947			32	32	1973	1,936	4,318	6,991	13,244
1948			110	110	1974	2,041	4,654	6,788	13,483
1949			235	235	1975	2,251	4,771	6,911	13,933
1950			369	369	1976	2,251	5,359	6,647	14,257
1951			549	549	1977	2,251	5,477	6,592	14,320
1952			800	800	1978	2,251	5,712	6,264	14,227
1953			1,000	1,000	1979	2,251	5,645	6,252	14,148
1954			1,500	1,500	1980	2,251	5,309	6,239	13,799
1955			2,200	2,200	1981	2,251	4,990	6,244	13,485
1956			3,000	3,000	1982	2,246	5,006	5,820	13,072
1957			4,200	4,200	1983	2,237	5,208	5,663	13,108
1958			5,700	5,700	1984	2,226	5,611	6,118	13,955
1959	6		7,000	7,006	1985	2,216	5,645	6,180	14,040
1960	13	34	6,954	7,000	1986	2,273	5,712	6,493	14,478
1961	60	84	6,730	6,874	1987	2,415	5,914	6,624	14,953
1962	213	151	6,847	7,211	1988	2,562	5,578	6,624	14,764
1963	627	168	6,303	7,098	1989	2,562	5,410	5,965	13,937
1964	952	403	6,471	7,827	1990	2,562	5,480	5,330	13,372
1965	897	773	6,567	8,237	1991	2,200	5,480	3,400	11,080
1966	1,054	1,327	6,633	9,014	1992	2,200	3,630	3,510	9,340
1967	1,096	1,630	6,861	9,587	1993	2,200	3,630	3,410	9,240
1968	1,096	1,630	6,590	9,316	1994	2,200	3,630	3,410	9,240
1969	1,096	1,630	6,421	9,147	1995	2,180	3,630	3,410	9,220
1970	1,306	1,630	6,465	9,401	1996	2,180	3,630	3,360	9,170

Bomber: Strategic airplane capable of long-range, intercontinental missions, designed for a tactical operating radius of over 2,500 nautical miles at design gross weight and design bomb load.
Intercontinental Ballistic Missile (ICBM): Strategic missile with a range capability from about 3,000 to 8,000 nautical miles.
Submarine-Launched Ballistic Missile (SLBM): Ballistic missile capable of being launched from fleet ballistic missile submarines.
Source: Natural Resources Defense Council, Inc.

10.30   Known Nuclear Tests Worldwide, 1945-1960

Year	United States		Soviet Union		United Kingdom		France		China		Total
	A	U	A	U	A	U	A	U	A	U	
1945	1	0	0	0	0	0	0	0	0	0	1
1946	2	0	0	0	0	0	0	0	0	0	2
1947	0	0	0	0	0	0	0	0	0	0	0
1948	3	0	0	0	0	0	0	0	0	0	3
1949	0	0	1	0	0	0	0	0	0	0	1
1950	0	0	0	0	0	0	0	0	0	0	0
1951	15	1	2	0	0	0	0	0	0	0	18
1952	10	0	0	0	1	0	0	0	0	0	11
1953	11	0	5	0	2	0	0	0	0	0	18
1954	6	0	10	0	0	0	0	0	0	0	16
1955	17	1	6	0	0	0	0	0	0	0	24
1956	18	0	9	0	6	0	0	0	0	0	33
1957	27	5	16	0	7	0	0	0	0	0	55
1958	62	15	34	0	5	0	0	0	0	0	116
1959	0	0	0	0	0	0	0	0	0	0	0
1960	0	0	0	0	0	0	3	0	0	0	3

A = atmospheric; U = underground.

10.31   Largest Armed Forces, 1998

Estimated active forces

Country	Army	Navy	Air	Total
China	2,090,000	280,000	470,000	2,840,000
U.S.	495,000	395,500	382,200	1,447,600*
Russia	420,000	220,000	130,000	1,240,000#
India	980,000	55,000	110,000	1,145,000
North Korea	923,000	47,000	85,000	1,055,000
South Korea	560,000	60,000	52,000	672,000
Turkey	525,000	51,000	63,000	639,000
Pakistan	520,000	22,000	45,000	587,000
Iran	350,000	18,000	30,000	518,000+
Vietnam	420,000	42,000	15,000	492,000

* Includes 174,900 Marine Corps
# Includes Strategic Deterrent Forces, Paramilitary, Nation Guard, etc.
+ Includes 120,000 Revolutionary Guards

In addition to the active forces listed here, many countries have substantial reserves on standby: South Korea's have been estimated at about 4,500,000, Vietnam's at 3-4,000,000, and China's at 1,200,000.

10.32   Largest Defense Budgets, 1997

Country	Budget ($)
U.S.	$259,400,000,000
Japan	43,300,000,000
UK	37,100,000,000
France	33,100,000,000
Russia	32,000,000,000
Germany	27,300,000,000
Italy	18,300,000,000
Saudi Arabia	17,900,000,000
South Korea	15,500,000,000
Taiwan	11,300,000,000

IV
ECONOMIC HISTORY

SECTION 11

Macroeconomic Trends

11.1 Real Gross Domestic Product, 1959-1998

By month in billions of chained 1992 dollars

Year	Month	GDP	Year	Month	GDP	Year	Month	GDP
1959	03	$2221.40	1972	04	3790.44	1986	01	5460.83
1959	04	2230.95	1973	01	3892.22	1986	02	5466.95
1960	01	2279.22	1973	02	3919.01	1986	03	5496.30
1960	02	2265.48	1973	03	3907.09	1986	04	5526.77
1960	03	2268.29	1973	04	3947.11	1987	01	5561.80
1960	04	2238.57	1974	01	3908.15	1987	02	5618.00
1961	01	2251.68	1974	02	3922.57	1987	03	5667.39
1961	02	2292.02	1974	03	3879.98	1987	04	5750.57
1961	03	2332.61	1974	04	3854.13	1988	01	5785.29
1961	04	2381.01	1975	01	3800.93	1988	02	5844.05
1962	01	2422.59	1975	02	3835.21	1988	03	5878.71
1962	02	2448.01	1975	03	3907.02	1988	04	5952.83
1962	03	2471.86	1975	04	3952.48	1989	01	6010.96
1962	04	2476.67	1976	01	4044.59	1989	02	6055.61
1963	01	2508.71	1976	02	4072.19	1989	03	6087.96
1963	02	2538.05	1976	03	4088.49	1989	04	6093.51
1963	03	2586.26	1976	04	4126.39	1990	01	6152.59
1963	04	2604.62	1977	01	4176.28	1990	02	6171.57
1964	01	2666.69	1977	02	4260.08	1990	03	6142.10
1964	02	2697.54	1977	03	4329.46	1990	04	6078.96
1964	03	2729.63	1977	04	4328.34	1991	01	6047.49
1964	04	2739.75	1978	01	4345.51	1991	02	6074.66
1965	01	2808.88	1978	02	4510.74	1991	03	6090.14
1965	02	2846.34	1978	03	4552.14	1991	04	6105.25
1965	03	2898.80	1978	04	4603.65	1992	01	6175.69
1965	04	2970.48	1979	01	4605.65	1992	02	6214.22
1966	01	3042.36	1979	02	4615.64	1992	03	6260.74
1966	02	3055.53	1979	03	4644.93	1992	04	6327.12
1966	03	3076.51	1979	04	4656.23	1993	01	6327.93
1966	04	3102.36	1980	01	4678.96	1993	02	6359.90
1967	01	3127.15	1980	02	4566.62	1993	03	6393.50
1967	02	3129.53	1980	03	4562.25	1993	04	6476.86
1967	03	3154.19	1980	04	4651.86	1994	01	6524.51
1967	04	3177.98	1981	01	4739.16	1994	02	6600.31
1968	01	3236.18	1981	02	4696.82	1994	03	6629.47
1968	02	3292.07	1981	03	4753.02	1994	04	6688.61
1968	03	3316.11	1981	04	4693.76	1995	01	6717.46
1968	04	3331.22	1982	01	4615.89	1995	02	6724.20
1969	01	3381.87	1982	02	4634.88	1995	03	6779.53
1969	02	3390.23	1982	03	4612.08	1995	04	6825.80
1969	03	3409.65	1982	04	4618.26	1996	01	6882.00
1969	04	3392.61	1983	01	4662.98	1996	02	6983.91
1970	01	3386.49	1983	02	4763.57	1996	03	7020.00
1970	02	3391.61	1983	03	4849.00	1996	04	7093.12
1970	03	3422.95	1983	04	4939.23	1997	01	7166.68
1970	04	3389.36	1984	01	5053.56	1997	02	7236.50
1971	01	3481.40	1984	02	5132.87	1997	03	7311.24
1971	02	3500.95	1984	03	5170.34	1997	04	7364.63
1971	03	3523.80	1984	04	5203.68	1998	01	7464.67
1971	04	3533.79	1985	01	5257.26	1998	02	7498.64
1972	01	3604.73	1985	02	5283.74	1998	03	7566.45
1972	02	3687.91	1985	03	5359.61	1998	04	7669.99
1972	03	3726.18	1985	04	5393.57			

Source: U.S. Department of Commerce.

11.2 GDP, Inflation and Unemployment Projections, 1998-2009

	1998	1999	2000	2001	2002	2003	2004	2005	2006	2007	2008	2009
Nominal GDP (Billions of dollars)	8,499	8,846	9,182	9,581	10,015	10,476	10,960	11,465	11,988	12,528	13,089	13,668
Nominal GDP (Percentage change)	4.8	4.1	3.8	4.3	4.5	4.6	4.6	4.6	4.6	4.5	4.5	4.4
Real GDP[1] (Percentage change)	3.7	2.3	1.7	2.2	2.4	2.4	2.4	2.4	2.4	2.3	2.3	2.3
Consumer Price Index[2] (Percentage change)	1.6	2.5	2.6	2.6	2.6	2.6	2.6	2.6	2.6	2.6	2.6	2.6
Unemployment Rate (Percent)	4.5	4.6	5.1	5.4	5.6	5.7	5.7	5.7	5.7	5.7	5.7	5.7
Three-Month Treasury Bill Rate (Percent)	4.8	4.5	4.5	4.5	4.5	4.5	4.5	4.5	4.5	4.5	4.5	4.5
Ten-Year Treasury Note Rate (Percent)	5.3	5.1	5.3	5.4	5.4	5.4	5.4	5.4	5.4	5.4	5.4	5.4

[1] Based on chained 1992 dollars.
[2] The consumer price index for all urban consumers.
Sources: Congressional Budget Office; Department of Commerce, Bureau of Economic Analysis; Department of Labor, Bureau of Labor Statistics; Federal Reserve Board.

11.3   Productivity Growth, 1947-1996

Output per worker per hour, 1992 = 100

1947	33.7		1972	76.0
1948	35.2		1973	78.4
1949	36.0		1974	77.1
1950	39.1		1975	79.8
1951	40.3		1976	82.5
1952	41.4		1977	83.9
1953	43.0		1978	84.9
1954	43.9		1979	84.5
1955	45.8		1980	84.2
1956	45.8		1981	85.7
1957	47.2		1982	85.3
1958	48.5		1983	88.0
1959	50.5		1984	90.2
1960	51.4		1985	91.7
1961	53.2		1986	94.0
1962	55.7		1987	94.0
1963	57.9		1988	94.6
1964	60.5		1989	95.4
1965	62.7		1990	96.1
1966	65.2		1991	96.7
1967	66.6		1992	100.0
1968	68.9		1993	100.2
1969	69.2		1994	100.6
1970	70.5		1995	100.5
1971	73.6		1996	102.0

11.4 The Great Depression

Events Leading to the Great Depression

—Massive build-up of business inventories.

—Lack of diversification in American economy—prosperity of 1920s largely a result of expansion of construction and automobile industries.

—Poor distribution of purchasing power among consumers. Many farmers and factory workers were unable to purchase cars and houses.

—Drop in farm income. Farm income declined 66% from 1920-1929.

—Unequal income distribution. By 1929 the top 10% of the nation's population received 40% of the nation's disposable income.

—Huge credit problems. Steady stream of bank failures in late 1920s as borrowers (many of them farmers) were unable to pay mortgages.

—Low margins encouraged speculative investment by banks, corporations, and individual investors.

—Decline in demand for American goods in international trade. Some European nations, particularly Germany, were so beset by financial crises and inflation that they could not afford to purchase American exports.

—High American protective tariffs discouraged trade.

Stock Market Crash, 1929

September 1929 Buying on margin reached all-time high. Stock prices began to fall.

October 24, 1929 (Black Thursday) Prices dropped sharply.

October 29, 1929 (Black Tuesday) Prices fell drastically as sellers panicked. Largest stock trading day in U.S. history.

December 1929 $40 billion in stock value lost between September and December. Hoover and business leaders attempted to calm Americans by assuring them that the country's economy was fundamentally sound.

1929-1933 Thousands of businesses failed as stock market crash fueled economic downturn. Corporate profits dropped from $10 billion to $1 billon.

1929-1933 Thousands of banks failed with more than nine million savings accounts lost ($2.5 billion).

1932 Ninety-five people died in New York City from starvation, Families scattered to look for work.

1933 Thirteen million workers were unemployed (25% of the work force) and many were underemployed. Malnutrition increased, as did tuberculosis, typhoid, and dysentery. Large numbers of homeless workers roamed the U.S. seeking work.

1932 Elections

Hoover rejected direct relief as undermining to character. He urged Americans to turn to community and church resources (Salvation Army, Community Chest, Red Cross) to meet the needs of the poor. Hoover gradually used federal agencies to address issues and set up the Reconstruction Finance Corporation in 1932 to make loans to stimulate economy. Hoover refused to accept any responsibility for the depression.

Franklin Roosevelt promoted liberalism, rejecting both Hoover's conservatism and the radical approach of the Socialists and Communists. He offered a New Deal for the "forgotten man" and promised a balanced budget along with economic reforms. Democrats supported repeal of Prohibition and an increase in federal relief. FDR won 57% of the popular vote and Democrats took control of both the House and Senate.

November 1932-March 1933 Hoover's lame duck administration.

March 1933 FDR launched Hundred Days of legislative and administrative changes. New Deal programs launched to relieve economic hardships.

11.5   Major New Deal Programs

Program, year established, purpose

Agricultural Adjustment Act (AAA) 1933 Provided crop subsidies to reduce production.

Civil Works Administration (CWA) 1933 Provided public works at $15/week for four million workers.

Civilian Conservation Corps (CCC) 1933 Sent young men to work at camps for conservation and restoration work.

Federal Emergency Relief Act (FERA) 1933 Distributed direct aid to unemployed workers.

Glass-Steagall Act 1933 Created federally insured bank (FDIC) to prevent bank failures.

National Industrial Recovery Act (NIRA) 1933 Created NRA to enforce minimum wage and collective bargaining for workers.

National Youth Administration (NYA) 1935 Provided part-time jobs for more than two million college and high school students.

Public Works Administration (PWA) 1933 Multi-billion dollar federal program public works projects.

Rural Electrification Administration (REA) 1935 Promoted cooperatives to bring electricity to farms and rural areas.

Securities and Exchange Commission (SEC) 1934 Regulated stock market and limited certain types of speculation; restricted margin buying.

Social Security Act 1935 Created system of pensions, unemployment insurance, and aid to the blind, deaf, and disabled, as well as dependent children.

Tennessee Valley Authority (TVA) 1933 Built series of dams to provide electricity.

Wagner Act 1935 Protected workers' rights to join unions.

Works Progress Administration (WPA) 1935 Employed nearly 10 million workers in construction and other jobs and provided work in arts project.

11.6   Important Supreme Court Cases on Monopolies

United States v. E. C. Knight Company, 156 U.S. 1 (1895)

Northern Securities Co. v. United States, 193 U.S. 197 (1904)

Swift and Company v. United States, 196 U.S. 375 (1905)

Loewe v. Lawlor, 208 U.S. 274 (1908)

Standard Oil Co. of New Jersey v. United States, 221 U.S. 1 (1911)

Houston East and West Texas Railway Company v. United States, 234 U.S. 342 (1914)

A. L. A. Schechter Poultry Corp. v. United States, 295 U.S. 495 (1935)

Ashwander v. Tennessee Valley Authority, 297 U.S. 288 (1936)

Bates v. State Bar of Arizona, 433 U.S. 350 (1977)

11.7   U.S. Business Cycle Expansions and Contractions, 1854-1999

Contractions (recessions) start at the peak of a business cycle and end at the trough. A recession is a recurring period of decline in total output, income, employment, and trade, usually lasting from six months to a year, and marked by widespread contractions in many sectors of the economy. A depression is a recession that is major in both scale and duration.

Trough	Peak	Trough	Peak
December 1854	June 1857	March 1919	January 1920
December 1858	October 1860	July 1921	May 1923
June 1861	April 1865	July 1924	October 1926
December 1867	June 1869	November 1927	August 1929
December 1870	October 1873	March 1933	May 1937
March 1879	March 1882	June 1938	February 1945
May 1885	March 1887	October 1945	November 1948
April 1888	July 1890	October 1949	July 1953
May 1891	January 1893	May 1954	August 1957
June 1894	December 1895	April 1958	April 1960
June 1897	June 1899	February 1961	December 1969
December 1900	September 1902	November 1970	November 1973
August 1904	May 1907	March 1975	January 1980
June 1908	January 1910	July 1980	July 1981
January 1912	January 1913	November 1982	July 1990
December 1914	August 1918	March 1991*	

* The determination that the last recession ended in March 1991 is the most recent decision of the Business Cycle Dating Committee of the National Bureau of Economic Research.
Source: U.S. Department of Commerce.

11.8   Consumer Price Index and Purchasing Power of the Consumer Dollar, 1913-1988

Year	CPI	Purchasing Power of the Dollar 1982 = $1.00	Year	CPI	Purchasing Power of the Dollar 1982 = $1.00
1913	9.9	10.077	1951	26.0	3.846
1914	10.0	9.942	1952	26.5	3.765
1915	10.1	9.842	1953	26.7	3.735
1916	10.9	9.152	1954	26.9	3.717
1917	12.8	7.793	1955	26.8	3.732
1918	15.1	6.635	1956	27.2	3.678
1919	17.3	5.779	1957	28.1	3.549
1920	20.0	4.989	1958	28.9	3.457
1921	17.9	5.585	1959	29.1	3.427
1922	16.8	5.962	1960	29.6	3.373
1923	17.1	5.857	1961	29.9	3.340
1924	17.1	5.845	1962	30.2	3.304
1925	17.5	5.701	1963	30.6	3.265
1926	17.7	5.647	1964	31.0	3.220
1927	17.4	5.755	1965	31.5	3.166
1928	17.1	5.833	1966	32.4	3.080
1929	17.1	5.833	1967	33.4	2.993
1930	16.7	5.986	1968	34.8	2.873
1931	15.2	6.563	1969	36.7	2.726
1932	13.7	7.317	1970	38.8	2.574
1933	13.0	7.712	1971	40.5	2.466
1934	13.4	7.464	1972	41.8	2.391
1935	13.7	7.281	1973	44.4	2.251
1936	12.6	7.213	1974	49.3	2.029
1937	14.4	6.961	1975	53.8	1.859
1938	14.1	7.093	1976	56.9	1.757
1939	13.9	7.195	1977	60.6	1.649
1940	14.0	7.126	1978	65.2	1.532
1941	14.7	6.788	1979	72.6	1.380
1942	16.3	6.132	1980	82.4	1.215
1943	17.3	5.779	1981	90.9	1.098
1944	17.6	5.680	1982	96.5	1.035
1945	18.0	5.552	1983	99.6	1.003
1946	19.5	5.115	1984	103.9	.961
1947	22.3	4.474	1985	107.6	.928
1948	24.1	4.151	1986	109.6	.913
1949	23.8	4.193	1987	113.6	.880
1950	24.1	4.151	1988	118.3	.846

11.9 Consumer Price Index—Urban Consumers (CPI-U), 1977-1998

Percent increase

1977	6.5
1978	7.6
1979	11.3
1980	13.5
1981	10.3
1982	6.2
1983	3.2
1984	4.3
1985	3.6
1986	1.9
1987	3.6
1988	4.1
1989	4.8
1990	5.4
1991	4.2
1992	3.0
1993	3.0
1994	2.6
1995	2.8
1996	3.0
1997	1.7
1998	1.2

Source: Bureau of Labor Statistics.

© 2000 by The Center for Applied Research in Education

11.10 Trends in Major Components of the CPI, 1989-1998

	1989	1990	1991	1992	1993	1994	1995	1996	1997	1998
Food and beverages	5.5	5.3	2.5	1.6	2.7	2.7	2.1	4.2	1.6	2.2
Housing	3.9	4.5	3.4	2.6	2.7	2.2	3.0	2.9	2.4	2.3
Apparel and upkeep	1.0	5.1	3.4	1.4	.9	−1.6	.1	−.2	1.0	−.5
Transportation	4.0	10.4	−1.5	3.0	2.4	3.8	1.5	4.4	−1.4	−1.3
Medical care	8.5	9.6	7.9	6.6	5.4	4.9	3.9	3.0	2.8	3.4
Entertainment	5.1	4.3	3.9	2.8	2.8	2.3	3.3	2.9	1.4	1.3
Other goods and services	8.2	7.6	8.0	6.5	2.7	4.2	4.3	3.6	5.2	6.4

Source: Bureau of Labor Statistics.

11.11   U.S. Trade Deficit, 1987-1997

$ Billions

Year	$ Billions
1987	$153.4
1988	115.9
1989	92.3
1990	81.2
1991	31.0
1992	39.2
1993	72.0
1994	104.4
1995	105.6
1996	111.0
1997	113.7

Source: U.S. Department of Commerce.

11.12   Ten Largest Banks in the U.S. by Deposits, 1999

Name of Bank	Total Deposits as of December 31, 1998 ($000)
Citibank, NA—New York	202,928,000
Bank of America National Trust and Savings Association—California	187,755,000
The Chase Manhattan Bank—New York	185,173,000
NationsBank, National Association—North Carolina	178,172,000
First Union National Bank—North Carolina	147,028,828
Wells Fargo Bank, National Association—California	69,415,000
Morgan Guaranty Trust Company of New York	56,220,962
Fleet National Bank—Rhode Island	50,454,000
U.S. Bank National Association—Minnesota	49,020,703
Bankboston NA	48,529,403

Source: FDIC.

11.13   Energy Expenditures by State, 1998

	Total		Per capita[1]	
	$ Millions	Rank	Dollars	Rank
United States	504,688	NA	1,938	NA
Alabama	8,912	20	2,114	13
Alaska	1,765	45	2,934	3
Arizona	7,545	24	1,844	39
Arkansas	5,147	33	2,097	17
California	50,216	1	1,601	48
Colorado	6,100	28	1,665	47
Connecticut	6,620	26	2,023	19
Delaware	1,510	48	2,133	10
District of Columbia	1,241	NA	2,184	NA
Florida	21,654	7	1,551	49
Georgia	13,777	10	1,951	28
Hawaii	2,065	42	1,761	43
Idaho	2,176	41	1,915	33
Illinois	22,632	6	1,929	30
Indiana	12,825	13	2,230	8
Iowa	5,944	29	2,099	16
Kansas	5,391	31	2,114	13
Kentucky	8,046	23	2,103	15
Louisiana	13,320	12	3,087	2
Maine	2,807	39	2,267	6
Maryland	8,692	21	1,738	44
Massachusetts	11,580	15	1,917	32
Michigan	17,777	8	1,874	36
Minnesota	8,502	22	1,859	38
Mississippi	5,282	32	1,979	24
Missouri	9,856	17	1,868	37
Montana	1,918	43	2,239	7
Nebraska	3,279	35	2,017	20
Nevada	3,099	37	2,117	11
New Hampshire	2,180	40	1,920	31
New Jersey	17,190	9	2,174	9
New Mexico	3,113	36	1,876	35
New York	31,041	3	1,706	46
North Carolina	13,677	11	1,932	29
North Dakota	1,645	47	2,571	4
Ohio	22,892	5	2,063	18
Oklahoma	6,450	27	1,982	23
Oregon	5,528	30	1,786	41
Pennsylvania	23,542	4	1,952	27
Rhode Island	1,894	44	1,902	34
South Carolina	7,245	25	1,989	22
South Dakota	1,429	49	1,973	25
Tennessee	10,203	16	1,972	26
Texas	47,246	2	2,563	5
Utah	2,959	38	1,550	50
Vermont	1,158	50	1,994	21
Virginia	11,858	14	1,811	40
Washington	9,185	18	1,716	45
West Virginia	3,858	34	2,117	11
Wisconsin	8,956	19	1,761	42
Wyoming	1,672	46	3,515	1

NA = Not applicable.
[1] Based on resident population estimated as of July 1.
Source: U.S. Bureau of the Census.

11.14   Farm Economics by State, 1997

	TOTAL			LIVESTOCK			CROPS	
	Rank	Cash Receipts $ Thousands	Rank	Cash Receipts $ Thousands		Rank	Cash Receipts $ Thousands	
Alabama	26	2,908,347	15	2,167,575		34	740,772	
Alaska	50	30,119	50	5,739		50	24,380	
Arizona	29	2,256,444	31	810,318		22	1,446,126	
Arkansas	13	5,065,456	9	3,023,223		18	2,042,233	
California	1	22,261,109	2	5,548,527		1	16,712,582	
Colorado	17	3,984,525	11	2,623,691		26	1,360,834	
Connecticut	41	484,490	43	256,811		40	227,679	
Delaware	40	675,613	39	516,489		44	159,124	
Florida	9	5,848,907	27	1,129,810		5	4,719,097	
Georgia	11	5,166,101	10	2,789,184		14	2,376,917	
Hawaii	42	483,468	47	71,812		38	411,656	
Idaho	22	3,166,248	26	1,221,044		19	1,945,204	
Illinois	5	7,887,034	18	1,710,126		2	6,176,908	
Indiana	14	4,981,458	17	1,741,352		10	3,240,106	
Iowa	3	10,958,874	4	5,067,752		3	5,891,122	
Kansas	6	7,521,311	5	4,692,784		12	2,828,527	
Kentucky	25	3,059,463	21	1,615,550		23	1,443,913	
Louisiana	32	2,024,862	34	629,837		25	1,395,025	
Maine	43	479,230	42	281,071		42	198,159	
Maryland	36	1,402,319	30	830,490		36	571,829	
Massachusetts	45	430,377	46	103,322		39	327,055	
Michigan	20	3,520,756	25	1,323,919		15	2,196,837	
Minnesota	7	7,001,667	8	3,450,724		7	3,550,943	
Mississippi	24	3,126,153	19	1,684,888		24	1,441,265	
Missouri	16	4,399,227	14	2,265,455		16	2,133,772	
Montana	33	1,845,168	32	797,914		30	1,047,254	
Nebraska	4	8,690,446	3	5,187,294		8	3,503,152	
Nevada	47	285,614	45	163,572		45	122,042	
New Hampshire	48	152,167	48	64,017		47	88,150	
New Jersey	38	773,151	44	200,478		35	572,673	
New Mexico	35	1,415,176	28	963,390		37	451,786	
New York	27	2,877,474	16	1,865,335		31	1,012,139	
North Carolina	8	6,986,814	7	3,735,338		9	3,251,476	
North Dakota	23	3,153,765	37	565,653		13	2,588,112	
Ohio	15	4,576,009	23	1,589,193		11	2,986,816	
Oklahoma	19	3,704,737	12	2,571,268		29	1,133,469	
Oregon	28	2,719,992	33	665,217		17	2,054,775	
Pennsylvania	18	3,738,250	13	2,552,046		28	1,186,204	
Rhode Island	49	80,059	49	10,008		49	70,051	
South Carolina	34	1,441,296	35	610,983		33	830,313	
South Dakota	21	3,383,637	20	1,676,297		20	1,707,340	
Tennessee	31	2,126,727	29	868,443		27	1,258,284	
Texas	2	13,287,680	1	8,453,836		4	4,833,844	
Utah	37	815,400	36	592,443		41	222,957	
Vermont	44	472,314	40	380,037		46	92,277	
Virginia	30	2,248,012	24	1,393,180		32	854,832	
Washington	12	5,157,957	22	1,594,376		6	3,563,581	
West Virginia	46	386,335	41	312,050		48	74,285	
Wisconsin	10	5,582,296	6	3,926,012		21	1,656,284	
Wyoming	39	725,987	38	543,918		43	182,069	

Source: USDA—National Agricultural Statistics Service.

11.15 Effective Tax Rates, 1901-1999

	President	Effective Tax Rate		President	Effective Tax Rate
1901-1909	Theodore Roosevelt	8.5	1969-1974	Richard Nixon	
1909-1913	William Taft	8.2	4/29/1969		32.5
1921-1923	Warren Harding	13.2	4/26/1970		31.5
1923-1929	Calvin Coolidge	10.1	4/23/1971		30.9
1929-1933	Herbert Hoover	10.8	4/27/1972		32.1
1933-1945	Franklin Roosevelt		4/27/1973		32.0
3/10/36		16.0	1974-1977	Gerald Ford	
3/8/1940		18.0	5/1/1974		32.9
3/18/1941		20.9	4/26/1975		31.6
3/19/1942		21.3	4/28/1976		32.3
4/7/1943		26.3	1977-1981	James Carter	
4/1/1944		25.0	4/30/1977		32.6
1945-1953	Harry Truman		4/29/1978		32.4
4/4/1945		25.7	4/29/1979		32.6
4/5/1946		25.8	4/30/1980		32.9
4/5/1947		25.9	1981-1989	Ronald Reagan	
3/29/1948		24.1	5/4/1981		33.7
3/25/1949		22.9	5/2/1982		33.3
4/3/1950		25.5	4/28/1983		32.3
4/10/1951		27.3	4/27/1984		32.1
4/10/1952		27.3	4/29/1985		32.5
1953-1961	Dwight Eisenhower		4/29/1986		32.8
4/9/1953		27.1	5/3/1987		33.5
4/4/1954		25.7	4/30/1988		33.1
4/7/1955		26.5	1989-1993	George Bush	
4/9/1956		27.3	5/2/1989		33.2
4/11/1957		27.5	5/1/1990		32.9
4/9/1958		26.9	5/1/1991		32.9
4/12/1959		27.9	4/29/1992		32.7
4/15/1960		28.9	1993-	William Clinton	
1961-1963	John Kennedy		4/30/1993		32.9
4/16/1961		29.0	5/2/1994		33.4
4/16/1962		29.0	5/4/1995		33.8
1963-1969	Lyndon Johnson		5/5/1996		34.4
4/18/1963		29.5	5/9/1997		35.1
4/13/1964		28.2	5/10/1998		35.4
4/13/1965		28.1			
4/16/1966		28.9			
4/18/1967		29.4			
4/23/1968		31.0			

Source: Tax Foundation.

11.16   Deficits, Surpluses and Debt, 1956-1998

	In Billions of Dollars			As a Percentage of GDP			GDP (Billions of dollars)		
	Deficit (–) or Surplus	Standardized-Employment Deficit (–) or Surplus[a]	Debt Held by the Public	Deficit (–) or Surplus	Standardized-Employment Deficit (–) or Surplus[ab]	Debt Held by the Public	Debt Held by the Public	Actual[c]	NAIRU[d] Potential (Percent)
1956	4	e	222	0.9	f	52.0	427	416	5.4
1957	3	1	219	0.8	0.2	48.7	451	445	5.4
1958	–3	1	226	–0.6	0.2	49.3	459	472	5.4
1959	–13	–10	235	–2.6	–2.1	47.9	490	497	5.4
1960	e	e	237	0.1	0.1	45.6	519	520	5.5
1961	–3	3	238	–0.6	0.5	45.0	530	548	5.5
1962	–7	–5	248	–1.3	–0.8	43.7	568	576	5.5
1963	–5	–3	254	–0.8	–0.5	42.4	599	607	5.5
1964	–6	–7	257	–0.9	–1.0	40.1	641	640	5.6
1965	–1	–5	261	–0.2	–0.8	38.0	687	678	5.6
1966	–4	–15	264	–0.5	–2.1	34.9	756	724	5.7
1967	–9	–20	267	–1.1	–2.6	32.9	810	780	5.8
1968	–25	–36	290	–2.9	–4.3	33.3	870	845	5.8
1969	3	–10	278	0.3	–1.1	29.3	948	919	5.8
1970	–3	–8	283	–0.3	–0.8	28.1	1,010	1,005	5.9
1971	–23	–20	303	–2.1	–1.8	28.1	1,078	1,094	5.9
1972	–23	–22	322	–2.0	–1.9	27.4	1,175	1,183	6.0
1973	–15	–31	341	–1.1	–2.4	26.0	1,310	1,275	6.1
1974	–6	–23	344	–0.4	–1.6	23.9	1,438	1,415	6.2
1975	–53	–37	395	–3.4	–2.3	25.4	1,554	1,613	6.2
1976	–74	–54	477	–4.3	–3.0	27.6	1,732	1,785	6.2
1977	–54	–46	549	–2.7	–2.3	27.9	1,971	1,996	6.2
1978	–59	–64	607	–2.7	–2.9	27.4	2,215	2,209	6.3
1979	–41	–56	640	–1.6	–2.3	25.6	2,497	2,472	6.3
1980	–74	–63	710	–2.7	–2.3	26.1	2,719	2,770	6.2
1981	–79	–65	785	–2.6	–2.1	25.8	3,048	3,117	6.2
1982	–128	–76	920	–4.0	–2.2	28.6	3,214	3,414	6.1
1983	–208	–139	1,132	–6.1	–3.8	33.1	3,423	3,654	6.1
1984	–185	–170	1,300	–4.9	–4.4	34.0	3,819	3,892	6.1
1985	–212	–196	1,500	–5.2	–4.7	36.5	4,109	4,137	6.0
1986	–221	–221	1,737	–5.1	–5.0	39.8	4,368	4,380	6.0
1987	–150	–158	1,889	–3.2	–3.4	41.0	4,609	4,638	6.0
1988	–155	–163	2,051	–3.1	–3.3	41.4	4,957	4,934	5.9
1989	–152	–157	2,190	–2.8	–3.0	40.9	5,356	5,282	5.9
1990	–221	–183	2,411	–3.9	–3.2	42.4	5,683	5,640	5.9
1991	–269	–202	2,688	–4.6	–3.4	45.9	5,862	6,014	5.9
1992	–290	–232	2,999	–4.7	–3.7	48.8	6,149	6,313	5.8
1993	–255	–237	3,247	–3.9	–3.6	50.1	6,478	6,604	5.8
1994	–203	–190	3,432	–3.0	–2.7	50.1	6,849	6,899	5.8
1995	–164	–187	3,603	–2.3	–2.6	50.1	7,194	7,222	5.7
1996	–107	–127	3,733	–1.4	–1.7	49.6	7,533	7,548	5.7
1997	–22	–86	3,771	–0.3	–1.1	47.3	7,972	7,897	5.7
1998	70	–1	3,720	0.8	f	44.3	8,404	8,218	5.6

[a] Excludes deposit insurance, receipts from auctions of the electromagnetic spectrum, timing adjustments, and contributions from allied nations for Operation Desert Storm (which were received in 1991 and 1992).

[b] The standardized-employment deficit is shown as a percentage of potential GDP.

[c] Values for 1956 through 1960 are estimated by CBO.

[d] The NAIRU is the non-accelerating inflation rate of unemployment. It is the benchmark for computing potential GDP.

[e] Less than $500 million.

[f] Less than 0.05 percent.

Source: Congressional Budget Office; Department of Commerce, Bureau of Economic Analysis.

11.17 Public Debt, 1791-1986

The national public debt is the total amount of money owed by the government; the federal budget deficit is the yearly amount by which spending exceeds revenue. The sum of all the deficits (and those few budget surpluses) for the past two centuries is the current public debt.

Date	Amount	Date	Amount
01/01/1791	$ 75,463,476.52	01/01/1838	$ 3,308,124.07
01/01/1792	77,227,924.66	01/01/1839	10,434,221.14
01/01/1793	80,358,634.04	01/01/1840	3,573,343.82
01/01/1794	78,427,404.77	01/01/1841	5,250,875.54
01/01/1795	80,747,587.39	01/01/1842	13,594,480.73
01/01/1796	83,762,172.07	01/01/1843	20,201,226.27
01/01/1797	82,064,479.33	07/01/1843	32,742,922.00
01/01/1798	79,228,529.12	07/01/1844	23,461,652.50
01/01/1799	78,408,669.77	07/01/1845	15,925,303.01
01/01/1800	82,976,294.35	07/01/1846	15,550,202.97
01/01/1801	83,038,050.80	07/01/1847	38,826,534.77
01/01/1802	80,712,632.25	07/01/1848	47,044,862.23
01/01/1803	77,054,686.40	07/01/1849	63,061,858.69
01/01/1804	86,427,120.88	07/01/1850	63,452,773.55
01/01/1805	82,312,150.50	07/01/1851	68,304,796.02
01/01/1806	75,723,270.66	07/01/1852	66,199,341.71
01/01/1807	69,218,398.64	07/01/1853	59,803,117.70
01/01/1808	65,196,317.97	07/01/1854	42,242,222.42
01/01/1809	57,023,192.09	07/01/1855	35,586,956.56
01/01/1810	53,173,217.52	07/01/1856	31,972,537.90
01/01/1811	48,005,587.76	07/01/1857	28,699,831.85
01/01/1812	45,209,737.90	07/01/1858	44,911,881.03
01/01/1813	55,962,827.57	07/01/1859	58,496,837.88
01/01/1814	81,487,846.24	07/01/1860	64,842,287.88
01/01/1815	99,833,660.15	07/01/1861	90,580,873.72
01/01/1816	127,334,933.74	07/01/1862	524,176,412.13
01/01/1817	123,491,965.16	07/01/1863	1,119,772,138.63
01/01/1818	103,466,633.83	07/01/1864	1,815,784,370.57
01/01/1819	95,529,648.28	07/01/1865	2,680,647,869.74
01/01/1820	91,015,566.15	07/01/1866	2,773,236,173.69
01/01/1821	89,987,427.66	07/01/1867	2,678,126,103.87
01/01/1822	93,546,676.98	07/01/1868	2,611,687,851.19
01/01/1823	90,875,877.28	07/01/1869	2,588,452,213.94
01/01/1824	90,269,777.77	07/01/1870	2,480,672,427.81
01/01/1825	83,788,432.71	07/01/1871	2,353,211,332.32
01/01/1826	81,054,059.99	07/01/1872	2,253,251,328.78
01/01/1827	73,987,357.20	07/01/1873	2,234,482,993.20
01/01/1828	67,475,043.87	07/01/1874	2,251,690,468.43
01/01/1829	58,421,413.67	07/01/1875	2,232,284,531.95
01/01/1830	48,565,406.50	07/01/1876	2,180,395,067.15
01/01/1831	39,123,191.68	07/01/1877	2,205,301,392.10
01/01/1832	24,322,235.18	07/01/1878	2,256,205,892.53
01/01/1833	7,001,698.83	07/01/1879	2,349,567,482.04
01/01/1834	4,760,082.08	07/01/1880	2,120,415,370.63
01/01/1835	33,733.05	07/01/1881	2,069,013,569.58
01/01/1836	37,513.05	07/01/1882	1,918,312,994.03
01/01/1837	336,957.83	07/01/1883	1,884,171,728.07

07/01/1884	$ 1,830,528,923.57	06/30/1936	$ 33,778,543,493.73
07/01/1885	1,863,964,873.14	06/30/1937	36,424,613,732.29
07/01/1886	1,775,063,013.78	06/30/1938	37,164,740,315.45
07/01/1887	1,657,602,592.63	06/30/1939	40,439,532,411.11
07/01/1888	1,692,858,984.58	06/29/1940	42,967,531,037.68
07/01/1889	1,619,052,922.23	06/30/1941	48,961,443,535.71
07/01/1890	1,552,140,204.73	06/30/1942	72,422,445,116.22
07/01/1891	1,545,996,591.61	06/30/1943	136,696,090,329.90
07/01/1892	1,588,464,144.63	06/30/1944	201,003,387,221.13
07/01/1893	1,545,985,686.13	06/30/1945	258,682,187,409.93
07/01/1894	1,632,253,636.68	06/28/1946	269,422,099,173.26
07/01/1895	1,676,120,983.25	06/30/1947	258,286,383,108.67
07/01/1896	1,769,840,323.40	06/30/1948	252,292,246,512.99
07/01/1897	1,817,672,665.90	06/30/1949	252,770,359,860.33
07/01/1898	1,796,531,995.90	06/30/1950	257,357,352,351.04
07/01/1899	1,991,927,306.92	06/29/1951	255,221,976,814.93
07/01/1900	2,136,961,091.67	06/30/1952	259,105,178,785.43
07/01/1901	2,143,326,933.89	06/30/1953	266,071,061,638.57
07/01/1902	2,158,610,445.89	12/31/1953	275,168,120,129.39
07/01/1903	2,202,464,781.89	12/31/1954	278,749,814,391.33
07/01/1904	2,264,003,585.14	12/30/1955	280,768,553,188.96
07/01/1905	2,274,615,063.84	12/31/1956	276,627,527,996.11
07/01/1906	2,337,161,839.04	12/31/1957	274,897,784,290.72
07/01/1907	2,457,188,061.54	12/31/1958	282,922,423,583.87
07/01/1908	2,626,806,271.54	12/31/1959	290,797,771,717.63
07/01/1909	2,639,546,241.04	12/30/1960	290,216,815,241.68
07/01/1910	2,652,665,838.04	12/29/1961	296,168,761,214.92
07/01/1911	2,765,600,606.69	12/31/1962	303,470,080,489.27
07/01/1912	2,868,373,874.16	12/31/1963	309,346,845,059.17
07/01/1913	2,916,204,913.66	12/31/1964	317,940,472,718.38
07/01/1914	2,912,499,269.16	12/31/1965	320,904,110,042.04
07/01/1915	3,058,136,873.16	12/30/1966	329,319,249,366.68
07/01/1916	3,609,244,262.16	12/29/1967	344,663,009,745.18
07/01/1917	5,717,770,279.52	12/31/1968	358,028,625,002.91
07/01/1918	14,592,161,414.00	12/31/1969	368,225,581,254.41
07/01/1919	27,390,970,113.12	12/31/1970	389,158,403,690.26
07/01/1920	25,952,456,406.16	12/31/1971	424,130,961,959.95
06/30/1921	23,977,450,552.54	12/29/1972	449,298,066,119.00
06/30/1922	22,963,381,708.31	12/31/1973	469,898,039,554.70
06/30/1923	22,349,707,365.36	12/31/1974	492,665,000,000.00*
06/30/1924	21,250,812,989.49	12/31/1975	576,649,000,000.00*
06/30/1925	20,516,193,887.90	12/31/1976	653,544,000,000.00*
06/30/1926	19,643,216,315.19	12/30/1977	718,943,000,000.00*
06/30/1927	18,511,906,931.85	12/29/1978	789,207,000,000.00*
06/30/1928	17,604,293,201.43	12/31/1979	845,116,000,000.00*
06/29/1929	16,931,088,484.10	12/31/1980	930,210,000,000.00*
06/30/1930	16,185,309,831.43	12/31/1981	1,028,729,000,000.00*
06/30/1931	16,801,281,491.71	12/31/1982	1,197,073,000,000.00*
06/30/1932	19,487,002,444.13	12/31/1983	1,410,702,000,000.00*
06/30/1933	22,538,672,560.15	12/31/1984	1,662,966,000,000.00*
06/30/1934	27,053,141,414.48	12/31/1985	1,945,941,616,459.88
06/29/1935	28,700,892,624.53	09/30/1986	2,125,302,616,658.42

* Rounded to millions.
The Outstanding Public Debt as of 04/09/99 is: $5,664,052,994,792.31.

11.18   History of the Federal Reserve

People who lived during the early 1900s deposited their money into savings accounts and borrowed money to build a home or start a business. When people borrowed money, banks issued them banknotes, and they spent these notes in the same way they would spend money. The public valued these banknotes as money because banks promised to exchange them for gold or silver on demand.

Occasionally the public feared that banks would not or could not honor the promise to redeem these notes, which led to bank runs. Believing that a particular bank's ability to pay was questionable, a large number of people in a single day would demand to have their banknotes exchanged for gold or silver. These bank runs created fear that often spread, causing runs on other banks and general financial panic.

Financial Panic and Bank Runs

During a run, even the healthiest and most conservative bank could not redeem all of its notes at once. Banks then, just as now, used most of the money deposited with them to make loans. As a result, the money was not sitting in the banks' vaults but was circulating in the community. In other words, the banks may have been solvent but not liquid. So when a bank run occurred, many times a bank had to close because it could not exchange the large number of notes presented in a single day.

Banks tried to prepare for increasing depositor withdrawals by building up their reserves of gold or silver and by restricting credit. They stopped making loans, and panic ensued as everyone scrambled to redeem notes. Businesses had difficulty operating normally. The country's economic activity slowed, and many people lost their jobs and life savings.

Financial panics such as these occurred frequently during the 1800s and early 1900s. A particularly severe banking panic in 1907 prompted cries for reform. People wanted a central banking authority to ensure the operation of healthy banks that might otherwise fail because of a bank panic and to supervise bank activities so banks would not engage in unsound business practices that might lead to more bank failures. The public also wanted a more elastic currency and an improved payments system, which would contribute to economic stability.

Creating the Fed

In response, Congress set up the National Monetary Commission to study the nation's financial system and pinpoint its weaknesses. One of the primary weaknesses identified was that the United States lacked an elastic currency. This meant the banking system did not have a way to supply currency if demand for it increased significantly in a short time, so panics occurred. In 1912, the commission presented Congress with a monetary reform plan that recommended the establishment of the National Reserve Association, which would hold the reserves of commercial banks and could make short-term loans to banks to ensure credit availability. Congress responded by drafting the Federal Reserve Act, creating the Federal Reserve System. President Woodrow Wilson signed the act into law on December 23, 1913.

Governors

Originally the Federal Reserve Board was composed of seven members, including five appointive members, the Secretary of the Treasury, who was ex-officio chairman of the Board, and the Comptroller of the Currency. In 1922 the number of appointive members was increased to six. The Banking Act of 1935, approved Aug. 23, 1935, changed the name of the Federal Reserve Board to the Board of Governors of the Federal Reserve System and provided that the Board should be composed of seven appointive members; that the Secretary of the Treasury and the Comptroller of the Currency should continue to serve as members until Feb. 1, 1936; that the appointive members in office on the date of that act should continue to serve until Feb. 1, 1936, or until their successors were appointed and had qualified; and that thereafter the terms of members should be fourteen years and that the designation of Chairman and Vice Chairman of the Board should be for a term of four years. Paul A. Volcker was chairman from Aug. 1979 to Aug. 1987 when Alan Greenspan became chairman.

Functions

Congress created the Federal Reserve System in 1913 to serve as the central bank of the United States and to provide the nation with a safer, more flexible and more stable monetary and financial system. Over the years, the Fed's role in banking and the economy has expanded, but its focus has remained the same. Today, the Fed's three functions are:

1. to conduct the nation's monetary policy,
2. to provide and maintain an effective and efficient payments system, and
3. to supervise and regulate banking operations.

Although all three roles are important in maintaining a stable growing economy, monetary policy is the most visible to many citizens. Monetary policy is the strategic action taken by the Federal Reserve to influence the supply of money and credit in order to foster price stability and maintain maximum sustainable economic growth.

Structure

The Federal Reserve System was structured by Congress as a distinctly American version of a central bank, established to carry out Congress' own constitutional mandate to "coin money and regulate the value thereof." The Fed is a decentralized central bank, with Reserve Banks and branches in 12 districts across the country, coordinated by the Board of Governors in Washington, D.C. The Fed has a unique public/private structure that operates independently within government but not independent of it. The Board of Governors, appointed by the President of the United States and confirmed by the Senate, represents the public sector, or governmental side of the Fed. The Reserve Banks and the local citizens on their boards of directors represent the private sector. This structure provides accountability while avoiding centralized, governmental control of banking and monetary policy.

Each Federal Reserve Bank has a board of directors, whose members work closely with their Reserve Bank President to provide grassroots economic information and input on management and monetary policy decisions. These boards are drawn from the general public and the banking community and oversee the activities of the organization. Banks that hold stock in the Fed are called member banks. All nationally chartered banks hold stock in the Federal Reserve.

Source: Federal Reserve.

11.19 Important Terms in U.S. Banking and Economics

absolute advantage A person, company or country has an absolute advantage if its output per unit of input of all goods and services produced is higher than that of another person, company or country.

amortization The process of fully paying off indebtedness by installments of principal and earned interest over a definite time.

Annual Percentage Rate (APR) The cost of credit on a yearly basis expressed as a percentage.

balance of payments An accounting statement of the money value of international transactions between one nation and the rest of the world over a specific time period. The statement shows the sum of transactions of individuals, businesses and government agencies located in one nation, against those of all other nations.

balance of trade That part of a nation's balance of payments dealing with imports and exports, that is trade in goods and services, over a given period. If exports of goods exceed imports, the trade balance is said to be "favorable"; if imports exceed exports, the trade balance if said to be "unfavorable."

bank regulation The formulation and issuance by authorized agencies of specific rules or regulations, under governing law, for the conduct and structure of banking.

bank run (bank panic) A series of unexpected cash withdrawals caused by a sudden decline in depositor confidence or fear that the bank will be closed by the chartering agency, i.e., many depositors withdraw cash almost simultaneously. Since the cash reserve a bank keeps on hand is only a small fraction of its deposits, a large number of withdrawals in a short period of time can deplete available cash and force the bank to close and possibly go out of business.

capital market The market in which corporate equity and longer-term debt securities (those maturing in more than one year) are issued and traded.

central bank The principal monetary authority of a nation, a central bank performs several key functions, including issuing currency and regulating the supply of credit in the economy. The Federal Reserve is the central bank of the United States.

certificate of deposit (CD) A form of time deposit at a bank or savings institution; a time deposit cannot be withdrawn before a specified maturity date without being subject to an interest penalty for early withdrawal. Small-denomination CDs are often purchased by individuals. Large CDs of $100,000 or more are often in negotiable form, meaning they can be sold or transferred among holders before maturity.

collateral Property that is offered to secure a loan or other credit and that becomes subject to seizure on default. (Also called security.)

comparative advantage Describes the ability of a person, company or country to produce a good or service at a lower cost relative to other goods and services. Even though a country may have an absolute advantage over another country, it still will be better off specializing in the good or service in which it has a comparative advantage and trading for goods and services it doesn't produce as efficiently.

credit The promise to pay in the future in order to buy or borrow in the present. The right to defer payment of debt.

current account balance The difference between the nation's total exports of goods, services, and transfers and its total imports of them. It excludes transactions in financial assets and liabilities.

currency appreciation An increase in the value of one currency relative to another currency. Appreciation occurs when, because of a change in exchange rates, a unit of one currency buys more units of another currency.

currency depreciation A decline in the value of one currency relative to another currency. Depreciation occurs when, because of a change in exchange rates, a unit of one currency buys fewer units of another currency.

currency devaluation A deliberate downward adjustment in the official exchange rate established, or pegged, by a government against a specified standard, such as another currency or gold.

currency revaluation A deliberate upward adjustment in the official exchange rate established, or pegged, by a government against a specified standard, such as another currency or gold.

default Failure to meet the terms of a credit agreement.

demand deposit A deposit payable on demand, or a time deposit with a maturity period or required notice period of less than 14 days, on which the depository institution does not reserve the right to require at least 14 days written notice of intended withdrawal. Commonly takes the form of a checking account.

depository institution Financial institution that obtains its funds mainly through deposits from the public. Includes commercial banks, savings and loan associations, savings banks, and credit unions.

discount rate The interest rate at which eligible depository institutions may borrow funds, usually for short periods, directly from the Federal Reserve Banks. The law requires the board of directors of each Reserve Bank to establish the discount rate every 14 days subject to the approval of the Board of Governors.

Eurodollars Deposits denominated in U.S. dollars at banks and other financial institutions outside the United States. Although this name originated because of the large amounts of such deposits held at banks in Western Europe, similar deposits in other parts of the world are also called Eurodollars.

exchange rate The price of a country's currency in terms of another country's currency.

Federal Deposit Insurance Corporation (FDIC) Agency of the federal government that insures accounts at most commercial banks and mutual savings banks. The FDIC also has primary federal supervisory authority over insured state banks that are not members of the Federal Reserve System.

federal funds Reserve balances that depository institutions lend each other, usually on an overnight basis. In addition, Federal funds include certain other kinds of borrowings by depository institutions from each other and from federal agencies.

federal funds rate ("funds rate") The interest rate at which banks borrow federal funds.

Federal Open Market Committee (FOMC) A 12-member committee consisting of the seven members of the Federal Reserve Board and five of the twelve Federal Reserve Bank presidents. The Committee sets objectives for the growth of money and credit that are implemented through purchases and sales of U.S. government securities in the open market. The FOMC also establishes policy relating to System operations in the foreign exchange markets.

Federal Reserve Bank One of the twelve operating arms of the Federal Reserve System, located throughout the nation, that together with their twenty-five Branches carry out various System functions.

Federal Reserve System The central bank of the United States created by Congress, consisting of a seven-member Board of Governors in Washington, D.C., 12 regional Reserve Banks, and depository institutions that are subject to reserve requirements. All national banks are members and state chartered banks may elect to become members. State member banks are supervised by the Board of Governors and the Reserve Banks. Reserve requirements established by the Federal Reserve Board apply to nonmember depository institutions as well as member banks. Both classes of institutions have access to Federal Reserve discount borrowing privileges and Federal Reserve services on an equal basis.

fiscal policy Government policy regarding taxation and spending. Fiscal policy is made by Congress and the Administration.

fixed exchange rate system Exchange rates between currencies that are set at predetermined levels and don't move in response to changes in supply and demand.

floating exchange rate system The flexible exchange rate system in which the exchange rate is determined by the market forces of supply and demand without intervention.

foreign exchange transactions Purchase or sale of the currency of one nation with that of another. Foreign exchange rates refer to the number of units of one currency needed to purchase one unit of another, or the value of one currency in terms of another.

forward exchange A type of foreign exchange transaction where by a contract is made to exchange one currency for another at a fixed date in the future at a specified exchange rate. By buying or selling forward exchange, businesses protect themselves against a decrease in the value of a currency they plan to sell at a future date.

futures Contracts that require delivery of a commodity of specified quality and quantity, at a specified price, on a specified future date. Commodity futures are traded on a commodity exchange and are used for both speculation and hedging.

gold standard A monetary system in which currencies are defined in terms of a given weight of gold.

Gross Domestic Product (GDP) Total value of goods and services produced in the economy.

inflation A rise, over time, in the average level of prices.

International Monetary Fund (IMF) An international organization with 146 members, including the United States. The main functions of the International Monetary Fund are to lend funds to member nations to finance temporary balance of payments problems, to facilitate the expansion and balanced growth of international trade, and to promote international monetary cooperation among nations. Member nations are required to subscribe to a Fund quota, paid mainly in their own currency. The IMF grew out of the Bretton Woods Conference of 1944.

lender of last resort As the nation's central bank, the Federal Reserve, has the authority and financial resources to act as "lender of last resort" by extending credit to depository institutions or to other entities in unusual circumstances involving a national or regional emergency, where failure to obtain credit would have a severe adverse impact on the economy.

margin With regard to securities, this term refers to a fractional amount of full value, or the equity outlay (down payment) required for an investment in securities purchased on credit.

money Anything that serves as a generally accepted medium of exchange, a standard of value, and a means to save or store purchasing power. In the United States, paper currency (nearly all of which consists of Federal Reserve notes), coin and funds in checking and similar accounts at depository institutions are examples of money.

monetary policy Federal Reserve actions to influence the availability and cost of money and credit, as a means of helping to promote high employment, economic growth, price stability, and a sustainable pattern of international transactions. Tools of monetary policy include open market operations, discount policy, and reserve requirements.

money stock

- M1—The sum of currency held by the public, plus travelers' checks, plus demand deposits, plus other checkable deposits (i.e., negotiable order of withdrawal [NOW] accounts, and automatic transfer service [ATS] accounts, and credit union share drafts).
- M2—M1 plus savings accounts and small denomination time deposits, plus shares in money market mutual funds (other than those restricted to institutional investors), plus overnight Eurodollars and repurchase agreements.
- M3—M2 plus large-denomination time deposits at all depository institutions, large denomination term repurchase agreements, and shares in money market mutual funds restricted to institutional investors.

open market operations Purchases and sales of government and certain other securities in the open market by the New York Federal Reserve Bank as directed by the FOMC in order to influence the volume of money and credit in the economy.

productivity The amount of physical output for each unit of productive input.

real GDP GDP adjusted for inflation. Real GDP provides the value of GDP in constant dollars, which is used as an indicator of the volume of the nation's output.

real interest rates Interest rates adjusted for the expected erosion of purchasing power resulting from inflation. Technically defined as nominal interest rates minus the expected rate of inflation.

recession A significant decline in general economic activity extending over a period of time.

reserves Funds set aside by depository institutions to meet reserve requirements. For member banks, reserve requirements are satisfied with holdings of vault cash and/or balances at the Federal Reserve Banks.

securities Paper certificates (definitive securities) or electronic records (book-entry securities) evidencing ownership of equity (stocks) or debt obligations (bonds).

Securities and Exchange Commission An independent agency of the U.S. government consisting of five members appointed by the President that administers comprehensive legislation governing the securities industry.

security interest The creditor's right to take property or a portion of property offered as security.

short-term interest rates Interest rates on loan contracts—or debt instruments such as Treasury bills, bank certificates of deposit, or commercial paper—having maturities of less than one year. Often called money market rates.

tender An application or offer to purchase a U.S. Treasury bill, note, or bond.

trade deficit Refers to the amount by which merchandise imports exceed merchandise exports.

Treasury bill Short-term U.S. Treasury security issued in minimum denominations of $10,000 and usually having original maturities of 3, 6, or 12 months. Investors purchase bills at prices lower than the face value of the bills; the return to the investors is the difference between the price paid for the bills and the amount received when the bills are sold or when they mature.

Treasury bond Long-term U.S. Treasury security usually having initial maturities of more than 10 years and issued in denominations of $1,000 or more, depending on the specific issue. Bonds pay interest semiannually, with principal payable at maturity.

Treasury note Intermediate-term coupon-bearing U.S. Treasury security having initial maturities from 1 to 10 years and issued in denominations of $1,000 or more, depending on the maturity of the issue. Notes pay interest semiannually, and the principal is payable at maturity.

Treasury securities Interest-bearing obligations of the U.S. government issued by the Treasury as a means of borrowing money to meet government expenditures not covered by tax revenues. Marketable Treasury securities fall into three categories—bills, notes, and bonds.

variable rate A variable rate agreement, as distinguished from a fixed rate agreement, calls for an interest rate that may fluctuate over the life of the loan.

velocity The rate at which money balances turn over in a period for expenditures on goods and services (often measured as the ratio of GNP to the money stock). A larger velocity means that a given quantity of money is associated with a greater dollar volume of transactions.

SECTION 12

Industrial and Technological Development

12.1 Important Dates in U.S. Industrial Development, 1830s-1900

1830s   Industrial stock issues begin to appear.

1840s   Shift to production by machine rather than by hand.

1840s-1860s   Expanded markets, no longer local and regional in scope.

1850s-1860s   Involvement of an increasing proportion of the work force in manufacturing, with production concentrated in large factories.

1850s-1870s   Increased capital accumulation for investment in expansion of production.

1850s-1870s   Telegraph systems link cities.

1860s   Rise of oil industry. First oil derrick drilled in Titusville, Pennsylvania, in 1859. Rockefeller organized Standard Oil Co.

1860s   National banking system is established.

1860s-1870s   Major steel production begins.

1870s-1890s   Railroad growth fueled industrial development. Investment bankers finance construction.

1870s   Rise of trade unions. Labor strife arose in the 1870s with frequent strikes.

1870s   Machines and new production processes, including the assembly line, reduced the demand for labor, employers cut costs further by hiring large numbers of women and children.

1880s   Telephones begin to replace telegraphs.

1900   Olds Company in Detroit opens first automobile factory. Henry Ford opens his first plant three years later.

12.2 Major Industrial and Technological Inventions and Achievements, 1713-1897

1713   In Massachusetts, Andrew Robinson builds the first schooner

1742   Benjamin Franklin invents the Franklin stove, heating rooms by circulating preheated air

1752   Benjamin Franklin invents the lightning rod

1784   Benjamin Franklin invents bifocal lenses

1787   The first demonstrations of steamboats take place: one invented by John Fitch on the Delaware River, the other by James Rumsey on the Potomac River

1787   Oliver Evans invents an automated process of grinding grain and sifting flour, thus simplifying the production of bread

1790   The industrial revolution begins in the U.S. with the opening of the first working cotton mill by engineer Samuel Slater and ironmaster David Wilkinson

1792   The United States Mint opens and begins to produce coins based on the decimal system

1792   Eli Whitney invents the cotton gin, a machine to quickly separate cotton fibers from seeds

1794   The Lancaster (PA) Road—the first U.S. toll road—opens

1795   The Springfield (MA) flintlock musket, the first official U.S. weapon, is devised

1798   Eli Whitney develops metal patterns called jigs which enable consistent duplication of parts and refine mass production

1799   Engineer James Finley builds the first suspension bridge using iron support chains

1802   Farmer Thomas Moore devises the icebox: one wooden box inside another, with charcoal or ash insulation in between

1805   Engineer Robert Fulton builds a steam-powered ship

1805   The first amphibious vehicle is invented

1805   America's first covered bridge opens over the Schuylkill River in Pennsylvania

1818   Elisha Collier and Artemis Wheeler patent the revolver

1819   The first phase of the Erie Canal opens between Rome and Utica in upstate New York

1822   Inventor William Church patents the first typesetting machine

1824   The Shakers build the first round barn in Hancock, New York

1824   Cherokee linguist Sequoia develops the written Cherokee alphabet

1825   The full 363-mile length of the Erie Canal links the Hudson River and the Great Lakes

1826   Five years after a Scotsman's original invention, Cyrus McCormick patents his design for a reaping machine

1827   A 12-seat horsedrawn bus ushers in the use of public transportation in New York City

1828   In Maryland, work begins on the Baltimore & Ohio, the first U.S. passenger service steam train

1829   Walter Hunt and Elias Howe independently invent the sewing machine, which is to be successfully marketed by Isaac Singer

1829   Peter Cooper's *Tom Thumb* is the first American-built locomotive

1830   Inventor Thaddeus Fairbanks develops the Fairbanks scale, the world's first platform scale

1831   Physicist Joseph Henry invents the electric motor

1831   The horse-drawn reaper is developed by Cyrus McCormick

1833   Builder Augustus Deodat Taylor designs the balloon frame house which will revolutionize house construction

1834   Jacob Perkins invents a compression machine that cools water

1836   Samuel Colt simplifies the revolver's cocking mechanism and begins to mass-produce them

1837   John and Hiram Pitts patent the first steam-powered thresher

1838   Samuel F.B. Morse sends the first message in Morse code

1839   The process of vulcanization, allowing rubber to retain its elasticity under all weather conditions, is discovered by Charles Goodyear

1843   The interlocking-stitch sewing machine is invented by Elias Howe

1844   Samuel Morse transmits the first telegraph message from Washington, D.C., to Baltimore, MD

1847   Tailor Ebenezer Butterick develops a process for cutting dressmaker patterns using the sewing machine

1847   Adhesive postage stamps are first used

1849   Inventor Walter Hunt patents the safety pin

1852   Mechanic Elisha Otis patents the safety elevator

1854   Abraham Gesner perfects a kerosene lamp oil from asphalt rock

1855   David Hughes devises a teleprinter to automatically decode an operator's hand-tapped message

1856   Gail Borden patents a process for condensing milk

1857   New York City's E.G. Hauaghwort Store is the first commercial building to use a passenger elevator

1858   Cabinetmaker George Pullman designs the two-tiered railroad sleeping car

1858   John Mason devises the Mason jar, revolutionizing home canning

1859   The first petroleum oil well is drilled by Edwin Drake in Titusville, PA

1861   Engineer Richard Jordan Gatling develops the multi-round, rapid-firing Gatling gun

1862   L.O. Colvin invents a milking machine

1865   Construction begins on the Union Pacific Railroad

1865   Machinists Francis Pratt and Amos Whitney open an industrial factory for the manufacture of interchangeable parts of rifles

1865   Inventor Linus Yale patents the Yale cylinder lock

1865   Inventor Thaddeus Lowe designs a compression ice-making machine

1866   Cyrus Field lays the first permanent transatlantic telegraph cable

1867   The first steam-operated elevated railway in America opens in New York City

1868   Using a vacuum tube, George Westinghouse designs the air brake for use in railroads

1868   Thomas Alva Edison invents the automatic stock ticker

1868   George Green develops an air-powered dental drill

1869   The Union Pacific and Central Pacific Railways are joined at Promontory Point, Utah, and America's transcontinental railroad is completed

1870   William Lyman designs the first mechanical can opener for personal use

1870   Richard Hoe develops a rotary press capable of printing two sides of a page at one time

1873   The world's first cable-car streetcar begins running in San Francisco

1873   Christopher Latham Sholes reduces key jams on the typewriter by devising the QWERTY keyboard arrangement. The Remington Company mass-markets it the following year

1874   Joseph F. Glidden's machine for making barbed wire (first invented in 1867) enables it to be mass-produced for the first time

1876   In Boston, Alexander Graham Bell transmits the first words over the telephone

1876	Thomas Alva Edison patents a wax-stencil duplicating process
1876	Shop owner Henry Sherwin popularizes ready-to-use paint by developing a process for mixing pigment and linseed oil
1877	The first telephone switchboard operation is put into use, in Boston
1877	Thomas Alva Edison tests the first phonograph, a machine which records sound onto indented metal cylinders
1878	Edison discovers that by adjusting electric current, electricity can be supplied for home use
1878	The Remington Arms Company develops a typewriter shift key to produce upper and lower case letters
1878	The first floating soap—called Ivory Soap—is invented by a Proctor & Gamble Company factory worker who accidentally injects air into a mixture
1879	The first commercial sugar substitute, saccharin, is developed by Ira Rensen and Constantine Fahlberg
1879	James Ritty invents the cash register
1879	Edison produces the first commercially viable, long-burning incandescent vacuum light bulb
1879	Margaret Knight invents a machine which makes square-bottomed paper bags
1879	A Brooklyn, NY, dairy is the first to use glass milk bottles
1881	Meat merchant Gustavus Swift develops the refrigerator train car
1883	The photoelectric cell is invented
1884	Insurance salesman Lewis Edson invents the first fountain pen with a regulated ink supply
1885	Engineer Benjamin Holt devises the "Caterpillar" crawling tractor
1885	George Westinghouse and William Stanley refine a workable transmitter for dispersing mass electrical power using alternating current
1886	Frederic Ives invents the half-tone photo-engraving process
1887	Thomas Edison invents a motorized phonograph using sound-imprinted wax cylinders
1888	George Eastman first markets the hand-held Kodak camera. Priced at $25, it can take up to one hundred photographs
1888	Inventor John Robert Gregg devises a new shorthand system called Light Line Phonography
1889	The I.M. Singer Company first markets electric sewing machines
1889	William Gray's coin-operated telephone first appears in a bank in Hartford, CT
1890	Engineer Herman Heollerith devises an electromechanical punch-card system for recording data
1891	Edward Goodrich Acheson develops carborundum
1891	Thomas Edison and W.K.L. Dickson patent the Kinetograph camera and Kinetoscope viewer, the world's first motion picture system
1891	The Carpenter Electric Company of St. Paul, MN, sells the first electric stoves to homes
1892	Almon Strowger invents the dial telephone and automatic telephone exchange
1892	William Painter patents a tin bottle cap with cork seal for bottled beverages
1893	Whitcomb Judson invents a zipper-like clasp locker
1893	Henry Ford test drives his first gasoline buggy
1896	The field of architectural acoustics is developed by physicist Wallace Sabine
1896	The Duryea Motor Wagon Company markets the first motorized car, the Haynes-Duryea
1896	Francis Edgar and Freelan O. Stanley market the Stanley Steamer motorcar
1897	Engineer Simon Lake's *Argonaut* is the first submarine to successfully navigate the open sea

12.3 Major Industrial and Technological Inventions and Achievements, 1900-1999

1900	Benjamin Holt invents the tractor
1900	Eastman Kodak markets the Brownie camera
1901	Engineer Peter Cooper Hewitt develops the mercury-vapor electric lamp
1902	The Horn & Hardart Baking Company opens the first automat, a "restaurant" that dispenses food from glass-walled compartments
1903	The newly-incorporated Ford Motor Company introduces the Model A
1903	The Harley-Davidson motorcycle is developed
1903	The Springfield rifle is developed
1903	In the first successful airplane flight, Orville Wright travels 120 feet, remaining in the air for twelve seconds, in the biplane built by him and brother Wilbur
1904	Merchant Thomas Sullivan invents the teabag
1905	Orville Wright makes the first turn and Wilbur the first complete circle in an airplane
1907	Lee DeForest invents the electron tube
1908	The Ford Motor Company introduces the Model T
1911	The Dyton Engineering Laboratories (Delco) develops the electric self-starter
1911	William Carrier invents an air conditioning system
1913	Henry Ford introduces the assembly line
1913	Physicist William David Coolidge invents the Coolidge tube, used to manufacture X-rays
1914	Lawrence and Elmer Sperry invent the automatic pilot
1915	Corning Glass Works introduces Pyrex, a heat and shock-resistant glassware for cooking
1917	Army Signal Corps Officer Edwin Armstrong develops a superheterodyne circuit, enabling amplitude modulation for AM radio
1918	Inventor Charles Strite patents the pop-up toaster
1919	Dial telephones are introduced by the American Telephone & Telegraph Company
1920	The American Racine Universal Motor Company introduces the hand-held hair dryer
1920	Army officer John T. Thompson invents the continuous-firing hand-held "Tommy" submachine gun
1921	University of California medical student John Larson develops the polygraph (lie detector) machine
1924	Two Army Air Corps biplanes complete the first round-the-world flight
1925	Clarence Birdseye and Charles Seabrook develop a deep-freezing process for cooked foods
1926	Richard Byrd and Floyd Bennett take the first (fifteen hour) flight over the North Pole
1926	A Bell Lab scientist develops the voice coder
1927	The Holland Tunnel, the first underwater passage between New York and New Jersey, is built
1927	An all mechanical cotton picker is developed by inventors John and Mack Rust
1927	Borden is the first dairy company to offer homogenized milk
1927	Flying *The Spirit of St. Louis,* aviator Charles Lindbergh makes the first solo nonstop transatlantic flight. It takes him 33 hours, 29 minutes to reach an airstrip outside Paris from take-off in Roosevelt Field, Long Island, New York
1928	Aviator Amelia Earhart is the first woman to pilot a solo transatlantic flight, traveling from New foundland to Wales
1928	Otto Frederick Rohwedder invents a commercial bread-slicing machine
1928	The Minnesota Mining and Manufacture Company introduces "Scotch Tape"
1929	Richard Byrd and his crew are the first to fly over the South Pole and back
1929	Eastman Kodak introduces the 16-millimeter movie camera, projector and film
1929	Pilot Jimmy Doolittle makes the first "blind" flight, relying completely on instruments to take off and land his plane
1930	Physicist Ernest Lawrence invents the cyclotron, a devise that uses a magnetic field to accelerate subatomic particles

1930   Wonder Bread, the first prepackaged loaf of sliced bread, is first sold by the Continental Bakery

1930   Electrical engineer Vann Bush develops the differential analyzer, the first partially electronic computer

1932   The parking meter is invented by Carlton Magee

1933   Edwin Land invents Polaroid film, the first synthetic light-polarizing film

1933   Edwin Armstrong refines the process of radio frequency modulation (FM)

1935   Eastman Kodak develops Kodachrome, a three-color process color film

1936   Boulder Dam (now known as Hoover Dam) is completed, providing southwestern U.S. with inexpensive electric power

1937   Nylon, the first fully synthetic fiber, is patented by DuPont chemist Wallace Hume Carothers

1937   Chester Carlson patents xerography

1938   DuPont chemist Roy Plunkett invents the non-stick material Teflon

1938   Owens-Illinois and Corning Glass develop fiberglass

1939   General Electric develops fluorescent lighting

1939   Pan American Airways debuts commercial passenger airline service

1940   The Joy machine, a deep-carving continuous digging machine, is invented by Carson Smith and Harold Silver

1940   Working for the Bantam Car Company, engineer Karl Pabst designs the Jeep

1940   The Pennsylvania Turnpike, the country's first superhighway with tunnels, opens

1941   Lyle Goodhue and William Sullivan adapt the aerosol spray can for commercial use

1942   The first jet plane flight takes place

1942   The U.S. military introduces the bazooka rocket launcher

1945   Frozen orange juice concentrate is developed

1946   The first successful, automatic computer called ENIAC (electronic numerical integrator and calculator) is built by John Eckert and John Mauchly at the University of Pennsylvania

1946   The microwave oven is invented by Percy LeBaron Spencer

1947   The transistor is first made by a Bell Laboratories research team headed by John Bardeen and Walter Brattain

1947   Edwin Land develops the one-step Polaroid camera

1947   B.F. Goodrich markets the first self-sealing tubeless car tires

1947   The Raytheon Company builds the Radarange, the first commercial microwave oven

1948   CBS engineer Peter Goldmark develops the long-playing vinyl phonograph, running at 33 1/3 rpm

1948   The first deodorant soap is developed

1950   DuPont introduces the polymer fiber Orlon

1951   Chrysler automobiles are the first to use power steering

1951   Remington Rand unveils the Univac computer for business use

1954   The first three-dimensional film is shown in theaters

1954   Color television sets are first sold commercially

1956   The Ampex Corporation sells the first video recorder for use by television stations

1958   Boeing Aircraft develops the Boeing 707, the first U.S. jet for passenger service

1959   Pantyhose is developed by a mill in North Carolina

1959   The microchip is invented by engineers at Fairchild Semiconductors and Texas Instruments

1959   The Xerox Corp markets the first copier

1960   Physicist Theodore Harold Maiman, working at Hughes Research Laboratories, builds the first working laser

1962   Bell Laboratories invent Telstar I, the first communications satellite able to re-broadcast a television image

1963   AT&T first markets touch-tone telephone service

1964   The first word processor, a screenless magnetic tape selectric typewriter, is developed at IBM

1967   The first practical satellite navigation systems—"Transit"—is made for the Navy to aid in steering ships away from rocks and reefs

1967   The first microwave for home use is marketed by the Amana Refrigeration Company

1967	Cellular mobile telephones are first developed in the U.S.

1967   Cellular mobile telephones are first developed in the U.S.

1968   Dialing 911 in event of emergency is first introduced, in New York

1968   Jacuzzi Brothers demonstrate the Jacuzzi whirling bath

1969   The first automated teller machine (ATM) appears

1969   Xerox's Gary Starkweather invents the laser printer

1970   IBM creates the floppy disk for data storage

1970   The first computerized supermarket, Telemart, opens in San Diego, CA

1971   The first pocket calculator is introduced in the U.S.

1972   Ralph Baer invents the first home video game, a simulation of table tennis called "Odyssey"

1972   RCA invents the compact disk

1972   Bell Systems introduces the first video telephone system

1972   Physicist Carl Sontheimer designs a food processor for home use

1974   Chemist Arthur Fry develops the process behind Post-It Notes

1975   Inventor Ed Roberts markets the Altair, the first personal computer

1975   Bill Gates and Paul Allen develop the computer language BASIC, the first software produced for a personal computer

1976   Fascimile (fax) machines become popular

1976   IBM introduces the ink-jet printer

1977   Stephen Wozniak's and Steve Jobs' Apple II computer becomes the first popular, mass-marketed personal computer

1979   LaserVision debuts

1979   The Gillette Company introduces the first erasable ballpoint pen

1979   Programmer John Barnaby creates Wordstar, the first popular word processing program for micro-computers

1979   Daniel Bricklin and Robert Frankston develop the first electronic spreadsheet for Apple II

1981   The stealth fighter Lockheed F-117A is the first aircraft designed to be invisible on enemy radar screens

1981   IBM introduces its first PC

1981   Microsoft introduces MS-DOS

1982   IBM develops a laser printer able to print thirty lines per second

1983   The first regular cellular telephone system in the U.S. begins operation

1983   Raymond Kurzweil invents the first computerized musical keyboard

1984   CD-ROMs become commercially available

1984   Apple introduces the user-friendly Macintosh computer

1986   Flown by Dick Rutan and Jeana Yeager, the *Voyager* is the first aircraft to fly around the world non-stop and without refueling

1987   Wide-screen, high-resolution television begins development

1988   Steven Jobs develops the Next computer, the first PC to incorporate an optical storage disc drive

1991   Go Corporation debuts PenPoint, an operating system for pen-based computers

1992   General Motors develops a one-hour charging device for car batteries

1992   Apple introduces the "Newton," its first pocket-size portable

1995   The electronic marketplace debuts on the World Wide Web

1995   Sun Microsystems introduces the Java programming language

1998   Marketing begins of HDTV television sets

1999   IBM produces a dual silicon chip with both logic and memory circuits

Sources: Bruno, Leonard C. *Science & Technology Firsts.* Detroit: Gale, 1996; Bunch, Bryan. *The Henry Holt Handbook of Current Science & Technology.* New York: Henry Holt and Company. 1992; Henderson, Harry. *Communications and Broadcasting.* New York: Facts on File, Inc., 1997; "Metro Business: I.B.M. Unveils Dual Chip," *New York Times.* Tuesday, February 23, 1999; Mount, Ellis and Barbara A. List. *Milestones in Science and Technology.* Second Edition; Phoenix, AZ: The Oryz Press, 1994; Ochoa, George and Melinda Corey. *The Timeline Book of Science.* New York: The Stonesong Press, Inc., 1995; Platt, Richard. *Smithsonian Visual Timeline Book of Inventions.* London: Dorling Kindersley Publishing, 1994; Riordan, Teresa. "Masters of the Mundane," *New York Times Magazine.* Sunday, January 3, 1999; Spencer, Donald D. *The Timetable of Computers: A Timetable of the Most Important People and Events in the History of Computers.* Ormond Beach, FL: Camelot Publishing Company, 1997.

12.4   Chronology of the U.S. Space Program

1926   American scientist Robert H. Goddard launched the world's first liquid-propellant rocket.

1958   The National Aeronautics and Space Administration (NASA) was formed.

1961   (May 5) Alan B. Shepard, Jr., became the first U.S. astronaut in space.

1962   (Feb. 20) John H. Glenn, Jr., became the first U.S. astronaut to orbit the earth.

1968   (Dec. 2) U.S. launched Apollo 8, the first manned space mission to orbit the moon.

1969   (July 20) U.S. astronauts Neil A. Armstrong and Edwin E. Aldrin, Jr., made the first manned lunar landing.

1975   (Aug. 20) The U.S. launched the probe Viking 1 to send back photos and data of Mars.

1977   (Aug. 20) The U.S. launched the probe Voyager 2.

1981   (April 12) The U.S. launched the space shuttle Columbia, the first reusable manned spacecraft.

1986   (Jan. 28) The U.S. space shuttle Challenger was destroyed in an accident shortly after launch, killing all seven crew members.

1990   (Aug. 10) The U.S. space probe Magellan began to orbit Venus and return radar images of the planet's surface.

1990   The Hubble Space Telescope (HST) was launched by the space shuttle Discovery.

1993   Astronauts aboard space shuttle Endeavor repaired the HST, enabling many discoveries, including the first observations of a black hole.

1995   (March 16) Norman Thagard, NASA astronaut and physicist, became the first American to board a Russian space station (space station Mir).

1997   U.S. began assembly, in space, of a permanent space station named the International Space Station (ISS), in cooperation with Canada, Russia, Japan and the 13-member European Space Agency. Due for completion in 2002.

1998   (Jan. 7) Lunar Prospector launched for a low polar orbit investigation of the Moon.

1998   (Oct. 29) Space Shuttle Discovery is launched with veteran astronaut John Glenn aboard.

1999   (Feb. 6) Stardust spacecraft DeHa II launched to fly close to a comet and collect cometary material for analysis.

12.5   Largest U.S. Manufacturing Plants, 1900

Name	Location	Product
8,000-10,000 Wage Earners		
Cambria Steel	Johnstown, Pa.	Steel
Carnegie Steel, Homestead plant	Homestead, Pa.	Steel
Jones & Laughlin	Pittsburgh, Pa.	Steel
Baldwin Locomotive	Philadelphia, Pa.	Locomotives
6,000-8,000 Wage Earners		
General Electric	Schenectady, N.Y.	Electrical machinery
Armour	Chicago, Ill.	Meat packing
Deering Harvester	Chicago, Ill.	Agricultural machinery
Illinois Steel, S. Chicago plant	Chicago, Ill.	Steel
National Tube, McKeesport plant	McKeesport, Pa.	Pipe
Westinghouse Electric	Pittsburgh, Pa.	Electrical machinery
William Cramp	Philadelphia, Pa.	Ships
Newport News Shipbuilding and Dry Dock	Newport News, Va.	Ships
Amoskeag Mills	Manchester, N.H.	Textiles
Pennsylvania Steel	Steelton, Pa.	Steel
4,000-6,000 Wage Earners		
Pullman Palace Car	Pullman, Ill.	Railroad cars
Singer Sewing Machine	Elizabeth, N.J.	Sewing machines
Alexander Smith	Yonkers, N.Y.	Carpets
Swift	Chicago, Ill.	Meat packing
McCormick Harvester	Chicago, Ill.	Agricultural machinery
Western Electric, Chicago plant	Chicago, Ill.	Electrical equipment
General Electric, Lynn plant	Lynn, Mass.	Electrical equipment
Pacific Mills	Lawrence, Mass.	Woolens
3,000-4,000 Wage Earners		
Arlington Mills	Lawrence, Mass.	Textiles
Western Electric, N.Y. plant	New York, N.Y.	Electrical equipment
Nelson Morris	Chicago, Ill.	Meat packing
Illinois Glass	Alton, Ill.	Glass
Pressed Steel Car	McKees Rocks, Pa.	Railroad cars
Bethlehem Steel	S. Bethlehem, Pa.	Steel
Merrimack Mills	Lowell, Mass.	Cotton
Lawrence Mills	Lowell, Mass.	Cotton
New York Shipbuilding	Camden, N.J.	Ships

Source: Daniel Nelson, *Managers and Workers: Origins of the New Factory System in the U.S.* Madison, Wis.: University of Wisconsin Press, 1975.

12.6 Average Number of Wage Earners per Plant in Manufacturing, 1870 and 1900

Industry	1870	1900
Cotton goods	142	287
Worsted goods	127	306
Iron and steel	103	333
Glass	79	149
Silk goods	77	135
Hosiery	60	91
Boots and shoes	57 (1880)	89
Carpets	56	214
Tobacco	38	67
Woolen goods	28	67
Paper	27	65
Shipbuilding	14	42
Agricultural implements	12	65
Slaughtering	11	61
Liquors, malt	6	26
Leather	5	40

Source: Daniel Nelson, *Managers and Workers: Origins of the New Factory System in the U.S.* Madison, Wis: University of Wisconsin Press, 1975.

12.7   Origins of Major U.S. Businesses, 1802-1999

1802   E.I. DuPont de Nemours and Co. is founded for manufacture of explosives.
1852   Anheuser-Busch is founded.
1870   Standard Oil of Ohio incorporates with John D. Rockefeller as president.
1875   R.J. Reynolds organizes as tobacco company.
1879   Scott Paper Co. is established.
1880   George Eastman establishes his business, which re-incorporates in 1901 as Eastman Kodak Co.
1885   American Telephone & Telegraph incorporates.
1886   Westinghouse Electric Corporation is founded.
1887   Johnson & Johnson incorporates.
1890   Procter & Gamble incorporates in New Jersey.
1892   Coca-Cola Co. is established in Georgia.
1892   General Electric Company is founded.
1894   Ralston Purina Co. incorporates.
1897   Dow Chemical Company forms.
1898   International Paper Co. incorporates in New York.
1898   Goodyear Tire & Rubber incorporates in Ohio.
1901   U.S. Steel Co. incorporates.
1902   Texaco organizes as The Texas Co.
1903   Ford Motor Company organizes in Michigan with Henry Ford as principal stockholder.
1904   Bethlehem Steel incorporates.
1906   Xerox Corporation is founded as Haloid Co. in New York.
1908   General Motors organizes as auto manufacturer.
1911   International Business Machines (IBM) incorporates as Computing Tabulating Recording Co.
1917   Union Carbide Corporation begins business.
1919   Loft, Inc., which changes its name to PepsiCo in 1965, incorporates.
1923   Archer-Daniels-Midland Co. incorporates.
1925   Chrysler incorporates.
1926   American Home Products Corp. incorporates.
1927   Honeywell, Inc. forms as Minneapolis-Honeywell Regulator Co.
1928   Motorola, Inc. incorporates.
1928   North American Aviation, Inc. begins business. In 1973 it adopts the name Rockwell International.
1932   Lockheed Aircraft Corp. incorporates in California.
1934   United Technologies Corporation incorporates.
1941   The South Street Co., later named Sara Lee, incorporates.
1947   Hewlett-Packard Co. incorporates in California.
1957   Digital Equipment incorporates.
1967   Textron, Inc. incorporates.
1969   James River Corp. of Virginia is founded.
1982   AT&T is ordered by federal court to break into AT&T Long Lines and regional companies, spawn-
           ing dozens of new phone companies.
1984   Unisys incorporates as successor to Burroughs Corporation.
1997   Microsoft Corp. faces federal anti-trust suit.
1998   Daimler and Chrysler merge to become fifth largest automaker worldwide.
1999   Amazon.com rises to stardom as e-commerce takes off.

12.8 Wealthiest Americans

1. John D. Rockefeller
2. Andrew Carnegie
3. Cornelius Vanderbilt
4. John Jacob Astor
5. William H. Gates III
6. Stephen Girard
7. A. T. Stewart
8. Frederick Weyerhaeuser
9. Jay Gould
10. Marshall Field
11. Sam Walton
12. Henry Ford
13. Warren Buffett
14. Andrew W. Mellon
15. Richard B. Mellon
16. James Huddleston
17. Moses Taylor
18. William Weightman
19. Russell Sage
20. John I. Blair
21. Cyrus Curtis
22. Paul G. Allen
23. John Pierpont Morgan
24. Edward Henry
25. Henry Stanford
26. Oliver Hazard Payne
27. Henry Clay Frick
28. Collis Potter
29. Peter A. Widener
30. Nicholas Longworth
31. Philip Danforth Armour
32. James C. Flood
33. Mark Hopkins
34. Edward Clark Harriman
35. Hetty Green
36. James J. Hill
37. William Rockefeller
38. Elias Huntington

Source: Forbes.

12.9 Notable American Bridges

Bridge	Location	Length[1] /Type of Bridge/ Completion Date	
Ambassador Bridge	Detroit River, Michigan/Canada	1,850 ft	Suspension, 1929
Arthur Kill Bridge	Arthur Kill, New Jersey/New York	558 ft	Vertical-lift, 1959
Astoria Bridge	Columbia River, Oregon	1,232 ft	Truss, 1966
Bayonne Bridge	Kill van Kull, New Jersey/New York	1,675 ft	Steel Arch, 1931
Bear Mountain Bridge	Hudson River, New York	1,623 ft	Suspension, 1924
Brooklyn Bridge	East River, New York City	1,595 ft	Suspension, 1883
Cape Cod Canal Bridge	Cape Cod Canal, Massachusetts	544 ft	Vertical-lift, 1935
Carquinez Strait Bridge	Carquinez Straits, California	2,200 ft	Cantilever, 1938
Chesapeake Bay Bridge	Chesapeake Bay, Maryland	22,968 ft	Combination[2], 1964
"Colossus" Bridge[3]	Schuylkill River, Philadelphia	340 ft	Truss, 1812
Delaware Memorial Bridge	Delaware River, Delaware/New Jersey	2,150 ft	Suspension, 1951, 1968
Eads Bridge	Mississippi River, St. Louis	1,524 ft	Steel Arch, 1874
George Washington Bridge	Hudson River, New York/New Jersey	3,500 ft	Suspension, 1931
Golden Gate Bridge	San Francisco Bay, California	4,200 ft	Suspension, 1937
Greater New Orleans Bridge	Mississippi River, New Orleans	1,575 ft	Cantilever, 1958
Hell Gate Bridge	East River, New York City	977 ft	Steel Arch, 1916
Henry Hudson Bridge	Harlem River, New York City	800 ft	Steel Arch, 1936
London Bridge[4]	Lake Havasu, Arizona	928 ft	Stone Arch, 1831, 1972
Mackinac Bridge	Straits of Mackinac, Michigan	3,800 ft	Suspension, 1957
New River Gorge Bridge	New River, West Virginia	1,700 ft	Steel Arch, 1978
Niagara-Clifton Bridge	Niagara River, New York/Canada	840 ft	Steel Arch, 1898
Peace Bridge	Niagara River, New York/Canada	3,575 ft	Pier, 1927
Lake Pontchartrain Causeway No. 2	Lake Pontchartrain, Louisiana	126,055 ft	Combination, 1969
Portage Railway Viaduct[5]	Genesee River, New York	876 ft	Trestle, 1852
Queensboro Bridge	East River, New York City	2,166 ft	Cantilever, 1909
Lewiston-Queenston Bridge	Niagara River, New York/Canada	1,000 ft	Steel Arch, 1962
Rainbow Bridge	Niagara River, New York/Canada	950 ft	Steel Arch, 1941

Bridge	Location	Length[1] /Type of Bridge/ Completion Date	
Rainbow Natural Arch	Rainbow Bridge National Monument, Utah	290 ft	Natural Stone Arch
Rockville Bridge	Susquehanna River, Pennsylvania	3,180 ft	Stone Arch, 1901
Royal Gorge Bridge	Arkansas River, Colorado	880 ft	Suspension, 1929
Oakland-San Francisco Bay Bridge	San Francisco Bay, California	43,560 ft	Combination, 1936
Sault Ste. Marie Bridge	Sault Ste. Marie Canal, Michigan/Canada	336 ft	Bascule, 1941
Tacoma Narrows Bridge[6]	The Narrows, Washington	2,800 ft	Suspension, 1940
Tappan Zee Bridge	Hudson River, New York	2,516 ft	Cantilever, 1955
Verrazano-Narrows Bridge	Hudson River, New York City	4,260 ft	Suspension, 1964
Lake Washington Bridge	Lake Washington, Seattle	12,596 ft	Pontoon, 1963
Wheeling Bridge[7]	Ohio River, Ohio/West Virginia	1,010 ft	Suspension, 1849
Williamsburg Bridge	East River, New York City	1,600 ft	Suspension, 1903

[1] The "length" of each bridge is the length of the actual span, not including approach roads and on-ramps.

[2] A "combination" bridge consists of several types of bridges and in some cases, includes a tunnel.

[3] Destroyed by fire in 1838 and replaced by a wire suspension bridge.

[4] Originally built in London in 1831. In 1972, the entire bridge was taken apart, brought to America, and rebuilt across Lake Havasu (the Colorado River).

[5] Destroyed by fire in 1875 and replaced by a metal structure.

[6] Also known as the famous "Galloping Gerdie." The roadway had very weak supports underneath, making it prone to bouncing up and down and to swinging—up to 28 feet—from side to side. Only four months after it was completed, the bridge collapsed after swinging too high in moderate winds. In 1950, a new bridge was built using the existing towers.

[7] Destroyed by winds in 1854, it was rebuilt two years later.

Sources: Beckett, Derrick. *Bridges.* London: Paul Hamlyn Publishing Group Ltd., 1969; Berlow, Lawrence H. *The Reference Guide to Famous Engineering Landmarks of the World.* Phoenix, AZ: Oryx, 1998; Brown, David J. *How Things Were Built.* New York: Random House, 1992; Browne, Lionel. *Bridges.* New York: Smithmark Publishers, 1996; Spangenburg, Ray and Diane K. Moser. *The Story of America's Bridges.* New York: Facts On File, Inc., 1991; Stephens, John H. *Towers, Bridges and Other Structures.* New York: Sterling Publishing Co., Inc., 1976; Whitney, Charles S. *Bridges.* New York: Greenwich House, 1983.

12.10   Important Canals

Canal	Location	Date Completed	Length
California	California	1974	385 miles
Cape Cod	Massachusetts	1914	17.5 miles
Chesapeake & Delaware	Maryland/Delaware	1829	19 miles
Chicago Sanitary and Ship	Illinois	1900	30 miles
C&O	Maryland/Pennsylvania	1850	341 miles
Erie	New York	1825	363 miles
Farmington	Connecticut	1828	86 miles
Houston Ship Channel	Texas	1914	50 miles
Lake Washington Ship	Washington	1916	8 miles
Leigh	Pennsylvania	1829	65 miles
Main Line	Pennsylvania	1824	395 miles
Middlesex	Massachusetts	1803	27 miles
Morris	New Jersey	1831	102 miles
New Orleans Industrial	Louisiana	1923	6 miles
New York State Barge	New York	1918	524 miles
Santee-Cooper	South Carolina	1800	22 miles
Sault Ste. Marie	Michigan	1919	1.6 miles
Soo	Michigan	1855	2 miles
St. Lawrence	New York/Canada	1959	182 miles

Sources: Bourne, Russel. *Floating West*. New York: W. W. Norton & Company, Inc., 1992. Stephens, John H. *Towers, Bridges and Other Structures*. New York: Sterling Publishing Co., 1976.

12.11 American Engineering: Important U.S. Skyscrapers, 1884-1999

**1884—The Washington Monument
(Washington DC)**
553 feet
Thomas L. Casey, architect

1885—Home Insurance Building (Chicago)
180 feet
William LeBaron Jenney, architect

1891—Wainwright Building (St. Louis)
135 feet
Louis Sullivan and Dankmar Adler, architects

1894—Reliance Building (Chicago)
200 feet
Daniel Burnham and John Wellborn Root, architects

1902—Flatiron (Fuller) Building (NYC)
285 feet
Daniel Burnham, architect

1908—Singer Building (NYC)
612 feet
Ernest Flagg, architect

1913—Woolworth Building (NYC)
792 feet
Cass Gilbert, architect

1924—American Radiator Building (NYC)
21 stories*
Howell & Hood, architects

1925—Tribune Tower (Chicago)
462 feet
Raymond Hood and John Howells, architects

1930—Chrysler Building (NYC)
1,046 feet
William van Alen, architect

1931—Empire State Building (NYC)
1,250 feet
Shreve, Lamb & Harmon, architects

* Height in feet not available.

1939—RCA Building, Rockefeller Center (NYC)
850 feet
Reinhard & Hofmeister; Corbett, Harrison & MacMurray; Hood & Foulhoux, architects

1952—Lever Brothers Building (NYC)
302 feet
Skidmore, Owings & Merrill, architects

1953—Alcoa Building (Pittsburgh)
410 feet
Harrison and Abramovitz, architects

1958—Seagram Building (NYC)
525 feet
Mies Van Der Rohe and Philip Johnson, architects

1969—John Hancock Center (Chicago)
1,127 feet
Skidmore, Owings & Merrill, architects

1972—Twin Towers, World Trade Center (NYC)
1362 and 1368 feet
Minoru Yamasaki and Emery Roth & Sons, architects

1973—Sears Tower (Chicago)
1,454 feet
Skidmore, Owings & Merrill, architects

1976—John Hancock Tower (Boston)
790 feet
I.M. Pei, architect

1977—Citicorp Center (NYC)
914 feet
Hugh Stubbins & Associates, architects

12.12   Leading U.S. Ports, 1997

(Millions of short tons)

South Louisiana, LA, Port of	106.8	Freeport, TX	5.1
Houston, TX	62.6	Huntington, WV	25.2
New York, NY and NJ	78.6	Chicago, IL	21.0
New Orleans, LA	2.4	Richmond, CA	16.5
Corpus Christi, TX	4.6	Marcus Hook, PA	10.0
Baton Rouge, LA	5.6	Boston, MA	9.9
Valdez, AK	70.1	Newport News, VA	6.1
Plaquemines, LA, Port of	47.0	Tacoma, WA	7.6
Long Beach, CA	18.9	Port Everglades, FL	12.0
Texas City, TX	19.2	Jacksonville, FL	9.3
Tampa, FL	36.7	Detroit, MI	12.0
Pittsburgh, PA	51.7	Cleveland, OH	14.8
Lake Charles, LA	21.6	Memphis, TN	18.0
Mobile, AL	24.3	Savannah, GA	3.2
Beaumont, TX	15.0	Charleston, SC	4.8
Norfolk Harbor, VA	10.9	Indiana Harbor, IN	16.0
Philadelphia, PA	15.0	Portland, ME	1.7
Los Angeles, CA	13.2	Lorain, OH	15.4
Baltimore, MD	14.8	Toledo, OH	7.5
Port Arthur, TX	7.6	San Juan, PR	9.1
St. Louis, MO and IL	31.3	Anacortes, WA	12.2
Pascagoula, MS	10.0	Two Harbors, MN	13.4
Portland, OR	3.0	Cincinnati, OH	12.9
Seattle, WA	7.9	Honolulu, HI	9.7

Source: U.S. Army Corps of Engineers, Navigation Data Center.

12.13 Largest Defense Contractors, 1998

Largest total dollar volume of Department of Defense prime contract awards during fiscal year 1998
Amounts in $ thousands

Rank	Contractor	Total Awards
1	LOCKHEED MARTIN CORPORATION	12,341,236
2	BOEING COMPANY	10,865,899
3	RAYTHEON COMPANY INC	5,661,161
4	GENERAL DYNAMICS CORPORATION	3,679,867
5	NORTHROP GRUMMAN CORPORATION	2,690,742
6	UNITED TECHNOLOGIES CORPORATION	1,983,147
7	TEXTRON INC	1,837,815
8	LITTON INDUSTRIES, INC	1,644,465
9	NEWPORT NEWS SHIPBUILDING INC	1,546,634
10	TRW INC	1,347,903
11	CARLYLE GROUP, THE	1,328,834
12	SCIENCE APPLICATIONS INTERNATIONAL	1,223,978
13	GENERAL ELECTRIC COMPANY INC	1,161,392
14	HUMANA INC	867,453
15	GTE CORPORATION	787,073
16	ITT INDUSTRIES, INC	780,794
17	THE GENERAL ELECTRIC CO. PLC	732,057
18	ALLIED SIGNAL INC	655,994
19	COMPUTER SCIENCES CORPORATION	646,655
20	FOUNDATION HEALTH SYSTEMS INC	592,990
21	CBS CORPORATION	567,485
22	DYNCORP	537,330
23	STANDARD MISSILE COMPANY, LLC	475,088
24	IT GROUP INC, THE	435,920
25	ROCKWELL INTERNATIONAL CORPORATION	435,264
26	TRIWEST HEALTHCARE ALLIANCE CO	419,973
27	AVONDALE INDUSTRIES INC	398,821
28	MITRE CORPORATION, THE	394,233
29	MASSACHUSETTS INSTITUTE OF TECHNOLOGY	371,883
30	TEXAS INSTRUMENTS INCORPORATED	349,120
31	ROLLS-ROYCE PLC	345,054
32	AEROSPACE CORPORATION, THE	339,055
33	LONGBOW LIMITED LIABILITY CORP	331,067
34	ALLIANT TECHSYSTEMS INC	316,569
35	WORLDCORP, INC	316,215
36	HIGHMARK, INC	314,923
37	BOOZ ALLEN & HAMILTON INC	311,704
38	JOHNS HOPKINS UNIVERSITY INC	305,842
39	PHILIPP HOLZMANN AKTIENGESELLS	304,869
40	NEW ENERGY VENTURES	297,075
41	FDX CORPORATION	288,999
42	HALLIBURTON COMPANY (INC)	285,623
43	UNISYS CORPORATION	281,197
44	OCEAN SHIPHOLDINGS, INC	278,784
45	GOVERNMENT OF THE UNITED STATES	265,291
46	ELECTRONIC DATA SYSTEMS CORPORATION	260,804
47	NASSCO HOLDINGS INC	257,650
48	SVERDRUP CORPORATION, THE	255,834
49	SHELL OIL COMPANY	254,625
50	NICHOLS RESEARCH CORPORATION	243,722

12.14 Largest U.S. Foundations, 1997

Rank	Name/(state)	Assets	Year End Date
1	Lilly Endowment Inc. (IN)	$11,459,588,283	12/31/97
2	The Ford Foundation (NY)	9,597,907,967	09/30/97
3	The David and Lucile Packard Foundaton (CA)	8,991,300,000	12/31/97
4	W. K. Kellogg Foundation (MI)	7,588,408,314	08/31/97
5	J. Paul Getty Trust (CA)	7,389,565,432	06/30/97
6	The Robert Wood Johnson Foundation (NJ)	6,734,918,302	12/31/97
7	The Pew Charitable Trusts (PA)	4,522,480,597	12/31/97
8	John D. and Catherine T. MacArthur Foundation (IL)	4,030,139,783	12/31/97
9	Robert W. Woodruff Foundation, Inc. (GA)	3,680,536,964	12/31/97
10	The Rockefeller Foundation (NY)	3,094,733,452	12/31/97
11	The Andrew W. Mellon Foundaton (NY)	3,080,437,000	12/31/97
12	The Annenberg Foundation (PA)	2,584,405,699	06/30/97
13	The Starr Foundation (NY)	2,541,595,582	12/31/97
14	The Kresge Foundation (MI)	2,102,976,862	12/31/97
15	The Duke Endowment (NC)	1,980,446,331	12/31/97
16	Charles Stewart Mott Foundation (MI)	1,963,825,032	12/31/97
17	The Harry and Jeanette Weinberg Foundation, Inc. (MD)	1,845,127,300	02/28/98
18	The William and Flora Hewlett Foundation (CA)	1,766,610,354	12/31/97
19	The California Endowment (CA)	1,759,533,900	02/28/98
20	The McKnight Foundation (MN)	1,709,867,516	12/31/97
21	Ewing Marion Kauffman Foundation (MO)	1,649,994,000	06/30/98
22	The New York Community Trust (NY)	1,588,174,769	12/31/97
23	Richard King Mellon Foundation (PA)	1,531,329,392	12/31/97
24	Robert R. McCormick Tribune Foundation (IL)	1,467,807,068	12/31/97
25	Carnegie Corporation of New York (NY)	1,441,675,860	09/30/98
26	W.M. Keck Foundation (CA)	1,437,083,000	12/31/97
27	Houston Endowment, Inc. (TX)	1,331,565,238	12/31/97
28	The Annie E. Casey Foundation (MD)	1,316,355,130	12/31/97
29	Doris Duke Charitable Foundation (NY)	1,306,684,800	12/31/97
30	The Cleveland Foundation (OH)	1,269,684,396	12/31/97
31	The Brown Foundation, Inc. (TX)	1,254,789,195	06/30/98
32	Joseph B. Whitehead Foundation (GA)	1,208,954,802	12/31/97
33	Donald W. Reynolds Foundation (OK)	1,194,912,087	06/30/97
34	John S. and James L. Knight Foundation (FL)	1,189,784,367	12/31/97
35	Alfred P. Sloan Foundation (NY)	1,101,586,214	12/31/97
36	The California Wellness Foundation (CA)	1,075,415,344	12/31/97
37	The James Irvine Foundation (CA)	1,051,258,644	12/31/97
38	The William Penn Foundation (PA)	1,005,604,178	12/31/97
39	Marin Community Foundation (CA)	929,264,255	06/30/98
40	The Chicago Community Trust and Affiliates (IL)	925,123,080	09/30/97
41	The Freeman Foundation (NY)	919,466,273	12/31/97
42	The Samuel Roberts Noble Foundation, Inc. (OK)	915,089,019	10/31/97
43	The Moody Foundation (TX)	904,699,976	12/31/97
44	The Freedom Forum (VA)	901,259,007	05/31/97
45	Howard Heinz Endowment (PA)	878,345,432	12/31/97
46	Longwood Foundation, Inc. (DE)	871,343,469	09/30/97
47	The Joyce Foundation (IL)	835,189,696	12/31/97
48	Weingart Foundation (CA)	804,204,288	06/30/98
49	DeWitt Wallace—Reader's Digest Fund, Inc. (NY)	797,790,903	12/31/98
50	Meadows Foundation, Inc. (TX)	787,852,438	12/31/97

Source: The Foundation Center.

12.15 U.S. Business Leaders, 1763-1999

John J. Astor (1763-1848)   Fur industry, real estate.

Eleuthere I. Du Pont (1771-1834)   Manufacturing gunpowder.

William Colgate (1783-1857)   Founder Colgate & Company (later Colgate-Palmolive Company).

Peter Cooper (1791-1883)   North American Telegraph Works. Manufacturing glue; ironworks.

Cornelius Vanderbilt (1794-1887)   Steamships and railroads.

Jay Cooke (1821-1905)   Investment bankings, mining.

Charles Crocker (1822-1888)   Railroads.

Meyer Guggenheim (1828-1905)   Metallic ores.

Philip D. Armour (1832-1901)   Meat-packing.

Marshall Field (1834-1906)   Marshall Field & Co. department stores.

Jay Gould (1836-1892)   Railroads.

John P. Morgan (1837-1913)   Financier.

John D. Rockefeller (1839-1937)   Founder of Standard Oil Company.

Marcus Daly (1841-1900)   Copper.

Henry C. Frick (1849-1919)   Cofounder of U.S. Steel Corporation (1901).

Frank W. Woolworth (1852-1919)   Founder of F.W. Woolworth & Co.

George Eastman (1854-1932)   Founder of Eastman Kodak Company (1884).

Andrew Mellon (1855-1937)   Banker. Founder of Aluminum Co. of America (Alcoa), Gulf Oil Corporation, and Union Steel Company.

James B. Duke (1856-1925)   Founder of American Tobacco Company (1890).

Will K. Kellogg (1860-1951)   Breakfast cereal tycoon.

William C. Durant (1861-1947)   Founder of Buick Motor Car Company (1905) and General Motors (1908).

Richard W. Sears (1863-1914)   Cofounder of Sears, Roebuck & Company.

Henry Ford (1863-1947)   Founder of Ford Auto Company (1903).

William R. Hearst (1863-1951)   Newspaper tycoon.

John D. Rockefeller, Jr. (1874-1960)   Oil tycoon.

Henry J. Kaiser (1882-1967)   Construction. Founder of Kaiser Aluminum Corp. (1946).

Charles E. Merrill (1885-1956)   Cofounder Merrill Lynch & Company.

Conrad N. Hilton (1888-1979)   Hotels.

H.L. Hunt (1889-1974)   Oil tycoon and founder of Hunt Oil Company (1936).

Jean Paul Getty (1892-1976)   Oil tycoon.

Samuel Irving Newhouse (1895-1979)   Publishing.

August Anheuser Busch, Jr. (1899-1969)   Brewing.

Walt Disney (1901-1966)   Entertainment.

William S. Paley (1901-)   Broadcasting.

Ray A. Kroc (1902-1984)   Founder of McDonald's.

Howard Hughes (1905-1976)   Tool company, real estate, airplanes.

Walter Hubert Annenberg (1908 -)   Publishing.

David Packard (1912-)   Cofounder of Hewlett-Packard Co. (1939).

William Redington Hewlett (1913-)   Cofounder of Hewlett-Packard Co. (1939).

Sam Moore Walton (1920-)   CEO of Wal-Mart Stores.

H. Ross Perot (1930-)   Founder Electronic Data Systems.

Carl Icahn (1936-)   Arbitrager and options specialist.

Robert Edward (Ted) Turner III (1938-)   Broadcasting.

William Henry Gates III (1956-)   Cofounder of Microsoft Corporation (1975).

12.16   Chronology of the U.S. Railroad Industry, 1815-1999

1815	First U.S. charter for railroad is granted to American inventor John Stevens.
1825	Inventor John Stevens builds locomotive that operates on short circular track in New Jersey.
1826	Horse-powered Granite Railway is built in Massachusetts.
1827	Charter granted for Baltimore & Ohio Railroad. First passengers ride in single, horse-drawn cars.
1828	Charles Carroll, the last surviving signer of the Declaration of Independence, lays the first rail of the Baltimore and Ohio Railroad on July 4.
1829	The Stourbridge Lion, the first steam locomotive ever seen in America, has its trial trip over the line of the Delaware and Hudson Canal and Railroad Company.
1830	Locomotive developed by inventor Peter Cooper makes its first run. South Carolina Canal and Rail Road offers first regular steam railway service.
1842	The whole of the Boston and Albany is completed, the first road to be operated as an important through route. The New York Central route to Buffalo is opened, though the various companies along the line are not consolidated until 11 years later.
1844	With the aid of the government, Samuel Morse builds his pioneer telegraph line between Baltimore and Washington.
1846	The Pennsylvania Railroad is chartered.
1850	Total track mileage exceeds 9,000 miles.
1853	New York Central Railroad is completed. First Texas railroad begins operation.
1856	Locomotive crosses Mississippi River on first railroad bridge. Railroad building begins in California.
1858	Railroad building is pushed as far West as the Missouri River, the Hannibal and St. Joseph reaching that river.
1859	First sleeping car is introduced for passenger service.
1860	Total track mileage reaches 30,000 miles.
1861-65	Railroads play significant role in Civil War.
1862	Congress authorizes construction of railroad from Missouri River to California on central route.
1868	George Westinghouse invents the air brake.
1869	The Union and Central Pacific lines are joined, making a through railroad route from the Atlantic to the Pacific. First U.S. transcontinental railroad is completed.
1870	Track mileage exceeds 53,000 miles.
1887	Interstate Commerce Commission is created by congressional act to establish maximum railroad rates.
1890	Conversion from iron rail to safer and stronger steel rail is largely complete.
1893	Steam locomotive, called "999," travels more than 100 mph outside Batavia, New York.
1902	Record New York-Chicago run in 20 hours by *20th Century Ltd.*
1917	President Woodrow Wilson establishes Railroad Administration to control and coordinate rail services until end of World War I. Government controls end in 1920.

1920	Congressional Transportation Act encourages consolidation of railroads and establishes Railroad Labor Board to determine wages and working conditions.
1926	Congress passes Railway Labor Act for mediation of labor disputes.
1930	First electric passenger train is tested in New Jersey.
1934	Diesel locomotive, developed in 1924, is first used for passenger service.
1941	Union Pacific Railroad builds the world's biggest steam locomotive, called "Big Boy," to carry freight over the Rocky Mountains. It is 130 feet long with a speed of 80 miles per hour.
1950s	Almost all railroad companies buy diesel locomotives. "Piggyback" system carrying truck trailers on flatcars is in use for high-value freight by this time.
1959	"Featherbedding" is issue in railroad labor relations. Management charges that unions require employment of unnecessary workers.
1960s	Railroad passenger ridership continues sharp decline as result of increasing emphasis on auto and airplane travel.
1968	Merger of New York Central and Pennsylvania railroads forms 21,000-mile Penn Central system. System files for bankruptcy in 1970.
1970	Burlington Northern System of 23,500 miles is formed by merger of Great Northern, Northern Pacific, and Chicago, Burlington and Quincy railroads.
1971	Federally sponsored National Railroad Passenger Corporation, later known as Amtrak, begins. It handles most northeastern passenger service.
1972	Centralized-traffic-control automatic signaling is in use on thousands of miles of track by this time.
1976	Federally funded corporation, Conrail, takes over bankrupt northeastern railroads.
1985	"Doublestack" freight trains carry containers across continent.
1999	Passenger travel continues to decline.

12.17   Twenty-Five Largest U.S. Corporations, 1999

<u>revenues in $ millions</u>

GENERAL MOTORS, Detroit, Mich.	161,315.0
FORD MOTOR, Dearborn, Mich.	144,416.0
WAL-MART STORES, Bentonville, Ark.	139,208.0
EXXON, Irving, Texas	100,697.0
GENERAL ELECTRIC, Fairfield, Conn.	100,469.0
INTL. BUSINESS MACHINES, Armonk, N.Y.	81,667.0
CITIGROUP, New York	76,431.0
PHILIP MORRIS, New York	57,813.0
BOEING, Seattle	56,154.0
AT&T, New York	53,588.0
BANKAMERICA CORP., Charlotte, N.C.	50,777.0
STATE FARM INSURANCE COS., Bloomington, Ill.	48,133.9
MOBIL, Fairfax, Va.	47,678.0
HEWLETT-PACKARD, Palo Alto	47,061.0
SEARS ROEBUCK, Hoffman Estates, Ill.	41,322.0
E.I. DU PONT DE NEMOURS, Wilmington, Del.	38,130.0
PROCTER & GAMBLE, Cincinnati, Ohio	37,154.0
TIAA-CREF, New York	35,889.1
MERRILL LYNCH, New York	35,853.0
PRUDENTIAL INS. CO. OF AMERICA, Newark, N.J.	34,427.0
KMART, Troy, Mich.	33,674.0
AMERICAN INTERNATIONAL GROUP, New York	33,296.0
CHASE MANHATTAN CORP., New York	32,379.0
TEXACO, White Plains, N.Y.	31,707.0
BELL ATLANTIC, New York	31,565.9

Source: *Fortune*, April 26, 1999.

12.18   History of the Internet

1969   ARPA (Advanced Research Projects Agency) goes online in December, connecting four major U.S. universities for research and education and joining them with government organizations. Its original purpose is to provide a communication network linking the country in the event that a military attack destroys conventional communications systems.

1972   Electronic mail is introduced.

1973   Transmillion Control Protocol/Internet Protocol (TCP/IP) is designed and in 1983 it becomes the standard for communicating between computers over the internet.

1989   The first effort to index the internet is created by Peter Deutsch at McGill University in Montreal, who devises Archie, an archive of FTP sites. Another indexing system, WAIS (Wide Area Information Server), is developed by Brewster Kahle of Thinking Machines Corp. Tim Bemers-Lee of CERN (European Laboratory for Particle Physics) develops a new technique for distributing information on the internet, which eventually is called the World Wide Web. The Web is based on hypertext, which permits the user to connect from one document to another at different sites on the Internet via hyperlinks (specially programmed words, phrases, buttons, or graphics).

1991   Gopher, the first user-friendly interface, is created at the University of Minnesota and named after the school mascot.

1993   Mosaic is developed by Marc Andreeson at the National Center for Supercomputing Applications (NCSA). It becomes the dominant navigating system for the World Wide Web, which at this time accounts for only 1% of all Internet traffic.

1994   U.S. White House launches Web page. Initial commerce sites are established and mass marketing campaigns are launched via email.

1996   Approximately 45 million people are using the Internet, with roughly 30 million of those in North America (United States and Canada), 9 million in Europe, and 6 million in Asia/Pacific.

1998   More than 20% of all U.S. households have access to the Internet, up from 13% at the end of 1996.

1999   E-business or e-commerce—doing business over the web—becomes a major trend in the U.S. and makes significant in-roads into both business-to-business and consumer sales.

Sources: *International Data Corporation; Internet Society.*

12.19   Largest Retailers in the U.S.

	Retailer	Sales $ (1997)
1.	Wal-Mart Stores	119,299,000,000
2.	Sears Roebuck and Co.	41,296,000,000
3.	Kmart Corp.	32,183,000,000
4.	J.C. Penney Co., Inc.	30,546,000,000
5.	Dayton Hudson	27,757,000,000
6.	The Kroger Co.	26,567,300,000
7.	Home Depot	24,146,000,000
8.	Safeway Stores	22,483,800,000
9.	Costco	21,874,000,000
10.	American Stores Co.	19,138,900,000

Source: *Fortune.*

12.20   Most Prolific Patentees in the U.S.

Patentee	No. of patents*
1. Thomas A. Edison	1,093
2. Francis H. Richards	619
3. Edwin Herbert Land	533
4. Marvin Camras	500
5. Jerome H. Lemelson	500
6. Elihu Thomson	444
7. Charles E. Scribner	374
8. Philo Taylor Farnsworth	300
9. Lee de Forest	300
10. Luther Childs Crowell	293

* Minimum number credited to each inventor.

12.21   First Ten Trademarks Issued in the U.S.

All of these trademarks were registered on the same day, October 25, 1870.

Issued to:	Product
Averill Chemical-Paint Company	Liquid paint
J.B. Baldy and Co.	Mustard
Ellis Branson	Retail Coal
Tracy Coit	Fish
William Lanfair Ellis and Co.	Oyster packing
Evands, Clow, Dalzell and Co.	Wrought-iron pipe
W.E. Garrett and Sons	Snuff
William G. Hamilton	Car Wheel
John K. Hogg	Soap
Abraham P. Olzendam	Woolen hose

12.22   First Ten Patents in the U.S.

Patentee	Patent	Date
1. Samuel Hopkins	Making pot and pearl ash	July 31, 1790
2. Joseph S. Sampson	Candle making	August 6, 1790
3. Oliver Evans	Flour and meal making	December 18, 1790
4. Francis Bailey	Punches for type	January 29, 1791
5. Aaron Putnam	Improvement in distilling	January 29, 1791
6. John Stone	Driving piles	March 10, 1791
7. Samuel Mullikin	Threshing machine	March 11, 1791
8. Samuel Mullikin	Breaking hemp	March 11, 1791
9. Samuel Mullikin	Polishing marble	March 11, 1791
10. Samuel Mullikin	Raising nap on cloth	March 11, 1791

12.23   First Women Patentees in the U.S.

Patentee	Patent	Date
Mary Kies	Straw weaving with silk or thread	May 5, 1809
Mary Brush	Corset	July 21, 1815
Sophia Usher	Carbonated liquid	September 11, 1819
Julia Planton	Foot stove	November 4, 1822
Lucy Burnap	Weaving grass hats	February 16, 1823
Diana H. Tuttle	Accelerating spinning-wheel heads	May 17, 1824
Catharine Elliot	Manufacturing moccasins	January 26, 1825
Phoebe Collier	Sawing wheel fellies (rims)	May 20, 1826
Elizabeth H. Buckley	Sheet-iron shovel	February 28, 1828
Henrietta Cooper	Whitening leghorn straw	November 12, 1828

12.24   Computer Fortunes Made in the U.S.

Name	Company	1998 wealth in $
Bill Gates	Microsoft	38,660,000,000
Paul Allen	Microsoft	14,770,000,000
Steve Ballmer	Microsoft	8,210,000,000
Larry Ellison	Oracle	8,200,000,000
Gordon Moore	Intel	7,970,000,000
Michael Dell	Dell	4,660,000,000
William Hewlett	Hewlett-Packard	4,200,000,000
Ted Waitt	Gateway	2,830,000,000
David Duffield	Peoplesoft	1,730,000,000
Charles B. Wang	Computer Associates	1,200,000,000

SECTION 13

Work Force

13.1 Civilian Labor Force, 1935-1998

Numbers in thousands

	Total population	Total labor force	%	Non-agricultural labor force	Agricultural labor force	Non-agricultural Employed	Unemployed	%	Not in labor force
Persons 14 years of age and over									
1935	(1)	52,870	(1)	42,260	10,110	32,150	10,610	20.1	(1)
1936	(1)	53,440	(1)	44,410	10,000	34,410	9,030	16.9	(1)
1937	(1)	54,000	(1)	46,300	9,820	36,480	7,700	14.3	(1)
1938	(1)	54,610	(1)	44,220	9,690	34,530	10,390	19.0	(1)
1939	(1)	55,230	(1)	45,750	9,610	36,140	9,480	17.2	(1)
1940	(1)	55,640	(1)	47,520	9,540	37,980	8,120	14.6	(1)
1941	(1)	55,910	(1)	50,350	9,100	41,250	5,560	9.9	(1)
1942	98,640	56,410	57.2	53,750	9,250	44,500	2,660	4.7	42,230
1943	94,640	55,540	58.7	54,470	9,080	45,390	1,070	1.9	39,100
1944	93,220	54,630	58.6	53,960	8,950	45,010	670	1.2	38,590
1945	94,090	53,860	57.2	52,820	8,580	44,240	1,040	1.9	40,230
1946	103,070	57,520	55.8	55,250	8,320	46,930	2,270	3.9	45,550
1947	106,018	60,168	56.8	57,812	8,256	49,557	2,356	3.9	45,850
Persons 16 years of age and over									
1947	101,827	59,350	58.3	57,038	7,890	49,148	2,311	3.9	42,477
1948	103,068	60,621	58.8	58,343	7,629	50,714	2,276	3.8	42,447
1949	103,994	61,286	58.9	57,651	7,658	49,993	3,637	5.9	42,708
1950	104,995	62,208	59.2	58,918	7,160	51,758	3,288	5.3	42,787
1951	104,621	62,017	59.2	59,961	6,726	53,235	2,055	3.3	42,604
1952	105,231	62,138	59.0	60,250	6,500	53,749	1,883	3.0	43,093
1953	107,056	63,015	58.9	61,179	6,260	54,919	1,834	2.9	44,041
1954	108,321	63,643	58.8	60,109	6,205	53,904	3,532	5.5	44,678
1955	109,683	65,023	59.3	62,170	6,450	55,722	2,852	4.4	44,660
1956	110,954	66,552	60.0	63,799	6,283	57,514	2,750	4.1	44,402
1957	112,265	66,929	59.6	64,071	5,947	58,123	2,859	4.3	45,336
1958	113,727	67,639	59.5	63,036	5,586	57,450	4,602	6.8	46,088
1959	115,329	68,369	59.3	64,630	5,565	59,065	3,740	5.5	46,960
1960	117,245	69,628	59.4	65,778	5,458	60,318	3,852	5.5	47,617
1961	118,771	70,459	59.3	65,746	5,200	60,546	4,714	6.7	48,312
1962	120,153	70,614	58.8	66,702	4,944	61,759	3,911	5.5	49,539
1963	122,416	71,833	58.7	67,762	4,687	63,076	4,070	5.7	50,583
1964	124,485	73,091	58.7	69,305	4,523	64,782	3,786	5.2	51,394
1965	126,513	74,455	58.9	71,088	4,361	66,726	3,366	4.5	52,058
1966	128,058	75,770	59.2	72,895	3,979	68,915	2,875	3.8	52,288
1967	129,874	77,347	59.6	74,372	3,844	70,527	2,975	3.8	52,527
1968	132,028	78,737	59.6	75,920	3,817	72,103	2,817	3.6	53,291
1969	134,335	80,734	60.1	77,902	3,606	74,296	2,832	3.5	53,602
1970	137,085	82,771	60.4	78,678	3,463	75,215	4,093	4.9	54,315
1971	140,216	84,382	60.2	79,367	3,394	75,972	5,016	5.9	55,834
1972	144,126	87,034	60.4	82,153	3,484	78,669	4,882	5.6	57,091
1973	147,096	89,429	60.8	85,064	3,470	81,594	4,365	4.9	57,667
1974	150,120	91,949	61.3	86,794	3,515	83,279	5,156	5.6	58,171
1975	153,153	93,775	61.2	85,846	3,408	82,438	7,929	8.5	59,377
1976	156,150	96,158	61.6	88,752	3,331	85,421	7,406	7.7	59,991
1977	159,033	99,009	62.3	92,017	3,283	88,734	6,991	7.1	60,025
1978	161,910	102,251	63.2	96,048	3,387	92,661	6,202	6.1	59,659
1979	164,863	104,962	63.7	98,824	3,347	95,477	6,137	5.8	59,900
1980	167,745	106,940	63.8	99,303	3,364	95,938	7,637	7.1	60,806
1981	170,130	108,670	63.9	100,397	3,368	97,030	8,273	7.6	61,460

	Total population	Total labor force	%	Non-agri-cultural labor force	Agricultural labor force	Non-agri-cultural Employed	Unemployed	%	Not in labor force
Persons 16 years of age and over									
1982	172,271	110,204	64.0	99,526	3,401	96,125	10,678	9.7	62,067
1983	174,215	111,550	64.0	100,834	3,383	97,450	10,717	9.6	62,665
1984	176,383	113,544	64.4	105,005	3,321	101,685	8,539	7.5	62,839
1985	178,206	115,461	64.8	107,150	3,179	103,971	8,312	7.2	62,744
1986	180,587	117,834	65.3	109,597	3,163	106,434	8,237	7.0	62,752
1987	182,753	119,865	65.6	112,440	3,208	109,232	7,425	6.2	62,888
1988	184,613	121,669	65.9	114,968	3,169	111,800	6,701	5.5	62,944
1989	186,393	123,869	66.5	117,342	3,199	114,142	6,528	5.3	62,523
1990	189,164	125,840	66.5	118,793	3,223	115,570	7,047	5.6	63,324
1991	190,925	126,346	66.2	117,718	3,269	114,449	8,628	6.8	64,578
1992	192,805	128,105	66.4	118,492	3,247	115,245	9,613	7.5	64,700
1993	194,838	129,200	66.3	120,259	3,115	117,144	8,940	6.9	65,638
1994	196,814	131,056	66.6	123,060	3,409	119,651	7,996	6.1	65,758
1995	198,584	132,304	66.6	124,900	3,440	121,460	7,404	5.6	66,280
1996	200,591	133,943	66.8	126,708	3,443	123,264	7,236	5.4	66,647
1997	203,133	136,297	67.1	129,558	3,399	126,159	6,739	4.9	66,837
1998	205,220	137,673	67.1	131,463	3,378	128,085	6,210	4.5	67,547

1 Not available.

13.2 Employment in Manufacturing, 1850

State	Number employed in manufacturing
ALABAMA	4,938
ARKANSAS	903
CALIFORNIA	3,964
CONNECTICUT	47,800
DELAWARE	3,888
FLORIDA	984
GEORGIA	8,378
ILLINOIS	12,060
INDIANA	15,242
IOWA	1,707
KENTUCKY	24,376
LOUISIANA	6,437
MAINE	28,078
MARYLAND	30,124
MASSACHUSETTS	165,938
MICHIGAN	9,398
MINNESOTA	63
MISSISSIPPI	3,113
MISSOURI	16,841
NEW HAMPSHIRE	27,092
NEW JERSEY	37,311
NEW YORK	199,349
NORTH CAROLINA	12,444
OHIO	51,480
PENNSYLVANIA	146,766
RHODE ISLAND	20,881
SOUTH CAROLINA	7,009
TENNESSEE	12,032
TEXAS	1,066
VERMONT	8,445
VIRGINIA	29,109
WISCONSIN	6,089
TOTAL U.S.	943,305

Source: U.S. Census Bureau.

13.3 Employment in Goods-Producing Industries, 1920-1999

(in millions)

Year	
1920	12.760
1925	12.489
1930	11.958
1935	10.893
1940	13.221
1945	17.507
1950	18.506
1955	20.513
1960	20.434
1965	21.926
1970	23.578
1975	22.600
1980	25.658
1985	24.842
1990	24.905
1995	24.265
1999	24.630 (p)

p : preliminary
Source: U.S. Bureau of Labor Statistics.

13.4   Employment in Manufacturing, 1919-1999

(in thousands)

Year

Year		Year	
1919	10,659	1960	16,796
1920	10,658	1961	16,326
1921	8,257	1962	16,853
1922	9,120	1963	16,995
1923	10,300	1964	17,274
1924	9,671	1965	18,062
1925	9,939	1966	19,214
1926	10,156	1967	19,447
1927	10,001	1968	19,781
1928	9,947	1969	20,167
1929	10,702	1970	19,367
1930	9,562	1971	18,623
1931	8,170	1972	19,151
1932	6,931	1973	20,154
1933	7,397	1974	20,077
1934	8,501	1975	18,323
1935	9,069	1976	18,997
1936	9,827	1977	19,682
1937	10,794	1978	20,505
1938	9,440	1979	21,040
1939	10,278	1980	20,285
1940	10,985	1981	20,170
1941	13,192	1982	18,780
1942	15,280	1983	18,432
1943	17,602	1984	19,372
1944	17,328	1985	19,248
1945	15,524	1986	18,947
1946	14,703	1987	18,999
1947	15,545	1988	19,314
1948	15,582	1989	19,391
1949	14,441	1990	19,076
1950	15,241	1991	18,406
1951	16,393	1992	18,104
1952	16,632	1993	18,075
1953	17,549	1994	18,321
1954	16,314	1995	18,524
1955	16,882	1996	18,495
1956	17,243	1997	18,657
1957	17,176	1998	18,716
1958	15,945	1999	18,419 (p)
1959	16,675		

p : preliminary
Source: U.S. Bureau of Labor Statistics.

13.5   Employment in Computer and Data Processing Services, 1972-1999

(in thousands)

Year		Year	
1972	106.7	1986	588.1
1973	119.5	1987	628.6
1974	134.6	1988	673.3
1975	143.0	1989	736.3
1976	159.4	1990	771.9
1977	186.6	1991	797.0
1978	223.8	1992	835.5
1979	270.8	1993	892.8
1980	304.3	1994	958.6
1981	336.6	1995	1,089.9
1982	364.6	1996	1,227.7
1983	415.6	1997	1,410.6
1984	474.4	1998	1,603.0
1985	541.5	1999	1,737.8

Source: U.S. Bureau of Labor Statistics.

13.6   Women in the Work Force, 1947-1998

Year	Percent of All Adult Women	Year	Percent of All Adult Women	Year	Percent of All Adult Women
1947	20.0	1965	34.7	1983	51.8
1948	22.0	1966	35.4	1984	52.8
1949	22.5	1967	36.8	1985	54.2
1950	23.8	1968	38.3	1986	54.6
1951	25.2	1969	39.6	1987	55.8
1952	25.3	1970	40.8	1988	56.5
1953	26.3	1971	40.8	1989	57.4
1954	26.6	1972	41.5	1990	57.5
1955	27.7	1973	42.2	1991	57.4
1956	29.0	1974	43.1	1992	57.8
1957	29.6	1975	44.4	1993	57.9
1958	30.2	1976	45.1	1994	58.8
1959	30.9	1977	46.6	1995	58.9
1960	30.5	1978	47.5	1996	59.3
1961	32.7	1979	49.3	1997	59.7
1962	32.7	1980	50.1	1998	59.9
1963	33.7	1981	51.0		
1964	34.4	1982	51.2		

Source: U.S. Bureau of Labor Statistics.

13.7   Strikes and Lockouts 1947-1998

Number of days of idleness in thousands for stoppages involving 1,000 workers or more.

The number of strikes and lockouts has declined dramatically over the past half century. The U.S. Bureau of Labor Statistics tracks the number of strikes and lockouts, the number of workers affected by each strike or lockout, and the number of days they are idle. To determine the "days of idleness," the Bureau multiplies the number of workers affected by the number of days they are off the job. The "days of idleness" measure of strikes and lockouts reflects not only the number of strikes and lockouts, but the size of the work force affected and the duration of the conflict.

1947	25,720		1973	16,260
1948	26,127		1974	31,809
1949	43,420		1975	17,563
1950	30,390		1976	23,962
1951	15,070		1977	21,258
1952	48,820		1978	23,774
1953	18,130		1979	20,409
1954	16,630		1980	20,844
1955	21,180		1981	16,908
1956	26,840		1982	9,061
1957	10,340		1983	17,461
1958	17,900		1984	8,499
1959	60,850		1985	7,079
1960	13,260		1986	4,481
1961	10,140		1988	4,381
1962	11,760		1989	16,996
1963	10,020		1990	5,926
1964	16,220		1991	4,584
1965	15,140		1992	3,989
1966	16,000		1993	3,981
1967	31,320		1994	5,021
1968	35,367		1995	5,771
1969	29,397		1996	4,889
1970	52,761		1997	4,497
1971	35,538		1998	5,116
1972	16,764			

Source: U.S. Bureau of Labor Statistics.

13.8   Chronology of the U.S. Labor Movement

1648	Boston shoemakers form guilds
1663	Maryland indentured servants strike
1676	Bacon's Rebellion in Virginia
1677	New York City carters strike
1741	New York City bakers strike
1768	New York City tailors strike
1774	Hibernia, New Jersey, ironworks strike
1778	Journeymen printers in New York combine to increase their wages
1786	Shay's Rebellion in western Massachussettes
1791	Philadelphia carpenters carry out the first strike in the building trades
1792	Philadelphia shoemakers form the first local union organized for collective bargaining
1794	Federal Society of Journeymen Cordwainers formed in Philadelphia
1806	Philadelphia shoemakers found guilty of criminal conspiracy after striking for higher wages
1824	Pawtucket, Rhode Island, textile strike
1825	The United Tailoresses of New York, a trade union organization for women, organized in New York City
1827	The Mechanics Union of Trade Associations, made up of skilled craftsmen in different trades, formed in Philadelphia—first city central federation
1828	The Workingmen's Party formed in Philadelphia
	Paterson, New Jersey, textile strike
1829	The Workingmen's Party of New York formed
1831	New England Association of Farmers, Mechanics and other Workingmen formed
1832	Boston Ship Carpenters' Ten-Hour Strike
1833	New York City carpenters strike
1834	National Trades Union, first attempt at a national labor federation, formed in New York
	Lowell, Massachusetts, Mill Women's strike
1835	Ten-hour movement among skilled workers
1835	Paterson, New Jersey, textile strike
1836	National Cooperative Association of Cordwainers, the first national union of a specific craft, formed in New York City
	Lowell, Massachusetts, Mill Women's strike
1840	President Martin Van Buren establishes the ten-hour day for employees on federal public works projects
1842	Massachusetts Supreme Court, in *Commonwealth v. Hunt,* rules that labor unions, as such, are not illegal conspiracies
	Anthracite coal strike
1844	Lowell Female Labor Reform Association formed
1847	New Hampshire passes first state law fixing ten hours as the legal workday
1848	Pennsylvania's child labor law makes twelve the minimum age for workers in commercial occupations
1850	New York City tailors strike
1852	Typographical Union founded
1859	Iron Molders' International Union founded
1860	New England shoemakers strike
1861	American Miners' Association, the first national coal miners' union, is formed in St. Louis, MO
1862	Congress passes the Homestead Act
1863	Brotherhood of Locomotive Engineers founded
1864	Cigar Makers' Union founded

1866   National Labor Union founded—an attempt at creating a national federation of unions

1867   Knights of St. Crispin founded—a union of factory workers in the shoe industry

1868   First federal eight-hour law passed—applied only to laborers, workmen, and mechanics employed
            by the government

        Anthracite coal strike

1869   Colored National Labor Union founded

        Knights of Labor organized in Philadelphia

1872   National Labor Reform Party formed

1874   Tompkins Square riot in New York City

1875   Conviction of Molly Maguires for anthracite coal field murders

        Anthracite coal strike

1876   Amalgamated Association of Iron, Steel, and Tin Workers founded

        Workingmen's Party founded—first Marxist party in the United States. Later becomes Socialist
            Labor Party

1877   Federal and state troops are called out to crush the first nationwide strike in U.S. history when rail-
            road workers walk off their jobs

1878   Socialist Labor Party founded

        Greenback Labor Party organized

        International Labor Union founded

1881   Federation of Organized Trades and Labor Unions of the United States and Canada founded—
            predecessor of the American Federation of Labor

        Brotherhood of Carpenters and Joiners founded

1882   First Labor Day celebration held in New York City

1883   International Working People's Association formed

1884   Federal Bureau of Labor established in the Department of the Interior

        Fall River, Massachusetts, textile strike

        Union Pacific Railroad Strike

1885   McCormick Harvesting Machine Company strike

        Southwest Railroad strike

1886   In Chicago, 350,000 workers demonstrate for the eight-hour workday, founding May Day as an
            international workers' holiday

        Eight-hour-day movement fails

        "Haymarket Massacre"—police attack Haymarket Square labor rally in Chicago, sparking violence
            and the frame-up of eight labor leaders

        American Federation of Labor founded with Samuel Gompers as first president

1887   Seven anarchists sentenced to death for the Haymarket bombing (five eventually executed).

        Port of New York longshoremen's strike

1888   First federal labor relations law enacted—applied only to railroads

        International Association of Machinists founded

1889   Fall River, Massachusetts, textile strike

1890   United Mine Workers of America founded in Columbus, Ohio

1892   International Longshoremen's Association founded

        Seamen's Union founded

        Strike in Homestead, Pennsylvania, by iron and steel workers gains national attention

        New Orleans general strike

1893   American Railway Union founded

        Western Federation of Miners founded

        Federal court in Louisiana applies the Sherman Antitrust Act to unions for the first time in finding
            a sympathy strike to be in restraint of trade

1894   Nationwide Rail Strike led by the American Railway Union in Pullman, Illinois, paralyzes nation's
            transportation

Coxey's Army of the unemployed marches on Washington, D.C.

Cripple Creek, Colorado, miners strike

Great Northern Railroad strike

Labor Day becomes an official U.S. holiday

1895　U.S. Supreme Court, in *In re Debs,* upholds an injunction restraining the Pullman strikers based on the power of the government to regulate interstate commerce

1897　Lattimer, Pennsylvania, massacre—a sheriff and deputies gun down 19 striking miners and wound 40 others during a peaceful protest

1898　Congress passes the Erdman Act providing for mediation and arbitration of railroad labor disputes

American Labor Union founded

1899　Brotherhood of Teamsters founded

New York City newsboys strike

1900　International Ladies' Garment Workers' Union founded

Anthracite coal strike

1901　Socialist Party of America founded

United Textile Workers founded

1902　Great Anthracite Coal Strike, miners walk off the job for 164 days

Chicago Teamsters strike

1903　Department of Commerce and Labor created by Congress

Women's Trade Union League founded

Cripple Creek, Colorado, miners strike

Telluride, Colorado, Miners Strike

1904　New York City Rapid Transit Strike

Packinghouse workers strike

1905　Industrial Workers of the World founded in Chicago

New York Supreme Court, in *Lochner v. New York,* declares maximum hours law for bakers unconstitutional

1906　Eight-hour day widely installed in the printing trades

1907　An explosion kills 361 miners in Monongah, West Virginia, in the nation's worst mining disaster

1908　U.S. Supreme Court, in *Danbury Hatters* case, holds a boycott by the United Hatters Union against a manufacturer to be a conspiracy in restraint of trade under the Sherman Antitrust Act

U.S. Supreme Court, in *Muller v. Oregon,* declares an Oregon law limiting working hours for women unconstitutional

1909　IWW free-speech fight in Spokane, Washington

"Uprising of the 20,000" garment strike in New York

1910　Bethlehem Steel strike

Philadelphia General strike

1911　U.S. Supreme Court, in *Gompers v. Bucks Stove and Range Company,* upholds an injunction ordering the AFL to remove the company from its unfair list and cease a boycott

Fire kills 146 workers at the Triangle Shirtwaist Factory in New York City

1912　Massachusetts adopts the first minimum wage act for women and minors

Chicago Newspaper strike

Lawrence, Massachusetts, textile strike—twenty thousand textile workers representing 26 different nationalities win the 60-day "Bread and Roses" strike

1913　U.S. Department of Labor established

Ludlow, Colorado, massacre

Paterson, New Jersey, textile strike

Rubber Workers strike

Studebaker Motors Auto Workers strike

1914　Congress passes the Clayton Antitrust Act—limits the use of injunctions in labor disputes

Amalgamated Clothing Workers founded

1915　Congress passes the LaFollette Seamen's Act—regulates working conditions for seamen

Standard Oil strike

Youngstown, Ohio, steel strike

Joe Hill, IWW union organizer, executed in Salt Lake City on murder charge

1916   Congress passes Federal Child Labor Law—later declared unconstitutional

Congress passes the Adamson Act establishing the eight-hour day for railroad workers

American Federation of Teachers founded

Standard Oil strike

1917   U.S. Supreme Court, in *Hitchman Coal and Coke v. Mitchell,* upholds the legality of yellow-dog contracts

Pacific Northwest Lumber strike

1918   War Labor Board is created

1919   Huge postwar strike wave sweeps across the nation

Red Scare begins

Seattle General strike

16,000 silk workers in Paterson, NJ, strike for a shorter workweek

Steel strike

1920   Trade Union Educational League founded

West Virginia Coal Wars begin; ten people killed in the Matewan Massacre in a battle over the right to organize the southern West Virginia coalfields

1921   Congress restricts immigration to the United States and establishes the national origin quota system

Seamen's strike

Battle of Blair Mountain—2,000 U.S. troops block miners' attempt to organize in southern West Virginia

1922   Anthracite coal strike

Bituminous coal strike

1924   Samuel Gompers dies. William Green becomes president of the American Federation of Labor

1925   Brotherhood of Sleeping Car Porters founded

1926   Congress passes the Railway Labor Act, which requires that employers bargain with unions and forbids discrimination against union members

Passaic, New Jersey, textile strike

1927   Nicolo Sacco and Bartolomeo Vanzetti, Massachussetts labor activists, are executed

Bituminous coal strike

1928   New Bedford, Massachusetts, textile strike

1929   Trade Union Unity League founded

Gastonia, North Carolina, textile strike

1930   National Unemployed Council formed

1931   Congress passes Davis-Bacon Act providing for payment of prevailing wages to workers employed on federal public works projects

Harlan County, Kentucky, miners strike

1932   Congress passes the Norris-LaGuardia Act, which prohibits federal injunctions in labor disputes and outlaws yellow-dog contracts

American Federation of Government Employees founded

Ford Hunger March in Detroit, Michigan

Four workers killed as protesters march on Ford Rouge Plant near Detroit seeking jobs during the Great Depression

1933   Congress passes the National Industrial Recovery Act, Section 7(a), which guarantees rights of employees to organize and bargain collectively

Frances Perkins becomes Secretary of Labor and the first woman named to a presidential cabinet

Newspaper Guild founded

California farmworkers strike

Hormel, Iowa, meat-packing strike

1934   Southern Tenant Farmers' Union founded
        Newark Star-Ledger newspaper strike begins
        Rubber Workers strike
        San Francisco Longshoremen & General strike
        Textile Workers strike
        Toledo, Ohio, Auto-Lite strike

1935   U.S. Supreme Court declares the National Industrial Recovery Act unconstitutional
        Congress passes the National Labor Relations Act (NLRA), which protects the rights of workers to
            organize and bargain collectively
        Roosevelt signs the labor-backed Social Security Act into law
        Committee for Industrial Organization (CIO) formed inside the American Federation of Labor
        Negro Labor Committee founded
        United Auto Workers founded
        Southern sharecroppers and farm laborers strike

1936   Steel Workers' Organizing Committee formed
        Rubber Workers begin the nation's first major sit-down strike at the Firestone tire plant in Akron,
            Ohio
        First sit-down strike by auto workers starts at Bendix Products in South Bend, Indiana
        Atlanta, Georgia, Auto Workers' Sit-Down Strike
        General Motors Sit-Down Strike
        RCA strike

1937   U.S. Supreme Court declares the NLRA constitutional
        American Federation of Labor expels the CIO unions
        American Federation of State, County and Municipal Employees union founded
        General Motors sit-down strikes in U.S. and Canada—strikes end after workers win first UAW
            contract
        Little Steel Strike and Memorial Day Massacre—ten strikers shot at Republic Steel in Chicago
        US Steel signs first contract with the Steel Workers Organizing Committee

1938   Congress passes the Fair Labor Standards Act, which establishes the forty-hour work week, the
            minimum wage, and bans child labor in interstate commerce
        Congress of Industrial Organizations (CIO) is founded with John L. Lewis as president
        Chicago Newspaper strike begins

1939   Chrysler Auto strike

1940   Philip Murray replaces John L. Lewis as CIO president
        Ford Motor strike

1941   United States enters World War II; AFL and CIO give no-strike pledges for the duration of the war
        Allis-Chalmers strike
        International Harvester strike

1942   National War Labor Board is established—establishes the "Little Steel Formula" for wartime wage
            adjustments
        United Steel Workers of America founded

1943   Fair Employment Practices Committee is established
        Congress passes the Smith-Connally Act to restrict strikes and union political activity during the
            war
        Bituminous coal strike, UMWA strike which triggered a U.S. government takeover of the mines,
            ends with a contract providing portal-to-portal pay and other benefits

1944   Philadelphia Transit strike

1945   Kelsey-Hayes strike
        New York City Longshoremen's strike

1946   Huge postwar strike wave sweeps across the nation
        Nationwide coal strike prompts U.S. government to seize the mines to continue production

General Motors strike

Railroad strike

Steelworkers launch 30-state strike against US Steel

1947   Congress passes the Taft-Hartley Act (Labor Management Relations Act) restricting union practices and permitting the states to ban union security agreements

1948   Progressive Party formed

1949   CIO expels two unions for alleged Communist domination

1950   CIO expels nine unions for alleged Communist domination

United Auto Workers and General Motors sign a contract that provides for pensions, automatic cost-of-living wage adjustments, and guaranteed increases over the life of the contract

1950   "Salt of the Earth" strike of New Mexico miners begins

1951   UAW president Walter Reuther elected president of CIO

1952   President Truman seizes the steel industry when the steel companies reject the Wage Stabilization Board recommendations. Supreme Court rules the action unconstitutional

George Meany becomes president of the AFL

Walter Reuther becomes president of the CIO

Steel strike

1953   AFL and CIO agree to a "no raiding" pact. AFL expels the International Longshoremen's Association for corruption

1955   United Auto Workers win supplementary unemployment benefits in bargaining with Ford

AFL and CIO merge with George Meany as first president; UMWA remains independent

1956   East Coast Longshoremen's strike

Steel strike

1957   AFL-CIO expels Teamsters, Bakery Workers, and Laundry Workers, for corruption

1959   Congress passes the Labor-Management Reporting and Disclosure Act (Landrum-Griffin), which regulates the internal affairs of unions Steel strike

1960   Negro American Labor Council founded

General Electric strike

Seamen's strike

1962   Presidential executive order gives federal employee's unions the right to bargain with government agencies

New York City newspaper strike

East Coast Longshoremen's strike

1963   Congress passes Equal Pay Act prohibiting wage differentials based on sex for workers covered by the Fair Labor Standards Act

1964   Title VII of the Civil Rights Act bars discrimination in employment on the basis of race, color, religion, sex or national origin

1965   United Farm Workers Organizing Committee formed

California Grape Workers' strike

1966   New York City mass-transit Workers' strike

1967   Copper strike begins

1968   New York City Teachers' strikes

1969   Charleston, South Carolina, Hospital Workers' strike

Black Lung compensation bill passes in West Virginia after mass demonstrations by UMWA members

1970   Postal strike is first nationwide strike of public employees

Hawaii becomes the first state to allow local and state government employees the right to strike

Congress passes the Occupational Safety and Health Act

General Motors strike

Postal Workers' strike, President Nixon declares a national emergency and orders 30,000 troops to New York City to break the first nationwide postal strike

Federal Coal Mine Health and Safety Act

1971	New York City Police strike
1972	Lordstown, Ohio, Auto Workers' strike
	Philadelphia Teachers' strike
	AFL-CIO breaks from Democratic Party by refusing to support George McGovern for president
1973	United Farm Workers, led by Cesar Chavez, is chartered by the AFL-CIO
1974	Coalition of Labor Union Women is founded (CLUW)
	Congress passes the Employment Retirement Income Security Act (ERISA) regulating all private pension plans
	Baltimore Police strike
	Oil, Chemical, and Atomic Workers union activist Karen Silkwood is killed during investigation of Kerr-McGee nuclear plant in Oklahoma
1975	First legal statewide public employees' strike in nation's history occurs in Pennsylvania
1977	Bituminous coal strike
	Coors Beer strike and boycott begins
	J.P. Stevens boycott begins
1978	Wilkes-Barre, Pennsylvania, newspaper strike
1979	George Meany retires; Lane Kirkland becomes president of the AFL-CIO
1980	Joyce Miller of the International Ladies' Garment Workers' Union becomes the first woman to sit on the AFL-CIO executive board
1981	President Ronald Reagan fires most of the nation's air traffic controllers for striking illegally and orders their union, the Professional Air Traffic Controllers Association, decertified
	400,000 unionists, the largest labor rally in American history, takes place in Washington in protest against the policies of the Reagan administration
1983	Phelps-Dodge Copper strike
1984	Yale University clerical workers' strike
1985	Hormel Meatpackers' strike
1986	Trans World Airlines flight attendants' strike
	USX (United States Steel) lockout begins
1987	Paperworkers' strike and lockout
	Professional football players' strike
1989	Eastern Airlines workers' strike
	Mine Workers' strike against Pittston Coal Company
1991	Three hundred thousand unionists march in Washington, DC to demand workplace fairness and health care reform
1993	Organized labor suffers major political setback when it fails to block the North American Free Trade Agreement in Congress
1995	Lane Kirkland comes under sharp attack from union leaders for policies that many believed hastened the decline of union power
	John Sweeney of the Service Employees International Union becomes president of the AFL-CIO
1998	GM strike
1999	James Hoffa, Jr., son of Teamster leader James Hoffa, becomes president of the Teamsters

13.9   Unions Affiliated with the AFL-CIO, 1999

Actors and Artists of America, Associated (4As)
Air Line Pilots Association (ALPA)
Amalgamated Transit Union (ATU)
American Federation of Government Employees (AFGE)
American Federation of Grain Millers (A.F.G.M.)
American Federation of Musicians (AFM)
American Federation of School Administrators (AFSA)
American Federation of State, County, & Municipal Employees (AFSCME)
American Federation of Teachers (AFT)
American Flint Glass Workers Union (AFGWU)
American Postal Workers Union (APWU)
American Train Dispatchers Association (ATDA)
American Radio Association (ARA)
Asbestos Workers, International Association of Heat & Frost Insulators and (AWIU)
Association of Flight Attendants (AFA)
Bakery, Confectionery and Tobacco Workers International Union (BC&T)
Boilermakers, Iron Ship Builders, Blacksmiths, Forgers &Helpers, International Brotherhood of (IBB)
Brotherhood of Locomotive Engineers (BLE)
Brotherhood of Maintenance of Way Employees (BMWE)
Brotherhood of Railroad Signalmen (BRS)
Communications Workers of America (CWA)
National Association of Broadcast & Technicians
Federation of Professional Athletes
Flight Engineers' International Association (FEIA)
Graphic Communications International Union (G.C.I.U.)
Hotel Employees & Restaurant Employees International Union (H.E.R.E.)
Glass, Molders, Pottery, Plastics and Allied Workers International Union
International Alliance of Theatrical Stage Employees (I.A.T.S.E.)
International Association of Bridge, Structural & Ornamental Iron Workers
International Association of Firefighters (I.A.F.F.)
International Association of Machinists & Aerospace Workers (IAM)
International Association of Operative Plasterers & Cement Masons
International Brotherhood of Electrical Workers (I.B.E.W.)
International Brotherhood of Painters and Allied Trades
International Brotherhood of Teamsters (IBT)
International Federation of Professional and Technical Engineers (I.F.P.T.E.)
International Longshoremen's Association (ILA)
International Organization of Masters, Mates & Pilots
International Longshore & Warehouse Union (ILWU)
International Union of Allied Novelty & Production Workers
International Union of Bricklayers and Allied Craftworkers
International Union of Electronic, Electrical, Salaried, Machine and Furniture Workers (IUE)
International Union of Elevator Constructors (I.U.E.C)
International Union of Journeymen Horseshoers of United States & Canada
International Union of Operating Engineers (IUOE)
International Union of Police Associations (I.U.P.A.)
Laborers International Union of North America (LIUNA)
National Postal Mail Handlers Union

Laundry & Dry Cleaning International Union
Marine Engineers' Beneficial Association (MEBA)
National Association of Letter Carriers (N.A.L.C.)
National Air Traffic Controllers Association
National Health & Human Service Employees Union
National Maritime Union (NMU)
Office & Professional Employees International Union (O.P.E.I.U.)
Oil, Chemical & Atomic Workers International Union (O.C.A.W.)
Plate Printers, Die Stampers & Engravers Union of North America
Retail, Wholesale & Department Store Union (R.W.D.S.U.)
Seafarers International Union (SIU)
Service Employees International Union (SEIU)
Sheet Metal Workers International Association
Transportation Communications Union (TCU)
Transport Workers Union
The Newspaper Guild
Union of Needletrades, Industrial and Textile Employees (UNITE!)
United Association of Plumbers and Pipefitters
United Auto Workers (UAW)
United Brotherhood of Carpenters and Joiners of America (UBC)
United Farm Workers of America (U.F.W.)
United Food and Commercial Workers International Union (UFCW)
United Mine Workers of America (UMWA)
United Paperworkers International Union (UPIU)
United Steelworkers of America (USWA)
United Transportation Union (UTU)
United Union of Roofers, Waterproofers and Allied Workers
Utility Workers Union of America (UWUA)
Writers Guild of America, East, Inc.

Source: AFL-CIO.

13.10 Union Membership in the United States, 1930-1998

% of non-agricultural work force

1930	11.6	1965	28.4
1931	12.4	1966	28.1
1932	12.9	1967	27.9
1933	11.3	1968	27.8
1934	11.9	1969	27.0
1935	13.2	1970	27.3
1936	13.7	1971	27.0
1937	22.6	1972	26.4
1938	27.5	1973	25.8
1939	28.6	1974	25.8
1940	26.9	1975	25.5
1941	27.9	1976	24.7
1942	25.9	1977	24.8
1943	31.1	1978	23.6
1944	33.8	1979	22.3
1945	35.5	1980	21.9
1946	34.5	1981	21.0
1947	33.7	1982	20.4
1948	31.9	1983	20.1
1949	32.6	1984	18.8
1950	31.5	1985	18.0
1951	33.3	1986	17.5
1952	32.5	1987	17.0
1953	33.7	1988	16.8
1954	34.7	1989	16.4
1955	33.2	1990	16.1
1956	33.4	1991	16.1
1957	32.8	1992	15.8
1958	33.2	1993	15.8
1959	32.1	1994	15.5
1960	31.4	1995	14.9
1961	30.2	1996	14.5
1962	29.8	1997	14.1
1963	29.1	1998	13.9
1964	28.9		

Source: U.S. Bureau of Labor Statistics.

13.11   Union Membership by Occupation and Industry, 1997

Occupation	% of total work force
Managerial and professional specialty	13.2
Executive, administrative, and managerial	5.1
Professional specialty	20.2
Technical, sales, and administrative support	9.1
Technicians and related support	10.4
Sales occupations	4.3
Administrative support, including clerical	12.3
Service occupations	13.2
Protective service	39.9
Service, except protective service	8.9
Precision production, craft, and repair	22.6
Operators, fabricators, and laborers	21.5
Machine operators, assemblers, and inspectors	21.9
Transportation and material moving occupations	24.3
Handlers, equipment cleaners, helpers, and laborers	18.1
Farming, forestry, and fishing	5.1

Industry	
Agricultural wage and salary workers	2.1
Private non-agricultural wage and salary workers	9.8
Mining	13.9
Construction	18.6
Manufacturing	16.3
Durable goods	17.5
Non-durable goods	14.5
Transportation and public utilities	26.0
Transportation	26.5
Communications and public utilities	25.1
Wholesale and retail trade	5.6
Wholesale trade	5.8
Retail trade	5.5
Finance, insurance, and real estate	2.2
Services	5.4
Government workers	37.2
Federal	32.0
State	29.5
Local	42.7

Source: U.S. Bureau of Labor Statistics.

13.12 Union Membership by State, 1997

	Union workers in 000s		Workers covered by union contract	
	1,000	Rank	Percent	Rank
United States	16,269.4	NA	16.2	NA
Alabama	200.7	22	12.8	27
Alaska	54.7	42	24.9	3
Arizona	106.8	32	7.5	48
Arkansas	74.4	36	8.4	44
California	2,060.6	1	18.8	15
Colorado	167.1	25	10.8	36
Connecticut	239.5	19	17.2	18
Delaware	40.0	46	14.0	26
District of Columbia	39.5	NA	19.4	NA
Florida	429.8	12	9.9	41
Georgia	242.1	18	9.1	43
Hawaii	111.9	30	24.5	4
Idaho	42.5	45	10.7	38
Illinois	1,043.1	3	21.5	8
Indiana	395.2	14	16.1	23
Iowa	168.7	24	15.7	24
Kansas	105.8	33	12.3	31
Kentucky	198.8	23	14.1	25
Louisiana	133.4	29	10.0	40
Maine	77.4	35	16.4	22
Maryland	353.5	16	17.4	17
Massachusetts	415.0	13	16.8	20
Michigan	983.3	4	25.4	2
Minnesota	437.4	11	21.2	9
Mississippi	62.0	39	8.1	45
Missouri	375.2	15	16.8	20
Montana	52.0	44	16.9	19
Nebraska	62.9	38	12.4	29
Nevada	147.3	26	24.3	5
New Hampshire	57.4	41	12.6	28
New Jersey	768.0	7	23.7	6
New Mexico	52.6	43	10.8	36
New York	1,942.0	2	28.2	1
North Carolina	134.0	28	5.0	49
North Dakota	24.4	48	10.5	39
Ohio	933.2	5	20.8	10
Oklahoma	135.5	27	12.4	29
Oregon	246.2	17	19.5	13
Pennsylvania	885.8	6	19.5	13
Rhode Island	81.0	34	20.1	11
South Carolina	58.2	40	5.0	49
South Dakota	23.0	49	9.2	42
Tennessee	219.2	20	11.1	34
Texas	527.7	8	8.0	46
Utah	71.1	37	11.1	34
Vermont	24.9	47	11.3	33
Virginia	200.8	21	8.0	46
Washington	464.2	10	21.8	7
West Virginia	109.7	31	17.9	16
Wisconsin	469.7	9	19.8	12
Wyoming	20.1	50	11.6	32

NA = Not applicable.

13.13   Ten Industries and Occupations with the Fastest Employment Growth, 1996-2006

Numbers in thousands of jobs

Employment Change, 1996-2006

Industry description	1996	2006	Number	Percent
Computer and data processing services	1,208	2,509	1,301	108
Health services	1,172	1,968	796	68
Management and public relations	873	1,400	527	60
Miscellaneous transportation services	204	327	123	60
Residential care	672	1,070	398	59
Personnel supply services	2,646	4,039	1,393	53
Water and sanitation	231	349	118	51
Individual and miscellaneous social services	846	1,266	420	50
Offices of health practitioners	2,751	4,046	1,295	47
Amusement and recreation services	1,109	1,565	457	41

Employment Change, 1996-2006

Occupation	1996	2006	Number	Percent
Database administrators, computer support specialists, and all other computer scientists	212	461	249	118
Computer engineers	216	451	235	109
Systems analysts	506	1,025	520	103
Personal and home care aides	202	374	171	85
Physical and corrective therapy assistants and aides	84	151	66	79
Home health aides	495	873	378	76
Medical assistants	225	391	166	74
Desktop publishing specialists	30	53	22	74
Physical therapists	115	196	81	71
Occupational therapy assistants and aides	16	26	11	69

Source: U.S. Bureau of Labor Statistics.

13.14 Value of the Federal Minimum Wage, 1954-1996

Minimum wage in 1996 dollars adjusted for inflation using the CPI-U.

Year	Nominal Dollars	1996 Dollars
1954	$0.75	$4.37
1955	0.75	4.39
1956	1.00	5.77
1957	1.00	5.58
1958	1.00	5.43
1959	1.00	5.39
1960	1.00	5.30
1961	1.15	6.03
1962	1.15	5.97
1963	1.25	6.41
1964	1.25	6.33
1965	1.25	6.23
1966	1.25	6.05
1967	1.40	6.58
1968	1.60	7.21
1969	1.60	6.84
1970	1.60	6.47
1971	1.60	6.20
1972	1.60	6.01
1973	1.60	5.65
1974	2.00	6.37
1975	2.10	6.12
1976	2.30	6.34
1977	2.30	5.95
1978	2.65	6.38
1979	2.90	6.27
1980	3.10	5.90
1981	3.35	5.78
1982	3.35	5.45
1983	3.35	5.28
1984	3.35	5.06
1985	3.35	4.88
1986	3.35	4.80
1987	3.35	4.63
1988	3.35	4.44
1989	3.35	4.24
1990	3.80	4.56
1991	4.25	4.90
1992	4.25	4.75
1993	4.25	4.61
1994	4.25	4.50
1995	4.25	4.38
1996	4.75	4.75

Source: U.S. Bureau of Labor Statistics

V

SOCIAL HISTORY

14. Demographics

15. Public Institutions

16. Ethnic, Social and Religious Groups

SECTION 14

Demographics

14.1   Urban Populations, 1790

Rank	Place	Population	Rank	Place	Population
1	New York city, NY	33,131	13	Newburyport town, MA	4,837
2	Philadelphia city, PA	28,522	14	Portsmouth town, NH	4,720
3	Boston town, MA	18,320	15	Sherburne town (Nantucket), MA	4,620
4	Charleston city, SC	16,359	16	Middleborough town, MA	4,526
5	Baltimore town, MD	13,503	17	New Haven city, CT	4,487
6	Northern Liberties township, PA	9,913	18	Richmond city, VA	3,761
7	Salem town, MA	7,921	19	Albany city, NY	3,498
8	Newport town, RI	6,716	20	Norfolk borough, VA	2,959
9	Providence town, RI	6,380	21	Petersburg town, VA	2,828
10	Marblehead town, MA	5,661	22	Alexandria town, VA	2,748
11	Southwark district, PA	5,661	23	Hartford city, CT	2,683
12	Gloucester town, MA	5,317	24	Hudson city, NY	2,584

Source: U.S. Census Bureau.

14.2   Urban Populations, 1800

Rank	Place	Population	Rank	Place	Population
1	New York city, NY	60,515	18	Schenectady city, NY	5,289
2	Philadelphia city, PA	41,220	19	Marblehead town, MA	5,211
3	Baltimore city, MD	26,514	20	New London city, CT	5,150
4	Boston town, MA	24,937	21	Savannah city, GA	5,146
5	Charleston city, SC	18,824	22	Alexandria town, DC	4,971
6	Northern Liberties township, PA	10,718	23	Middleborough town, MA	4,458
7	Southwark district, PA	9,621	24	New Bedford town, MA	4,361
8	Salem town, MA	9,457	25	Lancaster borough, PA	4,292
9	Providence town, RI	7,614	26	New Haven city, CT	4,049
10	Norfolk borough, VA	6,926	27	Portland town, ME	3,704
11	Newport town, RI	6,739	28	Hudson city, NY	3,664
12	Newburyport town, MA	5,946	29	Hartford city, CT	3,523
13	Richmond city, VA	5,737	30	Petersburg town, VA	3,521
14	Nantucket town, MA	5,617	31	Washington city, DC	3,210
15	Portsmouth town, NH	5,339	32	Georgetown town, DC	2,993
16	Gloucester town, MA	5,313	33	York borough, PA	2,503
17	Albany city, NY	5,289			

Source: U.S. Census Bureau.

14.3 Population at Selected Ranks from 1st to 100th of the Largest Urban Places, 1790-1990

	Rank								
Year	1st	2nd	3rd	4th	5th	10th	15th	20th	25th
1790	33,131	28,522	18,320	16,359	13,503	5,661	4,620	2,959	(X)
1800	60,515	41,220	26,514	24,937	18,824	6,926	5,339	5,150	4,292
1810	96,373	53,722	46,555	33,787	24,711	10,762	7,907	6,807	5,668
1820	123,706	63,802	62,738	43,298	27,176	12,731	8,581	7,327	7,147
1830	202,589	80,620	80,462	61,392	46,082	20,581	13,394	11,140	9,207
1840	312,710	102,313	102,193	93,665	93,383	29,261	22,314	20,153	15,218
1850	515,547	169,054	136,881	121,376	116,375	50,763	42,985	38,799	28,785
1860	813,669	565,529	266,661	212,418	177,840	81,129	56,802	45,246	37,910
1870	942,292	674,022	396,099	310,864	298,977	149,473	92,829	69,422	50,840
1880	1,206,299	847,170	566,663	503,185	362,839	216,090	136,508	104,857	63,600
1890	1,515,301	1,099,850	1,046,964	806,343	451,770	261,353	205,876	161,129	132,146
1900	3,437,202	1,698,575	1,293,697	575,238	560,892	325,902	278,718	175,597	133,859
1910	4,766,883	2,185,283	1,549,008	687,029	670,585	423,715	339,075	248,381	218,149
1920	5,620,048	2,701,705	1,823,779	993,078	796,841	576,673	414,524	315,312	256,491
1930	6,930,446	3,376,438	1,950,961	1,568,662	1,238,048	669,817	464,356	365,583	301,815
1940	7,454,995	3,396,808	1,931,334	1,623,452	1,504,277	671,659	494,537	386,972	319,077
1950	7,891,957	3,620,962	2,071,605	1,970,358	1,849,568	801,444	580,132	456,622	408,442
1960	7,781,984	3,550,404	2,479,015	2,002,512	1,670,144	750,026	627,525	532,759	482,872
1970	7,894,862	3,366,957	2,816,061	1,948,609	1,511,482	750,903	654,153	581,562	514,678
1980	7,071,639	3,005,072	2,966,850	1,688,210	1,595,138	786,775	638,333	562,994	455,651
1990	7,322,564	3,485,398	2,783,726	1,630,553	1,585,577	935,933	635,230	574,283	488,374

	Rank								
Year	30th	40th	50th	60th	70th	75th	80th	90th	100th
1790	(X)	(X)	(X)	(X)	(X)	(X)	(X)	(X)	(X)
1800	3,521	(X)	(X)	(X)	(X)	(X)	(X)	(X)	(X)
1810	4,948	3,462	(X)	(X)	(X)	(X)	(X)	(X)	(X)
1820	6,591	4,348	3,545	2,633	(X)	(X)	(X)	(X)	(X)
1830	8,322	6,822	5,566	4,530	4,073	3,529	3,194	2,623	(X)
1840	12,672	9,102	7,887	6,738	6,048	5,519	5,207	4,766	4,226
1850	21,019	17,049	14,010	11,334	9,408	8,728	8,291	8,012	7,250
1860	28,119	22,300	18,266	14,726	13,405	12,647	11,567	10,115	9,552
1870	41,105	31,584	26,766	21,830	20,038	19,229	18,434	16,103	14,930
1880	55,785	43,350	35,629	30,762	27,737	26,845	22,408	21,420	19,743
1890	88,150	74,398	57,458	48,682	42,837	39,385	37,718	33,300	30,801
1900	108,374	94,151	78,961	62,059	53,531	51,721	46,624	41,459	38,307
1910	168,497	125,600	100,253	88,926	77,403	73,312	69,647	58,833	53,684
1920	234,698	162,351	132,358	113,344	98,917	93,372	91,295	76,754	70,983
1930	284,063	209,326	156,492	138,513	115,514	112,597	106,597	101,463	85,864
1940	301,173	210,718	167,402	144,332	118,410	112,504	110,341	101,065	88,039
1950	369,129	251,117	203,486	163,143	134,042	130,803	128,009	115,911	106,756
1960	405,220	313,411	261,685	201,189	178,320	166,689	156,748	134,393	119,574
1970	448,003	358,633	277,767	241,178	179,260	175,415	170,516	154,168	138,764
1980	423,938	354,635	284,413	231,999	203,371	181,843	172,196	164,160	156,804
1990	437,319	369,879	328,123	265,968	225,366	207,951	193,187	181,519	170,936

(X) Not applicable. Number of urban places in this census year is less than this rank.
Source: U.S. Census Bureau.

14.4   Population of the United States by Census Year, 1790-1990

Census Year	Population
1790	3,929,214
1800	5,308,483
1810	7,239,881
1820	9,638,453
1830	12,866,020
1840	17,069,453
1850	23,191,876
1860	31,443,321
1870	39,818,449
1880	50,155,783
1890	62,947,714
1900	75,994,575
1910	91,972,266
1920	105,710,620
1930	122,775,046
1940	131,669,275
1950	151,325,798
1960	179,323,175
1970	203,211,926
1980	226,504,825
1990	248,709,873

Source: U.S. Census Bureau.

14.5   Three Most Populous States by Census Year, 1790-1990

Census Year	Three Most Populous States	Census Year	Three Most Populous States
1790	VA, PA, NC	1900	NY, PA, IL
1800	VA, PA, NY	1910	NY, PA, IL
1810	NY, VA, PA	1920	NY, PA, IL
1820	NY, PA, VA	1930	NY, PA, IL
1830	NY, PA, VA	1940	NY, PA, IL
1840	NY, PA, OH	1950	NY, CA, PA
1850	NY, PA, OH	1960	NY, CA, PA
1860	NY, PA, OH	1970	CA, NY, PA
1870	NY, PA, IL	1980	CA, NY, TX
1880	NY, PA, OH	1990	CA, NY, TX
1890	NY, PA, IL		

14.6 Distribution of the 10, 25, 50 and 100 Largest Urban Places by Region, 1790-1990

10 LARGEST

Region	1790	1800	1810	1820	1830	1840	1850	1860	1870	1880	1890	1900	1910	1920	1930	1940	1950	1960	1970	1980	1990
United States	10	10	10	10	10	10	10	10	10	10	10	10	10	10	10	10	10	10	10	10	10
North	8	7	7	6	7	7	8	8	7	7	8	8	9	8	8	8	7	6	5	4	4
Northeast	8	7	7	6	6	6	6	5	4	4	4	4	5	4	4	4	3	2	2	2	2
North Central	(X)	-	-	-	1	1	2	3	3	3	4	4	4	4	4	4	4	4	3	2	2
South	2	3	3	4	3	3	2	2	2	2	1	1	1	1	1	1	2	3	4	3	3
Southeast	2	3	2	3	2	2	1	1	1	1	1	1	1	1	1	1	2	2	2	2	-
South Central	-	-	1	1	1	1	1	1	1	1	-	-	-	-	-	-	-	1	2	1	3
West	(X)	(X)	(X)	(X)	(X)	(X)	-	-	1	1	1	1	-	1	1	1	1	1	1	3	3

25 LARGEST

Region	1790	1800	1810	1820	1830	1840	1850	1860	1870	1880	1890	1900	1910	1920	1930	1940	1950	1960	1970	1980	1990
United States	24	25	25	25	25	25	25	25	25	25	25	25	25	25	25	25	25	25	25	25	25
North	18	19	17	16	18	19	20	18	19	19	20	19	18	17	17	16	15	12	11	9	9
Northeast	18	19	17	15	17	17	17	12	13	12	10	9	9	8	8	7	6	5	4	3	3
North Central	(X)	-	-	1	1	2	3	6	6	7	10	10	9	9	9	9	9	7	7	6	6
South	6	6	8	9	7	6	5	6	5	5	4	4	4	3	4	5	6	8	8	9	10
Southeast	6	6	8	7	5	4	3	4	3	3	2	2	2	2	2	2	3	3	3	3	3
South Central	-	-	-	2	2	2	2	2	2	2	2	2	2	1	2	3	3	5	5	6	7
West	(X)	(X)	(X)	(X)	(X)	(X)	-	1	1	1	1	2	3	5	4	4	4	5	6	7	6

50 LARGEST

Region	1790	1800	1810	1820	1830	1840	1850	1860	1870	1880	1890	1900	1910	1920	1930	1940	1950	1960	1970	1980	1990
United States	24	33	46	50	50	50	50	50	50	50	50	50	50	50	50	50	50	50	50	50	50
North	18	24	35	36	36	38	39	38	39	39	39	37	34	33	31	27	26	23	20	18	17
Northeast	18	24	34	35	35	35	32	29	28	26	24	21	19	16	13	11	11	8	7	6	5
North Central	(X)	-	1	1	1	3	7	9	11	13	15	16	15	17	18	16	15	15	13	12	12
South	6	9	11	14	14	12	11	11	10	9	9	8	9	11	13	16	16	17	19	19	18
Southeast	6	9	11	12	12	9	11	7	9	6	5	4	4	4	4	6	9	11	12	13	7
South Central	-	-	-	2	2	3	-	4	1	3	4	4	5	7	9	10	7	6	7	6	11
West	(X)	(X)	(X)	(X)	(X)	(X)	-	1	1	2	2	5	7	6	6	7	8	10	11	13	15

100 LARGEST

Region	1790	1800	1810	1820	1830	1840	1850	1860	1870	1880	1890	1900	1910	1920	1930	1940	1950	1960	1970	1980	1990
United States	24	33	46	61	90	100	100	100	100	100	100	100	100	100	100	100	100	100	100	100	100
North	18	24	35	44	65	77	76	77	80	75	74	72	72	69	65	61	55	47	44	36	30
Northeast	18	24	34	43	59	67	64	60	54	48	45	46	45	40	36	33	28	19	16	12	9
North Central	(X)	-	1	1	6	10	12	17	26	27	29	26	27	29	29	28	27	28	28	24	21
South	6	9	11	17	25	23	24	21	18	20	18	19	18	18	21	21	23	29	30	38	40
Southeast	6	9	11	14	19	18	15	14	11	11	10	10	9	8	9	11	12	13	15	12	16
South Central	-	-	-	3	6	5	9	7	7	9	8	9	9	10	12	10	11	16	15	26	24
West	(X)	(X)	(X)	(X)	(X)	(X)	-	2	2	5	8	9	10	13	14	18	22	24	26	26	30

(-) Represents zero.
(X) Area not enumerated in the census. For information by state, see Table 26.
U.S. Census Bureau.

14.7   Population and Population Change, 1900-1997

Year	National Population	Population Change	Average Annual Percent Change
1997	267,636,061	2,456,650	0.92
1996	265,179,411	2,418,772	0.92
1995	262,760,639	2,468,202	0.94
1994	260,292,437	2,539,735	0.98
1993	257,752,702	2,750,875	1.07
1992	255,001,827	2,877,465	1.13
1991	252,124,362	2,684,817	1.07
1990	249,439,545	2,620,315	1.06
1989	246,819,230	2,320,248	0.94
1988	244,498,982	2,210,064	0.91
1987	242,288,918	2,156,031	0.89
1986	240,132,887	2,209,092	0.92
1985	237,923,795	2,098,893	0.89
1984	235,824,902	2,032,908	0.87
1983	233,791,994	2,127,536	0.91
1982	231,664,458	2,198,744	0.95
1981	229,465,714	2,241,033	0.98
1980	227,224,681	2,169,194	0.96
1979	225,055,487	2,470,942	1.10
1978	222,584,545	2,345,120	1.06
1977	220,239,425	2,204,261	1.01
1976	218,035,164	2,061,965	0.95
1975	215,973,199	2,119,271	0.99
1974	213,853,928	1,945,140	0.91
1973	211,908,788	2,012,767	0.95
1972	209,896,021	2,235,344	1.07
1971	207,660,677	2,608,503	1.26
1970	205,052,174	2,375,228	1.17
1969	202,676,946	1,970,894	0.98
1968	200,706,052	1,993,996	1.00
1967	198,712,056	2,151,718	1.09
1966	196,560,338	2,257,375	1.16
1965	194,302,963	2,414,172	1.25
1964	191,888,791	2,646,993	1.39
1963	189,241,798	2,704,061	1.44
1962	186,537,737	2,846,256	1.54
1961	183,691,481	3,020,323	1.66
1960	180,671,158	2,841,530	1.59
1959	177,829,628	2,947,724	1.67
1958	174,881,904	2,897,774	1.67
1957	171,984,130	3,081,099	1.81
1956	168,903,031	2,971,829	1.78
1955	165,931,202	2,905,348	1.77
1954	163,025,854	2,841,662	1.76
1953	160,184,192	2,631,452	1.66
1952	157,552,740	2,674,851	1.71
1951	154,877,889	2,606,472	1.70
1950	152,271,417	3,083,287	2.05
1949	149,188,130	2,556,828	1.73
1948	146,631,302	2,505,231	1.72

Year	National Population	Population Change	Average Annual Percent Change
1947	144,126,071	2,737,505	1.92
1946	141,388,566	1,460,401	1.04
1945	139,928,165	1,530,820	1.10
1944	138,397,345	1,657,992	1.21
1943	136,739,353	1,879,800	1.38
1942	134,859,553	1,457,082	1.09
1941	133,402,471	1,280,025	0.96
1940	132,122,446	1,242,728	0.95
1939	130,879,718	1,054,779	0.81
1938	129,824,939	1,000,110	0.77
1937	128,824,829	771,649	0.60
1936	128,053,180	802,948	0.63
1935	127,250,232	876,459	0.69
1934	126,373,773	795,010	0.63
1933	125,578,763	738,292	0.59
1932	124,840,471	800,823	0.64
1931	124,039,648	962,907	0.78
1930	123,076,741	1,309,741	1.07
1929	121,767,000	1,258,000	1.04
1928	120,509,000	1,474,000	1.23
1927	119,035,000	1,638,000	1.39
1926	117,397,000	1,568,000	1.34
1925	115,829,000	1,720,000	1.50
1924	114,109,000	2,162,000	1.91
1923	111,947,000	1,898,000	1.71
1922	110,049,000	1,511,000	1.38
1921	108,538,000	2,077,000	1.93
1920	106,461,000	1,947,000	1.85
1919	104,514,000	1,306,000	1.26
1918	103,208,000	−60,000	−0.06
1917	103,268,000	1,307,000	1.27
1916	101,961,000	1,415,000	1.40
1915	100,546,000	1,435,000	1.44
1914	99,111,000	1,886,000	1.92
1913	97,225,000	1,890,000	1.96
1912	95,335,000	1,472,000	1.56
1911	93,863,000	1,456,000	1.56
1910	92,407,000	1,917,000	2.10
1909	90,490,000	1,780,000	1.99
1908	88,710,000	1,702,000	1.94
1907	87,008,000	1,558,000	1.81
1906	85,450,000	1,628,000	1.92
1905	83,822,000	1,656,000	2.00
1904	82,166,000	1,534,000	1.88
1903	80,632,000	1,469,000	1.84
1902	79,163,000	1,579,000	2.01
1901	77,584,000	1,490,000	1.94
1900	76,094,000	—	—

NOTES: Population data as recorded on July 1 of each year.
(1) National population data for the years 1900 to 1929 are only available rounded to the nearest thousand.
(2) National population data for the years 1900 to 1949 exclude the population residing in Alaska and Hawaii.
(3) National population data for the years 1940 to 1979 cover the resident population plus Armed Forces overseas. National population data for all other years cover only the resident population.
Source: U.S. Census Bureau.

14.8   Population of the 100 Largest Urban Places, 1850

Rank	Place	Population	Rank	Place	Population
1	New York city, NY	515,547	51	Wilmington city, DE	13,979
2	Baltimore city, MD	169,054	52	Manchester city, NH	13,932
3	Boston city, MA	136,881	53	Hartford city, CT	13,555
4	Philadelphia city, PA	121,376	54	Lancaster city, PA	12,369
5	New Orleans city, LA	116,375	55	Oswego city, NY	12,205
6	Cincinnati city, OH	115,435	56	Springfield town, MA	11,766
7	Brooklyn city, NY	96,838	57	Fall River town, MA	11,524
8	St. Louis city, MO	77,860	58	Poughkeepsie village, NY	11,511
9	Spring Garden district, PA	58,894	59	Wheeling city, VA	11,435
10	Albany city, NY	50,763	60	Paterson township, NJ	11,334
11	Northern Liberties district, PA	47,223	61	Dayton city, OH	10,977
12	Kensington district, PA	46,774	62	Taunton town, MA	10,441
13	Pittsburgh city, PA	46,601	63	Nashville city, TN	10,165
14	Louisville city, KY	43,194	64	Portsmouth city, NH	9,738
15	Charleston city, SC	42,985	65	Newburyport town, MA	9,572
16	Buffalo city, NY	42,261	66	Newport town, RI	9,563
17	Providence city, RI	41,513	67	Auburn city, NY	9,548
18	Washington city, DC	40,001	68	Camden city, NJ	9,479
19	Newark city, NJ	38,894	69	Augusta city, GA	9,448
20	Southwark district, PA	38,799	70	Covington city, KY	9,408
21	Rochester city, NY	36,403	71	New London city, CT	8,991
22	Lowell city, MA	33,383	72	Schenectady city, NY	8,921
23	Williamsburgh town, NY	30,780	73	Memphis city, TN	8,841
24	Chicago city, IL	29,963	74	Alexandria town, VA	8,734
25	Troy city, NY	28,785	75	Montgomery city, AL	8,728
26	Richmond city, VA	27,570	76	Portsmouth town, VA	8,626
27	Moyamensing district, PA	26,979	77	Concord town, NH	8,576
28	Syracuse city, NY	22,271	78	Nantucket town, MA	8,452
29	Allegheny city, PA	21,262	79	Georgetown town, DC	8,366
30	Detroit city, MI	21,019	80	Chicopee town MA	8,291
31	Portland city, ME	20,815	81	Lawrence town, MA	8,282
32	Mobile city, AL	20,515	82	Augusta city, ME	8,225
33	New Haven city, CT	20,345	83	Dover town, NH	8,196
34	Salem city, MA	20,264	84	New Albany city, IN	8,181
35	Milwaukee city, WI	20,061	85	Lexington city, KY	8,159
36	Roxbury city, MA	18,364	86	Danvers town, MA	8,109
37	Columbus city, OH	17,882	87	Indianapolis city, IN	8,091
38	Utica city, NY	17,565	88	Lynchburg town, VA	8,071
39	Charlestown city, MA	17,216	89	Bath city, ME	8,020
40	Worcester city, MA	17,049	90	Madison city, IN	8,012
41	Cleveland city, OH	17,034	91	Dorchester town, MA	7,969
42	New Bedford city, MA	16,443	92	Zanesville city, OH	7,929
43	Reading city, PA	15,743	93	Harrisburg borough, PA	7,834
44	Savannah city, GA	15,312	94	Gloucester town, MA	7,786
45	Cambridge city, MA	15,215	95	Warwick town, RI	7,740
46	Bangor city, ME	14,432	96	North Providence town, RI	7,680
47	Norfolk city, VA	14,326	97	West Troy town (Watervliet), NY	7,564
48	Lynn city, MA	14,257	98	Pottsville borough, PA	7,515
49	Lafayette city (old), LA	14,190	99	Wilmington town, NC	7,264
50	Petersburg city, VA	14,010	100	Easton borough, PA	7,250

Excludes San Francisco, CA, for which 1850 census results were destroyed by fire. The population of San Francisco according to the 1852 state census was 34,776.
Source: U.S. Census Bureau.

14.9 Population of the 100 Largest Urban Places, 1900

Rank	Place	Population	Rank	Place	Population
1	New York city, NY	3,437,202	51	Wilmington city, DE	76,508
2	Chicago city, IL	1,698,575	52	Camden city, NJ	75,935
3	Philadalphia city, PA	1,293,697	53	Trenton city, NJ	73,307
4	St. Louis city, MO	575,238	54	Bridgeport city, CT	70,996
5	Boston city, MA	560,892	55	Lynn city, MA	68,513
6	Baltimore city, MD	508,957	56	Oakland city, CA	66,960
7	Cleveland city, OH	381,768	57	Lawrence city, MA	62,559
8	Buffalo city, NY	352,387	58	New Bedford city, MA	62,442
9	San Francisco city, CA	342,782	59	Des Moines city, IA	62,139
10	Cincinnati city, OH	325,902	60	Springfield city, MA	62,059
11	Pittsburgh city, PA	321,616	61	Somerville city, MA	61,643
12	New Orleans city, LA	287,104	62	Troy city, NY	60,651
13	Detroit city, MI	285,704	63	Hoboken city, NJ	59,364
14	Milwaukee city, WI	285,315	64	Evansville city, IN	59,007
15	Washington city, DC	278,718	65	Manchester city, NH	56,987
16	Newark city, NJ	246,070	66	Utica city, NY	56,383
17	Jersey City city, NJ	206,433	67	Peoria city, IL	56,100
18	Louisville city, KY	204,731	68	Charleston city, SC	55,807
19	Minneapolis city, MN	202,718	69	Savannah city GA	54,244
20	Providence city, RI	175,597	70	Salt Lake City city, UT	53,531
21	Indianapolis city, IN	169,164	71	San Antonio city, TX	53,321
22	Kansas City city, MO	163,752	72	Duluth city, MN	52,969
23	St. Paul city, MN	163,065	73	Erie city, PA	52,733
24	Rochester city, NY	162,608	74	Elizabeth city, NJ	52,130
25	Denver city, CO	133,859	75	Wilkes-Barre city, PA	51,721
26	Toledo city, OH	131,822	76	Kansas City city, KS	51,418
27	Allegheny city, PA	129,896	77	Harrisburg city, PA	50,167
28	Columbus city, OH	125,560	78	Portland city, ME	50,145
29	Worcester city, MA	118,421	79	Yonkers city, NY	47,931
30	Syracuse city, NY	108,374	80	Norfolk city, VA	46,624
31	New Haven city, CT	108,027	81	Waterbury city, CT	45,859
32	Paterson city, NJ	105,171	82	Holyoke city, MA	45,712
33	Fall River city, MA	104,863	83	Fort Wayne city, IN	45,115
34	St. Joseph city, MO	102,979	84	Youngstown city, OH	44,885
35	Omaha city, NE	102,555	85	Houston city, TX	44,633
36	Los Angeles city, CA	102,479	86	Covington city, KY	42,938
37	Memphis city, TN	102,320	87	Akron city, OH	42,728
38	Scranton city, PA	102,026	88	Dallas city, TX	42,638
39	Lowell city, MA	94,969	89	Saginaw city, MI	42,345
40	Albany city, NY	94,151	90	Lancaster city, PA	41,459
41	Cambridge city, MA	91,886	91	Lincoln city, NE	40,169
42	Portland city, OR	90,426	92	Brockton city, MA	40,063
43	Atlanta city, GA	89,872	93	Binghamton city, NY	39,647
44	Grand Rapids city, MI	87,565	94	Augusta city, GA	39,441
45	Dayton city, OH	85,333	95	Pawtucket city, RI	39,231
46	Richmond city, VA	85,050	96	Altoona city, PA	38,973
47	Nashville city, TN	80,865	97	Wheeling city, WV	38,878
48	Seattle city, WA	80,671	98	Mobile city, AL	38,469
49	Hartford city, CT	79,850	99	Birmingham city, AL	38,415
50	Reading city, PA	78,961	100	Little Rock city, AR	38,307

Source: U.S. Census Bureau.

14.10 Population and Density of the 100 Largest Places, 1950

Rank	Place	Population	Land area (sq. miles)	Population per sq. mile
1	New York city, NY	7,891,957	315.1	25,046
2	Chicago city, IL	3,620,962	207.5	17,450
3	Philadelphia city, PA	2,071,605	127.2	16,286
4	Los Angeles city, CA	1,970,358	450.9	4,370
5	Detroit city, MI	1,849,568	139.6	13,249
6	Baltimore city, MD	949,708	78.7	12,067
7	Cleveland city, OH	914,808	75.0	12,197
8	St. Louis city, MO	856,796	61.0	14,046
9	Washington city, DC	802,178	61.4	13,065
10	Boston city, MA	801,444	47.8	16,767
11	San Francisco city, CA	775,357	44.6	17,385
12	Pittsburgh city, PA	676,806	54.2	12,487
13	Milwaukee city, WI	637,392	50.0	12,748
14	Houston city, TX	596,163	160.0	3,726
15	Buffalo city, NY	580,132	39.4	14,724
16	New Orleans city, LA	570,445	199.4	2,861
17	Minneapolis city, MN	521,718	53.8	9,697
18	Cincinnati city, OH	503,998	75.1	6,711
19	Seattle city, WA	467,591	70.8	6,604
20	Kansas City city, MO	456,622	80.6	5,665
21	Newark city, NJ	438,776	23.6	18,592
22	Dallas city, TX	434,462	112.0	3,879
23	Indianapolis city, IN	427,173	55.2	7,739
24	Denver city, CO	415,786	66.8	6,224
25	San Antonio city, TX	408,442	69.5	5,877
26	Memphis city, TN	396,000	104.2	3,800
27	Oakland city, CA	384,575	53.0	7,256
28	Columbus city, OH	375,901	39.4	9,541
29	Portland city, OR	373,628	64.1	5,829
30	Louisville city, KY	369,129	39.9	9,251
31	San Diego city, CA	334,387	99.4	3,364
32	Rochester city, NY	332,488	36.0	9,236
33	Atlanta city, GA	331,314	36.9	8,979
34	Birmingham city, AL	326,037	65.3	4,993
35	St. Paul city, MN	311,349	52.2	5,965
36	Toledo city, OH	303,616	38.3	7,927
37	Jersey City city, NJ	299,017	13.0	23,001
38	Fort Worth city, TX	278,778	93.7	2,975
39	Akron city, OH	274,605	53.7	5,114
40	Omaha city, NE	251,117	40.7	6,170
41	Long Beach city, CA	250,767	34.7	7,227
42	Miami city, FL	249,276	34.2	7,289
43	Providence city, RI	248,674	17.9	13,892
44	Dayton city, OH	243,872	25.0	9,755
45	Oklahoma City city, OK	243,504	50.8	4,793
46	Richmond city, VA	230,310	37.1	6,208
47	Syracuse city, NY	220,583	25.3	8,719
48	Norfolk city, VA	213,513	28.2	7,571

Rank	Place	Population	Land area (sq. miles)	Population per sq. mile
49	Jacksonville city, FL	204,517	30.2	6,772
50	Worcester city, MA	203,486	37.0	5,500
51	Tulsa city, OK	182,740	26.7	6,844
52	Salt Lake City city, UT	182,121	53.9	3,379
53	Des Moines city, IA	177,965	54.9	3,242
54	Hartford city, CT	177,397	17.4	10,195
55	Grand Rapids city, MI	176,515	23.4	7,543
56	Nashville city, TN	174,307	22.0	7,923
57	Youngstown city, OH	168,330	32.8	5,132
58	Wichita city, KS	168,279	25.7	6,548
59	New Haven city, CT	164,443	17.9	9,187
60	Flint city, MI	163,143	29.3	5,568
61	Springfield city, MA	162,399	31.7	5,123
62	Spokane city WA	161,721	41.5	3,897
63	Bridgeport city, CT	158,709	14.6	10,870
64	Yonkers city, NY	152,798	17.2	8,884
65	Tacoma city WA	143,673	47.9	2,999
66	Paterson city, NJ	139,336	8.1	17,202
67	Sacramento city, CA	137,572	16.9	8,140
68	Arlington CDP, VA*	135,449	24.0	5,644
69	Albany city, NY	134,995	19.0	7,105
70	Charlotte city, NC	134,042	30.0	4,468
71	Gary city, IN	133,911	41.6	3,219
72	Fort Wayne city, IN	133,607	18.8	7,107
73	Austin city, TX	132,459	32.1	4,126
74	Chattanooga city, TN	131,041	28.0	4,680
75	Erie city, PA	130,803	18.8	6,958
76	El Paso city, TX	130,485	25.6	5,097
77	Kansas City city, KS	129,553	18.7	6,928
78	Mobile city, AL	129,009	25.4	5,079
79	Evansville city, IN	128,636	18.0	7,146
80	Trenton city, NJ	128,009	7.2	17,779
81	Shreveport city, LA	127,206	24.0	5,300
82	Baton Rouge city, LA	125,629	30.2	4,160
83	Scranton city, PA	125,536	24.9	5,042
84	Knoxville city, TN	124,769	25.4	4,912
85	Tampa city, FL	124,681	19.0	6,562
86	Camden city, NJ	124,555	8.6	14,483
87	Cambridge city, MA	120,740	6.2	19,474
88	Savannah city, GA	119,638	14.6	8,194
89	Canton city, OH	116,912	14.1	8,292
90	South Bend city, IN	115,911	20.2	5,738
91	Berkeley city, CA	113,805	9.5	11,979
92	Elizabeth city, NJ	112,817	11.7	9,642
93	Fall River city, MA	111,963	33.9	3,303
94	Peoria city, IL	111,856	12.9	8,671
95	Wilmington city, DE	110,356	9.8	11,261
96	Reading city, PA	109,320	8.8	12,423
97	New Bedford city, MA	109,189	19.1	5,717
98	Corpus Christi city, TX	108,287	21.5	5,037
99	Phoenix city, AZ	106,818	17.1	6,247
100	Allentown city, PA	106,756	15.9	6,714

Source: U.S. Census Bureau.

14.11   Population and Density of the 100 Largest Places, 1990

Rank	Place	Population	Land area (sq. miles)	Population per sq. mile
1	New York city, NY	7,322,564	308.9	23,705
2	Los Angeles city, CA	3,485,398	469.3	7,427
3	Chicago city, IL	2,783,726	227.2	12,252
4	Houston city, TX	1,630,553	539.9	3,020
5	Philadelphia city, PA	1,585,577	135.1	11,736
6	San Diego city, CA	1,110,549	324.0	3,428
7	Detroit city, MI	1,027,974	138.7	7,411
8	Dallas city, TX	1,006,877	342.4	2,941
9	Phoenix city, AZ	983,403	419.9	2,342
10	San Antonio city, TX	935,933	333.0	2,811
11	San Jose city, CA	782,248	171.3	4,567
12	Baltimore city, MD	736,014	80.8	9,109
13	Indianapolis city, IN	731,327	361.7	2,022
14	San Francisco city, CA	723,959	46.7	15,502
15	Jacksonville city, FL	635,230	758.7	837
16	Columbus city, OH	632,910	190.9	3,315
17	Milwaukee city, WI	628,088	96.1	6,536
18	Memphis city, TN	610,337	256.0	2,384
19	Washington city, DC	606,900	61.4	9,884
20	Boston city, MA	574,283	48.4	11,865
21	Seattle city, WA	516,259	83.9	6,153
22	El Paso city, TX	515,342	245.4	2,100
23	Cleveland city, OH	505,616	77.0	6,566
24	New Orleans city, LA	496,938	180.6	2,752
25	Nashville-Davidson, TN	488,374	473.3	1,032
26	Denver city, CO	467,610	153.3	3,050
27	Austin city, TX	465,622	217.8	2,138
28	Fort Worth city, TX	447,619	281.1	1,592
29	Oklahoma City city, OK	444,719	608.2	731
30	Portland city, OR	437,319	124.7	3,507
31	Kansas City city, MO	435,146	311.5	1,397
32	Long Beach city, CA	429,433	50.0	8,589
33	Tucson city, AZ	405,390	156.3	2,594
34	St. Louis city, MO	396,685	61.9	6,408
35	Charlotte city, NC	395,934	174.3	2,272
36	Atlanta city, GA	394,017	131.8	2,990
37	Virginia Beach city, VA	393,069	248.3	1,583
38	Albuquerque city, NM	384,736	132.2	2,910
39	Oakland city, CA	372,242	56.1	6,635
40	Pittsburgh city, PA	369,879	55.6	6,653
41	Sacramento city, CA	369,365	96.3	3,836
42	Minneapolis city, MN	368,383	54.9	6,710
43	Tulsa city, OK	367,302	183.5	2,002
44	Honolulu CDP, HI	365,272	82.8	4,411
45	Cincinnati city, OH	364,040	77.2	4,716
46	Miami city, FL	358,548	35.6	10,072
47	Fresno city, CA	354,202	99.1	3,574
48	Omaha city, NE	335,795	100.6	3,338

Rank	Place	Population	Land area (sq. miles)	Population per sq. mile
49	Toledo city, OH	332,943	80.6	4,131
50	Buffalo city, NY	328,123	40.6	8,082
51	Wichita city, KS	304,011	115.1	2,641
52	Santa Ana city, CA	293,742	27.1	10,839
53	Mesa city, AZ	288,091	108.6	2,653
54	Colorado Springs city, CO	281,140	183.2	1,535
55	Tampa city, FL	280,015	108.7	2,576
56	Newark city, NJ	275,221	23.8	11,564
57	St. Paul city, MN	272,235	52.8	5,156
58	Louisville city, KY	269,063	62.1	4,333
59	Anaheim city, CA	266,406	44.3	6,014
60	Birmingham city, AL	265,968	148.5	1,791
61	Arlington city, TX	261,721	93.0	2,814
62	Norfolk city, VA	261,229	53.8	4,856
63	Las Vegas city, NV	258,295	83.3	3,101
64	Corpus Christi city, TX	257,453	135.0	1,907
65	St. Petersburg city, FL	238,629	59.2	4,031
66	Rochester city, NY	231,636	35.8	6,470
67	Jersey City city, NJ	228,537	14.9	15,338
68	Riverside city, CA	226,505	77.7	2,915
69	Anchorage city, AK	226,338	1,697.6	133
70	Lexington-Fayette, KY	225,366	284.5	792
71	Akron city, OH	223,019	62.2	3,586
72	Aurora city, CO	222,103	132.5	1,676
73	Baton Rouge city, LA	219,531	73.9	2,971
74	Stockton city, CA	210,943	52.6	4,010
75	Raleigh city, NC	207,951	88.1	2,360
76	Richmond city, VA	203,056	60.1	3,379
77	Shreveport city, LA	198,525	98.6	2,013
78	Jackson city, MS	196,637	109.0	1,804
79	Mobile city, AL	196,278	118.0	1,663
80	Des Moines city, IA	193,187	75.3	2,566
81	Lincoln city, NE	191,972	63.3	3,033
82	Madison city, WI	191,262	57.8	3,309
83	Grand Rapids city, MI	189,126	44.3	4,269
84	Yonkers city, NY	188,082	18.1	10,391
85	Hialeah city, FL	188,004	19.2	9,792
86	Montgomery city, AL	187,106	135.0	1,386
87	Lubbock city, TX	186,206	104.1	1,789
88	Greensboro city, NC	183,521	79.8	2,300
89	Dayton city, OH	182,044	55.0	3,310
90	Huntington Beach city, CA	181,519	26.4	6,876
91	Garland city, TX	180,650	57.3	3,153
92	Glendale city, CA	180,038	30.6	5,884
93	Columbus city, GA	178,681	216.1	827
94	Spokane city, WA	177,196	55.9	3,170
95	Tacoma city, WA	176,664	48.0	3,681
96	Little Rock city, AR	175,795	102.9	1,708
97	Bakersfield city, CA	174,820	91.8	1,904
98	Fremont city, CA	173,339	77.0	2,251
99	Fort Wayne city, IN	173,072	62.7	2,760
100	Arlington CDP, VA	170,936	25.9	6,600

Source: U.S. Census Bureau.

14.12   Population of New York City, 1900-1990

In 1874 and 1895, New York City annexed parts of Westchester County. New York annexed Brooklyn in 1898 and "Greater New York" was formed consisting of five boroughs: Manhattan; Bronx (area annexed by New York County in 1874 and 1895); Brooklyn (Kings County, including Brooklyn city); Queens (Queens County excluding portion taken to form Nassau County); and Richmond (Richmond County). Bronx County, coextensive with Bronx borough, was formed in 1912, making New York County coextensive with Manhattan borough. Richmond borough was renamed Staten Island borough in 1975.

Year	Total	Bronx	Brooklyn	Manhattan	Queens	Staten Island (Richmond)
1900	3,437,202	200,507	1,166,582	1,850,093	152,999	67,021
1910	4,766,883	430,980	1,634,351	2,331,542	284,041	85,969
1920	5,620,048	732,016	2,018,356	2,284,103	469,042	116,531
1930	6,930,446	1,265,258	2,560,401	1,867,312	1,079,129	158,346
1940	7,454,995	1,394,711	2,698,285	1,889,924	1,297,634	174,441
1950	7,891,957	1,451,277	2,738,175	1,960,101	1,550,849	191,555
1960	7,781,984	1,424,815	2,627,319	1,698,281	1,809,578	221,991
1970	7,894,862	1,471,701	2,602,012	1,539,233	1,986,473	295,443
1980	7,071,639	1,168,972	2,230,936	1,428,285	1,891,325	352,121
1990	7,322,564	1,203,789	2,300,664	1,487,536	1,951,598	378,977

Source: U.S. Census Bureau.

14.13 Population Density by State, 1997

Persons per square mile of land area

STATE	1997 Number	1997 Rank	1990 Number	1990 Rank
United States	75.7	NA	70.3	NA
Alabama	85.1	25	79.6	25
Alaska	1.1	50	1.0	50
Arizona	40.1	37	32.3	37
Arkansas	48.4	34	45.1	35
California	206.9	12	191.0	12
Colorado	37.5	38	31.8	38
Connecticut	674.9	4	678.5	4
Delaware	374.2	7	340.8	7
District of Columbia	8,615.0	NA	9,884.4	NA
Florida	271.7	9	239.9	10
Georgia	129.3	20	111.8	21
Hawaii	184.7	13	172.5	13
Idaho	14.6	44	12.2	44
Illinois	214.0	11	205.6	11
Indiana	163.5	16	154.6	16
Iowa	51.1	33	49.7	33
Kansas	31.7	40	30.3	39
Kentucky	98.4	23	92.8	23
Louisiana	99.9	22	96.9	22
Maine	40.2	36	39.8	36
Maryland	521.2	5	489.1	5
Massachusetts	780.5	3	767.6	3
Michigan	172.0	14	163.6	14
Minnesota	58.9	31	55.0	31
Mississippi	58.2	32	54.9	32
Missouri	78.4	27	74.3	27
Montana	6.0	48	5.5	48
Nebraska	21.6	42	20.5	42
Nevada	15.3	43	10.9	45
New Hampshire	130.8	18	123.7	18
New Jersey	1,085.4	1	1,044.3	1
New Mexico	14.3	45	12.5	43
New York	384.1	6	381.0	6
North Carolina	152.4	17	136.1	17
North Dakota	9.3	47	9.3	46
Ohio	273.2	8	264.9	9
Oklahoma	48.3	35	45.8	34
Oregon	33.8	39	29.6	40
Pennsylvania	268.2	10	265.1	8
Rhode Island	944.9	2	960.3	2
South Carolina	124.9	21	115.8	20
South Dakota	9.7	46	9.2	47
Tennessee	130.2	19	118.3	19
Texas	74.2	29	64.9	29
Utah	25.1	41	21.0	41
Vermont	63.7	30	60.8	30
Virginia	170.1	15	156.3	15
Washington	84.3	26	73.1	28
West Virginia	75.4	28	74.5	26
Wisconsin	95.2	24	90.1	24
Wyoming	4.9	49	4.7	49

NA = Not applicable.
Source: U.S. Census Bureau.

14.14   Median Household Income by State, 1995-1997

State	1997 Median income	1997 Standard error	1996 Median income	1996 Standard error	1995 Median income	1995 Standard error
United States	$37,005	$ 171	$35,492	$ 179	$34,076	$ 197
Alabama	31,939	1,607	30,302	1,258	25,991	1,266
Alaska	47,994	1,258	52,779	1,907	47,954	2,008
Arizona	32,740	1,297	31,637	1,274	30,863	1,360
Arkansas	26,162	1,154	27,123	978	25,814	999
California	39,694	864	38,812	818	37,009	723
Colorado	43,233	1,944	40,950	1,329	40,706	1,552
Connecticut	43,985	1,989	42,119	3,087	40,243	2,269
Delaware	43,033	2,062	39,309	1,402	34,928	1,848
D.C.	31,860	984	31,966	1,578	30,748	1,182
Florida	32,455	583	30,641	513	29,745	612
Georgia	36,663	916	32,496	1,666	34,099	897
Hawaii	40,934	1,398	41,772	1,893	42,851	1,292
Idaho	33,404	1,339	34,709	1,341	32,676	1,116
Illinois	41,283	782	39,554	1,107	38,071	875
Indiana	38,889	1,183	35,147	1,298	33,385	1,444
Iowa	33,783	1,282	33,209	1,527	35,519	942
Kansas	36,471	1,614	32,585	1,460	30,341	921
Kentucky	33,452	1,660	32,413	1,439	29,810	1,149
Louisiana	33,260	1,551	30,262	1,290	27,949	1,090
Maine	32,772	1,301	34,696	1,211	33,858	1,088
Maryland	46,685	1,476	43,993	2,565	41,041	1,627
Massachusetts	42,023	1,383	39,494	1,932	38,574	1,475
Michigan	38,742	1,108	39,225	1,143	36,426	994
Minnesota	42,564	1,510	40,991	1,225	37,933	1,848
Mississippi	28,499	1,386	26,677	1,316	26,538	1,028
Missouri	36,553	2,060	34,265	1,513	34,825	1,373
Montana	29,212	1,144	28,684	1,566	27,757	1,105
Nebraska	34,692	1,528	34,014	1,500	32,929	1,155
Nevada	38,854	1,576	38,540	1,615	36,084	1,314
New Hampshire	40,998	1,605	39,407	1,734	39,171	1,556
New Jersey	48,021	1,424	47,468	1,217	43,924	1,400
New Mexico	30,086	1,156	25,086	1,091	25,991	1,100
New York	35,798	634	35,410	746	33,028	716
North Carolina	35,840	917	35,601	1,008	31,979	888
North Dakota	31,661	1,362	31,470	1,184	29,089	1,217
Ohio	36,134	894	34,070	1,063	34,941	988
Oklahoma	31,351	1,025	27,437	1,089	26,311	880
Oregon	37,247	1,788	35,492	1,274	36,374	970
Pennsylvania	37,517	964	34,899	974	34,524	683
Rhode Island	34,797	2,234	36,986	1,036	35,359	1,373
South Carolina	34,262	1,609	34,665	1,405	29,071	1,400
South Dakota	29,694	1,145	29,526	1,003	29,578	1,610
Tennessee	30,636	1,358	30,790	1,087	29,015	1,268
Texas	35,075	880	33,072	763	32,039	634
Utah	42,775	1,785	37,038	1,330	36,480	919
Vermont	35,053	1,726	32,358	1,250	33,824	1,242
Virginia	42,957	1,897	39,211	1,459	36,222	1,391
Washington	44,562	1,715	36,676	1,608	35,568	1,252
West Virginia	27,488	1,315	25,247	1,301	24,880	870
Wisconsin	39,595	1,150	40,001	1,780	40,955	1,318
Wyoming	33,423	1,441	30,953	858	31,529	1,136

14.15 Mean Income Received by Each Fifth and Top 5 Percent of Households, 1967-1997

Households as of March of the following year. Income in current and 1997 CPI-U adjusted dollars.

Year	Lowest fifth	Second fifth	Third fifth	Fourth fifth	Highest fifth	Top 5%
Current Dollars						
1997	$8,872	$22,098	$37,177	$57,582	$122,764	$215,436
1996	8,596	21,097	35,486	54,922	115,514	201,220
1995	8,350	20,397	34,106	52,429	109,411	188,828
1994	7,762	19,224	32,385	50,395	105,945	183,044
1993	7,412	18,656	31,272	48,599	101,253	173,784
1992	7,288	18,181	30,631	47,021	91,110	144,608
1991	7,263	18,149	30,147	45,957	88,130	137,532
1990	7,195	18,030	29,781	44,901	87,137	138,756
1989	7,021	17,401	28,925	43,753	85,529	138,185
1988	6,504	16,317	27,291	41,254	78,759	124,215
1987	6,167	15,584	26,055	39,383	74,897	118,000
1986	5,944	14,961	24,979	37,622	70,340	107,444
1985	5,797	14,330	23,735	35,694	65,841	98,946
1984	5,606	13,634	22,547	33,944	61,648	90,629
1983	5,239	12,796	21,105	31,667	57,303	83,943
1982	5,003	12,238	20,195	30,026	54,164	78,945
1981	4,836	11,589	19,141	28,512	49,942	71,095
1980	4,483	10,819	17,807	26,219	46,053	66,617
1979	4,114	10,021	16,495	24,193	42,990	64,197
1978	3,807	9,112	15,010	21,980	38,791	57,625
1977	3,513	8,291	13,671	20,018	35,091	51,792
1976	3,278	7,780	12,762	18,521	32,320	47,805
1975	3,034	7,204	11,787	17,117	29,809	43,940
1974	2,911	6,973	11,206	16,181	28,259	41,669
1973	2,568	6,366	10,402	14,954	26,521	40,417
1972	2,316	5,898	9,625	13,817	24,806	38,447
1971	2,126	5,529	8,965	12,745	22,583	34,637
1970	2,029	5,395	8,688	12,247	21,684	33,283
1969	1,957	5,216	8,335	11,674	20,520	31,586
1968	1,832	4,842	7,679	10,713	18,762	29,048
1967	1,626	4,433	7,078	9,903	17,946	28,605
1997 Dollars						
1997	$8,872	$22,098	$37,177	$57,582	$122,764	$215,436
1996	8,793	21,581	36,300	56,182	118,164	205,837
1995	8,794	21,481	35,919	55,216	115,226	198,864
1994	8,406	20,820	35,073	54,578	114,738	198,236
1993	8,233	20,722	34,735	53,980	112,464	193,027

Year	Lowest fifth	Second fifth	Third fifth	Fourth fifth	Highest fifth	Top 5%

1997 Dollars *(continued)*

Year	Lowest fifth	Second fifth	Third fifth	Fourth fifth	Highest fifth	Top 5%
1992	$8,337	$20,799	$35,041	$53,791	$104,228	$165,428
1991	8,559	21,387	35,526	54,156	103,854	162,070
1990	8,835	22,141	36,571	55,139	107,004	170,393
1989	9,088	22,523	37,439	56,632	110,705	178,860
1988	8,824	22,138	37,026	55,970	106,854	168,525
1987	8,713	22,018	36,812	55,642	105,818	166,717
1986	8,704	21,909	36,580	55,094	103,007	157,343
1985	8,647	21,375	35,404	53,242	98,211	147,591
1984	8,660	21,061	34,830	52,435	95,231	140,000
1983	8,442	20,620	34,010	51,030	92,341	135,270
1982	8,399	20,546	33,905	50,410	90,934	132,538
1981	8,615	20,644	34,097	50,790	88,964	126,645
1980	8,743	21,099	34,727	51,132	89,812	129,915
1979	8,923	21,735	35,776	52,473	93,242	139,238
1978	9,052	21,666	35,690	52,264	92,236	137,019
1977	8,921	21,055	34,718	50,837	89,116	131,529
1976	8,857	21,022	34,483	50,044	87,329	129,170
1975	8,665	20,574	33,662	48,884	85,131	125,487
1974	9,002	21,564	34,654	50,040	87,391	128,861
1973	8,732	21,647	35,371	50,850	90,183	137,435
1972	8,372	21,320	34,793	49,947	89,670	138,981
1971	7,917	20,589	33,385	47,461	84,097	128,985
1970	7,885	20,966	33,763	47,594	84,268	129,344
1969	7,972	21,248	33,953	47,555	83,590	128,669
1968	7,799	20,614	32,692	45,608	79,875	123,666
1967	7,189	19,600	31,295	43,786	79,348	126,477

14.16   Total Income Per Household Member by Race, 1980-1997

Race and year	Current dollars	1997 dollars
ALL RACES		
1997	$18,941	$18,941
1996	17,850	18,260
1995	16,943	17,844
1994	16,300	17,653
1993	15,501	17,217
1992	14,601	16,703
1991	14,455	17,034
1990	14,197	17,434
1989	13,871	17,954
1988	12,976	17,605
1987	12,160	17,180
1986	11,552	16,917
1985	10,884	16,235
1984	10,207	15,767
1983	9,377	15,111
1982	8,901	14,944
1981	8,389	14,944
1980	7,720	15,055
WHITE		
1997	$20,093	$20,093
1996	18,878	19,311
1995	18,011	18,968
1994	17,356	18,796
1993	16,516	18,345
1992	15,537	17,774
1991	15,322	18,056
1990	15,070	18,506
1989	14,720	19,053
1988	13,749	18,654
1987	12,897	18,222
1986	12,239	17,923
1985	11,531	17,200
1984	10,826	16,724
1983	9,947	16,029
1982	9,452	15,869
1981	8,896	15,847
1980	8,170	15,933
BLACK		
1997	$11,998	$11,998
1996	11,543	11,808
1995	10,449	11,004
1994	10,274	11,127
1993	9,386	10,425
1992	8,887	10,167
1991	8,924	10,516
1990	8,635	10,604
1989	8,344	10,800

Race and year	Current dollars	1997 dollars
BLACK (*continued*)		
1988	$7,979	$10,825
1987	7,231	10,216
1986	6,952	10,181
1985	6,676	9,958
1984	6,071	9,378
1983	5,534	8,918
1982	5,174	8,686
1981	4,975	8,862
1980	4,689	9,144
ASIAN AND PACIFIC ISLANDER		
1997	$18,569	$18,569
1996	17,928	18,339
1995	16,994	17,897
1994	16,867	18,267
1993	15,955	17,722
1992	14,828	16,963
1991	14,304	16,856
1990	13,694	16,816
1989	13,964	18,074
1988	12,696	17,225
HISPANIC ORIGIN		
1997	$10,137	$10,137
1996	9,545	9,764
1995	8,835	9,305
1994	8,979	9,724
1993	8,452	9,388
1992	8,143	9,315
1991	8,357	9,848
1990	8,134	9,989
1989	8,062	10,435
1988	7,699	10,445
1987	7,253	10,247
1986	6,767	9,910
1985	6,358	9,484
1984	6,147	9,496
1983	5,617	9,051
1982	5,380	9,032
1981	5,266	9,381
1980	4,806	9,373

14.17   Families in Poverty, 1959-1997

Number of families below the poverty level and poverty rate (numbers in thousands)

Year	Number of poor families	Poverty rate	Number of poor families with female householder	Poverty rate for female-headed families
1997	7,324	10.3	3,995	31.6
1996	7,708	11.0	4,167	32.6
1995	7,532	10.8	4,057	32.4
1994	8,053	11.6	4,232	34.6
1993	8,393	12.3	4,424	35.6
1992	8,144	11.9	4,275	35.4
1991	7,712	11.5	4,161	35.6
1990	7,098	10.7	3,768	33.4
1989	6,784	10.3	3,504	32.2
1988	6,874	10.4	3,642	33.4
1987	7,005	10.7	3,654	34.2
1986	7,023	10.9	3,613	34.6
1985	7,223	11.4	3,474	34.0
1984	7,277	11.6	3,498	34.5
1983	7,647	12.3	3,564	36.0
1982	7,512	12.2	3,434	36.3
1981	6,851	11.2	3,252	34.6
1980	6,217	10.3	2,972	32.7
1979	5,461	9.2	2,645	30.4
1978	5,280	9.1	2,654	31.4
1977	5,311	9.3	2,610	31.7
1976	5,311	9.4	2,543	33.0
1975	5,450	9.7	2,430	32.5
1974	4,922	8.8	2,324	32.1
1973	4,828	8.8	2,193	32.2
1972	5,075	9.3	2,158	32.7
1971	5,303	10.0	2,100	33.9
1970	5,260	10.1	1,951	32.5
1969	5,008	9.7	1,827	32.7
1968	5,047	10.0	1,755	32.3
1967	5,667	11.4	1,774	33.3
1966	5,784	11.8	1,721	33.1
1965	6,721	13.9	1,916	38.4
1964	7,160	15.0	1,822	36.4
1963	7,554	15.9	1,972	40.4
1962	8,077	17.2	2,034	42.9
1961	8,391	18.1	1,954	42.1
1960	8,243	18.1	1,955	42.4
1959	8,320	18.5	1,916	42.6

Source: U.S. Census Bureau.

14.18   State Populations and Growth, 1990-1997

When states share the same rank, the next lower rank is omitted. States may share the same value but have different ranks due to rounding.

STATE	Population				1990–1997			
	1997		1990		Net change		Percent change	
	1,000	Rank	1,000	Rank	1,000	Rank	Percent	Rank
United States	267,636	NA	248,765	NA	18,870.9	NA	7.6	NA
Alabama	4,319	23	4,040	22	278.8	22	6.9	23
Alaska	609	48	550	49	59.3	42	10.8	13
Arizona	4,555	21	3,665	24	889.6	5	24.3	2
Arkansas	2,523	33	2,351	33	172.2	28	7.3	20
California	32,268	1	29,786	1	2,482.4	1	8.3	18
Colorado	3,893	25	3,294	26	598.2	8	18.2	5
Connecticut	3,270	28	3,287	27	−17.3	50	−0.5	50
Delaware	732	46	666	46	65.4	40	9.8	16
District of Columbia	529	NA	607	NA	−77.9	NA	−12.8	NA
Florida	14,654	4	12,938	4	1,715.9	3	13.3	11
Georgia	7,486	10	6,478	11	1,008.1	4	15.6	6
Hawaii	1,187	41	1,108	41	78.4	38	7.1	22
Idaho	1,210	40	1,007	42	203.5	27	20.2	3
Illinois	11,896	6	11,431	6	465.2	13	4.1	38
Indiana	5,864	14	5,544	14	320.0	17	5.8	28
Iowa	2,852	30	2,777	30	75.6	39	2.7	42
Kansas	2,595	32	2,478	32	117.3	34	4.7	36
Kentucky	3,908	24	3,687	23	221.2	25	6.0	25
Louisiana	4,352	22	4,222	21	129.9	33	3.1	40
Maine	1,242	39	1,228	38	14.1	47	1.2	44
Maryland	5,094	19	4,781	19	313.5	18	6.6	24
Massachusetts	6,118	13	6,016	13	101.1	35	1.7	43
Michigan	9,774	8	9,295	8	478.6	11	5.1	34
Minnesota	4,686	20	4,376	20	309.9	19	7.1	21
Mississippi	2,731	31	2,575	31	155.0	30	6.0	25
Missouri	5,402	16	5,117	15	285.2	21	5.6	32
Montana	879	44	799	44	79.7	36	10.0	15
Nebraska	1,657	38	1,578	36	78.5	37	5.0	35
Nevada	1,677	37	1,202	39	475.1	12	39.5	1
New Hampshire	1,173	42	1,109	40	63.5	41	5.7	30
New Jersey	8,053	9	7,748	9	305.1	20	3.9	39
New Mexico	1,730	36	1,515	37	214.7	26	14.2	9
New York	18,137	3	17,991	2	146.4	31	0.8	47
North Carolina	7,425	11	6,632	10	792.7	6	12.0	12
North Dakota	641	47	639	47	2.1	48	0.3	48
Ohio	11,186	7	10,847	7	339.2	15	3.1	40
Oklahoma	3,317	27	3,146	28	171.5	29	5.5	33
Oregon	3,243	29	2,842	29	401.2	14	14.1	10
Pennsylvania	12,020	5	11,883	5	136.8	32	1.2	44
Rhode Island	987	43	1,003	43	−16.0	49	−1.6	49
South Carolina	3,760	26	3,486	25	273.9	24	7.9	19
South Dakota	738	45	696	45	42.0	43	6.0	25
Tennessee	5,368	17	4,877	17	491.0	10	10.1	14
Texas	19,439	2	16,986	3	2,453.0	2	14.4	8
Utah	2,059	34	1,723	35	336.3	16	19.5	4
Vermont	589	49	563	48	26.2	44	4.7	36
Virginia	6,734	12	6,189	12	544.8	9	8.8	17
Washington	5,610	15	4,867	18	743.7	7	15.3	7
West Virginia	1,816	35	1,793	34	22.3	46	1.2	44
Wisconsin	5,170	18	4,892	16	277.9	23	5.7	30
Wyoming	480	50	454	50	26.2	45	5.8	28

NA = Not applicable.
Source: U.S. Census Bureau.

14.19 State Populations by Race, 1996

STATE	White		Black		Asian or Pacific Islander		American Indian, Eskimo, or Aleut	
	Percent	Rank	Percent	Rank	Percent	Rank	Percent	Rank
United States	82.8	NA	12.6	NA	3.7	NA	0.9	NA
Alabama	73.2	44	25.8	6	0.7	43	0.4	26
Alaska	76.2	42	3.8	33	4.3	6	15.7	1
Arizona	88.9	23	3.5	34	2.0	19	5.6	6
Arkansas	82.7	34	16.1	12	0.7	43	0.5	23
California	80.0	38	7.4	24	11.6	2	1.0	16
Colorado	92.5	15	4.3	31	2.3	16	0.9	17
Connecticut	88.4	25	9.1	21	2.2	17	0.2	39
Delaware	79.0	39	18.8	9	1.9	20	0.3	33
District of Columbia	34.0	NA	62.7	NA	3.0	NA	0.3	NA
Florida	82.9	33	15.1	14	1.7	22	0.4	26
Georgia	69.8	45	28.2	4	1.8	21	0.2	39
Hawaii	33.5	50	3.0	37	63.0	1	0.6	21
Idaho	97.1	4	0.5	48	1.1	33	1.3	13
Illinois	81.4	36	15.3	13	3.2	11	0.2	39
Indiana	90.7	20	8.2	22	0.9	38	0.2	39
Iowa	96.6	5	1.9	40	1.2	29	0.3	33
Kansas	91.6	18	5.9	28	1.6	23	0.9	17
Kentucky	92.0	17	7.2	26	0.6	46	0.2	39
Louisiana	66.3	48	32.0	2	1.2	29	0.4	26
Maine	98.4	1	0.5	48	0.7	43	0.4	26
Maryland	68.9	46	27.1	5	3.7	8	0.3	33
Massachusetts	90.3	21	6.2	27	3.3	9	0.2	39
Michigan	83.6	31	14.3	16	1.5	24	0.6	21
Minnesota	93.6	12	2.7	38	2.4	14	1.2	15
Mississippi	62.7	49	36.3	1	0.6	46	0.4	26
Missouri	87.4	26	11.2	19	1.0	36	0.4	26
Montana	92.9	13	0.4	50	0.6	46	6.2	5
Nebraska	94.0	9	3.9	32	1.2	29	0.9	17
Nevada	86.6	29	7.4	24	4.2	7	1.8	9
New Hampshire	98.0	3	0.7	44	1.1	33	0.2	39
New Jersey	80.3	37	14.5	15	4.9	5	0.3	33
New Mexico	87.0	28	2.5	39	1.3	27	9.2	2
New York	76.9	40	17.6	10	5.1	4	0.4	26
North Carolina	75.4	43	22.2	7	1.2	29	1.3	13
North Dakota	94.0	9	0.6	45	0.8	40	4.6	7
Ohio	87.4	26	11.3	18	1.1	33	0.2	39
Oklahoma	83.2	32	7.7	23	1.3	27	7.9	3
Oregon	93.8	11	1.8	41	3.0	12	1.4	11
Pennsylvania	88.7	24	9.6	20	1.5	24	0.1	49
Rhode Island	92.6	14	4.8	30	2.2	17	0.5	23
South Carolina	68.8	47	30.2	3	0.8	40	0.2	39
South Dakota	91.0	19	0.6	45	0.6	46	7.8	4
Tennessee	82.4	35	16.4	11	0.9	38	0.2	39
Texas	84.7	30	12.2	17	2.6	13	0.5	23
Utah	95.4	8	0.8	42	2.4	14	1.4	11
Vermont	98.2	2	0.6	45	0.9	37	0.3	33
Virginia	76.6	41	19.8	8	3.3	9	0.3	33
Washington	89.4	22	3.4	35	5.4	3	1.8	9
West Virginia	96.2	6	3.2	36	0.5	50	0.1	49
Wisconsin	92.2	16	5.5	29	1.4	26	0.9	17
Wyoming	96.2	6	0.8	42	0.8	40	2.2	8

NA = Not applicable.
Source: U.S. Census Bureau.

14.20   Current Population

According to the U.S. Bureau of the Census, the resident population of the United States as of April 1, 1999, was 272,255,651.

One birth every ....8 seconds
One death every ....14 seconds
One international migrant (net) every...................29 seconds
One federal U.S. citizen (net) returning every.......4,764 seconds
Net gain of one person every ....12 seconds

Source: U.S. Census Bureau.

14.21   Most Popular Given Names, 1880-1997

Following are the ten most popular given names by year of birth and sex. At the left of each table is the rank. To the right of each name is the number in the sample with that name. At the bottom of each table is the total number of each sex in the sample.

1880

Rank	Male	Number	Female	Number
1.	John	464	Mary	176
2.	William	330	Anna	77
3.	Charles	218	Elizabeth	53
4.	George	214	Margaret	49
5.	James	199	Minnie	42
6.	Joseph	189	Emma	41
7.	Frank	149	Martha	38
8.	Henry	116	Alice	37
9.	Thomas	102	Marie	33
10.	Harry	89	Annie, Sarah (tie)	30

Total sample size in 1880: 4,770 males, 2,360 females

1960

Rank	Male	Number	Female	Number
1.	David	935	Mary	548
2.	Michael	897	Susan	428
3.	John	783	Maria	395
4.	James	774	Karen	388
5.	Robert	750	Lisa	360
6.	Mark	603	Linda	359
7.	William	510	Donna	341
8.	Richard	471	Patricia	337
9.	Thomas	411	Debra	285
10.	Steven	373	Deborah	277

Total sample size in 1960: 26,941 males, 25,024 females

1920

Rank	Male	Number	Female	Number
1.	John	693	Mary	747
2.	William	618	Dorothy	413
3.	James	563	Helen	390
4.	Robert	560	Margaret	343
5.	Joseph	358	Ruth	292
6.	Charles	341	Virginia	208
7.	George	328	Elizabeth	201
8.	Edward	237	Anna	190
9.	Thomas	208	Mildred	173
10.	Frank	202	Betty	169

Total sample size in 1920: 14,858 males, 15,091 females

1997

Rank	Male	Number	Female	Number
1.	Michael	225	Emily	145
2.	Jacob	177	Sarah	139
3.	Matthew	175	Taylor	111
4.	Christopher	159	Jessica	110
5.	Nicholas	151	Ashley	109
6.	Austin	145	Samantha	102
7.	Joshua	141	Madison	100
8.	Andrew	137	Hannah	95
9.	Joseph	129	Kayla	83
10.	Brandon	126	Alexis	81

Total sample size in 1997: 11,088 males, 10,489 females

Source: Social Security Administration.

14.22   Most Common Surnames in the U.S., 1997

	Name	Percentage of all Names
1	Smith	1.006
2	Johnson	0.810
3	Williams	0.699
4	Jones	0.621
5	Brown	0.621
6	Davis	0.480
7	Miller	0.424
8	Wilson	0.339
9	Moore	0.312
10	Anderson	0.311
11	Taylor	0.311
12	Thomas	0.311

The twelve most common U.S. surnames together make up over six percent of the entire U.S. population.

Source: Social Security Administration.

14.23   Most Common Causes of Death in the U.S., 1996

Cause		No. of deaths, 1996
1	Disease of the heart	733,834
2	Cancer	544,278
3	Cerebrovascular diseases	160,431
4	Chronic obstructive pulmonary diseases and allied conditions	106,146
5	Accidents and adverse effects	93,874
6	Pneumonia and influenza	82,579
7	Diabetes	61,559
8	Human immunodeficiency virus infection	32,655
9	Suicide	30,862
10	Chronic liver disease and cirrhosis	25,135

Preliminary figures are for 1996 based on a total number of 2,322,421 deaths estimated in the US for that year. "Accidents and adverse effects" includes 43,449 deaths resulting from motor vehicle accidents. The category "Homicide and legal intervention" remains 11th with 20,738 deaths.
Source: U.S. National Center for Health Statistics.

14.24   Major U.S. Epidemics, 1793-1997

1793	Philadelphia. More than 4,000 residents died from yellow fever.
1832	New York City. More than 3,000 people killed in a cholera epidemic. In New Orleans, cholera took the lives of 4,340 people.
1848	New York City. More than 5,000 deaths caused by cholera.
1853	New Orleans. Yellow fever killed 7,790.
1867	New Orleans. 3,093 perished from yellow fever.
1878	Southern States. More than 13,000 people died from yellow fever in lower Mississippi Valley.
1916	Nationwide over 7,000 deaths occurred and 17,363 cases were reported of polio (infantile paralysis) in America's worst polio epidemic.
1918	Nationwide outbreak of Spanish influenza killed over 500,000 people in the worst single U.S. epidemic.
1949	Nationwide, 2,720 deaths occurred from polio and 42,173 cases were reported.
1952	Nationwide, polio killed 3,300; 57,628 cases reported; worse epidemic since 1916.
1981-1997	Nationwide, total U.S. AIDS cases reported to Centers for Disease Control: 641,086; total AIDS deaths reported: 390,692.

SECTION 15

Public Institutions

15.1 Chronology of Public Education, 1635-1999

1635	Boston Latin School, the first public secondary school in the United States, begins classes.
1638	The first "reading" school in New Amsterdam (New York) opens.
1642	The Massachusetts General Court passes a law requiring parents and guardians to teach their children to read and understand the principles of religion. It is the first law of its kind in the English-speaking world.
1647	Massachusetts's "Old Deluder Satan Law" requires every town of fifty or more families to support an elementary school and appoint a teacher to teach children to read and write. Every town of one hundred or more families is required to establish a grammar school to teach Latin for the purpose of preparing its students for entry to the colonial college. The first textbook is the *Hornbook,* which contains the alphabet, vowels, syllables, the doctrine of the Trinity and the Lord's Prayer.
1640s-1650s	Two Latin grammar schools open in Virginia and a Catholic Latin grammar school opens in Maryland.
1689	The Friends Public School opens for boys in Philadelphia.
1690	One of the most popular textbooks of the colonial era, the *New England Primer,* is first published.
1704	The Church of England opens a school for blacks, American Indians, and whites in New York City.
1742	The Moravian Seminary, one of the few elite schools for girls, opens in Bethlehem, Pennsylvania.
1743	In Charleston, South Carolina, Anglicans open a school for blacks.
1749	The first academy, whose practical curriculum will eventually make it become more popular than the Latin Grammar School, is founded in Philadelphia by Benjamin Franklin.
1785	Georgia charters the first state university.
1795	The University of North Carolina becomes the first state university to hold classes.
1819	In the *Dartmouth College* case, the United States Supreme Court rules to protect private colleges from undue state control. The Office of Indian Affairs is established, enabling government-funded schools for the education of American Indians.
1820's	Normal schools (two-year institutions for teacher training) appear.
1821	The first public high school in the United States, the English Classical School of Boston, opens.
1827	Massachusetts becomes the first state to order compulsory support of public education through taxation.
1830s	States begin to organize public school systems open to all. State school taxes and statewide requirements for attendance, curriculum and teacher training begin to widely appear.
1836	*McGuffey's Eclectic Readers*, the enormously popular schoolbooks compiled by William H. McGuffey, first appear.
1837	The nation's first state Board of Education takes office in Massachusetts, with Horace Mann as secretary.
1847	At a grammar school in Quincy, Massachusetts, students are put into specific grade levels for the first time.
1852	Massachusetts passes the country's first compulsory school-attendance law.
1862	The Morrill Act gives federal land to support state agricultural and mechanical colleges.
1865	The federal government establishes the Freedmen's Bureau, a school system designed to educate former slaves.
1873	The first successful public kindergarten program in the country opens at the DesPeres School in St. Louis.
1874	In the *Kalamazoo* case, the Michigan Supreme Court rules that taxes could be levied for the support of public high schools, as well as for elementary schools and state universities.

1892	The National Education Association establishes its "Committee of Ten" to address problems of standarization in America's high schools. The Committee's recommendations include requiring eight years of attendance at elementary school followed by four years at secondary school. It also outlines specific high school curriculums.
1893	The National Education Association's "Committee of Fifteen" is established to address issues of organization, teaching training and curricula for the nation's elementary schools.
1896	In its *Plessy v. Ferguson* decision, the U.S. Supreme Court upholds the "separate but equal" doctrine concerning public facilities for black and whites, thus legalizing the practice of racial segregation in America's public schools.
1902	Joliet (IL) Junior College becomes the first public junior college in the United States.
1909	Berkeley, California, opens the nation's first junior high school.
1918	The National Education Association establishes the Commission on the Reoganization of Secondary Education to outline the objectives of the country's secondary schools.
1925	In the *Oregon* case, the Supreme Court holds that no state can require all children to attend public schools.
1953	The U.S. Department of Health, Education and Welfare is established.
1954	In the case of *Brown v. the Board of Education of Topeka,* the U.S. Supreme Court rules that public schools segregated according to race are inherently unequal and therefore unconstitutional, thus overthrowing its 1896 *Plessy v. Ferguson* decision. In finding that segregated public schools violate the 14th Amendment, which guarantees equal protection of the laws to all citizens, the Court forces the racial integration of the nation's public schools.
1957	In Arkansas, Governor Orval Faubus defies a federally mandated integration plan by ordering his State National Guard to bar nine black students from entering Little Rock Central High School. Following a court-ordered injunction, Faubus withdraws the Guard, but integration does not take place until President Dwight D. Eisenhower sends in federal troops to oversee the process. Faubus criticizes the move as "military occupation."
1962	After President John F. Kennedy orders the intervention of federal troops to quell a mob trying to block his entrance, James Meredith becomes the first black student to enroll at the University of Mississippi.
1964	The Civil Rights Act of 1964 gives federal district courts jurisdiction to act against discrimination in public education.
1979	President Jimmy Carter creates the Department of Education.
1982	In its *Phyler v. Doe* case, the U.S. Supreme Court rules that states cannot prohibit the children of illegal aliens from receiving a free public education.
1983	The National Commission on Excellence in Education issues a report called *A Nation at Risk* addressing and confirming the inadequacies of America's public schools and urging such reforms as more stringent high school graduation requirements, adoption of more rigorous academic standards and improved teaching.
1989	President George Bush convenes the first "education summit" to establish national education goals.
1994	Congress passes a bill authorizing several education goals as specified by the White House and the nation's governors.
1990s	Voucher programs begin, in which public funds are used to pay students' tuition at private schools. Also initiated at this time are options in school choice, charter schools and the hiring of private management companies to run public schools.

Sources: Button, H. Warren and Eugene F. Provenzo, Jr. *History of Education & Culture in America.* Englewood Cliffs, NJ: Prentice-Hall, 1983. Gutek, Gerald. *An Historical Introduction to American Education.* New York: Crowell Company, 1970.

15.2 Public Schools by State, 1850

ALABAMA	1,152
ARKANSAS	353
CALIFORNIA	2
CONNECTICUT	1,656
DELAWARE	194
FLORIDA	69
GEORGIA	1,251
ILLINOIS	4,054
INDIANA	4,822
IOWA	742
KENTUCKY	2,234
LOUISIANA	664
MAINE	4,042
MARYLAND	900
MASSACHUSETTS	3,679
MICHIGAN	2,714
MINNESOTA	0
MISSISSIPPI	782
MISSOURI	1,570
NEW HAMPSHIRE	2,381
NEW JERSEY	1,473
NEW YORK	11,580
NORTH CAROLINA	2,657
OHIO	11,661
PENNSYLVANIA	9,061
RHODE ISLAND	416
SOUTH CAROLINA	724
TENNESSEE	2,667
TEXAS	349
VERMONT	2,731
VIRGINIA	2,937
WISCONSIN	1,423
TOTAL U.S.	**80,940**

Source: U.S. Census Bureau.

15.3 Early American Colleges

1636–Harvard College Cambridge, Massachusetts (Congregational) Founded to provide a higher education for the ministers of the Congregational Church, over half its earliest graduates became Puritan ministers. The first curricula included grammar, rhetoric, logic, arithmetic, geometry, music, astronomy, ancient history, Hebrew and Greek. The college was named after John Harvard, a minister who bequeathed the School his library and half his estate.

1693–College of William and Mary Williamsburg, Virginia (Anglican) Founded with funds granted by King William III and Queen Mary II to educate the ministry of the Anglican Church. The honor system and the honor society Phi Beta Kappa both started here. The college's Sir Christopher Wren Building is the oldest American academic building still in use.

1701–Yale College New Haven, Connecticut (Congregational) Founded at a parsonage in Connecticut as the "Collegiate School" by ten ministers who felt Harvard had grown too liberal. In 1718, two years after the school moved to its present location, businessman Elihu Yale gave a gift of East India goods that the school sold to pay for books and buildings. In appreciation, the college named itself after this benefactor.

1746–College of New Jersey (Princeton) Princeton, New Jersey (Presbyterian) Founded by the Presbyterian synod to train ministers for the Great Awakening religious revival movement. Originally established in Elizabeth, New Jersey, it moved to Newark in 1748 and finally to Princeton four years later. The name was not changed to Princeton University until 1896.

1754–King's College (Columbia) New York, New York (Anglican) Founded as the College of the Province of New York, its first classes were held in an English charity schoolhouse with eight students attending. Its second president modeled the college after the English system and founded its medical school in 1767. During the American Revolution, the college was turned into a hospital and then re-established as Columbia College in 1784 under the Regents of the State of New York.

1755–College of Philadelphia (University of Pennsylvania) Philadelphia, Pennsylvania (Unaffiliated) The first college in America to offer a liberal, as opposed to theological, curriculum, it was also the first to offer professional training in medicine. It had its origins as a charity school and was founded as the Academy of Philadelphia in 1740 at the instigation of Benjamin Franklin. Its early curriculum included course offerings in agriculture, chemistry, mechanics, government, commerce and modern languages.

1764–College of Rhode Island (Brown) Providence, Rhode Island (Baptist) Named after its benefactor, Nicholas Brown, in 1804, it was originally called Rhode Island College. Founded in Warren, Rhode Island, it moved to Providence in 1770. During the Revolution, the college was closed and used as a barracks and hospital by American and French troops.

1766–Queen's College (Rutgers) New Brunswick, New Jersey (Dutch Reformed) Founded by leaders of the Dutch Reformed Church to educate youths in the liberal arts and sciences and to prepare them for the ministry. The college was re-named after its benefactor, Col. Henry Rutgers, in 1825.

1769–Dartmouth College Hanover, New Hampshire (Congregational) The last college in America founded by royal decree, it was opened as Moor's Indian Charity School in Lebanon, Connecticut, in 1755 by founder Rev. Eleazar Wheelock. With funds supplied partly by England's Earl of Dartmouth, Wheelock moved the school to Hanover in 1770 and added a college for whites.

15.4 Large U.S. Colleges and Universities, 1997

U.S. colleges and universities with undergraduate enrollments of 20,000 or more

College/University	Location	Enrollment
The University of Texas at Austin	Austin, TX	35,701
The Ohio State University	Columbus, OH	35,418
Texas A&M University	College Station, TX	33,926
Michigan State University	East Lansing, MI	33,032
Penn State University-University Park Campus	State College, PA	32,903
Arizona State University	Tempe, AZ	32,537
University of Florida	Gainesville, FL	30,100
Brigham Young University	Provo, UT	29,259
Perdue University	West Lafayette, IN	28,607
University of Phoenix	Phoenix, AZ	28,199
University of Wisconsin at Madison	Madison, WI	27,533
University of Illinois at Urbana-Champaign	Urbana, IL	26,391
University of Minnesota-Twin Cities Campus	Minneapolis, MN	26,072
Indiana University	Bloomington, IN	25,852
University of Washington	Seattle, WA	25,740
The University of Arizona	Tucson, AZ	24,769
San Diego State University	San Diego, CA	24,448
University of Michigan	Ann Arbor, MI	23,939
University of Maryland	College Park, MD	23,784
University of South Florida	Tampa, FL	23,489
University of Georgia	Athens, GA	22,983
University of California at Los Angeles	Los Angeles, CA	22,924
University of Central Florida	Orlando, FL	22,850
Florida State University	Tallahassee, FL	22,801
University of Houston	Houston, TX	22,369
California State University-Long Beach	Long Beach, CA	22,348
California State University- Northridge	Northridge, CA	21,808
San Jose State University	San Jose, CA	21,753
Louisiana State University and A&M College	Baton Rouge, LA	21,216
Florida International University	Miami, FL	21,166
San Francisco State University	San Francisco, CA	21,049
Virginia Polytechnic Institute and State University	Blacksburg, VA	20,996
Texas Tech University	Lubbock, TX	20,806
California State University-Fullerton	Fullerton, CA	20,743
Iowa State University of Science and Technology	Ames, IA	20,717
University of Colorado	Boulder, CO	20,271

Source: *Peterson's 1999 4 Year Colleges*. Twenty-ninth edition. Princeton, NJ: Peterson's, 1998.

15.5   Common 19th Century Medical Terms

ague: fever, or other recurrent symptom resulting from malaria; also known as a chill. It was a common term for intermittent fever.

amputation: removal of an appendage of the body, usually a limb. Most amputations were done within the first 24 hours of an injury.

anodynes: medicine that relieves pain.

apoplexy: stroke; sudden impairment due to a cranial hemorrhage. It could also refer to hemorrhaging in any organ.

asthenia: weakness.

bilious attack: certain diseases such as malaria or typhoid were sometimes designated as bilious fever. Applied to group of symptoms consisting of headache, abdominal pain, and constipation. Name commonly given to migraines or acute dyspepsia.

blue mass: also known as blue pill—a mercury mass used for many conditions.

Bright's disease: general term for kidney diseases.

Camp disease: included typhoid and many other diseases; a catch-all phrase.
   intermittent: recurring fevers; usually malaria was the cause.
   remittent: usually used to refer to malaria.
   typhoid: a disease characterized by chills, fever, abdominal distention, and an enlarged spleen.
   yellow: acute infectious disease transmitted by mosquitoes in which the symptoms are jaundice and fever.

catarrhus: inflammation of the mucus membranes.

cholera: acute infectious disease characterized by severe diarrhea with dehydration and electrolyte loss often leading to death; different types included Asiatic and morbus.

colica: acute abdominal pain

consumption: wasting away of the body; generally applied to tuberculosis.

debility: lack or loss of strength, considered generally to be lasting.

dementia: insanity; organic loss of intellectual function.

dengue: also known as "break bone fever." An infectious disease characterized by severe pains in the eyes, head, and extremities and accompanied by catarrhal symptoms; transmitted by the bite of a mosquito.

dysentery: inflammation of the intestines. The cause could be a chemical irritant, bacteria, or parasites.

dyspepsia: term used to describe epigastric discomfort after meals. It refers to a state in the stomach in which functions are disturbed.

dyspnea: difficulty in breathing.

erysipelas: a very contagious skin disease caused by a strep germ, characterized by redness and swelling of the affected areas and generally lasting between 10 and 14 days.

excision: removal by cutting; done usually instead of performing an amputation.

fevers: elevation of body temperature above normal.

grippe: also known as influenza; acute viral infection of the respiratory tract.

malaria: disease caused by a protozoa; parasitic of red blood cells and transmitted by mosquitoes. Symptoms included chills, fever, and sweating; often chronic and recurring.

mortification: death.

osteomyelitis: inflammation of bone; a common surgical fever.

peritonitis: often the cause of death in abdominal wounds. Inflammation of the internal membrane lining the abdomen and pelvic walls.

pneumonia: inflammation of the lungs. Different types included hypostatic, senile, and typhoid.

prostration: extreme exhaustion.

pyemia: referred to pus in blood, literally. Used during the Civil War to denote all types of blood poisoning. It was often fatal.

pyrosis: heartburn.

quinine: drug principally used to treat malaria and fevers including typhoid.

resection: same as excision. It was a recommended treatment for some types of fracture instead of amputation.

rheumatism: inflammation of the joints, muscles, and bursae.
  inflammatory: rheumatic fever. Could be fatal.

sloughing bone: necrotic bone that separates from portions that are viable.

suppuration: formation of pus; looked on as a good sign during the 1860s.

15.6   Health Expenditures

National health expenditures as a percent of gross domestic product: 13.6% (1995)

National health expenditures: $988.5 billion (1995)

National health expenditures, in private funds: $532.1 billion (1995)

National health expenditures, in public funds: $456.4 billion (1995)

Percent of national health expenditures in personal health care: 89% (1995)

Percent of national health expenditures in program administration and net cost of health insurance: 5% (1995)

Percent of national health expenditures in government public health activities: 3% (1995)

15.7   Violent Crimes by State, 1995

When states share the same rank, the next lower rank is omitted. States may share the same value but have different ranks due to rounding.

Violent crimes per 100,000 resident population, 1995

STATE	Murder		Forcible rape	
	Rate	Rank	Rate	Rank
United States	8.2	NA	37.1	NA
Alabama	11.2	5	31.7	32
Alaska	9.1	14	80.3	1
Arizona	10.4	9	33.6	26
Arkansas	10.4	9	37.2	21
California	11.2	5	33.4	27
Colorado	5.8	27	39.5	19
Connecticut	4.6	33	23.7	43
Delaware	3.5	40	80.2	2
District of Columbia	65.0	NA	52.7	NA
Florida	7.3	23	48.6	8
Georgia	9.5	12	35.3	24
Hawaii	4.7	32	28.3	36
Idaho	4.1	35	28.4	35
Illinois	10.3	11	36.5	23
Indiana	8.0	20	33.3	28
Iowa	1.8	47	21.8	47
Kansas	6.2	26	36.6	22
Kentucky	7.2	24	31.9	31
Louisiana	17.0	1	42.7	14
Maine	2.0	46	21.4	48
Maryland	11.8	4	42.2	16
Massachusetts	3.6	39	29.0	33
Michigan	8.5	18	62.0	3
Minnesota	3.9	37	56.2	7
Mississippi	12.9	2	39.1	20
Missouri	8.8	16	32.1	30
Montana	3.0	42	25.9	40
Nebraska	2.9	43	19.4	50
Nevada	10.7	7	61.2	4
New Hampshire	1.8	47	29.0	33
New Jersey	5.1	29	24.3	42
New Mexico	8.8	16	56.6	6
New York	8.5	18	23.7	43
North Carolina	9.4	13	32.2	29
North Dakota	.9	50	22.8	46
Ohio	5.4	28	43.4	13
Oklahoma	12.2	3	44.6	12
Oregon	4.1	35	41.7	17
Pennsylvania	6.3	25	25.2	41
Rhode Island	3.3	41	27.0	39
South Carolina	7.9	21	47.3	9
South Dakota	1.8	47	41.0	18
Tennessee	10.6	8	47.1	10
Texas	9.0	15	45.7	11
Utah	3.9	37	42.7	14
Vermont	2.2	44	28.2	37
Virginia	7.6	22	27.2	38
Washington	5.1	29	59.2	5
West Virginia	4.9	31	21.2	49
Wisconsin	4.3	34	23.3	45
Wyoming	2.1	45	34.4	25

NA = Not applicable.
Source: U.S. Bureau of the Census, State and Metropolitan Area Data Book 1997-98.

15.8   Most Common Reasons for Arrest in the U.S., 1996

	Offense	Rate per 100,000 residents	Arrests
1	Drug abuse violations	594.3	1,128,647
2	Larceny and theft	577.3	1,096,488
3	Driving under the influence	533.9	1,013,932
4	Disorderly conduct	330.1	626,918
5	Drunkenness	275.3	522,869
6	Liquor laws	258.6	491,176
7	Aggravated assault	204.1	387,571
8	Fraud	171.0	324,776
9	Burglary	139.1	264,193
10	Vandalisms	123.3	234,215
Total		5,838.2	11,088,352

15.9   Largest Prisons in the U.S., 1998

Prison	Capacity
Mississippi State Penitentiary, Parchman, Mississippi	5,369
Louisiana State Penitentiary, Angola, Louisiana	5,108
Coffield Unit, Colony, Texas	4,032
Men's Colony, San Luis Obispo, California	3,859
Federal Correctional Institution, Fort Dix, New Jersey	3,683
Beto Unit, Colony, Texas	3,364
California State Prison, San Quentin, California	3,286
Clements Unit, Amarillo, Texas	3,198
Eastern Correctional Institution, Westover, Maryland	3,180
Michael Unit, Colony, Texas	3,114

Source: American Correctional Association.

15.10 States with the Highest Rates of Prison Incarceration, 1997

Rate of sentenced prisoners in state and federal institutions per 100,000 residents, as of June 30, 1997.

State	Rate
District of Columbia	1,373
Texas	677
Louisiana	651
Oklahoma	599
South Carolina	542
Nevada	505
Mississippi	505
Alabama	499
Arizona	484
Georgia	476

Source: U.S. Department of Justice.

15.11 States with Most Prison Inmates, 1997

State	Inmates
California	153,010
Texas	136,599
New York	69,530
Florida	64,713
Ohio	47,248
Michigan	43,784
Illinois	40,425
Georgia	36,329
Pennsylvania	34,703
North Carolina	32,334

Source: U.S. Department of Justice.

15.12   Murders in U.S. Cities, 1986 and 1996

Top ten cities for murder.

1986		1996	
City	Murders	City	Murders
New York	1,582	New York	983
Los Angeles	834	Chicago	789
Chicago	744	Los Angeles	709
Detroit	648	Detroit	428
Houston	408	Philadelphia	414
Dallas	347	Washington	397
Philadelphia	343	New Orleans	351
Baltimore	240	Baltimore	328
New Orleans	197	Houston	261
Washington	194	Dallas	217

Source: FBI, Uniform Crime Reports.

15.13   Homicide Rates, 1950-1997

Homicides per 100,000 population.

Year	Homicide Rate	Year	Homicide Rate	Year	Homicide Rate
1950	4.6	1966	5.6	1982	9.1
1951	4.4	1967	6.2	1983	8.3
1952	4.6	1968	6.9	1984	7.9
1953	4.5	1969	7.3	1985	7.9
1954	4.2	1970	7.9	1986	8.6
1955	4.1	1971	8.6	1987	8.3
1956	4.1	1972	9.0	1988	8.4
1957	4.0	1973	9.4	1989	8.7
1958	4.8	1974	9.8	1990	9.4
1959	4.9	1975	9.6	1991	9.8
1960	5.1	1976	8.8	1992	9.3
1961	4.8	1977	8.8	1993	9.5
1962	4.6	1978	9.0	1994	9.0
1963	4.6	1979	9.7	1995	8.2
1964	4.9	1980	10.2	1996	7.4
1965	5.1	1981	9.8	1997	6.8

Source: FBI, Uniform Crime Reports, 1950-97.

15.14 States with Largest Number of Executions, 1977-1997

State	Executions 1977-1997
Texas	144
Virginia	46
Florida	39
Missouri	29
Louisiana	24
Georgia	22
Alabama	16
Arkansas	16
South Carolina	13
Illinois	10

Source: U.S. Department of Justice.

15.15 States with Largest Number of Prisoners under Death Sentence, 1997

State	Prisoners under death sentence
California	454
Texas	438
Florida	373
Pennsylvania	203
Ohio	170
Illinois	161
North Carolina	161
Alabama	151
Oklahoma	133
Arizona	121

A total of 3,219 U.S. prisoners were under sentence of death in 1997, a 5 percent increase from a year earlier.

Source: U.S. Department of Justice.

15.16   Earliest Electrocutions at Sing Sing Prison, New York, 1891-1893

The electric chair was installed in Sing Sing Prison, New York, in 1891. By the end of the 19th century, 29 inmates had been executed by this means.

Name	Electrocuted
Harris A. Smiler	July 7, 1891
James Slocum	July 7, 1891
Joseph Wood	July 7, 1891
Schihick Judigo	July 7, 1891
Martin D. Loppy	Dec. 7, 1891
Charles McElvaine	Feb. 8, 1892
Jeremiah Cotte	Mar. 28, 1892
Fred McGuire	Dec. 19, 1892
James L. Hamilton	Apr. 3, 1893
Carlyle Harris	May 8, 1893

15.17   Chronology of Development of Criminal Justice System

1789	New U.S. Constitution includes provision specifying trial by jury for crimes.
1790	First modern state penitentiary, Philadelphia's Walnut Street jail, is built.
1816	State prison built in Auburn, New York, which becomes model for U.S. prisons.
1847	Michigan abolishes death penalty—the first state to do so.
1871	U.S. federal prison systems is created.
1876	First U.S. reformatory for young offenders opens in Elmira, New York.
1890	Electric chair is used for death penalty for the first time in U.S.
1908	Bureau of Investigation, later FBI, is established.
1930	U.S. Federal Bureau of Prisons established.
1933	Alcatraz, a maximum-security federal prison, is opened.
1963	U.S. Supreme Court rules in *Gideon v. Wainwright* that accused criminals have right to free legal counsel.
1966	In *Miranda v. Arizona,* U.S. Supreme Court establishes requirement for Miranda warnings.
1971	Riot at Attica, New York prison marks beginning of unrest in U.S. prisons.
1972	U.S. Supreme Court, in *Furman v. Georgia,* rules against current state laws on capital punishment as cruel and unusual.

15.18   Prison and Jail Inmates, 1985-1997

At midyear 1997, an estimated 1,725,842 persons were incarcerated in U.S. prisons and jails. Federal and state prison authorities and local jail authorities held in their custody 645 persons per 100,000 U.S. residents. Prisoners in the custody of the 50 states, the District of Columbia, and the federal government accounted for two-thirds of the incarcerated population (1,158,763 inmates). The other third were held in local jails (567,079). Between July 1, 1996, and June 30, 1997, the U.S. prison population grew 4.7%, less than the annual average increase of 7.7% since 1990.

Number of persons held in state or federal prisons or in local jails, 1985 and 1990-97

Year	Total inmates in custody	Prisoners in custody held in			Incarceration rate*
		federal	state	local jail	
1985	744,208	35,781	451,812	256,615	313
1990	1,148,702	58,838	684,544	405,320	458
1991	1,219,014	63,930	728,605	426,479	481
1992	1,295,150	72,071	778,495	444,584	505
1993	1,369,185	80,815	828,566	459,804	528
1994	1,476,621	85,500	904,647	486,474	564
1995	1,585,586	89,538	989,004	507,044	600
1996	1,629,718	93,167	1,018,059	518,492	614
1997	1,725,842	99,175	1,059,588	567,079	645

* Total of persons in custody per 100,000 residents on July 1 of each reference year.

Source: U.S. Bureau of Justice.

15.19   Sex, Race and Hispanic Origin of Local Jail Inmates, Midyear 1985, 1990-1997

On average, the adult female jail population has grown 9.9% annually since 1985, while the adult male inmate population has grown annually by 6.4%. On June 30, 1997, local jails held nearly 1 in every 191 adult men and 1 in 1,732 women. At midyear 1997, a majority of local jail inmates were black or Hispanic. White non-Hispanics made up 40.6% of the jail population; black non-Hispanics, 42.0%; Hispanics, 15.7%; and other races (Asians, Pacific Islanders, American Indians, and Alaska Natives), 1.8%.

Percent of jail inmates

	1985	1990	1991	1992	1993	1994	1995	1996[a]	1997
Total	100	100	100	100	100	100	100	100	100
Sex									
Male	92	90.8	90.7	90.8	90.4	90	89.8	89.2	89.4
Female	8	9.2	9.3	9.2	9.6	10	10.2	10.8	10.6
Race/Hispanic origin[b]									
White, non-Hispanic	—	41.8	41.1	40.1	39.3	39.1	40.1	41.6	40.6
Black, non-Hispanic	—	42.5	43.4	44.1	44.2	43.9	43.5	41.1	42
Hispanic	—	14.3	14.2	14.5	15.1	15.4	14.7	15.6	15.7
Other[c]	—	1.3	1.2	1.3	1.3	1.6	1.7	1.7	1.8

Note: Detail may not add to total because of rounding.

— Not available.

[a] Data for 1996 based on all persons under jail supervision.

[b] Data on race/Hispanic origin were reported for 89.7% of all inmates in 1990, 91.1% in 1991, 97.6% in 1992, 85.1% in 1993, 95.8% in 1994, 97.1% in 1995, and 99.3% in 1996 and 1997.

[c] Includes American Indians, Alaska Natives, Asians, and Pacific Islanders.

	Estimated count	Number of jail inmates per 100,000 residents in each group
Total	567,079	212
White*	230,300	118
Black*	237,900	737
Hispanic	88,900	304
Other	10,000	87

* Non-Hispanic only.

15.20   Chronology of Alcatraz Prison

August 5, 1775 The pilot of a Spanish ship, Jose de Canizarer, and the ship's master, Juan Manuel de Ayala named the island, La Isla de los Alcatraces ("island of pelicans").

1848 Although the U.S. Army surveyed Alcatraz numerous times, possession of the island did not occur until 1848, when the Treaty of Guadalupe Hidalgo ended the Mexican-American War and ceded California to the U.S.

November 6, 1850 President Millard Fillmore signed an executive order that established Alcatraz as a military fort to protect the new boom city of San Francisco from possible invasion by hostile sea-faring vessels.

June 1, 1854 The lighthouse on the island was completed and became fully operational. This was the first lighthouse to be built on the Pacific Coast.

1861-1864 Alcatraz became a military prison. Its first inmates were two naval officers and two soldiers that would not take an oath of loyalty to the U.S.

April 15, 1865 A total of 39 civilians were jailed on Alcatraz for publicly cheering Lincoln's assassination.

1898 Spanish-American War brought a huge increase in prisoners on the island.

April 18, 1906 An earthquake hit Northern California and fire swept through San Francisco. Prisoners from the burned-out city jails had to be transferred to Alcatraz while the city rebuilt itself.

1912 Construction of the new cellhouse was completed and the inmates were moved into a cellhouse with spacious cells and central heating.

1920s News begins to circulate about unspeakable conditions the inmates had to endure on the island. Military decided to close the prison in 1933.

October 12, 1933 The U.S. Justice Department officially acquired Alcatraz from the military with plans to incorporate Alcatraz into the Bureau of Prisons and use it for high security prisoners, including members of organized crime rings. New security measures are added. The military's worst criminals remained on the island and became the first inmates of the U.S. Penitentiary, Alcatraz.

August 22, 1934 Al Capone, along with 52 other inmates, was transferred to the island, under heavy security, from a prison in Atlanta, Georgia.

September 4, 1934 George "Machine Gun" Kelly arrived on the island.

April 27, 1936 First escape attempt occurred as Joseph Bowers, serving a 25-year sentence for robbery, scaled the fence surrounding the cell house. Bowers was killed escaping.

December 16, 1937 Theodore Cole, serving time for kidnapping, and Ralph Roe, serving time for bank robbery, escaped from the island but were believed to have drowned in San Francisco Bay.

January 13, 1939 Four inmates attempted to escape; one was killed, three surrendered.

November 1940 Bureau of Prisons launched an investigation into the conditions on Alcatraz.

1942 Robert "The Birdman of Alcatraz" Stroud was transferred to Alcatraz from Leavenworth and spent his entire stay in solitary confinement.

May 2, 1946 An escape attempt ended with two officers and three of the escapees dead. The Siege of '46 was the bloodiest escape attempt to occur on Alcatraz.

June 11, 1962 An escape attempt by three inmates became the inspiration for many movies, including *Escape from Alcatraz* starring Clint Eastwood. The escape triggered new investigations of the prison. Faced with the huge expense of day-to-day operations, Alcatraz was closed on March 21, 1963.

1965 Nearly two years after the prison closed, five American Indian activists landed on the island and claimed Alcatraz as rightfully theirs. When federal marshals arrived on the island, the activists left willingly.

1969 Alcatraz was placed under the jurisdiction of the National Parks Service.

November 9, 1969 Four American Indian college students occupied the island, claiming it as Indian land, and were soon joined by 90 others. As the stalemate with the federal government dragged on, the majority of the occupiers began to slowly leave the island. The remaining 15 occupying the island were eventually arrested.

October 12, 1972 Alcatraz became part of the Golden Gate National Recreation Area and Alcatraz Island officially opened to the public a year later. Today, Alcatraz hosts more than 1.3 million visitors a year.

15.21 U.S. Supreme Court Decisions on the Death Penalty

Furman v. Georgia, 408 U.S. 238 (1972): Death penalty under current statutes is "abitrary and capricious" and therefore unconstitutional under the Eighth and Fourteenth Amendments.

Gregg v. Georgia, 428 U.S. 153 (1976): Reinstates the death penalty under a model of guided discretion. See also Jurek v. Texas, 428 U.S. 262 (1976) and *Proffitt v. Florida,* 428 U.S. 242 (1976).

Woodson v. North Carolina, 428 U.S. 280 (1976): Mandatory death penalty laws declared unconstitutional. See also Roberts v. Louisiana, 428 U.S. 325 (1976).

Coker v. Georgia, 433 U.S. 584 (1977): Death penalty for the rape of adult women declared unconstitutional because the sentence was disproportionate to the crime. Twenty prisoners from around the country were removed from death row as a consequence of this decision.

Lockett v. Ohio, 438 U.S. 586 (1978): Sentencing authorities must have the discretion to consider every possible mitigating factor, rather than being limited to a specific list of factors to consider. This decision resulted in the release of 99 prisoners from Ohio's death row. See also *Bell v. Ohio,* 438 U.S. 637 (1978).

Godfrey v. Georgia, 446 U.S. 420 (1980): Sent back for retrial on grounds of too broad and vague for an application of the provision stipulating the death penalty if the offense was "outrageously or wantonly vile, horrible, or inhumane, in that it involved torture, depravity of mind, or an aggravated battery to the victim."

Beck v. Alabama, 447 U.S. 625 (1980): Struck a portion of Alabama's death penalty law that blocked juries from convicting defendants of a lesser offense rather than the capital crime itself; juries were required to either convict a defendant of the capital crime or to acquit him.

Adams v. Texas, 448 U.S. 38 (1980): Prospective jurors cannot be excluded from service in capital trials because they would be "affected" by the possibility of a capital sentence.

Hopper v. Evans, 456 U.S. 605 (1982): Upheld the death sentence of a defendant convicted under the Alabama statute partially struck down in *Beck v. Alabama.* The court held that the conviction of a capital prisoner tried under a partially flawed statute need not be reversed unless it was actually touched by the imperfection. Evans was executed on April 22, 1983.

Enmund v. Florida, 458 U.S. 782 (1982): Struck down the death sentence of a defendant who had not intended, attempted, or actually killed the victim of a robbery in which he was an accomplice.

Pulley v. Harris, 465 U.S. 37 (1984): Upheld the death penalty in a California case, holding that there was no constitutional requirement for a proportionality review—that is, a review of sentences in comparable cases throughout a state to determine if similar cases are handled in a similar way—though many state death penalty laws provide for such a review.

Ford v. Wainwright, 477 U.S. 399 (1986): Held that it is unconstitutional to execute a person who is insane.

McCleskey v. Kemp, 481 U.S. 279 (1987): Rejected the claim that death penalty sentencing in Georgia was administered in a racially biased manner in violation of the Eighth and Fourteenth Amendments, despite statistical data on capital sentences in Georgia which showed that black defendants convicted of killing white victims were more likely to be given the death sentence than other defendants.

Thompson v. Oklahoma, 487 U.S. 815 (1988): Ruled that youths under 16 years of age at the time of their offense cannot be constitutionally executed.

Stanford v. Kentucky, 492 U.S. 361 (1989): Reaffirmed the court's opinion that it was not unconstitutional to execute youths at least 16 years old at the time of committing a capital offense. A number of states define minimum ages authorized for capital punishment.

15.22   Death Penalty Statistics, 1997

- Seventy-four persons in 17 states were executed—37 in Texas; 9 in Virginia; 6 in Missouri; 4 in Arkansas; 3 in Alabama; 2 each in Arizona, Illinois, and South Carolina; and 1 each in Colorado, Florida, Indiana, Kentucky, Louisiana, Maryland, Nebraska, Oklahoma, and Oregon.

- All of those executed were men:
—45 were white
—27 were black
—1 was American Indian
—1 was Asian

- Sixty-eight of the executions were carried out by lethal injection and 6 by electrocution.

- Thirty-eight states had capital punishment statutes.

- At year-end 1997, 34 states and the federal prison system held 3,335 prisoners under sentence of death, 3% more than at year-end 1996. All had committed murder.

- Of persons under sentence of death:
—1,876 were white
—1,406 were black
—28 were American Indian
—17 were Asian
—8 were classified as "other race"

- Forty-four women were under a sentence of death.

- The 283 Hispanic inmates under sentence of death accounted for 9.2% of inmates with a known ethnicity.

- Among inmates under sentence of death and with available criminal histories:
—2 in 3 had a prior felony conviction
—1 in 12 had a prior homicide conviction.

- Among persons for whom arrest information was available, the average age at time of arrest was 28; about 2% of inmates were age 17 or younger.

- At year-end, the youngest inmate under sentence of death was 18; the oldest was 81.

Source: U.S. Bureau of Justice.

15.23   Prisoners under Sentence of Death, 1968-1997

Number of prisoners on death row

	White	Black	Other		White	Black	Other		White	Black	Other
1968	243	271	3	1978	281	197	4	1988	1,235	848	34
1969	263	310	2	1979	354	236	3	1989	1,308	898	37
1970	293	335	3	1980	423	264	4	1990	1,368	940	38
1971	306	332	4	1981	498	354	8	1991	1,449	979	37
1972	167	166	1	1982	611	440	12	1992	1,511	1,031	38
1973	64	68	2	1983	692	505	12	1993	1,575	1,111	41
1974	110	128	6	1984	806	598	16	1994	1,653	1,203	49
1975	218	262	8	1985	896	664	15	1995	1,732	1,284	48
1976	225	195	0	1986	1,013	762	25	1996	1,833	1,358	51
1977	229	192	2	1987	1,128	813	26	1997	1,876	1,406	53

Source: U.S. Bureau of Justice.

SECTION 16

Ethnic, Social and Religious Groups

16.1   American Indian Populations in the U.S.

POPULATION

According to U.S. Census Bureau figures, there were 1,959,234 American Indians and Alaska Natives living in the United States in 1990 (1,878,285 American Indians, 57,152 Eskimos, and 23,797 Aleuts). This is a 37.9 percent increase over the 1980 recorded total of 1,420,400. The increase is attributed to improved census taking and more self-identification during the 1990 count. The BIA's 1990 estimate is that almost 950,000 individuals of this total population live on or adjacent to federal Indian reservations.

RESERVATIONS

The number of Indian land areas in the U.S. administered as Federal Indian reservations (reservations, pueblos, rancherias, communities, etc.) total 278. The largest is the Navajo Reservation of some 16 million acres of land in Arizona, New Mexico and Utah. Many of the smaller reservations are less than 1,000 acres with the smallest less than 100 acres. On each reservation, the local governing authority is the tribal government. The states in which the reservations are located have limited powers over them, and only as provided by federal law. On some reservations, however, a high percentage of the land is owned and occupied by non-Indians. Some 140 reservations have entirely tribally owned land.

TRUST LANDS

A total of 56.2 million acres of land are held in trust by the United States for various Indian tribes and individuals. Much of this is reservation land; however, not all reservations land is trust land. On behalf of the United States, the Secretary of the Interior serves as trustee for such lands with many routine trustee responsibilities delegated to BIA officials.

TRIBES

There are 510 federally recognized tribes in the United States, including about 200 village groups in Alaska. "Federally-recognized" means these tribes and groups have a special, legal relationship to the U.S. government and its agent, the BIA, depending upon the particular situation of each tribe.

BIRTH RATE—Birth rates were 28.0 births per 1,000 in 1986-88. The U.S. all-races rate was 15.7 births per 1,000 in 1987. The infant death rate was 9.7 per 1,000 live births in 1986-88, while the U.S. all-races was 10.1 per 1,000 births in 1987.

LIFE EXPECTANCY—In 1979-81, life expectancy was 71.1 years (males, 67.1 years and females 75.1 years). These figures are based on 1980 census information. Diseases of the heart and accidents continue to be the two major causes of death among American Indians and Alaska Natives. The 1988 age-adjusted death rate for diseases of the heart was 138.1 per 100,000 of the population and 166.3 per 100,000 for all U.S. races. In the same period, the age-adjusted death rate from accidents was 80.8 percent per 100,000, including 44.7 related to motor vehicle accidents and 36.1 from other accidents. The U.S. all-races 1988 age-adjusted rate was 35.0 per 100,000, including 19.7 related to motor vehicle accidents and 15.3 related to other accidents. The age-adjusted suicide death rate for the population has decreased 29 percent since its peak in 1975 (21.1 deaths per 100,000 population). The Indian rate for 1988 was 14.5 compared to the U.S. all-races rate of 11.4.

PRIMARY FEDERAL AGENCY

The Bureau of Indian Affairs (BIA) in the U.S. Department of the Interior, is the federal agency with primary responsibility for working with federally recognized Indian tribal governments and with Alaska Native village communities. A principal BIA responsibility is administering and managing some 56.2 million acres of land held in trust by the United States for American Indians. The BIA was established in 1824 in the War Department. It became an agency of the Department of the Interior when the Department was created in 1849.

FEDERAL APPROPRIATIONS

Over the past decade, the annual budget for the BIA has averaged approximately $1 billion. The fiscal year 1991 appropriation for the BIA is $1.5 billion for the principal program categories of: Education, $554.5 million; Tribal Services (including social services and law enforcement), $338.9 million; Economic Development, $14.6 million; Navajo-Hopi Settlement, $1.4 million; Natural Resources, $139.7 million; Trust Responsibilities, $74.7 million; Facilities Management, $94.2 million; General Administration $112.0 million; Construction, $167.6 million; Indian Loan Guaranty, $11.7 million; Miscellaneous Payments to Indians, $56.1 million; and Navajo Rehabilitation Trust Fund, $3.0 million.

LANGUAGE

At the end of the 15th century, more than 300 languages were spoken by the native population of what is now the United States. Some were linked by "linguistic stocks" which meant that widely scattered tribal groups had some similarities in their languages. Today, some 250 tribal languages are still spoken, some by only a few individuals and others by many. Most American Indians now use English as their main language for communicating with non-tribal members. For many, it is a second language.

MILITARY SERVICE

American Indians have the same obligations for military service as other U.S. citizens. They have fought in all American wars since the Revolution. In the Civil War, they served on both sides. Eli S. Parker, Seneca from New York, was at Appamattox as aide to Gen. Ulyssess S. Grant when Lee surrendered, and the unit of Confederate Brigadier General Stand Watie, Cherokee, was the last to surrender. It was not until World War I that Indians' demonstrated patriotism (6,000 of the more than 8,000 who served were volunteers) moved Congress to pass the Indian Citizenship Act of 1924. In World War II, 25,000 Indian men and women, mainly enlisted Army personnel, fought on all fronts in Europe and Asia, winning (according to an incomplete count) 71 Air Medals, 51 Silver Stars, 47 Bronze Stars, 34 Distinguished Flying Crosses, and two Congressional Medals of Honor. The most famous Indian exploit of World War II was the use by Navajo Marines of their language as a battlefield code, the only such code which the enemy could not break. In the Korean conflict, there was one American Indian Congressional Medal of Honor winner. In the Vietnam War, 41,500 Indians served in the military forces. In 1990, prior to Operation Desert Storm, some 24,000 Indian men and women were in the military. Approximately 3,000 served in the Persian Gulf with three among those killed in action. One out of every four American Indian males is a military veteran and 45 to 47 percent of tribal leaders today are military veterans.

VOTING RIGHTS

In 1948, the Arizona Supreme Court declared unconstitutional disenfranchising interpretations of the state constitution and Indians were permitted to vote as in most other states. A 1953 Utah state law stated that persons living on Indian reservations were not residents of the state and could not vote. That law was subsequently repealed. In 1954, Indians in Maine who were not then federally recognized were given the right to vote, and in 1962, New Mexico extended the right to vote to Indians.

OFFICE HOLDING

American Indians have been elected to the U.S. Congress from time to time for more than 80 years. Ben Reifel, a Sioux Indian from South Dakota, served five terms in the U.S. House of Representatives. Ben Nighthorse Campbell, a member of the Northern Cheyenne Tribe of Montana, was elected to the U.S. House of Representatives in 1986 from the Third District of Colorado, and is currently serving in his third term. He is the only American Indian currently serving in Congress.

Indians also served and now hold office in a number of state legislatures. Others currently hold or have held elected or appointive positions in state judiciary systems and in county and city governments including local school boards.

TREATIES

Congress ended treaty-making with Indian tribes in 1871. Since then, relations with Indian groups are by congressional acts, executive orders, and executive agreements. The treaties that were made often contain obsolete commitments which have either been fulfilled or superseded by congressional legislation. The provision of educational, health, welfare, and other services by the government to tribes often has extended beyond treaty requirements. Many large Indian groups have no treaties, yet share in the many services for Indians provided by the federal government.

The specifics of particular treaties signed by government negotiators with Indians are contained in one volume (Vol. II) of the publication, "Indian Affairs, Laws and Treaties," compiled, annotated and edited by Charles Kappler. Published by the Government Printing Office in 1904, it is now out of print, but can be found in most large law libraries. More recently, the treaty volume has been published privately under the title, "Indian Treaties, 1778-1883."

Originals of all the treaties are maintained by the National Archives and Records Service of the General Services Administration. A duplicate of a treaty is available upon request for a fee. The agency will also answer questions about specific Indian treaties. Write to: Diplomatic Branch, National Archives and Records Service, Washington, D.C. 20408.

TRIBAL GOVERNMENT

Most tribal governments are organized democratically, that is, with an elected leadership. The governing body is generally referred to as a "council" and is comprised of persons elected by vote of the eligible adult tribal members. The presiding official is the "chairman," although some tribes use other titles such as "principal chief," "president" or "governor." An elected tribal council, recognized as such by the Secretary of the Interior, has authority to speak and act for the tribe and to represent it in negotiations with federal, state, and local governments.

Tribal governments generally define conditions of membership, regulate domestic relations of members, prescribe rules of inheritance for reservation property not in trust status, levy taxes, regulate property under tribal jurisdiction, control conduct of members by tribal ordinances, and administer justice.

Many tribes are organized under the Indian Reorganization Act (IRA) of 1934. This includes a number of Alaska Native villages, which adopted formal governing documents (Constitutions) under the provisions of a 1936 amendment to the IRA. The passage in 1971 of the Alaska Native Claims Settlement Act, however, provided for the creation of village and regional corporations under state law to manage the money and lands granted by the Act. The Oklahoma Indian Welfare Act of 1936 provided for the organization of Indian tribes within the State of Oklahoma. Some tribes do not operate under any of these acts, but are nevertheless organized under documents approved by the Secretary of the Interior. Some tribes continue their traditional forms of governments.

Prior to reorganization, the tribes maintained their own, often highly developed, systems of self-government.

Source: U.S. Bureau of Indian Affairs.

16.2 Resources on American Indians

Library, U.S. Department of the Interior, 1849 C St., NW, Rm. 1041, Washington, DC 20240. The Interior Library has a large collection of books on Indians available to the public or through inter-library loan, as well as research periodicals for current information about Indians.

Indian Arts and Crafts Board, U.S. Department of the Interior, 1849 C St. NW, Rm. 4004-MIB, Washington, DC 20240 (202) 208-3773. The Board publishes information related to contemporary American Indian arts and crafts, including directories of sources for these products, available upon request.

Indian Health Service, U.S. Department of Health and Human Services, Parklawn Building, 5600 Fishers Lane, Rockville, MD 20857 (301) 443-1397. The IHS has information on Indian health matters, including programs supported by the federal government, and statistics.

Bureau of the Census, U.S. Department of Commerce, Racial Statistics Branch, Population Division, Washington, DC 20233 (301) 763-2607. The Liaison with American Indians office provides 1990 Census information including statistical profiles of the American Indian, Eskimo and Aleut population for the United States.

National Archives and Records Service, U.S. General Services Administration, Civil Reference Branch, 7th St. and Pennsylvania Ave., NW, Washington, DC 20480 (202) 523-3238. The Archives assists scholarly research into the history of the federal-Indian relationship and those concerned with the legal aspect of Indian administration. Pertinent materials are among the old records of the Department of War, the Bureau of Indian Affairs, and the General Land Office. They include papers related to Indian treaty negotiations; annuity, per capita and other payment records; tribal census rolls; records of Indian agents; and maps of Indian lands and reservations.

Smithsonian Institution, Public Affairs Office, Department of Anthropology, National Museum of Natural History, 10th Street and Constitution Ave., NW, Washington, DC 20560 (202) 357-1592. The Handbook Office is preparing a 20-volume series on the history, culture and contemporary circumstances of North American Indians. The series is entitled, Handbook of North American Indians, of which nine volumes have thus far been published. Library of Congress, General Reading Room Division, 10 First St., SE, Washington, DC 20540 (202) 707-5522. Its resources are collections of over 84 million items—books, maps, music, photographs, motion pictures, prints, manuscripts—some of which contain much material for research on American Indians.

Newberry Library Center for the History of the American Indian, 60 West Walton St., Chicago, IL 60610 (312) 943-9090. One of America's foremost research libraries, the Newberry makes its resources available to academic and lay scholars. The library has more than 100,000 volumes on American Indian history.

National Indian Law Library, Native American Rights Fund, 1522 Broadway, Boulder, CO 80302 (303) 447-8760. A clearinghouse for Indian law-related materials, the Library contains 14,000 court proceedings in every major Indian case since the 1950s and 4,000 non-court materials. It has a government documents and tribal codes and constitutions collection.

The National Native American Cooperative, PO Box 1000, San Carlos, Arizona 85550-0301 (602) 230-3399, periodically publishes a directory that includes a calendar of American Indian events and celebrations and information on arts and crafts.

National Anthropological Archives, Smithsonian Institution, Museum of Natural History, Washington, DC 20560 (202) 357-1986, has a large collection of photographs dating back to the early 1800s. Inquiries should specify names of individuals, tribe name, historical events, etc. Researchers with broad or numerous interests should visit the NAA which has, in addition to photographs, manuscripts, field notes, sound tapes, linguistic data, and other documents including vocabularies of Indian and Inuit languages and drawings.

Library of Congress, Prints and Photographs Division, Washington, DC 20540 (202) 707-6394, has available an historic collection of prints and photographs of American Indians.

National Museum of the American Indian, Smithsonian Institution, Photograph Department, 3735 Broadway, New York, NY 10032, (212) 283-2420, has a large collection of objects and photographs of Native Americans. Much of the Museum's collection will be moved to Washington, DC, when the National Museum of the American Indian is built on the Mall to house the the collections currently located in New York City.

Native American Public Broadcasting Consortium, PO Box 8311, Lincoln, NB 68501 (402) 472-3522, maintains the Nation's largest quality library of American Indian video programs for public television, instructional and information use. Topics range from history, culture and education to economic development and the arts.

16.3 Books on American Indians

Commissioner of Indian Affairs, 1849-1967, *Annual Reports to the Secretary of the Interior,* Washington, D.C. U.S. Government Printing Office (Reprinted by AMS Press, New York, 1976-1977.)

Kvasnicka, Robert M., and Herman J. Viola, eds. 1979, *The Commissioners of Indian Affairs, 1824-1977.* Lincoln, Nebraska: University of Nebraska Press.

Meriam, Lewis, et. al., 1928, *The Problem of Indian Administration.* Report of a survey made at the request of the Honorable Hubert Work, Secretary of the Interior, and submitted to him, February 21, 1927. (Originally published by the U.S. Government Printing Office). Baltimore, Maryland: John Hopkins University Press.

Taylor, Theodore W., 1984, *The Bureau of Indian Affairs.* Boulder, Colorado: Westview Press.

ECONOMIC DEVELOPMENT:

Lovett, Vincent, et al., 1984, *American Indians (U.S. Indian Policy, Tribes and Reservations, BIA: Past and Present, Economic Development)* Washington, D.C.: U.S. Government Printing Office.

Presidential Commission on Indian Reservation Economies, 1984, Report and Recommendations to the President of the United States. Washington, D.C.: U.S. Government Printing Office.

White, Robert H., 1991, *Tribal Assets, The Rebirth of Native America, 1990.* New York: Henry Holt & Co.

EDUCATION:

Fuchs, Estelle, and Robert J. Havinghurst, 1972, *To Live on This Earth: American Indian Education.* Garden City, New York: Doubleday.

Indian Nations at Risk Task Force, 1991, *Final Report to the Secretary of Education.* Washington, D.C.: U.S. Department of Education.

National Advisory Council on Indian Education, U.S. Department of Education, Annual Reports, Washington, D.C.: U.S. Government Printing Office.

Prucha, Francis Paul, 1979, *The Churches and the Indian Schools,* Lincoln, Nebraska: University of Nebraska Press.

Szasz, Margaret, 1975, *Education and the American Indian: the Road to Self-Determination, 1928-1973.* Albuquerque, New Mexico: University of New Mexico Press.

United States Congress, Senate Committee on Interior and Insular Affairs, 1970, Comprehensive Indian Education Act. Hearings, 92nd Congress, 2nd session, on S. 2724. Washington, D.C.: U.S. Government Printing Office.

United States Congress, Senate Special Subcommittee on Indian Education, 1969, Indian Education: A National Tragedy, A National Challenge. 91st Congress, 1st Session. Senate Report No. 91-501. Washington, D.C.: U.S. Government Printing Office.

GUIDES AND DIRECTORIES:

Fleming, Paula R., and Judith Luskey, 1986, *The North American Indian in Photographs from 1850 to 1920.* New York: Harper & Row.

Hill, Edward E., 1974, *The Office of Indian Affairs, 1824-1880: Historical Sketches,* New York, Clearwater Publishing Company.

Hill, Edward E., comp., 1981, Guide to Records in the National Archives of the United States Relating to American Indians. Washington, D.C.: National Archives Trust Fund Board, U.S. General Services Administration.

Hirschfelder, Arlene B., et al., 1983, *Guide to Research on North American Indians.* Chicago: American Library Association.

National Archives Trust Fund Board, 1984, *American Indians: A Select Catalog of National Archives Microfilm Publications.* Washington, D.C.: National Archives Trust Fund Board, U.S. General Services Administration.

Prucha, Francis Paul, 1990, *Atlas of American Indian Affairs,* Lincoln, Nebraska: University of Nebraska Press.

U.S. Department of Commerce, 1974, Federal and State Indian Reservations and Indian Trust Areas. Washington, D.C.: U.S. Government Printing Office.

Waldman, Carl, 1985, *Atlas of the North American Indians*. Facts on File Publications.

HEALTH:

Dorris, Michael, 1989, *The Broken Cord*. New York: Harper & Row.

Nabokov, Peter, 1981, *Indian Running*. Santa Barbara, California: Capra Press.

Trends in Indian Health, 1991. Rockville, Maryland: U.S. Department of Health and Human Services, Indian Health Service.

Vogel, Virgil J., 1970, *American Indian Medicine*. Norman, Oklahoma: University of Oklahoma Press. (Reprint, in paperback, 1973, New York: Ballantine Books).

INDIAN POLICIES:

Abernethy, Thomas Perkins, 1959, *Western Lands and the American Revolution*. New York: Russell and Russell.

American Indian Policy Review Commission, 1977, Final Report, Submitted to Congress May 17, 1977. Washington, D.C.: U.S. Government Printing Office.

Deloria, Vine Jr., and Clifford M. Lytly, 1984, *The Nations Within: The Past and Future of American Indian Sovereignty*. New York: Pantheon Books.

Johanson, Bruce, E., 1982, *Forgotten Founders: Benjamin Franklin, The Iroquois and the Rationale for the American Revolution*. Ipswich, Massachusetts: Gambit.

Kelly, Lawrence C., 1983, *The Assault of Assimilation: John Collier and the Origins of Indian Policy Reform*. Albuquerque, New Mexico: University of New Mexico Press.

Philip, Kenneth R., 1977, *John Collier's Crusade for Indian Reform: 1920-1954*. Tucson: University of Arizona Press.

Prucha, Francis P., 1984, *The Great Father: The United States and the American Indians*. 2 vols. Lincoln, Nebraska: University of Nebraska Press.

Prucha, Francis P., 1990, *Documents of United States Indian Policy*. (2nd edition, expanded). Lincoln/London: University of Nebraska Press.

Schaaf, Gregory, 1990, *Wampum Belts and Peace Treaties, George Morgan, Native Americans and Revolutionary Diplomacy*. Golden, Colorado: Fulcrum Publishing.

Taylor, Theodore W., 1972, *The States and Their Indian Citizens*, Washington, D.C.: U.S. Department of the Interior, Bureau of Indian Affairs.

Taylor, Theodore, 1983, *American Indian Policy*. Mt. Airy, Maryland: Lomond Publications, Inc.

Tyler, S. Lyman, 1973, *A History of Indian Policy*. Washington, D.C.: U.S. Department of the Interior, Bureau of Indian Affairs.

Washburn, Wilcomb E., 1973, *The American Indian and the U.S., A Documentary History*. 4 vols. New York: Random House.

INDIAN-WHITE RELATIONS:

1982, Indian-White Relations in the United States: A Bibliography of Works Published, 1975-1980. Lincoln, Nebraska: University of Nebraska Press.

Berkhofer, Robert F., Jr., 1978, *The White Man's Indian: Images of the American Indian from Columbus to the Present*. New York: Alfred A Knopf.

Deloria, Vine, Jr., 1974, *Behind the Trail of Broken Treaties*, New York: Dell Publishing Company.

Hagan, William T., 1979, *American Indians* (Revised edition). Chicago: The University of Chicago Press.

Haynie, Nancy A., comp., 1984, *Native Americans and the Military, Today and Yesterday*. Fort McPherson, Georgia: U.S. Army Forces Command Information Branch.

Josephy, Alvin M., Jr., 1973, *The Indian Heritage of America*. New York: Alfred A. Knopf.

Matthiessen, Peter, 1983, *In the Spirit of Crazy Horse.* New York: Viking Press.

Prucha, Francis P., 1971, *Indian Peace Medals in American History* (State Historical Society of Wisconsin, Madison). Lincoln, Nebraska: University of Nebraska Press.

Prucha, Francis P., 1977, *A Bibliographical Guide to the History of Indian-White Relations in the United States.* Chicago: University of Chicago Press.

Rosenstiel, Annette, 1983, *Red and White: Indian Views of the White Man, 1492-1982.* New York: Universe Books.

Stedman, Raymond W., 1982, *Shadows of the Indian: Stereotypes in American Culture.* Norman, Oklahoma: University of Oklahoma Press.

Utley, Robert M., and Wilcomb E. Washburn, 1977, *The American Heritage History of the Indian Wars.* New York: American Heritage Publishing Company.

Washburn, Wilcomb E., 1974, *The Indian in America (The New American Nation Series).* New York: Harper & Row.

Viola, Herman J., 1990, *After Columbus, The Smithsonian Chronicle of the North American Indians.* Washington, D.C.: Smithsonian Books.

Washburn, Wilcomb E., 1987, *History of Indian-White Relations.* Handbook of North American Indians, Vol. 4, William C. Sturtevant, gen. ed. Washington, D.C.: Smithsonian Institution.

LAND:

Kickingbird, Kirke, and Karen Ducheneaux, 1973, *One Hundred Million Acres* (The social, historical and legal significance of Indian land problems). New York: Macmillan Company.

O'Donnell, Janet, 1991, *The Dispossession of the American Indian, 1887-1934.* Bloomington: University of Indiana Press.

Ross, Norman A., comp., 1973, *Index to Expert Testimony Before the Indian Claims Commission: The Written Reports* (The Library of American Indian Affairs). New York: Clearwater Publishing Company.

Sutton, Imre, 1975, *Indian Land Tenure, Bibliographical Essays and a Guide to the Literature.* New York: Clearwater Publishing Company.

Sutton, Imre, 1985, *Irredeemable America: The Indians' Estate and Land Claims.* Albuquerque: University of New Mexico Press.

United States Indian Claims Commission, 1980, Final Report, 1 (79. 96th Congress, 2nd Session, House Document No. 96-383. (Serial No. 13354). Washington, D.C.: U.S. Government Printing Office.

LANGUAGES:

Campbell, Lyle, and Marianne Mithun, eds., 1979, *The Languages of Native America: Historical and Comparative Assessment.* Austin, Texas: University of Texas Press.

INDIAN LAW:

Brakel, Samuel J., 1978, *American Indian Tribal Courts: The Costs of Separate Justice.* Chicago: American Bar Foundation.

Cohen, Felix S., 1942, *Handbook of Federal Indian Law.* Albuquerque: University of New Mexico Press. (Reprinted: The Michie Company, Law Publishers, Charlottsville, Virginia, 1982).

Deloria, Vine, Jr., and Clifford M. Lytle, 1983, *American Indians, American Justice.* Austin, Texas: University of Texas Press.

Peavar, Stephen, 1983, *The Rights of Indians and Tribes* (ACLU Handbook). New York: Bantam Books.

Native American Rights Fund, 1985, *Indian Cases: The 1984-1985 Supreme Court Term.* The NARF Legal Review, Spring. Boulder, Colorado.

U.S. Commission on Civil Rights, 1980, *American Indian Civil Rights Handbook,* 2nd ed., Clearinghouse Publications, No. 35. Washington, D.C.: U.S. Government Printing Office.

1981, *Indian Tribes: A Continuing Quest for Survival.* Washington, D.C.: U.S. Government Printing Office.

PROFILES AND BIOGRAPHY:

Dockstader, Frederick J., 1977, *Great North American Indians: Profiles in Life and Leadership.* New York: Van Nostrand Reinhold Company.

Eastman, Charles A. (Ohiyesa), 1918, *Indian Heroes and Great Chieftains* (Reprint, 1991. Lincoln, Nebraska: Bison Books, University of Nebraska Press).

Neithammer, Carolyn, 1977, *Daughters of the Earth: The Lives and Legends of American Indian Women.* New York: Macmillan.

RELIGION:

Deloria, Vine, Jr., 1973, *God Is Red.* New York: Grosset & Dunlap.

Huyltkranz, Ake, 1987, *Native Religions of North America.* New York: Harper & Row.

Hurdy, John M., 1970, *American Indian Religions.* Los Angeles: Sherbourne Press.

Native American Rights Fund, 1979, *We Also Have a Religion: The American Indian Religious Freedom Act and the Religious Freedom Project of the Native American Rights Fund.* Announcements (Winter) 5(1). Boulder, Colorado.

United States Federal Agencies Task Force, 1979, *American Indian Religious Freedom Act Report* (P.L. 95-341). Chairman, Cecil D. Andrus, Secretary of the Interior, Washington. D.C.

Peterson, Scott, 1990, *Native American Prophecies; Examining the History, Wisdom and Startling Predictions of Visionary Native Americans.* New York: Paragon House.

TREATIES:

Kappler, Charles J., comp., 1904-1941, *Indian Affairs: Laws and Treaties.* 5 vols. Washington, D.C.: U.S. Government Printing Office (Reprinted: AMS Press, New York, 1971).

TRIBAL GOVERNMENT:

Lopach, James J., Brown, Margery Hunter, and Clow, Richmond L., 1990, *Tribal Government Today, Politics on Montana Indian Reservations.* San Francisco, Boulder, London: Westview Press.

O'Brien, Sharon, 1989, *American Indian Tribal Governments.* Norman, Oklahoma: University of Oklahoma Press.

Taylor, Graham D., 1980, *The New Deal and American Indian Tribalism.* Lincoln, Nebraska: University of Nebraska Press.

TRIBES:

Hodge, Frederick W., ea., 1907-1910, *Handbook of American Indians North of Mexico.* 2 vols. Bureau of American Ethnology Bulletin 30 (Reprinted 1971. New York: Rowman and Littlefield).

Sturtevant, William C., gen. ea., 1978, *Handbook of North American Indians.* 20 vols. Washington, D.C.: Smithsonian Institution. 1978 vol. 8, California; 1978 Vol. 15, Northeast; 1979 Vol. 9, Southwest (Pueblos); 1981 Vol 6, Subarctic; 1983 Vol. 10, Southwest (Navajo, Apache, etc.); 1984 Vol. 5, Arctic; 1986 Vol. 11, Great Basin; 1989 Vol. 4, History of Indian-White Relations; 1990 Vol. 7, Northwest Coast; (1992 Vol. 13, Plains).

Swanton, John R., 1952, *The Indian Tribes of North America.* Bureau of American Ethnology Bulletin 145, Washington, D.C.

Source: U.S. Bureau of Indian Affairs.

16.4   Largest Indian Reservations

Reservation/State	Population
1. Navajo, Arizona/New Mexico/Utah	143,405
2. Pine Ridge, Nebraska/South Dakota	11,182
3. Fort Apache, Arizona	9,825
4. Gila River, Arizona	9,116
5. Papago, Arizona	8,480
6. Rosebud, South Dakota	8,043
7. San Carlos, Arizona	7,110
8. Zuni Pueblo, Arizona/New Mexico	7,073
9. Hopi, Arizona	7,061
10. Blackfeet, Montana	7,025

16.5   American Indian Tribes with Populations Greater than 30,000

1990 U.S. Census figures

American Indian Tribe	Number
American Indian population total	1,878,285
Cherokee	308,132
Navajo	219,198
Chippewa	103,826
Sioux	103,255
Chioclaw	82,299
Pueblo	52,939
Apache	50,051
Lumbee	49,038
Creek	43,550
Blackfoot	32,234

16.6   Excerpts from Geronimo, *His Own Story*

The Coming of the White Men

About the time of the massacre of "Kaskiyeh" (1858) we heard that some white men were measuring land to the south of us. In company with a number of other warriors I went to visit them. We could not understand them very well, for we had no interpreter, but we made a treaty with them by shaking hands and promising to be brothers. Then we made our camp near their camp, and they came to trade with us. . . . These were the first white men I ever saw.

About ten years later some more white men came. These were all warriors. They made their camp on the Gila River south of Hot Springs. At first they were friendly and we did not dislike them, but they were not as good as those who came first.

After about a year some trouble arose between them and the Indians, and I took the warpath as a warrior, not as a chief. I had not been wronged, but some of my people had been, and I fought with my tribe; for the soldiers and not the Indians were at fault.

Not long after this some of the officers of the United States troops invited our leaders to hold a conference at Apache Pass (Fort Bowie). Just before noon the Indians were shown into a tent and told that they would be given someting to eat. When in the tent they were attacked by soldiers. Our chief, Mangus-Colorado, and several other warriors, by cutting through the tent, escaped; but most of the warriors were killed or captured. After this treachery the Indians went back to the mountains and left the fort entirely alone. I believe it was entirely planned by the soldiers.

From the very first the soldiers sent out to our western country, and the officers in charge of them did not hesitate to wrong the Indians. They never explained to the Government when an Indian was wronged, but always reported the misdeeds of the Indians. Much that was done by mean white men was reported at Washington as the deeds of my people.

The Indians always tried to live peaceably with the white soldiers and settlers. One day during the time that the soldiers were stationed at Apache Pass I made a treaty with the post. This was done by shaking hands and promising to be brothers. Cochise and Mangus-Colorado did likewise. I do not know the name of the officer in command, but this was the first regiment that ever came to Apache Pass. This treaty was made about a year before we were attacked in a tent, as above related. In a few days after the attack at Apache Pass we organized in the mountains and returned to fight the soldiers. There were two tribes—the Bedonkohe and the Chokonen Apaches, both commanded by Cochise. After a few days' skirmishing we attacked a freight train that was coming in with supplies for the Fort. We killed some of the men and captured the others. These prisoners our chief offered to trade for the Indians whom the soldiers had captured at the massacre in the tent. This the officers refused, so we killed our prisoners, disbanded, and went into hiding in the mountains. Of those who took part in this affair I am the only one now living.

In a few days troops were sent out to search for us, but as we were disbanded, it was, of course, impossible for them to locate any hostile camp. During the time they were searching for us many of our warriors (who were thought by the soldiers to be peaceable Indians) talked to the officers and men, advising them where they might find the camp they sought, and while they searched we watched them from our hiding places and laughed at their failures.

After this trouble all of the Indians agreed not to be friendly with the white men any more. There was no general engagement, but a long struggle followed. Sometimes we attacked the white men, sometimes they attacked us. First a few Indians would be killed and then a few soldiers. I think the killing was about equal on each side. The number killed in these troubles did not amount to much, but this treachery on the part of the soldiers had angered the Indians and revived memories of other wrongs, so that we never again trusted the United States troops.

16.7   Chronology of Black America, 1861-1999

1861   The Civil War begins in Charleston, S.C., as the Confederates open fire on Fort Sumter.

1862   Future U.S. Congressman Robert Smalls and 12 other slaves seize control of a Confederate armed frigate in Charleston harbor. They turn it over to a Union naval squadron blockading the city.

1862   The second Confiscation Act is passed, stating that slaves of civilian and military Confederate officials "shall be forever free," enforceable only in areas of the South occupied by the Union Army.

1863   President Abraham Lincoln signs the Emancipation Proclamation on January 1.

1865   Civil War ends on April 26 after the surrender of the Confederate generals Robert E. Lee and J.E. Johnston. Congress establishes the U.S. Bureau of Refugees, Freedmen, and Abandoned Lands to aid four million black Americans in transition from slavery to freedom.

1866   The states of the former Confederacy pass "black code" laws to replace the social controls removed by the Emancipation Proclamation and the Thirteenth Amendment.

1866   The U.S. Army forms black cavalry and infantry regiments. Serving in the West from 1867 to 1896 and fighting Indians on the frontier, they are nicknamed "buffalo soldiers" by the Indians.

1867   Howard University, a predominantly black university, is founded in Washington, D.C. It is named for General Oliver Otis Howard, head of the post–Civil War Freedmen's Bureau.

1870   Joseph Hayne Rainey is the first black elected to the U.S. House of Representatives.

1870   Hiram R. Revels of Mississippi takes the former seat of Jefferson Davis in the U.S. Senate, becoming the only black in the U.S. Congress and the first elected to the Senate.

1872   John R. Lynch, speaker of the Mississippi House of Representatives, is elected to the U.S. Congress.

1877   Reconstruction ends as the last Federal troops are withdrawn. Southern conservatives regain control of their state governments through fraud, violence, and intimidation.

1881   Tuskegee Normal and Industrial Institute in Alabama is founded on July 4 with Booker T. Washington as the school's first president.

1887   Florida A&M University is founded as the State Normal (teacher-training) School for Colored Students.

1895   A merger of three major black Baptist conventions leads to the formation of the National Baptist Convention, U.S.A., Inc., in Atlanta, Ga.

1896   Mary Church Terrell becomes the first president of the National Association of Colored Women, working for educational and social reform and an end to racial discrimination.

1899   Composer and pianist Scott Joplin publishes "The Maple Leaf Rag," one of the most important and popular compositions during the era of ragtime, precursor to jazz.

1901   Booker T. Washington dines with President Theodore Roosevelt at the White House. The dinner meeting is bitterly criticized by many whites, who view it as a marked departure from racial etiquette.

1903   W.E.B. Du Bois publishes *The Souls of Black Folk,* which declares that "the problem of the Twentieth Century is the problem of the color-line," and discusses the dual identity of black Americans.

1905   The Niagara Movement is founded as a group of black intellectuals from across the nation meet near Niagara Falls, Ont., adopting resolutions demanding full equality in American life.

1906   After educator John Hope becomes its president, Atlanta Baptist College expands its curriculum and is renamed Morehouse College.

1907   Black Primitive Baptist congregations formed by emancipated slaves after the Civil War organize the National Primitive Baptist Convention, Inc.

1909   A group of whites shocked by the Springfield riot of 1908 merge with W.E.B. Du Bois's Niagara Movement, forming the National Association for the Advancement of Colored People (NAACP).

1910   *The Crisis,* a monthly magazine published by the NAACP, is founded. W.E.B. Du Bois edits the magazine for its first 24 years.

1911   The National League on Urban Conditions Among Negroes (National Urban League) is formed in New York City with the mission to help migrating blacks find jobs and housing and adjust to urban life.

1914   George Washington Carver of the Tuskegee Institute reveals his experiments concerning peanuts and sweet potatoes, popularizing alternative crops and aiding the renewal of depleted land in the South.

1914   The Universal Negro Improvement Association is founded by Marcus Garvey in his homeland of Jamaica to further racial pride and economic self-sufficiency and to establish a black nation in Africa.

1915   A schism in the National Baptist Convention yields the National Baptist Convention of America, the largest black church in the United States.

1917   Racial antagonism toward blacks newly employed in war industries leads to riots that kill 40 blacks and 8 whites in East Saint Louis, Ill.

1919   During the "Red Summer" following World War I, 13 days of racial violence on the South Side of Chicago leave 23 blacks and 15 whites dead, 537 people injured, and 1,000 black families homeless.

1922   Louis Armstrong leaves New Orleans, arriving in Chicago to play second trumpet in cornetist King Oliver's Creole Jazz Band. Armstrong's work in the 1920s would revolutionize jazz.

1923   Charles Clinton Spaulding becomes president of the North Carolina Mutual Life Insurance Company. He builds it into the nation's largest black-owned business by the time of his death in 1952.

1923   Poet and novelist Jean Toomer publishes his masterpiece, *Cane,* an experimental novel often considered one of the greatest achievements of the Harlem Renaissance.

1923   Blues singer Bessie Smith, discovered by pianist-composer Clarence Williams, makes her first recording. She will eventually become known as "Empress of the Blues."

1925   In an era when Ku Klux Klan membership exceeds 4,000,000 nationally, a parade of 50,000 unmasked members takes place in Washington, D.C.

1925   A. Philip Randolph, trade unionist and civil-rights leader, founds the Brotherhood of Sleeping Car Porters, which becomes the first successful black trade union.

1925   At a historic literary awards banquet during the Harlem Renaissance, Langston Hughes earns first place in poetry with "The Weary Blues," which is read aloud by James Weldon Johnson.

1930   Benjamin Oliver Davis, Sr., becomes the first black colonel in the U.S. Army. He later oversees race relations and the morale of black soldiers in World War II and becomes the first black general in 1940.

1931   Nine black youths accused of raping two white women on a freight train go on trial for their lives in Scottsboro, Ala. The case becomes a cause célèbre among Northern liberal and radical groups.

1931   Walter White begins his tenure as executive secretary of the NAACP, his principal objective being the abolition of lynching.

1936   Track-and-field athlete Jesse Owens wins four gold medals in the 1936 Olympic Games in Berlin. His victories derail Adolf Hitler's intended use of the games as a show of Aryan supremacy.

1938   In a knockout in the first round of their rematch, heavyweight champion Joe Louis wreaks vengeance on Max Schmeling of Germany, the only boxer to have knocked out Louis in his prime.

1939   The NAACP Legal Defense and Education Fund is organized. Charles Hamilton Houston spearheads the effort to consolidate some of the nation's best legal talents in the fight against legally sanctioned bias.

1940   Author Richard Wright publishes his masterpiece, *Native Son.* The stark, tragic realism of this novel immediately places Wright in the front ranks of contemporary American writers.

1941   Bayard Rustin organizes the New York branch of the Congress on Racial Equality.

1941   Following considerable protest, the War Department forms the all-black 99th Pursuit Squadron of the U.S. Army Air Corps, later known as the Tuskegee Airmen, commanded by Benjamin Oliver Davis, Jr.

1942   The interracial Congress of Racial Equality (CORE) is founded in New York City. Its direct-action tactics achieve national prominence during the Freedom Rides of 1961.

1945   Adam Clayton Powell, Jr., pastor of the Abyssinian Baptist Church in Harlem, is elected to the U.S. House of Representatives as a Democrat from Harlem, serving 11 successive terms.

1947   Jackie Robinson joins the Brooklyn Dodgers, becoming the first black baseball player in the major leagues.

1950   Ralph Bunche is awarded the Nobel Peace Prize for his work as United Nations mediator in the Arab-Israeli dispute in Palestine.

1950   After refusing to disavow his membership in the Communist Party, Paul Robeson—singer, actor, and activist—has his passport withdrawn by the U.S. State Department.

1952   Ralph Ellison publishes his masterpiece, *Invisible Man,* which receives the National Book Award in 1953.

1954   On May 17, the U.S. Supreme Court rules unanimously in *Brown v. Board of Education of Topeka* that racial segregation in public schools violates the Fourteenth Amendment to the Constitution.

1955   Lynchings continue in the South with the brutal slaying of a 14-year-old Chicago youth, Emmett Till, in Money, Miss. *Jet* magazine publishes a picture of the mutilated corpse.

1955   Rosa Parks, secretary of the Montgomery Ala., chapter of the NAACP, refuses to surrender her seat when ordered by a local bus driver, leading to the Mongomery bus boycott of 1955-56.

1957   The Southern Christian Leadership Conference is established by Reverend Martin Luther King, Jr., and others to coordinate and assist local organizations working for the full equality of African Americans.

1957   President Dwight D. Eisenhower orders federal troops into Little Rock, Ark., after unsuccessfully trying to persuade Governor Orval Faubus to give up efforts to block desegregation at Central High.

1958   The Alvin Ailey American Dance Theater is formed. Composed primarily of African Americans, the dance company tours extensively both in the United States and abroad.

1959   Trumpeter Miles Davis records "Kind of Blue" often considered his masterwork, with composer-arranger-pianist Bill Evans and tenor saxophonist John Coltrane.

1959   *Raisin in the Sun,* by Lorraine Hansberry, becomes the first drama by a black woman to be produced on Broadway. The 1961 film version features Sidney Poitier and receives a special award at Cannes.

1960   The sit-in movement is launched at Greensboro, N.C., when black college students insist on service at a local segregated lunch counter.

1963   Medgar Evers, Mississippi field secretary for the NAACP, is shot and killed in an ambush in front of his home, following a historic broadcast on the subject of civil rights by President John F. Kennedy.

1963   In Birmingham, Ala., Police Commissioner Eugene "Bull" Connor uses water hoses and dogs against civil-rights protesters, many of whom are children, increasing pressure on President John F. Kennedy to act.

1963   The Reverend Martin Luther King, Jr., writes "Letter from a Birmingham Jail" to eight clergymen who attacked his role in Birmingham. Widely reprinted, it soon becomes a classic of protest literature.

1963   The Civil Rights Movement reaches its climax with a massive march on Washington, D.C. Among the themes of the march "for jobs and freedom" was a demand for passage of the Civil Rights Act.

1964   President Lyndon Johnson signs the Civil Rights Act into law, giving federal law enforcement agencies the power to prevent racial discrimination in employment, voting, and the use of public facilities.

1964 The Reverend Martin Luther King, Jr., is awarded the Nobel Prize for Peace in Oslo, Norway.

1965 The Voting Rights Act is passed following the Selma-to-Montgomery March, which garnered the nation's attention when marchers were beaten mercilessly by state troopers at the Edmund Pettus Bridge.

1965 The Watts area of Los Angeles explodes into violence following the arrest of a young male motorist charged with reckless driving. At the riot's end, 34 are dead, 1,032 injured, and 3,952 arrested.

1966 The Black Panther Party for Self-Defense is founded in Oakland, Calif., by Huey Newton and Bobby Seale, with the original purpose of protecting residents from acts of police brutality.

1966 Charting a new course for the Civil Rights Movement, Stokely Carmichael, chairman of the Southern Christian Leadership Conference, uses the phrase "black power" at a rally during the James Meredith March that summer in Mississippi.

1966 The African American holiday of Kwanzaa, patterned after various African harvest festivals, is created by Maulana Karenga, a black-studies professor at California State University at Long Beach.

1967 Huey P. Newton, co-founder of the Black Panther Party, is convicted on a charge of manslaughter in the death of an Oakland policeman, leading to the rapid expansion of the party nationwide.

1968 Eldridge Cleaver, the Black Panther Party's minister of information, publishes his autobiographical volume, *Soul on Ice*.

1968 On April 4, the Reverend Martin Luther King, Jr., is assassinated in Memphis, Tenn. The assassination is followed by a week of rioting in at least 125 cities across the nation, including Washington, D.C.

1968 Following the assassination of Martin Luther King, Jr., Ralph Abernathy succeeds him as president of the Southern Christian Leadership Conference, carrying out the SCLC's Poor People's Campaign.

1968 Shirley Chisholm becomes the first black American woman to be elected to the U.S. Congress, defeating civil-rights leader James Farmer.

1971 Angela Davis is arraigned on charges of murder, kidnapping, and conspiracy for her alleged participation in a violent attempted escape from the Hall of Justice in Marin county, Calif., in 1970.

1976 Barbara Jordan, congressional representative from Texas, delivers the keynote address at the Democratic National Convention, confirming her reputation as one of the most eloquent public speakers of her era.

1978 In Regents of the *University of California v. Bakke,* the Supreme Court rules against fixed racial quotas but upholds the use of race as a factor in making decisions on admissions for professional schools.

1983 Writer Alice Walker receives the Pulitzer Prize for *The Color Purple.*

1983 Harold Washington wins the Democratic nomination by upsetting incumbent Mayor Jane Byrne and Richard M. Daley and is elected the first African American mayor of Chicago.

1983 Civil-rights leader Jesse Jackson announces his intention to run for the Democratic presidential nomination, becoming the first African American to make a serious bid for the presidency.

1989 President George Bush nominates Colin Powell Chairman of the Joint Chiefs of Staff, making him the first black officer to hold the highest military post in the United States.

1992 Riots break out in Los Angeles, sparked by the acquittal of four white police officers caught on videotape beating Rodney King, a black motorist. The riots cause at least 55 deaths and $1 billion in damage.

1995 Minister Louis Farrakhan, leader of the Nation of Islam, rises to the height of his influence as the most prominent organizer of the "Million Man March" of African American men in Washington, D.C.

Source: Amistad Research Center.

16.8   Slave Populations by State, 1850

State	Number of Slaves	State	Number of Slaves
ALABAMA	342,844	MISSISSIPPI	309,878
ARKANSAS	47,100	MISSOURI	87,422
DELAWARE	2,290	NEW JERSEY	236
FLORIDA	39,310	NORTH CAROLINA	288,548
GEORGIA	381,682	SOUTH CAROLINA	384,984
KENTUCKY	210,981	TENNESSEE	239,459
LOUISIANA	244,809	TEXAS	58,161
MARYLAND	90,368	VIRGINIA	472,528
		U.S. total	3,200,600

16.9   Major Events in the 20th Century Civil Rights Movement

1909   National Association for the Advancement of Colored People (NAACP) founded in New York.

1915   Ku Klux Klan inaugurated under legal charter in Georgia.

1920   Foundation of American Civil Liberties Union.

1929   Two thousand–strong lynch mob in Mississippi burns alleged black rapist to death; jury returns verdict of death "due to unknown causes."

1941   Founding of Congress of Racial Equality (CORE).

1944   Supreme Court rules that no American can be denied the right to vote because of color.

1948   Executive Order 9981 ends racial segregation in armed forces.

1955   U.S. Supreme Court orders desegregation of all public places.

1956   Martin Luther King, Jr.'s home in Montgomery bombed; southern congressmen issue a manifesto pledging to use "all lawful means" to disrupt the Supreme Court's desegregation ruling.

1957   Federal troops sent in to Central High School, Little Rock, Arkansas, when crowds prevent nine black children from entering the school; Civil Rights Commission established.

1962   Riots break out at University of Mississippi when black student James Howard Meredith attempts to take his place.

1963   Martin Luther King Jr., makes his historic "I Have a Dream" speech in Washington, D.C.; more than 200,000 black and white demonstrators march on Washington, D.C. in support of civil rights reforms.

1964   Southern senators filibuster for 75 days to block Civil Rights Bill but fail and bill becomes law; bodies of three civil-rights workers, killed by white supremacists, discovered in Philadelphia, Mississippi.

1965   Malcolm X shot dead as he prepares to speak on racial harmony.

1966   First black senator elected in Massachusetts.

1967   First black Supreme Court Justice sworn in.

1968   Martin Luther King, Jr. assassinated; Chicago's Mayor Daley gives police a "shoot to kill" order to quell riots following King's death.

1971   Rioting in New York's Attica Correctional Facility, after inmates discover differences in sentences and parole decisions that appear to have a racial basis.

1986   Martin Luther King Jr.'s birthday becomes a national holiday.

1992   Acquittal of policemen charged with beating of unarmed black motorist Rodney King in 1991 prompts the worst riots in U.S. history.

16.10   Chronology of the Life of Martin Luther King, Jr.

January 15, 1929 - Michael King (later known as Martin Luther King, Jr.) is born in Atlanta, Georgia.

September 1944 - King begins his freshman year at Morehouse College.

February 1948 - King is ordained and appointed associate pastor at Ebenezer Church.

June 1948 - King receives his bachelor of arts degree in sociology from Morehouse.

May 1951 - King graduates from Crozer with a bachelor of divinity degree, as valedictorian and student body president.

September 1951 - King begins graduate work in theology at Boston University.

June 18, 1953 - King marries Coretta Scott at the Scott home near Marion, Alabama.

October 1954 - King is ordained pastor of Dexter Avenue Baptist Church in Montgomery, Alabama.

June 1955 - King is awarded a doctorate from Boston University.

December 1955 - The Montgomery Bus Boycott begins and King is elected president of the Montgomery Improvement Association (MIA) after Rosa Parks' arrest for refusing to obey the city's policy mandating segregation on buses.

January 30, 1956 - The Kings' home is bombed.

February 1956 - An all-white grand jury indicts King and 88 black leaders of the MIA for violating a state anti-labor law prohibiting boycotts.

December 1956 - Montgomery buses are integrated after the U.S. Supreme Court declares Alabama's segregation laws unconstitutional and King is among the first people to ride an integrated Montgomery bus.

August 8-9, 1957 - One hundred fifteen black leaders meet in Montgomery and form the Southern Christian Leadership Conference (SCLC).

June 23, 1958 - King meets with President Eisenhower.

September 1958 - King publishes his first book, *Stride Toward Freedom: The Montgomery Story*.

September 20, 1958 - King is stabbed in Harlem.

February 1959 - King departs for India as guest of Prime Minister Nehru.

June 22, 1960 - King meets privately with presidential candidate John F. Kennedy.

October 1960 - King is arrested for a sit-in at Rich's Department store in Atlanta, refuses to post bail, and goes to jail with student protestors.

October 16, 1962 - King meets with President Kennedy and urges him to issue a second Emancipation Proclamation to end racial segregation.

April 1963 - King is jailed in Birmingham and writes "Letter from a Birmingham Jail."

August 28, 1963 - King delivers the "I Have a Dream" speech at the March on Washington for Jobs and Freedom.

September 22, 1963 - King eulogizes four girls killed in 16th Street Baptist Church bombing in Birmingham, Alabama.

September 1963 - *Strength to Love* is published.

October 1963 - Robert Kennedy authorizes the FBI to wiretap King's telephone in Atlanta, and subsequently approves taps on SCLC's phones.

December 1964 - King receives the Nobel Peace Prize

March 21-25, 1965 - King leads Selma to Montgomery March.

August 6, 1965 - King is present when President Johnson signs the Voting Rights Act.

August 1965 - King publicly opposes the Vietnam War, urging negotiation and a halt to the bombing of North Vietnam.

March 28, 1968 - King leads a march of approximately 6,000 protestors in support of striking Memphis sanitation workers.

April 3, 1968 - King delivers his last speech, "I've Been to the Mountaintop," at the Mason Temple in Memphis.

April 4, 1968 - King is assassinated in Memphis.

Source: Amistad Research Center.

16.11   King's "I Have a Dream" Speech, 1963

Martin Luther King's "I Have a Dream" speech, delivered August 28, 1963.

I am happy to join with you today in what will go down in history as the greatest demonstration for freedom in the history of our nation.

Five score years ago, a great American, in whose symbolic shadow we stand today, signed the Emancipation Proclamation. This momentous decree came as a great beacon of hope to millions of slaves, who had been seared in the flames of withering injustice. It came as a joyous daybreak to end the long night of their captivity. But one hundred years later, the colored America is still not free. One hundred years later, the life of the colored American is still sadly crippled by the manacle of segregation and the chains of discrimination.

One hundred years later, the colored American lives on a lonely island of poverty in the midst of a vast ocean of material prosperity. One hundred years later, the colored American is still languishing in the corners of American society and finds himself an exile in his own land. So we have come here today to dramatize a shameful condition.

In a sense we have come to our Nation's Capitol to cash a check. When the architects of our great republic wrote the magnificent words of the Constitution and the Declaration of Independence, they were signing a promissory note to which every American was to fall heir.

This note was a promise that all men, yes, black men as well as white men, would be guaranteed to the inalienable rights of life, liberty, and the pursuit of happiness.

It is obvious today that America has defaulted on this promissory note insofar as her citizens of color are concerned. Instead of honoring this sacred obligation, America has given its colored people a bad check, a check that has come back marked "insufficient funds."

But we refuse to believe that the bank of justice is bankrupt. We refuse to believe that there are insufficient funds in the great vaults of opportunity of this nation.

So we have come to cash this check, a check that will give us upon demand the riches of freedom and security of justice.

We have also come to this hallowed spot to remind America of the fierce urgency of Now. This is not time to engage in the luxury of cooling off or to take the tranquilizing drug of gradualism.

Now is the time to make real the promise of democracy.

Now is the time to rise from the dark and desolate valley of segregation to the sunlit path of racial justice.

Now is the time to lift our nation from the quicksands of racial injustice to the solid rock of brotherhood.

Now is the time to make justice a reality to all of God's children.

It would be fatal for the nation to overlook the urgency of the moment and to underestimate the determination of its colored citizens. This sweltering summer of the colored people's legitimate discontent will not pass until there is an invigorating autumn of freedom and equality. Nineteen sixty-three is not an end but a beginning. Those who hope that the colored Americans needed to blow off steam and will now be content will have a rude awakening if the nation returns to business as usual.

There will be neither rest nor tranquility in America until the colored citizen is granted his citizenship rights. The whirlwinds of revolt will continue to shake the foundations of our nation until the bright day of justice emerges.

We can never be satisfied as long as our bodies, heavy with the fatigue of travel, cannot gain lodging in the motels of the highways and the hotels of the cities.

We cannot be satisfied as long as the colored person's basic mobility is from a smaller ghetto to a larger one.

We can never be satisfied as long as our children are stripped of their selfhood and robbed of their dignity by signs stating "for white only."

We cannot be satisfied as long as a colored person in Mississippi cannot vote and a colored person in New York believes he has nothing for which to vote.

No, no we are not satisfied and we will not be satisfied until justice rolls down like waters and righteousness like a mighty stream.

I am not unmindful that some of you have come here out of your trials and tribulations. Some of you have come from areas where your quest for freedom left you battered by storms of persecutions and staggered by the winds of police brutality.

You have been the veterans of creative suffering. Continue to work with the faith that unearned suffering is redemptive.

Go back to Mississippi, go back to Alabama, go back to South Carolina, go back to Georgia, go back to Louisiana, go back to the slums and ghettos of our modern cities, knowing that somehow this situation can and will be changed.

Let us not wallow in the valley of dispair. I say to you, my friends, we have the difficulties of today and tomorrow.

I still have a dream. It is a dream deeply rooted in the American dream.

I have a dream that one day this nation will rise up and live out the true meaning of its creed. We hold these truths to be self-evident that all men are created equal.

I have a dream that one day, out in the red hills of Georgia, the sons of former slaves and the sons of former slaveowners will be able to sit down together at the table of brotherhood.

I have a dream that one day even the state of Mississippi, a state sweltering with the heat of oppression, will be transformed into an oasis of freedom and justice.

I have a dream that my four little children will one day live in a nation where they will not be judged by the color of their skin but by their character.

I have a dream today.

I have a dream that one day down in Alabama, with its vicious racists, with its governor having his lips dripping with the words of interposition and nullification, that one day right down in Alabama little black boys and black girls will be able to join hands with little white boys and white girls as sisters and brothers.

I have a dream today.

I have a dream that one day every valley shall be engulfed, every hill shall be exalted and every mountain shall be made low, the rough places will be made plains and the crooked places will be made straight and the glory of the Lord shall be revealed and all flesh shall see it together.

This is our hope. This is the faith that I will go back to the South with. With this faith we will be able to hew out of the mountain of despair a stone of hope.

With this faith we will be able to transform the jangling discords of our nation into a beautiful symphony of brotherhood.

With this faith we will be able to work together, to pray together, to struggle together, to go to jail together, to climb up for freedom together, knowing that we will be free one day.

This will be the day when all of God's children will be able to sing with new meaning "My country 'tis of thee, sweet land of liberty, of thee I sing. Land where my fathers died, land of the Pilgrim's pride, from every mountainside, let freedom ring!"

And if America is to be a great nation, this must become true. So let freedom ring from the hilltops of New Hampshire. Let freedom ring from the mighty mountains of New York.

Let freedom ring from the heightening Alleghenies of Pennsylvania.

Let freedom ring from the snow-capped Rockies of Colorado.

Let freedom ring from the curvaceous slopes of California.

But not only that, let freedom ring from Stone Mountain of Georgia.

Let freedom ring from every hill and molehill of Mississippi and every mountainside.

When we let freedom ring, when we let it ring from every tenement and every hamlet, from every state and every city, we will be able to speed up that day when all of God's children, black men and white men, Jews and Gentiles, Protestants and Catholics, will be able to join hands and sing in the words of the old spiritual, "Free at last, free at last. Thank God Almighty, we are free at last."

16.12   Chronology of Asian American History

1600s   Chinese and Filipinos reach Mexico on ships of the Manila galleon.

1830s   Chinese "sugar masters" working in Hawaii. Chinese sailors and peddlers in New York.

1835   U.S. and China sign first treaty.

1848   Gold discovered in California. Chinese begin to arrive.

1852   First group of Chinese contract laborers lands in Hawaii. Over 20,000 Chinese enter California.

1854   U.S. and Japan sign first treaty.

1858   California passes a law to bar entry of Chinese and "Mongolians."

1860   Japan sends a diplomatic mission to U.S.

1865   Central Pacific Railroad Co. recruits Chinese workers for the transcontinental railroad.

1868   U.S. and China sign Burlingame-Seward Treaty recognizing rights of their citizens to emigrate.

1877   Anti-Chinese violence in Chico, California.

1878   *In re Ah Yup* rules Chinese not eligible for naturalized citizenship.

1879   California state legislature passes law requiring all incorporated towns and cities to remove Chinese outside of city limits, but U.S. circuit court declares the law unconstitutional.

1880   U.S. and China sign treaty giving the U.S. the right to limit but "not absolutely prohibit" Chinese immigration. California's Civil Code prohibits issuing of licenses for marriages between whites and "Mongolians, Negroes, mulattoes and persons of mixed blood."

1882   Chinese Exclusion Law suspends immigration of laborers for ten years. U.S. and Korea sign first treaty.

1885   San Francisco builds new segregated "Oriental School." Anti-Chinese violence at Rock Springs, Wyoming Territory. First group of Japanese contract laborers arrives in Hawaii.

1886   Residents of Tacoma, Seattle, and many places in the American West forcibly expel the Chinese immigrants to Hawaii.

1889   *Chae Chang Ping v. U.S.* upholds constitutionality of Chinese exclusion laws.

1892   Geary Law renews exclusion of Chinese laborers for another ten years and requires all Chinese to register. *Fong Yue Ting v. U.S.* upholds constitutionality of Geary Law.

1898   *Wong Kim Ark v. U.S.* decides that Chinese born in the U.S. can't be stripped of their citizenship. U.S. annexes Hawaii.

1913   California passes alien land law prohibiting "aliens ineligible to citizenship" from buying land or leasing it for longer than three years.

1917   Arizona passes an Alien Land law.

1917   Immigration Law defines a geographic "barred zone" (including India) from which no immigrants can come.

1918   Servicemen of Asian ancestry who had served in World War I receive right of naturalization.

1922   *Takao Ozawa v. U.S.* declares Japanese not eligible for naturalized citizenship. New Mexico passes an alien land law.

1923   *U.S. v. Bhagat Singh Thind* declares Asian Indians not eligible for naturalized citizenship. Idaho, Montana, and Oregon pass alien land laws.

1924   Immigration Act denies entry to virtually all Asians.

1930   Anti-Filipino riot in Watsonville, California.

1934   Tydings-McDuffie Act spells out procedure for eventual Philippine independence and reduces Filipino immigration to 50 persons a year.

1941   After declaring war on Japan, 2,000 Japanese community leaders along Pacific Coast states and Hawaii are rounded up and interned in Department of Justice camps.

1942   President Franklin D. Roosevelt signs Executive Order 9066 authorizing the Secretary of War to delegate a military commander to designate military areas "from which any and all persons may be excluded"—primarily enforced against Japanese.

1943   Congress repeals all Chinese exclusion laws, grants right of naturalization and a small immigration quota to Chinese.

1946   Luce-Celler bill grants right of naturalization and small immigration quotas to Asian Indians and Filipinos. Wing F. Ong becomes first Asian American to be elected to state office in the Arizona House of Representatives.

1947   Amendment to 1945 War Brides Act allows Chinese American veterans to bring brides into the U.S.

1949   5,000 highly educated Chinese in the U.S. granted refugee status after China institutes a Communist government.

1952   One clause of the McCarran–Walter Act grants the right to naturalization and a small immigration quota to Japanese.

1956   California repeals its alien land laws. Dalip Singh from the Imperial Valley, California, is elected to Congress.

1962   Daniel K. Inouye becomes U.S. Senator and Spark Matsunaga becomes U.S. Congressman from Hawaii.

1964   Patsy Takemoto Mink becomes first Asian American woman to serve in Congress as representative from Hawaii.

1965   Immigration Law abolishes "national origins" as basis for allocating immigration quotas to various countries—Asian countries now on equal footing.

1974   *Lau v. Nichols* rules that school districts with children who speak little English must provide them with bilingual education.

1975   More than 130,000 refugees enter the U.S. from Vietnam, Kampuchea and Laos as Communist governments are established there.

1976   President Gerald Ford rescinds Executive Order 9066.

1978   National convention of the Japanese American Citizens League adopts resolution calling for redress and reparations for the internment of Japanese Americans.

1979   Resumption of diplomatic relations between the People's Republic of China and the United States of America reunites members of long-separated Chinese American families.

1980   The Socialist Republic of Vietnam and the United Nations High Commissioner for Refugees set up an Orderly Departure Program to enable Vietnamese to immigrate legally.

1986   Immigration Reform and Control Act imposes civil and criminal penalties on employers who knowingly hire undocumented aliens.

1987   The U.S. House of Representatives votes 243 to 141 to make an official apology to Japanese Americans and to pay each surviving internee $20,000 in reparations.

1989   U.S. reaches agreement with Vietnam to allow political prisoners to emigrate to the U.S.

Source: Sucheng Chan, *Asian Americans, An Interpretive History,* 1991, Twayne Publishers, Boston.

16.13 Notable Black Americans

Abolitionists
Amos G. Beman
Henry Bibb
Mary Ann Shadd Cary
Samuel E. Cornish
Martin R. Delany
Frederick Douglass
A. N. Freeman
Henry Highland Garnet
Josiah Henson
Jermain Wesley Loguen
J. Sella Martin
James W. C. Pennington
Charles B. Ray
Christopher Rush
James McCune Smith
Samuel Ringgold Ward
Theodore S. Wright

Reconstruction Politicians
Francis L. Cardoza (South Carolina)
Thomas Cardoza (Mississippi)
Pierre Landry (Louisiana)
Hiram Rhoades Revels (Mississippi)
Jonathan J. Wright (South Carolina)

Black Organization Officials
NAACP:
Gloster B. Current
William E. B. DuBois
Benjamin O. Hooks
James Weldon Johnson
Clarence Mitchell
Henry Moon
William Pickens
Walter White
Roy Wilkins

Urban League:
George Edmund Haynes
Eugene Kinckle Jones
Vernon Jordon
Whitney Young
John E. Jacob
Hugh Price

College Presidents
Rufus E. Clement (Atlanta University)
John W. Davis (West Virginia State College)
Joseph Gayles (Talladega College)
Hugh Gloster (Morehouse College)
John Hope (Morehouse College & Atlanta University)
Charles S. Johnson (Fisk University)
Mordecai W. Johnson (Howard Universty)
James Lawson (Fisk University)
Albert E. Manley (Spelman College)
Benjamin E. Mays (Morehouse College)
Robert R. Moton (Tuskegee Institute)
Frederick D. Patterson (Tuskegee Institute)
Benjamin Payton (Benedict College, Tuskegee Institute)
Booker T. Washington (Tuskegee Institute)
Stephen J. Wright (Fisk University)

Civil Rights Attorneys
Robert L. Carter (later appointed a federal judge)
William T. Coleman (later appointed U.S. Secretary of Transportation)
Robert Collins (later appointed a federal judge)
William H. Hastie (later appointed a federal judge)
A. Leon Higginbotham (later appointed a federal judge)
Thurgood Marshall (later appointed to the U.S. Supreme Court)
Constance Baker Motley (later appointed a federal judge)

Civil Rights Activists
Ella Baker
Stokley Carmichael
Martin Luther King
Rosa Parks
A. Philip Randolph
Bayard Rustin
Andrew Young
Malcolm X

Literary Figures
William E. B. DuBois
Alex Haley
Langston Hughes
Alain Leroy Locke
Dorothy West
Richard Wright

Source: Amistad Research Center.

16.14   Notable American Women

Anne Hutchinson (1591-1643)—Early champion of religious liberty and free speech, this midwife was put on trial in 1637 for her outspoken views. The Massachusetts General Court found her guilty of sedition and banished her from the Colony.

Hannah Adams (1755-1831)—Historian and the first professional woman writer in the United States, she published *A Summary History of New England* in 1799.

Deborah Sampson Gannett (1760-1827)—Signing up for the 4th Massachusetts Regiment under an assumed male name, she became the first woman to enlist as a soldier in the American army. After being wounded nineteen months later, she received an honorable medical discharge and, later, a military pension.

Emma Willard (1787-1870)—Foremost 19th century proponent of higher education for women. She founded the Troy (NY) Female Academy, an all-girls' school, where she daringly taught her students science and math and educated hundreds of future teachers. Her efforts on behalf of equal educational opportunities for women helped lead to coeducational school systems.

Sacajawea (c.1789-c.1812)—A Shoshone Indian, she was captured by an enemy tribe who eventually sold her to the French Canadian trapper she later married. In 1804, Meriweather Lewis and William Clark hired her to help lead them as they explored the western United States. Bringing along her newborn son, she acted as interpreter and guide and was later credited by the men with the success of their expedition.

Sarah Moore Grimke (1792-1873) and **Angelina Emily Grimke** (1805-1879)—Sisters from a wealthy slave-owning family in South Carolina, they were the only white southerners to be leaders in the American Anti-Slavery Society. In an 1838 abolitionist speech before the Massachusetts State Legislature, Angelina became the first American woman to address a legislative body. Their work inspired leading women's rights figures.

Lucretia Mott (1793-1880)—Ordained Quaker minister and pioneering activist in the women's suffrage movement who addressed the first women's rights convention at Seneca Falls (NY). She was also an outspoken abolitionist whose staunch beliefs caused her to boycott all goods produced by slave labor.

Sojourner Truth (c.1797-1883)—A former slave, she became a leading proponent of human rights and a spokesperson for abolition and women's rights. Her question "and ain't I a woman?" posed during a speech before a women's rights convention sought to align the plights of poor and black women with those of white suffragists.

Dorothea Dix (1802-1887)—Crusader of rights for the mentally ill in North America and Europe, she founded or improved over thirty hospitals for the mentally ill and influenced government legislation with her research. In 1861, she was appointed first Superintendent of U.S. Army Nurses.

Margaret Fuller (1810-1850)—Leading female intellectual of her day and author of the pioneering feminist work *Women in the Nineteenth Century* (1845). She edited Ralph Waldo Emerson's paper *The Dial* and, while writing literary and social criticism in Europe for the *New York Tribune,* became America's first female correspondent.

Harriet Beecher Stowe (1811-1896)—Author of short stories, poetry and the biggest best-seller of the nineteenth century, *Uncle Tom's Cabin.* The novel, which first appeared in serialized version in *National Era* magazine, was the first major American work in which a black man appeared as the central hero. The book had a remarkable impact on pre–Civil War society, stirring the nation's opposing passions regarding slavery and hastening the conflict. When President Abraham Lincoln later met Stowe, he addressed her as "the little woman who made this great war."

Harriet Tubman (1815-1913)—As a "conductor" on the Underground Railroad, this fugitive slave helped thousands of blacks escape north prior to the Civil War. During the War, she served as a Union nurse and military spy.

Elizabeth Cady Stanton (1815-1902)—Known, along with Susan B. Anthony, as one of the foremost figures of the movement for women's equality. Her outrage at being excluded from an anti-slavery convention because of her gender inspired her to co-organize the 1948 Seneca Falls (NY) Women's Rights Convention.

There, she drafted her famous Declaration of Sentiments, modeled on the Declaration of Independence. Her accomplishments included co-founding the newspaper *Revolution,* heading the National Woman Suffrage Association for twenty years and being first president of the National American Woman Suffrage Association.

Amelia Bloomer (1818-1894)—Social reformer, suffragist, and publisher of the temperance paper *The Lily,* she was ridiculed by nineteenth century men for the liberated "pants" outfits she popularized.

Maria Mitchell (1818-1889)—The first American woman astronomer and the director of the observatory at Vassar College, she was the first female member of the American Academy of Arts and Sciences and the American Association for the Advancement of Science.

Lucy Stone (1818-1893)—Pioneering leader in the women suffrage movement and founder of the American Woman Suffrage Association. Her 1855 marriage ceremony to Henry Blackwell exemplified her commitment to her cause: the standard promise of obedience was eliminated and, drawing inspiration from the example she and her husband set, the word *stoner* became a common 19th century word for women who kept their maiden names after marriage.

Julia Ward Howe (1819-1911)—Abolitionist, suffragist, and social reformer, she was also a poet whose most famous work became the anthem, *The Battle Hymn of the Republic.*

Susan Brownell Anthony (1820-1906)—Leader in the American Anti-Slavery Society, she later turned her life's devotion to women's suffrage and, with Elizabeth Cady Stanton, founded the National Woman Suffrage Association and the newspaper *Revolution.* She was so widely considered a symbol of the women's suffrage movement that the 19th Amendment finally giving women the right to vote was commonly referred to as the Anthony Amendment and her likeness was later etched on an American silver dollar.

Mary Baker Eddy (1821-1910)—Founder of Christian Science, the international religious movement which advocates spiritual healing in the belief that the body is governed not by physical cause and effect but by the powers of the mind and spirit. In 1879, she organized the First Church of Christ, Scientist in Boston, and in 1908, established the internationally known newspaper, *The Christian Science Monitor.*

Elizabeth Blackwell (1821-1910)—The first American woman to receive a medical doctor degree (1849), she opened the New York Infirmary for Women and Children and co-founded the Women's Medical College in 1868.

Clara Barton (1824-1912)—Called the "Angel of the Battlefield" for her first aid heroism during the Civil War, she was instrumental in founding the American Red Cross.

Antoinette Louisa Brown (1825-1921)—Social reformer, abolitionist and suffragist, she was the nation's first ordained female minister, one of the first American women to attend college, and an author of books on evolution and social theory.

Emily Dickinson (1839-1886)—Reclusive poet of hundreds of inventive, original poems, she was the most famous woman poet in nineteenth-century America.

Mary Harris "Mother" Jones (1830-1930)—Labor organizer who championed the cause of social justice and devoted herself to the struggle against the poor hours, pay and working conditions of railroad, textile and mine workers.

Mary Cassatt (1844-1926)—World-renown artist, she introduced Impressionism to America and is famous especially for her paintings and prints depicting mothers and children.

Carry Nation (1846-1930)—Prohibitionist reformer, she gained fame for wielding a hatchet while destroying saloons.

Carrie Chapman Catt (1859-1947)—Editor of the *National Suffrage Bulletin* and a leader in the women's suffrage movement, she was instrumental in achieving voting rights for women in America's West and was president of the National American Woman Suffrage Association at the time the 19th Amendment was finally passed. She also served as president of the International Woman Suffrage Alliance and founded the National League of Women Voters to help teach women how to intelligently use their vote. Her 1890 marriage included a prenuptial agreement giving her four months in each year to travel for the cause of women's equality.

Martha Thomas Carey (1857-1935)—Suffragist and educator long associated with Bryn Mawr College, she was the first female college faculty member in the country to hold the title "dean," started the first graduate program at any women's school, and established the country's first graduate scholarships. She was also a founder of the Association to Promote Scientific Research by Women and of the International Federation of University Women.

Annie Oakley (Phoebe Anne Oakley Mozee) (1860-1926)—Known as "Lady Sure Shot," this markswoman made a living demonstrating her amazing ability to hit her target. As star of Buffalo Bill's Wild West Show, she traveled the world, dazzling audiences with such feats as shooting the flames off a revolving wheel of candles, splitting a playing card held edge-on and, while on tour in Berlin, knocking the ash off a cigarette held between the lips of Germany's Crown Prince William.

Charlotte Perkins Gilman (1860-1935)—Writer and lecturer on women's role in society, she was a leading feminist theorist and instrument of change.

Jane Addams (1860-1935)—Co-founder of the famous Chicago settlement house "Hull House," she was a pacifist, a suffragist, an advocate of social reform and, in 1931, the first American woman to win the Nobel Peace Prize. She turned her prize winnings over to the Woman's International League for Peace and Freedom, of which she was president.

Ida B. Wells (1862-1931)—Black journalist and militant civil rights leader, she was a co-founder of the NAACP and the first president of the Negro Fellowship League.

Sarah Breedlove "Madame C.J." Walker (1867-1919)—A southern sharecropper's daughter, she became the first female black millionaire by successfully selling hair preparations for black woman. She also founded several factories and beauty colleges and actively supported many charitable and educational institutions.

Emma Goldman (1869-1940)—Outspoken feminist, pacifist and lifelong anarchist, this lecturer and author founded *Mother Earth* newspaper and was noted for her radicalism in aiding the world's oppressed.

Mary McLeod Bethune (1875-1955)—Writer and educator, and daughter of former slaves, she was a champion of humanitarian causes and an advocate of civil rights and education for Blacks. Among her accomplishments were establishing Florida's Bethune-Cookman College and serving as Director of the Division of Negro Affairs in the National Youth Administration during Franklin D. Roosevelt's presidency, at that time the highest position ever held in government by a black woman.

Isadora Duncan (1878-1927)—Pioneer of modern dance in America and Europe, she elevated dance to an art form practiced by serious artists and gained huge popularity for her innovative, expressive style.

Margaret Sanger (1879-1966)—Pioneering crusader for the legalization of birth control, this social reformer battled the nation's government and courts to open America's first birth control clinic. Founder of the Natural Birth Control League and Planned Parenthood of America, she later took her campaign to provide safe contraceptions worldwide and formed the International Planned Parenthood Federation.

Helen Keller (1880-1968)—Triumphing over an early childhood illness which left her blind and deaf, she went on to graduate with honors from Radcliffe College and become a world-famous lecturer, author, and advocate of rights for people with disabilities.

Frances Perkins (1880-1965)—Social and political reformer, she became the first woman appointed to the New York State Industrial Commission and the first woman member of a United States Cabinet, heading the Department of Labor.

Jeanette Rankin (1880-1973)—In 1916, this suffragist became the first female elected to the House of Representatives. A Republican from Montana, she campaigned on a platform of peace and voted against the United States' entry into World War I.

Eleanor Roosevelt (1884-1962)—Political and social reformer, humanitarian, and outspoken crusader, this First Lady championed causes of social justice worldwide and as a United Nations delegate, chaired the United Nations Commission on Human Rights.

Alice Paul (1885-1977)—Activist and suffragist who organized the 1913 women's rights march through Washington, D.C. and founded the Congressional Union for Women's Suffrage, a militant branch of the National American Woman Suffrage Association.

Georgia O'Keeffe (1887-1986)—Known as the greatest American woman artist of the 20th century, her iconoclastic paintings are noted for their lyrical use of abstract color and shape in depicting flowers, nature and the American landscape.

Marian Anderson (1897-1993)—The first black to become a member of the Metropolitan Opera Company, this internationally renowned opera singer pushed aside racial discrimination and obstacles to achieve worldwide fame. In 1939, she made history when her scheduled concert at Washington D.C.'s Constitution Hall was blocked by the hall's owners, the Daughters of the American Revolution. In response, Eleanor Roosevelt publicly resigned from that organization and a public concert at the Lincoln Memorial was arranged instead. Its attendance by a mixed crowd of 75,000 people, including numerous dignitaries, became a national symbol of social justice and hope.

Martha Graham (1894-1991)—Founder and longtime principal dancer of the Martha Graham Dance Company and School of Contemporary Dance, this most influential twentieth century choreographer revolutionized the medium through her use of American themes and original scores. Her innovative choreography, expressing raw emotion and inner tension, often incorporated Asian dance, Greek myth and Zen philosophy.

Amelia Earhart (1898-1937)—Pioneering female aviator and the first woman to fly solo across the Atlantic Ocean, she achieved many aviation firsts and set numerous transcontinental records before disappearing in the South Pacific while attempting to fly around the world.

Zora Neale Hurston (1901-1960)—Novelist, essayist and playwright associated with the Harlem Renaissance movement, she also gained fame as an anthropologist of black culture and was the first black to compile a book of African American folklore.

Margaret Mead (1901-1978)—This internationally known social scientist, environmentalist, and spokesperson for social and intellectual issues introduced the world to anthropology through her 1928 bestseller *Coming of Age in Samoa,* based on her study of cultures in the South Pacific. Her pioneering research and new techniques of fieldwork revolutionized the field of anthropology. Her many accomplishments included serving as President of the American Academy for the Advancement of Science and Curator of Ethnology at the American Museum of Natural History and authoring countless books and articles on society and culture.

Margaret Bourke-White (1904-1971)—Pioneering photojournalist, she gained fame for her photographs of millworkers and sharecroppers and was famous for her association with *Life* magazine.

Rachel Carson (1907-1964)—Biologist and author of numerous books about the sea. Her pioneering book, *Silent Spring,* which alerted the country to the environmental dangers of pesticides, had an immediate impact on governmental regulations and is widely, considered to have started the modern environmental protection movement.

Rosa Parks (b.1913)—By refusing to give up her seat on a city bus to a white man in 1955 Montgomery, Alabama because she "was just plain tired," this hard-working seamstress set off a thirteen-month bus boycott and a long chain of civil rights protests. The result: national attention for Dr. Martin Luther King, Jr., a Supreme Court ruling outlawing segregation on buses and the title "Mother of the Civil Rights Movement" for Parks, who went on to continue her fight against racial injustice.

Mildred "Babe" Didrikson (1914-1956)—This remarkable and prodigious athlete, a six-time winner of the Associated Press "Woman Athlete of the Year" award, competed in baseball, basketball, golf and billiards on a national level and was a medal-winning track star, swimmer and skater. Among her many achievements were winning every available golf title in the 1940's, thrice winning the U.S. Women's (Golf) Open, founding the Ladies Professional Golf Association and winning three gold medals in track events at the 1932 Olympics.

Betty Friedan (b.1921)—Founder of the National Organization of Women, her 1963 best-selling book, *The Feminine Mystique,* changed women's lives worldwide and is credited with inspiring the start of the modern women's liberation movement.

Shirley Chisholm (b.1924)—The first black woman elected to Congress, she fought hard for the country's disadvantaged, championing such causes as child welfare, job training, health care, and education.

Maya Angelou (b.1928)—Pulitzer Prize–winning author, poet and playwright. In January 1993, she became the first black to compose a poem for a presidential inauguration, which she delivered as *On the Pulse of Morning* at Bill Clinton's swearing-in.

Jacqueline Kennedy Onassis (1929-1994)—A cultural icon to millions of Americans, she restored the White House and elevated America's image here and abroad during her years as First Lady to President John F. Kennedy. After his assassination, her own courage helped support the country in its grief. In her later life, she was admired as a mother, historic preservationist, and book editor.

Sandra Day O'Connor (b. 1930)—This Arizona lawmaker-turned-judge and the first woman to hold the office of majority leader in a state senate, made history in 1981 through Ronald Reagan's appointment and subsequent Senate confirmation as Associate Justice of the U.S. Supreme Court, the first woman to sit on this body in its 191-hear history.

Toni Morrison (b.1931)—Author of *The Song of Solomon, Beloved,* and *Tar Baby,* among others, this African American writer, the second American woman to receive the Nobel Prize for literature, gained fame for her powerful writing on black American issues.

Gloria Steinem (b. 1934)—Founding editor of *Ms.* magazine and co-founder of the Women's Action Alliance, this journalist and essayist is a leading activist and spokesperson for the contemporary feminist movement.

Geraldine Ferraro (b. 1935)—As a member of the U.S. Congress, she introduced the Private Pension Reform Act, was a member of the Select Committee on Aging and chaired the House Democratic Caucus Task Force on Women's Economic Issues. In 1984, she made American history when Democratic Presidential candidate Walter Mondale tapped her to become the nation's first female vice presidential running mate.

Barbara Jordan (1936-1996)—Lawyer by training, she was the first African American woman to serve in the Texas Legislature. She went on to become the first black woman from the South ever elected to the U.S. Congress where she served on the House Judiciary Committee and fought for voting rights, school funding and the creation of the Consumer Protection Agency. In 1976 she became the first woman to give the keynote address at the Democratic National Convention.

Billie Jean King (b. 1943)—Champion of women's tennis and founder of the Women's Tennis Association, the Women's Sport Foundation, and *WomenSports* magazine, this twenty-time Wimbledon titlist became the first woman athlete to earn over $100,000 in a single year. She has earned worldwide fame and respect both for her athletic ability and her record-breaking earnings as well as her efforts to promote equity between male and female sports.

Antonia Novello (b. 1944)—A physician and public health professional, she was the first woman and the first Hispanic to be appointed U.S. Surgeon General. In this capacity, she led the campaign for stronger warnings on cigarette labels, worked to increase public awareness of AIDS and fought against alcohol advertisements aimed at children.

Wilma Mankiller (b.1945)—Advocate for American Indian causes, she championed programs for job training, housing, property rights, education and community development and was elected the first woman chief of the Cherokee Nation.

Candy Lightner (b.1946)—The death of her thirteen-year-old daughter at the hands of a drunk driver inspired this one-woman crusader to found the now nationwide organizations Mothers Against Drunk Driving (MADD) and Students Against Driving Drunk (SADD). Her campaigns have effected tougher drunk driving laws, helped ensure the passage of the National Minimum Drinking Age Act and led to the establishment of the National Commission on Drunk Driving.

Sally Ride (b. 1951)—Beating out more than 8,300 applicants, she became a mission specialist for NASA's space program. In 1983, abroad the space shuttle *Challenger,* this astrophysicist became the first American woman to fly in space.

Sources: Ashby, Ruth and Deborah Gore Ohrn, editors. *Herstory: Woman who Changed the World.* New York: Viking, 1995. Browne, Ray B., editor. *Contemporary Heroes and Heroines.* Detroit, MI: Gale Research Inc., 1990. Cirker, Hayward and Blanche. *Dictionary of American Portraits.* New York: Dover Publications, 1967. deMille, Agnes. *America Dances.* New York: Macmillan Publishing Company, Inc., 1980. Hopkins, Jospeh G.E., editor. *Concise Dictionary of American Biography.* New York: Charles Scribner's Sons, 1964. Jacobs, William Jay. *Great Lives: Human Rights.* New York: Charles Scribner's Sons, 1990. James, Edward T. *Notable American Women 1607-1950: A Biographical Dictionary.* Cambridge, MA: Harvard University Press, 1971. Kostman, Samuel. *20th Century Women of Achievement.* New York: Richards Rosen Press, Inc., 1976. Raven, Susan and Alison Weir. *Women of Achievement: Thirty-five Centuries of History.* New York: Harmony Books, 1981. Weatherford, Doris. *A History of the American Suffragist Movement.* Santa Barbara, CA: ABC CLIO, Inc., 1998.

16.15   First U.S. Women in Space

Sally K. Ride STS*-7 June 18-24, 1983 (b. May 26, 1951) was the first American woman in space.

Judith A. Resnik STS-41-D Aug 30-Sep+ 5, 1984 (b. Apr 5, 1949) was later killed in the STS-51-L *Challenger* disaster, Jan 28, 1986.

Kathryn D. Sullivan STS-41-G Oct 5-13, 1984 (b. Oct 3, 1951) was the first American woman to walk in space.

Anna L. Fisher STS-51-A Nov 8-16, 1984 (b. Aug 24, 1949) was the first American mother in space.

Margaret Rhea Seddon STS-51-D Apr 12-19, 1985 (b. Nov 8, 1947) flew again in STS-40 (June 5-14, 1991) and STS-58 (Oct 18-Nov 1, 1993).

Shannon W. Lucid STS-51-G June 17-24, 1985 (b. Jan 14, 1943) also flew in STS-34 (Oct 18-23, 1989), STS-43 (Aug 2-11, 1991), and STS-58 (Oct 18-Nov 1, 1993). From STS-76 she transferred to the Russian Mir space station, then returned to Earth with STS-79 (Mar 22- Sept 26, 1996).

Bonnie J. Dunbar STS-61-A Oct 30-Nov 6, 1985 (b. Mar 3, 1949) also flew in STS-32 (Jan 9-20, 1990), STS-50 (June 25-July 9, 1992), and STS-71 (June 27-July 7, 1995)

Mary I. Cleave STS-61-B Nov 26-Dec 3, 1985 (b. Feb 5, 1947) also flew in STS-30 (May 4-8, 1989).

Eileen M. Collins (b. 1957) was the first woman to command a shuttle mission, launched July 24, 1999.

S. Christa McAuliffe STS 51-L *Challenger*-Jan 28, 1986 (b. Sept 2, 1948), a New Hampshire school teacher, was chosen by NASA as the first American teacher in space. She was also the first American civilian in space. She and six astronauts were killed when *Challenger* exploded moments after liftoff.

*STS = SPACE TRANSPORTATION SYSTEM. In flight STS-41A, "4" refers to the last digit of the fiscal year the shuttle was to be launched; "1" refers to the launch site (Kennedy Space Center is 1; Vandenberg Air Force Base is 2); "A" denotes the first launch scheduled that year (B would be the second launch). Before STS-41B, flights were numbered in order as STS-1 through STS-9. STS-9 became STS-41A in the new numbering system. Sequential flight numbers were resumed in 1986 with Challenger STS-25, the 25th shuttle launch.

16.16   Chronology of the Women's Rights Movement, 1848-1999

© 2000 by The Center for Applied Research in Education

1848   The world's first women's rights convention is held in Seneca Falls, New York, on July 19 and 20. A Declaration of Sentiments and Resolutions is debated and ultimately signed by 68 women and 32 men, setting the agenda for the women's rights movement that followed.

1849   Amelia Jenks Bloomer publishes and edits *Lily,* the first prominent women's rights newspaper.

1850   The first national women's rights convention attracts over 1,000 participants to Worcester, Massachusetts, from as far away as California. Only lack of space kept hundreds from attending. Annual national conferences are held through 1860 (except 1857).

1851   Sojourner Truth gives her spontaneous "Ain't I a Woman?" speech at the women's rights convention in Akron, Ohio.

1855   Lucy Stone becomes first woman on record to keep her own name after marriage, setting a trend among women who are consequently known as "Lucy Stoners."

1855   The University of Iowa becomes the first state school to admit women. In 1858, the board of managers tries, but fails, to exclude women.

1859   American Medical Association announces its opposition to abortion. In 1860, Connecticut is the first state to enact laws prohibiting all abortions, both before and after quickening.

1862   Mary Jane Patterson is the first African American woman to receive a full baccalaureate degree, from Oberlin College. Three European American women had been graduated in 1841 from Oberlin College: Mary Hosford, Elizabeth Smith Prall, and Caroline Mary Rudd.

1862   Congress passed the Morrill Act, which established land grant colleges in rural areas. Through them, millions of women earn low-cost degrees.

1866   14th Amendment is passed by Congress (ratified by the states in 1868), the first time "citizens" and "voters" are defined as "male" in the Constitution.

1866   The American Equal Rights Association is founded, the first organization in the U.S. to advocate national women's suffrage.

1868   The National Labor Union supports equal pay for equal work.

1868   Elizabeth Cady Stanton and Susan Anthony begin publishing *The Revolution,* an important women's movement periodical.

1869   The first woman suffrage law in the U.S. passed in the territory of Wyoming.

1869   In disagreement over the 15th Amendment, Anthony and Stanton withdraw from the Equal Rights Association to found the National Woman Suffrage Association. Its wide-ranging goals include achieving a federal amendment for the women's vote.

1869   The American Woman Suffrage Association is formed to secure the vote through each state constitution.

1870   In March, for the first time in the history of jurisprudence, women serve on juries in the Wyoming Territory.

1870   The 15th Amendment receives final ratification. By its text, women are not specifically excluded from the vote. During the next two years, approximately 150 women will attempt to vote in almost a dozen different jurisdictions.

1872   Through the efforts of lawyer Belva Lockwood, Congress passes a law to give women federal employees equal pay for equal work.

1872   November 5: Susan B. Anthony and fourteen women register and vote in the presidential election to test whether the recently adopted Fourteenth Amendment can be interpreted as protecting women's rights. Anthony is arrested, tried, found guilty, and fined $10, which she refuses to pay.

1873   The Association for the Advancement of Women is formed to promote both higher education and professional possibilities for women.

1873 *Bradwell v. Illinois:* Supreme Court affirms that states can restrict women from the practice of any profession to preserve family harmony and uphold the law of the Creator.

1873 Congress passes the Comstock Law, defining contraceptive information as "obscene material." As postal inspector, moralist Anthony Comstock seizes mail and shuts down newspapers carrying such information.

1874 The Woman's Christian Temperance Union is founded by Annie Wittenmyer. The WCTU later becomes an important force for woman suffrage.

1875 Through her will, Sophia Smith is the first woman to found and endow a women's college. Smith College was chartered in 1871, opened in 1875.

1875 *Minor v. Happersett:* Supreme Court refuses to extend the 14th amendment protection to women's rights, denying voting rights to women.

1877 Helen Magill is the first woman to receive a Ph.D. at a U.S. school, a doctorate in Greek from Boston University.

1878 The Susan B. Anthony Amendment, to grant women the vote, is first introduced in the U.S. Congress.

1884 Belva Lockwood, presidential candidate of the National Equal Rights Party, is the first woman to receive votes in a presidential election (approximately 4,000 in six states).

1887 For the first and only time in this century, the U.S. Senate votes on woman suffrage. It loses, 34 to 16. Twenty-five Senators do not bother to participate.

1889 The work of educated women serving the Chicago poor at Hull House establishes social work as a paid profession for women.

1890 National Woman Suffrage Association and American Woman Suffrage Association merge to form the National American Woman Suffrage Association (NAWSA), becoming the movement's mainstream organization.

1893 Colorado is the first state to adopt a state amendment enfranchising women.

1896 The National Association of Colored Women, founded by Margaret Murray Washington, unites Black women's organizations, with Mary Church Terrell its first president. The NACW becomes a major vehicle for attempted reform during the next forty years.

1903 Middle-class reformers and women labor organizers join forces to form the national Women's Trade Unions League (WTUL), to bring public attention to the concerns of women workers.

1908 *Muller v. Oregon*: U.S. Supreme Court declares unconstitutional protective legislation for women workers.

1910 In Washington State, women win the vote.

1910 The first large suffrage parade in New York City is organized by the Women's Political Union.

1912 Juliette Gordon Low founds first American group of Girl Guides, in Atlanta, Georgia. Later renamed the Girl Scouts of the U.S.A., the organization brings girls into the outdoors, encourages their self-reliance and resourcefulness, and prepares them for varied roles as adult women.

1914 Margaret Sanger calls for legalization of contraceptives in her new, feminist publication, the *Woman Rebel,* which the Post Office bans from the mails.

1915 40,000 march in New York City suffrage parade, the largest parade ever held in that city.

1917 During World War I, women move into many jobs working in heavy industry in mining, chemical manufacturing, automobile and railway plants. They also run street cars, conduct trains, direct traffic, and deliver mail.

1917 Jeannette Rankin of Montana becomes the first woman elected to the U.S. Congress.

1919 The House of Representatives passes the woman suffrage amendment, 304 to 89; the Senate passes it with just two votes to spare.

1920 The Women's Bureau of the Department of Labor is formed to advocate for and keep statistics on women in the workforce.

1920 On August 26, the 19th Amendment to the Constitution is ratified, guaranteeing American women citizens the right to vote. It is quietly signed into law in a ceremony to which the press and suffragists were not invited.

1920 Suffrage passed, Carrie Chapman Catt founds the League of Women Voters to educate the newly enfranchised voters about the issues.

© 2000 by The Center for Applied Research in Education

1921   The American Association of University Women is formed.

1921   Margaret Sanger organizes the American Birth Control League, which evolves into the Federation of Planned Parenthood in 1942.

1923   Alice Paul and the National Woman's Party succeed in having a constitutional amendment introduced in Congress which said: "Men and women shall have equal rights throughout the United States and every place subject to its jurisdiction." In 1943 the wording was revised to what we know today as the Equal Rights Amendment.

1924   Nellie Tayloe Ross of Wyoming becomes the first woman elected governor of a state.

1926   Bertha Knight Landes is the first woman elected mayor of a sizable U.S. city (Seattle).

1932   Hattie Wyatt Caraway is the first woman elected to U.S. Senate. She represents Arkansas for three terms.

1933   Frances Perkins, the first woman in a Presidential Cabinet, serves as Secretary of Labor during the entire Roosevelt presidency.

1935   Margaret Mead's *Sex and Temperament in Three Primitive Societies* challenges sex-role assumptions.

1935   Mary McLeod Bethune organizes the National Council of Negro Women as a lobbying coalition of black women's groups, and serves as president until 1949. The NCNW becomes foremost at fighting job discrimination, racism, and sexism.

1940   One-fifth of white women and one-third of black women are wage earners; 60% of the black women are still domestics, compared with 10% of white women.

1941   A massive government and industry media campaign persuades women to take jobs during the war. Almost 7 million women respond, 2 million as industrial "Rosie the Riveters" and 400,000 joining the military.

1945   The Equal Pay for Equal Work bill is again introduced into Congress (see 1872). It passes in 1963.

1945   Women industrial workers begin to lose their jobs in large numbers to returning service men, although surveys show 80% want to continue working.

1948   Margaret Chase Smith (R-ME) becomes first woman elected to the U.S. Senate in her own right. In 1964, she becomes the first woman to run for the U.S. Presidency in the primaries of a major political party (Republican). She serves in the Senate until 1973.

1950   30% of all women are in the paid labor force—more than half of all single women and more than a quarter of married women.

1955   Women earn an average of 63 cents for every dollar earned by men.

1957   The number of women and men voting is approximately equal for the first time.

1960   The Food and Drug Administration approves birth control pills.

1960   Women now earn only 60 cents for every dollar earned by men, a decline since 1955. Women of color earn only 42 cents.

1963   The Equal Pay Act, proposed twenty years earlier, establishes equal pay for men and women performing the same job duties. It does not cover domestics, agricultural workers, executives, administrators or professionals.

1963   Betty Friedan's best-seller, *The Feminine Mystique,* detailed the "problem that has no name." Five million copies are sold by 1970, laying the groundwork for the modern feminist movement.

1964   Title VII of the Civil Rights Act bars employment discrimination by private employers, employment agencies, and unions based on race, sex, and other grounds. To investigate complaints and enforce penalties, it establishes the Equal Employment Opportunity Commission (EEOC), which receives 50,000 complaints of gender discrimination in its first five years.

1964   Patsy Mink (D-HI) is the first Asian American woman elected to the U.S. Congress.

1965   In *Griswold v Connecticut,* the Supreme Court overturns one of the last state laws prohibiting the prescription or use of contraceptives by married couples.

1965   Lyndon Johnson's Executive Order 11246 takes the 1964 Civil Rights Act a step further, requiring federal agencies and federal contractors to take "affirmative action" in overcoming employment discrimination.

1966   In response to EEOC inaction on employment discrimination complaints, twenty-eight women found the National Organization for Women (called NOW) to function as a civil rights organization for women.

1967   Chicago Women's Liberation Group organizes, considered the first to use the term "liberation."

1967   New York Radical Women is founded. The following year the group begins a process of sharing life stories, which becomes known as "consciousness raising." Groups immediately take root coast to coast.

1967   California becomes the first state to re-legalize abortion.

1968   EEOC rules that unless employers can show a bona fide occupational qualification exists, sex-segregated help-wanted newspaper ads are illegal.

1968   Shirley Chisholm (D-NY) is first black woman elected to the U.S. Congress.

1969   The Boston Women's Health Book Collective publishes the self-help manual *Our Bodies, Ourselves: A Book by and for Women,* incorporating medical information with personal experiences. Nearly 4 million copies sold as of 1997.

1969   California adopts the nation's first "no-fault" divorce law, allowing couples to divorce by mutual consent. Other states follow rapidly.

1970   *Sexual Politics,* by Kate Millett, is published.

1970   San Diego State College in California establishes the first official, integrated women's studies program.

1970   Women's wages fall to 59 cents for every dollar earned by men. Although nonwhite women earn even less, the gap is closing between white women and women of color.

1970   The Equal Rights Amendment is reintroduced into Congress.

1971   *Ms.* magazine first appears as an insert in *New York* magazine. Gloria Steinem, *Ms.* co-founder and editor, becomes a leading journalist.

1972   Title IX of the Education Amendments requires that "No person in the United States shall, on the basis of sex, be excluded from participation in, be denied the benefits of, or be subjected to discrimination under any education program or activity receiving federal financial assistance."

1972   Congress extends the Equal Pay Act to include executives, administrative and professional personnel.

1972   Congress passes the Equal Employment Opportunity Act, giving the EEOC power to take legal action to enforce its rulings.

1972   After languishing since 1923, the ERA is passed by Congress on March 22 and sent to the states for ratification. Hawaii approves it within the hour. By the end of the week, so have Delaware, Nebraska, New Hampshire, Idaho and Iowa.

1972   Barbara Jordan (D-TX) becomes first Black woman elected to Congress from a Southern state.

1973   Billie Jean King scores an enormous victory for female athletes when she beats Bobby Riggs in "The Battle of the Sexes," a televised tennis tournament watched by nearly 48,000,000 people.

1973   9to5: National Association of Working Women, is founded by Karen Nussbaum in Boston. Nussbaum later becomes Director of the Women's Bureau, U.S. Department of Labor.

1973   The Civil Service Commission eliminates height and weight requirements that have discriminated against women applying for police, park service, and firefighting jobs.

1973   The U.S. military is integrated when the women-only branches are eliminated.

1973   In *Roe v. Wade,* the Supreme Court establishes a woman's right to an abortion, effectively canceling the anti-abortion laws of 46 states.

1974   Little League agrees to include girls "in deference to a change in social climate," but creates a softball branch specifically for girls to draw them from baseball.

1974   The Coalition for Labor Union Women is founded, uniting blue-collar women across occupational lines.

1974   The number of women in public office begins to rise. Women now hold 8% of state legislative seats and 16 seats in Congress. By 1986: 14.8% of legislative seats, and 24 seats in Congress. In 1997: 21% of legislative seats, 62 seats in Congress.

1976   Dr. Benjamin Spock eliminates sex bias in his revised *Baby and Child Care.*

1976   The United Nations' "Decade for Women" begins.

1976   U.S. military academies open admissions to women.

1976   In a groundbreaking law, marital rape becomes a crime in Nebraska.

1977   Between 1969 and 1977, the Supreme Court issues full opinions on 21 women's rights cases.

1978   100,000 march in support of the Equal Rights Amendment in Washington, D.C..

1978   For the first time in history, more women than men enter college.

1978   The Pregnancy Discrimination Act amends the 1964 Civil Rights Act to ban employment discrimination against pregnant women.

1978   The first national feminist conference on pornography is held in San Francisco, with a large "Take Back the Night" march. Soon thousands of women across the country stage similar marches.

1980   New EEOC guidelines list sexual harassment as a form of prohibited sexual discrimination.

1980   The "gender gap" first shows up at the election polls as women report different political priorities from men.

1981   Sandra Day O'Connor is the first woman ever appointed to the U.S. Supreme Court. In 1993, she is joined by Ruth Bader Ginsberg.

1982   Ratification efforts for an Equal Rights Amendment fail despite a solid majority of the public—63%—supporting it. It is promptly reintroduced into Congress.

1982   Over 900 women hold positions as state legislators, compared with 344 a decade earlier.

1984   Sex discrimination in the admission policies of organizations such as the Jaycees is forbidden by the Supreme Court in *Roberts v. United States Jaycees,* opening many previously all-male organizations to women.

1984   Geraldine Ferraro is the first woman vice presidential candidate of a major political party (Democratic Party).

1984   The non-partisan National Political Congress of Black Women is founded by Shirley Chisholm to address women's rights issues and encourage participation in the electoral process at every level.

1985   Tracey Thurman of Connecticut is first woman to win a civil suit as a battered wife.

1985   Wilma Mankiller becomes first woman installed as principal chief of a major Native American tribe, the Cherokee in Oklahoma.

1986   The Supreme Court declares sexual harassment is a form of illegal job discrimination.

1986   The *New York Times* is the last among major dailies to allow use of "Ms." as a title.

1986   About 25% of scientists are now women, but they are still less likely than men to be full professors or on a tenure track in teaching. Only 3.5% of the National Academy of Sciences members are women (51 members); since the academy's 1863 founding, only 60 women have been elected.

1989   300,000 marchers demonstrate for women's reproductive rights in Washington, D.C.

1990s Women in their twenties, calling themselves "the third wave," form myriad on- and off-campus organizations to tackle their generation's particular concerns and vulnerabilities.

1992   Women are now paid 71 cents for every dollar paid to men. The range is from 64 cents for working-class women to 77 cents for professional women with doctorates. Black women earned 65 cents, Latinas 54 cents.

1992   "The Year of the Woman." A record number of women run for public office, and win. Twenty-four are newly elected to the House of Representatives.

1993   The Family Medical Leave Act finally goes into effect. Vetoed by President Bush, it is the first bill signed by President Clinton.

1993   Women hold a record number of positions in state as well as federal government: 20.4% of state legislators; 3 governors; 11 lieutenant governors; 8 attorneys general; 13 secretaries of state; 19 state treasurers; 6 women in the Senate; and 48 in the House of Representatives.

1996   *United States v. Virginia* affirms that the male-only admissions policy of the state-supported Virginia Military Institute violates the Fourteenth Amendment.

1997   Elaborating on Title IX, the Supreme Court rules that college athletics programs must actively involve roughly equal numbers of men and women to qualify for federal support.

Source: National Women's History Project.

16.17   Seneca Falls Resolutions, 1848

Resolutions passed at the Women's Rights Convention held at Seneca Falls, N.Y., July 19th and 20th, 1848:

Whereas, the great precept of nature is conceded to be; "that man shall pursue his own true and substantial happiness." Blackstone, in his Commentaries, remarks, that this law of Nature being coeval with mankind, and dictated by God himself, is of course superior in obligation to any other. It is binding over all the globe, in all countries, and at all times; no human laws are of any validity if contrary to this, and such of them as are valid, derive all their force, and all their validity, and all their authority, mediately and immediately, from this original; Therefore,

Resolved, That such laws as conflict, in any way, with the true and substantial happiness of woman, are contrary to the great precept of nature, and of no validity; for this is "superior in obligation to any other."

Resolved, That all laws which prevent woman from occupying such a station in society as her conscience shall dictate, or which place her in a position inferior to that of man, are contrary to the great precept of nature, and therefore of no force or authority.

Resolved, That woman is man's equal—was intended to be so by the Creator, and the highest good of the race demands that she should be recognized as such.

Resolved, That the women of this country ought to be enlightened in regard to the laws under which they live, that they may no longer publish their degradation, by declaring themselves satisfied with their present position, not their ignorance, by asserting that they have all the rights they want.

Resolved, That inasmuch as man, while claiming for himself intellectual superiority, does accord to woman moral superiority, it is pre-eminently his duty to encourage her to speak, and teach as she has an opportunity, in all religious assemblies.

Resolved, That the same amount of virtue, delicacy, and refinement of behavior, that is required of woman in the social state, should also be required of man, and the same transgressions should be visited with equal severity on both man and woman.

Resolved, That the objection of indelicacy and impropriety, which is so often brought against woman when she addresses a public audience, comes with a very ill grace from those who encourage, by their attendance, her appearance on the stage, in the concert, or in the feats of the circus.

Resolved, That woman has too long rested satisfied in the circumscribed limits which corrupt customs and a perverted application of the Scriptures have marked out for her, and that it is time she should move in the enlarged sphere which her great Creator has assigned her.

Resolved, That it is the duty of the women of this country to secure to themselves their sacred right to the elective franchise.

Resolved, That the equality of human rights results necessarily from the fact of the identity of the race in capabilities and responsibilities.

Resolved, Therefore, That, being invested by the Creator with the same capabilities, and the same consciousness of responsibility for their exercise, it is demonstrably the right and duty of woman, equally with man, to promote every righteous cause, by every righteous means; and especially in regard to the great subjects of morals and religion, it is self-evidently her right to participate with her brother in teaching them, both in private and in public, by writing and by speaking, by any instrumentalities proper to be used, and in any assemblies proper to be held; and this being a self-evident truth, growing out of the divinely implanted principles of human nature, and custom or authority adverse to it, whether modern or wearing the hoary sanction of antiquity, is to be regarded as self-evident falsehood, and at war with the interests of mankind.

16.18   Declaration of Sentiments, 1848

Deliberately modeled on the U.S. Declaration of Independence, this Declaration of Sentiments was written and adopted at the first Women's Rights Convention in U.S., held in Seneca Falls, New York, July 19-20, 1848.

When, in the course of human events, it becomes necessary for one portion of the family of man to assume among the people of the earth a position different from that which they have hitherto occupied, but one to which the laws of nature and of nature's God entitle them, a decent respect to the opinions of mankind requires that they should declare the causes that impel them to such a course.

We hold these truths to be self-evident; that all men and women are created equal; that they are endowed by their Creator with certain inalienable rights; that among these are life, liberty, and the pursuit of happiness; that to secure these rights governments are instituted, deriving their just powers from the consent of the governed. Whenever any form of Government becomes destructive of these ends, it is the right of those who suffer from it to refuse allegiance to it, and to insist upon the institution of a new government, laying its foundation on such principles, and organizing its powers in such form as to them shall seem most likely to effect their safety and happiness. Prudence, indeed, will dictate that governments long established should not be changed for light and transient causes; and accordingly, all experience hath shown that mankind are more disposed to suffer, while evils are sufferable, than to right themselves, by abolishing the forms to which they are accustomed. But when a long train of abuses and usurpations, pursuing invariably the same object, evinces a design to reduce them under absolute despotism, it is their duty to throw off such government, and to provide new guards for their future security. Such has been the patient sufferance of the women under this government, and such is now the necessity which constrains them to demand the equal station to which they are entitled.

The history of mankind is a history of repeated injuries and usurpations on the part of man toward woman, having in direct object the establishment of an absolute tyranny over her. To prove this, let facts be submitted to a candid world.

He has never permitted her to exercise her inalienable right to the elective franchise.

He has compelled her to submit to laws, in the formation of which she had no voice.

He has withheld from her rights which are given to the most ignorant and degraded men—both natives and foreigners.

Having deprived her of this first right of a citizen, the elective franchise, thereby leaving her without representation in the halls of legislation, he has oppressed her on all sides.

He has made her, if married, in the eye of the law, civilly dead.

He has taken from her all right in property, even to the wages she earns.

He has made her, morally, an irresponsible being, as she can commit many crimes, with impunity, provided they be done in the presence of her husband. In the covenant of marriage, she is compelled to promise obedience to her husband, he becoming, to all intents and purposes, her master—the law giving him power to deprive her of her liberty, and to administer chastisement.

He has so framed the laws of divorce, as to what shall be the proper causes of divorce; in case of separation, to whom the guardianship of the children shall be given, as to be wholly regardless of the happiness of women—the law, in all cases, going upon the false supposition of the supremacy of man, and giving all power into his hands.

After depriving her of all rights as a married woman, if single and the owner of property, he has taxed her to support a government which recognizes her only when her property can be made profitable to it.

He has monopolized nearly all the profitable employments, and from those she is permitted to follow, she receives but a scanty remuneration.

He closes against her all the avenues to wealth and distinction, which he considers most honorable to himself. As a teacher of theology, medicine, or law, she is not known.

He has denied her the facilities for obtaining a thorough education—all colleges being closed against her.

He allows her in Church as well as State, but a subordinate position, claiming Apostolic authority for her exclusion from the ministry, and with some exceptions, from any public participation in the affairs of the Church.

He has created a false public sentiment, by giving to the world a different code of morals for men and women, by which moral delinquencies which exclude women from society, are not only tolerated but deemed of little account in man.

He has usurped the prerogative of Jehovah himself, claiming it as his right to assign for her a sphere of action, when that belongs to her conscience and her God.

He has endeavored, in every way that he could to destroy her confidence in her own powers, to lessen her self-respect, and to make her willing to lead a dependent and abject life.

Now, in view of this entire disfranchisement of one-half the people of this country, their social and religious degradation, in view of the unjust laws above mentioned, and because women do feel themselves aggrieved, oppressed, and fraudulently deprived of their most sacred rights, we insist that they have immediate admission to all the rights and privileges which belong to them as citizens of these United States.

In entering upon the great work before us, we anticipate no small amount of misconception, misrepresentation, and ridicule; but we shall use every instrumentality within our power to effect our object. We shall employ agents, circulate tracts, petition the State and national Legislatures, and endeavor to enlist the pulpit and the press in our behalf. We hope this Convention will be followed by a series of Conventions, embracing every part of the country.

Firmly relying upon the final triumph of the Right and the True, we do this day affix our signatures to this declaration.

Lucretia Mott	Cynthia Davis	Rhoda Palmer
Harriet Cady Eaton	Hannah Plant	Margaret Jenkins
Margaret Pryor	Lucy Jones	Cynthia Fuller
Elizabeth Cady Stanton	Sarah Whitney	Mary Martin
Eunice Newton Foote	Mary H. Hallowell	P. A. Culvert
Mary Ann McClintock	Elizabeth Conklin	Susan R. Doty
Margaret Schooley	Sally Pitcher	Rebecca Race
Martha C. Wright	Mary Conklin	Sarah A. Mosher
Jane C. Hunt	Susan Quinn	Mary E. Vail
Amy Post	Mary S. Mirror	Lucy Spalding
Catharine F. Stebbins	Phebe King	Lavinia Latham
Mary Ann Frink	Julia Ann Drake	Sarah Smith
Lydia Mount	Charlotte Woodward	Eliza Martin
Delia Mathews	Martha Underhill	Maria E. Wilbur
Catharine C. Paine	Dorothy Mathews	Elizabeth D. Smith
Elizabeth W. McClintock	Eunice Barker	Caroline Barker
Malvina Seymour	Sarah R. Woods	Ann Porter
Phebe Mosher	Lydia Gild	Experience Gibbs
Catharine Shaw	Sarah Hoffman	Antoinette E. Segur
Deborah Scott	Elizabeth Leslie	Hannah J. Latham
Sarah Hallowell	Martha Ridley	Sarah Sisson
Mary Gilbert	Rachel D. Bonnel	
Sophrone Taylor	Betsey Tewksbury	

The following are the names of the gentlemen present in favor of the movement:

Richard P. Hunt
Samuel D. Tillman
Justin Williams
Elisha Foote
Frederick Douglass
Henry Seymour
Henry W. Seymour
David Spalding
William G. Barker
Elias J. Doty
John Jones
William S. Dell
James Mott
William Burroughs
Robert Smallbridge
Jacob Mathews

Charles L. Hoskins
Thomas McClintock
Saron Phillips
Jacob P. Chamberlain
Jonathan Metcalf
Nathan J. Milliken
S. E. Woodworth
Edward F. Underhill
George W. Pryor
Joel D. Bunker
Isaac Van Tassel
Thomas Dell
E. W. Capron
Stephen Shear
Henry Hatley
Azaliah Schooley

16.19   Chronology of the Life of Susan B. Anthony

1820   Susan Brownell Anthony born on February 15 in Adams, Mass., the second of seven children.

1845   The Anthony family moves to Rochester, N.Y., on the Erie Canal. Their house becomes a meeting-place for anti-slavery activists, including Frederick Douglass.

1846   Susan B. Anthony begins teaching at Canajoharie Academy for a yearly salary of $110.

1851   Anthony travels to Syracuse anti-slavery convention. She visits Amelia Bloomer, hears William Lloyd Garrison and George Thompson, and meets Elizabeth Cady Stanton.

1852   Anthony attends her first women's rights convention.

1854   Anthony circulates petitions for married women's property rights and woman suffrage. She is refused permission to speak at the Capitol and Smithsonian in Washington. She begins her New York State campaign for woman suffrage in Mayville, Chatauqua County, speaking and traveling alone.

1856   Anthony becomes agent for the American Anti-Slavery Society.

1861   Anthony conducts anti-slavery campaign from Buffalo to Albany—"No Union with Slaveholders. No Compromise."

1863   Anthony and Elizabeth Stanton write the "Appeal to the Women of the Republic."

1868   Anthony begins publication of *The Revolution.*

1869   Anthony calls the first Woman Suffrage Convention in Washington D.C.

1872   Anthony is arrested for voting and is indicted in Albany. She continues to lecture and attend conventions.

1873   Anthony is tried and fined $100 with costs after the judge ordered the jury to find her guilty. Anthony refuses to pay but is not imprisoned so cannot appeal the verdict.

1881   Anthony, Stanton, and Matilda Joslin Gage publish Volume I of *History of Woman Suffrage,* followed by Volumes II, III and IV in 1882, 1885 and 1902.

1898   *The Life and Work of Susan B. Anthony, A Story of the Evolution of the Status of Women* is published. Anthony establishes a press bureau to feed articles on woman suffrage to the national and local press.

1905   Anthony meets with President Theodore Roosevelt in Washington, D.C., about submitting a suffrage amendment to Congress.

1906   Anthony attends suffrage hearings in Washington, D.C. She gives her "Failure is Impossible" speech at her 86th birthday celebration. Anthony dies at her Madison Street home on March 13.

1920   The 19th Amendment to the U.S. Constitution, also known as the Susan B. Anthony Amendment, grants the right to vote to all U.S. women over 21.

16.20   Books on the U.S. Suffrage Movement

Alberti, Johanna. *Beyond Freedom: Feminists in War and Peace.* (NY: St. Martin's Press, 1989).

Anthony, Katharine. *Susan B. Anthony: Her Personal History and Her Era.* (NY: Doubleday, 1954).

Bacon, Margaret Hope. *Valiant Friend: The Life of Lucretia Mott.* (NY: Walker, 1980).

Barry, Kathleen. *Susan B. Anthony: A Biography of a Singular Feminist.* (NY: New York University Press, 1988).

Beeton, Beverly. *Women Vote in the West: The Woman Suffrage Movement, 1869-1896.* (NY: Garland, 1986).

Benjamin, Anne M. *A History of the Anti-Suffrage Movement in the United States from 1895 to 1920: Women Against Equality.* (Lewiston, NY: Edwin Mellen Press, 1991).

Blatch, Harriet Stanton. *Challenging Years: The Memoirs of Harriet Stanton Blatch.* (NY: Putnam, 1940).

Buechler, Steven M. *The Transformation of the Woman Suffrage Movement: The Case of Illinois, 1850-1920.* (New Brunswick, NJ: Rutgers University Press, 1986).

Buechler, Steven. *Women's Movements in the United States: Woman Suffrage, Equal Rights, and Beyond.* (New Brunswick, NJ: Rutgers University Press, 1990).

Catt, Carrie Chapman and Nettie Rogers Shuler. *Woman Suffrage and Politics: The Inner Story of the Suffrage Movement.* (NY: Scribner, 1923).

Daley, Caroline and Melanie Nolan. *Suffrage and Beyond: International Feminist Perspectives.* (NY: New York University Press, 1994).

DuBois, Ellen Carol. *Elizabeth Cady Stanton/Susan B. Anthony: Correspondence, Writings, Speeches.* (Boston: Northeastern University Press, 1992). Revised edition.

DuBois, Ellen Carol. *Feminism and Suffrage: The Emergence of an Independent Women's Movement in America, 1848-1869.* (Ithaca, NY: Cornell University Press, 1978).

Flexner, Eleanor. *Century of Struggle: The Women's Rights Movement in the United States.* (Cambridge, MA: Harvard University Press, 1975).

Frost, Elizabeth and Kathryn Cullen-DuPont. *Women's Suffrage in America: An Eyewitness History.* (NY: Facts on File, 1992).

Griffith, Elisabeth. *In Her Own Right: The Life of Elizabeth Cady Stanton.* (NY: Oxford University Press, 1984).

Harper, Ida Husted. *The Life and Work of Susan B. Anthony.* (Indianapolis: Bowen-Merrill, 1899, 1908). 3 volumes.

Hays, Elinor. *Morning Star: A Biography of Lucy Stone, 1818-1893.* (NY: Harcourt, Brace and World, 1961).

Kraditor, Aileen. *Ideas of the Woman Suffrage Movement, 1890-1920.* (NY: Columbia University Press, 1965).

Lunardini, Christine A. *From Equal Suffrage to Equal Rights: Alice Paul and the National Woman's Party, 1910-1928.* (NY: New York University Press, 1986).

Lutz, Alma. *Susan B. Anthony: Rebel, Crusader, Humanitarian.* (Boston: Beacon, 1959).

Melder, Keith E. *Beginnings of Sisterhood: The American Woman's Rights Movement 1800-1850.* (NY: Schocken, 1977).

Morgan, David. *Suffragists and Democrats: The Politics of Woman Suffrage in America.* (East Lansing, MI: Michigan State University Press, 1972).

Sherr, Lynn. *Failure is Impossible: Susan B. Anthony in Her Own Words.* (New York: Times Books, 1995).

Solomon, Martha M., editor. *A Voice of Their Own: The Woman Suffrage Press, 1840-1910.* (Tuscaloosa, AL: University of Alabama Press, 1991).

Stanton, Elizabeth Cady, Susan B. Anthony, and Matilda Joslyn Gage. *History of Woman Suffrage.* Volumes 1-3 (Rochester: 1887); Volume 4 by Susan B. Anthony and Ida Husted Harper (Rochester: 1902); Volumes 4-5 by Ida Husted Harper (NY: 1922).

Stanton, Elizabeth Cady. *Eighty Years And More: Reminiscences 1815-1897.* (NY: Schocken Books, 1971). First published in 1898.

Van Voris, Jacqueline. *Carrie Chapman Catt: A Public Life.* (NY: Feminist Press, 1987).

Waggenspack, Beth M. *The Search for Self-Sovereignty: The Oratory of Elizabeth Cady Stanton.* (NY: Greenwood Press, 1989).

Ware, Susan. *Beyond Suffrage: Women in the New Deal.* (Cambridge, MA.: Harvard University Press, 1981).

Wheeler, Marjorie Spruill. *New Women of the New South: The Leaders of the Woman Suffrage Movement in the Southern States.* (NY: Oxford University Press, 1993).

16.21   Major Events in American Religious Life

1620   Puritan Separatists, later called Pilgrim Fathers, arrive in North America on the ship *Mayflower.*

1633   Puritan clergyman John Cotton begins to preach in Boston, Massachusetts.

1634   Maryland founded as a Catholic colony with religious tolerance.

1636   Puritan Roger Williams banished from Massachusetts and founds Providence Plantation Colony (Rhode Island) as a pure democracy with religious freedom.

1639   Roger Williams establishes first Baptist Church in North America.

1646   John Cotton produces *Spiritual Milk for Babes.*

1648   First documented witch trial in North America: Margaret Jones hanged at Plymouth, Massachusetts.

1654   First Jews arrive in New Amsterdam (later New York).

1661-1663 John Eliot translates Bible into Algonquian language to gain converts among the Pequot people; first Bible printed in America.

1678   John Bunyan publishes *The Pilgrim's Progress.*

1689   Witch mania in Salem, Massachusetts: of around 150 accused from 1689-93, 19 are hanged and four die in jail. Cotton Mather, American clergyman, encourages witch-hunters.

1702   Cotton Mather produces Magnalia Christi Americana, an ecclesiastical history of New England.

1727   American Philosophical Society founded in Philadelphia.

1732   Seventh Day Baptists (Ephrata Community) established at Germantown, Pennsylvania.

1733   Corporation for the Propagation of the Gospel in New England founded.

1734   Moravian Brethren establish Moravian Church in North America and begin missionary activity, especially among American Indians and Inuits.

1736   Massachusetts makes accusation of witchcraft a criminal offense.

1737   John Wesley's *Psalms and Hymns* is published in Charleston, South Carolina.

1738   George Whitefield, English methodist evangelist, follows John Wesley to Georgia in North America, to take part in the "Great Awakening," a religious revival.

1741   American theologian, Jonathan Edwards publishes *Sinners in the Hands of an Angry God,* the text of a sermon delivered at Enfield, Massachusetts, during the Great Awakening.

1761   American Quakers bar slave traders from their society.

1800   Church of United Brethren in Christ is founded in the U.S.

1807   The American Evangelical Association holds its first convention.

1816   American Bible Society established.

1819   Unitarianism is founded by Boston Congregationalist pastor William Channing.

1824   American Sunday School union formed.

1827   U.S. evangelist Alexander Campbell founds Disciples of Christ evangelical group.

1830   Joseph Smith, American religious leader, founds the Church of Jesus Christ of Latter-Day Saints (Mormons).

1831	William Miller begins Adventist preachings in the U.S.
1832	Church of Christ (Disciples) organized in the United States.
1840	Mormons establish Nauvoo community in Hancock County, Illinois; some 20,000 Mormons in the area by 1843.
1843	William Miller, American founder of the Second Adventists, proclaims April 3 to be Doomsday; about 100,000 Millerites gather in New England.
1846-47	Brigham Young leads Mormons from Nauvoo, Illinois, to Utah, where Salt Lake City is founded.
1848	Modern Spiritualism begins in the U.S. and rapidly expands.
1857	"Mormon War" in Utah: troops sent to suppress Mormon polygamists.
1858	Father Isaac Thomas Hecker, U.S. priest, founds Missionary Priests of St. Paul (Paulist Fathers).
1863	Ellen Gould White, U.S. visionary, founds Seventh-Day Adventists.
1872	American Charles Taze Russell founds Jehovah's Witnesses.
1875	Theosophical Society founded in New York City by Helen Blavatsky and H.S. Olcott.
1879	Mary Baker Eddy founds the Church of Christ, Scientist in Boston.
1885	Mormons split into polygamous and monogamous sections.
1901	Pentacostal movement begins in Topeka, Kansas.
1918	Foundation of the Native American Church, combining Christian practices with ritual use of the hallucinatory peyote cactus.
1931	International Bible Students' Association changes its name to Jehovah's Witnesses.
1953	Church of Scientology founded in Los Angeles by L. Ron Hubbard. The church, describing itself as "the modern science of mental health," combines therapy with doctrines similar to those of Buddhism.
1954	Korean evangelist Sun Myung Moon founds the Unification Church, whose members come to be known as the Moonies.
1957	United Church of Christ established in the U.S.
1966	Swami Prabhupada (A.C. Bhaktivedants) founds the international Society for Krishna Consciousness (Hare Krishna) in the U.S.
1974	U.S. evangelist Jim Bakker founds the *Praise The Lord* television ministry.
1975	Four women are ordained to the Episcopal priesthood in the U.S.
1978	Mass suicide of members of the People's Temple Church, led by Jim Jones, at Jonestown, Guyana.
1979	American Jerry Falwell founds the Moral Majority movement with airtime on 300 U.S. television stations.
1993	Branch Davidian cult community is destroyed by federal authorities at Waco, Texas, with many deaths.
1999	Pope John Paul II visits U.S.

16.22 Fastest Growing Religious Affiliations in the U.S., 1970 and 1995

Affiliation	Members 1970	1995	% growth
Sikh	1,000	190,000	18,900.0
Hindu	100,000	910,000	810.0
Muslim	800,000	5,100,000	537.5
Buddhist	200,000	780,000	290.0
Baha'i	133,000	300,000	117.4
Evangelical Christians	50,688,000	72,363,000	42.8
Orthodox	4,387,000	5,631,000	28.4
Roman Catholic	48,391,000	55,259,000	14.2
Jews	6,700,000	5,602,000	−16.4
Anglican	3,234,000	2,350,000	−27.3

16.23 Christian Denominations in the U.S., 1998

Denomination	Members
Roman Catholic Church	61,207,914
Southern Baptist Convention	15,692,964
The United Methodist Church	8,495,378
National Baptist Convention, US, Inc.	8,200,000
Church of God in Christ	5,499,875
Evangelical Lutheran Church in America	5,180,910
Church of Jesus Christ of Latter-Day Saints	4,800,000
Presbyterian Church (US)	3,637,375
African Methodist Episcopal Church	3,500,000
National Baptist Convention of America	3,500,000

Source: National Council of the Churches of Christ.

16.24   Notable American Families, 1620-1999

Adams

Samuel (1722-1803)—Revolutionary leader. Signer of the Declaration of Independence. Member, Massachusetts legislature. Leader of the Boston Tea Party. Delegate to the First and Second Continental Congresses. Governor of Massachusetts

John (1735-1826)—Pamphleteer, lawyer, first American minister to England, member of the First and Second Continental Congresses and the Committee to Draft the Declaration of Independence. Considered the Father of the Navy. First United States Vice President and second President

Hannah (1755-1831)—Historian and author of *A Summary History of New England* and several books on religion

John Quincy (1767-1848)—Diplomat, foreign minister, legislator, Secretary of State, Massachusetts Congressman and Senator, sixth American President

Charles Francis (1807-1886)—U.S. Minister to Great Britain, member, Massachusetts legislature and U.S. Congress

Charles Francis Jr. (1835-1915)—Author, businessman, Massachusetts historian and president of the Union Pacific Railroad

Henry (1838-1918)—Pulitzer Prize–winning author, American historian and Harvard professor

Brooks (1848-1927)—Writer, law professor, historian and theoretician

Astor

John Jacob (1763-1848)—Leading New York City land speculator and American fur trader. His 1811 fur-trading post in Astoria, Oregon, was the first white settlement west of the Rockies

William Backhouse (1792-1875)—Capitalist and real estate speculator known as the Landlord of New York

John Jacob III (1822-1890)—Capitalist, real estate speculator and great library benefactor

William Waldorf (1848-1919)—U.S. Minister to Italy

John Jacob IV (1864-1912)—Real estate developer, author, inventor

Beecher

Lyman (1775-1863)—Outspoken Presbyterian clergyman, social reformer and president of the Lane Theological Seminary in Ohio

Catherine (1800-1878)—An anti-suffragist and early home economist, author of books promoting women's role as homemaker, advocate of educational opportunities for women and founder of the American Woman's Educational Association

Edward (1803-1895) Abolitionist, Congregational clergyman, President of Illinois College and founder of the *Congregationalist*

Harriet Stowe (1811-1896)—Abolitionist, novelist and author of *Uncle Tom's Cabin*

Henry Ward (1813-1887)—Congregational clergyman, orator, leading abolitionist

Charles (1815-1900)—Congregational clergyman, reformer, abolitionist, President of Illinois College

Thomas Kinnicut (1824-1900)—Congregational clergyman, pioneer in church social work

Frederick Perkins (1828-1899)—Author, editor, librarian of the San Francisco Public Library

Charlotte Perkins Gilman (1860-1935)—Novelist, short-story writer ("The Yellow Wallpaper"), women's rights advocate

Biddle

William (?-1712)—Member, New Jersey Governor's Council and General Assembly

Edward (1738-1779)—Lawyer, Speaker of the Pennsylvania Assembly, Member, First and Second Continental Congresses

Clement (1740-1814)—Distinguished Revolutionary soldier, businessman

Thomas (?-1857)—Founder, private investment bank

John (?-1826)—Founder, the Philadelphia Saving Fund Society
Owen (?-1779)—Astronomer, mathematician, clockmaker, importer
Charles (1745-1821)—Seafarer, Lieutenant Governor of Pennsylvania
Nicholas (1750-1778)—Distinguished naval officer
James (1783-1848)—Naval officer, diplomat
Nicholas (1786-1844)—Financier, author, poet, editor (of the journals of Lewis and Clark's expedition and the *Port Folio,* an early intellectual magazine), diplomat, president of the Bank of the United States and the youngest graduate of (now) Princeton University
John (1792-1859)—Mayor of Detroit, president of the Michigan Constitutional Convention
Anthony Jr. (1896-1961)—U. S. Ambassador to Poland and to Spain

Booth

Junius Brutus (1796-1852)—Foremost tragic actor of his day
Edwin Thomas (1833-1893)—Founder of Booth's Theatre and the Players Club, great Shakespearean interpreter and leading actor
John Wilkes (1838-1865)—Great Shakespearean actor and fanatical Southern sympathizer. Originally foiled in a March 1865 plot to abduct Abraham Lincoln, he assassinated the President the following month in Washington's Ford's Theater

Bradford

William (1663-1752)—Founder of Philadelphia's first printing press (1685), he printed the first New York paper currency (1709), the first printed American play, *Androboros* (1714), New York's first newspaper, *New-York Gazette* (1725) and the first history of New York (1727)
Andrew (1686-1742)—Pioneer printer and publisher. Publisher of *American Weekly Mercury,* Philadelphia's first and the country's third newspaper
William III (1722-1791)—"Patriot-printer of 1776," appointed printer to Congress in 1775. His publications include *Weekly Advertiser* and *American Magazine and Monthly Chronicle*
Thomas (1745-1838)—Printer and publisher, started Philadelphia's *Merchant Daily Advisor* in 1797
William (1755-1795)—Revolutionary soldier, jurist, United State Attorney General

Byrd

William I (1652-1704)—Tobacco planter, importer, fur trader, slave trader, land speculator. Member, House of Burgesses and the Council of State and auditor-general of Virginia
William II (1674-1744)—Tobacco magnate, author and collector of one of the largest libraries in colonial America. Member of the House of Burgesses and the Council of State
William III (1729-1777)—Commander of the 2nd Virginia Regiment in French and Indian War. Member of the House of Burgesses and the Council of State
Richard (1888-1957)—Naval officer, aviator and explorer, he helped create the Navy Bureau of Aeronautics, invented numerous aerial navigational aids, led several Arctic expeditions and flew the first flights over both the North (1926) and South (1929) Poles. An author, he wrote several accounts of his flights and expeditions

du Pont

Eleuthere Irenee (1771-1834)—Founder of a powder works on the Brandywine River near Wilmington, Delaware, in 1802, now the present day E.I.du Pont de Nemours & Company.
Samuel Francis (1803-1865)—Civil War rear Admiral and commander of the South Atlantic Blockading Squadron
Henry Algernon (1838-1926)—West Point–trained army officer, Republican U.S. Senator from Delaware and Chairman of the Senate Military Committee
Thomas Coleman (1863-1930)—Iron and coal industrialist, president of the expanding du Pont chemical company, Republican U.S. Senator from Delaware
Pierre Samuel (1870-1954)—Philanthropist, President and Chairman of DuPont & Company

Guggenheim

Meyer (1828-1905)—Industrialist who established the family's conglomerate of smelting companies and refineries

Daniel (1856-1930)—President of the American Smelting and Refining Company and overseer of the international expansion of the family's holdings and operations. Philanthropic ventures included establishing the School of Aeronautics at New York University and funding a foundation for the promotion of aeronautics

Solomon (1861-1949)—Industrialist and noted patron of modern art, founder of New York City's Guggenheim Museum

Simon (1867-1941)—President of the American Smelting and Refining Company, United States Senator from Colorado and founder of The Guggenheim Foundation

Harry (1890-1971)—Ambassador to Cuba and newspaper publisher

Peggy (1898-1980)—Leading modern art patron and proponent and gallery owner

Kennedy

Joseph (1888-1969)—Banker and entrepreneur, Chairman of the Securities and Exchange Commission and U.S. Ambassador to Great Britain

John Fitzgerald (1917-1963)—World War II navy commander, Pulitzer Prize–winning author (*Profiles in Courage*), Democratic Congressman and Senator from Massachusetts, and the 35th President of the United States, the youngest man and first Catholic ever elected

Eunice Shriver (b. 1921)—Founder of the Special Olympics

Robert Francis (1925-1968)—U.S. Attorney General, Democratic Senator from New York, presidential candidate

Edward Moore (b.1932)—Democratic Senator from Massachusetts

Kathleen Townsend (b.1951)—Lawyer, writer, political activist, lieutenant governor of Maryland

Joseph Patrick II (b.1952)—U.S. Congressman from Massachusetts

Robert Francis Jr. (b.1954)—Lawyer, author, and activist in conservation causes

Maria Shriver (b.1955)—Television correspondent

Caroline (b.1958)—Lawyer, author of books on constitutional issues

Kerry (b.1959)—Human rights activist

John Fitzgerald Jr. (1960-1999)—Lawyer, magazine publisher

Patrick Joseph (b.1967)—U.S. Congressman from Rhode Island

Lee

Richard (1610-1664)—Virginia tobacco planter, Attorney General, Secretary of State and member of Council

Thomas (1690-1750)—Acting Governor of the Virginia Colony, western real estate speculator

Richard Henry (1732-1794)—Revolutionary leader, signer of the Declaration of Independence, member of the Virginia legislature, president of the First Continental Congress, U.S. Senator from Virginia

Francis Lightfoot (1734-1797)—Signer of the Declaration of Independence, member of the Virginia House of Burgesses, delegate to the Continental Congress

Arthur (1740-1792)—Member of the Virginia House of Delegates and the Continental Congress, commissioner of the U.S. Treasury Board

Thomas Sim (1745-1819)—Delegate to the Continental Congress and second Governor of the state of Maryland

Henry ("Light-Horse Harry") (1756-1818)—Leading Calvary commander in the Revolutionary Army, member of the Continental Congress and Virginia House of Delegates, Congressman and Governor of Virginia

Robert Edward (1807-1870)—Noted soldier, Commander-in-Chief of the Confederate Army, Superintendent of West Point and President of (the now) Washington and Lee University

Fitzhugh (1835-1905)—Governor of Virginia, Consul General for Havana

Livingston
Robert (1654-1728)—Secretary of Indian Affairs for New York, Speaker of the New York Provincial Assembly
Peter (1710-1792)—Patriot and leading NYC merchant
Philip (1716-1778)—Signer of the Declaration of Independence, member of Continental Congress
Robert (1718-1775)—Member, New York Assembly, New York Supreme Court judge, delegate to the Stamp Act Congress
William (1723-1790)—Member of First and Second Continental Congresses, delegate to the Constitutional Convention, and the first Governor of New Jersey
Robert (1746-1813)—Member of the Continental Congress, the committee to draft the Declaration of Independence and the U.S. House of Representatives. Minister to France and the technical and financial advisor for the first commercially successful steamboat, Robert Fulton's *Clermont.* As the first Chancellor of New York, he administered the oath of office to President George Washington
Henry Brockholst (1757-1823)—United States Supreme Court Justice
Edward (1764-1836)—New York City Mayor, U.S. Congressman from New York and Louisiana, U.S. Senator from Louisiana, Secretary of State under Andrew Jackson and Minister to France
Robert (b. 1943)—U.S. Congressman (Republican) from Louisiana

Lodge
Henry Cabot (1850-1924)—Historian, editor, essayist, Republican Congressman and Senator from Massachusetts
George Cabot (1873-1909)—Poet and dramatist
Henry Cabot Jr. (1902-1985)—Senator from Massachusetts, U.S. Ambassador to the United Nations under President Eisenhower and Richard Nixon's vice-presidential running mate in the 1960 presidential election

Lowell
Robert Traill Spence (1816-1891)—Poet, novelist, teacher, Episcopal clergyman
James Russell (1819-1891)—Poet, critic, Harvard professor, first editor of the *Atlantic Monthly,* Ambassador to Spain and Great Britain
Percival (1855-1916)—Astronomer
Abbot Lawrence (1856-1943)—Educator, political economist, President of Harvard University
Amy (1874-1925)—Noted free verse imagist poet and critic
Robert (1917-1977)—Playwright, essayist, Pulitzer Prize–winning poet

Mather
Richard (1596-1669)—Leading Congregational clergyman and author of numerous books on religion, including *The Bay Psalm Book* (1640)
Increase (1639-1723)—Noted clergyman, author, political activist, pastor of Boston's North Church and President of Harvard College. His book *Cases of Conscience Concerning Evil Spirits* helped end the execution of suspected Salem witches
Cotton (1663-1728)—Pastor of North Church and a founder of Yale College. Noted scholar, educator and prolific author, he entered Harvard at age twelve, later organized a school for the education of blacks and was the first American elected a fellow of the Royal Society in London
Hannah Crocker (1752-1829)—Writer and patriot, she authored *Observations on the Real Rights of Women*
Mather Brown (1761-1831)—Portrait painter
Stephen (1867-1930)—A leading conservationist, he organized the Interior Department's National Park Service and was instrumental in determining the criteria for naming land to the national park system

Mellon
Thomas (1813-1908)—Judge, founder of Thomas Mellon and Sons, Bankers (later Mellon National Bank)
Andrew (1855-1937)—Financier and industrialist, Secretary of the Treasury under three presidents, Ambassador to Britain and philanthropist who created the National Gallery of Art in Washington, DC and founded Pittsburgh's Mellon Institute

Paul (1907-1999)—Philanthropist, notably for artistic, literary and environmental causes, he created the Yale Center for British Art, established the Bollingen Prize for American poetry, and further endowed and guided the National Gallery

Peale
Charles Willson (1741-1827)—Artist especially known for his portraits and natural history scenes, he founded art and natural history museums and the first American art academy
James (1749-1831)—Artist especially known for his miniatures
Raphaelle (1774-1825)—Still life and portrait painter and director of the Peale Museums
Rembrandt (1778-1860)—Co-founder of the Pennsylvania Academy of the Fine Arts, portrait artist and painter of historical scenes
Rubens (1784-1864)—Manager of Peale Museums in Philadelphia, New York and Baltimore and still life and landscape artist
Maria (1787-1866)—Still life artist
James Jr. (1789-1876)—Artist especially known for his watercolor seascapes
Margaretta (1795-1882)—Still life artist
Titian (1799-1885)—Director of the Philadelphia Museum, naturalist and natural history painter
Sarah (1800-1885)—Portrait painter
Mary Jean (1826-1902)—Still life and portrait artist

Rockefeller
John D. (1839-1937)—Businessman, industrialist, philanthropist, and oil tycoon, he founded the Standard Oil Company and endowed the University of Chicago and Spelman College
John D. Jr. (1874-1960)—Businessman, environmentalist, and real estate developer, he restored Williamsburg, VA, established the United Services Organization and built Rockefeller Center in New York City
John D III (1906-1978)—Businessman and philanthropist
Nelson Aldrich (1908-1979)—Leading Republican politician, Governor of New York, U.S. Vice President under Gerald R. Ford
Laurance (b.1910)—Entrepreneur, business developer, conservationist
Winthrop (1912-1973)—Oil executive, rancher, Governor of Arkansas
David (b.1915)—Financier, head of the Chase Manhattan Bank
John D. IV "Jay" (b. 1937) Governor of West Virginia

Roosevelt
Nicholas (1658-1742)—Fur trader, flour miller, New York alderman
Nicholas Jr. (1687-1771)—Goldsmith and silversmith
Isaac (1726-1794)—Member, Committee of One Hundred, New York state senator, delegate to New York's Constitutional Convention, second president of the Bank of New York
Cornelius (1794-1871)—New York City real estate speculator, co-founder of the Chemical National Bank
James J. (1795-1875)—U.S. Congressman
Robert B. (1829-1906)—U.S. Congressman
Theodore (1858-1919)—New York Governor, Assistant Secretary of the Navy, Vice President, two-term U.S. President
Franklin Delano (1882-1945)—New York Governor, Assistant Secretary of the Navy, four-term U.S. President
(Anna) Eleanor (1884-1962)—Humanitarian, First Lady, United Nations delegate
Kermit (1889-1943)—Soldier, travel book author
James (1907-1991)—U.S. Congressman (California)
Franklin Delano Jr. (1914-1988)—U.S. Congressman (New York), U.S. Under-Secretary of Commerce

Vanderbilt

Cornelius (1794-1877)—Financier, businessman and shipping and railroad tycoon, the "Commodore" was the first president of the New York Central Railroad and endowed Vanderbilt University
William Henry (1821-1885)—Railroad tycoon and financier
Cornelius II (1843-1899)—Railroad tycoon and philanthropist
William (1849-1920)—Railroad tycoon
George Washington (1862-1914)—Pioneer in forestry science, noted agriculturist, capitalist, philanthropist
Cornelius III (1873-1942)—Railroad tycoon, banker
Harold Stirling (1884-1970)—Railroad executive, experimental farmer, one of the country's foremost yachtsmen, philanthropist and the developer of the game of contract bridge
Cornelius Jr. (1898-1974)—Reporter, columnist, author
Amy (1908-1974)—Leading authority on etiquette, author and syndicated columnist
Gloria (b. 1924)—Fashion designer, businesswoman

Winslow

Edward (1595-1655)—A founder and three-term Governor of Plymouth Colony who authored such famous accounts of the Colony as *Good News From New England* (1624). He arranged the first treaty with the Massasoit Indians and was a successful trader with the Native Americans
Josiah (1629-1680)—First native-born colonial governor in America. Founder of the first public school in Plymouth (1674) and commander of the United Colonies forces in King Philip's war (1675).

Winthrop

John (1588-1649)—Noted colonial leader and first Governor of the Massachusetts Bay Colony. He founded the settlement that became Boston and authored *The History of New England*
John Jr. (1606-1676)—A colonial Governor of Connecticut, he founded New London, Connecticut
John III (1638-1707)—A colonial Governor of Connecticut, he fought against the Dutch and Indians
John (1714-1779)—Leading scholar, astronomer, scientist and mathematician, he received the first honorary doctorate ever awarded by Harvard
Robert Charles (1809-1894)—Noted orator, U.S. Congressman and Speaker of the House from Massachusetts, he briefly served in the Senate and for years was president of the Massachusetts Historical Society
Theodore (1828-1861)—Businessman, poet, novelist

Wolcott

Roger (1679-1767)—Poet, military officer, Chief Justice of Connecticut's Superior Court, and Governor of that state
Oliver (1726-1797)—Delegate to the Continental Congress, signer of the Declaration of Independence, military commander, commissioner of Indian affairs and Governor of Connecticut
Oliver (1760-1833)—Secretary of the U.S. Treasury, Governor of Connecticut

Sources: American Heritage Junior Library. *The Pilgrims and Plymouth Colony.* Harper & Row, 1961. Bowman, John S. editor. *The Cambridge Dictionary of American Biography.* Cambridge, England: Cambridge University Press, 1995. Bumiller, Elisabeth. "Putting Family Ahead of a Senate Seat," *The New York Times.* November 24, 1998. Burt, Nathaniel. *First Families: The Making of an American Aristocracy.* Boston: Little, Brown and Company, 1970. Chen, David W. "A Livingston Legacy Revived," *The New York Times.* November 23, 1998. Chernow, Ron. "Mystery of the Generous Monopolist," *The New York Times.* November 18, 1998. Cirker, Hayward and Blanche. *Dictionary of American Portraits.* New York: Dover Publications, 1967. Goodwin, Doris Kearns. *The Fitzgeralds and the Kennedys.* New York: Simon & Schuster, 1986. Hopkins, Joseph G.E., editor. *Concise Dictionary of American Biography.* New York: Charles Scribner's Sons, 1964. Middlekauff, Robert. *The Mathers: Three Generations of Puritan Intellectuals 1596-1728.* New York: Oxford University Press, 1971. Morgan, Edmund S. *The Puritan Family.* New York: Harper & Row, Publishers, 1966. Perkins, George, Barbara Perkins and Phillip Leininger, editors. *Benet's Reader's Encyclopedia of American Literature.* New York: Harper Collins Publishers, 1991. *Prominent Families in America with British Ancestry.* New York: London House & Maxwell, 1977. Russell, John. "Paul Mellon, Patrician Champion of Art and National Gallery, Dies," *The New York Times.* February 3, 1999. Stetler, Susan L., editor. *Biography Almanac.* Second Edition. Detroit: Gale Research Company, 1983. Van Doren, Charles, editor. *Webster's American Biographies.* Springfield, MA: G.&C. Merriam Company, 1974. Vidal, Gore, V.S. Pritchett, et al. *Great American Families.* New York: W W. Norton & Company, 1977. *Who Was Who in America.* Chicago: Marquis Who's Who Inc., 1967. *Who Was Who in America.* Chicago: The A.N. Marquis Company, 1943.

VI
INTELLECTUAL AND CULTURAL HISTORY

SECTION 17

American Writers

17.1 Important American Authors

Authors are listed chronologically by date of birth.

Washington Irving (1783-1859)
1809—*A History of New York*
1820—*The Sketch Book*
1832—*The Legends of the Alhambra*

James Fenimore Cooper (1789-1851)
1821—*The Spy*
1826—*The Last of the Mohicans*
1827—*The Red Rover*
1841—*The Deerslayer*

Ralph Waldo Emerson (1803-1882)
1836—*Nature*

Nathaniel Hawthorne (1804-1864)
1837—*Twice-Told Tales*
1846—*Mosses from an Old Manse*
1850—*The Scarlet Letter*
1851—*House of the Seven Gables*
1853—*Tanglewood Tales*
1860—*The Marble Faun*

Harriet Beecher Stowe (1811-1896)
1852—*Uncle Tom's Cabin*
1859—*The Minister's Wooing*
1869—*Oldtown Folks*

Henry David Thoreau (1817-1862)
1854—*Walden, or Life in the Woods*

Frederick Douglass (1818-1895)
1845—*Narrative of the Life of Frederick Douglass,
    An American Slave: Written by Himself*

Herman Melville (1819-1891)
1846—*Typee: A Peep at Polynesian Life*
1847—*Omoo: A Narrative of Adventures in the
    South Seas*
1851—*Moby Dick; or, The Whale*

Edward Everett Hale (1822-1909)
1865—*The Man Without a Country*

Louisa May Alcott (1832-1888)
1863—*Hospital Sketches*
1868—*Little Women*
1871—*Little Men*
1886—*Jo's Boys*

Horatio Alger (1832-1899)
1867—*Ragged Dick, or Street Life in New York*
1869—*Luck and Pluck series*
1871—*Tattered Tom series*

Mark Twain (Samuel Clemens) (1835-1910)
1876—*The Adventures of Tom Sawyer*
1882—*The Prince and the Pauper*
1883—*Life on the Mississippi*
1884—*The Adventures of Huckleberry Finn*
1889—*A Connecticut Yankee in King Arthur's Court*

Bret Harte (1836-1902)
1867—*Condensed Novels*
1868—*The Luck of Roaring Camp*

William Dean Howells (1837-1920)
1882—*A Modern Instance*
1885—*The Rise of Silas Lapham*
1890—*A Hazard of New Fortunes*

Henry James (1843-1916)
1878—*Daisy Miller*
1881—*The Portrait of a Lady*
1886—*The Bostonians*
1898—*The Turn of the Screw*
1902—*The Wings of the Dove*

Sarah Orne Jewett (1849-1909)
1877—*Deephaven*
1896—*The Country of the Pointed Firs*

Kate Chopin (1851-1904)
1899—*The Awakening*

Booker T. Washington (1856-1915)
1900—*Up From Slavery*

L. Frank Baum (1856-1919)
1900—*The Wonderful Wizard of Oz*

Charlotte Perkins Gilman (1860-1935)
1890—*The Yellow Wallpaper*
1910—*What Diana Did*
1916—*With Her in Ourland*

O. Henry (William Sidney Porter) (1862-1910)
1904—*Cabbages and Kings*
1906—*The Gift of the Magi*
1907—*The Last Leaf*
1908—*The Voice of the City*

Edith Wharton (1862-1937)
1905—*The House of Mirth*
1911—*Ethan Frome*
1920—*The Age of Innocence*

Booth Tarkington (1869-1946)
1914—*Penrod*
1916—*Seventeen*
1918—*The Magnificent Ambersons*
1921—*Alice Adams*

Stephen Crane (1871-1900)
1893—*Maggie: A Girl of the Streets*
1895—*The Red Badge of Courage*
1898—*The Open Boat and Other Tales of Adventure*

James Weldon Johnson (1871-1938)
1912—*The Autobiography of an Ex-Colored Man*

Theodore Dreiser (1871-1945)
1900—*Sister Carrie*
1925—*An American Tragedy*

Willa Cather (1873-1947)
1913—*O Pioneers!*
1918—*My Antonia*
1927—*Death Comes to the Archbishop*

Ellen Glasgow (1874-1945)
1925—*Barren Ground*
1926—*The Romantic Comedians*
1941—*In This Our Life*

Gertrude Stein (1874-1946)
1914—*Tender Buttons*
1925—*The Making of Americans*
1933—*The Autobiography of Alice B. Toklas*

Jack London (1876-1916)
1903—*The Call of the Wild*
1904—*The Sea Wolf*
1906—*White Fang*

Sherwood Anderson (1876-1941)
1919—*Winesburg, Ohio*
1921—*The Triumph of the Egg*

Carl Sandburg (1878-1967)
1926—*Abraham Lincoln: The Prairie Years*
1939—*Abraham Lincoln: The War Years*

Upton Sinclair (1878-1968)
1906—*The Jungle*
1917—*King Coal*
1934—*Dragon's Teeth*

Sinclair Lewis (1885-1951)
1920—*Main Street*
1922—*Babbitt*
1925—*Arrowsmith*
1927—*Elmer Gantry*
1935—*It Can't Happen Here*

Will (1885-1981) **and Ariel** (1898-1981) **Durant**
1935-67—*The Story of Civilization series*

Edna Ferber (1887-1968)
1924—*So Big*
1930—*Cimarron*
1952—*Giant*

Henry Beston (1888-1968)
1928—*The Outermost House*

Katherine Anne Porter (1890-1980)
1930—*Flowering Judas*
1939—*Pale Horse, Pale Rider*
1962—*Ship of Fools*

Zora Neale Hurston (1891-1960)
1934—*Jonah's Gourd Vine*
1937—*Their Eyes Were Watching God*

Henry Miller (1891-1980)
1934—*Tropic of Cancer*
1939—*Tropic of Capricorn*

Pearl S. Buck (1892-1973)
1931—*The Good Earth*

James Thurber (1894-1961)
1940—*Fables for Our Time*
1942—*My World and Welcome to It*
1943—*Men, Women and Dogs*

Jean Toomer (1894-1967)
1923—*Cane*

F. Scott Fitzgerald (1896-1940)
1920—*This Side of Paradise*
1925—*The Great Gatsby*
1934—*Tender Is the Night*

Marjorie Kinnan Rawlings (1896-1953)
1938—*The Yearling*

John Dos Passos (1896-1970)
1921—*Three Soldiers*
1930-1937—*U.S.A. (trilogy)*
1939-1949—*District of Columbia (trilogy)*

William Faulkner (1897-1962)
1929—*The Sound and the Fury*
1929—*As I Lay Dying*
1932—*Light in August*
1936—*Absalom, Absalom!*

Thornton Wilder (1897-1975)
1927—*The Bridge of San Luis Rey*
1967—*The Eighth Day*
1973—*Theophilus North*

Ernest Hemingway (1899-1961)
1926—*The Sun Also Rises*
1929—*A Farewell to Arms*
1940—*For Whom the Bell Tolls*
1952—*The Old Man and the Sea*

E.B. White (1899-1985)
1945—*Stuart Little*
1952—*Charlotte's Web*

Janet Lewis (1899-1998)
1941—*The Wife of Martin Guere*

Thomas Wolfe (1900-1938)
1925—*Look Homeward Angel*
1935—*Of Time and the River*
1940—*You Can't Go Home Again*

Laura Z. Hobson (1900-1986)
1947—*Gentleman's Agreement*

Margaret Mitchell (1900-1949)
1936—*Gone with the Wind*

John Steinbeck (1902-1968)
1937—*Of Mice and Men*
1939—*The Grapes of Wrath*

1945—*Cannery Row*
1947—*The Pearl*
1952—*East of Eden*

Arna Bontemps (1902-1973)
1935—*Black Thunder*
1939—*Dreams at Dusk*

Erskine Caldwell (1903-1987)
1932—*Tobacco Road*
1933—*God's Little Acre*

Nathanael West (1904-1940)
1933—*Miss Lonely-Hearts*
1939—*The Day of the Locust*

Dr. Seuss (Theodor Seuss Geisel) (1904-1991)
1937—*And To Think I Saw it on Mulberry Street*
1957—*The Cat in the Hat*

John O'Hara (1905-1970)
1934—*Appointment in Samarra*
1935—*Butterfield 8*
1940—*Pal Joey*

Robert Penn Warren (1905-1989)
1939—*Night Rider*
1947—*All the King's Men*

William Saroyan (1906-1981)
1934—*The Daring Young Man on the Flying Trapeze*
1942—*The Human Comedy*

Henry Roth (1906-1995)
1934—*Call It Sleep*

Anne Morrow Lindbergh (b.1906)
1955—*Gift from the Sea*

Robert Heinlein (1907-1988)
1961—*Stranger in a Strange Land*

Dorothy West (1907-1998)
1948—*The Living is Easy*
1995—*The Wedding*

James Michener (1907-1997)
1947—*Tales of the South Pacific*
1959—*Hawaii*
1965—*The Source*

Richard Wright (1908-1960)
1940—*Native Son*
1945—*Black Boy*

James Agee (1909-1955)
1941—*Let Us Now Praise Famous Men*
1957—*A Death in the Family*

Wallace Stegner (1909-1993)
1943—*The Big Rock Candy Mountain*
1971—*Angle of Repose*
1976—*The Spectator Bird*

Eudora Welty (b.1909)
1942—*The Robber Bridegroom*
1972—*The Optimist's Daughter*

Paul Bowles (b.1910)
1949—*The Sheltering Sky*
1950—*The Delicate Prey and Other Stories*

John Cheever (1912-1982)
1957—*The Wapshot Chronicle*
1960—*Bullet Park*
1977—*Falconer*
1978—*The Stories of John Cheever*

Mary McCarthy (1912-1989)
1952—*The Groves of Academe*
1957—*Memoirs of a Catholic Girlhood*
1963—*The Group*

Bernard Malamud (1914-1986)
1952—*The Natural*
1957—*The Assistant*
1958—*The Magic Barrel*
1966—*The Fixer*

John Hersey (1914-1993)
1944—*A Bell for Adano*
1946—*Hiroshima*

Ralph Ellison (1914-1994)
1952—*Invisible Man*

William Burroughs (1914-1997)
1959—*Naked Lunch*

Saul Bellow (b.1915)
1959—*Henderson the Rain King*
1964—*Herzog*
1975—*Humboldt's Gift*

Herman Wouk (b.1915)
1951—*The Caine Mutiny*
1955—*Marjorie Morningstar*
1962—*Youngblood Hawke*

Carson McCullers (1917-1967)
1940—*The Heart Is a Lonely Hunter*
1941—*Reflections in a Golden Eye*
1946—*Member of the Wedding*
1951—*The Ballad of the Sad Cafe*

Shirley Jackson (1919-1965)
1948—*The Road Through the Wall*
1949—*The Lottery*
1962—*We Have Always Lived in the Castle*

J.D. Salinger (b.1919)
1951—*The Catcher in the Rye*
1961—*Franny and Zooey*

Ray Bradbury (b.1920)
1953—*Fahrenheit 451*
1962—*Something Wicked This Way Comes*

Alex Haley (1921-1992)
1964—*Autobiography of Malcolm X*
1976—*Roots*

James Jones (1921-1977)
1951—*From Here to Eternity*
1957—*Some Came Running*
1962—*The Thin Red Line*

Jack Kerouac (1922-1969)
1957—*On the Road*

William Gaddis (1922-1998)
1955—*The Recognitions*
1975—*J R*
1985—*Carpenter's Gothic*

Kurt Vonnegut (b.1922)
1963—*Cat's Cradle*
1969—*Slaughterhouse-Five*
1973—*Breakfast of Champions*

Joseph Heller (b.1923)
1962—*Catch 22*
1979—*Good as Gold*

Norman Mailer (b.1923)
1948—*The Naked and the Dead*
1979—*The Executioner's Song*

Truman Capote (1924-1984)
1948—*Other Voices, Other Rooms*
1958—*Breakfast at Tiffany's*
1965—*In Cold Blood*

James Baldwin (1924-1987)
1953—*Go Tell It on the Mountain*
1955—*Notes of a Native Son*
1961—*Nobody Knows My Name*
1962—*Another Country*

Flannery O'Connor (1925-1964)
1955—*A Good Man Is Hard to Find*
1960—*The Violent Bear it Away*
1965—*Everything That Rises Must Converge*
1978—*Letters*

William Styron (b.1925)
1951—*Lie Down in Darkness*
1967—*The Confessions of Nat Turner*
1979—*Sophie's Choice*

Harper Lee (b.1926)
1960—*To Kill a Mockingbird*

Alice Adams (b.1926)
1984—*Superior Women*
1989—*After You've Gone*

Maya Angelou (b.1928)
1970—*I Know Why the Caged Bird Sings*

William Kennedy (b.1928)
1983—*Ironweed*

Harold Brodkey (1930-1996)
1958—*First Love and Other Sorrows*
1988—*Stories in an Almost Classical Mode*

John Barth (b.1930)
1960—*The Sot-Weed Factor*
1971—*Chimera*

Donald Barthelme (1931-1989)
1964—*Come Back Dr. Caligari*
1981—*Sixty Stories*

E.L. Doctorow (b. 1931)
1975—*Ragtime*
1980—*Loon Lake*
1986—*World's Fair*
1989—*Billy Bathgate*

Toni Morrison (b. 1931)
1970—*The Bluest Eye*
1977—*Song of Solomon*
1981—*Tar Baby*
1987—*Beloved*

Tom Wolfe (b.1931)
1965—*The Kandy-Kolored Tangerine-Flake Streamline Baby*
1968—*The Electric Kool-Aid Acid Test*
1987—*The Bonfire of the Vanities*

Sylvia Plath (1932-1963)
1963—*The Bell Jar*

John Updike (b.1932)
1959—*Poorhouse Fair*
1960—*Rabbit Run*
1963—*The Centaur*
1970—*Bech: A Book*
1981—*Rabbit Is Rich*
1990—*Rabbit at Rest*

Philip Roth (b.1933)
1959—*Goodbye, Columbus*
1962—*Letting Go*
1969—*Portnoy's Complaint*

Joan Didion (b.1934)
1970—*Play It As It Lays*
1977—*A Book of Common Prayer*

Ken Kesey (b.1935)
1962—*One Flew Over the Cuckoo's Nest*
1964—*Sometimes a Great Notion*

Eldridge Cleaver (1935-1998)
1968—*Soul on Ice*

Thomas Pynchon (b.1937)
1963—*V.*
1967—*The Crying of Lot 49*
1973—*Gravity's Rainbow*

Raymond Carver (1938-1989)
1976—*Will You Be Quiet Please?*
1983—*Cathedral*
1988—*Where I'm Calling From*

Joyce Carol Oates (b.1938)
1978—*Son of the Morning*
1980—*Bellefleur*
1985—*Solstice*

Bobbie Ann Mason (b.1940)
1982—*Shiloh and Other Stories*
1985—*In Country*

Paul Theroux (b.1941)
1982—*Mosquito Coast*

Anne Tyler (b. 1941)
1982—*Dinner at the Homesick Restaurant*
1985—*The Accidental Tourist*
1989—*Breathing Lessons*

John Irving (b.1942)
1978—*The World According to Garp*
1981—*The Hotel New Hampshire*
1989—*A Prayer for Owen Meany*
1998—*A Widow for One Year*

Frederick Barthelme (b.1943)
1990—*Natural Selection*

Alice Walker (b.1944)
1982—*The Color Purple*
1988—*The Temple of My Familiar*

Annie Dillard (b.1945)
1974—*Pilgrim at Tinker Creek*
1985—*An American Childhood*
1989—*The Writing Life*

Ann Beattie (b.1947)
1976—*Chilly Scenes of Winter*
1980—*Falling in Place*
1986—*Where You'll Find Me*

Mary Gordon (b.1950)
1978—*Final Payments*
1985—*Men and Angels*

Louise Erdich (b.1954)
1984—*Love Medicine*
1996—*Tales of Burning Love*

Amy Tan (b.1952)
1989—*The Joy Luck Club*
1991—*The Kitchen God*

17.2   Chronology of the Life of Ralph Waldo Emerson

1803	Born May 25, in Boston
1811	Father, William Emerson, dies
1812-17	Attends Boston Latin School
1817-21	Attends Harvard College
1821-25	Teaches school
1826	Trip to St. Augustine
1828	Engaged to Ellen Tucker
1829	Ordained minister of Second Church in Boston; marries Ellen Tucker, September 10
1831	Ellen dies, February 8
1832	Resigns from Second Church; first trip to Europe and England
1834	Starts new career lecturing; brother Edward dies, October 1
1835	Moves to Concord, Massachusetts; marries Lydia Jackson, September 14
1836	Brother Charles dies, May 9; *Nature* published; son Waldo born, October 30
1837	"The American Scholar" address at Harvard
1838	"Divinity School Address"
1839	Daughter Ellen born, February 24
1840-44	*The Dial*
1841	*Essays* published; daughter Edith born, November 22
1842	Son Waldo dies, January 27
1844	Son Edward born, July 10
1847-48	Second trip to England and France
1850	*Representative Men* published; first western lecture tour
1853	Mother, Ruth Haskins Emerson dies, November 16
1855	Meets Walt Whitman
1856	*English Traits* published
1859	Brother Bulkeley dies, May 27
1860	*The Conduct of Life* published
1862	Henry Thoreau dies, May 6
1863	Aunt Mary Moody Emerson dies, October 3
1867	*May-Day and Other Pieces* published
1868	Brother William dies, September 13
1870	*Society and Solitude* published; "Natural History of Intellect" lectures at Harvard
1871	Trip to California
1872	House burns, July 24
1873	Third trip to Europe, including England and Egypt
1874	*Parnassus* published
1875	*Letters and Social Aims* published
1882	Dies in Concord, April 27

Source: Robert D. Richardson, Jr., *Emerson: The Mind on Fire.* Los Angeles: University of California Press, 1995.

17.3   Chronology of the Life of Edgar Allan Poe

1809   Born to actors David Poe and Elizabeth Arnold Poe on January 19 in Boston, Massachusetts. One older brother, Henry

1810   Sister, Rosalie, born

1811   David Poe abandons family. Elizabeth dies of tuberculosis at the age of twenty-four. Poe is taken into the Richmond home of Scottish tobacco exporter John Allan and his wife, Frances.

1820   Returns to Richmond and enters a local school run by a classical scholar

1825   Becomes secretly engaged to fifteen-year-old Elmira Royster

1826   Enters the University of Virginia.

1827   Elmira Royster, whose father has been intercepting Poe's letters to her, believes she has been jilted and becomes engaged to another man. Poe enlists in the United States Army and self-publishes *Tamerlane and Other Poems* anonymously

1829   Publishes *Al Aaraaf, Tamerlane,* and *Minor Poems*

1830   Enters the United States Military Academy

1831   Unhappy with the rigors and restrictions of the Military Academy, Poe deliberately gets himself court martialed and dismissed. Moves to New York and publishes *Poems.* Moves to Baltimore. Renews relationship with brother, Henry. Henry dies of tuberculosis

1832   Poe's first five short stories are published by the Philadelphia *Saturday Courier*

1833   Publication in the *Baltimore Saturday Visitor* for the short story "MS. Found in a Bottle"

1835   Becomes assistant editor of the Richmond (VA) magazine *Southern Literary Messenger.* Marries thirteen-year-old cousin Virginia Clemm.

1837   Loses job because of heavy drinking and depression. Moves to New York City

1838   Moves to Philadelphia. Publishes *The Narrative of Arthur Gordon Pym*

1839   Becomes the associate editor of *Burton's Gentleman's Magazine.* Writes *The Fall of the House of Usher*

1840   Is fired from *Burton's.* Publishes the two-volume *Tales of the Grotesque and Arabesque,* which receives mixed reviews and sells poorly

1841   Becomes literary editor of *Graham's Magazine,* in which he publishes "A Descent into the Maelstrom," "The Murders in the Rue Morgue," and "The Masque of the Red Death." Suffering from tuberculosis, Virginia Poe begins hemorrhaging and never fully regains her health. Poe meets Charles Dickens, who offers to help find him an English publisher, and Nathaniel Hawthorne, whose works Poe reviews in *Graham's Magazine*

1842   Resigns from *Graham's*

1843   Achieves first real fame for his short story "The Gold Bug," published in Philadelphia's *Dollar Newspaper.* Begins lecturing for fees to sold-out audiences. Writes "The Tell-Tale Heart"

1844   Moves to New York where he is appointed editor of the New York *Evening Mirror.* In the next two years, writes "The Purloined Letter," "The Pit and the Pendulum," and "The Cask of Amontillado"

1845   Gains greater fame with the printing of "The Raven" in the *Evening Mirror* and the *Whig Review.* Becomes co-editor of the *Broadway Journal*

1846   Publishes "The Cask of Amontillado" in *Godey's Lady's Book.* Wife's health worsens

1847   Virginia Clemm Poe dies of tuberculosis at the age of twenty-four at the Poes' cottage in Fordham, New York. Writes poem "Ulalume"

1848   Is briefly engaged to poet Sarah Helen Whitman

1849   Writes "Annabel Lee" and "The Bells." Is arrested in Philadelphia for public drunkenness and begins suffering from delusions. Travels to Baltimore, where he again begins to drink heavily and hallucinate. On October 1, he is found in the street unconscious and ill and is taken to Washington College Hospital. Six days later (October 7), after uttering his last words, "Lord, help my poor soul," Edgar Allan Poe dies. He is buried in Presbyterian Cemetery in Baltimore the next day

17.4   Excerpts from *Moby Dick*, 1851

The first British edition of the novel we know as *Moby Dick* was first entitled *The Whale* and published in three volumes on October 18, 1851, by Richard Bentley, London. The first American edition was published November 14, 1851, by Harper & Brothers, New York. The excerpts are included here as examples of writing from what many experts consider the quintessential American novel, and one of the greatest novels written.

Call me Ishmael. Some years ago—never mind how long precisely—having little or no money in my purse, and nothing particular to interest me on shore, I thought I would sail about a little and see the watery part of the world. It is a way I have of driving off the spleen, and regulating the circulation. Whenever I find myself growing grim about the mouth; whenever it is a damp, drizzly November in my soul; whenever I find myself involuntarily pausing before coffin ware-houses, and bringing up the rear of every funeral I meet; and especially whenever my hypos get such an upper hand of me, that it requires a strong moral principle to prevent me from deliberately stepping into the street, and methodically knocking people's hats off—then, I account it high time to get to sea as soon as I can. This is my substitute for pistol and ball. With a philosophical flourish Cato throws himself upon his sword; I quietly take to the ship. There is nothing surprising in this. If they but knew it, almost all men in their degree, some time or other, cherish very nearly the same feelings towards the ocean with me.—*Opening paragraph*

Already several fatalities had attended his chase. But though similar disasters, however little bruited ashore, were by no means unusual in the fishery; yet, in most instances, such seemed the White Whale's infernal aforethought of ferocity, that every dismembering or death that he caused, was not wholly regarded as having been inflicted by an unintelligent agent. Judge, then, to what pitches of inflamed, distracted fury the minds of his more desperate hunters were impelled, when amid the chips of chewed boats, and the sinking limbs of torn comrades, they swam out of the white curds of the whale's direful wrath into the serene, exasperating sunlight, that smiled on, as if at a birth or a bridal.

His three boats stove around him, and oars and men both whirling in the eddies; one captain, seizing the line-knife from his broken prow, had dashed at the whale, as an Arkansas duellist at his foe, blindly seeking with a six inch blade to reach the fathom-deep life of the whale. That captain was Ahab. And then it was, that suddenly sweeping his sickle-shaped lower jaw beneath him, Moby Dick had reaped away Ahab's leg, as a mower a blade of grass in the field. . . . Small reason was there to doubt, then, that ever since that almost fatal encounter, Ahab had cherished a wild vindictive-ness against the whale, all the more fell for that in his frantic morbidness he at last came to identify with him, not only all his bodily woes, but all his intellectual and spiritual exasperations. The White Whale swam before him as the mono-maniac incarnation of all those malicious agencies which some deep men feel eating in them, till they are left living on with half a heart and half a lung. That intangible malignity which has been from the beginning; to whose dominion even the modern Christians ascribe one-half of the worlds; which the ancient Ophites of the east reverenced in their statue devil;—Ahab did not fall down and worship it like them; but deliriously transferring its idea to the abhorred white whale, he pitted himself, all mutilated, against it. All that most maddens and torments; all that stirs up the lees of things; all truth with malice in it; all that cracks the sinews and cakes the brain; all the subtle demonisms of life and thought; all evil, to crazy Ahab, where visibly personified, and made practically assailable in Moby Dick. He piled upon the whale's white hump the sum of all the general rage and hate felt by his whole race from Adam down; and then, as if his chest had been a mortar, he burst his hot heart's shell upon it.—*Chapter 41 (Moby Dick)*

The hatch, removed from the top of the works, now afforded a wide hearth in front of them. Standing on this were the Tartarean shapes of the pagan harpooneers, always the whale-ship's stokers. With huge pronged poles they pitched hiss-ing masses of blubber into the scalding pots, or stirred up the fires beneath, till the snaky flames darted, curling, out of the doors to catch them by the feet. The smoke rolled away in sullen heaps. To every pitch of the ship there was a pitch of the boiling oil, which seemed all eagerness to leap into their faces. Opposite the mouth of the works, on the further side of the wide wooden hearth, was the windlass. This served for a sea-sofa. Here lounged the watch, when not other-wise employed, looking into the red heat of the fire, till their eyes felt scorched in their heads. Their tawny features, now all begrimed with smoke and sweat, their matted beards, and the contrasting barbaric brilliancy of their teeth, all these were strangely revealed in the capricious emblazonings of the works. As they narrated to each other their unholy adventures, their tales of terror told in words of mirth; as their uncivilized laughter forked upwards out of them, like the flames from the furnace; as to and fro, in their front, the harpooneers wildly gesticulated with their huge pronged forks and dippers; as the wind howled on, and the sea leaped, and the ship groaned and dived, and yet steadfastly shot her red hell further and further into the blackness of the sea and the night, and scornfully champed the white bone in her mouth, and viciously spat round her on all sides; then the rushing Pequod, freighted with savages, and laden with fire, and burning a corpse, and plunging into that blackness of darkness, seemed the material counterpart of her monomaniac commander's soul.—*Chapter 96 (The Try-Works)*

It was a clear steel-blue day. The firmaments of air and sea were hardly separable in that all-pervading azure; only, the pensive air was transparently pure and soft, with a woman's look, and the robust and man-like sea heaved with long, strong, lingering swells, as Samson's chest in his sleep.

Hither, and thither, on high, glided the snow-white wings of small, unspeckled birds; these were the gentle thoughts of the feminine air; but to and fro in the deeps, far down in the bottomless blue, rushed mighty leviathans, sword-fish, and sharks; and these were the strong, troubled, murderous thinkings of the masculine sea. But though thus contrasting within, the contrast was only in shades and shadows without; those two seemed one; it was only the sex, as it were, that distinguished them.

Aloft, like a royal czar and king, the sun seemed giving this gentle air to this bold and rolling sea; even as bride to groom. And at the girdling line of the horizon, a soft and tremulous motion—most seen here at the equator—denoted the fond, throbbing trust, the loving alarms, with which the poor bride gave her bosom away.

Tied up and twisted; gnarled and knotted with wrinkles; haggardly firm and unyielding; his eyes glowing like coals, that still glow in the ashes of ruin; untottering Ahab stood forth in the clearness of the morn; lifting his splintered helmet of a brow to the fair girl's forehead of heaven.—*Chapter 132 (The Symphony)*

Like noiseless nautilus shells, their light prows sped through the sea; but only slowly they neared the foe. As they neared him, the ocean grew still more smooth; seemed drawing a carpet over its waves; seemed a noon-meadow, so serenely it spread. At length the breathless hunter came so nigh his seemingly unsuspecting prey, that his entire dazzling hump was distinctly visible, sliding along the sea as if an isolated thing, and continually set in a revolving ring of finest, fleecy, greenish foam. He saw the vast, involved wrinkles of the slightly projecting head beyond. Before it, far out on the soft Turkish-rugged waters, went the glistening white shadow from his broad, milky forehead, a musical rippling playfully accompanying the shade; and behind, the blue waters interchangeably flowed over into the moving valley of his steady wake; and on either hand bright bubbles arose and danced by his side. But these were broken again by the light toes of hundreds of gay fowl softly feathering the sea, alternate with their fitful flight; and like to some flagstaff rising from the painted hull of an argosy, the tall but shattered pole of a recent lance projected from the white whale's back; and at intervals one of the cloud of soft-toed fowls hovering, and to and fro skimming like a canopy over the fish, silently perched and rocked on this pole, the long tail feathers streaming like pennons. . . .

On each soft side—coincident with the parted swell, that but once laving him, then flowed so wide away—on each bright side, the whale shed off encitings. No wonder there had been some among the hunters who namelessly transported and allured by all this serenity, had ventured to assail it; but had fatally found that quietude but the vesture of tornadoes. Yet calm, enticing calm, oh, whale! thou glidest on, to all who for the first time eye thee, no matter how many in that same way thou may'st have bejuggled and destroyed before.—*Chapter 134 (The Chase—First Day)*

As if to strike a quick terror into them, by this time being the first assailant himself, Moby Dick had turned, and was now coming for the three crews. Ahab's boat was central; and cheering his men, he told them he would take the whale head-and-head—that is, pull straight up to his forehead—a not uncommon thing; for when within a certain limit, such a course excludes the coming onset from the whale's sidelong vision. But ere that close limit was gained, and while yet all three boats were plain as the ship's three masts to his eye; the White Whale churning himself into furious speed, almost in an instant as it were, rushing among the boats with open jaws, and a lashing tail, offered appalling battle on every side; and heedless of the irons darted at him from every boat, seemed only intent on annihilating each separate plank of which those boats were made. But skilfully manoeuvred, incessantly wheeling like trained chargers in the field; the boats for a while eluded him; though, at times, but by a plank's breadth; while all the time, Ahab's unearthly slogan tore every other cry but his to shreds.—*Chapter 134 (The Chase—Second Day)*

17.5   Herman Melville's Death Notice, 1891

As this obituary from the *New York Times* makes clear, Herman Melville, one of the greatest American novelists, died in obscurity and poverty.

New York Times, October 2, 1891

There has died and been buried in this city, during the current week, at an advanced age, a man who is so little known, even by name, to the generation now in the vigor of life that only one newspaper contained an obituary account of him, and this was but of three or four lines. Yet forty years ago the appearance of a new book by Herman Melville was esteemed a literary event, not only throughout his own country, but so far as the English-speaking race extended. To the ponderous and quarterly British reviews of that time, the author of *Typee* was about the most interesting of literary Americans, and men who made few exceptions to the British rule of not reading an American book not only made Melville one of them, but paid him the further compliment of discussing him as an unquestionable literary force. Yet when a visiting British writer a few years ago inquired at a gathering in New York of distinctly literary Americans what had become of Herman Melville, not only was there not one among them who was able to tell him, but there was scarcely one among them who had ever heard of the man concerning whom he inquired, albeit that man was then living within a half mile of the place of the conversation. Years ago the books by which Melville's reputation had been made had long been out of print and out of demand. The latest book, now about a quarter of a century old, *Battle Pieces and Aspects of the War,* fell flat, and he has died an absolutely forgotten man.

In its kind this speedy oblivion by which a once famous man so long survived his fame is almost unique, and it is not easily explicable. Of course, there are writings that attain a great vogue and then fall entirely out of regard or notice. But this is almost always because either the interest of the subject matter is temporary, and the writings are in the nature of journalism, or else the workmanship to which they owe their temporary success is itself the produce or the product of a passing fashion. This was not the case with Herman Melville. Whoever, arrested for a moment by the tidings of the author's death, turns back now to the books that were so much read and so much talked about forty years ago has no difficulty in determining why they were then read and talked about. His difficulty will be rather to discover why they are read and talked about no longer. The total eclipse now of what was then a literary luminary seems like a wanton caprice of fame. At all events, it conveys a moral that is both bitter and wholesome to the popular novelists of our own day.

Melville was a born romancer. One cannot account for the success of his early romances by saying that in the Great South Sea he had found and worked a new field for romance, since evidently it was not his experience in the South Sea that had led him to romance, but the irresistible attraction that romance had over him that led him to the South Sea. He was able not only to feel but to interpret that charm, as it never had been interpreted before, as it never has been interpreted since. It was the romance and the mystery of the great ocean and its groups of islands that made so alluring to his own generation the series of fantastic tales in which these things were celebrated. Typee and Omoo and Mardi remain for readers of English the poetic interpretation of the Polynesian Islands and their surrounding seas. Melville's pictorial power was very great, and it came, as such power always comes, from his feeling more intensely than others the charm that he is able to present more vividly than others. It is this power which gave these romances the hold upon readers which it is surprising that they have so completely lost. It is almost as visible in those of his books that are not professed romances, but purport to be accounts of authentic experiences—in *White Jacket,* the story of life before the mast in an American man-of-war; in *Moby Dick,* the story of a whaling voyage. The imagination that kindles at a touch is as plainly shown in these as in the novels, and few readers who have read it are likely to forget Melville's poetizing of the prosaic process of trying out blubber in his description of the old whaler wallowing through the dark and "burning a corpse." Nevertheless, the South Pacific is the field that he mainly made his own, and that he made his own, as those who remember his books will acknowledge, beyond rivalry.

17.6   Works by Henry James, 1875-1919

Henry James (1843-1916) began writing on a serious basis at the age of 22, and wrote almost constantly for the next fifty years. He personifies the best of the nineteenth century "men of letters," and, as this list of his works shows, was a truly prolific writer.

A Passionate Pilgrim and Other Tales, 1875

Transatlantic Sketches, 1875

Roderick Hudson, 1876

The American, 1877

Watch and Ward, 1878 (James's first novel, serialized in 1871)

French Poets and Novelists, 1878

The Europeans, 1878

Daisy Miller, 1878

An International Episode, 1879

The Madonna of the Future and Other Tales, 1879

Hawthorne, 1879

The Diary of a Man of Fifty, and A Bundle of Letters, 1880

Confidence, 1880

Washington Square, 1881

The Portrait of a Lady, 1881

The Siege of London, The Pension Beaurepas, and The Point of View, 1883

Portraits of Places, 1883

Tales of Three Cities, 1884

A Little Tour in France, 1885

Stories Revived, 1885

The Bostonians, 1886

The Princess Casamassima, 1886

Partial Portraits, 1888

The Aspen Papers, 1888

Louisa Pallant, and The Modern Warning, 1888

Wheel of Time, 1893

The Real Thing and Other Tales, 1893

Picture and Text, 1893

Essays in London and Elsewhere, 1893

Theatricals: Two Comedies—Tenants, and Disengaged, 1894

Theatricals, Second Series, 1895

Terminations, The Death of the Lion, etc, 1895

Embarrassments, 1896

The Other House, 1896

The Spoils of Poynton, 1897

What Maisie Knew, 1897

The Two Magics, The Turn of the Screw, and Covering End, 1898

In the Cage, 1898

The Awkward Age, 1899

The Soft Side, 1900

The Sacred Fount, 1901

The Wings of the Dove, 1902

William Wetmore Story and His Friends, 1903

The Better Sort, 1903

The Ambassadors, 1903

The Golden Bowl, 1904

The Question of Our Speech, and The Lesson of Balzac, 1905

English Hours, 1905

The American Scene, 1907

Views and Reviews, 1908

Julia Bride, 1909

Italian Hours, 1909

The Finer Grain, 1910

The Outcry, 1911

A Small Boy and Others, 1913

Notes on Novelists, 1914

Notes of a Son and Brother, 1914

The Ivory Tower, 1917

The Middle Years, 1917

The Sense of the Past, 1917

Within the Rim and Other Essays, 1914-1915, 1918

Gabrielle de Bergerac, 1918

Travelling Companions, 1919

17.7   Famous Quotations from Mark Twain

On aristocracy:

The blunting effects of slavery upon the slaveholder's moral perceptions are known and conceded the world over; and a privileged class, an aristocracy, is but a band of slaveholders under another name.—*A Connecticut Yankee in King Arthur's Court*

Any kind of royalty, however modified, any kind of aristocracy, however pruned, is rightly an insult.—*A Connecticut Yankee in King Arthur's Court*

Essentially, nobilities are foolishness, but if I were a citizen where they prevail I would do my best to get a title, for the consideration it furnishes—that is what we want. In Republics we strive for it with the surest means we have—money.—*Notebook*

On democracy:

Men write many fine and plausible arguments in support of monarchy, but the fact remains that where every man in a state has a vote, brutal laws are impossible.—*A Connecticut Yankee in King Arthur's Court*

We adore titles and heredities in our hearts and ridicule them with our mouths. This is our democratic privilege.—*Autobiography*

Whenever you find yourself on the side of the majority, it is time to reform (or pause and reflect).—*Notebook*

On government:

The government of my country snubs honest simplicity, but fondles artistic villainy, and I think I might have developed into a very capable pickpocket if I had remained in the public service a year or two.—*Roughing It*

There is a phrase which has grown so common in the world's mouth that it has come to seem to have sense and meaning—the sense and meaning implied when it is used: that is the phrase which refers to this or that or the other nation as possibly being "capable of self-government;" and the implied sense of it is, that there has been a nation somewhere, some time or other, which wasn't capable of it—wasn't as able to govern itself as some self-appointed specialists were or would be to govern it. The master minds of all nations, in all ages, have sprung, in affluent multitude, from the mass of the nation, and from the mass of the nation only—not from its privileged classes; and so, no matter what the nation's intellectual grade was, whether high or low, the bulk of its ability was in the long ranks of its nameless and its poor, and so it never saw the day that it had not the material in abundance whereby to govern itself. Which is to assert an always self-proven fact: that even the best governed and most free and most enlightened monarchy is still behind the best condition attainable by its people; and that the same is true of kindred governments of lower grades all the way down to the lowest.—*A Connecticut Yankee in King Arthur's Court*

On slavery:

The skin of every human being contains a slave.—*Notebook*

Man is the only Slave. And he is the only animal who enslaves. He has always been a slave in one form or another, and has always held other slaves in bondage under him in one way or another. In our day he is always some man's slave for wages, and does that man's work; and this slave has other slaves under him for minor wages, and they do his work. The higher animals are the only ones who exclusively do their own work and provide their own living.—*The Damned Human Race,* "The Lowest Animal"

. . . the "poor whites" of our South who were always despised, and frequently insulted, by the slave lords around them, and who owed their base condition simply to the presence of slavery in their midst, were yet pusillanimously ready to side with the slave lords in all political moves for the upholding and perpetuating of slavery, and did also finally shoulder their muskets and pour out their lives in an effort to prevent the destruction of that very institution which degraded them. And there was only one redeeming feature connected with that pitiful piece of history; and that was, that secretly the "poor white" did detest the slave lord, and did feel his own shame. That feeling was not brought to the surface, but the fact that it was there and could have been brought out, under favoring circumstances, was something—in fact it was enough; for it showed that a man is at bottom a man, after all, even if it doesn't show on the outside.—*A Connecticut Yankee in King Arthur's Court*

© 2000 by The Center for Applied Research in Education

On patriotism:

Patriotism is usually the refuge of the scoundrel. He is the man who talks the loudest.—*Speech, 1908*

In the beginning of a change the patriot is a scarce man, and brave, and hated and scorned. When his cause succeeds, the timid join him, for then it costs nothing to be a patriot.—*Notebook*

The soul and substance of what customarily ranks as patriotism is moral cowardice—and always has been.—*Notebook*

Man is the only Patriot. He sets himself apart in his own country, under his own flag, and sneers at the other nations, and keeps multitudinous uniformed assassins on hand at heavy expense to grab slices of other people's countries, and keep them from grabbing slices of his. And in the intervals between campaigns he washes the blood of his hands and works for "the universal brotherhood of man"—with his mouth.—*The Damned Human Race,* "The Lowest Animal"

On knowledge and truth:

All schools, all colleges, have two great functions: to confer, and to conceal, valuable knowledge. The theological knowledge which they conceal cannot justly be regarded as less valuable than that which they reveal. That is, when a man is buying a basket of strawberries it can profit him to know that the bottom half of it is rotten.—*Notebook*

For all the talk you hear about knowledge being such a wonderful thing, instinct is worth forty of it for real unerringness.—*Tom Sawyer Abroad*

We have not the reverent feeling for the rainbow that the savage has, because we know how it is made. We have lost as much as we gained by prying into that matter.—*A Tramp Abroad*

Sir, I have been through it from Alpha to Omega, and I tell you that the less a man knows the bigger the noise he makes and the higher the salary he commands.—*How I Edited an Agricultural Paper,* 1870

We are always hearing of people who are around seeking after the Truth. I have never seen a (permanent) specimen. I think he has never lived. But I have seen several entirely sincere people who thought they were (permanent) Seekers after the Truth. They sought diligently, persistently, carefully, cautiously, profoundly, with perfect honesty and nicely adjusted judgment—until they believed that without doubt or question they had found the Truth. That was the end of the search. The man spent the rest of his hunting up shingles wherewith to protect his Truth from the weather.—*What is Man?*

No real gentleman will tell the naked truth in the presence of ladies.—*A Double-Barreled Detective Story*

Familiarity breeds contempt. How accurate that is. The reason we hold truth in such respect is because we have so little opportunity to get familiar with it.—*Notebook*

If you tell the truth you don't have to remember anything.—*Notebook*

On virtue:

. . . Virtue has never been as respectable as money.—*Innocents Abroad*

Be virtuous and you will be eccentric.—*Mental Photographs, A Curious Dream,* 1872

A crime persevered in a thousand centuries ceases to be a crime, and becomes a virtue.—*Following the Equator,* 1897

17.8   Chronology of the Life of William Faulkner

1897   Born Sept. 25 in New Albany, Mississippi, the great-grandson of a Civil War colonel.

1902   Family moves to Oxford.

1905   Enters first grade, Oxford Grade School.

1908   Faulkner is believed to have witnessed the lynching of a black man on the square in Oxford. The themes of race, violence and the complexities of the American South appear in most of his works as a writer.

1915   Quits Oxford High School.

1916   Works briefly at grandfather's bank as a clerk; often visits the University of Mississippi campus, and begins to write verse.

1918   Tries to enlist in U.S. Army but is turned down. Moves to New Haven, Conn., and begins working as a ledger clerk. Joins Canadian Royal Air Force as cadet, but is discharged after six months and returns to Oxford. Begins heavy drinking.

1919   Poem "L'Apres-Midi d'un Faune" appears in *The New Republic*. Enters the University of Mississippi in September as a special student; begins publishing poems in *The Mississippian* and the *Oxford Eagle*. His first poems are noticed by Sherwood Anderson, who suggests that Faulkner try his hand at fiction.

1921   Takes job as postmaster at the University of Mississippi post office.

1922   Poem "Portrait" published in *The Double-Dealer* (New Orleans).

1925   Begins to contribute to New Orleans *Times-Picayune*.

1926   *Soldiers' Pay* published.

1927   *Mosquitoes* published.

1929   *Sartoris* published. Marries Estelle Franklin. *The Sound and the Fury* published Oct. 7.

1930   Begins publishing stories in national magazines. *As I Lay Dying* published.

1931   Daughter Alabama born Jan. 11 but dies nine days later. *Sanctuary* published Feb. 9. *These 13* published Sept. 21.

1932   Arrives in Culver City, Calif., as MGM contract writer. *Light in August* published Oct. 6.

1933   *A Green Bough* published April 20. Daughter Jill born June 24.

1934   *Doctor Martino and Other Stories* published April 16.

1935   *Pylon* published. Brother Dean killed in plane crash Nov. 10. Leaves for five-week assignment at Twentieth Century-Fox where he meets Meta Dougherty Carpenter and begins intimate relationship that would last intermittently for fifteen years.

1936   *Absalom, Absalom!* published.

1937   Leaves on three-and-a-half-week trip to New York in mid-October, where he suffers a severe burn during a drinking spree.

1938   *The Unvanquished* published and screen rights are sold to MGM.

1939   Elected to National Institute of Arts and Letters. *The Wild Palms* published.

1940   *The Hamlet* published.

1942   *Go Down, Moses* published. Begins long-term Warner Brothers contract.

1946   Viking Press publishes *The Portable Faulkner*, edited by Malcolm Cowley. The publication of this collection marks Faulkner as an important novelist, master of a highly symbolic style, and the greatest novelist of the post–Civil War South.

1948   Screen rights to *Intruder in the Dust* sold to MGM; story is published Sept. 27. Elected to American Academy of Arts and Letters.

1949   *Knight's Gambit* published.

1950   Receives American Academy's Howells Medal for Fiction in May. *Collected Stories* published. Wins the Nobel Prize for Literature.

1951   Receives National Book Award for Fiction in March for *Collected Stories*. *Requiem for a Nun* published.

1954   *A Fable* published.

1955   Accepts National Book Award for Fiction for *A Fable*, which also wins the Pulitzer Prize. *Big Woods* published.

1957   *The Town* published.

1959   American debut of *Requiem for a Nun* on Broadway. *The Mansion* published.

1960   Accepts appointment to University of Virginia.

1963   *The Reivers* is published and wins the Pulitzer Prize. Dies of heart attack on July 6; buried in Oxford.

17.9   Winners of the Pulitzer Prize for Fiction, 1918-1998

The Pulitzer Prizes were endowed by Joseph Pulitzer (1847-1911), publisher of the *New York World,* in a bequest to Columbia University. The prizes honor work in 20 categories of journalism and letters, along with a prize for music. They are awarded annually by the president of Columbia on the recommendation of the Pulitzer Prize Board. The Pulitzer Prize for fiction is seen as the highest accolade for American writers. It is awarded for fiction in book form by an American author, preferably for work dealing with American life. Winners to date are:

1918   Ernest Poole. *His Family.*

1919   Booth Tarkington. *The Magnificent Andersons.*

1921   Edith Wharton. *The Age of Innocence.*

1922   Booth Tarkington. *Alice Adams.*

1923   Willa Cather. *One of Ours.*

1924   Margaret Wilson. *The Able McLaughlins.*

1925   Edna Ferber. *So Big.*

1926   Sinclair Lewis. *Arrowsmith.* (refused prize)

1927   Louise Bromfield. *Early Autumn.*

1928   Thornton Wilder. *The Bridge of San Luis Rey.*

1929   Julia M. Peterkin. *Scarlet Sister Mary.*

1930   Oliver LaFarge. *Laughing Boy.*

1931   Margaret Ayer Barnes. *Years of Grace.*

1932   Pearl S. Buck. *The Good Earth.*

1933   T. S. Stribling. *The Store.*

1934   Caroline Miller. *Lamb in His Bosom.*

1935   Josephine W. Johnson. *Now in November.*

1936   Harold L. Davis. *Honey in the Horn.*

1937   Margaret Mitchell. *Gone With the Wind.*

1938   John P. Marquand. *The Late George Apley.*

1939   Marjorie Kinnan Rawlings. *The Yearling.*

1940   John Steinbeck. *The Grapes of Wrath.*

1942   Ellen Glasgow. *In This Our Life.*

1943   Upton Sinclair. *Dragon's Teeth.*

1944   Martin Flavin. *Journey in the Dark.*

1945   John Hersey. *A Bell for Adano.*

1947   Robert Penn Warren. *All the King's Men.*

1948   James A. Michener. *Tales of the South Pacific.*

1949   James Gold Cozzen. *Guard of Honor.*

1950   A. B. Guthrie, Jr. *The Way West.*

1951   Conrad Richter. *The Town.*

1952   Herman Wouk. *The Cain Mutiny.*

1953   Ernest Hemingway. *The Old Man and the Sea*

1955   William Faulkner. *A Fable.*

1956   MacKinlay Cantor. *Andersonville.*

1958   James Agee. *A Death in the Family.*

1959   Robert Lewis Taylor. *The Travel of Jamie McPheeters.*

1960   Allen Drury. *Advise and Consent.*

1961   Harper Lee. *To Kill a Mockingbird.*

1962   Edwin O'Connor. *The Edge of Sadness.*

1963   William Faulkner. *The Reivers.*

1965   Shirley Ann Grau. *The Keepers of the House.*

1966   Katherine Anne Porter. *The Stories of Katherine Anne Porter.*

1967   Bernard Malamud. *The Fixer.*

1968   William Styron. *The Confessions of Nat Turner.*

1969   N. Scott Momaday. *House Made of Dawn.*

1970   Jean Stafford. *Collected Stories.*

1972   Wallace Stegner. *Angle of Repose.*

1973   Eudora Welty. *The Optimist's Daughter.*

1975   Michael Shaara. *The Killer Angels.*

1976   Saul Bellow. *Humboldt's Gift.*

1978   James Alan McPherson. *Elbow Room.*

1979   John Cheever. *The Stories of John Cheever.*

1980   Norman Mailer. *The Executioner's Song.*

1981   John Kennedy Toole. *A Confederacy of Dunces.*

1982   John Updike. *Rabbit Is Rich.*

1983   Alice Walker. *The Color Purple.*

1984   William Kennedy. *Ironweed.*

1985   Alison Lurie. *Foreign Affairs.*

1986   Larry McMurtry. *Lonesome Dove.*

1987   Peter Taylor. *A Summons to Memphis.*

1988   Toni Morrison. *Beloved.*

1989   Anne Tyler. *Breathing Lessons.*

1990   Oscar Hijuelos. *The Mambo Kings Play Songs of Love.*

1991   John Updike. *Rabbit at Rest.*

1992   Jane Smiley. *A Thousand Acres.*

1993   Robert Olen Butler. *A Good Scent from a Strange Mountain.*

1994   E. Annie Proulx. *The Shipping News.*

1995   Carol Shields. *The Stone Diaries.*

1996   Richard Ford. *Independence Day.*

1997   Steven Millhauser. *Martin Dressler: The Tale of an American Dreamer.*

1998   Philip Roth. *American Pastoral.*

17.10 Bestsellers in the 1960s

This list of bestsellers in the 1960s, with books as wildly divergent as Miller's *Tropic of Cancer* and Graham's *World Aflame,* illustrates the conflicts that wracked American life throughout the decade.

1960

Fiction

1. *Advise and Consent,* Allen Drury
2. *Hawaii,* James A. Michener
3. *The Leopard,* Giuseppe di Lampedusa
4. *The Chapman Report,* Irving Wallace
5. *Ourselves To Know,* John O'Hara
6. *The Constant Image,* Marcia Davenport
7. *The Lovely Ambition,* Mary Ellen Chase
8. *The Listener,* Taylor Caldwell
9. *Trustee from the Toolroom,* Nevil Shute
10. *Sermons and Soda-Water,* John O'Hara

Nonfiction

1. *Folk Medicine,* D. C. Jarvis
2. *Better Homes and Gardens First Aid for Your Family*
3. *The General Foods Kitchens Cookbook*
4. *May This House Be Safe from Tigers,* Alexander King
5. *Better Homes and Gardens Dessert Book*
6. *Better Homes and Gardens Decorating Ideas*
7. *The Rise and Fall of the Third Reich,* William L. Shirer
8. *The Conscience of a Conservative,* Barry Goldwater
9. *I Kid You Not,* Jack Paar
10. *Between You, Me and the Gatepost,* Pat Boone

1961

Fiction

1. *The Agony and the Ecstasy,* Irving Stone
2. *Franny and Zooey,* J. D. Salinger
3. *To Kill a Mockingbird,* Harper Lee
4. *Mila 18,* Leon Uris
5. *The Carpetbaggers,* Harold Robbins
6. *Tropic of Cancer,* Henry Miller
7. *Winnie Ille Pu,* Alexander Lenard, trans.
8. *Daughter of Silence,* Morris West
9. *The Edge of Sadness,* Edwin O'Connor
10. *The Winter of Our Discontent,* John Steinbeck

Nonfiction

1. *The New English Bible: The New Testament*
2. *The Rise and Fall of the Third Reich,* William Shirer
3. *Better Homes and Gardens Sewing Book*
4. *Casserole Cook Book*
5. *A Nation of Sheep,* William Lederer
6. *Better Homes and Gardens Nutrition for Your Family*
7. *The Making of the President, 1960,* Theodore H. White
8. *Calories Don't Count,* Dr. Herman Taller
9. *Betty Crocker's New Picture Cook Book: New Edition*
10. *Ring of Bright Water,* Gavin Maxwell

1962

Fiction

1. *Ship of Fools,* Katherine Anne Porter
2. *Dearly Beloved,* Anne Morrow Lindbergh
3. *A Shade of Difference,* Allen Drury
4. *Youngblood Hawke,* Herman Wouk
5. *Franny and Zooey,* J. D. Salinger
6. *Fail-Safe,* Eugene Burdick and Harvey Wheeler
7. *Seven Days in May,* Fletcher Knebel and Charles W. Bailey II
8. *The Prize,* Irving Wallace
9. *The Agony and the Ecstasy,* Irving Stone
10. *The Reivers,* William Faulkner

Nonfiction

1. *Calories Don't Count,* Dr. Herman Taller
2. *The New English Bible: The New Testament*
3. *Better Homes and Gardens Cook Book: New Edition*
4. *O Ye Jigs & Juleps!,* Virginia Cary Hudson
5. *Happiness Is a Warm Puppy,* Charles M. Schulz
6. *The Joy of Cooking: New Edition,* Irma S. Rombauer and Marion Rombauer Becker
7. *My Life in Court,* Louis Nizer
8. *The Rothschilds,* Frederic Morton
9. *Sex and the Single Girl,* Helen Gurley Brown
10. *Travels with Charley,* John Steinbeck

1963

Fiction

1. *The Shoes of the Fisherman,* Morris L. West
2. *The Group,* Mary McCarthy
3. *Raise High the Roof Beam, Carpenters, and Seymour—An Introduction,* J. D. Salinger
4. *Caravans,* James A. Michener
5. *Elizabeth Appleton,* John O'Hara
6. *Grandmother and the Priests,* Taylor Caldwell
7. *City of Night,* John Rechy
8. *The Glass-Blowers,* Daphne du Maurier
9. *The Sand Pebbles,* Richard McKenna
10. *The Battle of the Villa Fiorita,* Rumer Godden

Nonfiction

1. *Happiness Is a Warm Puppy,* Charles M. Schulz
2. *Security Is a Thumb and a Blanket,* Charles M. Schulz
3. *J.F.K.: The Man and the Myth,* Victor Lasky
4. *Profiles in Courage: Inaugural Edition,* John F. Kennedy
5. *O Ye Jigs & Juleps!,* Virginia Cary Hudson
6. *Better Homes and Gardens Bread Cook Book*
7. *The Pillsbury Family Cookbook*
8. *I Owe Russia $1200,* Bob Hope
9. *Heloise's Housekeeping Hints*
10. *Better Homes and Gardens Baby Book*

1964

Fiction

1. *The Spy Who Came in from the Cold,* John Le Carré
2. *Candy,* Terry Southern and Mason Hoffenberg
3. *Herzog,* Saul Bellow
4. *Armageddon,* Leon Uris
5. *The Man,* Irving Wallace
6. *The Rector of Justin,* Louis Auchincloss
7. *The Martyred,* Richard E. Kim
8. *You Only Live Twice,* Ian Fleming
9. *This Rough Magic,* Mary Stewart
10. *Convention,* Fletcher Knebel and Charles W. Bailey II

Nonfiction

1. *Four Days,* American Heritage and United Press International
2. *I Need All the Friends I Can Get,* Charles M. Schulz
3. *Profiles in Courage: Memorial Edition,* John F. Kennedy
4. *In His Own Write,* John Lennon

5. *Christmas Is Together-Time,* Charles M. Schulz
6. *A Day in the Life of President Kennedy,* Jim Bishop
7. *The Kennedy Wit,* compiled by Bill Adler
8. *A Moveable Feast,* Ernest Hemingway
9. *Reminiscences,* General Douglas MacArthur
10. *The John F. Kennedys,* Mark Shaw

1965

Fiction

1. *The Source,* James A. Michener
2. *Up the Down Staircase,* Bel Kaufman
3. *Herzog,* Saul Bellow
4. *The Looking Glass War,* John Le Carré
5. *The Green Berets,* Robin Moore
6. *Those Who Love,* Irving Stone
7. *The Man with the Golden Gun,* Ian Fleming
8. *Hotel,* Arthur Hailey
9. *The Ambassador,* Morris West
10. *Don't Stop the Carnival,* Herman Wouk

Nonfiction

1. *How To Be a Jewish Mother,* Dan Greenburg
2. *A Gift of Prophecy,* Ruth Montgomery
3. *Games People Play,* Eric Berne, M.D.
4. *World Aflame,* Billy Graham
5. *Happiness Is a Dry Martini,* Johnny Carson
6. *Markings,* Dag Hammarskjöld
7. *A Thousand Days,* Arthur Schlesinger Jr.
8. *My Shadow Ran Fast,* Bill Sands
9. *Kennedy,* Theodore C. Sorensen
10. *The Making of the President, 1964,* Theodore H. White

1966

Fiction

1. *Valley of the Dolls,* Jacqueline Susann
2. *The Adventurers,* Harold Robbins
3. *The Secret of Santa Vittoria,* Robert Crichton
4. *Capable of Honor,* Allen Drury
5. *The Double Image,* Helen MacInnes
6. *The Fixer,* Bernard Malamud
7. *Tell No Man,* Adela Rogers St. Johns
8. *Tai-Pan,* James Clavell
9. *The Embezzler,* Louis Auchincloss
10. *All in the Family,* Edwin O'Connor

Nonfiction

1. *How to Avoid Probate,* Norman F. Dacey
2. *Human Sexual Response,* William Howard Masters and Virginia E. Johnston

3. *In Cold Blood,* Truman Capote
4. *Games People Play,* Eric Berne, M.D.
5. *A Thousand Days,* Arthur M. Schlesinger Jr.
6. *Everything but Money,* Sam Levenson
7. *The Random House Dictionary of the English Language*
8. *Rush to Judgment,* Mark Lane
9. *The Last Battle,* Cornelius Ryan
10. *Phyllis Diller's Housekeeping Hints,* Phyllis Diller

1967

Fiction

1. *The Arrangement,* Elia Kazan
2. *The Confessions of Nat Turner,* William Styron (tie)
3. *The Chosen,* Chaim Potok (tie)
4. *Topaz,* Leon Uris
5. *Christy,* Catherine Marshall
6. *The Eighth Day,* Thornton Wilder
7. *Rosemary's Baby,* Ira Levin
8. *The Plot,* Irving Wallace
9. *The Gabriel Hounds,* Mary Stewart
10. *The Exhibitionist,* Henry Sutton

Nonfiction

1. *Death of a President,* William Manchester
2. *Misery Is a Blind Date,* Johnny Carson
3. *Games People Play,* Eric Berne, M.D.
4. *Stanyan Street & Other Sorrows,* Rod McKuen
5. *A Modern Priest Looks at His Outdated Church,* Father James Kavanaugh
6. *Everything but Money,* Sam Levenson
7. *Our Crowd,* Stephen Birmingham
8. *Edgar Cayce—The Sleeping Prophet,* Jess Stearn (tie)
9. *Better Homes and Gardens Favorite Ways with Chicken* (tie)
10. *Phyllis Diller's Marriage Manual,* Phyllis Diller (tie)

1968

Fiction

1. *Airport,* Arthur Hailey
2. *Couples,* John Updike
3. *The Salzburg Connection,* Helen MacInnes
4. *A Small Town in Germany,* John Le Carré
5. *Testimony of Two Men,* Taylor Caldwell
6. *Preserve and Protect,* Allen Drury
7. *Myra Breckinridge,* Gore Vidal

8. *Vanished,* Fletcher Knebel
9. *Christy,* Catherine Marshall
10. *The Tower of Babel,* Morris L. West

Nonfiction

1. *Better Homes and Gardens New Cook Book*
2. *The Random House Dictionary of the English Language: College Edition,* Laurence Urdang, editor
3. *Listen to the Warm,* Rod McKuen
4. *Between Parent and Child,* Haim G. Ginott
5. *Lonesome Cities,* Rod McKuen
6. *The Doctor's Quick Weight Loss Diet,* Erwin M. Stillman and Samm Sinclair Baker
7. *The Money Game,* Adam Smith
8. *Stanyan Street & Other Sorrows,* Rod McKuen
9. *The Weight Watcher's Cook Book,* Jean Nidetch
10. *Better Homes and Gardens Eat and Stay Slim*

1969

Fiction

1. *Portnoy's Complaint,* Philip Roth
2. *The Godfather,* Mario Puzo
3. *The Love Machine,* Jacqueline Susann
4. *The Inheritors,* Harold Robbins
5. *The Andromeda Strain,* Michael Crichton
6. *The Seven Minutes,* Irving Wallace
7. *Naked Came the Stranger,* Penelope Ashe
8. *The Promise,* Chaim Potok
9. *The Pretenders,* Gwen Davis
10. *The House on the Strand,* Daphne du Maurier

Nonfiction

1. *American Heritage Dictionary of the English Language,* William Morris, editor
2. *In Someone's Shadow,* Rod McKuen
3. *The Peter Principle,* Laurence J. Peter and Raymond Hull
4. *Between Parent and Teenager,* Dr. Haim G. Ginott
5. *The Graham Kerr Cookbook,* the Galloping Gourmet
6. *The Selling of the President 1968,* Joe McGinniss
7. *Miss Craig's 21-Day Shape-Up Program for Men and Women,* Marjorie Craig
8. *My Life and Prophecies,* Jeanne Dixon with René Noorbergen
9. *Linda Goodman's Sun Signs,* Linda Goodman
10. *Twelve Years of Christmas,* Rod McKuen

17.11 Notable American Poets

Poets are listed chronologically by date of birth.

Anne Bradstreet (1612-1672)
1650—"The Tenth Muse, Lately Sprung up in
        America"

Mercy Otis Warren (1728-1814)
1790—*Poems Dramatic and Miscellaneous*

Philip Freneau (1752-1832)
1770—"The Power of Fancy"
1776—"The Beauties of Santa Cruz"
1786—"The Wild Honey Suckle"
1788—"The Indian Burying Ground"

Francis Scott Key (1779-1843)
1814—"The Star-Spangled Banner"

Clement Moore (1779-1863)
1823—"'Twas the Night Before Christmas"

William Cullen Bryant (1794-1878)
1811—"Thanatopsis"
1815—"To a Waterfowl"
1832—"A Forest Hymn"

Henry Wadsworth Longfellow (1807-1882)
1841—"The Wreck of the Hesperus"
1842—"Evangeline: A Tale of Acadie"
1842—"The Village Blacksmith"
1855—"The Song of Hiawatha"
1858—"The Courtship of Miles Standish"
1863—"Paul Revere's Ride"

John Greenleaf Whittier (1807-1892)
1843—*Lays of My Home and Other Poems*
1846—*Voices of Freedom*
1850—*Songs of Labor*
1854—"Maud Muller"
1855—"The Barefoot Boy"
1866—"Snow-Bound"

Edgar Allan Poe (1809-1849)
1827—*Tamerlane and Other Poems*
1845—"The Raven"
1847—"Ulalume"
1849—"Annabel Lee"
1949—"The Bells"

Oliver Wendell Holmes (1809-1894)
1830—"Old Ironsides"
1833—"The Last Leaf"
1858—"The Chambered Nautilus"

James Russell Lowell (1819-1891)
1848—"The Vision of Sir Launfal"
1849—"A Fable for Critics"
1870—*The Cathedral*

Walt Whitman (1819-1892)
1855-92—*Leaves of Grass* collections ("Song of
        Myself," "I Sing the Body Electric,"
        "Oh Captain, My Captain")

Julia Ward Howe (1819-1910)
1861—"Battle Hymn of the Republic"

Emily Dickinson (1830-1886)
1861—"I'm Nobody! Who Are You?"
1890—"I Heard a Fly Buzz When I Died"
1890—"Because I Could Not Stop For Death"

Sidney Lanier (1842-1881)
1875—*The Symphony*
1877—*The Song of the Chattahoochee*
1878—*The Marshes of Glynn*

Emma Lazarus (1849-1887)
1882—*Songs of a Semite*
1883—"The New Colossus"
1887—*By the Waters of Babylon*

Edgar Lee Masters (1868-1950)
1915—*Spoon River Anthology*
1920—*Domesday Book*
1941—*Illinois Poems*

Edwin Arlington Robinson (1869-1935)
1897—"Richard Cory"
1916—"The Man Against the Sky"
1921—*Collected Poems*
1925—*The Man Who Died Twice*
1927—*Tristam*

James Weldon Johnson (1871-1938)
1917—*Fifty Years and Other Poems*
1927—*God's Trombones*

Paul Lawrence Dunbar (1872-1906)
1896—*Lyrics of Lowly Life*
1905—*Lyrics of Sunshine and Shadow*

Amy Lowell (1874-1925)
1914—*Sword Blades and Poppy Seed*
1919—*Pictures of the Floating World*
1925—*What's O'Clock?*

Robert Frost (1874-1963)
1914—"Mending Wall"
1916—"The Road Not Taken"
1923—"Stopping by Woods on a Snowy Evening"
1923—"Acquainted With the Night"

Carl Sandburg (1878-1967)
1914—"Chicago"
1916—*Chicago Poems*
1918—*Cornhuskers*
1920—*Smoke and Steel*
1950—*Complete Poems*

Vachel Lindsay (1879-1931)
1908—"A Gospel of Beauty"
1913—*General William Booth Enters into Heaven and Other Poems*
1914—"Abraham Lincoln Walks at Midnight"
1923—*Collected Poems*

Wallace Stevens (1879-1955)
1915-23—"Sunday Morning"
1923—"Peter Quince at the Clavier"
1936—"The Idea of Order at Key West"
1942—"Connoisseur of Chaos"

William Carlos Williams (1883-1963)
1917—"Tract"
1921—*Sour Grapes*
1923—"Red Wheelbarrow"
1946-51—*Paterson*
1954—*Desert Music*

Sara Teasdale (1884-1933)
1907—*Sonnets to Duse and Other Poems*
1915—*Rivers to the Sea*
1918—*Love Songs*
1926—*Dark of the Moon*

Elinor Wylie (1885-1928)
1921—*Nets to Catch the Wind*
1923—*Black Armour*
1928—*Trivial Breath*
1929—*Angels and Earthly Creatures*

Ezra Pound (1885-1972)
1926—*Personae*
1934—*Homage to Sextus Propertius*
1948—*The Cantos of Ezra Pound*

Joyce Kilmer (1886-1918)
1913—*Trees and Other Poems*
1917—*Main Street and Other Poems*

Hilda Doolittle (1886-1961)
1916—*Sea Garden*
1944—*Trilogy*
1972—*Hermetic Definition*

Robinson Jeffers (1887-1962)
1924—*Tamar and Other Poems*
1928—*Cawdor*
1929—*Dear Judas*

Marianne Moore (1887-1972)
1921—"Poetry"
1924—"A Grave"
1924—*Observations*
1944—*Nevertheless*
1951—*Collected Poems*

Claude McKay (1889-1948)
1911—*Songs of Jamaica*
1922—*Harlem Shadows*

Conrad Aiken (1889-1973)
1914—*Earth Triumphant*
1931—*Preludes for Memnon*
1971—*Collected Poems 1916-1970*

Edna St. Vincent Millay (1892-1950)
1922—*A Few Figs From Thistles*
1923—*The Harp-Weaver and Other Poems*
1937—*Observations at Midnight*

Archibald MacLeish (1892-1982)
1932—*Conquistador*
1958—*J.B.*
1985—*Collected Poems, 1917-1982*

Dorothy Parker (1893-1967)
1927—*Enough Rope*
1931—*Death and Taxes*
1936—*Not So Deep as a Well*

e.e. cummings (1894-1962)
1923—*Tulips and Chimneys*
1925—*XLI Poems*
1926—*is 5*
1935—*No thanks*
1938—*Collected Poems*

Jean Toomer (1894-1967)
1923—*Cane*

Mark Van Doren (1894-1972)
1924—*Spring Thunder*
1939—*Collected Poems*

Stephen Vincent Benet (1898-1943)
1915—*Five Men and Pompey*
1928—"John Brown's Body"
1944—"Western Star"

Hart Crane (1899-1932)
1926—*White Buildings*
1930—*The Bridge*

Allen Tate (1899-1979)
1926—"Ode to the Confederate Dead"
1928—*Mr. Pope, and Other Poems*
1944—"Seasons of the Soul"
1977—*Collected Poems, 1919-1976*

Janet Lewis (1899-1998)
1981—*Poems Old and New; 1918-1978*

Langston Hughes (1902-1967)
1926—*The Weary Blues*
1932—*The Dream Keeper*
1943—*Freedom's Plow*
1951—"Harlem"

Ogden Nash (1902-1971)
1931—*Free Wheeling*
1938—*I'm a Stranger Here Myself*
1959—*Verses From 1929 On*

Countee Cullen (1903-1946)
1928—*Ballad of the Brown Girl*
1947—*On These I Stand*

Robert Penn Warren (1905-1989)
1943—"Bearded Oaks"
1953—*Brother to the Dragons*
1957—*Promises: Poems 1954-1956*
1960—*You, Emperors, and Others*

Theodore Roethke (1908-1963)
1941—*Open House*
1953—*The Waking: Poems 1933-1953*
1954—*Words For the Wind*

Elizabeth Bishop (1911-1979)
1946—*North & South*
1955—*Cold Spring*
1976—*Geography III*

Karl Shapiro (b.1913)
1944—*V-Letter and Other Poems*
1978—*Collected Poems, 1940-1977*

Randall Jarrell (1914-1965)
1945—*Little Friend, Little Friend*
1965—*The Lost World*

John Berryman (1914-1972)
1956—"Homage to Mistress Bradstreet"
1964—*77 Dream Songs*

Robert Lowell (1917-1977)
1946—*Lord Weary's Castle*
1959—*Life Studies*
1964—*For the Union Dead*

Gwendolyn Brooks (b.1917)
1945—*A Street in Bronzeville*
1950—*Annie Allen*

Lawrence Ferlinghetti (b.1919)
1955—*Pictures of the Gone World*
1958—*A Coney Island of the Mind*
1976—*Who Are We Now?*
1979—*Landscapes of Living & Dying*

Amy Clampitt (1920-1994)
1983—*The Kingfisher*
1990—*Westward*

James Dickey (1923-1997)
1967—*Poems 1957-1967*
1981—*Falling, May Day Sermon, and Other Poems*

Kenneth Koch (b.1925)
1959—*Ko, or A Season on Earth*
1985—*Selected Poems, 1950-1982*

Maxine Kumin (b.1925)
1956—*Some Trees*
1975—*Self-Portrait in a Convex Mirror*

Adrienne Rich (b. 1927)
1951—*A Change of World*
1963—*Snapshots of a Daughter-in-Law*
1973—*Diving into the Wreck*

Anne Sexton (1928-1974)
1960—*To Bedlam and Part Way Back*
1966—*Live or Die*
1971—*Transformations*

Maya Angelou (b.1928)
1978—*And Still I Rise*
1983—*Shaker, Why Don't You Sing?*
1992—"On the Pulse of Morning"

Gregory Corso (b.1930)
1958—*Gasoline*
1960—*The Happy Birthday of Death*
1970—*Elegiac Feelings American*

Sylvia Plath (1932-1963)
1960—*The Colossus*
1965—*Ariel*
1981—*Collected Poems*

Amiri Baraka (LeRoi Jones) (b.1934)
1961—*Preface to a Twenty Volume Suicide Note*

Robert Pinsky (b.1940)
1975—*Sadness and Happiness*
1990—*The Want Bone*

Nikki Giovanni (b.1943)
1968—*Black Feeling, Black Talk*
1970—*Re: Creation*

Rita Dove (b.1952)
1980—*The Yellow House on the Corner*
1986—*Thomas and Beulah*

17.12   American Poet Laureates

In 1985 the U.S. Congress established an American Poet Laureateship, elevating what had previously been the position of poetry consultant of the Library of Congress. The post is awarded yearly by the librarian of Congress to an American poet of eminent stature.

1986-1987
Robert Penn Warren

1987-1988
Richard Wilbur

1988-1990
Howard Nemerov

1990-1991
Mark Strand

1991-1992
Joseph Brodsky

1992-1993
Mona Van Duyn

1993-1995
Rita Dove

1995-1996
Robert Hass

1997-1999
Robert Pinsky

17.13 Important American Playwrights

Authors are listed chronologically by date of birth.

Edna Ferber (1887-1968)
1932—*Dinner at Eight*
1936—*Stage Door*

Eugene O'Neill (1888-1953)
1921—*Anna Christie*
1928—*Strange Interlude*
1931—*Mourning Becomes Electra*
1933—*Ah, Wilderness!*
1946—*The Iceman Cometh*
1947—*A Moon for the Misbegotten*
1956—*Long Day's Journey Into Night*

Maxwell Anderson (1888-1959)
1924—*What Price Glory?*
1933—*Both Your Houses*
1935—*Winterset*
1955—*The Bad Seed*

Elmer Rice (1892-1967)
1914—*On Trial*
1923—*The Adding Machine*
1929—*Street Scene*

Philip Barry (1896-1949)
1929—*Holiday*
1939—*The Philadelphia Story*

Robert Sherwood (1896-1955)
1935—*The Petrified Forest*
1936—*Idiot's Delight*
1938—*Abe Lincoln in Illinois*
1940—*There Shall Be No Night*

Thornton Wilder (1897-1975)
1938—*Our Town*
1942—*The Skin of Our Teeth*
1954—*The Matchmaker*

Lillian Hellman (1905-1984)
1934—*The Children's Hour*
1939—*The Little Foxes*
1941—*Watch on the Rhine*

Clifford Odets (1906-1963)
1935—*Waiting for Lefty*
1937—*Golden Boy*
1950—*The Country Girl*

William Saroyan (1908-1981)
1939—*My Heart's in the Highlands*
1939—*The Time of Your Life*

Tennessee Williams (1911-1983)
1945—*The Glass Menagerie*
1948—*A Streetcar Named Desire*
1948—*The Rose Tattoo*
1951—*Summer and Smoke*
1953—*Camino Real*
1955—*Cat on a Hot Tin Roof*
1959—*Sweet Bird of Youth*

William Inge (1913-1973)
1950—*Come Back, Little Sheba*
1953—*Picnic*
1955—*Bus Stop*
1957—*The Dark at the Top of the Stairs*

Arthur Miller (b.1915)
1947—*All My Sons*
1949—*Death of a Salesman*
1953—*The Crucible*
1955—*A View From the Bridge*
1964—*After the Fall*

Robert Anderson (b.1917)
1953—*Tea and Sympathy*
1968—*I Never Sang For My Father*

Paddy Chayefsky (1923-1981)
1953—*Marty*

Neil Simon (b.1927)
1963—*Barefoot in the Park*
1965—*The Odd Couple*
1968—*Plaza Suite*
1977—*Chapter Two*
1983—*Brighton Beach Memoirs*

Edward Albee (b.1928)
1959—*Zoo Story*
1962—*Who's Afraid of Virginia Woolf?*
1964—*Tiny Alice*
1966—*A Delicate Balance*

Lorraine Hansberry (1930-1965)
1959—*A Raisin in the Sun*

A.R. Gurney (b.1930)
1982—*The Dining Room*
1988—*The Cocktail Hour*
1992—*Later Life*
1999—*Far East*

Lanford Wilson (b.1937)
1973—*The Hot L Baltimore*
1978—*Fifth of July*
1979—*Talley's Folly*

John Guare (b.1938)
1971—*The House of Blue Leaves*
1971—*Two Gentlemen of Verona*
1990—*Six Degrees of Separation*

Terence McNally (b.1939)
1991—*Lips Together, Teeth Apart*
1995—*Master Class*

David Rabe (b. 1940)
1967—*The Basic Training of Pavlo Hummel*
1968—*Sticks and Bones*
1976—*Streamers*

Sam Shepard (b.1943)
1978—*Buried Child*
1980—*True West*
1983—*Fool For Love*

August Wilson (b.1945)
1984—*Ma Rainey's Black Bottom*
1987—*Fences*
1988—*The Piano Lesson*

David Mamet (b. 1947)
1977—*American Buffalo*
1983—*Glengarry Glen Ross*
1988—*Speed-the-Plow*

Wendy Wasserstein (b.1950)
1977—*Uncommon Women and Others*
1988—*The Heidi Chronicles*
1993—*The Sisters Rosensweig*

David Henry Hwang (b.1957)
1981—*FOB*
1988—*M. Butterfly*

Tony Kushner (b.1957)
1992—*Angels in America, Part I: Millenium Approaches*
1993—*Perestroika*

17.14   Chronology of the Life of Allen Ginsberg

1926   Born June 3 to Louis and Naomi Ginsberg in Newark, New Jersey. Is introduced to poetry by his fa-
              ther, a high school teacher and poet

1930s-early 1940s   Educated in the public schools of Paterson, NJ where he meets his mentor, poet William
              Carlos Williams

1943   Enters New York City's Columbia University to study law. Changes major to English and wins several
              poetry prizes. Is temporarily suspended from school for a time

1948   Graduates from Columbia. Alone in New York over the summer, he experiences an auditory hallucina-
              tion in which William Blake recites poetry to him. Ginsberg considers the experience a personal revela-
              tion and is to refer to it often

Late 1940s-early 1950s   Holds series of jobs, including dishwasher, welder in Brooklyn Navy Yard, reviewer for
              Newsweek and *Merchant Marine.* Begins to associate with such avant-garde writers as Jack Kerouac,
              William Burroughs and Gregory Corso. Hospitalized for eight months as a psychiatric patient. Moves to
              San Francisco where he works as a market-researcher and meets his long-time companion, Peter
              Orlovsky

1950   Appears as a fictional character in Kerouac's *The Town and the City*

1952   Appears as a fictional character in John Clellon Holme's *Go*

1955   Becomes known as leader of the Beat Generation. Attends graduate school at the University of Califor-
              nia at Berkeley. Gives first reading of "Howl," his best known poem and Beat anthem

1956   Obscenity charges are leveled against his first book, *Howl and Other Poems,* which is published by
              Lawrence Ferlinghetti's City Lights Bookstore. The first edition is confiscated and Ferlinghetti ar-
              rested, but is later cleared of charges of distributing obscene material in San Francisco Municipal
              Court. Naomi Ginsberg dies, after spending years in a mental institution

1960   Publishes *Empty Mirror*

Early 1960's   Gives poetry readings in South America, India and England

1961   Publishes *Kaddish and Other Poems, 1958-1960.* The title poem is a eulogy to his mother

1962-63   Lives in the Far East. In India, is introduced to meditation and yoga which he later declares to be supe-
              rior to the drugs he used earlier for raising levels of consciousness

1963   Publishes *Reality Sandwiches*

1965   Appears in the movie *Wholly Communion.* Introduces idea of "flower power" to peace marchers in
              Berkeley

1965-66   Wins Guggenheim Fellowship in Poetry. Travels to Europe, Russia and Cuba, giving readings

1966   Appears in the movie *Chappaqua*

1967   Publishes *Ankor-Wat*

1968   Publishes *Planet News: 1961-1967.* Goes on speaking tour of U.S. colleges, lecturing on American
              military and industrial power. Leads demonstrators at the Democratic National Convention in Chicago

1972   Play *Kaddish* opens. Ginsberg is arrested in Miami for demonstrating against Richard Nixon at the Re-
              publican National Convention

1973   Publishes *The Fall of America: Poems of These States, 1965-1971*

Mid-1970s   Curtails his political activism and returns to Buddhism

1985   Publishes *Collected Poems 1957-1980*

1986   Publishes *White Shroud: Poems 1980-1985*

1994   Publishes *Cosmopolitan Greetings*

1997   Ginsberg dies on April 6 of liver cancer at age seventy. He is memorialized with readings and tributes
              in a church in Manhattan's Lower East Side

© 2000 by The Center for Applied Research in Education

17.15   Important American Print and Broadcast Journalists

© 2000 by The Center for Applied Research in Education

Journalists are listed chronologically by date of birth.

William Bradford (1663-1752)—Founder of the first paper mill in the United States, he began New York's first newspaper, the *New York Gazette,* on November 8, 1725.

William Bradford (1686-1742)—Printer and publisher who founded the first newspaper outside Boston and New York, the *American Weekly Mercury* (1728-54) and the first American magazine, the *American Magazine.* He also held the positions of Printer to the Commonwealth of Pennsylvania (1712-1730) and Postmaster (1728-37).

Cornelia Smith Bradford (NA-1775)—One of the few women in the field, she published the *American Weekly Mercury.*

John Peter Zenger (1697-1746)—New York City print shop owner who printed the first arithmetic textbook in New York and who gained lasting fame as an early advocate of freedom of the press. In 1734, in reaction to articles appearing in his publication, the *New-York Weekly Journal,* in which criticisms were leveled at the Governor of New York, Zenger was arrested on grounds of seditious libel. In his 1735 trial, his lawyer, Alexander Hamilton, argued that people have a "natural right" to complain against the government. This defense won Zenger an acquittal and was a turning point in America's history, setting the stage for the First Amendment to the Constitution guaranteeing freedom of the press.

Benjamin Franklin (1706-1790)—Inventor, scientist, public official and leading intellectual, he was appointed public printer to four middle Atlantic colonies, was one of the first Americans to both write and print a newspaper (*The Pennsylvania Gazette* of 1729-1766). Franklin received wide acclaim throughout the colonies by publishing *Poor Richard's Almanack,* a series of twenty-six almanacs (1732-1757).

Thomas Paine (1737-1809)—Author of the most sensational pamphlet of its time, *Common Sense* (1776), as well as *The Crisis* (1776-92), his writings forced Americans to take stock of their political situation, rallied public opinion in support of the Revolutionary War and helped prepare them for their fight for independence.

Margaret Green Draper (1727-1804)—Publisher of the *Massachusetts Gazette* and *Boston Weekly News-Letter* (1774-76), the Loyalist newspaper which condemned the Boston Tea Party and attacked the Continental Congress. After the end of the Revolutionary War, with her home and print shop confiscated by the new American government, she left for Britain where she received a pension in recognition of her loyalty to the Crown.

Isaiah Thomas (1749-1831)—Founder of the Whig paper the *Massachusetts Spy,* this minuteman was the official printer for the patriots and, in 1810, compiled the authoritative *History of Printing in America.*

John Fenno (1751-1798)—Editor and publisher, his *Gazette of the United States* (1789-98) supported the Federalist Party and promoted the administration and programs of George Washington and Alexander Hamilton.

Philip Freneau (1752-1832)—Editor of many newspapers and journals, his *National Gazette* (1792-03) gained fame for its support of the politics of Thomas Jefferson and James Madison. Such Republican viewpoints pitted Freneau's paper against Fenno's *Gazette of the United States,* against which it waged a newspaper war.

Sarah Josepha Hale (1788-1879)—Editor of *American Ladies Magazine* and of *Godey's Lady's Book,* the first magazine edited by and for women.

William Cullen Bryant (1794-1878)—Defender of free speech and editor of the *New York Evening Post.*

Elias Boudinot (born Galagina Oowatie) (1803-1839)—An American Indian, he edited the *Cherokee Phoenix* (1828-32), a newspaper printed in the English and Cherokee languages.

William Lloyd Garrison (1805-1879)—Founder of the *Liberator,* the nation's leading abolitionist newspaper.

Margaret Fuller (1810-1850)—Editor (*The Dial*) and journalist (*New York Tribune*), she was the country's first professional book reviewer and first female correspondent.

Benjamin Henry Day (1810-1889)—Father of the "penny press," he founded the *New York Sun* (1883) which sold for one cent to the middle and working class.

Horace Greeley (1811-1872)—Founder and editor of the *New York Tribune.*

Frederick Douglass (1817-1895)—Famous black antislavery figure, he was the editor of the abolitionist newspaper *The North Star.*

Joseph Medill (1823-99)—Editor of the *Chicago Tribune* (and later elected mayor of that city); the Medill School of Journalism at Northwestern University is named after him.

Bill Arp (Charles Henry Smith) (1826-1903)—Adopting a folksy yet philosophical persona, this Southern journalist used a letter-writing format to express his opinions on leading issues of the day. His popularity later helped him attain elective office in Georgia.

William Dean Howells (1837-1920)—As editor-in-chief of the *Atlantic Monthly,* this literary critic enormously influenced America's literary scene and was instrumental in encouraging the careers of such authors as Stephen Crane, Emily Dickinson, Mark Twain and Henry James.

Joseph Pulitzer (1847-1911)—As publisher of the *New York World* (1881-1907) and *St. Louis Post-Dispatch* (1878-1907), he pioneered the use of banner headlines and editorial cartoons. He endowed Columbia University's School of Journalism and the Pulitzer Prizes for Journalism and Literature.

Jacob Riis (1849-1914)—Writing for the *New York Tribune* (1877-88) and the *New York Sun* (1888-99), he called the public's attention to urban poverty issues, particularly slum conditions in New York City. His exposés helped bring about government reform in such areas as housing for the poor, the clean-up of city water supplies and the passage of child labor laws.

Ida Tarbell (1857-1944)—A writer on several magazine staffs, her serialized expose of the unfair business practices of John D. Rockefeller's Standard Oil Company captured the nation's attention and helped bring about government regulation and the break-up of business monopolies.

Adolph Ochs (1858-1935)—In 1896, he bought the *New York Times* and, using the motto *All the News That's Fit to Print,* established it as the nation's leading newspaper.

William Randolph Hearst (1863-1951)—A giant in the publishing world and rival of Joseph Pulitzer in sensationalistic journalism, his media empire included news services, syndications, radio stations and such newspapers as the *New York Journal,* the *San Francisco Examiner,* the *Detroit Times,* the *Los Angeles Herald-Express,* the *New York Mirror* and the *Chicago Herald-American,* and *Cosmopolitan, Good Housekeeping* and *Harper's Bazaar* magazines.

Nellie Bly (Elizabeth Cochrane Seaman) (1864-1922)—Columnist, social reformer and investigative reporter most associated with the *New York World* (1887-96). By traveling around the world in seventy-two days in an attempt to best the time it took Phileas Fogg, hero of Jules Verne's 1872 novel *Around the World in Eighty Days,* she gained worldwide fame and greatly increased readership for her newspaper.

Lincoln Steffens (1866-1936)—Through such assignments as managing editor at *McClure's Magazine* (1901-06), and co-publisher of the *American Magazine* (1906-07), this famous muckraker used investigative reporting to uncover and expose government and business corruption.

William Allen White (1868-1944)—Muckraking journalist who won a Pulitzer Prize for his editorial writing, he used his (Kansas) *Emporia Daily* and *Weekly Gazette* to espouse liberal Republican views in editorials which were widely re-printed throughout the nation.

H. L. Menken (1880-1956)—Noted literary critic and writer for the *Baltimore Evening Sun,* he gained fame for his reporting on the Scopes Monkey Trial. He was co-founder and editor of the intellectual periodical *American Mercury* (1924-33) and edited the periodical *The Smart Set* (1908-23).

George Nathan (1882-1958)—This co-founder of the *American Mercury* and *American Spectator* arts magazines was enormously influential in elevating the standards of American theater.

Walter Lippmann (1889-1974)—Syndicated columnist for such magazines and newspapers as *Newsweek, Vanity Fair,* the *New York Herald Tribune* and the *Washington Post,* he gained fame as a political journalist whose columns held influence over American politicians and policy.

Claude Barnett (1890-1967)—Founder and director of the Associated Negro Press (1919-1964), the first successful news service for newspapers.

Harold Ross (1892-1951)—The founding editor of and leading force behind *The New Yorker* magazine, renown for its high level of writing, reporting and cartooning.

Lowell Thomas (1892-1981)—Originally a war correspondent and foreign correspondent, he broadcast the news for CBS for almost fifty years.

Dorothy Thompson (1893-1961)—This syndicated columnist, foreign correspondent and bureau chief for various newspapers and magazines is sometimes referred to as the "First Lady of American Journalism."

Dorothy Parker (1893-1967)—As book reviewer for *The New Yorker* and *Esquire* magazines and drama critic at *Vanity Fair,* her often-quoted comments, sarcastic and clever, earned her a reputation as a biting, powerful literary wit.

Walter Winchell (1897-1972)—This modern "gossip columnist" and syndicated columnist for almost forty years began his career writing about show business and later became a successful radio commentator.

Henry Luce (1898-1967)—Founder and editor-in-chief of *Time, Fortune, Life* and *Sports Illustrated* magazines.

Ernie Pyle (1900-1945)—Famous World War II war correspondent for the Scripps-Howard newspaper chain, he won a Pulitzer Prize for his sensitive reporting on the experience of war.

Margaret Bourke-White (1904-1971)—Globe-trotting, pioneering photojournalist for *Fortune* and *Life* magazines, she was the first woman to be accredited as a war correspondent to the U.S. army.

James Reston (1909-1995)—Respected journalist best known for his association with the *New York Times,* he gained fame with his World War II reporting and collected two Pulitzer Prizes for national coverage.

Edward R. Murrow (1908-1965)—Working for CBS, he was one of the first foreign radio correspondents during World War II. In the 1950s, his "See It Now" television series provided insightful analyses of current events while his "Person to Person" series presented highly popular informal interviews of the leading personalities of the day.

Walter Cronkite (b.1916)—Anchor for almost twenty years of the CBS Evening News and an advocate of hard fact, unbiased reporting, he was voted "the most trusted man in America" in public opinion polls.

Katharine Graham (b.1917)—Former reporter and editorial writer, and owner of the *Washington Post* and *Newsweek,* she has been called one of the most powerful women in America.

Eric Severeid (1912-1992)—Foreign correspondent for CBS radio during World War II and national correspondent for the *CBS Evening News,* he was best known as a scholarly commentator and news analyst.

Fred Friendly (1915-1998)—Noted radio and television news journalist and producer, he was an important figure in the evolution of television news coverage. Long associated with both Edward R. Murrow (with whom he produced CBS-TV's "See It Now" program) and Walter Cronkite, he served as president of CBS News and later became a professor of journalism at Columbia University, where he directed "Seminars on Media and Society."

Nancy Dickerson (1920-1997)—A pioneer in the area of women broadcasters, she was the first female correspondent for CBS news (1960), the first woman to have a daily network television news program (NBC, 1963), and NBC's first woman floor reporter at the political conventions (1964). Renowned for her interviews, *Radio-TV Daily* voted her 1964 Woman of the Year for her coverage of President Kennedy's assassination.

Helen Thomas (b.1920)—White House bureau chief for United Press International and the recipient of numerous journalism awards, she was the first woman to head the presidential coverage for a major news service, the first woman elected head of the White House Correspondents Association and the first woman elected to the Gridiron Club.

Allen Neuharth (b.1924)—As Chairman and Chief Executive Office of the Gannet newspaper chain, he started *USA Today,* a national newspaper incorporating many graphics and color images designed for a mass audience used to relying on television, rather than newspapers, for their news.

Mike Royko (1932-1997)—Named Best Newspaper Columnist in America four times by the Washington Journalism Review, this chronicler of Chicago wrote for the *Chicago Daily News,* the *Chicago Sun-Times* and the *Chicago Tribune.* Among the many honors he received for his writing were the H.L. Menken Award, the Ernie Pyle Award, the National Press Club's Lifetime Achievement Award and the Pulitzer Prize for commentary.

Gloria Steinem (b. 1934)—Founding editor of *Ms.,* the leading magazine of the modern feminist movement

Carl Bernstein (b. 1944) and **Bob Woodward** (b. 1943)—As investigative reporters for the *Washington Post,* their story uncovering the break-in of the Democratic headquarters at Washington's Watergate Hotel by Republican Party operatives earned a Pulitzer Prize for their newspaper and led to the resignation of President Richard Nixon.

SECTION 18

Visual Arts

18.1 Important American Painters

Painters are listed chronologically by date of birth.

John Singleton Copley (1738-1815)
1770—Paul Revere
1773—Mr. And Mrs. Thomas Mifflin (Sarah Morris)
1778—Watson and the Shark

Benjamin West (1738-1820)
1771—The Death of General Wolfe
1771—Penn's Treaty With the Indians
1802—Death on a Pale Horse

Charles Willson Peale (1741-1827)
1767—Washington After Trenton
1781—George Washington at the Battle of Princeton
1822—The Artist in His Museum

Gilbert Stuart (1755-1828)
1797—Athenaeum Head (George Washington)
1815—Mrs. John Adams

John Trumbull (1756-1843)
1784—The Battle of Bunker's Hill
1787-1820—The Declaration of Independence
1824—Washington Resigning His Commission

Raphaelle Peale (1774-1825)
1822—Venus Rising From the Sea-A Deception

Rembrandt Peale (1778-1860)
1805—Thomas Jefferson
1820—Court of Death

Edward Hicks (1780-1849)
1845—The Peaceable Kingdom
1849—The Cornell Farm

Thomas Sully (1783-1872)
1819—Washington at the Passage of the Delaware
1840—Mother and Son

John James Audubon (1785-1851)
1826-1838—The Birds of America

Asher Brown Durand (1796-1886)
1849—Kindred Spirits
1859—The Catskills

Thomas Cole (1801-1848)
1827—Expulsion from the Garden of Eden
1840—The Voyage of Life
1844—American Lake Scene

William Sidney Mount (1807-1868)
1831—Dancing on the Barn Floor
1856—The Banjo Painter

George Caleb Bingham (1811-1879)
1845—Fur Traders Descending the Missouri
1946—The Jolly Flatboatmen
1847—Raftsmen Playing Cards
1855—The Verdict of the People

George Inness (1825-1894)
1880—The Coming Storm
1893—The Home of the Heron
1894—Sundown

Frederic Church (1826-1900)
1855—The Andes of Equador
1857—Niagara
1859—Heart of the Andes
1860—Heart of the Wilderness

Albert Bierstadt (1830-1902)
1862—The Bombardment of Fort Sumter
1863—The Rocky Mountains
1867—Donner Lake From the Summit
1889—The Last of the Buffalo

James Abbott McNeill Whistler (1834-1903)
1862—The White Girl: Symphony in White No.1
1871—Arrangement in Gray and Black: The Artist's Mother
1872-1875—Nocturne in Blue and Gold, Old Battersea Bridge
1874—Nocturne in Black and Gold: The Falling Rocket

John LaFarge (1835-1910)
1862—Flowers on a Window Ledge
1891—Afterglow, Tantira River, Tahiti

Winslow Homer (1836-1910)
1871—Country School
1872—Snap the Whip
1884—The Lifeline
1895—The Northeaster
1899—After the Hurricane, Bahamas

Thomas Eakins (1844-1916)
1871—The Champion Single Sculls
1875—The Gross Clinic
1889—The Agnew Clinic
1900—Mrs. William D. Frishmuth

Mary Cassatt (1845-1926)
1891—The Bath
1894—The Boating Party
1900—Mother and Child
1902—The Caress

Albert Pinkham Ryder (1847-1917)
1885—Moonlight
1887—The Flying Dutchman
1890—Siegfried

William Harnett (1848-1892)
1879—The Artist's Card Rack
1885—After the Hunt
1886—The Old Violin

William Merritt Chase (1849-1916)
1885—James A. McNeill Whistler
1895—Shinnecock Hills

John Henry Twachtman (1853-1902)
1885—Arques-la-Bataille

John Singer Sargent (1856-1925)
1884—Madame X
1888—Isabella Stewart Gardner
1889—The Daughters of Edward Darley Boit
1911—Repose

Maurice Prendergast (1859-1924)
1910—Central Park
1913—The Promenade
1915—On the Beach

Childe Hassam (1859-1935)
1886—Boston Common at Twilight
1887—Grand Prix Day
1918—Celebration Day

Henry Ossawa Tanner (1859-1937)
1893—The Banjo Lesson
1896—Daniel in the Lions Den
1897—The Raising of Lazarus

Grandma Moses (Anna Mary Robertson) (1860-1961)
1941—Black Horses
1946—From My Window
1957—First Snow

Fredric Remington (1861-1909)
1895—The Bronco Buster
1903—His First Lesson

Arthur Davies (1862-1928)
1890—Along the Erie Canal
1906—Unicorns
1910—Crescendo

Edmund Tarbell (1862-1938)
1891—In the Orchard
1922—Mother and Mary

Robert Henri (1865-1929)
1902—New York Street in Winter
1904—Young Woman in White

George Luks (1867-1933)
1905—The Wrestlers
1918—Armistice Night

William Glackens (1870-1938)
1905—Chez Mouquin
1935—The Soda Fountain

John Marin (1870-1953)
1920—Lower Manhattan
1922—Maine Islands
1949—The Fog Lifts

John Sloan (1871-1951)
1907—Sixth Avenue and Thirtieth Street
1922—The City From Greenwich Village

Lyonel Feininger (1871-1956)
1913—Bridge One
1921—Gelmeroda VIII
1946—Church on the Hill

Marsden Hartley (1877-1943)
1914—Portrait of a German Officer
1915—Painting Number 5
1937—Smelt Brook Falls

Joseph Stella (1877-1946)
1913—Battle of Lights, Coney Island, Mardi Gras
1922—The Voice of the City of New York Interpreted: The Bridge

Arthur Dove (1880-1946)
1910—Abstractions
1924—Portrait of Ralph Dusenberry
1930—Sand Barge
1944—That Red One

Hans Hofmann (1880-1866)
1939—Red Trickle
1962—Autumn Chill and Sun

Max Weber (1881-1961)
1910—Composition with Three Figures
1915—Athletic Contest
1955—Flute Soloist

George Bellows (1882-1925)
1908—North River
1909—Pennsylvania Station Excavation
1909—Both Members of This Club
1924—The Dempsey-Firpo Fight

Edward Hopper (1882-1967)
1929—The Lighthouse at Two Lights
1930—Early Sunday Morning
1942—Nighthawks
1955—Carolina Morning

Charles Demuth (1883-1935)
1927—My Egypt
1928—I Saw the Figure 5 in Gold

Charles Sheeler (1883-1965)
1920—Church Street El
1930—American Landscape
1946—Ballardvale
1954—Midwest

Morgan Russell (1886-1953)
1914—Synchromy in Orange: To Form

Georgia O'Keeffe (1887-1986)
1919—Blue and Green Music
1926—Black Iris
1927—The Radiator Building-Night, New York, 1927
1931—Cow's Skull

Horace Pippin (1888-1946)
1943—Domino Players

Josef Albers (1888-1976)
1959—Homage to the Square
1963—Manhattan

Thomas Hart Benton (1889-1975)
1935—Social History of Missouri
1938—Cradling Wheat

Stanton MacDonald-Wright (1890-1973)
1914—Abstraction on Spectrum
1920—Canyon Synchromy

Man Ray (1890-1976)
1916—The Rope Dancer Accompanies Herself with Her Shadows
1932—Observatory Time—The Lovers

Grant Wood (1892-1942)
1930—Stone City, Iowa
1930—American Gothic
1931—Midnight Ride of Paul Revere

Milton Avery (1893-1965)
1945—Swimmers and Sunbathers
1954—Green Sea

Charles Burchfield (1893-1967)
1932—Old House By Creek
1955—An April Mood

Stuart Davis (1894-1964)
1932—Men Without Women
1938—Swing Landscape
1954—Colonial Cubism

Ivan Albright (1897-1983)
1941—That Which I Should Have Done I Did Not Do

Reginald Marsh (1898-1954)
1930—Why Not Use the "L"?
1935—Coney Island Beach

Ben Shahn (1898-1969)
1931—The Passion of Sacco and Vanzetti
1945—Liberation
1949—Death of a Minor

Raphael Soyer (1899-1987)
1959—Farewell to Lincoln Square
1965—Homage to Eakins

Richard Lindner (1901-1978)
1953—The Visitor
1963—Moon Over Alabama
1966—Ice

Mark Rothko (1903-1970)
1946—Entombment
1947—Red Rock Falls
1950—Number 10
1957—Slate Blue and Brown on Plum

Adolph Gottlieb (1903-1974)
1951—The Frozen Sounds, Number 1
1958—Exclamation
1959—Thrust
1965—Chrome

Arshile Gorky (1904-1948)
1943—Sochi
1944—The Liver is the Cock's Comb
1947—Plumage Landscape

Clyfford Still (1904-1980)
1949—Number 2
1951—Painting
1958—Untitled

Willem deKooning (1904-1997)
1950—Excavation
1950s—Women series
1951—Night Square
1981—Pirate (Untitled)

Barnett Newman (1905-1970)
1945—Gea
1948—Onement I
1950—Vir Heroicus Sublimis
1965—Triad

Fairfield Porter (1907-1975)
1966—The Mirror
1969—Island Farmhouse
1971—Under the Elms

Franz Kline (1910-1962)
1953—New York
1959—Orange and Black Wall
1960—Meryon
1961—Andrus

Morris Graves (b.1910)
1939—Bird Singing in the Moonlight
1941—Bird in the Spirit

Jackson Pollack (1912-1956)
1943—Pasiphae
1947—Full Fathom Five
1948—Composition Number 1
1950—Autumn Rhythm
1953—Portrait and a Dream

Morris Louis (1912-1962)
1960—Where
1960—Aleph Series I
1961—Moving In

William Baziotes (1912-1963)
1955—The Beach
1958—Dusk

Agnes Martin (b.1912)
1963—Night Sea

Romare Bearden (1912-1988)
1964—The Dove
1980—The Falling Star
1983—The Piano Lesson

Ad Reinhardt (1913-1967)
1948-49—Number 18
1952—Abstract Painting, Blue
1952—Red Painting

Philip Guston (1913-1980)
1955—The Room
1961—Duo
1969—Studio

Robert Motherwell (1915-1991)
1943—Pancho Villa, Dead and Alive
1949—At Five in the Afternoon
1961—Elegy to the Spanish Republic LXX

Jacob Lawrence (b.1917)
1941—The Migration of the Negro
1943—Life in Harlem

Andrew Wyeth (b.1917)
1949—A Crow Flew By
1948—Christina's World

Wayne Thibaud (b.1920)
1963—Pie Counter
1980—Down Eighteenth Street (Corner Apartments)

Richard Diebenkorn (1922-1993)
1957—Man and Woman in Large Room
1972—Ocean Park No.54

Sam Francis (1923-1994)
1958—Shining Back
1962—Around the Blues
1973—Untitled, No.11

Roy Lichtenstein (1923-1997)
1962—Whaam!
1974—Artist's Studio: The Dance
1978—Goldfish Bowl II

Ellsworth Kelly (b.1923)
1951—Brush Strokes Cut into 49 Squares and
Arranged by Chance
1951—Colors for a Large Wall
1962—Blue, Red, Green

Larry Rivers (b.1923)
1953—Washington Crossing the Delaware
1955—Double Portrait of Birdie
1963—Dutch Masters and Cigars II

Kenneth Noland (b.1924)
1961—Turnsole
1964—Bend Sinister
1966—Par Transit

Philip Pearlstein (b.1924)
1966—Woman Reclining on Couch
1973—Standing Female Model and Mirror

Robert Rauchenberg (b.1925)
1955-1959—Monogram
1956—Odalisque
1959—Bed
1963—Estate

Alex Katz (b.1927)
1965—Smile Again
1974—Good Morning #2
1978—The Red Band

Andy Warhol (1928-1987)
1962—Marilyn Monroe
1965—Campbell's Soup Can
1972—Mao
1986—Camouflage Self-Portrait

Helen Frankenthaler (b.1928)
1952—Mountains and Sea
1964—Small's Paradise
1967—The Human Edge

Robert Indiana (b.1928)
1963—The Demuth American Dream No. 5
1966—LOVE

Cy Twombly (b.1928)
1969—Untitled

Jasper Johns (b.1930)
1955—Flag
1955—White Flag
1955—Target With Four Faces
1961—Numbers 0 Through 9
1964—Field Painting

James Rosenquist (b.1933)
1965—F-111
1970—Horizon Home Sweet Home

Jim Dine (b.1935)
1963—Hatchet with Two Palettes
1964—Double Isometric Self-Portrait (Serape)

Frank Stella (b.1936)
1959—The Marriage of Reason and Squalor
1964—Adelante
1965—Tuftonboro II

Brice Marden (b.1938)
1966—The Dylan Painting
1983—Green (Earth)
1988—Cold Mountain I (Path)

Chuck Close (b. 1940)
1968—Self-Portrait
1991—Self-Portrait

Elizabeth Murray (b.1940)
1976—Beginner
1981—Art Part
1995-96—Careless Love

Jennifer Bartlett (b.1941)
1976—Rhapsody

Mark Tansey (b.1949)
1992—The Enunciation

Keith Haring (1958-1990)
1983—New York City Subway Drawing

18.2 Notable American Photographers

Photographers are listed chronologically by date of birth.

Matthew Brady (1823-1896)
Known for his portraits of Abraham Lincoln and images of the Civil War

Eadweard Muybridge (1830-1904)
Pioneer in stop-action photography

Timothy O'Sullivan (1840-1882)
Noted for his images depicting the Civil War and his landscapes documenting the American West

William Henry Jackson (1843-1942)
Photographer of scenes of American Indians and the American West

Alfred Stieglitz (1864-1946)
His Photo-Secession movement stressed the personal expression possible in photography, approached as a serious art movement. Advocate of the "straight" photography of Pictorialism, he was also instrumental in championing emerging artists

Edward Steichen (1879-1973)
"Art for art's sake" proponent who equated the importance of photography with that of painting and whose work greatly influenced modern art

Imogen Cunningham (1883-1976)
Portrait photographer of many leading figures in the arts; also known for her plant studies

Edward Weston (1886-1958)
Proponent of pure photography, he was also known for his nature studies of California and the far West

Man Ray (1890-1976)
Experimental Dada artist and creator of the Rayogram, a collage of objects placed on photographic paper and exposed to light without the use of a lens

Paul Strand (1890-1976)
Major avant-garde photographer especially known for his geometrically composed compositions

Dorothea Lange (1895-1965)
Documentary photographer famous for her Depression scenes of the Dust Bowl and California migrant workers

Berenice Abbott (1898 -1991)
Her studies of old New York helped preserve images of a changing city

Eliot Porter (1901-1990)
Best known for his color scenes of wildlife and nature

Ansel Adams (1902-1984)
Foremost nature and landscape photographer, especially noted for his black and white images

Walker Evans (1903-1975)
"Straight" photographer famous for the Depression-era images he produced for the Works Project Agency

Margaret Bourke-White (1904-1971)
Life magazine's famous premiere photojournalist, her work focused on both monumental subjects as well as human images

Minor White (1908-1976)
Known for his "sequencing" of images and his use of photography as a visual representation of spiritual concepts

Diane Arbus (1923-1971)
Famous for her evocative portraits of society's outsiders

Richard Avedon (b.1923)
Innovative fashion photographer and creator of revealing, close-up portraits of well-known personalities

Garry Winogrand (1928-1984)
Using wit and mystery, his photographs document American life

Lee Friedlander (b.1934)
A "street" photographer and documentor of contemporary, everyday events

Bruce Davidson (b.1934)
Known for photo essays depicting the relationship between people and their environment

Robert Mapplethorpe (1946-1989)
Famous for photographic explorations of flowers and human sexuality

Cindy Sherman (b. 1954)
Combining photography and performance art, she makes use of costumes, props and lighting to transform herself into her own subjects, portrayals that comment on relationships between history, image and culture

18.3   Important Sculptors and Conceptual Artists in America

Sculptors are listed chronologically by date of birth.

William Rush (1756-1833)
1808—Comedy
1808—Tragedy
1809—Water Nymph

Horatio Greenough (1805-1852)
1841—George Washington (U.S. Capitol)
1841—Venus
1851—Castor and Pollox

Hiram Powers (1805-1873)
1843—Greek Slave
1858—Daniel Webster

William Story (1819-1895)
1861—Libyan Sibyl
1869—Cleopatra

Augustus Saint-Gaudens (1848-1907)
1881—Admiral David Farragut
1887—Abraham Lincoln
1892—Diana

Daniel Chester French (1850-1935)
1873—Minute Man
1882—John Harvard
1907—Four Continents
1917—Abraham Lincoln (Lincoln Memorial)

Fredric Remington (1861-1909)
1895—The Bronco Buster
1902—Coming Through the Rye

Gutzon Borglum (1867-1941)
1925-1941— Mount Rushmore

Elie Nadelman (1882-1946)
1909—Standing Female Nude
1915—Man in the Open Air
1917—Woman at the Piano

Jacques Lipchitz (1891-1973)
1930—Figure
1936—Prometheus Strangling the Vulture
1972—Bellerophon

Alexander Calder (1898-1976)
1928—Romulus and Remus
1932—Circus
1939—Lobster Trap and Fish Tail
1958—The Spiral

Louise Nevelson (1899-1988)
1956—The Royal Voyage
1958—The Moon Garden Plus One
1960—Young Shadows
1964—Sun Garden, No.1

Joseph Cornell (1903-1973)
1942—Medici Slot Machine
1942-1953—Object (Roses des Vents)
1945—The Hotel Eden

Isamu Noguchi (1904-1988)
1939—Capital
1941—Plaque at Rockefeller Center
1945—Kuros
1958—Bird E-Square Bird

David Smith (1906-1965)
1948—The Royal Bird
1950—The Letter
1951—Hudson River Landscape
1956-1961—Sentinel series
1961-1965—Cubi series

Tony Smith (1912-1980)
1962—Die
1962—Free Ride
1967—Smoke

George Segal (b. 1924)
1962—The Bus Driver
1964—The Gas Station
1964-66—The Diner

Duane Hanson (1925-1996)
1969—Motorcycle Accident
1970—Tourists
1977—Woman With Dog

Donald Judd (1928-1994)
1965—Untitled
1977—Untitled
1982-1986—Untitled

Sol Lewitt (b.1928)
1966—Serial Project #1
1967—Sculpture Series "A"

Claes Oldenburg (b. 1929)
1962—Floor Cake
1966—Soft Toilet
1970—Giant Icebag
1981—Flashlight

Marisol (b.1930)
1962—The Family
1963—The Bicycle Race
1966—The Party

Robert Morris (b.1931)
1961—Box with the Sound of its Own Making
1964—Slab
1968—Untitled

Dan Flavin (1933-1996)
1968—Pink and Gold
1992—Untitled (to Tracy to celebrate the love of
    a lifetime)

Mark di Suvero (b.1933)
1960—Hankchampion
1965—Loveseat
1970—XDelta

Red Grooms (b. 1937)
1967—City of Chicago
1970—Discount Store
1976—Ruckus Manhattan

Robert Smithson (1938-1973)
1969-70—Spiral Jetty

Robert Indiana (b.1938)
1972—LOVE

Judy Chicago (b.1939)
1974-79—The Dinner Party

Richard Serra (b.1939)
1969—Skullcracker series
1981—Tilted Arc
1992—Intersection II

Kiki Smith (b.1954)
1990—Untitled
1992-93—Mother

Maya Lin (b. 1959)
1982—Vietnam Veterans Memorial
1989—Civil Rights Memorial
1991—TOPO
1993—The Women's Table

18.4   Notable Craftspeople in America

Craftspeople are listed in alphabetical order under each craft category.

Ceramics
Robert Arneson (1930-1992)
Rudy Autio (b.1926)
Clarisse Cliff (1899-1972)
Maija Grotell (1899-1973)
Wayne Higby (b.1943)
Karen Karnes (b.1925)
Hui Ka Kwong (b.1922)
Glen Lukens (1887-1967)
Maria Montoya Martinez (1887-1980)
Gertrud (1935-1971) **and Otto** (b.1908) **Natzler**
Paul Soldner (b.1921)
Toshiko Takaezu (b.1929)
Peter Voulkos (b.1924)
Beatrice Wood (1893-1998)

Glass
Dale Chihuly (b.1941)
Dominick Labino (b.1910)
John LaFarge (1835-1910)
Harvey Littleton (b.1922)
Joel Philip Myers (b.1934)
Josh Simpson (b.1949)
Louis Comfort Tiffany (1848-1933)
Mary Ann (Toots) Zynsky (b.1951)

Fiber
Anni Albers (1899-1994)
Sheila Hicks (b.1934)
Jack Lenor Larsen (b.1927)
Dorothy Liebes (1899-1972)
Faith Ringgold (b.1930)
Edward Rossbach (b.1914)
Lenore Tawney (b.1907)
Carol Westfall (b.1938)
Claire Zeisler (1903-1991)

Decorative Arts
Elbert Hubbard (1856-1915)
Gustave Stickley (1858-1942)

Wood
Arthur Carpenter (b.1920)
Wendell Castle (b.1932)
Wharton Esherick (1887-1970)
Sam Maloof (b.1916)
George Nakashima (1905-1990)

Metalwork/Jewelry
Deborah Agundo (b.1939)
Mary Lee Hu (b.1943)
Sam Kramer (1913-1964)
Stanley Lechtzin (b.1936)
Albert Paley (b.1944)
John Prip (b.1922)
Mary Ann Scherr (b.1931)

18.5   Important American Architects

Architects are listed chronologically by date of birth.

Peter Harrison (1716-1775)
1750—Redwood Library (Newport, RI)
1754—King's Chapel (Boston)
1760—Christ Church (Cambridge, MA)
1761—Truro Synagogue (Newport, RI)

Thomas Jefferson (1743-1826)
1768-1809—Monticello (Charlottesville, VA)
1785—Virginia State Capitol (Richmond)
1822-1826—University of Virginia (Charlottesville)

Pierre L'Enfant (1754-1825)
1789—Federal Hall (NYC)
1791—City plan (Washington, DC)

Samuel McIntire (1757-1811)
1779—Pierce-Nichols House (Salem, MA)
1793—Theodore Lyman House (Waltham, MA)
1794—Elias Derby House (Salem, MA)

William Thornton (1759-1828)
1798—Octagon House (Washington, DC)

James Hoban (1762-1831)
1793—The White House (Washington, DC)

Charles Bulfinch (1763-1844)
1793—Connecticut State House (Hartford)
1797—Massachusetts State House (Boston)
1805—Faneuil Hall (Boston)
1827—U.S. Capitol (completion) (Washington, DC)
1832—Maine State House (Augusta)

Benjamin Latrobe (1764-1820)
1798—Bank of Pennsylvania (Philadelphia)
1803—U.S. Capitol (Washington, DC)
1818—St. Mary's Roman Catholic Cathedral (Baltimore)

Robert Mills (1781-1855)
1804—Sansom Street Church (Philadelphia)
1814—Washington Monument (Baltimore)
1836—Washington Monument (Washington, DC)
1836—U.S. Treasury Building (Washington, DC)
1839—U.S. Post Office Building (Washington, DC)
1839—U.S. Patent Office (Washington, DC)

Richard Upjohn (1802-1878)
1841—Trinity Episcopal Church (NYC)
1848—St. Mary's Episcopal Church (Burlington, NJ)

Alexander Jackson Davis (1803-1892)
1866—Lyndhurst (Tarrytown, NY)

James Renwick (1818-1895)
1843—Grace Church (NYC)
1858—St. Patrick's Cathedral (NYC)
1846—Smithsonian Institution (Washington, DC)
1859—Corcoran Gallery of Art (Washington, DC)
1865—Vassar College (Poughkeepsie, NY)
1887—All Saints Church (NYC)

Richard Morris Hunt (1827-1895)
1875—Tribune Building (NYC)
1886—Base, Statue of Liberty (NYC)
1891—Marble House (Newport, RI)
1895—The Breakers (Newport, RI)
1895—Biltmore House (Ashville, NC)
1895—Metropolitan Museum of Art (NYC)

Richard Mitchell Upjohn (1828-1903)
1861—Greenwood Cemetery (Brooklyn, NY)
1872—Connecticut State Capitol (Hartford)

William LeBaron Jenney (1832-1907)
1885—Home Insurance Building (Chicago)
1889—Leiter Building (Chicago)
1890—Fair Store (Chicago)

Henry Hobson Richardson (1838-1886)
1866—First Unitarian Church (Springfield, MA)
1866—Episcopal Church (West Medford, MA)
1872—Brattle Square Church (Boston)
1877—Trinity Episcopal Church (Boston)
1880—Sever Hall, Harvard (Cambridge, MA)
1884—Pittsburgh Jail and Court House (PA)
1887—Marshall Field Warehouse Building (Chicago)

Daniel Burnham (1846-1912) and John Root (1850-1891)
1882—Montauk Building (Chicago)
1886—The Rookery (Chicago)
1891—Monadnock Building (Chicago)
1902—Flatiron Building (NYC)

Charles McKim (1847-1909)
1887—Boston Public Library
1892—Rhode Island State Capitol (Providence)
1895—Columbia University Buildings (NYC)
1902—White House restoration (Washington, DC)
1903—Pennsylvania Station (NYC)
1906—Pierpont Morgan Library (NYC)

Henry Hardenbergh (1847-1918)
1884—The Dakota (NYC)
1885—Astor Building (NYC)
1892-1897—Waldorf-Astoria Hotel (NYC)
1906—Plaza Hotel (NYC)

Stanford White (1853-1906)
1885—Villard Houses (NYC)
1889—Madison Square Garden (NYC)
1889—Washington Arch (NYC)
1893—New York Herald Building (NYC)

Louis Sullivan (1856-1924)
1889—Walker Warehouse (Chicago)
1890—Auditorium Theater (Chicago)
1890—Wainwright Building (St. Louis)
1896—Guaranty Building (Buffalo, NY)
1906—Carson, Pirie & Scott Building (Chicago)

Ernest Flagg (1857-1947)
1891—Corcoran Art Gallery (Washington, DC)
1898-1908—Singer Building (NYC)
1899—United States Naval Academy (Annapolis, MD)

Cass Gilbert (1859-1934)
1896—Minnesota State Capitol (Minneapolis)
1904—Art Building (St. Louis)
1913—Woolworth Building (NYC)
1935—Supreme Court (Washington, DC)

Bernard Maybeck (1862-1957)
1907—Lawson House (Berkeley, CA)
1910—First Church of Christ Scientist (Berkeley, CA)
1915—Palace of Fine Arts (San Francisco)
1924—Packard Salesroom Building (San Francisco)

Charles (1868-1957) and Henry (1870-1954) Greene
1907—R.R. Blacker House (Pasadena, CA)
1908—Gamble House (Pasadena)
1909—Pratt House (Ojai, CA)

Frank Lloyd Wright (1869-1959)
1906—Unity Temple (Oak Park, IL)
1908—Robie House (Chicago)
1911—Taliesin (Spring Green, WI)
1936—Fallingwater (Bear Run, PA)
1938—Taliesin West (Paradise Valley, AZ)
1939—Johnson Wax Company Factory Complex (Racine, WI)
1959—The Guggenheim Museum (NYC)

Irving Gill (1870-1936)
1909—Bentham Hall and Tower (La Jolla, CA)
1916—Dodge House (Los Angeles)

Eliel Saarinen (1873-1950)
1926-1943—Cranbrook Academy (Bloomfield Hills, MI)
1942—Tabernacle Church of Christ (Columbus, IN)
1948—Smithsonian Institution Annex (Washington, DC)
1950—Christ Lutheran Church (Minneapolis)

Raymond Hood (1881-1934)
1923—Chicago Tribune Building
1924—American Radiator Building (NYC)
1931—McGraw-Hill Building (NYC)
1933—Rockefeller Center (NYC)

William Van Alen (1882-1954)
1930—Chrysler Building (NYC)

Walter Gropius (1883-1969)
1937—Architect's Residence (Lincoln, MA)
1941—Aluminum City (New Kensington, PA)
1950—Harvard University Graduate Center (Cambridge, MA)
1958—Pan Am Building (NYC)

Ludwig Mies Van Der Rohe (1886-1969)
1949-51—Lake Shore Drive Apartments (Chicago)
1950—Farnsworth House (Plano, IL)
1956—Crown Hall, Illinois Institute of Technology
1958—Seagram Building (with Philip Johnson) (NYC)

Richard Neutra (1892-1970)
1929—Lovell House (Hollywood CA)
1947—Kaufman House (Palm Springs, CA)
1962—Garden Grove Community Church (Garden Grove, CA)

Buckminster Fuller (1895-1983)
1927—Dymaxion House
1946—Wichita House
1967—United States Pavilion, Expo '67 (Montreal)

Louis Skidmore (1897-1953), Nathaniel Ownings (1903-1984) & John Ogden Merrill (1896-1975)
1951—Manufacturers Hanover Trust Building (NYC)
1956—Air Force Academy (Colorado Springs, CO)
1963—Beinecke Rare Book Library at Yale University (New Haven, CT)
1971—Lyndon Johnson Library at the University of Texas (Austin, TX)

Louis Kahn (1901-1974)
1952—Yale University Art Gallery (New Haven, CT)
1965—Richards Medical Center, University of Pennsylvania (Philadelphia)
1965—Salk Institute (La Jolla, CA)
1972—Kimball Art Museum (Fort Worth, TX)
1974—Yale Center for British Art (New Haven, CT)

Marcel Breuer (1902-1981)
1953-1968—Saint John's Abbey and University (Collegeville, MN)
1965—Armstrong Rubber Company Building (West Haven, CT)
1966—Whitney Museum of American Art (NYC)
1968—Department of Housing and Urban Development Office Building (Washington, DC)

Edward Durrell Stone (1902-1978)
1935—Mandel House (Mt. Kisco, NY)
1937—Museum of Modern Art (NYC)
1955—Commercial Museum (Philadelphia)
1971—Kennedy Center for the Performing Arts (Washington, DC)

Philip Johnson (b. 1906)
1949—Glass House (New Caanan, CT)
1954—Museum of Modern Art Annex and Sculpture Garden (NYC)
1954—Port Chester Synagogue (NY)
1958—Seagram Building (with Ludwig Mies Van Der Rohe) (NYC)
1964—New York State Theater at Lincoln Center (NYC)
1976—Penzoil Place (with John Burgee) (Houston)
1980—The Crystal Cathedral (Garden Grove, CA)
1983—AT&T Headquarters (with John Burgee) (NYC)

Eero Saarinen (1910-1961)
1956—Ingalls Hockey Rink at Yale University (New Haven, CT)
1962—Trans World Airlines Terminal, John F. Kennedy International Airport (NYC)
1962—Dulles International Airport (Washington, DC)
1963—Vivian Beaumont Theatre at Lincoln Center (NYC)
1964—Jefferson National Expansion Memorial Arch (St. Louis)

Minoru Yamasaki (1912-1986)
1955—Lambert Field-St. Louis Municipal Airport (MO)
1956—American Concrete Institute (Detroit)
1962—Science Pavilion, Seattle World's Fair
1966—Northwestern Life Insurance Company Building (Minneapolis)
1972—World Trade Center (NYC)

Edward Larrabee Barnes (b.1915)
1951—Reid House (Purchase, NY)
1983—IBM Building (NYC)
1970—Walker Art Center Building (Minneapolis)

I.M. Pei (b.1917)
1961—National Airline Terminal, Kennedy International Airport (NYC)
1967—L'Enfant Plaza (Washington, DC)
1968—Everson Museum of Art (Syracuse, NY)
1978—East Wing, National Gallery of Art (Washington, DC)
1986—First Interstate Bank Tower (Dallas)
1995—Rock and Roll Hall of Fame Museum (Cleveland)

Kevin Roche (b.1922)
1968—Oakland Museum (CA)
1968—Ford Foundation Headquarters (NYC)
1968—New Haven Coliseum and Convention Center (CT)
1969—College Life Insurance Building (Columbus, IN)
1988—Morgan Bank Headquarters Building (NYC)

Charles Moore (1925-1993)
1965—Sea Ranch Condominium (CA)
1975-80—Piazza d'Italia (New Orleans)
1982—Beverly Hills Civic Center (CA)

Robert Venturi (b.1925)
1962-64—Vanna Venturi House (Chestnut Hill, PA)
1980—Gordon Wu Hall, Princeton University
1984—Seattle Art Museum
1989—Bard College Library (Annandale-on-Hudson, NY)

Frank Gehry (b.1929)
1978—Gehry House
1983—Museum of Contemporary Art (Los Angeles)
1984—California Aerospace Museum (Los Angeles)
1991—Chiat/Day Building (Venice, CA)
1993—Walt Disney Concert Hall (Los Angeles)

Richard Meier (b.1934)
1971—Douglas House (Harbor Springs, MI)
1975-79—The Atheneum (New Harmony, IN)
1977—Bronx Developmental Center (NYC)
1983—High Museum of Art (Atlanta)
1997—Getty Museum (Los Angeles)

Michael Graves (b.1934)
1969—Benacerraf House (Princeton, NJ)
1981-83—Portland Public Services Building (OR)
1982—San Juan Capistrano Library (CA)
1982-87—Humana Medical Corporation HQ (Louisville, KY)

Charles Gwathmey (b.1938)
1976—Whig Hall, Princeton University (NJ)
1981—East Campus, Columbia University (NYC)
1982—de Menil residence (East Hampton NY)
1988—Westover School (Middlebury, CT)

Robert A.M. Stern (b.1939)
1979—Residence (East Hampton, NY)
1991—Ohrstrom Library, St. Paul's School (Concord, NH)
1995—Walt Disney Feature Animation Building (Burbank, CA)
1996—Celebration (master plan) (Orlando, FL)
1999—Tribeca Park Apartments, Battery Park City (NYC)

Andres Duany (b.1949) and Elizabeth Plater-Zyberk (b.1950)
1982—Atlantis Condominium (Miami)
1980s—Seaside (master plan) (Florida)

SECTION 19

Academic Disciplines

19.1 Major American Philosophers

Carnap, Rudolf (1891-1970) German-American philosopher. Leading member of the Vienna Circle.

Dewey, John (1859-1952) American philosopher and educator. Believed that intelligence needed to be stimulated by new experiences and that education should also ensure the moral development of children.

Edwards, Jonathan (1703-58) U.S. theologian. Foremost theologian of American Puritanism.

Godel, Kurt (1906-78) Austrian-born U.S. mathematician and logician. "Godel's theorem" (1931) demonstrated that there can be no proof of the consistency of a formal mathematical system from within that system.

James, William (1842-1910) U.S. philosopher and psychologist. Describing himself as a "radical Empiricist," he argued that beliefs are true if and because they work.

Mather, Cotton (1663-1728) Colonial clergyman and author. Was noted as a fiery preacher and as a major defender of orthodox Puritanism in Boston and throughout New England. Founded Yale University (1701).

Mead, George Herbert (1863-1931) U.S. philosopher and author. Although known initially for his philosophical work he later became associated with social psychology.

Peirce, Charles (1839-1914) American philosopher who founded pragmatism, the view that the practical significance of a concept determines its meaning, and pragmaticism. Also a founder of semiotics and a great logician.

Quine, W.V.O. (1908-) U.S. philosopher who wrote the seminal essay *Two Dogmas of Empiricism* (1951); studied under Alfred Whitehead and Carnap and taught at Harvard.

Santayana, George (1863-1952) Spanish-born philosopher who taught at Harvard and authored a number of books.

Tillich, Paul (1886-1965) German-born U.S. philosopher and theologian. Attempted to correlate biblical faith with modern philosophical Rationalism.

19.2 Major American Economists

Arrow, Kenneth Joseph (b. 1921) His primary field of study is collective decisions based on uncertainty and risk. Awarded the Nobel Prize in 1972 with Sir John Richard Hicks.

Buchanan, James McGill (b. 1919) Awarded the Nobel Prize in 1986 for his work on theories of public choice.

Chamberlain, Edward Hastings (1899-1967) Turned the attention of economists away from analysis of an industry as a whole to focus on individual firms within that industry.

Debreu, Gerard (b. 1921) Awarded the Nobel Prize in 1983 for his work on equilibrium between prices, production and consumer demand.

Feldstein, Martin (b. 1939) Macroeconomic theory.

Friedman, Milton (b. 1912) A leading figure in the Chicago School of economics, noted for his monetarist theories. Nobel Prize winner in 1976.

Galbraith, John Kenneth (b. 1908) His criticisms of social provision under capitalism have acted as a counterweight to the monetarism of Friedman.

Klein, Lawrence Robert (b. 1920) Economic adviser to President Carter (1976-81), awarded the Nobel Prize in 1980 for his work on forecasting business fluctuations.

Kuznets, Simon Smith (1901-85) Emigrated to the U.S. in 1922; his work contained original ideas on economic growth and social change, such as the 20-year "Kuznets cycle" of economic growth. Awarded the Nobel Prize in 1971.

Modigliani, Franco (b. 1918) General economic theory. Awarded the Nobel Prize in 1985.

Rostow, Walt (b. 1916) Adviser to President Kennedy and President Johnson. Noted for his theory of five stages of economic growth.

Samuelson, Paul (b. 1915) General economic theorist and educator, whose text books on economics are used in many U.S. colleges and universities. Received the Nobel Prize in 1970.

Schumpeter, Joseph (1883-1950) Harvard professor known for theories of capitalist development and business cycles.

Simon, Herbert Alexander (b. 1916) Awarded the Nobel Prize in 1978 for pioneering work on the decision-making process within commercial organizations.

Tobin, James (b. 1918) Awarded the Nobel Prize in 1981 for his "portfolio selection theory" of investment practices.

Veblen, Thorstein B. (1857-1919) As an economist and social philosopher, he scrutinized U.S. social mores, coining the term "conspicuous consumption" and criticizing those who practice it.

19.3 Major American Archaeologists, Anthropologists and Linguists

Albright, William Foxwell (1891-1971) U.S. biblical scholar. One of the first academics to apply archaeological and linguistic disciplines to the study of biblical history. His most famous work is *The Archaeology of Palestine and the Bible* (1932-1935).

Benedict, Ruth (1887-1948) U.S. anthropologist. Developed important theories on culture and personality with books such as *Patterns of Culture* (1934) and *The Chrysanthemum and the Sword* (1946) and was an early supporter of cultural relativism.

Binford, Lewis (b. 1930) U.S. archaeologist. Pioneer of anthropologically oriented "processual" school (New Archaeology).

Bloomfield, Leonard (1887-1949) U.S. linguist. Profoundly influenced U.S. studies of linquistics with his work on Algonquian and other languages. His textbook *Language* (1933) remains a classic.

Boas, Franz (1858-1942) German-born U.S. anthropologist. Established modern anthropology in the U.S. Author of the seminal *Race, Language, and Culture* (1940) and extensive writings on Eskimos and indigenous British Columbian peoples.

Chomsky, Noam (b. 1928) U.S. linguist and political activist. His *Syntactic Structures* (1957) introduced a new theory of language and began a revolution in linguistics.

Geertz, Clifford (b. 1923) U.S. cultural anthropologist. He advocates an interpretive stance in which cultures are compared to literary texts.

Herskovits, Melville (1895-1963) U.S. anthropologist. Overturned many prejudices about African Americans with his *The Myth of the Negro Past* (1941) and in 1961 founded the first department of African studies at a U.S. university (Northwestern).

Johanson, Donald Carl (b. 1943) U.S. paleoanthropologist. His finds of fossil hominids 3-4 million years old in Hadar, Ethiopia, include "Lucy."

Mead, Margaret (1901-1978) U.S. anthropologist. Her writings such as *Male and Female* (1949) and *Growth and Culture* (1951) have made anthropology accessible to a wide public.

Montagu, Ashley (b. 1905) U.S. anthropologist whose work covers evolution, culture, and child care. Famous for debunking old ideas about race, notably in *Man's Most Dangerous Myth: The Fallacy of Race* (1942).

Morgan, Lewis (1818-1881) U.S. ethnologist. He made extensive investigations into the cultures of American Indians. His best known work is *Ancient Society* (1877).

Sahlins, Marshall David (b. 1930) U.S. cultural anthropologist. Made major contributions in the field of Oceanian anthropology, cultural evolution, and the analysis of symbolism.

Whorf, Benjamin (1897-1941) U.S. linguist. He contrasted the language and vocabulary of the North American Hopi Indians with Standard Average European to show how language fundamentally influences peoples' perception of the world.

19.4 Notable American Historians

William Hickling Prescott (1796-1859)—Educated at Harvard. Focused his research and writing on Spanish, Mexican, and Peruvian history.

George Bancroft (1800-1891)—Called "the father of American history." Held several political offices and wrote a comprehensive history of the United States.

Charles Francis Adams (1835-1915)—Former Union Army officer, railroad commissioner of Massachusetts and president of the American Historical Society.

Henry Brooks Adams (1838-1918)—Harvard-educated historian, philosopher of history, and culture critic and son of the elder Charles Francis Adams. Wrote outstanding American biographies of Jefferson and Madison.

Alfred Thayer Mahan (1840-1914)—Naval officer and historian educated at the U.S. Naval Academy. Wrote several influential works on sea power, the first of which had a great influence on the policies of nations such as the U.S. and Germany.

John Fiske (1842-1901)—Educated at Harvard. Philosopher and historian responsible for spreading in the U.S. the ideas of British philosopher Herbert Spencer and Charles Darwin. Also wrote a nearly complete colonial history of the U.S.

Brooke Adams (1848-1927)—Harvard-educated lawyer. Wrote religious, political and economic histories of his times. A son of Charles Francis Adams Sr. and brother of Charles Francis Adams.

Frederick Jackson Taylor (1861-1932)—Educated at the University of Wisconsin and Johns Hopkins. Taught at Wisconsin and Harvard. Thought American society was shaped not by European influences, but by the Western frontier. Wrote relatively few works, but won a Pulitzer Prize in history in 1933.

James Henry Breasted (1865-1935)—Educated at Chicago Theological Seminary, Yale and The University of Berlin. An Orientalist best known for archaeological studies of Egypt and his founding of the Oriental Institute at the University of Chicago.

Charles A. Beard (1874-1948)—Leading progressive historian known for economic determinism. Professor of politics at Columbia and one of the founders of the New School for Social Research.

Carter Godwin Goodson (1875-1950)—Studied at Berea College, University of Chicago and Harvard. A dean of Howard University and West Virginia Institute. Devoted life to improving the image of the African American in history.

Mary Ritter Beard (1876-1958)—Educated at DePauw University. A prominent suffragist who organized women textile workers in New York City and authored several books on women. Also authored history books with husband Charles Austin Beard.

James Truslow Adams (1878-1949)—Educated at Brooklyn Polytech and Yale, won Pulitzer Prize in history for *The Founding of New England* (1921); his *Epic of America* (1931) was a bestseller.

Will Durant (1885-1981)—Educated at St. Peter's College and Columbia, taught philosophy at Columbia. Wrote extensively on philosophy and world history, including a popular series that began with *The Story of Civilization*. Won the Pulitzer Prize in 1968 for *Rousseau and the Revolution*. Collaborated in later years with wife Ariel Durant.

Samuel Eliot Morison (1887-1976)—Educated at Harvard. Member of the American Commission to Negotiate Peace that helped draft the Versailles Treaty. Received Presidential Medal of Freedom, wrote the official history of the U.S. Navy in World War II and won a Pulitzer Prize in 1960 for his biography of John Paul Jones.

Arthur Meier Schlessinger, Jr. (1888-1965)—Educated at Ohio State and Columbia, taught at Ohio State, State University of Iowa, then Harvard. Served as President of the American Historical Society. His several works focused on the sociological forces that shaped American history.

Bruce Catton (1899-1978)—Educated at Oberlin College. Editor of *American Heritage* magazine and author of books on the Civil War. In 1954 he won a Pulitzer Prize in history and the National Book Award in history and biography for *A Stillness at Appomattox*.

Henry Steele Commager (1902-)—Historian and educator who taught at Harvard, Columbia, and Amherst College; regarded as one of the foremost authorities on American history.

Barbara Tuchman (1912-1989)—Educated at Radcliffe. Author,self-trained historian and two-time Pulitzer Prize winner. Covered Spanish Civil War for *The Nation*, her father's magazine. Editor at U.S. Office of War Information.

19.5 Notable American Sociologists

Henry Charles Carey (1793-1879) Works include: *Essay on the Rate of Wages, Principles of Political Economy, The Past, the Present and the Future, the Harmony of Interests, The Principles of Social Science, the Unity of Law, The Slave Trade, Domestic and Foreign: Why It Exists and How It May Be Extinguished.*

Lewis Henry Morgan (1818-1881) Studied Native Americans and the evolution of the family. Works include: *Ancient Society.*

Lester Frank Ward (1841-1913) Works include: *Dynamic Sociology* (2 vols.), *Outline of Sociology, Pure Sociology* and *Applied Sociology.*

Albion Woodbury Small (1854-1926) Started the first sociology department (University of Chicago); works include: first textbook in sociology, *General Sociology* and *Origins of Sociology.*

George Herbert Mead (1863-1931) Well-known for theories which are today associated with symbolic interactionism and for the theories and methodologies he advanced in the Chicago school of sociological thought. Works include: *The Social Self, Scientific Method and the Moral Sciences,* and *The Genesis of the Self and Social Control.*

Charles Horton Cooley (1864-1929) Works include: *Social Organization: A Study of the Larger Mind* and *Human Nature and the Social Order.*

Raymond Pearl (1879-1940) Works include: *The Natural History of Population.*

William Fielding Ogburn (1886-1959) Works include: *Social Change With Respect to Culture and Original Nature, American Marriage and Family Relationships* (with Ernest Rutherford Groves), *Recent Social Trends in the United States, American Society in Wartime,* and *Technology and International Relations.*

Talcott Parsons (1902-1979) A functionalist concerned with the order of society, he was considered by many to be the most influential sociologist of the 20th century. Works include: *Structure of Social Action, Essays in Sociological Theory, Pure and Applied, The Social System,* and *Toward a General Theory of Action.*

Robert King Merton (1910-) A structural functionalist and student of Talcott Parsons who pioneered middle range sociology. Works include: *Social Theory and Social Structure.*

Charles Wright Mills (1916-1962) Proponent of the historical sociological perspective and critical of Parsons' branch of functionalism. Works include: *The New Men of Power, America's Labor Leaders, Character and Social Structure: The Psychology of Social Institutions* (with Hans Gerth), *Mass Society and Liberal Education, The Power Elite, The Causes of World War Three, The Sociological Imagination.*

19.6 American Winners of the Nobel Prize for Chemistry

1914	Theodore W. Richards	1965	Robert B. Woodward	1983	Henry Taube
1932	Irving Langmuir	1966	Robert S. Muliken	1984	Bruce Merrifield
1934	Harold C. Urey	1968	Lars Onsager	1985	Herbert A. Hauptman
1946	James B. Sumner	1972	Christian B. Anfinsen		Jerome Karle
	John H. Northrop		Stanford Moore	1986	Dudley R. Herschbach
	Wendell M. Stanley		Liam H. Stein		Yuan T. Lee
1949	William F. Giauque	1974	Paul J. Flory	1987	Donald J. Cram
1951	Edwin M. McMillan	1976	William N. Lipscomb		Charles Pederson
	Glenn T. Seaborg	1977	Ilya Prigogine	1989	Sidney Altman
1954	Linus C. Pauling	1979	Herbert C. Brown		Thomas R. Cech
1955	Vincent Du Vigneaud	1980	Paul Berg		
1960	Willard F. Libby		Walter Gilbert		
1961	Melvin Calvin				

19.7 American Winners of the Nobel Prize for Physics

1907	Albert A. Michelson	1968	Luis W. Alvarez
1923	Robert A. Milikan	1969	Murray Gell-Mann
1927	Arthur H. Compton	1972	John Bardeen
1936	Carl D. Anderson		John R. Schrieffer
1937	Clinton J. Davisson		Leon N. Cooper
1939	Ernest O. Lawrence	1973	Ivar Giaever
1943	Otto Stern	1975	James Rainwater
1944	Isidor I. Rabi	1976	Burton Richter
1945	Wolfgang Pauli		Samuel Chao Ching Ting
1946	Percy W. Bridgman	1977	John H. Van Vleck
1952	Felix Bloch		Philip W. Anderson
	Edward M. Purcell	1978	Amo A. Penzias
1955	Willis E. Lamb, Jr.		Robert W. Wilson
	Polykarp Kusch	1979	Sheldon L. Glashow
1956	William B. Shockley		Steven Weinberg
	John Bardeen	1980	James W. Cronin
	Walter H. Brattain		Val I. Fitch
1959	Emilio G. Segre	1981	Arthur L. Schawlow
	Owen Chamberlain		Nicholas Bloembergen
1960	Donald A. Glaser	1982	Kenneth Wilson
1961	Rudolf L. Mossbauer	1983	William A. Fowler
	Robert Hofstadter		Subrahmanyan Chandrasekhar
1963	Maria Mayer	1988	Leon Lederman
	Eugene P. Wigner		Melvin Schwartz
1964	Charles H. Townes		Jack Steinberger
1965	Richard Feynman	1989	Norman Ramsey
1967	Hans A. Bethe		Hans Dehmelt

19.8 Major Scientific Discoveries and Accomplishments, 1746-1999

1746   John Winthrop, author of *Notes on Sunspots* (1739) establishes the country's first laboratory for experimental physics at Harvard.

1751   Benjamin Franklin proves that lightning is electricity by flying a kite attached to a metal key during a thunderstorm.

1800   Fossil footprints of Triassic dinosaurs are found in the Connecticut Valley.

1831   Chemist Samuel Guthrie discovers chloroform.

1839   The country's first official observatory is founded at Harvard College.

1847   First American woman astronomer Maria Mitchell discovers a comet.

1850   William Bond makes the first photograph of a star, establishing the field of stellar photography.

1856   Dinosaur fossils are first identified in the Western Hemisphere by paleontologist Joseph Leidy.

1869   The developer of theoretical astrophysics, Jonathan Lane is the first to mathematically investigate the sun as a gaseous body.

1869   Astronomer Charles Young is the first to photograph the spectrum of the sun's corona.

1870   The U.S. Weather Bureau is established.

1872   Yellowstone is declared the first U.S. National Park.

1872   Astronomer Henry Draper is the first to photograph a stellar spectrum.

1875   Paleontologist O.C. Marsh presents evidence of a link between birds and reptiles.

1876   In New York State, geologist Charles Doolittle Walcott makes the first American discovery of a trilobite with preserved appendages.

1876   Using a white spot he discovers on the surface of Saturn, astronomer Asaph Hall determines the planet's period of rotation.

1877   Asaph Hall discovers the first satellite of Mars.

1879   Astronomer E.C. Pickering invents the meridian photometer.

1880   Astronomer Henry Draper is the first to photograph a nebula.

1881   A pioneer in celestial photography, astronomer Edward Emerson Barnard makes the first photographic discovery of a comet.

1889   Edward Barnard takes the first photograph of the Milky Way.

1890   The Harvard Classification System for classifying stars is introduced by astronomers Edward Pickering and Williamina Paton Fleming.

1892   Edward Barnard discovers a fifth satellite around Jupiter.

1895   Astronomer James Keeler observes that the rings around Saturn consist of (non-solid) particles.

1897   The world's largest refracting telescope is installed at the Yerkes Observatory in Williams Bay, WI.

1899   In the first instance of using photography to discover satellites, William Pickering discovers Phoebe, Saturn's ninth satellite.

1903   Astronomer George Ellery Hale begins creating an observatory on Mount Wilson, near Pasadena, CA.

1905   Percival Lowell predicts the presence of Pluto.

1908   George Hale is the first to detect the magnetic field of an extraterrestrial body.

1914   Astronomer Seth Barnes Nicholson discovers four satellites of Jupiter.

1918   Astronomer Harlow Shapley uses the reflecting telescope on Mount Wilson to measure the size of our galaxy.

1921   Helium is first used as a lifting gas in the U.S. Navy C-7 Dirigible.

1922   Physicist William Weber Coblentz uses his invention, the thermocouple, to determine the surface temperature of the planet Mercury.

1924   Astronomer Edwin Hubble devises the first system for the classification of galaxies according to shape.

1926   Robert Goddard launches the world's first liquid-fuel rocket.

1929   The theory of the expanding universe is begun by Edwin Hubble's formulation of the law that galaxies recede from our galaxy at speeds proportional to their distances.

1930   The planet Pluto is discovered by astronomer Clyde Tompaugh.

1930   Chemist Thomas Midgley Jr. discovers freon, to be used as a coolant in air conditioning and refrigeration.

1930   Physicist Artur Compton offers the first indication that earth's magnetic field influences cosmic radiation.

1931   Harold Urey discovers heavy hydrogen.

1931   Radio astronomy is founded, following the accidental discovery by Bell Laboratories' Karl Jansky of radio radiation coming from the sky.

1932   Phycisist Carl David Anderson discovers the positron, the first known form of antimatter.

1935   Seismologist Charles Richter develops the Richter scale for measuring the severity of earthquakes.

1941   President Franklin D. Roosevelt approves the Manhattan Project to develop a nuclear fission bomb.

1942   The first radio maps of the universe are made by astronomer Grote Reber.

1944   The first nuclear reactor begins operation in Washington State.

1945   Grand Rapids, Michigan is the site of the first fluoridation of water supplies.

1945   Robert Oppenheimer directs the construction of the atomic bomb.

1945   The first man-made atomic bomb is exploded at a test site in New Mexico.

1947   Carbon dating is invented by chemist Willard Frank Libby.

1947   Chuck Yeager breaks the sound barrier in the first piloted supersonic airplane flight.

1948   The Hale telescope, the largest reflecting telescope in the world, is built at Mount Palomar, CA.

1948   Physicist Richard Feynman develops the theory of quantum electrodynamics.

1949   Genes are first photographed at the University of Southern California.

1949   Physicist Harold Lyons invents the atomic clock.

1949   The first multi-stage rocket is launched from Cape Canaveral, Florida.

1950   DuPont introduces the polymer fiber Orlon.

1951   Astronomer William Morgan discovers the spiral structure of the Milky Way galaxy.

1951   Electricity is first generated by nuclear power.

1952   Astronomers Harold and Horace Babcock use their solarmagnetograph to localize magnetic fields on the surface of the sun.

1952   The U.S. detonates the first hydrogen bomb in the Pacific.

1952   Astronomer Walter Baade discovers that the distance of the Andromeda galaxy is over two million light-years away.

1954   The field ion microscope is invented by physicist Erwin Mueller.

1957   The fiber-optic endoscope is developed by physician Basil Hischowitz and physicists Lawrence Curtis and C. Wilbur Peters.

1958   James Van Allen discovers radiation belts surrounding Earth.

1960   The U.S. launches the first weather satellite.

1960   The laser is invented by physicist Theodore Maiman.

1960   The first quasars are discovered by American and Australian astronomers.

1961   Alan Shepard is the first American to fly in space.

1962   Astronomers Roland Carpenter and Richard Goldstein determine the rotation of Venus.

1963   The first commercial nuclear reactor opens in New Jersey.

1964   John Glenn is the first American to orbit the earth.

1964   Physicist Hong Yee Chiu coins the term *quasar.*

1964   Physicist Murray Gell-Mann introduces the concept of "quarks."

1965   Edward White is the first American to walk in space.

1965   Scientist Emmet Leith tests holography.

1966   The *Surveyor 1* is the first (unmanned) U.S. spacecraft to land on the moon.

1969   Neil Armstrong, emerging from Apollo 11, becomes the first human being to set foot on the moon.

1969   Three American astronomers make the first optical identification of a pulsar.

1971   Mars probe *Mariner 9* is the first man-made object to be placed in orbit about another planet.

1973   *Skylab,* America's first orbiting space station, is launched.

1973   Paul Berg and Stanley Cohen produce the first successful gene splicing.

1974   Astronomer Carles Kowall discovers Leda, Jupiter's thirteenth satellite.

1974   F. Sherwood Rowland and Mario Molina are the first to point out ozone depletion caused by chlorofluoro-carbons.

1977   Charles Kowal discovers Charon, an asteroid orbiting between Saturn and Uranus.

1977   James Elliot discovers rings around Uranus.

1978   The U.S. launches *Seasat I,* the first satellite dedicated to the gathering of oceanic data.

1979   The Three Mile Island (PA) nuclear reactor experiences a partial meltdown.

1980   Geologic discoveries by physicist Luis Walter Alvarez lead to the first linking of asteroids and dinosaur extinction.

1982   The first wind farm, generating 2.5 megawatts of power, is built by the U.S. Department of Energy at the Goldendale Columbia River Gorge in Washington State.

1984   Astronaut Bruce McCandless II makes the first untethered space walk during a mission of the *Challenger* space shuttle.

1986   *Pioneer 10* becomes the first man-made spacecraft to leave the solar system.

1987   John Stanford of Cornell University devises a gene gun that can fire new genetic material directly into a cell at high speed.

1988   Geneticist Henry Erlich devises DNA fingerprinting from a single hair.

1990   The Hubble Space Telescope is the first telescope to be placed in outer space.

1991   The *Magellan* spacecraft completes the first map of the surface of Venus.

1991   Geologists Dennis Kent and Paul Olsen are the first to demonstrate a link between periodic changes in the earth's orbit and its longer climate cycles.

1991   The first bacteria to be recovered from an extinct animal are found in the remains of a mastodon discovered in Newark, Ohio.

1992   American researchers produce the first solid compound of helium.

1992   Irradiated food first becomes available in American groceries.

1993   Climatologist Reginald Newell first identifies atmospheric rivers of water vapor.

1994   American seismologists first sense the largest deep earthquake ever reported.

1995   Physicists Carl Wieman and Eric Cornell produce a new state of matter, a Bose-Einstein condensate.

1997   Scientists at Oregon Regional Primate Research Center create two rhesus monkeys using DNA taken from cells of developing monkey embryos.

Sources: Bruno, Leonard C. *Science & Technology Firsts.* Detroit: Gale, 1996. Bunch, Bryan. *The Henry Holt Handbook of Current Science & Technology.* New York: Henry Holt and Company. 1992. Hellemans, Alexander and Bryan Bunch. *The Timetables of Science.* New York: Simon & Schuster, Inc., 1988. Mount, Ellis and Barbara A. List. *Milestones in Science and Technology.* Second Edition. Phoenix, AZ: The Oryz Press, 1994. Ochoa, George and Melinda Corey. *The Timeline Book of Science.* New York: The Stonesong Press, Inc., 1995. Platt, Richard. *Smithsonian Visual Timeline Book of Inventions.* London: Dorling Kindersley Publishing, 1994.

SECTION 20

Performing Arts and Popular Culture

20.1 Chronology of the Performing Arts: Music, Theater and Dance, 1640-1999

1640 The *Bay Psalm Book,* the first book printed in America, includes instructions as to the tunes to which the psalms might be sung

1665 William Darby's *Ye Bare and Ye Cubb,* performed at Cowles Tavern in Accomac County, Virginia, is the first English-language play on record to be presented in America

1680s Boston ministers complain about mixed dancing and discussion of "play-acting"

c.1700 Richard Hunter petitions the acting governor of the Province of New York for a license to present plays in New York City

1721 Cotton Mather writes *The Accomplished Singer* to help New Englanders learn how to sing properly

1730 A production of *Romeo and Juliet,* in New York City, is the first known presentation in America of a Shakespeare play

1735 An opera performed in Charleston, South Carolina, is probably the first presentation of a musical piece on an American stage

1736 Students at the College of William and Mary in Williamsburg, Virginia, perform *Cato,* a tragedy by Joseph Addison

1746 America's first composer, William Billings, is born

1750 Boston passes a law against dramatic performances

1751 The Virginia Company of Comedians, originally based in Philadelphia, is the first professional theater company in America. Their opening performance is *Richard III*

1762 The St. Cecilia Society, the nation's oldest musical society, is founded in Charleston, South Carolina

1766 The Southwark Theatre in Philadelphia is the first permanent theater building built in America. The American Company of Comedians, housed there, is the first professional company to produce native drama

1767 Andrew Barton's *The Disappointment, or The Force of Credulity* is the first opera to be written by an American composer

1771 An early circus act, using horses, is staged in Salem, Massachusetts

1774 Congress signs a resolution that plays be abandoned during the Revolutionary War period

1779 The Pennsylvania Legislature passes a law prohibiting all forms of theatrical entertainment
In New York, the British stage a series of performances

1787 Royall Tyler's comedy, *The Contrast,* is the first American play professionally produced in New York

1789 The prohibition against theater in Philadelphia is repealed

1790 America's first professional dancer, John Durang, makes his stage debut with the Old American theatre company at the Baltimore (MD) Theatre
The first foreign-language opera is performed in New York

1792 Boston repeals its anti-theater law

Late 1700s Theaters and theater companies spring up in major American cities

Early 1800s Theater troupes begin traveling west and south to put on performances

1820s Blackfaced white song and dance men, known as Ethiopian Delineators, become popular
The practice of scheduling theatrical perfomances six nights of the week is adopted

1826 America's first star and major tragedian actor, Edwin Forrest, stars in Philadelphia in *Othello*

1835 America's largest opera theatre, the St. Charles, is built in New Orleans

1842 The New York Philharmonic Society is founded

1843 The first minstrel show is performed by the Virginia Minstrels in New York City. One year later, a minstrel troupe performs in the White House

1849 The Eagle Theatre, California's first, opens in Sacramento

1850s-1860s Stephen Foster composes such songs as "Camptown Races," "Old Black Joe," "My Old Kentucky Home" and "Jeanie with the Light Brown Hair"
The growth of the nation's railroads enable leading theatrical and musical performers to tour the country and increase their following
New York City establishes its position as headquarters for American theatre

1852 Numerous and widely successful productions of Harriet Beecher Stowe's *Uncle Tom's Cabin* mark the first time issues of race and slavery are introduced on the American stage

1858   Notable actor Joseph Jefferson appears in Tom Taylor's *Our American Cousin*

1859   Dan Emmett composes *Dixie*

1860s   Black spirituals begin to receive recognition

Variety shows, precursors to vaudeville, come into being

Blacks begin acting in minstrel shows

Melodramas are popular theater fare

Conservatories of music are founded in Boston, Baltimore, Cincinnati, and Oberlin, Ohio

1864   The three members of the acting Booth family, Junius, Edwin and John Wilkes, appear together at a benefit perfomance of *Julius Caesar* in New York's Winter Garden

1865   John Wilkes Booth assassinates President Abraham Lincoln during a performance at Ford's Theatre, Washington, DC

1866   Dion Boucicault's version of Washington Irving's *Rip Van Wrinkle,* with Joseph Jefferson in the title role, opens on the New York stage with great success. Jefferson portrays this character for the next half century

1869   Booth's Theatre, designed with the latest mechanical and design innovations to enable easier movement of scenery, opens in New York City

1877   Thomas Alva Edison invents the phonograph

1878   Americans take to Gilbert and Sullivan's light opera, *H.M.S. Pinafore*

1879   Character actor Otis Skinner makes his New York City debut

1880s   Touring female burlesque shows become popular

Vaudeville, as acceptable family entertainment, comes into being

Opera houses are built across America

1880   Barnum and Bailey's Circus is formed

1881   The Boston Symphony Orchestra is founded

1883   The Metropolitan Opera House opens in New York City

1884   The Lyceum Theatre in New York City begins an acting school, the precursor to the American Academy of Dramatic Art

1885   The Pittsburgh Symphony Orchestra is founded

1888   Edwin Booth founds The Players theater group

1889   The Auditorium Building, Chicago's opera house, opens

1890s   Broadway theater marquees are electrified and Broadway becomes known as "The Great White Way"

The cakewalk, an old slave dance, is popularized by the black dance team of Charlie Johnson and Dora Dean and the leading black vaudeville team of Bert Williams and George Walker

Antonin Dvorak, head of the National Conservatory of Music in New York, announces his admiration for black spirituals and advises his American colleagues to incorporate them in their concert music

1891   Bronson Howard founds the American Dramatists Club, forerunner of the Dramatists' Guild

1892   John Philip Sousa forms his band

1893   Theater stagehands form a union

1894   *Prince Ananias,* Victor Herbert's first comic opera, opens

Billboard magazine is founded

1896   *Oriental America at Mrs. Waldorf's Fifth Anniversary* is the first black opera on Broadway

1897   Scott Joplin writes "Maple Leaf Rag," ushering in the era of Ragtime

John Philip Sousa composes "The Stars and Stripes Forever"

1900   The Philadelphia Orchestra is founded

1900s   Tap dancing comes into being

The Shubert Brothers begin to gain control of theaters nationwide

1902   Bert Williams and George Walker produce and star in *In Dahomey,* Broadway's first big all-black musical

Victor Herbert composes *Babes in Toyland*

Ethel Barrymore stars in *The Girl with the Green Eyes*

1904   George M. Cohan's first major work, *Little Johnny Jones,* opens on Broadway. The show includes such songs as "Give My Regards to Broadway" and "Yankee Doodle Dandy"

1905   The Juilliard School of Music opens in New York City

Maude Adams stars in *Peter Pan*

Variety is founded

1907   Florenz Ziegfeld stages his first *Follies* on the roof of the New York Theatre

1908   Charles Ives, America's first important nationalist composer of symphonic and chamber music, composes "Unanswered Question" for two orchestras

1910s   Tin Pan Alley, a group of New York based songwriters and music publishers including Sammy Kahn, Irving Berlin and Jerome Kern, gains popularity

1910   Victor Herbert composes the Broadway show *Naughty Marietta*

Comedian Bert Williams is the first black to perform in the *Ziegfeld Follies*

1910s   The Tango (dance) gains popularity

Fanny Brice first appears in the *Ziegfeld Follies*

1911   Bessie Smith is discovered by "Ma" Rainey

Irving Berlin composes "Alexander's Ragtime Band"

The San Francisco Symphony Orchestra is founded

1912   Vernon and Irene Castle, popularizers of ballroom dancing and the first performers to dance not in costume but in contemporary clothes, become the rage of New York

Actors' Equity Association is founded

1913   The Palace Theatre, symbolic of vaudeville, opens on Broadway

The Houston Symphony Orchestra is founded

1914   The American Society of Composers, Authors and Publishers (ASCAP) is founded to protect copyrights and performing rights

"Father of the Blues" W.C. Handy publishes "The St. Louis Blues"

The Detroit Symphony Orchestra is founded

1915   America's first nonprofit regional theater, the Cleveland Playhouse, opens

Scott Joplin arranges a performance of his innovative opera, *Treemonisha*

Modern dance theorist Ruth St. Denis and her husband Ted Shawn open their Denishawn dance school, where prominent students are to include dance legend Martha Graham

1916   Katharine Cornell first appears with the Washington Square Players

Two Eugene O'Neill plays are staged on Cape Cod by the Provincetown Players

America's first actors' strike closes every Broadway theater

1918   The New York Philharmonic Society bans compositions by living German composers

The Yiddish Art Theatre opens in New York

The Cleveland Orchestra is founded

1919   The Los Angeles Philharmonic Orchestra gives its first concert

Elmer Rice's *The Adding Machine* is the first production of the newly founded Theatre Guild

George Gershwin writes *La, La Lucille,* his first musical

1920   Jazz conductor Paul Whiteman opens the Palais Royale on Broadway, inaugurating the decade's "Jazz Age"

Eugene O'Neill's first full-length play, *Beyond the Horizon,* is produced on Broadway

Rudolph Valentino appears in *The Four Horsemen of the Apocalypse*

1920s   Harlem's Cotton Club, offering black talent to a white audience, becomes popular

1920s   The Lindy, a dance named after Charles Lindbergh, becomes popular

Richard Rodgers and Lorenz Hart write their first musical, *The Poor Little Ritz Girl*

Strip teases and burlesque gain in popularity

1921   The all-black Broadway musical, *Shuffle Along* with music by Eubie Blake, opens, helping to usher in the Harlem Renaissance

1922   *Abie's Irish Rose* begins its record-breaking five-year Broadway run

Fred and Adele Astaire's appearance on Broadway in *For Goodness Sake* receives national acclaim

Paul Robeson appears in O'Neill's *Emperor Jones* at the Provinceton Playhouse

1923   George Gershwin composes *Rhapsody in Blue*

Bessie Smith, "Empress of the Blues," makes her first record, "Down Hearted Blues"

1924   Martha Graham establishes her dance school in New York City

Louis Armstrong records his first record, "Everybody Loves My Baby"

1925   The Charleston (dance) becomes popular

The Lawrence Welk Band begins playing

1926   Actress Eva LeGallienne founds the Civic Reperatory Theater in New York

Jazz innovator Jelly Roll Morton organizes his band, Jelly Roll Morton's Red Hot Peppers

Louis Armstrong and blues singer Sippie Wallace make a series of records together

The Carter family, pioneers of modern country music, begin to perform

Hoagy Carmichael writes "Stardust"

1927   *Show Boat,* a musical adaptation of Edna Ferber's novel with music and lyrics by Jerome Kern and Oscar Hammerstein II, opens on Broadway

1928   George Gershwin composes *An American in Paris,* with lyrics by his brother, Ira

The Front Page, by Ben Hecht and Charles MacArthur opens on Broadway

Bill "Bojangles" Robinson gains popularity with white audiences

Doris Humphrey forms a dance school and company

1929   Four-year-old Sammy Davis, Jr. enters show business

The Chicago Civic Opera House opens

Early 1930s   The Federal Theater Project, funded by the Works Progress Administration, is the country's first government-subsidized producing organization

Nashville, Tennessee, and the Grand Ole Opry become the center of country music

Duke Ellington releases *Mood Indigo*

1931   Helmsley Winfield founds The New Negro Art Theatre Dance Group, the first professional black dance group

Of Thee I Sing by George and Ira Gershwin and George S. Kaufman is the first musical to win a Pulitzer Prize

Cole Porter's "Let's Do It" launches his song-writing career

1932   New York's Palace Theater, the ultimate vaudeville house, becomes a movie theater

San Francisco's War Memorial Opera House opens

1933   The American Ballet (becoming, in 1948, the New York City Ballet) is founded by Lincoln Kirstein and choreographer George Balanchine

1934   Kirstein and Balanchine found the School of American Ballet

Virgil Thomson's opera *Four Saints in Three Acts,* with libretto by Gertrude Stein, is first performed

1935   George Gershwin composes *Porgy and Bess,* based on DuBose Heyward's book, with lyrics by Ira Gershwin

1936   Ella Fitzgerald achieves acclaim as a scat singer

Samuel Barber composes *Adagio for Strings*

Billie Holliday gains fame as a jazz and blues singer

1937   George S. Kaufman and Moss Hart's *You Can't Take it With You* wins the Pulitzer Prize

1937-54   The National Broadcasting Company forms the NBC Symphony Orchestra for conductor Arturo Toscanini and a host of virtuoso musicians

1938   The first big band jazz, or swing, concert, with Benny Goodman, Harry James, Gene Krupa, Lionel Hampton and Count Basie takes place in New York's Carnegie Hall

Glenn Miller forms his band

Aaron Copeland composes the ballet *Billy the Kid*

1939   Ballet Theatre is founded by Richard Pleasant and Lucia Chase

Irving Berlin writes "God Bless America"

John Cage composes *Constructions in Metal*

Marian Anderson sings to an audience of 75,000 at the Lincoln Memorial

Life With Father, written by Russel Crouse and Howard Lindsay based on the book by Clarence Day, Jr., opens its eight-year Broadway run

1940   *Pal Joey* by Rodgers and Hart opens on Broadway

Artie Shaw records Cole Porter's "Begin the Beguine"

Folk singing legend Woody Guthrie makes his first record

1940s   The Jitterbug (dance) becomes popular

A new jazz movement called *bebop* develops, characterized by the music of Charlie "Bird" Parker

1941   The San Francisco Ballet is formed

1942   Breaking his contract with the Tommy Dorsey Band, Frank Sinatra is booked into an eight-week engagement at New York's Paramount Theatre and becomes a bobby-soxer idol

Bing Crosby introduces Irving Berlin's "White Christmas"

Aaron Copeland composes the ballet *Rodeo,* choreographed by Agnes de Mille

Katherine Dunham, known for her use of black-inspired movements and rhythms, choreographs *Tropical Revue,* her first Broadway production

1943 *Oklahoma!,* choreographed by Agnes de Mille, with lyrics by Oscar Hammerstein II and music by Richard Rogers, premieres. A landmark in American musical theater, it is the first musical in which the songs and dances advance the story

Paul Robeson stars on Broadway in *Othello*

At age twenty-five, Leonard Bernstein is appointed assistant conductor of the New York Philharmonic

New York City establishes the City Center of Music and Drama

1944 Jerome Robbins' first ballet staging, *Fancy Free,* made for the Ballet Theatre, with music by Leonard Bernstein, expands into Broadway's *On the Town*

Aaron Copeland composes the ballet *Appalachian Spring,* choreographed and danced by Martha Graham

1945 *The Glass Menagerie* establishes Tennessee Williams as a major new talent

1947 Lee Strasberg founds the Actors Studio in New York City

Alan Jay Lerner and Frederick Loewe's *Brigadoon* opens on Broadway with choreography by Agnes de Mille

1948 Maria Tallchief joins the New York City Ballet

Country legend Hank Williams (1923-1953) has his first number one hit

Columbia Records introduces long-playing 33-1/3 phonograph records, RCA-Victor debuts the 45 rpm record

1949 Rodgers and Hammerstein's *South Pacific,* directed by Joshua Logan, opens on Broadway

Death of a Salesman starring Lee J. Cobb opens on Broadway, establishing Arthur Miller as a major new playwright

Miles Davis leads a nonet in a series of cool jazz recordings

Folk legend Pete Seeger forms the Weavers

The Off-Broadway Theatre League is formed

1950 Broadway's first theater-in-the-round opens

Nat "King" Cole sings "Mona Lisa"

1951 Gian-Carlo Menotti composes his opera *Amahl and the Night Visitors*

American Ballet Theatre School is founded

1952 Circle-in-the-Square Theater opens in New York City

1953 Avant-garde composer John Cage, the father of chance music, composes "4'33"

Merce Cunningham founds his dance company

1954 The Newport (Rhode Island) Jazz Festival is held for the first time

Cleveland disc jockey Alan Freed begins playing rhythm and blues records for white teenagers, ushering in the era of rock and roll

Joseph Papp founds the New York Shakespeare Festival

Paul Taylor forms his dance company

Elvis Presley makes his first record

1955 Bob Fosse choreographs *Damn Yankees*

Ned Rorem composes *Design for Orchestra* and *The Poet's Requiem*

Beverly Sills begins her association with the New York City Opera

Ray Charles has his first hit

The Miles Davis Quintet becomes a leading jazz group

Fats Domino popularizes New Orleans rhythm and blues

Country music legend Johnny Cash cuts his first record

1956 Robert Joffrey founds the Joffrey Ballet

Ballet Theatre becomes the American Ballet Theatre

Lerner and Lowe's *My Fair Lady* opens on Broadway

Doris Day sings "Que Sera, Sera"

Frankie Valli forms the white doo-wop group The Four Seasons

Ringling Brothers and Barnum & Bailey Circus plays its final performance under a big canvas tent

Elvis Presley's hit singles include "Hound Dog," "Don't Be Cruel," and "Love Me Tender"

1957   *West Side Story* opens on Broadway with music by Leonard Bernstein, lyrics by Stephen Sondheim and choreography by Jerome Robbins
Meredith Willson's *The Music Man* opens
Leontyne Price makes her operatic stage debut with the San Francisco Opera
John Coltrane and Thelonius Monk begin playing jazz together
Rock pioneer Buddy Holly records "That'll Be the Day"
Sarah Caldwell founds the Boston Opera Group
Sam Cooke has his first big hit

1958   Alvin Ailey founds the Alvin Ailey American Dance Theatre
Leonard Bernstein becomes musical director of the New York Philharmonic
Chuck Berry releases his first album
James Brown has his first hit record

1959   *A Raisin in the Sun,* by Lorraine Hansberry, opens, the first Broadway premiere of a play by an African American woman
Rodgers and Hammerstein's *The Sound of Music* opens
The Columbia-Princeton Electronic Music Center is established in Manhattan
Virgil Thomson composes his *Requiem Mass*

1960   Chubby Checker popularizes the Twist (dance)
Roy Orbison has his first hit record
The Fantasticks by Tom Jones and Harvey Schmidt premieres in New York, where it is still running

1961   Bob Dylan moves to New York City where he begins to sing in Greenwich Village coffee houses and makes his first record. Joan Baez joins him in concert bills, singing protest songs
Leontyne Price debuts with the Metropolitan Opera
Johnny Mercer and Henry Mancini write "Moon River"
Milton Babbitt composes *Composition for Synthesizer*
Peter, Paul and Mary form their folk trio

1962   Leopold Stokowski founds the American Symphony Orchestra in New York
Country and western singer/songwriter Willie Nelson writes "Crazy" for Patsy Cline
Soul music gains popularity
The Limbo becomes a popular dance

1963   Rock's California Sound, as exemplified by the Beach Boys, gains popularity

1964   Go-go dances, such as the monkey, watusi, frug, become popular
Fiddler on the Roof, choreographed by Jerome Robbins, opens on Broadway
Barbra Streisand stars in *Funny Girl*
New York's Lincoln Center Arts Center is completed
Bob Dylan records "The Times They Are a-Changin'"

1965   The National Endowment for the Arts is created

Mid-1960s   Motown music, founded by Berry Gordy and exemplified by such groups as the Supremes, the Temptations, the Four Tops and Stevie Wonder, becomes popular
Folk-rock music becomes popular
Paul Simon and Art Garfunkel release "The Sounds of Silence"

1966   Samuel Barber composes *Antony and Cleopatra*
Sweet Charity, choreographed by Bob Fosse, opens

1967   Eliot Feld makes his choreographic debut with *Harbinger* perfomed by the American Ballet Theatre
The rock musical *Hair* opens
Soul singer Aretha Franklin begins selling millions of records
Country rock becomes popular
White blues singer Janis Joplin stops the show at the Monterey (CA) International Pop Festival, the first major rock festival
The Grateful Dead, of psychedelic rock fame, release their debut album
Janis Ian sings "Society's Child" on television accompanied by Leonard Bernstein and the New York Philharmonic

1968   Lar Lubovitch founds his modern-dance company
Reggae music is introduced
Singer/songwriter Joni Mitchell records her first album

1969   The rock festival Woodstock attracts 400,000 young music fans to upstate Bethel, New York
            78,000 concert-goers attend the Newport (RI) Jazz Festival
            Arthur Mitchell, the first black to achieve stardom in modern American ballet, founds the Dance Theater of Harlem
1970   James Taylor releases "Sweet Baby James"
1971   Moses Pendleton and Jonathan Wolken found the Pilobolus Dance Theater
            Leonard Bernstein composes *Mass*
            Washington, D.C.'s John F. Kennedy Center for the Performing Arts opens
            Joni Mitchell releases "Blue"
1973   Twyla Tharp choreographs *Deuce Coupe* for the Joffrey Ballet
1975   Michael Bennett's *A Chorus Line* opens on Broadway
            Bruce Springsteen releases "Born to Run"
Mid 1970s   Punk rock and disco music become popular
1976   Philip Glass's minimalist opera, *Einstein on the Beach,* performs to sold-out houses
            Sarah Caldwell is the first woman to appear as conductor with the Metropolitan Opera
1977   Martha Graham choreographs *The Scarlet Letter* at age eighty-four
1978   The Metropolitan Opera transmits its first live telecast
            Bob Fosse's *Dancin'* opens
1979   Mikhail Baryshnikov becomes head of the American Ballet Theatre
            Stephen Sondheim's *Sweeney Todd* opens
1981   MTV debuts
            Ned Rorem composes his Double Concerto for Cello and Piano
1980   Mark Morris establishes his Dance Group
1980s   Break dancing becomes popular
            Rap music becomes popular
            Foreign musicals, particularly those of Britain's Andrew Lloyd Webber, dominate Broadway stages
1982   Compact discs introduce digital music
            Michael Jackson releases "Thriller"
1983   Harvey Fierstein's *Torch Song Trilogy* opens
1984   Madonna releases "Like a Virgin"
1985   New York City Ballet star Edward Villella becomes founding artistic director of the Miami City Ballet
1988   Gian Carlo Menotti becomes artistic director of Spoleto Festival USA
1989   Compact discs edge out vinyl records
1990s   Broadway openings include *The Lion King, Ragtime* and *Rent*
            Theatrical fare includes performance artists such as Laurie Anderson, Meredith Monk, Anna Devere Smith and Spaulding Gray
            New York City revitalizes its Times Square theater district
            Broadway ticket prices top out at $80.00
            Hip-hop music gains popularity
            Ringling Brothers and Barnum & Bailey Circus returns to performing under a (polyvinyl) tent

© 2000 by The Center for Applied Research in Education

Sources: Barnouw, Erik. *Tube of Plenty: The Evolution of American Television.* New York: Oxford University Press, 1975. Carman, Joseph. "Baby Steps Meet Invention As a Dance Grows," *New York Times.* February 28, 1999. Chase, Gilbert. *America's Music From the Pilgrims to the Present.* New York: McGraw-Hill Book Company, 1966. Collins, Glenn. "Ringling Goes Upscale Under the Little Top," *The New York Times.* February 9, 1999. deMille, Agnes. *America Dances.* New York: Macmillan Publishing Company, Inc., 1980. Dizikes, John. *Opera in America: A Cultural History.* New Haven, CT: Yale University Press, 1993. Dunning, Jennifer. "City Ballet: 50 Years of Thrills for Stars," *The New York Times.* January 8, 1999. Ganzl, Kurt. *The Musical: A Concise History.* Boston: Northeastern University Press, 1997. Gruen, John. *The World's Great Ballets.* New York: Harry Abrams, Inc., 1981. Hitchcock, H. Wiley, editor. *Music in the United States: A Historical Introduction.* Englewood Cliffs, NJ: Prentice Hall, 1988. Hughes, Glenn. *A History of the American Theatre (1700-1950).* New York: Samuel French, 1951. Kerman, Joseph. *Listen: Second Brief Edition.* New York: Worth Publishers, 1992. Kisselgoff, Anna. "Jerome Robbins: Dancing Outside the Box," *The New York Times Magazine.* January 3, 1999. Londre, Felicia Hardison and Daniel J. Watermeier. *The History of North American Theater.* New York: Continuum, 1998. *The New York Public Library Performing Arts Desk Reference.* New York: Macmillan, 1994. Ochoa, George and Melinda Corey. *The Timeline Book of the Arts.* New York: Ballantine Books, 1995. Pareles, Jon and Patricia Romanowski, editors. *The Rolling Stone Encyclopedia of Rock & Roll.* New York: Rolling Stone Press/Summit Books, 1983. Perkins, George, Barbara Perkins and Phillip Leininger, editors. *Benet's Reader's Encyclopedia of American Literature.* New York: Harper Collins Publishers, 1991. Rowen, Beth, editor. *1998 A&E Entertainment Almanac.* Boston: Information Please, 1997. Stambler, Irwin. *Encyclopedia of Popular Music.* New York: St. Martin's Press, 1965. Tobias, Tobi. "Dance: Happy Anniversary," *New York Magazine.* November 23, 1998. Toll, Robert C. *On With the Show.* New York: Oxford University Press, 1975.

20.2   Chronology of American Movie-Making, 1891-1999

1891	Thomas Edison and W.K.L. Dickson patent the Kinetograph camera and the Kinetoscope viewer, the first motion picture apparatus.
1893	W.K.L. Dickson makes the earliest movies at Edison's Black Maria Studio in East Orange, New Jersey.
1894	Dickson's thirty-to-sixty second length movies are viewed in Kinescope parlors nationwide.
1896	During a vaudeville show at Koster and Bial's Music Hall in New York City, a Vitascope machine is used to project Kinetoscope film onto a large screen for the first time.
Late 1890s	A number of companies start producing short films. These are first shown at vaudeville shows, then at nickelodeon theaters where admission is five cents.
1903	Edwin S. Porter completes *The Great Train Robbery.*
1904	The nation's first movie theater opens near Pittsburgh, Pennsylvania.
1909	The Motion Picture Patent Company, a monopoly trust of major film companies, is formed.
1910-15	The film industry moves its base of operations from the East Coast to Hollywood, California.
1912	Mack Sennett joins the Keystone Film Company.
1914	Cecil B. DeMille co-directs his first movie, a popular six-reel western called *The Squaw Man.*
1915	Former actor and scriptwriter D.W. Griffith directs the epic *Birth of a Nation,* using now-modern camera techniques. The movie is met with protests by those who cite its racist depiction of blacks. Charlie Chaplin stars in *The Tramp.*
1916	D.W. Griffith directs the twenty-hour long *Intolerance.*
1918	The Motion Picture Patent Company is dissolved.
1919	The Buster Keaton Studio is formed. The first air-conditioned movie theater opens.
1921	Rudolph Valentino is elevated to stardom by his role in *The Four Horsemen of the Apocalypse.*
1922	Robert Flaherty's *Nanook of the North* is the first American documentary.
1924	Cecil B. DeMille directs *The Ten Commandments.* Buster Keaton stars in *The General.*
1925	Charlie Chaplin makes *The Gold Rush* for United Artists.
1927	*The Jazz Singer,* starring Al Jolson, premieres. The first full-length movie using sound dialogue, it signals in the end of the silent film era. The Academy of Motion Picture Arts and Sciences is founded. The 6,200-seat Roxy Theater, the epitome of the new style of elaborate new movie theaters, opens in New York City.
1928	Walt Disney produces the first Mickey Mouse cartoons.
1929	The first Academy Awards are presented.
1930s	American moviegoers turn to the movies in large numbers to escape from the worries and realities of the nation's economic Depression.
1930	The Motion Pictures Producers and Distributors of America develops "The Hays Code" system of censorship in films. Hal Wallis' *Little Caesar* is the first of many popular gangster movies.
1933	Busby Berkeley's *42nd Street* is an example of the new style of intricately choreographed musicals.
1934	Frank Capra's *It Happened One Night,* with Clark Gable and Claudette Colbert, typifies the era's popular screwball comedy. Shirley Temple makes *Stand Up and Cheer,* her first full-length movie.
1935	*Becky Sharp,* the first three-color Technicolor feature film, is produced.
1936	*Modern Times,* starring Charlie Chaplin, opens.
1937	Walt Disney makes the Disney Studio's first feature-length cartoon, *Snow White and the Seven Dwarfs.*
1939	The eagerly-awaited *Gone With the Wind* opens.
1940	Alfred Hitchcock makes *Rebecca,* his first American film.
1941	John Huston directs his first hit, *The Maltese Falcon.* Orson Welles releases *Citizen Kane.*
1942	Spencer Tracy and Katharine Hepburn co-star together for the first time in *Woman of the Year.*
1943	Maya Deren's *Meshes of the Afternoon* ushers in the avant-garde New American Cinema.

1948   The Supreme Court's Paramount Decision, prohibiting studies from owning the theaters that show their films, indicates the end of the studio system.

Late 1940s-early 1950s   Led by Wisconsin Senator Joseph McCarthy, the House Committee on Un-American Activities impels the movie industry to blacklist anyone suspected of being or associating with Communists. The Committee's impact on individuals' film careers takes on varying degrees of devastation.

1950   As a result of her role in *All About Eve,* Marilyn Monroe is offered a contract by Twentieth Century Fox.

1950s   The rise of television cuts into movie audiences.

1951   Elia Kazan's *A Streetcar Named Desire,* starring Marlon Brando, features the "method-acting"of New York's Actors Studio.

1953   Premiere of Henry Koster's *The Robe,* the first movie filmed in the widescreen process known as CinemaScope. The first commercial 3-D film, Arch Oboler's *Bwana Devil,* opens.

1954   Elia Kazan directs *On the Waterfront.*

1956   John Ford's *The Searchers* exemplifies a new style of westerns.

1960   Alfred Hitchcock directs *Psycho.*

1960s   Large conglomerates begin their takeover of movie studios.

1963   Sidney Poitier's Best Actor award for *Lilies of the Field* marks the first Oscar win for a black actor.

1967   Arthur Penn's *Bonnie and Clyde* and Mike Nichols's *The Graduate* represent new trends in contemporary filmmaking.

1968   The Motion Picture ratings system goes into effect.
            Stanley Kubrick's *2001: A Space Odyssey* takes special effects to new heights.

1969   Peter Fonda and Dennis Hopper's *Easy Rider* is an influential protest film.

Early 1970s   Movie distribution patterns change, as films begin to be released simultaneously in hundreds of theaters across the country rather than the more gradual and limited distribution of earlier years.

1972   Francis Ford Coppola makes *The Godfather, Part I.*
            Charlie Chaplin, denied re-entry to the United States twenty years earlier because of alleged Communist sympathies, returns to accept a special Academy Award.

1974   *Carnal Knowledge* is ruled not obscene by the U.S. Supreme Court.

1976   Martin Scorsese makes *Taxi Driver.*

1977   George Lucas' *Star Wars* (and, five years later, Steven Spielberg's *E.T.-The Extraterrestrial*) ushers in the vogue for computer-enhanced science fiction fantasy films appealing to children and adult audiences.
            Woody Allen makes *Annie Hall.*

1981   Video camcorder technology is introduced.

1985   Actor Robert Redford founds the Sundance Film Festival as an outlet for independent films and an alternative to Hollywood.
            SONY introduces consumer camcorders.

1986   Media mogul Ted Turner acquires the MGM film library and begins to (controversially) colorize some black-and-white movie classics which he will air on his cable television network.

1988   Spike Lee's *School Daze* helps establish him as a leading black movie maker.

1990s   Increasingly, American filmmaking is divided between big-budget blockbusters and smaller, independent releases.
            Theatrical releases become video releases in ever-decreasing amounts of time.
            Multiplex theaters proliferate.
            Independent films increasingly win Academy Award nominations.
            Average ticket prices nationally are around $5.00; those in New York City hit $9.50.
            Disney's *Toy Story,* released in 1995, is the world's first completely computer-animated film.
            James Cameron's *Titanic,* released in 1997 and costing between $250 and $300 million to produce and market, breaks all box-office records, becoming the biggest money-making movie of all time.
            The American film industry prepares for the advent of "electronic cinema,"[1] as digital movie projectors and movies in digital formats are being readied to replace 35-millimeter movie reels. The new technology is expected to improve film quality and consistency and to revolutionize the way studios distribute their products.

Sources: Henderson, Harry. *Communications and Broadcasting.* New York, New York: Facts on File, Inc., 1997. Mount, Ellis and Barbara A. List. *Milestones in Science and Technology.* Second Edition. Phoenix, AZ. The Oryz Press, 1994. *New York Times Index 1997.* New York, NY: The New York Times Company, 1998. Ochoa, George and Melinda Corey. *The Timeline Book of the Arts.* New York: Ballantine Books, 1995. Sterngold, James. "A Preview of Coming Attractions: Digital Projectors Could Bring Drastic Changes to Movie Industry." *The New York Times.* February 22, 1999.

[1] Sterngold, James. "A Preview of Coming Attractions: Digital Projectors Could Bring Drastic Changes to Movie Industry," *The New York Times.* Monday, February 22, 1999.

20.3 American Television Broadcasting: A History of the Medium

© 2000 by The Center for Applied Research in Education

1907—The term *television* is used in an article in the June issue of the journal *Scientific American.*

1920—Experiments on television technology resume, having been halted during World War I.

1923—Vladimir Zworykin patents the first television scanning camera.

1924—Zworykin patents the television picture tube.

1925—GE engineer Ernst Alexanderson conducts his first demonstration in which a picture is reproduced at the receiving end. According to Alexanderson, "the test demonstrated the operativeness of all the principles which we consider necessary for development of practical television."[1]

1926—Philo Farnsworth transmits the first (still) all-electronic television picture.

1927—The first transmission by wire of still and moving pictures with synchronized sound takes place when images of then-Secretary of Commerce Herbert Hoover are transmitted from Washington, D.C., to an audience in New York.

Television magazine debuts in New York.

1928—General Electric receives the first license for an experimental TV broadcasting station to be operated by radio station WGY in Schenectady, NY. Alexanderson announces "the starting point of practical and popular television"[2] and demonstrates the experimental system by telecasting programs which are viewed by engineers, reporters and GE officials on 3″ × 4″-screened sets.

1929—Zworykin applies to patent his Kinescope receiver tube.

Bell Labratories gives the first demonstration of color television in America.

1930—The future of television technology shifts focus from the mechanical system devised by Alexanderson to Zworykin's cathode-ray receiving tube and electronic system.

Philo Farnsworth devises a new scanning and synchronizing system.

1931—Zworykin successfully tests his one-sided camera tube, the Iconoscope.

NBC begins experimental telecasts from a transmitter on top of the Empire State Building.

CBS begins regular television broadcasts on a station in New York City.

1933—Educational television debuts on an Iowa station.

1934—Philo Farnsworth demonstrates electronic television at Philadelphia's Franklin Institute.

1937—NBC readies a television mobile unit in New York City.

1939—NBC debuts regular television broadcasting.

NBC airs the first televised sports event.

Franklin D. Roosevelt is the first President to appear on television.

RCA TV sets, with 5″, 9″ and 12″ tubes and priced from $200-$600, are displayed at the New York World's Fair.

1940—Peter Carl Goldmark invents the first system for commercial color TV broadcasting. The first experimental color broadcast is made from CBS's transmitter in New York City.

1940s—Cable TV begins as a means of bringing programming to remote locations unable to receive broadcast signals.

1941—The FCC approves recommendations made by the National Television Systems Committee regarding industry standards and authorizes commercial broadcasting to begin. NBC's WNBT and CBS's WCBW are licensed as the country's first commercial television stations.

1942—Commercial television begins, only to be halted soon thereafter with the advent of World War II.

1943—The American Broadcasting Company (ABC) is formed.

1946—Television sets go on sale.

The Dumont Television Network is formed.

CBS and NBC demonstrate color television.

The Academy of Television Arts and Sciences is founded.

[1] Fisher, David E. and Marshall Jon Fisher. *Tube: The Invention of Television.* Washington, DC: Counterpoint. 1996. p. 71.
[2] *Ibid.* p. 87.

1947—Harry S. Truman gives the first major television address by a President.
> Congress is televised in session for the first time.

1948—The *CBS-TV News* with Douglas Edwards is the first regularly scheduled television network news program.
> Nielsen ratings are first reported.
> The Democratic and Republican conventions, in Philadelphia, are televised nationwide for the first time, using an AT&T co-axial cable linking New York and Washington.
> The popularity of Milton Berle on NBC's *Texaco Star Theater* earns him the nickname "Mr. Television."

1949—The presidential inauguration is telecast for the first time.
> The Emmy Awards are first presented in Los Angeles, becoming national three years later.

1950s—Television's rising popularity has nationwide implications on American culture: a drop in movie-watching leads to theater closings, libraries and book stores report drops in circulation and sales, and restaurants and night clubs experience a loss of patronage on popular television-watching nights.
> The base of operations for television programming moves from New York to Los Angeles.
> CBS's *I Love Lucy,* made by Desilu Studios, pioneers the practice of recording a program on film, using multi-cameras, in front of a studio audience.

1951—The FCC reserves 242 television channels for educational use.
> President Truman appears in the first coast-to-coast televised broadcast.
> *Amos and Andy* debuts on CBS, the first series with an all-black cast.

1952—Walter Annenberg founds *TV Guide.*

1953—The first educational-TV station goes on the air in Houston, Texas.

1954—A telecast of Pasadena's Rose Bowl parade is the first program broadcast in color on a nationwide network.
> RCA markets the first color television sets, a 12″ screen model costing $1,000.

1955—Dumont Television Network ceases operation.
> The presentation of the Emmys are broadcast nationally for the first time.

1956—Zenith Corporation develops the first practical wireless remote control device.

1957—The videotape process, which records both picture and sound magnetically, is used for the first time in filming Dwight D. Eisenhower's presidential inauguration and comes to replace the previously used kinescope film.

1960—The nation's presidential election is strongly influenced by a televised debate in which the camera decidedly favors "telegenic" candidate John Kennedy over his opponent, Richard Nixon.

1961—The first live television coverage of a presidential news conference is broadcast.

1962—Telstar is launched, making possible live telecasts between Europe and the U.S.

1963—TV viewers witness Jack Ruby shooting and killing President Kennedy's assassin, Lee Harvey Oswald.
> Roone Arledge, head of ABC sports, uses videotape to devise "instant replay."
> Television news programs expand from fifteen minutes to a half-hour in length.

1964—Subscription TV debuts.

1965—Early Bird, the first commercial communications satellite, is launched, enabling worldwide broadcasting.

1966—All three major networks offer all-color prime-time programming.

1967—The FCC applies the Fairness Doctrine to commercials for the first time and requires stations to run anti-smoking spots to "balance" cigarette advertising.
> The Corporation for Public Broadcasting is created.
> The Children's Television Workshop is created to produce *Sesame Street.*

1968—*"Julia,"* starring Diahann Carroll, is the first television series to feature a black professional woman as the lead character.
> CBS' *60 Minutes* debuts, inaugurating the news magazine genre.

1970s—Minicam video cameras revolutionize local television news.
> Television closed-captioning is introduced.

1971—Cigarette advertising is banned on network television.
> *All in the Family* debuts on CBS, ushering in a new era in which television characters and programming directly address controversial and socially relevant matters.

1972—Home Box Office (HBO), the first cable network, is established by Time, Inc.
> Color televisions begin to outnumber black and white sets.

1975—The first home VCR, the Betamax, is introduced by the Sony Corporation.

Cable TV companies begin offering programming from satellites.

Late 1970s—Ted Turner's Atlanta station WTBS is the first satellite-delivered independent station.

1977—ABC airs its miniseries *Roots* to the highest ratings in television history.

1978—Cable's Showtime debuts.

1979—C-SPAN is launched by the House of Representatives.

1980s—Projection television systems are introduced.

MTV and rock videos become popular television fare.

Stereo sound is added to some broadcasts.

Distinctions begin to blur between news and entertainment programs.

The skyrocketing popularity of VCRs affects television viewership.

With theatrical movies now available to viewers on videocassette, HBO begins to stress original programming.

1981—Turner Broadcasting System's Cable News Network (CNN) is launched.

1982—The FCC authorizes a new satellite service called direct broadcast satellite (DBS).

1986—General Electric buys NBC.

1987—The FCC creates the Advisory Committee on Advanced Television Service to develop "HDTV," a wide-screen, high-resolution television system already in regular use in Japan. Congress issues a federally mandated schedule setting in place the timetable for the introduction of high definition television in America.

1988—Turner Network Television (TNT) is launched.

1989—Commercialism enters America's classrooms with the debut of Whittle Communications' *Channel One,* a controversial telecast of news and advertisements delivered via satellite hook-up.

1990—General Instrument's announcement of the production of the first all-digital television system ushers in a new era in television technology and capability. Based on computerized digital code rather than analog wavelengths, digital television (or "DTV") will enable Internet connections and provide the information-gathering capabilities of a computer.

1990s—Major networks continue to lose viewers to cable channels.

WebTV delivers Internet information directly to television sets.

Infomercials and home shopping networks gain popularity.

1993—Fox becomes the first new national network since the 1950s.

1995—Westinghouse acquires CBS.

Cap Cities/ABC is acquired by The Walt Disney Company.

Ted Turner's cable network empire merges with Time Warner.

1996—Congress passes the Telecommunications Act of 1995, paving the way for digital television.

1998—The FCC approves a new television ratings system and requires manufacturers to include V-chip technology in new TV sets that can be set to block specified programs.

Retailers begin selling new wide-screen TV sets and commercial network broadcasting of digital, high-definition television begins.

1999—According to FCC ruling, digital broadcasting must begin in the nation's top ten metropolitan areas by May and in the top thirty areas by November. The remainder are to receive the service by the year 2003. Eventually, analog airwave signals are to be silenced as the nation's current television system is completely replaced by digital technology.

Sources: Alexander, Oscar. *Media in the 20th Century.* San Mateo, CA: Bluewood Books, 1997. Barnouw, Erik. *Tube of Plenty: The Evolution of American Television.* New York: Oxford University Press, 1975. Fisher, David E. and Marshall Jon. *Tube: The Invention of Television.* Washington, DC: Counterpoint, 1996. Henderson, Harry. *Communications and Broadcasting.* New York: Facts on File, Inc., 1997. Hudson, Robert V. *Mass Media: A Chronological Encyclopedia of Television, Radio, Motion Pictures, Magazines, Newspapers, and Books in the United States.* New York: Garland Publishing Co., 1987. Kisseloff, Jeff. "In the Beginning, There Was Risk Taking," *The New York Times.* Sunday, November 29, 1998. Lampton, Christopher. *Telecommunications: From Telegraphs to Modems.* New York: Franklin Watts, 1991. Lichty, Lawrence W. and Malachi C. Topping. *A Source Book on the History of Radio and Television.* New York: Hastings House, Publishers, 1975. Mount, Ellis and Barbara A. List. *Milestones in Science and Technology.* Second Edition. Phoenix, AZ: The Oryz Press, 1994. Newcomb, Horace, editor. *Museum of Broadcast Communications Encyclopedia of Television.* Chicago: Fitzroy Dearborn Publishers, 1997. Ochoa, George and Melinda Corey. *The Timeline Book of the Arts.* New York: Ballantine Books, 1995. *Who's Who in America 1999.* New Providence, NJ: Marquis Who's Who, 1998.

20.4   Top 100 Nielsen Markets, 1998

1. New York, NY
2. Los Angeles, CA
3. Chicago, IL
4. Philadelphia, PA
5. San Francisco/Oakland/San Jose, CA
6. Boston, MA
7. Washington, DC/Hagerstown, MD
8. Dallas/Ft. Worth, TX
9. Detroit, MI
10. Atlanta, GA
11. Houston, TX
12. Seattle/Tacoma, WA
13. Cleveland, OH
14. Minneapolis/St. Paul, MN
15. Tampa/St. Petersburg/Sarasota, FL
16. Miami/Ft. Lauderdale, FL
17. Phoenix, AZ
18. Denver, CO
19. Pittsburgh, PA
20. Sacramento/Stockton/Modesto, CA
21. St. Louis, MO
20. Orlando/Daytona Beach/Melbourne, FL
23. Baltimore, MD
24. Portland, OR
25. Indianapolis, IN
26. San Diego, CA
27. Hartford/New Haven, CT
28. Charlotte, NC
29. Raleigh/Durham, NC
30. Cincinnati, OH
31. Milwaukee, WI
32. Kansas City, MO
33. Nashville, TN
34. Columbus, OH
35. Greenville/Spartanburg/Anderson, SC, and
     Asheville, NC
36. Salt Lake City, UT
37. Grand Rapids/Kalamazoo/Battle Creek, MI
38. San Antonio, TX
39. Norfolk/Portsmouth/Newport News, VA
40. Buffalo, NY
41. New Orleans, LA
42. Memphis, TN
43. West Palm Beach/Ft. Pierce, FL
44. Oklahoma City, OK
45. Harrisburg/Lancaster/Lebanon/York, PA
46. Greensboro/High Point/Winston-Salem, NC
47. Wilkes-Barre/Scranton, PA
48. Albuquerque/Santa Fe, NM
49. Providence, RI and New Bedford, MA
50. Louisville, KY

51. Birmingham, AL
52. Albany/Schenectady/Troy, NY
53. Dayton, OH
54. Jacksonville, FL, and Brunswick, GA
55. Fresno/Vasalia, CA
56. Little Rock/Pine Bluff, AR
57. Charleston/Huntington, WV
58. Tulsa, OK
59. Richmond/Petersburg, VA
60. Austin, TX
61. Las Vegas, NV
62. Mobile, AL, and Pensacola, FL
63. Flint/Saginaw/Bay City, MI
64. Knoxville, TN
65. Wichita/Hutchinson, KS
66. Toledo, OH
67. Lexington, KY
68. Roanoke/Lynchburg, VA
69. Des Moines/Ames, IA
70. Green Bay/Appleton, WI
71. Honolulu, HI
72. Syracuse, NY
73. Spokane, WA
74. Omaha, NE
75. Rochester, NY
76. Shreveport, LA
77. Springfield, MO
78. Tucson (Nogales), AZ
79. Paducah, KY, Cape Girardeau, MO, and
     Harrisburg/Mt. Vernon, IL
80. Portland/Auburn, ME
81. Champaign/Springfield/Decatur, IL
82. Huntsville/Decatur/Florence, AL
83. Ft. Myers/Naples, FL
84. Madison, WI
85. South Bend/Elkhart, IN
86. Chattanooga, TN
87. Cedar Rapids/Waterloo/Dubuque, IA
88. Columbia, SC
89. Davenport, IA, and Rock Island/Moline, IL
90. Jackson, MS
91. Burlington, VT, and Plattsburgh, NY
92. Johnstown/Altoona, PA
93. Tri-Cities, TN, and Tri-Cities, VA
94. Colorado Springs/Pueblo, CO
95. Evansville, IN
96. Waco/Temple/Bryan, TX
97. Youngstown, OH
98. Baton Rouge, LA
99. El Paso, TX
100. Savannah, GA

20.5 Chronology of American Radio Broadcasting, 1895-1999

1895   Guglielmo Marconi first sends radio communication signals through the air.

1906   Using continuous radio waves, inventor Reginald Fessanden broadcasts music and voice from an alternator in Brant Rock, Massachusetts, to ship operators at sea.

1907   Inventor Lee De Forest begins making broadcasts using his newly patented "Audion" triode vacuum tube, capable of detecting, amplifying and generating radio waves.

1912   Edwin Armstrong, an undergraduate student at Columbia University, invents a dual-purpose feedback circuit, the basis of radio transmitters.
A new federal law requires broadcasting licenses.

1915   David Sarnoff, chief inspector for the Marconi Wireless Telegraph Company and later president of RCA, proposes a "radio music box" which could broadcast music, news and sporting events.

1917   Amplitude modulation (AM radio) is pioneered by Edwin Armstrong.
During the duration of World War I, the U.S. government orders a moratorium on radio patent activity.

1918   Edwin Armstrong invents the superheterodyne circuit to improve long-distance reception and amplification.

1919   General Electric forms the Radio Corporation of America (RCA).
Speaking from sea to World War I troops aboard other ships, President Woodrow Wilson becomes the first President to use radio.

1920   Westinghouse Corporation's KDKA in Pittsburgh becomes the world's first commercial radio station.
The election of Warren G. Harding is the first presidential election result to be broadcast over the air. Detroit's WWJ also begins broadcasting at this time.

1921   RCA makes the first broadcast of a sporting event.
The popular-priced ($25) home radio receiver, the Aeriola, Jr., is first marketed.

1922   WEAF in New York City, an AT&T station, airs the first commercial announcement, an advertisement selling apartments in Queens.
The American Society of Composers, Authors, and Performers (ASCAP) begins demanding radio stations pay royalties for use of their music.
President Warren Harding installs the first radio in the White House.

1926   The National Broadcasting Company (NBC), a network of radio stations, is founded by David Sarnoff and RCA.

1927   NBC is divided into two separate networks: the Red Network (today's NBC) and the Blue Network (today's ABC).
Congress establishes the Federal Radio Commission to control the airways and regulate broadcasts.
William Paley forms the Columbia Broadcasting System (CBS).
Philco produces the first car radio.

1929   *Amos and Andy,* the first hit radio show, debuts as America's first situation comedy.
The first broadcast rating service is established for the Association of National Advertisers.

Early 1930s   Radio stations debut such programming as comedy variety hours, amateur contests, serial dramas, action adventures and detective shows.

1933   Frequency Modulation (FM) radio, which eliminates static, is developed by Edwin Armstrong.
President Franklin D. Roosevelt uses radio to talk directly to the American public in his weekly "fire side chats."

1934   The Federal Communications Commission replaces the Radio Commission.
The Mutual Broadcasting System is formed.
WNEW's program *The Make-Believe Ballroom,* presenting popular American dance music, begins its fifty-eight year run.

Late 1930s   Quiz shows and suspense thrillers become popular radio programming.

1937   NBC-affiliate announcer Herbert Morrison's coverage of the *Hindenberg* disaster in Lakehurst, New Jersey, is radio's first example of impromptu, on-the-spot reporting of a dramatic event.

1938   Orson Welles and his Mercury Theatre's all-too convincing radio drama based on H.G. Wells's novel *War of the Worlds* leads to nationwide panic over the supposed invasion by Martians.

Edward R. Murrow begins broadcasting news from London during Nazi bombing raids.

Edwin Armstrong's experimental FM station, WXMN, begins broadcasting.

1940   The Federal Communications Commission authorizes commercial FM radio to begin.

FM radios are first sold commercially.

Texaco begins sponsorship of weekly radio broadcasts of the Metropolitan Opera.

1941   Ninety million listeners hear President Roosevelt address the nation following the attack on Pearl Harbor.

Early 1940s   Radio is used extensively to broadcast news of World War II and to garner support for war efforts.

1943   The FCC forces NBC to sell one of its two networks, leading to the formation of the American Broadcasting Company (ABC).

1945   New York Mayor Fiorello LaGuardia uses radio to "read" the Sunday comics to children during a city newspaper strike.

1948   The transistor, which will allow for smaller televisions and radios, is developed by Bell Laboratories.

Early 1950s   Todd Storz, at KOWH in Omaha, Nebraska, begins the concept of limited-play, top 40 music programming. Disc jockeys become an integral part of this innovation. DJ Alan Freed's "Moondog Matinee" program first plays black R & B records to a white teenage audience, a breakthrough for rock and roll radio.

1952   Hand-held transistor radios are first marketed in the United States by the Sony Corporation.

Early 1950s   Television's increasing popularity puts an end to the comedies and dramas of radio's "Golden Age of Broadcasting," replacing them instead with music, talk and news programming.

1960   Presidential candidates John Kennedy and Richard Nixon hold the first radio and television debates.

1961   The first live radio (and television) coverage of a presidential news conference is broadcast.

1960s   Stereo broadcasting begins and FM radio takes off.

1969   The Earth picks up radio signals from the astronauts on the moon.

1970   National Public Radio is founded.

1970s   Album-oriented radio (AOR) becomes a leading FM radio format.

1982   AM radio stations begin stereo broadcasting.

1986   RCA and NBC are acquired by General Electric.

1990s   The programming of commercial FM radio is largely formatted, with disc jockeys or engineers playing a pre-determined roster of songs. More independent, varied programming now occurs on commercial public and college stations, generally located below 92 on the radio dial.

Audience-participatory talk radio continues to be a popular AM format.

Internet broadcasters begin to offer competition for radio listeners.

The FCC removes limits on the number of stations a single corporation can own.

Digital audio broadcasting is developed.

© 2000 by The Center for Applied Research in Education

Sources: Alexander, Oscar. *Media in the 20th Century*. San Mateo CA: Bluewood Books. 1997. Dizikes, John. *Opera in America: A Cultural History*. New Haven, CT: Yale University Press, 1993. Henderson, Harry. *Communications and Broadcasting*. New York: Facts on File, Inc., 1997. Hudson, Robert V. *Mass Media: A Chronological Encyclopedia of Television, Radio, Motion Pictures, Magazines, Newspapers, and Books in the United States*. New York: Garland Publishing Co., 1987. Lackman, Ron. *Same Time . . . Same Station*. New York: Facts on File, Inc., 1996. Lampton, Christopher. *Telecommunications: From Telegraphs to Modems*. New York: Franklin Watts, 1991. Lichty, Lawrence W. and Malachi C. Topping. *A Source Book on the History of Radio and Television*. New York: Hastings House, Publishers, 1975. Pareles, Jon. "Fracturing the Formula: A Hope for the Offbeat on Small FM," *New York Times*. Tuesday, February 9, 1999.

20.6 Protest Songs—Woodie Guthrie

Woody Guthrie's "Deportees" is a prime example of the protest music that played a central role in American political movements from the 1940s through the 1970s. The song dates from the late forties and was reportedly written after Guthrie read a news report about a plane crash over California's Los Gatos canyon in which the deaths were dismissed as unimportant because they were all (excepting the pilot) "deportees."

Deportees

The crops are all in, and the peaches are rotting,
The oranges are piled in their creseote dumps,
You're flying them back to the Mexico border
To pay all their money to wade back again.

Goodbye to my Juan, goodbye Rosalita,
Adios mis amigos, Jesus and Maria.
You won't have a name when you ride the big airplane,
And all they will call you will be deportee.
My father's own father he waded that river,
They took all the money he made in his life.
My brothers and sisters come working the fruit trees
They rode the truck till they took down and died.

Some of us are illegal and some are not wanted,
Our work contracts out and we have to move on.
Six hundred miles to that Mexico border,
They chase us like outlaws, and rustlers, and thieves.

We died in your hills; we died in your deserts;
We died in your valleys and died on your plains;
We died neath your trees, we died in your bushes,
Both sides of the river, we died just the same.

The skyplane caught fire over Los Gatos Canyon,
A fireball of lightning, it scarred all our hills,
Who are these friends all scattered like dry leaves?
The radio says they are just deportees.

Is this the best way we can grow our big orchards?
Is the is the best way we can grow our good fruit?
To fall like dry leaves, to rot on the topsoil,
And be known by no name except deportee?

20.7   Protest Songs of the 1960s and 1970s

"Abraham, Martin and John" Dion (Laurie, 1968) written about Abraham Lincoln, Martin Luther King, Jr. and John F. Kennedy

"If I Had a Hammer (The Hammer Song)" Peter, Paul and Mary (Warner, 1962)

"The Lonesome Death of Hattie Carroll" Bob Dylan (Columbia, 1964)

"Keep On Pushing" Curtis Mayfield and The Impressions (ABC-Paramount, 1964)

"People Got to Be Free" The Rascals (Atlantic, 1968)

"Respect Yourself" The Staple Singers (Stax, 1971)

"Say It Loud—I'm Black and I'm Proud(Part 1)" James Brown (King, 1968)

"Stand" Sly and the Family Stone (Epic, 1969)

"Think" Aretha Franklin (Atlantic, 1968) recorded April 15, 1968; Franklin was a personal friend of Martin Luther King, Jr. and had performed at a number of events with Dr. King

"We Shall Overcome" Joan Baez (Vanguard, 1963) recorded live at Miles College in Birmingham, Alabama; based on music from a 1794 hymn

"Blowin' in the Wind" Bob Dylan (Columbia, 1963)

"Alice's Rock & Roll Restaurant" Arlo Guthrie (Reprise, 1969)—short version of his 18-minute tale "Alice's Restaurant Massacre"

"Draft Dodger Rag" Phil Ochs (Elektra, 1965)

"For What It's Worth (Stop, Hey What's That Sound)" Buffalo Springfield (Atco, 1966)

"Fortunate Son" Creedence Clearwater Revival (Fantasy, 1969)

"Give Peace a Chance" John Lennon and the Plastic Ono Band (Apple, 1969) recorded in a hotel suite in Montreal, Canada; new version by the Peace Choir (featuring son, Sean) charted, 1991

"Ohio" Crosby, Stills, Nash and Young (Atlantic, 1970) written by Young after four students were killed at Kent State University

"Viet Nam" Jimmy Cliff (A&M, 1970)

20.8   Inductees in the Rock 'n Roll Hall of Fame

Ackerman, Paul
Allman Brothers Band, The
Animals, The
Armstrong, Louis
Baker, La Vern
Ballard, Hank
Band, The
Bartholomew, Dave
Bass, Ralph
Beach Boys, The
Beatles, The
Bee Gees, The
Berry, Chuck
Bland, Bobby "Blue"
Booker T. and the M.G.'s
Bowie, David
Brown, James
Brown, Ruth
Buffalo Springfield
Byrds, The
Cash, Johnny
Charles, Ray
Chess, Leonard
Christian, Charlie
Clark, Dick
Coasters, The
Cochran, Eddie
Cooke, Sam
Cream
Creedence Clearwater Revival
Crosby, Stills and Nash
Darin, Bobby
Diddley, Bo
Dion
Dixon, Willie
Domino, Fats
Donahue, Tom
Doors, The
Drifters, The
Dylan, Bob
Eagles, The
Eddy, Duane
Ertegun, Ahmet
Ertegun, Nesuhi
Everly Brothers, The
Fender, Leo
Fleetwood Mac
Four Seasons, The
Four Tops, The
Franklin, Aretha
Freed, Alan
Gabler, Milt
Gaye, Marvin
Goffin, Gerry and Carole King

Gordy, Berry
Graham, Bill
Grateful Dead
Green, Al
Guthrie, Woody
Haley, Bill
Hammond, John
Holland, Dozier, and Holland
Holly, Buddy
Hooker, John Lee
Howlin' Wolf
Impressions, The
Ink Spots, The
Isley Brothers, The
Jackson Five, The
Jackson, Mahalia
James, Elmore
James, Etta
Jefferson Airplane
Jimi Hendrix Experience
Joel, Billy
John, Elton
John, Little Willie
Johnson, Robert
Joplin, Janis
Jordan, Louis
King, B.B.
King, Carole and Gerry Goffin
Kinks, The
Knight, Gladys and the Pips
Leadbelly
Led Zeppelin
Leiber, Jerry and Mike Stoller
Lennon, John
Lewis, Jerry Lee
Lymon, Frankie and the Teenagers
Mamas and the Papas
Marley, Bob
Martin, George
Mayfield, Curtis
McCartney, Paul
McPhatter, Clyde
Mitchell, Joni
Monroe, Bill
Morrison, Van
Morton, Jelly Roll
Nathan, Syd
Nelson, Rick
Orbison, Roy
Orioles, The
Otis, Johnny
Parliament-Funkadelic
Paul, Les
Perkins, Carl

Phillips, Sam
Pickett, Wilson
Pink Floyd
Platters, The
Pomus, Doc
Presley, Elvis
Price, Lloyd
Professor Longhair
Rainey, Ma
(Young) Rascals, The
Redding, Otis
Reed, Jimmy
Richard, Little
Robinson, Smokey
Rodgers, Jimmie
Rolling Stones, The
Sam and Dave
Santana
Seeger, Pete
The Shirelles
Shannon, Del
Simon and Garfunkel
Sly and the Family Stone
Smith, Bessie
Soul Stirrers, The
Spector, Phil
Springfield, Dusty
Springsteen, Bruce
Staple Singers, The
Stewart, Rod
Stoller, Mike, and Jerry Leiber
Supremes, The
Temptations, The
Toussaint, Allen
Turner, Big Joe
Turner, Ike and Tina
Vandellas, The
Velvet Underground, The
Vincent, Gene
Walker, T-Bone
Washington, Dinah
Waters, Muddy
Wexler, Jerry
Who, The
Williams, Hank
Wills, Bob and His Texas Playboys
Wilson, Jackie
Wonder, Stevie
Yancey, Jimmy
Yardbirds, The
Young, Neil
Zappa, Frank

20.9 Most Played U.S. Jukebox Singles of All Times

Rank	Artist/song	Year
1.	Patsy Cline, *Crazy*	1962
2.	Bob Seger, *Old Time Rock 'n Roll*	1979
3.	Elvis Presley, *Hound Dog/Don't Be Cruel*	1956
4.	Bobby Darin, *Mack The Knife*	1959
5.	Steppenwolf, *Born To Be Wild*	1968
6.	Frank Sinatra, *New York, New York*	1980
7.	Bill Haley and His Comets, *Rock Around The Clock*	1955
8.	Marvin Gaye, *I Heard It Through The Grapevine*	1968
9.	Otis Redding, *(Sittin' on) The Dock of the Bay*	1968
10.	The Doors, *Light My Fire*	1967

Source: Amusement and Music Operators Association.

20.10 Largest Public Libraries in the U.S.

Library/No. of branches	Location	Founded	Books
New York Public Library (82)	New York, NY	1895	10,505,079
Queens Borough Public Library (62)	Jamaica, NY	1896	9,681,898
Chicago Public Library (81)	Chicago, IL	1872	6,840,109
Boston Public Library (26)	Boston, MA	1852	6,529,998
Carnegie Library of Pittsburgh (18)	Pittsburgh, PA	1895	6,409,300
County of Los Angeles Public Library (147)	Los Angeles, CA	1872	6,102,920
Free Library of Philadelphia (52)	Philadelphia, PA	1891	5,933,711
Public Library of Cincinnati and Hamilton County (41)	Cincinnati, OH	1853	4,655,050
Houston Public Library (37)	Houston, TX	1901	4,113,095
Buffalo and Erie County Public Library (53)	Buffalo, NY	1836	4,096,516

Source: American Library Association.

20.11 Earliest Public Libraries in the U.S.

Library	Founded
Peterboro Public Library, Peterboro, New Hampshire	1833
New Orleans, Public Library, New Orleans, Louisiana	1843
Boston Public Library, Boston, Massachusetts	1852
Public Library of Cincinnati and Hamilton County, Cincinnati, Ohio	1853
Springfield City Library, Springfield, Massachusetts	1857
Worcester Public Library, Worcester, Massachusetts	1859
County Library, Portland, Oregon	1864
Detroit Public Library, Detroit, Michigan	1865
St. Louis Public Library, St. Louis, Missouri	1865
Atlanta-Fulton Public Library, Atlanta, Georgia	1867

Source: American Library Association.

20.12　Longest Published Magazines in the U.S.

Magazine	First published
Scientific American	1845
Town and Country	1846
Harper's[1]	1850
The Moravian	1856
The Atlantic[2]	1857
Armed Forces Journal[3]	1863
The Nation	1865
American Naturalist	1867
Harper's Bazaar	1867
Animals	1868

[1] Originally *Harper's New Monthly Magazine*
[2] Originally *The Atlantic Monthly*
[3] Originally *Army and Navy Journal*

Source: Magazine Publishers of America.

20.13　Oldest Newspapers in the U.S.

Newspaper	Year established
The Hartford Courant, Hartford, CT	1764
Poughkeepsie Journal, Poughkeepsie, NY	1785
The Augusta Chronicle, Augusta, GA	1785
Register-Star, Hudson, NY	1785
Pittsburgh Post Gazette, Pittsburgh, PA	1786
Daily Hampshire Gazette, Northampton, MA	1786
The Berkshire Eagle, Pittsfield, MA	1789
Norwich Bulletin, Norwich, CT	1791
The Recorder, Greenfield, MA	1792
Intelligencer Journal, Lancaster, PA	1794

Source: Editor and Publisher Year Book.

20.14　Daily Newspapers with Largest Circulations, 1997

Newspaper	Average daily circulation
1. *Wall Street Journal*	1,774,880
2. *USA Today*	1,629,665
3. *New York Times*	1,074,741
4 *Los Angeles Times*	1,050,176
5. *Washington Post*	775,894
6. *New York Daily News*	721,256
7. *Chicago Tribune*	653,554
8. *Long Island Newsday*	568,914
9. *Houston Chronicle*	549,101
10. *Dallas Morning News*	484,379

NOTES

NOTES

NOTES

NOTES

NOTES

NOTES